Including Students with Special Needs

A Practical Guide for Classroom Teachers

MARILYN FRIEND

University of North Carolina at Greensboro

WILLIAM D. BURSUCK

University of North Carolina at Greensboro

Boston   Columbus   Indianapolis   New York   San Francisco   Upper Saddle River
Amsterdam   Cape Town   Dubai   London   Madrid   Milan   Munich   Paris   Montreal   Toronto
Delhi   Mexico City   São Paulo   Sydney   Hong Kong   Seoul   Singapore   Taipei   Tokyo

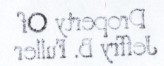
Vice President and Editor in Chief:
Jeffery W. Johnston
Executive Editor: Ann Castel Davis
Editorial Assistant: Penny Burleson
Senior Development Editor: Alicia Reilly
Vice President, Director of Marketing:
Margaret Waples
Marketing Manager: Joanna Sabella
Senior Managing Editor: Pamela D. Bennett
Senior Production Editor: Sheryl Glicker Langner
Senior Operations Supervisor:
Matthew Ottenweller

Senior Art Director: Diane C. Lorenzo
Text Designer: Candace Rowley
Photo Researcher: Lori Whitley
Permissions Coordinator: Sonia Martin
Cover Designer: Ali Mohrman
Cover image: SuperStock
Media Producer: Rebecca Norsic
Media Project Manager: Autumn Benson
Composition: S4Carlisle Publishing Services
Printer/Binder: Quebecor World Color/Versailles
Cover Printer: Lehigh-Phoenix Color
Text Font: Garamond

Credits and acknowledgments for material borrowed from other sources and reproduced, with permission, in this textbook appear on appropriate page within text.

Every effort has been made to provide accurate and current Internet information in this book. However, the Internet and information posted on it are constantly changing, so it is inevitable that some of the Internet addresses listed in this textbook will change.

Photo Credits: photo credits are on page xxiv.

Library of Congress Cataloging-in-Publication Data

Friend, Marilyn Penovich
Including students with special needs : a practical guide for classroom teachers / Marilyn Friend, William D. Bursuck.—6th ed.
    p. cm.
Includes bibliographical references and index.
ISBN-13: 978-0-13-217972-0
ISBN-10: 0-13-217972-5
1. Inclusive education—United States. 2. Mainstreaming in education—United States. 3. Special education—United States. 4. Children with disabilities—Education—United States. I. Title.
LC1201.F75 2012
371.9'046—dc22

2010049471

10 9 8 7 6 5 4 3 2 1

www.pearsonhighered.com

ISBN 10:   0-13-217972-5
ISBN 13: 978-0-13-217972-0

To BETH and BRUCE

our spouses and often unacknowledged collaborators—for their support of our work.

About the Authors

MARILYN FRIEND has worked in the field of education for over 30 years in a variety of roles. In addition to teaching in both special education and general education, she has worked as a teacher educator, consultant, and staff developer and currently is chair and professor in the Department of Specialized Education Services at the University of North Carolina at Greensboro. Her particular areas of expertise—the focus of her research, grants, teaching, writing, and work in the field—include inclusive schooling, co-teaching and other collaborative school practices, systems change, urban education, and family–school partnerships.

WILLIAM BURSUCK began his career as a general education teacher, and as a special education teacher and university teacher educator he has maintained an active interest in inclusive practices, publishing numerous research articles, successfully obtaining grants to conduct research, and publishing two books. Dr. Bursuck takes particular pleasure in providing classroom and future teachers with practical, evidence-based strategies to improve educational outcomes for students with special needs in this age of teacher accountability. He is a professor in the Department of Specialized Education Services at the University of North Carolina at Greensboro.

Preface

THE PAST DECADE has been characterized by significant changes in expectations related to students with disabilities and other special needs. Like all students, those who struggle to learn because of intellectual, physical, sensory, emotional, communication, or learning disabilities or other special needs must be taught using research-based practices, and nearly all are expected to reach the same high academic standards as other students. Importantly, teachers, administrators, and other professionals are more accountable than ever for ensuring that these challenging but appropriate goals are accomplished.

In many ways, the current educational climate is consonant with the beliefs on which *Including Students with Special Needs: A Practical Guide for Classroom Teachers* is based. In this sixth edition, we have expanded our efforts to integrate today's expectations for students with our own continued strong commitment to inclusive practices, a commitment tempered by our knowledge and experience of the realities of day-to-day teaching. We know that teachers cannot do the job themselves; they must also have strong and sustained administrative support and adequate resources. We cannot guarantee that key supports will always be in place, but we can provide teachers with a firm grounding in special education concepts, an understanding of the professionals who support these students and the procedures followed to ensure their rights are upheld, and a wealth of research-based strategies and interventions that can foster their success.

The textbook is divided into four main sections. The first section provides fundamental background knowledge about the field of special education as well as current information on how students with disabilities are served within inclusive school environments. The second section of the book provides a framework for thinking about effective instructional practices for students who struggle to learn. The third section of the book introduces readers to students with specific disabilities and other special needs. The material in the fourth section of the text represents the heart of any course on inclusive practices: instructional approaches that emphasize teaching students effectively both in academic and in social and behavior domains, regardless of disability or special need.

We have brought to this project our own diversity: Marilyn with expertise in elementary and secondary education, especially in urban settings, and in collaboration, inclusive practices, and co-teaching; Bill with expertise in secondary education, literacy, instructional strategies, assessment, and grading practices. Importantly, the organization of the book and the amount of space devoted to various topics reflect our priorities for preparing general education teachers to effectively instruct all their students. These priorities are based on our research; our analysis of the scholarly literature on instruction, teacher preparation, and professional development; and our experiences teaching undergraduate and graduate educators. Our understanding, though, ultimately is grounded in our many conversations with general education and special education teachers who are diligently working, often in difficult circumstances, to make a difference in the lives of their students. We truly hope that we have managed to find the right blend of both reader friendly and research-based information. Above all, we hope this sixth edition is responsive to the many instructional dilemmas confronting today's teachers.

Changes to the Sixth Edition

In addition to the following chapter-by-chapter changes, we've added to this edition a new feature called *Instructional Edge*. Each installment of this feature focuses on evidence-based practices that teachers can use with confidence.

- Chapter 1 includes the most current information on the **No Child Left Behind Act** (now the Elementary and Secondary Education Act—ESEA) and **IDEA 2004.** It also includes updates on related court cases and a discussion of inclusive practices based on the most salient factors affecting education today.
- Chapter 2 explains **response to intervention (RtI)** as an alternative to traditional approaches for determining whether students have learning disabilities. It places increased emphasis on **parents' rights in making decisions** regarding their children who may have disabilities. This chapter's discussion of the professional in special education has been streamlined, with those with whom elementary and secondary teachers usually work highlighted.
- Chapter 3 explores the **increasing importance of professional collaboration** in the delivery of special education services, including those related to RtI. It directly addresses the complexity of collaboration when disagreements occur, especially those between school professionals and parents. Strong emphasis is placed on co-teaching, teaming, and consultation.
- Chapter 4 has added coverage in math and writing to its already comprehensive section on curriculum-based assessment. The chapter also provides important coverage of the use of **universal screening assessments in RtI.**
- Chapter 5 presents a timely new special feature on how to select and use evidence-based practices. Expanded coverage of the use of **evidence-based practices in RtI** also is provided.
- Chapter 6 highlights the characteristics and needs of students with **autism spectrum disorders** and other low-incidence disabilities. Strong emphasis is placed on the use of technology to meet the needs of students with these special needs.
- Chapter 7 includes a new technology feature on the use of **assistive technology in reading** as well as expanded coverage on identifying students with learning disabilities using RtI.
- Chapter 8 includes updated data related to students with special needs other than disabilities. It focuses on students with **attention deficit–hyperactivity disorder** and the best ways to accommodate students with ADHD in the general education classroom. It also covers students who have special gifts and talents, and it examines the role of RtI in preventing the need for special education for some at-risk students.
- Chapter 9's practical, research-based coverage of **differentiated instruction** has been updated and includes a new feature on how to differentiate instruction within **Tier 2 in RtI.**
- New strategies have been added to the popular learning strategies section of Chapter 10. Ways to differentiate instruction in **Tier 3 of RtI** also are described.
- In addition to an expanded section on testing accommodations, Chapter 11 presents a new feature on **progress monitoring in RtI.**
- Chapters 12 and 13 have been blended so that students' social, emotional, and behavioral needs are addressed in a single, unified chapter. Emphasis is placed on preventing behavior problems, addressing serious problems through the use of **behavior intervention plans**, and fostering positive social interactions among students with disabilities and their classmates.

Every chapter of this text includes features designed to help readers learn more effectively, as well as to add to the general discussion and in-depth information about topics such as teaching strategies, cultural diversity, and technology.

PROFESSIONALISM

PROFESSIONAL EDGE
Thinking About Roles and Responsibilities in Collaboration

This activity is designed to help you think about collaborating with special educators. Complete the activity by yourself, and then compare responses with classmates. If possible, ask individuals preparing to be special educators to complete the task as well. Then discuss areas of agreement and disagreement and the implications for working together, whether in the classroom or at other times.

First, review the list of responsibilities for general and special educators. Then decide which professional is responsible for each of them. List each responsibility in the appropriate section of the Venn diagram.

Shared Responsibilities

GE Teacher Responsibilities   SE Teacher Responsibilities

TEACHER RESPONSIBILITIES RELATED TO STUDENTS WITH DISABILITIES

1. Plan for instruction
2. Write the IEP
3. Complete student assessments
4. Communicate with parents
5. Provide report card grades
6. Evaluate student work (for example, assignments, tests)
7. Provide supervision for work of paraprofessionals
8. Implement the classroom supports needed by student (for example, provide calculators, allow students to work on a computer)
9. Provide specially designed instructions to students, that is, learning options not usually found in the general education setting
10. Reteach instruction that students do not understand
11. Gather data about student learning and behavior
12. Prepare materials that take student needs into account (for example, create a word bank; rearrange test items to be clearer)
13. Respond to student behavior issues
14. Raise concerns about student achievement or behavior
15. Place the student's achievement in the context of the curriculum standards
16. Facilitate social interactions between students with and without disabilities
17. Assist students to identify postschool goals and arrange instruction to help them achieve those goals.

PROFESSIONAL EDGE features provide information on a variety of key topics related to each chapter's main focus. For example, Chapter 1 includes a checklist that educators can use to reflect on the extent to which a school might be considered inclusive.

TECHNOLOGY NOTES
Using Assistive Technology (AT) in Reading

Most students with learning and behavioral disabilities have reading problems, and unfortunately, the reading problems persist into their preteen and adolescent years. At the same time, these students are spending more time in general education classes where access to content depends on reading independently textbooks written at their frustration level. While attempts to remediate their reading skills need to continue, AT can help students with learning and behavioral disabilities access content independently by bypassing their reading disability. A text-to-speech screen reader can be helpful for students who are unable to read their content textbooks, but have good listening skills. The particular screen reading tool required depends on how it is used. The various uses for screen-reader programs, along with corresponding examples of AT tools are shown below (Bisagno & Haven, 2002; Bursuck & Damer, 2011).

Use	AT Tool
Read aloud	Simple text (Apple)
large volumes of straight text from the computer screen	ReadPlease (PC)
Navigate and search the Internet	eReader (CAST.org) Home Page Reader (IBM)
Provide real-time aural feedback on written text that student types	Co:Writer 4000 (Don Johnston) WordSmith (textHELP)
Provide customized visual presentation of text as well as read-aloud	Kurzweil 3000 (Kurzweil Educational Systems) Freedom Scientific
Read aloud large volumes of straight text from hand-held eReader	Kindle (Amazon) Sony 505 Digital Reader Apple IPAD

Here are some additional suggestions when using AT for print access (Bisagno & Haven, 2002; Bursuck & Damer, 2011):

- Using a screen writer requires having an electronic version of the text to be read. E-text can be obtained from other sources such as Bookshare.org.
- To convert course readers and text not available electronically to e-text, a scanner, OCR software, and adequate editing time are needed.
- For students who prefer a human to a computerized voice, prerecorded audiofiles, CDs, or MP3 downloads are available from organizations such as Recordings for the Blind and Dyslexic or public and college libraries.
- If a recorded version of a book is not available, have the book read by a volunteer or paid reader.
- For more technical texts such as science and math, using a human reader who has knowledge of the subject is preferable.
- Bypass strategies using AT are not a substitute for learning how to read. Be sure your students are receiving systematic explicit instruction in reading decoding and comprehension as needed.

TECHNOLOGY NOTES features illustrate the application of many types of technology available to support students with disabilities in inclusive schools. In Chapter 9, research on the effectiveness of the latest computer software on improving the writing skills of students with disabilities provides teachers with the most current information.

WORKING TOGETHER
The Reluctant Co-Teacher

Juanita Kirk, a math teacher, initially was excited about co-teaching with Susan Harris, the special educator assigned to the seventh-grade team. Now, though, she is disillusioned. Although Susan was offered paid planning time during the summer, she declined to participate, explaining that she had made her family the focus of her summers and that she would not make professional commitments during that time. Juanita could understand that, but then, at their first meeting in the fall, Susan explained to Juanita that she had always disliked math and had not studied it since she was in high school. She said that she would be most comfortable adjusting to co-teaching by spending the first semester taking notes for students, learning the curriculum, and then helping individual students after instruction had occurred. She stated clearly that she did not have much time for preparing outside class given all her other responsibilities, and she also made it clear that she did not consider it her responsibility to grade student work.

Juanita was surprised. This was not at all what she expected co-teaching to be. She envisioned a partnership in which she and her colleague not only could make instruction more intensive but also could energize math instruction by using various grouping arrangements and brainstorming new ways to reach their students. Now six weeks into the school year, she is beginning to think that co-teaching is more like having an assistant in the classroom—an assistant who is highly paid for not doing very much work. She wonders if this is how co-teaching looks in English, the other seventh-grade course to which Susan is assigned.

ADDRESSING THE DILEMMA

If you were Juanita, how might you address this situation by using ideas in this chapter and in chapter 3?

WORKING TOGETHER features present cases in which professional and family collaboration is needed and provide tips for optimizing collaborative efforts. For example, the Chapter 12 Working Together includes an example of what may occur when parents and professionals disagree.

dimensions of DIVERSITY

Diversity has many faces. It includes ethnic, cultural, economic, linguistic, religious, ability, gender, and racial differences among the students you may teach.

www resources

The Family Village School website (www.familyvillage .wisc.edu/ education/inclusion.html) provides a wide variety of information about associations, instructional resources, legal issues, projects, and research related to inclusion.

fyi

A primary disability is one that most adversely affects a student's educational performance. A secondary disability is an additional disability that also affects a student's education but to a lesser degree. For example, a student identified with a learning disability as a primary disability could have an emotional disability or health impairment as a secondary disability.

RESEARCH NOTE

Dunn, Chambers, and Rabren (2004) found that students with learning disabilities are less likely to drop out of school if they perceive that (1) a connection exists between what they are learning and life after high school, (2) someone in school is trying to help them, and (3) at least one class in high school is helpful to them.

MARGINAL ANNOTATIONS
are designed to stimulate higher-level thinking and provide additional information on cultural and linguistic diversity, research, and useful websites. They provide readers access to the most current research related to teaching students with disabilities.

INSTRUCTIONAL PRACTICE

INSTRUCTIONAL EDGE features provide numerous evidence-based practices for teachers to use. In the Sixth Edition, Chapter 5 provides an Instructional Edge on strategies for enhancing instruction for students with special needs in Tier 1 of RtI.

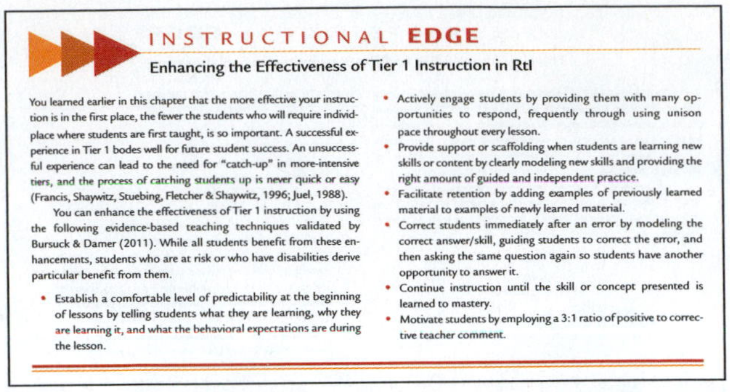

INSTRUCTIONAL EDGE
Enhancing the Effectiveness of Tier 1 Instruction in RtI

You learned earlier in this chapter that the more effective your instruction is in the first place, the fewer the students who will require individual-place where students are first taught, is so important. A successful experience in Tier 1 bodes well for future student success. An unsuccessful experience can lead to the need for "catch-up" in more-intensive tiers, and the process of catching students up is never quick or easy (Francis, Shaywitz, Stuebing, Fletcher & Shaywitz, 1996; Juel, 1988).

You can enhance the effectiveness of Tier 1 instruction by using the following evidence-based teaching techniques validated by Bursuck & Damer (2011). While all students benefit from these enhancements, students who are at risk or who have disabilities derive particular benefit from them.

- Establish a comfortable level of predictability at the beginning of lessons by telling students what they are learning, why they are learning it, and what the behavioral expectations are during the lesson.

- Actively engage students by providing them with many opportunities to respond, frequently through using unison pace throughout every lesson.
- Provide support or scaffolding when students are learning new skills or content by clearly modeling new skills and providing the right amount of guided and independent practice.
- Facilitate retention by adding examples of previously learned material to examples of newly learned material.
- Correct students immediately after an error by modeling the correct answer/skill, guiding students to correct the error, and then asking the same question again so students have another opportunity to answer it.
- Continue instruction until the skill or concept presented is learned to mastery.
- Motivate students by employing a 3:1 ratio of positive to corrective teacher comment.

CASE IN PRACTICE

Intervening to Promote Positive Social Interactions

Ms. Giano, a middle school teacher, is in a quandary. This afternoon she received a phone call from Ms. Perez concerning Jesse, her son. Ms. Perez related that Jesse had come home from school looking disheveled and with torn books and papers. At first he wouldn't tell his mother what had happened, but eventually he related the story. Jesse has albinism. He has very little pigment in his skin, hair, and eyes. His skin is very pale, and his hair seems almost white. In addition, Jesse has a serious vision problem related to his albinism, and he also has been identified as having a learning disability. He told his mother that several of his classmates had begun making fun of him on the walk to the bus and then continued on the bus. They had been doing this almost since the beginning of the school year, but things had been getting worse lately. Today, Jesse explained, he couldn't stand it anymore and he lunged at the boys. The bus driver intervened, but all the boys now were to be brought back to school by their parents for fighting.

Ms. Perez was upset. She also mentioned to Ms. Giano that Jesse had asked her not to call school, saying that he would deal with the situation and accept the discipline for fighting on the bus. He was afraid that his classmates' teasing would become even worse if it was made an issue. Ms. Perez is not satisfied; she wants something done to stop the teasing and protect her son. She is concerned that Jesse is becoming discouraged and has read about the association between such teasing and depression, especially among middle and high school students.

REFLECTION

How does this story relate to the topic of bullying? If you were Ms. Giano, what would you say to Ms. Perez? What is the role of the general education teachers in ensuring that students are treated respectfully? How would you address this issue with Jesse? With the other boys? If you think they should have an additional consequence, what should it be? What might you try as an all-homeroom activity to foster better understanding among your diverse students? Would your response to the situation and interventions be significantly different if you plan to teach elementary students? High school students? How so?

CASE IN PRACTICE features clarify key principles by providing brief case studies related to chapter concepts and teaching scripts as models. Chapter 12, for example, has a Case in Practice on intervening to promote positive social interactions in the case of a student with special needs being teased on the school bus.

CHAPTER-OPENING VIGNETTES serve as introductory material to help readers think about how the content of chapters relates to teachers and students. They conclude with critical-thinking questions. These cases serve as examples throughout the chapters and are revisited in the Back to the Cases feature at the end of each chapter. The opening vignettes have been designed to introduce novice educators to the very real and sometimes complex needs of students.

THOMAS is one of those students who makes his presence known very quickly. He announced on the first day in his seventh-grade social studies class that the color of the walls was *xantho* (yellow). For several days later that fall, he came to school wearing only socks on his feet, because, as his mother explained, he had completely outgrown his old shoes but would not wear new, better-fitting ones because he said they "had knots in the toes." In all his classes, Thomas tends to keep to himself, and when group projects are assigned, he has difficulty knowing how to talk to his classmates about anything except the subjects he enjoys—French words commonly used in the English language and Alfred Hitchcock movies. When Thomas began elementary school, he was enrolled in a special education class for students with autism. However, most of his classmates had significant intellectual disabilities, and the teacher and Thomas's parents quickly realized that he needed to be challenged academically in a way that could not happen in that class. Since second grade, he has spent most of his time in general education classrooms. In some situations, a special education teacher worked in his classroom with the general education teacher, or a paraprofessional was present to assist the teacher and all the students. Now such support generally is not necessary. Thomas meets with his special education

and math in a special education resource class, but she is a member of a general education class for science and social studies as well as for art, music, library/media, physical education, and technology skills classes. Spending time in both special education and general education settings was determined by a team to be the best option for Patricia. As Ms. Schwarz, her general education teacher, worries that the other students do not have enough interactions with Patricia to really get to know and value her and that Patricia's learning is actually made more difficult because she comes and goes from the classroom. Ms. Schwarz favors reducing the amount of time Patricia spends in the special education classroom. Ms. Ramos, the special educator, agrees; this topic will be addressed at a meeting to decide

How likely are you to teach a student like Patricia? What is an intellectual disability? What factors have led teachers to advocate for educating students like Patricia in typical classrooms for all or much of the school day instead of in special education classrooms?

AARON has a learning disability that was identified when he was in second grade. He also takes medication for attention deficit-hyperactivity disorder (ADHD). Aaron is continuing to learn the academic difficulties he is at about his learning disability about a seventh-grade level, like that of a student in second talk about his learning disability other students to make fun emly because he has LD. He is asked to talk about why he though his doctor has caused-dication exactly as prescribed, he's taking it to see if he can get As. history class, Aaron is most he answers questions orally; accepts even if it sometimes hought. Because he doesn't wever, he sometimes refuses to peers. Explain why you think these methods would be helpful for Josh, onal assistance during study is lower than they could be. Aaron is an excellent athlete, and on the basketball court, he feels equal to his friends. However, his parents are concerned that his interest in sports is distracting him from schoolwork.

How often will you meet students like Aaron? What is a learning disability? What types of supports and services do Aaron and other students with LD need to succeed in school?

BACK TO THE CASES features bring content into clearer focus by showing how principles, concepts and strategies explained in the chapter can be applied to the students described in the chapter-opening vignettes. For example, in Chapter 5 students are shown how to accommodate and then monitor the progress of a student with learning disabilities included in a content area class.

WRAPPING IT UP
BACK TO THE CASES

This section provides opportunities for you to apply the knowledge gained in this chapter to the cases described at the beginning of this chapter. The questions and activities that follow demonstrate how the principles and concepts you have learned about in this chapter connect to the everyday activities of all teachers.

MR. RODRIGUEZ has provided a digital copy of the text and a daily review of previously presented content, outlines of lectures, and small-group discussions to support Manuel's learning of content. Step 7 of the INCLUDE strategy asks teachers to evaluate student

progress. Using information in this chapter and Chapter 4, suggest two assessment methods that Mr. Rodriguez might use to monitor Manuel's progress. Explain why you selected these two methods.

JOSH may face peers who have difficulty adjusting to his speech. As a result, they may stay away from interactions with him. Based on information provided in this chapter, describe two ways Ms. Steward can use classroom management, grouping, instructional materials, or specific teaching methods to support Josh's interactions with peers. Explain why you think these methods would be helpful for Josh.

lived in six foster homes because her mother was unable to take care of her and gave up custody. Happily, her current foster family has decided to adopt Patricia, a time-consuming process that should be completed before the end of this school year. In school, Patricia receives highly specialized instruction in language arts

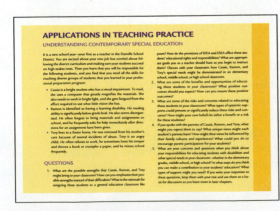

APPLICATIONS IN TEACHING PRACTICE
UNDERSTANDING CONTEMPORARY SPECIAL EDUCATION

It is a new school year—your first as a teacher in the Danville School District. You are excited about your new job but worried about following the district curriculum and making sure your students succeed on high-stakes tests. Then you learn that you will be responsible for the following students, and you find that you need all the skills for reaching diverse groups of students that you learned in your professional preparation program:

- Cassie is a bright student who has a visual impairment. To read, she uses a computer that greatly magnifies the materials. She also needs to work in bright light, and she gets fatigued from the effort required to use what little vision she has.
- Ramon is identified as having a learning disability. His reading ability is significantly below grade level. He also seems disorganized. He often forgets to bring materials and assignments to school, and he frequently asks for help immediately after directions for an assignment have been given.
- Tory lives in a foster home. He was removed from his mother's care because of several incidents of abuse. Tory is an angry child. He often refuses to work, he sometimes loses his temper and throws a book or crumples a paper, and he misses school frequently.

QUESTIONS

1. What are the possible strengths that Cassie, Ramon, and Tory might bring to your classroom? How can you emphasize their possible strengths instead of their difficulties? What is the rationale for assigning these students to a general education classroom like

yours? How do the provisions of IDEA and ESEA affect these students' educational rights and responsibilities? What are appropriate goals you as a teacher should have as you begin to instruct them? Discuss with your classmates how Cassie, Ramon, and Tory's special needs might be demonstrated in an elementary school, middle school, or high school classroom.

2. What are some of the benefits and opportunities of educating these students in your classroom? What positive outcomes should you expect? How can you ensure these positive outcomes?

3. What are some of the risks and concerns related to educating these students in your classroom? What types of systemic supports could prevent or significantly reduce these risks and concerns? How might your own beliefs be either a benefit or a risk for these students?

4. If you spoke with the parents of Cassie, Ramon, and Tory, what might you expect them to say? What unique views might each student's parents have? How might their views be influenced by their family cultures and experiences? What could you do to encourage parent participation for your students?

5. What are your concerns and questions when you think about your responsibilities for educating students with disabilities and other special needs in your classroom—whether in the elementary grades, middle school, or high school? In what ways do you think you can make a contribution to your students' education? Write these questions, keep them with your text and use them as a basis for discussion as you learn more in later chapters.

APPLICATIONS IN TEACHING PRACTICE cases and activities at the end of each chapter are designed to encourage students to apply the chapter contents to real-life classroom situations. For example, in Chapter 1, students are asked to assume the role of a teacher at the beginning of the year and plan for 3 students with disabilities to be included in their class.

New! CourseSmart eTextbook Available

CourseSmart is an exciting new choice for students looking to save money. As an alternative to purchasing the printed textbook, students can purchase an electronic version of the same content. With a CourseSmart eTextbook, students can search the text, make notes online, print out reading assignments that incorporate lecture notes, and bookmark important passages for later review. For more information, or to purchase access to the CourseSmart eTextbook, visit www.coursesmart.com.

Supplements

This edition boasts the most comprehensive and integrated collection of supplements to date to assist students and professors alike in maximizing learning and instruction. All instructor supplements are available at the Pearson Instructor's Resource Center. Go to **www.pearsonhighered.com** and click on the "Educators" link. Here you will be able to login or complete a one-time registration for a user name and password to gain access to the following supplements.

Online Instructor's Manual and Test Bank

The Online Instructor's Manual and Test Bank synchronize all of the resources available for each chapter and can be used for traditional courses as well as online or online-supported courses. The Instructor's Manual is fully integrated with the MyEducationLab that accompanies this text and includes many ideas and activities to help instructors teach the course. The Test Bank provides hundreds of multiple-choice, short-answer, and essay questions, all with answer keys.

Pearson MyTest

Pearson MyTest is a powerful assessment generation program that helps instructors easily create and print quizzes and exams. Questions and tests are authored online, allowing ultimate flexibility and the ability to efficiently create and print assessments anytime, anywhere! Instructors can access Pearson MyTest and their test bank files by going to www.pearsonmytest.com to log in, register, or request access. Features of Pearson MyTest include:

Premium assessment content
- Draw from a rich library of assessments that complement your Pearson textbook and your course's learning objectives.
- Edit questions or tests to fit your specific teaching needs.

Instructor-friendly resources
- Easily create and store your own questions, including images, diagrams, and charts using simple drag-and-drop and Word-like controls.
- Use additional information provided by Pearson, such as the question's difficulty level or learning objective, to help you quickly build your test.

Time-saving enhancements
- Add headers or footers and easily scramble questions and answer choices—all from one simple toolbar.
- Quickly create multiple versions of your test or answer key, and when ready, simply save to MS-Word or PDF format and print!
- Export your exams for import to Blackboard 6.0, CE (WebCT), or Vista (WebCT)!

Online PowerPoint Slides/Transparency Masters
These visual aids display, summarize, and help explain core information presented in each module. All PowerPoint slides have been updated for consistency and to reflect content in the new edition.

PEARSON
myeducationlab   The power of classroom practice

In *Preparing Teachers for a Changing World*, Linda Darling-Hammond and her colleagues point out that grounding teacher education in real classrooms—among real teachers and students and among actual examples of students' and teachers' work—is an important, and perhaps even an essential, part of training teachers for the complexities of teaching in today's classrooms. MyEducationLab is an online learning solution that provides contextualized interactive exercises, simulations, and other resources designed to help develop the knowledge and skills teachers need. All of the activities and exercises in MyEducationLab are built around essential learning outcomes for teachers and are mapped to professional teaching standards. Utilizing classroom video, authentic student and teacher artifacts, case studies, and other resources and assessments, the scaffolded learning experiences in MyEducationLab offer pre-service teachers and those who teach them a unique and valuable education tool.

For each topic covered in the course you will find most or all of the following features and resources:

Connection to National Standards

Now it is easier than ever to see how coursework is connected to national standards. Each topic on MyEducationLab lists intended learning outcomes connected to the appropriate national standards. And all of the activities and exercises in MyEducationLab are mapped to the appropriate national standards and learning outcomes as well.

Assignments and Activities

Designed to enhance student understanding of concepts covered in class and save instructors preparation and grading time, these assignable exercises show concepts in action (through video, cases, and/or student and teacher artifacts). They help students deepen content knowledge and synthesize and apply concepts and strategies they read about in the book. (Correct answers for these assignments are available to the instructor only under the Instructor Resource tab.)

Building Teaching Skills and Dispositions

These learning units help students practice and strengthen skills that are essential to quality teaching. After presenting the steps involved in a core teaching process, students are given an opportunity to practice applying this skill via videos, student and teacher artifacts, and/or case studies of authentic classrooms. Providing multiple opportunities to practice a single teaching concept, each activity encourages a deeper understanding and application of concepts, as well as the use of critical thinking skills.

IRIS Center Resources

The IRIS Center at Vanderbilt University (http://iris.peabody.vanderbilt.edu)—funded by the U.S. Department of Education's Office of Special Education Programs (OSEP) develops training enhancement materials for pre-service and in-service teachers. The Center works with experts from across the country to create challenge-based interactive modules, case study units, and podcasts that provide research-validated information about working with students in inclusive settings. In your MyEducationLab course we have integrated this content where appropriate.

Teacher Talk

This feature emphasizes the power of teaching through videos of master teachers, each speaker telling their own compelling stories of why they teach. These videos help teacher candidates see the bigger picture and consider why what they are learning is important to their career as a teacher. Each of these featured teachers has been awarded the Council of Chief State School Officers Teachers of the Year award, the oldest and most prestigious award for teachers.

Study Plan Specific to Your Text

A MyEducationLab Study Plan is a multiple choice assessment tied to chapter objectives, supported by study material. A well-designed Study Plan offers multiple opportunities to fully master required course content as identified by the objectives in each chapter:

- *Chapter Objectives* identify the learning outcomes for the chapter and give students targets to shoot for as you read and study.
- *Multiple Choice Assessments* assess mastery of the content. These assessments are mapped to chapter objectives, and students can take the multiple-choice quiz as many times as they want. Not only do these quizzes provide overall scores for each objective, but they also explain why responses to particular items are correct or incorrect.
- *Study Material: Review, Practice and Enrichment* give students a deeper understanding of what they do and do not know related to chapter content. This material includes text excerpts, activities that include hints and feedback, and interactive multi-media exercises built around videos, simulations, cases, or classroom artifacts.
- *Flashcards* help students study the definitions of the key terms within each chapter.

Course Resources

The Course Resources section on MyEducationLab is designed to help students, put together an effective lesson plan, prepare for and begin their career, navigate their first year of teaching, and understand key educational standards, policies, and laws. The Course Resources Tab includes the following:

- The **Lesson Plan Builder** is an effective and easy-to-use tool that students can use to create, update, and share quality lesson plans. The software also makes it easy to integrate state content standards into any lesson plan.
- The **IEP Tutorial** shows how to develop appropriate IEPs and how to conduct effective IEP conferences.
- The **Preparing a Portfolio** module provides guidelines for creating a high-quality teaching portfolio.
- **Beginning Your Career** offers tips, advice, and other valuable information on:
  - *Resume Writing and Interviewing:* Includes expert advice on how to write impressive resumes and prepare for job interviews.
  - *Your First Year of Teaching:* Provides practical tips to set up a first classroom, manage student behavior, and more easily organize for instruction and assessment.
  - *Law and Public Policies:* Details specific directives and requirements teachers need to understand under the ESEA (formerly No Child Left Behind Act) and the Individuals with Disabilities Education Improvement Act of 2004.
- **Special Education Interactive Timeline**. Use this tool to build your own detailed timelines based on different facets of the history and evolution of special education.

Certification and Licensure

The Certification and Licensure section is designed to help students pass their licensure exam by giving them access to state test requirements, overviews of what tests cover, and sample test items.
The Certification and Licensure tab includes the following:

- **State Certification Test Requirements:** Here students can click on a state and will then be taken to a list of state certification tests.

- Students can click on the **Licensure Exams** they need to take to find:
  - Basic information about each test
  - Descriptions of what is covered on each test
  - Sample test questions with explanations of correct answers
- **National Evaluation Series**™ by Pearson: Here students can see the tests in the NES, learn what is covered on each exam, and access sample test items with descriptions and rationales of correct answers. They can also purchase interactive online tutorials developed by Pearson Evaluation Systems and the Pearson Teacher Education and Development group.
- **ETS Online Praxis Tutorials:** Here students can purchase interactive online tutorials developed by ETS and by the Pearson Teacher Education and Development group. Tutorials are available for the Praxis I exams and for select Praxis II exams.

Visit www.myeducationlab.com for a demonstration of this exciting new online teaching resource.

Acknowledgments

We are grateful to the many individuals who helped us during the preparation of the sixth edition of *Including Students with Special Needs*. Without their assistance and encouragement the project undoubtedly would have stalled. First and most important, we express our gratitude to our families. They have listened to us worry about how to meet the deadlines that sometimes seemed impossibly near and obsess about the material to include in the book as well as that which must be relegated to the "maybe next time" file. They helped us sort through the conundrums, offered suggestions with the perspective of outsiders who deeply cared, and tolerated our need to hide in our offices as we wrote and rewrote. We cannot possibly say thank you in enough ways for their support.

We also thank the individuals who helped us with all the innumerable details of revising a textbook. Graduate assistants Cynthia Shamberger and Gretchen Smallwood patiently combed through sources and helped us to find obscure pieces of information. Sonia Martin, department administrative assistant at University of North Carolina at Greensboro an invaluable colleague, assisted in checking the manuscript for accuracy, including making sure all the references were included and any typos corrected. She also completed with meticulous care the arduous task of obtaining permissions for others' work used in the textbook. We especially thank her for lending a sympathetic ear and for her inimitable sense of humor.

The professionals at Pearson also have supported this effort with both words and actions. Executive Editor Ann Davis has steered this sixth edition through the many steps of its creation, offering guidance and insights with encouragement and patience. Developmental Editor Alicia Reilly was, as always, diligent in her efforts to help us keep the book clear, responsive to the needs of the field, and on target with the correct number of pages—and she demonstrated once again that nagging about deadlines and tasks still awaiting attention can be accomplished in a way that is neither overly intrusive nor offensive. Thanks, Alicia.

Special thanks go to the reviewers for this edition: Genevieve H. Hay, College of Charleston; Diane Evans Kelley, Cardinal Stritch University; Myung-Sook Koh, Eastern Michigan University; and Debra Pratt, Purdue University, North Central. We were impressed with the care with which they reviewed the manuscript and the insightful suggestions they made. We tried to incorporate most of their suggestions, and they definitely helped us create a better textbook.

Finally, we continue to be grateful to all of our colleagues and students who influence our thinking about educating students with special needs in general education classrooms. Their questions about best practices, their challenges to our thinking, and their ideas for better communicating our message have been invaluable.

Brief Contents

chaps 4-5
6-7

Contents

Assessing Student Needs 98

Planning Instruction by Analyzing Classroom and Student Needs 128

Students with Low-Incidence Disabilities 166

Students with High-Incidence Disabilities 202

Students with Special Needs Other Than Disabilities 232

Responding to Student Behavior 368

Features at a Glance

Features at a Glance *(continued)*

	Professional Edge	Instructional Edge	
CHAPTER 8 **Students with Special Needs Other Than Disabilities**	· Section 504 Accommodations, 237 · Gifted Underachievers, 249 · Levels of Language Proficiency, 254	English-Language Learners and Reading, 253	
CHAPTER 9 **Differentiating Instruction**	How to Develop Study Guides, 284	· Providing Differentiated Instruction in Tier 2 in RtI, 274 · Strategies for Teaching Science to English-Language Learners, 279	
CHAPTER 10 **Strategies for Independent Learning**	· Developing Your Own Learning Strategies, 308 · The Key Word Strategy for Solving Math Word Problems: Is There a Better Way?, 327	Providing Differentiated Instruction in Tier 3 in RtI, 309	
CHAPTER 11 **Evaluating Student Learning**	· Teaching Test-Taking Strategies for Taking Objective Tests, 343 · Modifications in Test Construction for Students with Disabilities, 345 · Using Grading Rubrics with Students, 347 · The Legalities of Grading Students with Disabilities, 361	· Testing English-Language Learners in Math-Problem Solving, 346 · Using Progress Monitoring to Evaluate Student Performance in RtI, 354	
CHAPTER 12 **Responding to Student Behavior**	· Preventing School Violence, 370 · Response to Intervention and Positive Behavior Supports, 372 · Strategies for Managing Students' Surface Behaviors, 382 · Bullying: The Problems and Some Interventions, 387	Cooperative Learning in Action, 379	

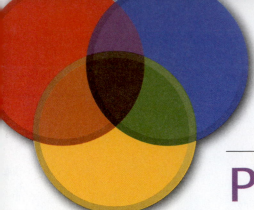

Photo Credits

Pierre Tremblay/Masterfile Stock Image Library, p. 2; Elizabeth Crews/The Image Works, p. 5; Don Cravens/Getty Images/Time Life Pictures, p. 9; Mac H. Brown/Merrill, p. 15; © Jeff Greenberg/Alamy, p. 20; Courtesy of AbleNet, Inc., p. 25; Masterfile Royalty Free Division, p. 30; Jupiter Images – Food Pix – Creatas, pp. 33 (top left), 154; iStockphoto.com, p. 33 (top right); © Bob Daemmrich/ Alamy, pp. 33 (center), 64, 76, 380; Katelyn Metzger/Merrill, pp. 33 (center left), 237, 266; Anthony Magnacca/Merrill, pp. 33 (center right), 33 (bottom left), 171; Ellen B. Senisi/The Image Works, pp. 33 (bottom right), 178; Lori Whitley/Merrill, p. 34; © Ilene MacDonald/Alamy, p. 38; Syracuse Newspapers/The Image Works, p. 48; EXCEED® is a registered trademark of Spectrum K12 School Solutions, Inc., p. 53; Getty Images, Inc., p. 69; Pearson Learning Photo Studio, p. 72; Stone/Getty Images, p. 79; Michael Newman/PhotoEdit Inc., pp. 86, 100, 142, 192 (top), 202, 251, 330, 349, 372; Bob Daemmrich/PhotoEdit Inc., pp. 98, 128, 166; Cleve Bryant/PhotoEdit Inc., p. 105; Robin Sachs/PhotoEdit Inc., p. 110; David Young-Wolff/PhotoEdit Inc., pp. 112, 222; Ken Karp/ Prentice Hall School Division, p. 119; Liz Strenk/SuperStock, Inc., p. 131; Shahn Kermani, p. 136; Elizabeth Crews/The Image Works, p. 161; Model Me Kids, LLC http://www.modelmekids.com, p. 176 (bottom); Doug Menuez/Getty Images, Inc. PhotoDisc, p. 176 (right); Comstock Royalty Free Division, p. 176 (left); Richard Hutchings/PhotoEdit Inc., p. 177; Courtesy of the Attainment Company, p. 182 (left); Courtesy of AbleNet, Inc., p. 182 (right); © Paul Doyle/Alamy, p. 185; Courtesy of Harpo, p. 186 (top left); Marilyn Friend, p. 186 (center left); Image owned by Maxi-Aids Inc. www.maxiaids.com; p. 186 (top right); Spencer Grant/PhotoEdit Inc., p. 186 (center right), 192 (bottom right); Caltrox Educational Software, p. 186 (bottom); John W. McDonough/Oticon Inc., p. 192 (center); Mark Benjamin/Rochester Institute of Technology, p. 192 (bottom left); Alix/Photo Researchers, Inc., p. 195; Mary Kate Denny/Getty Images Inc. – Stone Allstock, p. 224; © Steve Skjold/Alamy, p. 232; © Design Pics/SuperStock, p. 241; Patrick White/Merrill, p. 243; David Mager/Pearson Learning Photo Studio, p. 246; Tony Freeman/PhotoEdit Inc., p. 261; Courtesy of Ningbo AST Industry Co., Ltd., p. 262; Will Faller, p. 278; Paul Conklin/PhotoEdit Inc., p. 286; © Jim West/Alamy, pp. 296, 400; Getty Images Inc. – Image Source Royalty Free, p. 302; Shutterstock, p. 310; © Kathy deWitt/Alamy, p. 317; Charles Gupton/ Corbis – NY, p. 338; Tom Watson/Merrill, p. 341; Laima Druskis/PH College, p. 360; © Enigma/Alamy, p. 368; © Ian Shaw/Alamy, p. 377; Supplied by the author, p. 389; Mary Kate Denny/ PhotoEdit Inc., p. 395

chapter 1

The Foundation for Educating Students with Special Needs

LEARNING Objectives

After you read this chapter, you will be able to

1. Explain key terms and concepts that describe special education.
2. Trace the historical events that have shaped contemporary special education services.
3. Outline the laws that govern current practices for educating students with disabilities.
4. Analyze your beliefs related to inclusive practices, taking into account contemporary knowledge and expectations about effective instruction and educational access, as well as parent perspectives.
5. Describe the categories of disabilities addressed in federal law.
6. Explain special needs other than disability that your students may have.

THOMAS is one of those students who makes his presence known very quickly. He announced on the first day in his seventh-grade social studies class that the color of the walls was *xantho* (yellow). For several days later that fall, he came to school wearing only socks on his feet, because, as his mother explained, he had completely outgrown his old shoes but would not wear new, better-fitting ones because he said they "had knots in the toes." In all his classes, Thomas tends to keep to himself, and when group projects are assigned, he has difficulty knowing how to talk to his classmates about anything except the subjects he enjoys—French words commonly used in the English language and Alfred Hitchcock movies. When Thomas began elementary school, he was enrolled in a special education class for students with autism. However, most of his classmates had significant intellectual disabilities, and the teacher and Thomas's parents quickly realized that he needed to be challenged academically in a way that could not happen in that class. Since second grade, he has spent most of his time in general education classrooms. In some situations, a special education teacher worked in his classroom with the general education teacher, or a paraprofessional was present to assist the teacher and all the students. Now such support generally is not necessary. Thomas meets with his special education teacher, Ms. Meyer, once each day with several other students who have learning and behavior disabilities to learn strategies related to their schoolwork, and he receives social skills instruction from a counselor. If an issue arises in a general education class, Ms. Meyer problem solves with the teacher to address it. Thomas would like to be a linguist when he grows up.

What is autism? Why is it so important for Thomas to access the same curriculum as his peers? What provisions in current laws ensure that Thomas has the right to be educated in general education as much as possible?

PATRICIA is a fourth-grade student who was identified as having an intellectual disability (sometimes called mental retardation) when she was in the first grade. The cause of her disability cannot be pinpointed nor does it have a specific name, but there is a high likelihood that it was at least partly the result of her mother's drinking and drug use during pregnancy. Patricia already has lived in six foster homes because her mother was unable to take care of her and gave up custody. Happily, her current foster family has decided to adopt Patricia, a time-consuming process that should be completed before the end of this school year. In school, Patricia receives highly specialized instruction in language arts

and math in a special education resource class, but she is a member of a general education class for science and social studies as well as for art, music, library/media, physical education, and technology skills classes. Spending time in both special education and general education settings was determined by a team to be the best option for Patricia, but Ms. Schwarz, her general education teacher, worries that the other students do not have enough interactions with Patricia to really get to know and value her and that Patricia's learning is actually made more difficult because she comes and goes from the classroom. Ms. Schwarz favors reducing the amount of time Patricia spends in the special education classroom. Ms. Ramos, the special educator, agrees; this topic will be addressed at a meeting to be held soon.

How likely are you to teach a student like Patricia? What is an intellectual disability? What factors have led teachers to advocate for educating students like Patricia in typical classrooms for all or much of the school day instead of in special education classrooms?

AARON has a learning disability that was identified when he was in second grade. He also takes medication for attention deficit–hyperactivity disorder (ADHD). Now in eleventh grade, Aaron is continuing to learn how to compensate for the academic difficulties he experiences. Although he is a bright and personable young man, he reads at about a seventh-grade level, and his writing is much like that of a student in second grade. He doesn't like to talk about his learning disabilities (LD); he doesn't want other students to make fun of him or treat him differently because he has LD. He is even more sensitive when asked to talk about why he takes medication. Even though his doctor has cautioned him to take the medication exactly as prescribed, he sometimes secretly skips taking it to see if he can get along without it. In his U.S. history class, Aaron is most successful on tests when he answers questions orally; he understands the concepts even if he sometimes cannot write down his thoughts. Because he doesn't like to be singled out, however, he sometimes refuses to take tests or get additional assistance during study period, so his grades are lower than they could be. Aaron is an excellent athlete, and on the basketball court, he feels equal to his friends. However, his parents are concerned that his interest in sports is distracting him from schoolwork.

How often will you meet students like Aaron? What is a learning disability? What types of supports and services do Aaron and other students with LD need to succeed in school?

Students like Thomas, Patricia, and Aaron are not unusual. They are among the 6.1 million school-age students in the United States who have disabilities that make them eligible for special education (U.S. Department of Education, 2009). But their disabilities do not tell you who they are: They are children or young adults and students first. Like all students, they have positive characteristics and negative ones, they have great days and not-so-great days, and they have likes and dislikes about school and learning. As a teacher, you probably will instruct students like Thomas, Patricia, and Aaron along with other students with disabilities or other special needs.

The purpose of this book is to help you understand these students and learn strategies for addressing their needs. Ultimately, you can be the teacher who makes a profound positive difference in a student's life. With the knowledge and skills you learn for teaching learners with exceptional needs, you will be prepared for both the challenges and the rewards of helping them achieve their potential.

What Key Concepts Guide Special Education?

As you begin your study of special education and think about your responsibility for teaching students like Thomas, Patricia, and Aaron, it is important that you understand that the field is guided by a number of critical concepts, some based directly on federal laws and the courts' interpretation of those laws and some based on a combination of research and recommended practices. What these key concepts illustrate clearly is the centrality of your role in the education of students with disabilities.

Special Education Services

When teachers refer to students with *disabilities*, they mean students who are eligible to receive special education services according to federal and state guidelines. **Special education** is the **specially designed instruction** provided by the school district or other local education agency that meets the unique needs of students identified as disabled according to federal and state eligibility criteria. Special education is a set of services that may include instruction in a general education or special education classroom, education in the community for students who need to learn life and work skills, and specialized assistance in areas such as physical education and vocational preparation.

Students with disabilities also may receive **related services,** that is, assistance required to enable students to benefit from special education. Examples of related services include speech/language therapy, transportation to and from school in a specialized van or school bus, and physical therapy. Additionally, students with disabilities are entitled to **supplementary aids and services.** This means they must receive, as needed, supports such as preferential seating, access to computer technology, and instructional adjustments (for example, more time to complete tests, simplified assignments) that enable them to be educated with their peers who do not have disabilities. All special education, related services, and supplementary aids and services are provided to students by public schools at no cost to parents.

You may encounter one additional set of terms relates to students' services. Students with disabilities are entitled to receive accommodations and modifications related to their instruction. **Accommodations** are changes in *how* the student learns key curriculum. For example, a student may be assigned fewer math problems because he takes longer than other students to complete each one. Another student may respond to an essay question on a history test by writing bullet points instead of paragraphs, because it reduces the writing task and the goal is to determine what she has learned about history. In each case, the curriculum has remained the same. **Modifications** refer to *what* the student learns and usually implies that some curriculum is removed. For example, a student with a significant intellectual disability may not learn all the vocabulary in a science unit, focusing instead on words that he is likely to encounter in day-to-day life. As you might surmise, many students with disabilities need accommodations, but only those with significant intellectual disabilities usually require modifications.

Least Restrictive Environment

As you read this textbook and complete the activities designed for your course, you will learn many important facts and skills related to working with students with disabilities. However, one of the most important concepts for you to understand as a general educator is **least restrictive environment (LRE),** a provision in the federal law that has governed special education for nearly four decades. The LRE provision guarantees a student's right to be educated in the setting most like that for peers without disabilities in which the student can be successful with appropriate supports provided (Palley, 2006). For most students, the least restrictive environment is full-time or nearly full-time participation in a general education classroom (Schwarz, 2007). In fact, in 2004–2005, approximately 51.9 percent of all school-age students with disabilities received 79 percent or more of their education in general education classrooms (U.S. Department of Education, 2009). This is true for Thomas, Patricia, and Aaron, who were introduced at the beginning of this chapter. Thomas and Patricia also receive instruction in a special education classroom each day. Aaron, who can succeed in social studies class when he gives test answers aloud, may leave his classroom for that purpose only. His LRE is a general education classroom; the test procedure is a supplementary service.

For some students—for example, some who have emotional or behavioral disabilities or autism—being in a general education classroom nearly all day may be academically and emotionally inappropriate. For these students, the LRE may be a general education classroom for part of the day and a special education classroom, sometimes called a *resource room,* for the remainder of the day. Yet other students' LRE may be a special education setting for most of the day, sometimes referred to as a *self-contained class.* Students with significant behavior problems and students who require intensive supports may be educated in this way. Finally, just a few students with disabilities attend separate or residential schools or learn in a home or hospital setting. These very restrictive options usually are necessary only for students with the most significant or complex disabilities.

Identifying an LRE other than a general education setting is a serious decision that usually is made by a team of professionals and a student's parents only after

In inclusive schools, all students are welcomed members of their learning communities.

intensive supports have been provided in the general education classroom without success. These supports can include alternative materials or curriculum, assistance from a paraprofessional (that is, a teaching assistant) or a special education teacher, adaptive equipment such as a computer, or consultative assistance from a psychologist or counselor. However, a few students' needs are so great that a setting outside general education is the only one considered. Chapter 2 presents more detail about the range of LRE settings considered for students with disabilities. Here, the points to remember are these: The LRE for most students with disabilities is general education, and you, as a professional educator, have a crucial role to play in these students' education.

Inclusive Practices

Over the past two decades, the entire structure of special education services has undergone significant change (Fuchs, Fuchs, & Stecker, 2010). Although federal law continues to stipulate that a range of settings must be made available to meet the needs of students with disabilities, many professionals now seriously question the assumption that students who need more intensive services should routinely receive them in a restrictive setting such as a special education classroom. The concept of inclusive practices, while not directly addressed in federal special education law, implies that students are more alike than different and that all students are welcomed members of their learning communities (for example, Connor & Ferri, 2007; Downing & Eichinger, 2003; Fitch, 2003; Valle & Conner, 2011). In the past, many students with disabilities were only temporary guests in general education classrooms, and few efforts were made to provide assistance so they could be successfully educated with their nondisabled peers (for example, Artiles, Harris-Murri, & Rostenberg, 2006).

Many educators now find that all or most supports for students with disabilities can be provided effectively in general education classrooms when teachers are prepared to work with such students and related concerns are addressed (Dukes & Lamar-Dukes, 2009; McLeskey & Waldron, 2007a). They further maintain that if students cannot meet traditional academic expectations, the expectations should be changed, not the setting. These educators reject the assumption that the setting dictates the type and intensity of services, and they support instead inclusive practices (Roach & Salisbury, 2006).

The concept of **inclusive practices** is founded on the belief or philosophy that students with disabilities should be fully integrated into their school learning communities, usually in general education classrooms, and that their instruction should be based on their abilities, not their disabilities. Inclusive practices have three dimensions:

1. *Physical integration:* Placing students in the same classroom as nondisabled peers should be a strong priority, and removing them from that setting should be done only when absolutely necessary.
2. *Social integration:* Relationships should be nurtured between students with disabilities and their classmates and peers as well as adults.
3. *Instructional integration:* Most students should be taught in the same curriculum used for students without disabilities and helped to succeed by adjusting how teaching and learning are designed (that is, with accommodations) and measured. For some students with significant intellectual disabilities, instructional integration means anchoring instruction in the standard general curriculum but appropriately adjusting expectations (that is, making modifications).

Ultimately, the concept of inclusive practices as used in this book means that all learners are welcomed full members at their schools and in their classrooms and that they are seen as the responsibility of all educators (Frattura & Capper, 2006; Skilton-Sylvester & Slesaransky-Poe, 2009). It further implies that educators' strong preference is for these students to be educated with their peers without disabilities.

We also would like to note that we prefer the phrase *inclusive practices* to the term *inclusion* because the latter can imply that there is a single model or program that can serve all students' needs, while the former more accurately conveys that inclusiveness is made up of many strategies and options. Later in this chapter, we address in more detail how inclusive practices increasingly form the basis for contemporary education practices.

One more term should be mentioned in this discussion of how students with disabilities receive services. When the LRE concept became part of special education laws during the 1970s, the LRE for most students with disabilities was a part-time or full-time special education class. When such students were permitted to participate in general education, it was called mainstreaming. **Mainstreaming** involves placing students with disabilities in general education settings only when they can meet traditional academic expectations with minimal assistance or when those expectations are not relevant (for example, participation only in recess or school assemblies for access to social interactions with peers). In most locales, *mainstreaming* now is considered a dated term and has been replaced with the phrase *inclusion* or *inclusive practices*. However, as you participate in field experiences and speak to experienced educators, you may find that in some schools, the vocabulary of inclusion is used, but the practices implemented seem more like mainstreaming. That is, teachers may say that their school is inclusive but then explain that students like Aaron, featured in the beginning of the chapter, need to be in separate classes because of their below-grade reading levels. This practice is actually mainstreaming.

Finally, you also may find that teachers in your locale use words such as *LRE*, *mainstreaming*, and *inclusion* interchangeably, or they might have yet different terms to describe special education services. They may refer to *integrated classes* or *collaborative classes* when describing the general education classes in which students with disabilities participate. To assist you with the vocabulary of special education programs and instructional approaches, a glossary is provided at the back of this textbook. Keep in mind, though, that knowing the terms used in special education is not nearly as important as learning about your students, developing skills for addressing their needs, and celebrating your role in enabling them to achieve success.

How Did Today's Special Education Services Come to Exist?

Special education as it exists today has been influenced by a number of different factors. Although people with disabilities have been identified and treated for centuries, special education grew rapidly only in the twentieth century (Kode, 2002; Winzer, 1993). As special education has evolved, it has been shaped by federal law, the civil rights movement and related court cases, and changing social and political beliefs. Figure 1.1 illustrates some factors that have influenced the evolution of special education.

The Development of Education for Students with Disabilities

When compulsory public education began near the turn of the twentieth century, almost no school programs existed for students with disabilities (Kode, 2002; Scheerenberger, 1983). Students with disabilities that were relatively mild—that is, learning or behavior problems or minor physical impairments—were educated along with other students because their needs were not considered extraordinary. Many children with significant intellectual or physical disabilities did not attend school at all, and others were educated by private agencies or lived in institutions. In fact, for the first half of the twentieth century, many states explicitly legislated permission for school districts to prohibit some students with disabilities from attending (Yell, Rogers, & Rogers, 1998).

However, as compulsory education became widespread during the 1920s and 1930s, the number of special classes in public schools grew. Schools were expected

The Council for Exceptional Children (CEC), founded in 1922 by Elizabeth Farrell, is a professional organization for teachers, administrators, parents, and other advocates for the rights of students with disabilities (http://www.cec.sped.org).

www.resources

http://idea.ed.gov/explore/view/p/%2Croot%2Cdynamic%2CVideoClips%2C
At Building the Legacy: IDEA 2004 you can learn more detail about the requirements of federal special education law through a series of brief video clips.

FIGURE 1.1 **Influences on Current Special Education Practices**

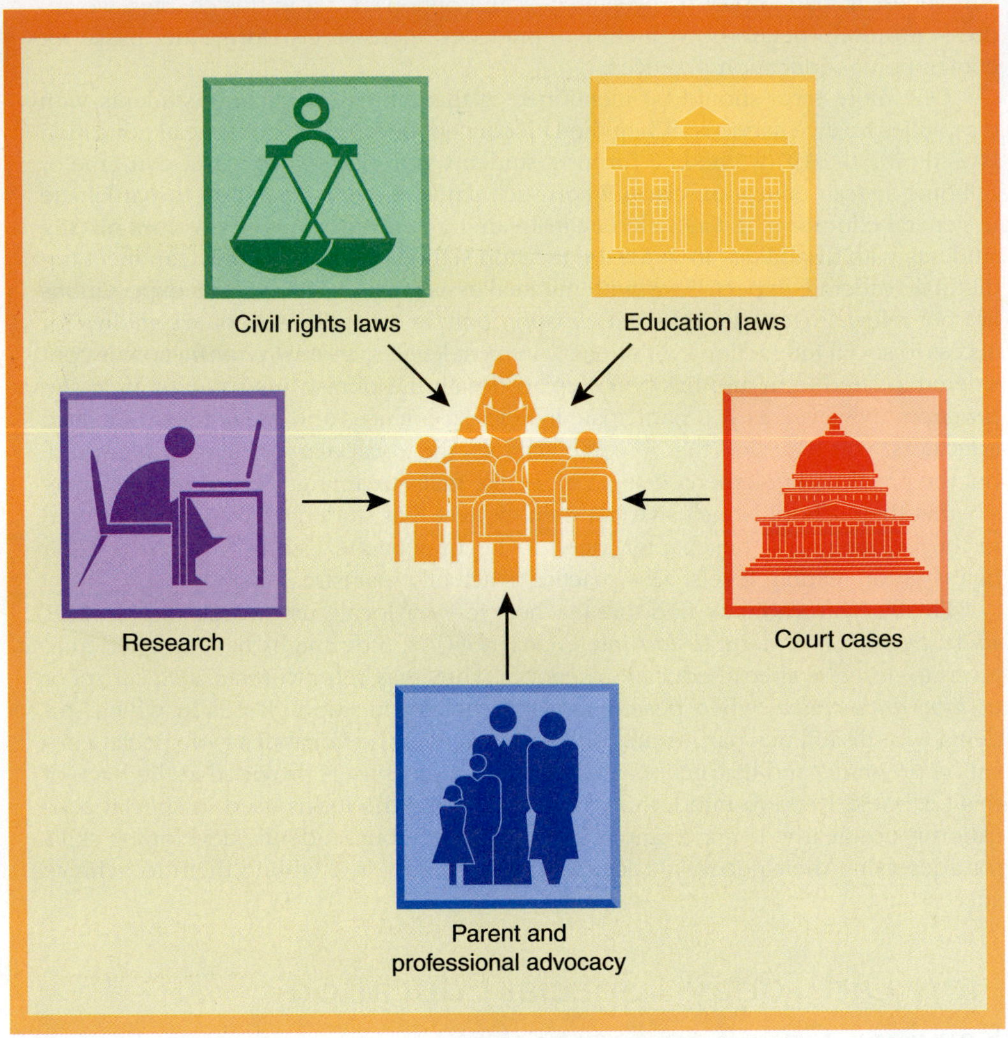

Civil rights laws

Education laws

Research

Court cases

Parent and
professional advocacy

to be like efficient assembly lines, with each class of students moving from grade to grade and eventually graduating from high school as productive citizens prepared to enter the workforce (Patton, Payne, & Beirne-Smith, 1986; Scheerenberger, 1983). Special classes were developed as a place for students who could not keep up with their classmates. Because many students with disabilities still were not in school, most of the students sent to special classes probably had mild or moderate learning or intellectual disabilities. Educators at the time believed that such students would learn better in a protected setting and that the efficiency of the overall educational system would be preserved (Bennett, 1932; Pertsch, 1936).

By the 1950s, special education programs were available in many school districts, but some undesirable outcomes were becoming apparent. For example, students in special classes often were considered incapable of learning academic skills. They spent their school time practicing what were called "manual skills" such as weaving and bead stringing. Researchers began questioning this practice and conducted studies to explore the efficacy of special education. When they compared students with disabilities who were in special education classes to similar students who had remained in general education, they found the latter group often had learned more than the former (Blatt, 1958; Goldstein, Moss, & Jordan, 1965). Parents at this time also became active advocates for better educational opportunities for their children (Blatt, 1987). By the late 1960s, many authorities in the field agreed

dimensions of
DIVERSITY

As you prepare to be an educator, you will learn about the importance of developing *cultural competence*. Doing so involves valuing diversity, assessing your own views of diversity, being aware of the dynamics of intercultural interactions, developing cultural knowledge, and adjusting your teaching and other professional activities based on that knowledge (King, Sims, & Osher, 2007).

that segregated special classes were not the most appropriate educational setting for many students with disabilities (Blatt, 1958; Christopolos & Renz, 1969; Dunn, 1968; Hobbs, 1975; Lilly, 1971).

The Impact of the Civil Rights Movement on Special Education

During the 1950s and 1960s, another force began contributing to the development of new approaches for special education. The civil rights movement, although initially focused on the rights of African Americans, expanded and began to influence thinking about people with disabilities (Chaffin, 1975; Fleischer & Zames, 2001). In the ***Brown v. Board of Education*** decision in 1954, the U.S. Supreme Court ruled that it was unlawful under the Fourteenth Amendment to discriminate arbitrarily against any group of people. The Court then applied this concept to the education of children, ruling that the state-mandated separate education for African American students could not be an equal education. This court decision introduced the concept of *integration* into public education, the notion that the only way to protect students' constitutional right to equal opportunity was to ensure that diverse student groups learned together. Soon people with disabilities were recognized as another group whose rights often had been violated because of arbitrary discrimination. For children, the discrimination occurred when they were denied access to schools because of their disabilities. Beginning in the late 1960s and continuing through today, parents and others have used the court system to ensure that the civil and educational rights of children with disabilities are preserved (Blanchett, Brantlinger, & Shealey, 2005; Rueda, Klingner, Sager, & Velasco, 2008). Figure 1.2 summarizes several influential court cases that have helped shape special education concepts and services.

The civil rights movements of the 1950s and 1960s strongly contributed to the recognition of the rights of individuals with disabilities.

Section 504   One of the outcomes of the civil rights movement was legislation designed to prevent discrimination against individuals with disabilities, whether children in schools or adults in the workforce. **Section 504** of the Vocational Rehabilitation Act of 1973 is a civil rights law that prevents discrimination against all individuals with disabilities in programs that receive federal funds, as do all public schools. For children of school age, Section 504 ensures equal opportunity for participation in the full range of school activities (Walker, 2006; Zirkel, 2009a). Through Section 504, some students not eligible for services through special education may be entitled to receive specific types of assistance to help them succeed in school.

For example, Sondra is a student with a severe attention problem. She cannot follow a lesson for more than a few minutes at a time; she is distracted by every noise in the hallway and every car that goes by her classroom window. Her teacher describes her as a student who "acts first and thinks later." Sondra does not have a disability as established in special education law, but she does need extra assistance and is considered disabled according to Section 504 because her significant attention problem negatively affects her ability to function in school. The professionals at her school are required to create and carry out a plan to help Sondra access education. Special education teachers may assist because they know techniques that will help Sondra, but Sondra does not receive special education services, and responsibility for the plan lies with the principal and teachers. Some of the other students who might receive assistance through Section 504 include those with health problems such as asthma and extreme allergies and those with physical disabilities who do not need special education (Zirkel, 2009b). More detail on Section 504 is presented in Chapter 8.

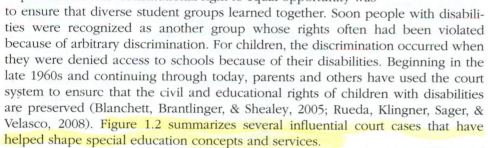

RESEARCH NOTE

In a qualitative study, Lindstrom, Doren, Metheny, Johnson, and Zane (2007) found that positive family relationships, involvement, advocacy, career aspirations, and career-related activities led to better employment for young adults with learning disabilities.

FIGURE 1.2   Court Cases Affecting Special Education

Since 1954, hundreds of legal decisions have clarified the rights of students with disabilities and the responsibilities of schools for educating them. The following cases have had a significant impact on special education.

Brown v. Board of Education (347 U.S. 483) (1954)

- U.S. Supreme Court case
- School segregation denies students equal educational opportunity
- Although referring primarily to racial segregation, this decision has since become the cornerstone for ensuring equal rights for students with disabilities

Pennsylvania Association for Retarded Children v. Commonwealth of Pennsylvania (343 F. Supp. 279) (1972)

- U.S. District Court of the Eastern District of Pennsylvania decision
- Schools may not refuse to educate students with mental retardation
- A free public education must be provided to *all* students

Larry P. v. Wilson Riles (793 F.2d 969) (1986)

- U.S. District Court for the Northern District of California decision
- Intelligence (IQ) tests cannot be used to determine whether African-American students have mental retardation because of the tests' racial and cultural bias
- In 1986, the ruling was expanded to include IQ testing of these students for any disability

Board of Education of Hendrick School District v. Rowley (632 F. 2d 945) (1982)

- U.S. Supreme Court decision
- Special education services must provide an appropriate education; the law does not require optimum services
- Parent request for an interpreter for their daughter with a hearing loss, who was achieving at an average level, was denied

Daniel R. R. v. State Board of Education (874 F.2d 1036) (1989)

- U.S. Court of Appeals for the Fifth Circuit decision
- Appropriate placement for students with disabilities depends on whether (1) a student can be satisfactorily educated in the general education setting with supplementary supports provided and (2) the student is mainstreamed to the maximum extent appropriate in cases in which the general education setting is not successful
- For Daniel, a student with Down syndrome, the school district did not violate his rights when he was moved from general education after an unsuccessful attempt to include him

Oberti v. Board of Education of Clementon School District (995 F.2d 204) (1993)

- U.S. Court of Appeals for the Third Circuit decision
- School districts must make available a full range of supports and services in the general education setting to accommodate students with disabilities, including the student with Down syndrome involved in the suit
- Just because a student learns differently from other students does not necessarily warrant that student's exclusion from general education

Doe v. Withers (20 IDELR 422, 426–427) (1993)

- West Virginia Circuit Court decision
- Michael Withers, a high school history teacher, refused to make oral testing accommodations needed by Douglas Doe, a student with learning disabilities, resulting in a failing grade and athletic ineligibility
- The family was awarded $5,000 in compensatory damages and $30,000 in punitive damages, illustrating general education teachers' very real responsibility to make a good faith effort to provide required accommodations for students with disabilities

Schaffer v. Weast (126 S. Ct. 528) (2005)

- U.S. Supreme Court decision
- The burden of proof in any disagreement about a student's individualized education plan lies with the party bringing suit—in this case, the Schaffer family
- Until this case, it typically had been assumed that a school district had to prove that its position in a suit was correct, even if the district had not filed the suit

Winkelman v. Parma City School District (2007 U.S. LEXIS 5902; 75 U.S.L.W. 4329) (2007)

- U.S. Supreme Court decision
- Parents of children with disabilities (in this case, the Winkelmans) have rights through IDEA and thus are entitled to represent themselves (and hence their children) in court
- Parents are not obligated to hire an attorney to represent them in court

Sources: Adapted from "Reflections on the 25th Anniversary of the Individuals with Disabilities Education Act," by A. Katisyannis, M. L. Yell, and R. Bradley, 2001, *Remedial and Special Education, 22,* pp. 324–334; "Medical Services: The Disrupted Related Service," by L. Bartlett, 2000, *Journal of Special Education, 33,* pp. 215–223; *Legal Issues in Special Educations,* by A. G. Osborne, 1996, Boston: Allyn & Bacon; "Adequate Access or Equal Treatment: Looking beyond the IDEA to Section 504 in a Post-Schaffer Public School," by C. J. Walker, 2006, *Stanford Law Review, 58,* pp. 1563–1622; and *Winkelman v. Parma City School District,* 2007, U.S. LEXIS 5902, 75 U.S.L.W. 4329.

Americans with Disabilities Act   In July 1990, President George H. W. Bush signed into law the **Americans with Disabilities Act (ADA).** This civil rights law was based on the Rehabilitation Act of 1973, but it further extended the rights of individuals with disabilities. This law, amended and updated through the **Americans with Disabilities Act Amendments** (ADAA) in 2008, is the most significant disability legislation ever passed (National Council on Disability, 2006; Zirkel, 2009b). It protects all individuals with disabilities from discrimination, and it requires most employers to make reasonable accommodations for them. Although ADA does not deal directly with the education of students with disabilities, it does clarify the civil rights of all individuals with disabilities and thus has an impact on special education. This law also ensures that transportation, buildings, the workplace, and many places open to the public are accessible to people with disabilities. If you are a teacher with a disability, you might be influenced by ADA in the same way that it affects you in other situations. For example, if your school is not accessible to wheelchairs and undergoes renovation, then ramps, elevators, and wide entries with automatic doors probably will have to be installed. If you have a disability, this law also protects you from discrimination when you look for a teaching position.

The Legislative Basis for Contemporary Special Education

Influenced by researchers' growing doubts about the effectiveness of special education classes and by civil rights court cases, many states by the early 1970s had begun to address special education issues by passing laws to guarantee that students with disabilities would receive an appropriate education. Federal law soon mirrored this trend and continues to do so today (Valle & Conner, 2011). You can review the original core principles of and key subsequent additions to federal special education law in Figure 1.3.

The First Federal Special Education Legislation   In 1975, Congress passed **Public Law (P.L.) 94-142,** the Education for All Handicapped Children Act (EHCA), thereby setting federal guidelines for special education and laying the foundation on which current special education practice rests. It took into account many of the early court decisions that established the civil rights of students with disabilities, and it mandated the concept of least restrictive environment (LRE). This law also specifically described categories of disabilities that make students eligible to receive special education and clarified the related services to which students might be entitled. In addition, it established procedures for identifying a student as needing special education and outlined the rights of parents who disapprove of the educational services offered to their children.

Revisions and Refinements to Special Education Legislation   Since 1975, P.L. 94-142 has been reauthorized several times. As each reconsideration of the law has occurred, its core principles have been upheld. At the same time, the law has been extended and its provisions clarified. For example, in 1990 the name of the law was changed to the Individuals with Disabilities Education Act (IDEA) to reflect more contemporary person-first language. In addition, the term *handicapped* was removed from the law and the preferred term *disability* was substituted. This law also added significantly to the provisions for children from birth to age 5 with disabilities who had first been included in the law in 1986. It also bolstered provisions for supporting students with disabilities preparing to transition from school to work, postsecondary education, and other postschool options. One other important 1990 change in this law was the addition of two new categories of disability: autism and traumatic brain injury (TBI).

    IDEA was revised again in 1997. Perhaps most important for general education teachers, this law recognized that most students with disabilities spend all or

dimensions of DIVERSITY

Guiberson (2009) found that Hispanic students are underrepresented in certain disability categories (e.g., intellectual and emotional/behavioral disabilities) and overrepresented in others (learning disability and speech-language impairment).

FIGURE 1.3 Provisions of the Individuals with Disabilities Education Improvement Act (IDEA)

Core Principles

- *Free appropriate public education (FAPE).* Students with disabilities are entitled to attend public schools and receive the educational services they need. This education is provided at no cost to parents.

- *Least restrictive environment (LRE).* Students with disabilities must be educated in the least restrictive environment in which they can succeed with appropriate supports provided. For most students, this environment is the general education classroom.

- *Individualized education.* The instructional services and other assistance for a student with disabilities must be tailored to meet his needs according to a prepared individualized education program (IEP) that is reviewed and updated annually. IEPs are discussed in detail in Chapter 2.

- *Nondiscriminatory evaluation.* Students must be assessed using instruments that do not discriminate on the basis of race, culture, or disability. In considering eligibility for special education services, a student must be assessed by a multidisciplinary team in her native language using tests that are relevant to the area of concern. Eligibility cannot be decided on the basis of only one test.

- *Due process.* If a disagreement occurs concerning a student's eligibility for special education placement or services, whether raised by parents or the school district, no changes can be made until the issue has been resolved by an impartial hearing and, if necessary, the appropriate court, a procedure referred to as *due process.*

- *Zero reject–child find.* No student may be excluded from public education because of a disability. Further, each state must take action to locate children who may be entitled to special education services.

Additional Major Provisions

- *Transition services.* Transition services that prepare students for leaving school (for higher education, vocational training, or a job) must be addressed in IEPs for students beginning at age 16. Transition plans must include strategies to improve academic and functional achievement to foster student success and must be based on student strengths. These plans must be updated annually and be written to include measurable goals for the postsecondary years.

- *General education teacher roles and responsibilities.* At least one general education teacher must participate as a member of the team that writes a student's IEP, unless school professionals and parents agree for some reason that this would not be beneficial to the student. In addition, the IEP must directly address student participation in general education and justify any placement that is not in general education.

- *Highly qualified special education teachers.* Special education teachers who teach core academic subjects must obtain two types of credentials. First, they must have a special education teaching credential. In addition, in secondary schools, unless special education teachers work only with students with significant intellectual disabilities, they must be documented as being highly qualified in every core subject area in which they teach. However, in most states, if they work in general education classrooms, ensuring that students with disabilities receive their needed supports there, they are not obligated to have the highly qualified status in those core academic areas. Elementary special educators usually are considered highly qualified to teach core subject areas at that level.

- *Parent participation.* Parents must be part of the decision-making team for determining eligibility for special education services as well as for determining the appropriate educational placement for their children. Furthermore, schools must report to parents on the progress of their children with disabilities at least as often as they report progress for students without disabilities.

- *Evaluation and eligibility.* School districts generally have 60 days from the time a parent agrees that the child can be evaluated until a decision must be reached about the child's eligibility for special education. Students are not eligible for special education simply because of poor math or reading instruction or because of language differences. For some students, the requirement that a complete reassessment be completed every three years can be modified. That is, for older students already existing information can be used in lieu of repeatedly administering standardized tests.

- *Disproportionate representation.* School districts must take specific steps to ensure that students from minority groups are not overidentified as being eligible for special education services. If disproportionate representation exists, districts must take steps to correct this problem.

- *Assessment of students.* States are required to measure the academic progress of students who have disabilities, either by including them in the standardized assessments other students take or, for students with significant intellectual disabilities, by using an alternate assessment process. Students are entitled to appropriate accommodations during assessment (for example, extended time, large-print materials).

- *Discipline.* As needed, strategies for addressing a student's behavior must be included as part of the IEP. If a student is suspended or placed in an alternative interim placement, a behavior plan must be developed. In some cases (for example, when students bring weapons or drugs to school), schools may place students with disabilities in alternative interim placements for up to 45 days, pending a meeting to determine the next steps. Students must continue to receive special education services during this time.

- *Paraprofessionals.* Paraprofessionals, teaching assistants, and other similar personnel must be trained for their jobs and appropriately supervised.

- *Procedural safeguards.* States must make mediation available to parents as an early and informal strategy for resolving disagreements about the identification of, placement of, or provision of services for students with disabilities. Parents are not obligated to mediate, and mediation may not delay a possible hearing. Unless waived with parent approval, the school district also must convene a dispute resolution session prior to a formal hearing regarding disagreements related to special education.

most of their school time in general education settings, and so it included a provision that the general education teacher usually should be a member of the team that writes the student's educational plan. Another important change occurred regarding assessment. Acknowledging that students with disabilities often were excluded from local and state assessments, the law added a requirement that students with disabilities be assessed like other students, using either the same assessment instrument employed with typical learners or some type of alternative instrument.

Current Special Education Legislation   The most recent reauthorization of IDEA, signed into law in 2004 and sometimes called the **Individuals with Disabilities Education Improvement Act,** mandated yet further refinements in special education. For example, this legislation streamlined some procedures and paperwork, and it also specified that all students with disabilities must participate in all assessment conducted by local school districts with needed supports provided (Hyatt, 2007). The law also established that special education teachers must be **highly qualified** if they teach core academic content to students with disabilities. Yet another provision is this: IDEA now permits school districts to use some of the funds allotted to special education to design strategies for prevention. That is, by providing intensive teaching, behavior interventions, and other supports, it may be possible to prevent some students from needing special education at all.

The element of the current reauthorization of IDEA that may have the most direct impact on general education teachers is called response to intervention (RtI). RtI is a new and alternative way for students to be identified as having a learning disability. Rather than relying just on test scores, RtI permits states to decide to base that decision on whether or not increasingly intensive interventions implemented to address the student's academic problems have a positive impact on learning (Zirkel & Thomas, 2010). If they do, no disability exists. If little or no improvement occurs after research-based strategies and programs are carefully used more frequently and for longer periods of time, the student may be found to have a learning disability. Since its initial development, RtI also has been applied to student behavior problems. The principles on which RtI was developed are outlined in the Instructional Edge, and you will learn more about this concept in Chapter 2 and the rest of this text. For now what is essential for you to remember is that RtI is implemented by general education teachers, reading specialists, and others; it is not a special education service. This means that it is likely you will have a role in an RtI process, and this is so whether you plan a career in elementary, middle, or high school.

www.resources

http://www.rti4success.org/
The National Center on Response to Intervention provides a straight-forward explanation of RtI, training modules and other resources, and a free monthly newsletter.

Elementary and Secondary Education Act of 1965 (ESEA)   Most recently reauthorized in 2002 and sometimes referred to as the **No Child Left Behind Act** (NCLB), it is the law that has the goal of ensuring that all students, including those who live in poverty, have equal access to a high quality education. Although the law directly addresses only schools whose students live in poverty, it generally mandates higher academic standards and increased accountability for all students, including those with disabilities. These are some of the law's key provisions:

- All students must be assessed to determine their academic progress. Nearly all students with disabilities take the same annual standardized assessments as their peers without disabilities; a few students, those with significant intellectual disabilities, take alternate tests designed to measure their learning.
- Each state must make adequate yearly progress (AYP) toward the goal of achievement at grade level for all students by 2014, and the scores of students with disabilities and other special needs (for example, those who live in poverty, those whose native language is not English) are part of this calculation.

INSTRUCTIONAL **EDGE**

Understanding Response to Intervention (RtI)

Response to intervention (RtI), part of IDEA, has rapidly become central to most schools' efforts to reach struggling learners. General education teachers, literacy and math specialists, administrators, and many other professionals have responsibility for implementing RtI, which is based on these core principles:

- An unwavering belief that all students can learn
- A focus on prevention in the academic, behavioral, and social domains
- Universal screening, that is, checking the academic, behavior, and social functioning of all students to determine which students are at-risk for failure so that interventions can be implemented
- A collaborative problem-solving approach to identifying and effectively addressing student learning, behavior, and social problems, one that includes professionals and parents/families

- Emphasis on implementing interventions with consistency (sometimes called fidelity of implementation)
- Decision making based on student data (rather than impressions or perceptions)
- Evidence-based practices, that is, academic, behavioral, and other supports implemented are only those demonstrated through research to be effective
- Continuous monitoring of student progress during interventions to determine in a timely manner whether those interventions are effective
- Multiple tiers of intervention; that is, increasingly intensive interventions matched to student needs implemented if evidence demonstrates those already in place are not reducing gaps
- If multiple tiers of intervention are not successful, referral for additional assessment and possibly special education services

www.resources

http://www.nichcy.org/Pages/Home.aspx
The National Dissemination Center for Children with Disabilities provides extensive information on disabilities and disability-related issues for families, teachers, and others. The website includes fact sheets and research briefs on specific disabilities as well as special education law. Most pages are available in Spanish as well as English.

At the school level, this means that if students with disabilities are not improving enough in terms of achievement, the school is identified as failing to make AYP, and sanctions may be applied.

- Assessments must include reporting individual student scores (not just aggregated scores) so that parents can be informed of their children's achievement.
- All students must be taught core academic subjects by teachers who are highly qualified in the content areas. This provision has helped to ensure that students with disabilities, especially those in middle school and high school, have more access to general education settings and teachers who generally have more extensive knowledge about the core academic subjects than do some special education teachers. This component of NCLB further strengthens the least restrictive environment provision of IDEA.
- Teaching practices and instructional programs, particularly those in reading and math, must be based on rigorous research. That is, they should have a strong basis in studies that demonstrate their positive impact on student learning. Consistent with this provision of the law, you will find as you read this textbook that the strategies presented for improving student achievement are grounded in such research.

Special education has evolved on the basis of many factors. When special education began, essentially no services were offered in public schools. Today comprehensive services in a wide variety of settings are supplied, and both very young children and young adults, as well as students in elementary and secondary schools, benefit from them. As the rights and needs of students with disabilities have been better understood and federal legislation has set higher standards for their education, general education teachers—in traditional core academic areas as well as in the essential related areas such as art, music, and physical education—have become increasingly involved in their education, a trend that surely will continue.

What Factors Influence Inclusive Practices in Today's Schools?

Now that you have learned about the key concepts that guide special education, the development of the field, and the litigation and legislation that have shaped special education services, it is important to return one more time to the topic of inclusion. The purpose of the following discussion is to draw your attention to the complexity of inclusive practices by briefly exploring several factors that have a significant influence on their implementation, including current and likely future legislation and policies; understanding of the concept of inclusive practices; the impact on stakeholders—students, parents, and educators; and resource limits that affect essential matters such as scheduling and staffing.

Legislation and Related Policies

Although the term *inclusion* does not appear in federal laws governing special education, provisions in those laws as well as other education and civil rights legislation you have read about in this chapter provide a strong foundation for inclusive practices (McLaughlin, 2010). This foundation is unlikely to be abandoned as new laws are enacted. For example, IDEA requires that students be educated in the least restrictive environment, and ESEA mandates access to the curriculum for all students. Together, these provisions have led state and local policymakers to stress inclusive practices. Similar comments could be made related to provisions such as the requirement for all students to participate in assessments and to make adequate yearly progress (AYP) and those related to teachers being highly qualified in core content areas. A useful activity is to scan back through all the information presented thus far to identify additional legislative provisions that probably have led to more inclusive practices in schools. This trend is not likely to vanish. Educational reformers maintain their commitment to holding all students, including those with disabilities, to high standards so that they leave school well-prepared for college or a vocation (U.S. Department of Education, 2010).

Not all the legislative influences are positive, however. For example, the requirements of ESEA have resulted in tremendous pressure for all students to reach achievement goals. In some schools, teachers fear that having students with disabilities in their classes may lower their average class scores. Others note that proposals to link teacher pay to the performance of their students may result in teachers resisting instructing students with disabilities out of concern they may miss out on bonuses and other financial incentives (Gratz, 2009). Concerns such as these should not be the basis for decisions about students' education, but they reflect the rather complicated situation that exists in schools today.

Understanding of Inclusive Practices

Although it is a bit surprising after so many years of discussion, a second influence on inclusive practices concerns its definition. Too often, research on inclusive practices and essays on their relative merits and drawbacks focus almost exclusively on where students are seated, that is, the amount of time they spend in general education classrooms (Friend & Shamberger, 2008; Idol, 2006). As a result, some professionals argue that students with disabilities sometimes need a small group, highly structured environment that is difficult to create in

General education teachers are accountable for the education of all the students in their classrooms, including those with disabilities.

PROFESSIONAL **EDGE**

Characteristics of Inclusive Schools

As you learn about your responsibilities as a teacher for students with disabilities, this list of characteristics can help you understand in a real-world way what an inclusive school is like.

- Every person who works in the school is committed to the goal of helping all students achieve their potential; inclusiveness is a school-level belief system.
- The principal is a strong and vocal advocate for all students, adamant that they access the general curriculum with a system of supports around them.
- Professionals and other staff routinely use respectful, person-first language.
- Emphasis is on abilities rather than disabilities.
- Special education and other services are seamless—their benefit to students is maximized and their cost to students is minimized.
- Special education and other services do not exist as separate entities (for example, "we have inclusion, resource, and

self-contained programs; speech and ESL are pullout programs").

- Differentiation is considered the rule, not the exception.
- Assistive technology enhances access to the general curriculum.
- Parents are not just welcomed partners in the schools; their participation and collaboration are actively sought.
- A variety of support services are available to students, including instruction in a separate setting—but only when it is the last choice and only for as long as data indicate it is effective.
- Inclusiveness is communicated in many ways—materials displayed, books and other media available, adult interactions with students and each other, schedules, room assignments, and so on.
- The term *inclusion* is rarely needed because it is such an integral part of the school culture.

---

the general education classroom, and they conclude that inclusion—sometimes using the phrase *full inclusion*—is not sound educational practice.

Alternatively, in many school districts and among some authors (for example, Handler, 2003; McLeskey & Waldron, 2007), inclusive practices are conceptualized as a belief system that emphasizes welcoming all students in a school learning community (Frattura & Capper, 2006). Just as important, inclusiveness is not judged solely on the location of a student's education. In these schools, factors such as those listed in the Professional Edge are stressed. As you have learned, this broader view is the one taken in this textbook. In highly inclusive schools, professionals and parents realize that instruction sometimes must occur in a separate setting. However, their goal is to return the student to instruction with peers as soon as possible and for as much time as possible. Further, they judge the effectiveness of inclusive practices on a student-by-student basis, monitoring progress and making instructional decisions according to the student's individual needs and educational program (for example, Brigham, Morocco, Clay, & Zigmond, 2006).

Impact on Students, Parents, and Educators

Discussion about the best ways to educate students with disabilities should consider the key stakeholders. That is, consideration must be given to students and their parents and families. In addition, the perspectives of teachers and administrators should be taken into account.

Student Outcomes   Any discussion of inclusive practices must consider the effect on student achievement (Yell et al., 2006). That is, if students with disabilities in inclusive settings do not adequately progress in their learning, then inclusion is not in their best interests. At the same time, inclusive practices should not interfere with the achievement of other students. Generally, academic outcomes in inclusive schools have been found to be positive for students (Hang & Rabren, 2009; Idol, 2006). For example, in a statewide study, researchers found that students with disabilities who spent more time in general education passed the eighth-grade assessment at a higher rate than similar students with disabilities who were educated in special education settings. Students educated in general education settings also graduated at a higher rate from high school with a standard diploma (Luster & Durrett, 2003). Another

---

fyi

Although this textbook focuses on special education for students in kindergarten through twelfth grade, young children—those birth to age 5—also may be determined to be eligible for special education services.

statewide study found that school districts reporting the greatest achievement gains for students with disabilities focused on educating those students with nondisabled peers so that all had access to the same core curriculum (Silverman, Hazelwood, & Cronin, 2009).

Yet other researchers have found positive effects of inclusive practices on mathematics achievement (Kunsch, Jitendra, & Sood, 2007), language development (Rafferty, Piscitelli, & Boettcher, 2003), problem-solving skills (Agran, Blanchard, Wehmeyer, & Hughes, 2002; Ryndak, Ward, Alper, Storch, & Montgomery (2010), and discipline referrals (Cawley, Hayden, Cade, & Baker-Kroczynski, 2002). Although only a few studies have been reported on the impact of inclusive practices on typical students, they suggest that these students' achievement is not hindered (for example, McDonnell et al., 2003).

Few studies of students' perceptions of inclusive education have been reported, but those available generally indicate that students prefer to receive their education with their peers. For example, Connor (2006) reported on the experience of a student named Michael who was identified as being learning disabled and also lived in poverty. Michael discussed extensively the stigma of being labeled as disabled and receiving services in the special education classroom. He strongly preferred remaining in general education. Wilson and Michaels (2006) surveyed high school students with disabilities and their typical peers in a general education classroom with both a special education and a general education teacher. Both groups of students perceived the class as positive in terms of their access to multiple learning styles and assistance as needed.

Parent Perspectives Parents generally are positive about special education services, and they often prefer that their children be educated with peers in general education classrooms (Leach & Duffy, 2009; Purcell, Turnbull, & Jackson, 2006). They believe that inclusive practices are beneficial for academic achievement, and they also strongly believe that their children learn critical social skills when they spend most or all of the school day with their typical peers (Salend, 2006; Williams & Reisberg, 2003). One parent commented that when her fourth-grade son with autism was integrated into a general education classroom for most of the day, his behavior improved both at school and at home. She also noted that the other students in the class were clearly kind to her son, and she was grateful that they sought him out on the playground and chose him as a lunch partner.

When parents are uneasy about inclusive practices, their concerns usually relate to problems they have experienced or anticipate (for example, Hanline & Daley, 2002). For example, parents of children with physical disabilities have found that many teachers are poorly prepared to work with students with special needs and that these educators have not prepared students to have a classmate with a disability (Pivik, McComas, & Laflamme, 2002). Some parents find that their children seem more comfortable in a special education classroom that has fewer students and more structure (Johnson & Duffett, 2002). For all parents, perceptions of inclusive practices are more positive when they participate in collaborative decision making concerning their children's educational services (Matuszny, Banda, & Coleman, 2007).

Perspectives of Professionals The perceptions of teachers and administrators regarding inclusive practices can be represented along a continuum (for example, DeSimone & Parmar, 2006; Pavri & Monda-Amaya, 2001; Rea, McLaughlin, & Walther-Thomas, 2002). In some studies, general education teachers in elementary, middle, and high schools are found to believe strongly in inclusive practices based on high standards for students (King & Youngs, 2003; McLeskey et al., 2001). Teachers who support inclusive practices report making instructional accommodations to facilitate student learning and feeling positive about their work with students with disabilities (for example, Clayton, Burdge, Denham, Kleinert, & Kearns, 2006).

At the same time, some teachers' perceptions of inclusive practices are more ambivalent (for example, Kozik, Cooney, Vinciguerra, Gradel, & Black, 2009; Sze, 2009).

RESEARCH NOTE

Technology can improve outcomes for students with disabilities. Myles, Ferguson, and Hagiwara (2007) found that when they taught an adolescent with Asperger syndrome to use a personal digital assistant (PDA), he was motivated by the use of technology and significantly increased the number of times he independently recorded homework assignments.

They recognize the value of inclusive practices but are uncertain about implementation. In one study of mathematics teachers (DeSimone & Parmar, 2006), the educators indicated that they had not learned enough about students with disabilities in their professional preparation programs and were uncertain about students' needs and how to address them. As you think about teaching students with disabilities and other special needs, what knowledge and skills do you anticipate needing? Among the items frequently mentioned are a commitment to inclusive practices and knowledge of effective instructional strategies (Stanovich & Jordan, 2002).

In addition to the views of teachers, principals' support of inclusive practices is essential, because principals are responsible for keeping the vision focused, fostering among staff an understanding of inclusion, and nurturing the development of the skills and practices needed to implement these practices (Horrocks, White, & Roberts, 2008; Salisbury & McGregor, 2002). Generally, principals report positive attitudes toward inclusive practices (for example, Praisner, 2003). Like teachers, though, they express concern that general education teachers may not have the skills to effectively instruct students with disabilities in their classrooms (for example, Oluwole, 2009).

Limited Resources

The most immediate influences on inclusive practices and those often the most daunting challenges to them seldom relate directly to instruction. Instead they often relate to practical matters and other pressures that exist in schools (Sindelar, Shearer, Yendol-Hoppey, & Liebert, 2006). These are common concerns:

- *Adequate personnel:* Because inclusive schooling relies so heavily on the strong collaborative relationships among educators, staffing often is a critical issue. First, in many locales the overall size of classes has increased because of budget constraints. This leads to teachers having less time to spend with any individual student, including those with disabilities. Similarly, many special educators' caseloads have increased, and so their time has to be distributed among more students, and the same often can be said for other special service providers such as speech-language pathologists.

- *Scheduling:* The limited number of educators leads directly to problems in scheduling the inclusive programs and services needed by students with disabilities. For example, some students are best educated when their special education teacher joins the general education teacher in the general education and they co-teach, a topic addressed in Chapter 3. If one special educator is providing services to students in four, five, six, or even more classrooms, such partnerships are difficult to arrange. Similarly, in rural areas special education teachers and other service providers may may need to travel from school to school, limiting their availability for programs based on inclusive practices. In schools where teacher turnover is high, it is difficult to sustain efforts to support students with disabilities in general education classrooms.

- *Time for shared planning:* The success of inclusive practices ultimately relies on the extent to which general and special education teachers can collaborate to design instructional strategies and discuss student learning and behavior. Nearly every study of inclusive practices includes mention of planning time as a barrier to implementation (Horne & Timmons, 2009; Scruggs, Mastropieri, & McDuffie, 2007).

Putting the Pieces Together

In some ways, the various positive and negative influences on inclusive practices are like puzzle pieces. In today's schools some of the pieces may be missing and others difficult to fit into place; yet others may be readily addressed and fit easily into the larger picture. Even in your own course, classmates may have a wide range of opinions about inclusive practices and what is affecting them, and they may come across studies on inclusive practices that present contradictory results. In your field experiences, you are likely to discover that in some schools inclusive practices are the norm, while in others very traditional approaches are still in place. You may find yourself struggling to reconcile all these views.

One way that you can put the puzzle together is to learn to teach in a way that is responsive to a wide range of student needs (Sobel & Taylor, 2006; Zascavage & Winterman, 2009) and to use collaboration with colleagues and parents, as described in the Working Together, as a means for extending your expertise. As you will learn in the chapters that follow, much is known about effective ways to instruct students with disabilities, and many of those strategies will help other students learn as well (for example, Meo, 2008; McGuire, Scott, & Shaw, 2006; Pisha & Stahl, 2005). By welcoming all your students and making these strategies an integral part of your instruction, your pieces of the inclusive practices puzzle will fit right into place.

Finally, as you read about inclusive practices, keep in mind that the results researchers obtain and the viewpoints authors present are influenced by many variables in addition to those just discussed, including the abilities and disabilities, ages, and cultural backgrounds of students; the attitudes, knowledge, and skills of general and special education teachers; the commitment and participation of parents; school administration; policies and procedures; the type of outcomes measured; and even the predisposition of researchers and authors toward particular views of inclusive practices. As you develop your own understanding of inclusive practices, keep all these factors in mind to help you make sense of what you read. In this way, you will learn to be inclusive in your thinking but flexible in your approach to educating students with disabilities.

Working TOGETHER

The Importance of Collaboration for Meeting Student Needs

As you read this textbook and learn about your responsibilities for educating students with disabilities, you will find that *collaboration*—working together with others—is one of the keys to successful inclusive practices. Here are just a few examples of how you will collaborate on behalf of students:

- *Meeting with special education teachers:* You will meet frequently with special education teachers, both formally and informally. A special educator may contact you to see how a student is doing in your class, or you may contact a special educator to ask for new ideas for responding to a student's behavior. You and the special educator may share responsibility for meeting with parents during open houses or parent conferences.

- *Co-teaching:* Depending on local programs and services, you may co-teach with a special education teacher or related services professional such as a speech/language pathologist. In co-teaching, you share teaching responsibilities, with both educators working with all students. This topic is addressed in detail in Chapter 3.

- *Working with paraprofessionals:* If your class includes a student with a significant disability or several students who need support (but not co-teaching), you may collaborate with

a paraprofessional. You will guide the work of that individual in your class to ensure that student support is appropriately provided.

- *Meeting on teams:* Various school teams support inclusive practices. Your grade-level or middle or high school department team will likely spend part of its time discussing students with disabilities and problem solving to address their needs. You also may be part of a team that tries to address student learning and behavior problems prior to any consideration of the need for special education. If a student in your class is being assessed to determine whether special education is needed, you will be part of that team. The latter two teams are discussed in Chapter 2.

- *Interacting with parents:* Perhaps the most important part of collaborating on behalf of students with disabilities is working with parents. You may communicate with parents through notes sent home and through e-mail; meet with them occasionally as they express concerns about their children; confer with them at formal team meetings; and work with them as they volunteer at school, help with field trips, and participate in other school activities and initiatives.

A disability label protects a student and gives access to resourses, but it does not provide information about a student's abilities and potential.

Who Receives Special Education and Other Special Services?

Throughout this chapter, we have used the phrase *students with disabilities*. At this point, we will introduce you to the specific types of disabilities that may entitle students to receive special education services, as well as other special needs that may require specialized assistance. As you read the following definitions, remember that a disability label can only provide general guidelines about a student. Labels are a form of shorthand that professionals use, but no label can accurately describe a student. Your responsibility is to understand your students with disabilities in ways that extend beyond what any label communicates so you can help them reach their potential.

Categories of Disability in Federal Law

When we say that students have disabilities, we are referring to the specific categories of exceptionality prescribed by federal law. Each state has additional laws that clarify special education practices and procedures, and the terms used to refer to disabilities in state laws may differ from those found in federal law. For example, although federal law specifies the label *emotional disturbance* for some students, in some states, the term *behavior disorder* or *behavioral and emotional disability* is used. Similarly, although IDEA uses the term *mental retardation*, some states use the alternative *cognitive disability* or *intellectual disability*. Check with your instructor or your state department of education website for the terms used in your state.

According to IDEA, students with one or more of the following thirteen disabilities that negatively affect their educational performance are eligible for special education services. These disabilities also are summarized in Figure 1.4 on the next page.

fyi

Although childhood obesity is not a disability specifically addressed in IDEA, it is becoming a major health concern: According to the Centers for Disease Control and Prevention (2010), 19.6 percent of children ages 6 to 11 and 18.1 percent of adolescents ages 12 to 19 are obese.

Learning Disabilities   Students with *learning disabilities (LD)* have dysfunctions in processing information typically found in language-based activities. They have average or above-average intelligence, but they often encounter significant problems learning how to read, write, and compute. They may not see letters and words in the way others do; they may not be able to pick out important features in a picture they are looking at; and they may take longer to process a question or comment directed to them. They also may have difficulty following directions, attending to tasks, organizing assignments, and managing time. Sometimes these students appear to be unmotivated or lazy when in fact they are trying to the best of their ability. Aaron, described at the beginning of this chapter, has one type of learning disability, but many other types also exist, and no single description characterizes all students with LD. Learning disabilities are by far the most common special need: Slightly fewer than half of all students receiving special education services in public schools in 2004–2005 had a learning disability (U.S. Department of Education, 2009).

Speech or Language Impairments   When a student has extraordinary difficulties communicating with others for reasons other than maturation, a *speech or language impairment* is involved. Students with this disability may have trouble with *articulation*, or the production of speech sounds. They may omit words or mispronounce common words when they speak. They also may experience difficulty in *fluency*, such as a significant stuttering problem. Some students have far-reaching speech or language disorders, in which they have significant problems receiving and producing language. They may communicate through pictures or sign language.

FIGURE 1.4 IDEA Disability Categories

Federal Disability Term[1]	Brief Description[2]
Learning disability (LD)	A disorder related to processing information that leads to difficulties in reading, writing, and computing; the most common disability, accounting for almost half of all students receiving special education.
Speech or language impairment (SLI)	A disorder related to accurately producing the sounds of language or meaningfully using language to communicate.
Mental retardation (MR)	Significant limitations in intellectual ability and adaptive behavior; this disability occurs in a range of severity.
Emotional disturbance (ED)	Significant problems in the social-emotional area to a degree that learning is negatively affected.
Autism	A disorder characterized by extraordinary difficulty in social responsiveness; this disability occurs in many different forms and may be mild or significant.
Hearing impairment (HI)	A partial or complete loss of hearing.
Visual impairment (VI)	A partial or complete loss of vision.
Deaf-blindness	A simultaneous significant hearing loss and significant vision loss.
Orthopedic impairment (OI)	A significant physical limitation that impairs the ability to move or complete motor activities.
Traumatic brain injury (TBI)	A medical condition denoting a serious brain injury that occurs as a result of accident or injury; potentially affecting learning, behavior, social skills, and language.
Other health impairment (OHI)	A disease or health disorder so significant that it negatively affects learning; examples include cancer, sickle-cell anemia, and diabetes.
Multiple disabilities	The simultaneous presence of two or more disabilities such that none can be identified as primary; the most common is the combination of intellectual and physical disabilities.
Developmental delay (DD)	A nonspecific disability category that states may choose to use as an alternative to specific disability labels for students up to age 9.

[1]The terms used in your state may vary from those specified in federal special education law.
[2]More complete federal definitions of each category are presented in Chapters 6 and 7.

Some students' primary disability is a speech or language disorder, and they may receive services for this. For other students with disabilities, speech/language services supplement their other educational services. For example, a student with a learning disability also might receive speech/language services, as might a student with autism or traumatic brain injury. In these instances, speech/language services are often considered a related service, as defined earlier in this chapter.

Mental Retardation   Students with *mental retardation (MR)* have significant limitations in intellectual ability and adaptive behaviors. They learn at a slower pace than do other students, and they may reach a point at which their learning levels off. Although the federal description of disability categories does not distinguish between students with mild mental retardation and those with more significant intellectual disabilities, many state descriptions do. Most individuals with this disability can lead independent or semi-independent lives as adults and can hold appropriate jobs. Because the term *mental retardation* can be very stigmatizing, the alternative term *intellectual disability* is becoming more common. In this text, the two terms are used interchangeably. Patricia, one of the students you met in the introduction to this chapter, has an intellectual disability.

RESEARCH NOTE

Although many researchers have studied the effects of children with significant disabilities on their families, few have examined the effects of children with learning disabilities. Dyson (2010) found a surprising number of negative effects, including general stress, parent disagreements, and negative reactions from extended family members.

Emotional Disturbance   When a student has significant difficulty in the social-emotional domain—serious enough to interfere with the student's learning—*emotional disturbance (ED)*, also sometimes called an *emotional and behavior disorder (EBD)*, exists. Students with this disability may have difficulty with interpersonal relationships and may respond inappropriately in emotional situations. That is, they may have extraordinary trouble making and keeping friends; they may get extremely angry when peers tease or play jokes on them; and they may repeatedly and significantly show little or inappropriate emotion when it is expected, such as when a family pet dies. Some students with ED are depressed; others are aggressive. Students with ED display these impairments over a long period of time, across different settings, and to a degree significantly different from their peers. Students with emotional disabilities are not just students whose behavior in a classroom is challenging to address; rather, they have chronic and extremely serious emotional or behavioral problems.

Autism   Students with *autism*, sometimes referred to as *autism spectrum disorder* because of its many variations, usually lack appropriate social responsiveness from a very early age. They generally avoid physical contact (for example, cuddling and holding), and they may not make eye contact. Problems with social interactions persist as these children grow; they appear unaware of others' feelings and may not seek interactions with peers or adults. They may have unusual language patterns, speaking without inflection, repeating what others say, or repeating something heard on television over and over. To feel comfortable, they may need highly routinized behavior, such as a formalized procedure for putting on their clothes or eating their meals. Some students with autism have above-average intelligence; others have intellectual disabilities. The causes of autism are not well understood, and the best approaches for working with students with autism are still emerging.

Asperger syndrome, usually considered a type of autism, is receiving increased attention among professionals. Individuals with this disorder usually experience difficulty in social interactions and communication, and they often have a very narrow range of interests. However, with appropriate supports and teacher understanding, students with Asperger syndrome can be highly successful in school. Thomas, one of the students you met at the beginning of the chapter, is identified as having autism, and his characteristics are consistent with having Asperger syndrome. You can learn a little more about autism by reading the Case in Practice in which teachers meet to problem solve regarding another student with this disability.

Hearing Impairments   Disabilities that concern inability or limited ability to receive auditory signals are called *hearing impairments (HI)*. When students are *hard of hearing*, they have a significant hearing loss but are able to capitalize on residual hearing by using hearing aids and other amplifying systems. Students who are *deaf* have little or no residual hearing and therefore do not benefit from traditional devices that aid hearing. Some students with hearing loss may be assisted through the use of advanced technology such as a cochlear implant, a small, complex electronic device implanted near the ear that can provide a sense of sound. Depending on the extent of the disability, students with hearing impairments may use sign language, speech reading, or other ways to help them communicate.

Visual Impairments   Disabilities that concern the inability or limited ability to receive information visually are called *visual impairments (VI)*. Some students have *partial sight* and can learn successfully using magnification devices and other adaptive materials; students who are *blind* do not use vision as a means of learning and instead rely primarily on touch and hearing. Depending on need, students with visual impairments may use braille, specialized computers, and other aids to assist in learning. In addition, some students with vision loss need specialized training to help them learn to move around successfully in their environment.

www.resources

http://www.familyvillage.wisc.edu/school.htm
The Family Village School website provides a wide variety of information about associations, instructional resources, legal issues, projects, and research related to inclusion.

CASE IN PRACTICE

Problem Solving in Inclusive Schools: The Classroom Teacher's Role

At Adams Middle School, staff members are meeting to discuss John, a seventh-grade student who has a formal diagnosis from a pediatric psychologist of pervasive developmental disorder (PDD) and who has many characteristics associated with autism. Ms. Diaz is David's English teacher, and Ms. Horton is the special educator who provides needed support. Mr. Powell, the school psychologist, also is present.

Ms. Diaz: John is a student with many dimensions. He usually does fairly well in class, and his behavior is much less disruptive than it was at the beginning of the school year, but whenever we transition from one activity to another, there is a fairly strong chance that John will refuse to change. If I insist, even using the strategies you've given me, Ms. Horton, John often starts rocking and singing in a loud voice and essentially shutting me out. I've had two calls from other parents who said their children reported that John takes up too much of my time in class. It was difficult to respond because I think that perception is fairly accurate. I hope we can come up with some ideas to improve the whole situation.

Ms. Horton: I know you also discussed John at your last team meeting. What did his other teachers have to say?

Ms. Diaz: Everyone except Mr. Bryant is experiencing the same problems. Mr. Bryant said that John really likes science and that his behavior problems might not be as pronounced there because John really wants to do the labs. He also said that sometimes he can tell by watching John's facial expression that John is trying very hard to transition between activities without a problem—and that it's very difficult for him.

Mr. Powell: You've mentioned the problem of transitioning between activities as one concern. Before we start addressing that, are there any other problems we should be aware of?

Ms. Diaz: No. Right now, it's the behavior during transitions—and I want to be clear that all of us on the team know John is quite capable of learning what we're teaching, and our data tell us he is making very strong gains academically. We are committed to finding more solutions before the problem becomes more serious.

Ms. Horton: One contribution I can make is to get into your classroom—and also into the classrooms of other teachers on your team—to gather some additional information. It will help to gather data on the sequence of events in class that seem to prevent or lead to his behavior. For example, I'd like to observe how other students respond when he has a problem during a transition.

Ms. Diaz: That would be helpful, but I hope you can observe him within the next couple of days so we come up with new strategies. There is no time to waste. I've been cuing him as you suggested—it's not working now. I also tried to ignore him, but that made it worse.

Mr. Powell: Maybe we should focus for a minute or two on what is going well for John in your class.

Ms. Diaz: Let's see . . . He's usually fine and makes a good contribution when we're talking about assignments that are very concrete or literal. For example, he knows the nuances of parts of speech better than nearly any of the other students and always knows the answers and wants to share when an objective like that is the focus.

Mr. Powell: Our meeting time is nearly up—the bell is about to ring. Are we all clear on next steps? Ms. Horton, will you be able to observe in Ms. Diaz's class by the end of the week? I know you need answers right away, but I hope we can get a clearer sense of the pattern of John's behavior so we can find the right strategy for addressing it. If we can get in to observe this week, could we meet next Tuesday to try to generate some strategies?

Ms. Diaz: That would be great. Let's work out the details on observing.

REFLECTION

Why was this meeting a positive example of teachers addressing a student problem in an inclusive school? What did they do that has set them up for success? If you were trying to understand John better, what other questions would you ask about him? What would you like others to observe in the classroom in relation to him? In relation to you as the teacher? What do you think will happen at the next meeting? On the basis of this case, how would you describe the role of general education teachers in addressing the challenges of inclusion?

Deaf-Blindness Students who have both significant vision and hearing loss sometimes are eligible for services as *deaf-blind*. These students have extraordinarily unique learning needs, particularly in the domain of communication, and because of the highly specialized services they require. The degree of the vision and hearing loss may vary from moderate to severe and may be accompanied by other disabilities. Students in this category are likely to receive special education services beginning at birth or very soon thereafter.

Orthopedic Impairments Students with *orthopedic impairments (OI)* have physical conditions that seriously impair their ability to move about or complete motor activities. Students who have cerebral palsy are included in this group, as are those with other diseases that affect the skeleton or muscles. Students with physical limitations resulting from accidents also may be orthopedically impaired. Students with orthopedic impairments are difficult to describe as a group because their strengths and needs vary tremendously. For example, some students with this disability are unable to move about without a wheelchair and may need special transportation to get to school and a ramp to enter the school building. Others may lack the fine motor skills needed to write and may require extra time or adapted equipment to complete assignments.

Traumatic Brain Injury Students with *traumatic brain injury (TBI)* have a wide range of characteristics and special needs, including limited strength or alertness, developmental delays, short-term memory problems, hearing or vision losses that may be temporary or permanent, irritability, and sudden mood swings. Their characteristics depend on the specific injuries they experienced, and their needs often change over time. Because TBI is a medical condition that affects education, diagnosis by a physician is required along with assessment of learning and adaptive behavior. Students who experience serious head trauma from automobile accidents, falls, and sports injuries are among those who might be eligible for services as TBI.

Other Health Impairments Some students have a disease or disorder so significant that it affects their ability to learn in school. The category of disability addressing their needs is called *other health impairments (OHI)*. Students who have chronic heart conditions necessitating frequent and prolonged absences from school might be eligible for special education in this category, as might those with severe and chronic asthma. Students with diseases such as acquired immune deficiency syndrome (AIDS) and sickle cell anemia also may be categorized as having other health impairments, depending on the impact of their illnesses on learning. Some students—but not all—with attention deficit–hyperactivity disorder (ADHD) also receive special education services in this category.

Multiple Disabilities The category used when students have two or more disabilities is called *multiple disabilities*. Students in this group often have an intellectual disability as well as a physical disability, but this category also may be used to describe any student with two or more disability types (with the exception of deaf-blindness as noted above). However, this classification is used only when the student's disabilities are so serious and interrelated that none can be identified as a primary disability. Students with multiple disabilities often benefit from *assistive technology,* that is, simple or complex devices that facilitate their learning, as explained in the Technology Notes.

Developmental Delays The category *developmental delays (DD)* is somewhat different than the other disabilities recognized in IDEA. It is an option that states may use for children ages 3 through 9. This category includes youngsters who have significant delays in physical, cognitive, communication, social-emotional, or adaptive development, but it is applied instead of one of the more specific disability categories. This option has two advantages: First, it avoids the use of more stigmatizing labels for young children, and second, it acknowledges the difficulty of determining the nature of a specific disability when children are rapidly growing and changing.

A Cross-Categorical Approach to Special Education

Federal and state education agencies and local school districts use the categories of disability described in the previous section for counting the number of students receiving special education services and allocating money to educate them. When you prepare to teach a student, however, you probably will find that the specific category

---

fyi

A *primary disability* is one that most adversely affects a student's educational performance. A *secondary disability* is an additional disability that also affects a student's education but to a lesser degree. For example, a student identified with a learning disability as a primary disability could have an emotional disability as a secondary disability.

The Opportunities of Assistive Technology

Whether the students you teach have mild or significant disabilities, they can use technology to help them to communicate, complete assignments, and fully participate in school and community. *Assistive technology*, which students with disabilities are entitled to access, refers to any device (that is, piece of equipment, product, or other item) used to increase, maintain, or improve the functional capabilities of an individual with a disability. Here are examples of the levels of assistive technology students might use.

NO TECHNOLOGY OR LOW TECHNOLOGY

No technology (no-tech) or *low technology (low-tech)* refers to items that do not include any type of electronics. Examples:

- A rubber pencil grip that enables a student with a disability to better grasp a pencil or pen
- A nonslip placemat on a student's desk that makes it easier for her to pick up items because it stops them from sliding
- A study carrel that helps a student pay closer attention to the schoolwork at hand

MID-TECHNOLOGY

Devices in the *mid-technology (mid-tech)* category use simple electronics. Examples:

- An audio recorder that a student uses to record lectures
- A calculator that assists a student in completing math computations
- A timer that lets a student know it is time to change from one activity to another

HIGH TECHNOLOGY

Items considered *high technology (high-tech)* incorporate more sophisticated, sometimes costly technology. Examples:

- Voice-recognition software that allows a student to use a microphone to dictate information that then appears in print on the computer
- Electronic communication boards on which a student can touch a picture and a prerecorded voice communicates for

Electronic communication boards are an example of high-tech assistive technology that benefits students with communication disorders.

him. For example, a student touches a picture of himself and a voice says "Hello. My name is Danny. What is your name?"

Are you interested in assistive technology? These video clips demonstrate its use:

- http://teachertube.com/viewVideo.php?video_id=75646&title=Assistive_Technology_for_Writing_Low_High_Tech_Options
  This video demonstrates low-tech options for assisting students with writing tasks.

- http://teachertube.com/viewVideo.php?video_id=165020&title=Assistive_Technology
  This video shows both a younger and an older student using a communication device called a Dynovox.

- http://www.youtube.com/watch?v=fAdEOXD9Tvk
  In this video, Ellen, a college student with significant physical disabilities, demonstrates how she uses switches she touches with her head to control her wheelchair and communication device.

●●●

of disability does not guide you in discovering that student's strengths and devising appropriate teaching strategies. Further, students in different categories often benefit from the same instructional adjustments. Therefore, throughout this book, students generally are discussed in terms of only the following two groups:

1. *High-incidence disabilities* are those that are most common, including learning disabilities, speech or language impairments, mild intellectual disabilities, and emotional disturbance. Together these disabilities account for more than 80 percent of the disabilities reported in 2004–2005, the most recent year for which data are available (U.S. Department of Education, 2009).
2. *Low-incidence disabilities* are those that are less common and include all the other categories: moderate to severe intellectual disabilities, multiple disabilities, hearing impairments, orthopedic impairments, other health impairments, visual impairments, deaf-blindness, autism, traumatic brain injury, and developmental delays.

Consistent with a **cross-categorical approach,** characteristics of students with disabilities are discussed in more detail in Chapters 6 and 7, where more attention is paid to students' learning needs than to their labels. In addition, although some strategies specific to categorical groups are outlined in those chapters (for example, the use of large-print books for students with visual impairments), most of the strategies presented throughout the text can be used effectively with most students. If you adopt a cross-categorical approach in your own thinking about teaching students with disabilities, you will see that many options are available for helping all students succeed.

Other Students with Special Needs

Not all students who have special learning and behavior needs are addressed in special education laws. The instructional strategies you learn in this book also can assist you in teaching many other students who may struggle in school, including those described in the following sections.

Students Who Are Gifted or Talented   Students who demonstrate ability far above average in one or several areas—including overall intellectual ability, leadership, specific academic subjects, creativity, athletics, and the visual or performing arts—are considered *gifted* or *talented*. Erin is included in this group; she seems to learn without effort, and she also is eager to learn about almost everything. Evan is considered talented; still in elementary school, he has participated in state and national piano recitals, and his parents have requested that he have access to the music room during recess so he can practice. Students who are gifted or talented are not addressed in federal special education law, but many states have separate laws that provide guidelines for identifying and educating students with special talents. Adequate funds are not always provided to implement these laws, however, and so the availability and scope of services for students with particular talents vary across the country and even within each state.

Students Protected by Section 504   Some students not eligible to receive special education services are entitled to protection through Section 504 and receive specialized assistance because of their functional disabilities, as described previously in this chapter. Among those likely to be included in this group are some students with attention deficit–hyperactivity disorder (ADHD). These students have a medical condition often characterized by an inability to attend to complex tasks for long periods of time, excessive motor activity, and/or impulsivity. The impact of this disorder on students' schoolwork can be significant. Students with ADHD may take medication, such as Ritalin or Strattera, that helps them focus their attention. Many students with learning disabilities or emotional disturbance also have ADHD, but these students receive assistance through IDEA, as do students with ADHD whose disorder is so significant that they are determined to be eligible for special education. Other students who may be protected by Section 504 include those with asthma, severe allergies, or epilepsy.

Students at Risk   Often, the general term *at risk* refers to students whose characteristics, environment, or experiences make them more likely than others to fail in school (and they also may have disabilities). Students whose primary language is not English—sometimes referred to as *English-language learners (ELLs)*—sometimes are considered at risk, and they may need assistance in school learning. They may attend bilingual education programs or classes for English as a second language (ESL) to have opportunities to learn English while also learning the standard curriculum, or they may receive assistance in their general education classrooms. Some ELLs also have disabilities; when this is the case, both English-language instruction and special education are provided. The checklist presented in the Professional Edge is a tool you can use to analyze your readiness to work with students and families from diverse backgrounds, including those who are English language learners.

dimensions of DIVERSITY

Diversity has many faces. It includes ethnic, cultural, economic, linguistic, religious, ability, gender, and racial differences among the students you may teach.

PROFESSIONAL EDGE

Promoting Cultural Competence: A Self-Assessment

Cultural competence refers to your understanding of and responses to diversity. Here is an excerpt from a tool designed to help professionals reflect on their awareness of a variety of factors that contribute to cultural competence. You can find the complete self-assessment checklist at http://nccc.georgetown.edu/documents/ChecklistCSHN.pdf.

DIRECTIONS: Please select A, B, or C for each item listed below

A = Things I do frequently, or statement applies to me to a great deal.

B = Things I do occasionally, or statement applies to me to a moderate degree

C = Things I do rarely or never, or statement applies to me to a minimal degree or not at all

- For children who speak languages or dialects other than English, I attempt to learn and use key words in their language so that I am better able to communicate with them during assessment, treatment, or other interventions.
- I use visual aids, gestures, and physical prompts in my interactions with children who have limited English proficiency.
- When interacting with parents who have limited English proficiency, I always keep in mind that:
  - Limitation in English proficiency is in no way a reflection of their level of intellectual functioning.
  - Their limited ability to speak the language of the dominant culture has no bearing on their ability to communicate effectively in their language of origin.
  - They may or may not be literate neither in their language of origin or English.
- I use alternative formats and varied approaches to communicate and share information with children and/or their family members who experience disability.
- I avoid imposing values that may conflict or be inconsistent with those of cultures or ethnic groups other than my own.
- I recognize and accept that individuals from culturally diverse backgrounds may desire varying degrees of acculturation into the dominant culture.

- I accept and respect that male-female roles in families may vary significantly among different cultures (e.g., who makes major decisions for the family, play and social interactions expected of male and female children).
- I recognize and understand that beliefs and concepts of emotional well-being vary significantly from culture to culture.
- I accept that religion and other beliefs may influence how families respond to illnesses, disease, disability and death.
- I recognize and accept that folk and religious beliefs may influence a family's reaction and approach to a child born with a disability or later diagnosed with a physical/emotional disability or special health care needs.
- I understand that traditional approaches to disciplining children are influenced by culture.
- I understand that families from different cultures will have different expectations of their children for acquiring toileting, dressing, feeding, and other self-help skills.
- I accept and respect that customs and beliefs about food, its value, preparation, and use are different from culture to culture.

NOTE: This checklist is intended to heighten the awareness and sensitivity of personnel to the importance of cultural diversity and cultural competence in human service settings. There is no answer key with correct responses. However, if you frequently responded "C," you may not necessarily demonstrate values and engage in practices that promote a culturally diverse and culturally competent service delivery system for children with disabilities or special health care needs and their families.

Checklist excerpts are included with express permission from the National Center for Cultural Competence.

Source: Goode, T. D. (2009). *Promoting cultural diversity and cultural competency: Self-assessment checklist for personnel providing services and supports to children with disabilities & special health needs and their families.* Washington, DC: Georgetown University Center for Child and Human Development. Retrieved October 23, 2010, from http://nccc.georgetown.edu/documents/ChecklistCSHN.pdf.

A second group of at-risk students includes *slow learners* whose educational progress is below average but who do not have a disability. These students are learning to the best of their ability, but they often cannot keep pace with the instruction in most general education classrooms without assistance. They are sometimes described as "falling between the cracks" of the educational system because while most professionals agree they need special assistance, they are not eligible for special education. They are likely to access and benefit from response to intervention (RtI) services described earlier in this chapter.

Other students who might be considered at risk include those who are homeless; those who live in poverty or move frequently; those who are born to mothers abusing drugs or alcohol or who abuse drugs or alcohol themselves; and those who are victims of physical or psychological abuse. Students in these groups are at risk for school failure because of the environment or circumstances in which they live.

fyi

Using *person-first language* is a way to ensure that you focus on students and not their labels. For example, say "students with disabilities" instead of "disabled students" and "my student who has autism" instead of "my autistic student."

You may find it challenging to find effective strategies to reach your students who have special needs but who do not have disabilities according to special education law. However, current trends in education can help you. First, you can access response to intervention procedures, explained more fully in Chapter 2, for research-based interventions for your struggling learners. In addition, as students with disabilities spend increasing amounts of time in general education classes, special education teachers and other special services providers often informally assist teachers in planning and adapting educational activities for them. Thus, other students with special needs often benefit from the trend toward inclusive education for students with disabilities.

WRAPPING IT UP

BACK TO THE CASES

This section provides opportunities for you to apply the knowledge gained in this chapter to the cases described at the beginning of this chapter. The questions and activities that follow demonstrate how the concepts you have learned about connect to the everyday activities of all teachers.

THOMAS, as you may remember from the beginning of the chapter, is a student with autism. If you believe that being a member of a general education classroom has been successful for Thomas, explain what factors led you to that conclusion and how they may contribute to success for other students with disabilities. If you believe Thomas would be more successful learning in a special education setting, explain what factors led you to that conclusion and how they may prevent success for other students with disabilities.

PATRICIA, the elementary student with an intellectual disability, receives some of her education in general education and some in a special education setting. Why might this be a preferred option for some students? What could be the drawbacks to this approach for Patricia, her classmates, and her teachers? Which of the laws and court cases you learned about in this chapter led to the educational options Patricia has?

AARON, as you may recall, is troubled by his learning disability. Several of the assistive technologies mentioned in the Technology Notes on page 25 could provide support for Aaron's problems with attention and written tests. Select at least two technologies that you would recommend to Aaron. Remembering that Aaron does not want to stand out or be treated differently, what would you say to him to help him accept these assistive supports?

SUMMARY

- *Special education* refers to the specialized instruction received by the millions of students in the United States who have disabilities and is guided by the concept of the least restrictive environment (LRE).

- Current special education practices have evolved from a combination of historical factors, including the inception of compulsory public education early in the twentieth century, research questioning instructional practices for students with disabilities, the civil rights movement and related court cases, and a series of federal civil rights and education laws, including Section 504, P.L. 94-142, ADA, IDEA, and ESEA/NCLB.

- Inclusive practices today have been shaped by the historical, legislative, and litigative dimensions of special education. Although the primary goal of inclusion is to improve student outcomes by ensuring their rights, its implementation can be complicated by uncertainty about its meaning; professional understanding, attitude, and skill; and practical dilemmas related to funding and other resources.

- Federal law identifies 13 categories of disability that may entitle students to special education services: learning disabilities, speech or language impairments, mental retardation (increasingly called *intellectual disabilities*), emotional disturbance, autism, hearing impairments, visual impairments, deaf-blindness, orthopedic impairments, traumatic brain injury, other health impairments, multiple disabilities, and developmental delays.

- Many students have special needs not addressed through special education, including those who are gifted or talented; who have ADHD; who are at risk, including English-language learners and slow learners; and whose life situations comprise high risk for school failure. Students with disabilities also may have these special needs.

- Central to twenty-first-century education is the understanding that nearly all public school teachers are responsible for instructing students with disabilities and other special needs.

APPLICATIONS IN TEACHING PRACTICE
UNDERSTANDING CONTEMPORARY SPECIAL EDUCATION

It is a new school year—your first as a teacher in the Danville School District. You are excited about your new job but worried about following the district curriculum and making sure your students succeed on high-stakes tests. Then you learn that you will be responsible for the following students, and you find that you need all the skills for reaching diverse groups of students that you learned in your professional preparation program:

- Cassie is a bright student who has a visual impairment. To read, she uses a computer that greatly magnifies the materials. She also needs to work in bright light, and she gets fatigued from the effort required to use what little vision she has.

- Ramon is identified as having a learning disability. His reading ability is significantly below grade level. He also seems disorganized. He often forgets to bring materials and assignments to school, and he frequently asks for help immediately after directions for an assignment have been given.

- Tory lives in a foster home. He was removed from his mother's care because of several incidents of abuse. Tory is an angry child. He often refuses to work, he sometimes loses his temper and throws a book or crumples a paper, and he misses school frequently.

QUESTIONS

1. What are the possible strengths that Cassie, Ramon, and Tory might bring to your classroom? How can you emphasize their possible strengths instead of their difficulties? What is the rationale for assigning these students to a general education classroom like yours? How do the provisions of IDEA and ESEA affect these students' educational rights and responsibilities? What are appropriate goals you as a teacher should have as you begin to instruct them? Discuss with your classmates how Cassie, Ramon, and Tory's special needs might be demonstrated in an elementary school, middle school, or high school classroom.

2. What are some of the benefits and opportunities of educating these students in your classroom? What positive outcomes should you expect? How can you ensure these positive outcomes?

3. What are some of the risks and concerns related to educating these students in your classroom? What types of systemic supports could prevent or significantly reduce these risks and concerns? How might your own beliefs be either a benefit or a risk for these students?

4. If you spoke with the parents of Cassie, Ramon, and Tory, what might you expect them to say? What unique views might each student's parents have? How might their views be influenced by their family cultures and experiences? What could you do to encourage parent participation for your students?

5. What are your concerns and questions when you think about your responsibilities for educating students with disabilities and other special needs in your classroom—whether in the elementary grades, middle school, or high school? In what ways do you think you can make a contribution to your students' education? What types of support might you need? If you write your responses to these questions, keep them with your text and use them as a basis for discussion as you learn more in later chapters.

Go to Topic 1: Inclusive Practices and Topic 2: Law, in the MyEducationLab (http://www .myeducationlab.com) for your course, where you can:

- Find learning outcomes for Inclusive Practices and Law along with the national standards that connect to these outcomes.

- Complete Assignments and Activities that can help you more deeply understand the chapter content.

- Apply and practice your understanding of the core teaching skills identified in the chapter with the Building Teaching Skills and Dispositions learning units.

- Examine challenging situations and cases presented in the IRIS Center Resources. (optional)

- Access video clips of CCSSO National Teachers of the Year award winners responding to the question, "Why Do I Teach?" in the Teacher Talk section. (optional)

- Check your comprehension on the content covered in the chapter by going to the Study Plan in the Book Resources for your text. Here you will be able to take a chapter quiz, receive feedback on your answers, and then access Review, Practice, and Enrichment activities to enhance your understanding of chapter content. (optional.)

2

Special Education Procedures and Services

LEARNING Objectives

After you read this chapter, you will be able to

1. Explain the roles and responsibilities of the individuals who may participate in educating students with disabilities.

2. Describe the process through which a student may become eligible to receive special education services.

3. Name the components of individualized education programs (IEPs) and provide examples of them.

4. Describe the types of services that students with disabilities may receive and the settings in which they may receive them.

5. Discuss how parents participate in special education decision making and what occurs when parents and school district representatives disagree.

6. Outline the role of general education teachers in the procedures and services of special education, reflecting on their critical contributions to positive outcomes for students with disabilities.

MS. KUCHTA continues to worry about Christopher, one of her first-grade students, and she is preparing for a meeting with her school's Student Intervention Team (SIT) to discuss his slow learning progress. Christopher was identified as being at risk for school failure early in kindergarten. With intensive instruction and frequent monitoring of his progress, his learning accelerated. But now in first grade, problems are occurring again. Ms. Kuchta has been implementing what are referred to as Tier 1 interventions, research-based reading strategies, but Ms. Kuchta's data indicate they are insufficient. At today's meeting, Ms. Kuchta anticipates that the team—which includes the school psychologist, the assistant principal, the literacy coach, and another teacher—will decide to move Christopher to Tier 2. This means he will receive additional reading instruction three times each week for 40 minutes. If, after 10 weeks, that intervention is not increasing his learning rate, he will receive even more intensive interventions at Tier 3. The goal, if at all possible, is to address Christopher's academic deficits before they become so significant that special education might be needed. This process of data-driven and increasingly intensive interventions is referred to as *response to intervention*.

What actions do Ms. Kuchta and other teachers take when their students are struggling? How do educators decide whether Christopher's (and other students') learning challenges are so significant that they may constitute a disability and require special education services?

MS. LEE, a high school English teacher, has just pulled from her mailbox something titled "IEP at a Glance." As she reads through it, she realizes that it is a summary of the individualized education program (IEP) for Jennifer, one of her students. The summary includes a list of test accommodations Jennifer should receive, and it mentions steps being taken to help Jennifer prepare for a vocational program she will attend after high school. For example, Jennifer needs to complete unit tests in a small, structured environment. That means she will go to the special education classroom on test days instead of reporting to Ms. Lee's room. Ms. Lee notes that the speech/language therapist, the transition specialist, and the social worker are mentioned in the document, but the special education teacher is listed as the person to contact to answer questions.

What roles do general education teachers play in the writing and implementation of IEPs? How are they responsible for ensuring that IEP accommodations are available in the classroom? Who are the other service providers that teachers may work with as they educate students with disabilities?

MS. TURNER teaches science to seventh graders. Toward the end of the last school year, she was invited to become a member of her school's inclusive practices leadership team. At a summer professional development seminar, she learned that many of the students in her school still leave general education classes for a significant part of each day to receive special education services and that renewed effort is being made to ensure that these students have access to the same curriculum as other students by receiving more of their core academic instruction with their nondisabled peers. Ms. Turner and her colleagues are charged with planning professional development for all the professionals at their school on differentiation of instruction; designing ways to support students with disabilities in general education classes; and enlisting the assistance of administrators, parents, and teachers in refining the school's services.

What options exist for students with disabilities to receive the services to which they are entitled? To what extent does this occur in the general education setting? How are such decisions made? How do general education teachers and other school staff contribute to the education of students with disabilities?

Regardless of the ages of the students you plan to teach, you will encounter students who struggle to learn. Some may appear to do everything they can *not* to learn. Others may try their best but still not be successful. Yet other students may have challenging behaviors, and you may find that the strategies effective with most students do not work with them. You may wonder whether some of these students should be receiving special education services and who will provide them.

This chapter introduces you to people who specialize in working with students with disabilities and procedures for deciding whether a student is eligible for special education services. You also will learn how students' individualized education programs (IEPs) are designed and monitored and which services students with disabilities use. You will discover that parents play a crucial role in special education procedures and that when they or students disagree with school professionals about special services, procedures exist to help them resolve these differences. Most important, you will learn about your role in working with other professionals and parents to determine student eligibility for special education, carrying out students' educational programs, and monitoring student learning.

Who Are the Professionals in Special Education?

Students with disabilities are entitled to a wide range of supports and services. Not surprisingly, many different individuals can be involved in the delivery of these services. You probably will interact with some of these professionals, such as special education teachers, almost every day. Others you might work with only occasionally. Some of these professionals serve students indirectly or work only with the few students who have the most challenging disabilities. Together, however, these educators create, implement, and evaluate the special education that students with disabilities receive.

General Education Teachers

As the *general education teacher,* you are the first professional discussed in this section because for many students with suspected or documented disabilities, you are the person who has the most detailed knowledge of their day-to-day needs in your classroom.

Your responsibilities span several areas. You are the person most likely to bring to the attention of other professionals a student whom you suspect may have a disability (Egyed & Short, 2006; McClanahan, 2009). That is, you may encounter a student who is reading significantly below grade level, a student whose behavior is so different from that of other students that you suspect an emotional disorder, or a student who has extraordinary difficulty focusing on learning. When you suspect a disability, you document the student's characteristics and behaviors that led to your concern by gathering samples of the student's work, compiling descriptions of his behavior, and keeping notes of how you have attempted to address the problem (Walker-Dalhouse et al., 2009). You work with special education colleagues and other professionals to systematically implement interventions in your classroom to clarify whether the student's problems need further exploration (Mercier-Smith, Fien, Basaraba, & Travers, 2009; Reutebuch, 2008). If the student is referred for assessment for special education, you contribute information about his academic and social functioning in your classroom and help identify the student's strengths, needs, and educational program components. For example, you might help others understand the curricular expectations in your classroom and the types of accommodations that may be necessary for the student to succeed there. If special education services are deemed necessary, you participate in deciding appropriate goals and, for some students, objectives. You also might assist special services staff members in updating parents on their

dimensions of DIVERSITY

Culturally and linguistically diverse students are more likely to succeed in school when their teachers create compassionate and flexible classroom environments, help students persist in spite of life challenges, and teach with "urgency." (Cartledge & Kourea, 2008).

child's quarterly and yearly progress. Most important, you are expected to work with special services staff to provide appropriate instruction within your classroom (Carter, Prater, Jackson, & Marchant, 2009; Munk, Gibb, & Caldarella, 2010). Several of the key responsibilities of a general education teacher are summarized in Figure 2.1.

When all your responsibilities are listed, your role in planning and providing special services to students may seem overwhelming. However, studies of general education teachers typically indicate that they are willing and able to contribute to the education of students with disabilities as long as some conditions are met. The most important conditions include having administrative leadership and staff preparation, sufficient time for teacher planning, and adequate funding and other resources for program support (Conderman, & Johnston-Rodriguez, 2009; Elhoweris & Alsheikh, 2006; Idol, 2006).

FIGURE 2.1 **General Education Teacher Responsibilities Related to Implementing IDEA**

Identify students with learning, behavior, or other needs serious enough to seek input from colleagues.

Contribute to discussions of students as a member of an intervention assistance team.

Implement strategies and gather data as part of a response to intervention (RtI) procedure.

Provide evidence–based day–to–day instruction.

Collaborate with colleagues regarding students with disabilities.

Communicate with parents regarding their child's strengths and needs.

Participate in writing IEPs as a member of the multidisciplinary team.

Special Education Teachers

Special education teachers are the professionals with whom you are most likely to have ongoing contact in teaching students with disabilities, and these professionals have increasingly complex roles (Fuchs, Fuchs, & Stecker, 2010). They are responsible for managing and coordinating the services a student receives, including writing and implementing the individualized education program (IEP). They typically also provide direct and indirect instruction to students who are assigned to them. In addition, they may consult with you regarding a student suspected of having a disability and work with you to determine whether a referral for assessment for possible special education is warranted, a process explained later in this chapter.

Depending on the state in which you teach and the disabilities of the students in your classroom, you may work with different types of special education teachers. Sometimes special education teachers are assigned to work with all of the students with disabilities in your class. For example, a special education teacher may support a student with learning disabilities and also a student with a moderate intellectual disability or a speech or language impairment. That professional may work indirectly with other special education professionals to ensure that each student's educational plan is being implemented and monitored. Sometimes, special education teachers work only with specific categories of students. For example, a teacher for students with visual impairments or hearing loss generally will be responsible only for students with those disabilities. In states that do not use categorical labels for students, some teachers work with students with high-incidence disabilities or low-incidence disabilities.

In other situations, special education teachers may be designated by the type of services they provide. For example, for some students with high-incidence disabilities in your class, you may work with a *consulting teacher* or perhaps an *inclusion facilitator* (Friend & Cook, 2010). This professional might meet with you regularly to monitor students' progress, problem solve with you about student concerns, and coordinate students' services, in some cases working directly with students but in other situations working indirectly by supporting teachers. You also might work with a *resource teacher* who divides time among directly instructing students, working with teachers regarding student needs, and co-teaching, a topic addressed in Chapter 3 (Friend, Cook, Hurley-Chamberlain, & Shamberger, 2010). In some high schools, special education teachers now are assigned to work with a particular department, attending department meetings and providing supports for all students with disabilities enrolled in that department's courses.

General educators, whether in core academic areas or related arts, are most likely to work with special educators to ensure that students with disabilities receive the specialized services to which they are entitled.

For some groups of students, the special educator with whom you interact might be an *itinerant teacher.* Itinerant teachers often have roles like the professionals just described, but they travel between two or more school sites to provide services to students (For example, Dinnebeil, McInerney, & Hale, 2006). Teachers for students with vision or hearing disabilities often are itinerant. However, if you work in a school district where each school has only a few students with disabilities, even the special educator for students with high-incidence disabilities may deliver services this way.

One other type of special education teacher is a *transition specialist.* This professional typically works in a high school setting and helps prepare students to leave school for vocational training, employment, or postsecondary education (Brooke, Revell, & Wehman, 2009; Hartman, 2009). No matter what subject you teach in high school, you might work very closely with a transition specialist,

fyi

The most recent data available indicate that there are 403,971 special education teachers in the United States (U.S. Department of Education, 2009).

but this is especially likely in business education, consumer sciences, industrial and other vocational arts, and similar areas. This professional also spends time working directly with students to assess their skills and interests related to life after school. A transition specialist works with community businesses to arrange student job sites and resolve problems related to student workers. This professional also may serve as a *job coach,* accompanying a student to a job site and helping her master the skills needed to do the job successfully.

As the nature of special education services changes, so do the job responsibilities and titles of special educators. For example, you might find that the professionals in your school who used to be called *special education teachers* are now referred to as *intervention specialists (ISs).* This change in title represents an effort to delabel teachers and parallels the effort to deemphasize students' labels—that is, to focus on student strengths and needs rather than the language of disability. Regardless of the type of special education teachers with whom you work, you will find that they are important instructional partners who are no longer relegated to teaching just in the special education classroom. They support students by creating adapted materials, teaching with you in the general education classroom, working directly and separately with students who have disabilities, and often serving as coordinators for all the services any single student may receive.

Related Service Providers and Other Specialists

In addition to working with special education teachers, you will have contact with a variety of other service providers (National Dissemination Center for Children with Disabilities, n.d.). They, too, play important roles in educating students with disabilities. The following list includes the individuals with whom you are most likely to work.

School Psychologists   *School psychologists* offer at least two types of expertise related to educating students with disabilities. First, school psychologists often have a major responsibility for determining a student's intellectual, academic, social, emotional, and/or behavioral functioning. They typically contribute a detailed written analysis of the student's strengths and areas of need; in many school districts, this document is referred to as a "psych report" (that is, a psychological report). In a related role, school psychologists sometimes chair the multidisciplinary team that meets to decide whether a student has a disability and, if so, what types of services are needed (Arivett, Rust, Brissie, & Dansby, 2007).

A second major task for school psychologists is designing strategies to address students' academic and social or behavior problems, whether students have been identified as having a disability or not (Kaniuka, 2009). For example, these professionals typically are part of the team that designs and implements interventions prior to a decision about referral for possible special education services. Sometimes they serve as behavior consultants. Occasionally, they assist a teacher by working with an entire class group on social skills. They also might provide individual assistance to students with emotional or behavioral problems who are not eligible for special education.

Counselors   Although *counselors* most often advise high school students and assist students with disabilities as they transition from school to postschool options (Milsom & Hartley, 2005), they also work at other school levels and contribute to the education of students with disabilities (Mitcham, Portman, & Dean, 2009). For example, counselors in some school districts assess students' social and emotional functioning, including areas such as self-concept; motivation; attitude toward school, peers, and teachers; and social skills. Counselors also can provide services to both teachers and students. For teachers, they might suggest ways to draw out a student who is excessively shy, to incorporate activities designed to enhance students' self-concept into day-to-day classroom instruction, or to create an emotionally safe classroom environment. For students,

dimensions of DIVERSITY

When middle school teachers were shown videos of students displaying "traditional walking" or stylized "strolling," they concluded the latter students had lower achievement, were more aggressive, and were more likely to need special education than the former students (Neal, McCray, Webb-Johnson, & Bridgest, 2003). The race or ethnicity of the student did not make a difference in the results.

counselors might provide individual assistance to a student struggling to understand a parent's death or unexplained departure from the family or other stressful events, arrange group sessions with several students who share specific needs, or work with an entire class on how to interact with a peer who has a disability.

Speech/Language Therapists   Many students with disabilities have communication needs. Some have mild problems in pronouncing words or speaking clearly. Others have an extremely limited vocabulary. Yet others rely on alternative means of communication, such as communication boards. The professionals who specialize in meeting students' communication needs are *speech/language therapists*, and they have a tremendously diverse range of school responsibilities (Harris, Prater, Dyches, & Heath, 2009). At the early elementary level, they might work with an entire class on language development or with an individual student on pronouncing sounds. At the intermediate elementary level, they might work on vocabulary with a group of students and might also help a student with a moderate cognitive disability pronounce some words more clearly or combine words into sentences. At the middle or high school level, they often focus on functional vocabulary and work mostly with students with low-incidence disabilities. For example, they might help a student with an intellectual disability learn to read common signs and complete tasks such as ordering in a restaurant or asking for assistance.

Social Workers   *Social workers'* expertise is similar to that of counselors in terms of being able to help teachers and students address social and emotional issues (Sabatino, 2009). Thus, social workers may serve as consultants to teachers and also may provide individual or group assistance to students. However, social workers have additional expertise. They often are liaisons between schools and families. For example, they can create a family history by interviewing parents and visiting a student's home; this information may be critical in determining whether a student needs special education services. Similarly, they may help other school professionals work with families on matters such as gaining access to community health services. The school social worker often follows up on teacher reports about the suspected abuse or neglect of students.

Administrators   The school principal, assistant principal, and sometimes a department chairperson or team leader are the *administrators* most likely to participate actively in the education of students with disabilities (Angelle & Bilton, 2009; Lasky & Karge, 2006). Their role is to offer knowledge about the entire school community and provide perspective on school district policies regarding special education and also to help address parents' concerns. Every team that determines whether a student is eligible for special education must have administrative representation. In one school, the mother of Marisha, a student with severe language delays, requested that her daughter receive speech/language therapy for 40 minutes daily. School professionals were in agreement that this amount of therapy was not appropriate. Dr. Wade, the principal, worked with the team and the parent to negotiate the amount of speech therapy needed to accomplish Marisha's goals.

In some locales, especially large urban and suburban districts where it is difficult to ensure that all required special education procedures are followed, a *special education coordinator* or *supervisor* is part of the district's administration. This professional specializes in understanding the sometimes complex procedures of special education. Coordinators help alleviate the pressure on principals and assistant principals to accurately interpret and follow guidelines. They also explain services and options to parents, problem solve with teachers when issues arise, and assist in monitoring to ensure that students with disabilities receive needed supports.

Paraprofessionals   Individuals who assist teachers and others in the provision of services to students with disabilities are *paraprofessionals* (Giangreco, Suter, & Doyle, 2010). These individuals usually have a certificate based on completing a community college or similar training program; some are even licensed teachers.

PROFESSIONAL **EDGE**

Working with Paraprofessionals

No matter what grade level you teach, you will likely find yourself at some point working closely with paraprofessionals, also called *paraeducators*. These individuals are employed by school districts to provide support to students with disabilities either by working with particular students one to one or by working in general or special education classrooms with several students.

Generally, paraprofessionals work under the direction of teachers or other professionals, and they do not have sole responsibility for any aspect of a student's educational program. If a paraprofessional is assigned to your classroom in order to support students with disabilities, these are some of the responsibilities that individual may carry out:

- Locate, arrange, or construct instructional materials.
- Assist students with eating, dressing, personal care, and bathroom use.
- Help prepare the classroom for students and keep work areas neat.
- Instruct students with disabilities individually, in small or large groups, and/or with typical peers, supervised by licensed educators and as specified in students' IEPs or by professionals on the service delivery team. Such instruction generally is review or reteaching rather than initial core instruction.
- Collect student data for professional team members regarding student progress toward goals.
- Score tests and certain papers using a key or rubric.
- Maintain files or records about students.
- Supervise playgrounds, halls, lunchrooms, buses, and loading zones.
- Address students' specific health needs (for example, suction tracheotomy tubes as assigned and trained by a school nurse).
- Assist and facilitate appropriate peer interactions.

- Assist students using adaptive equipment or devices (for example, a communication board).
- Support student behavior and social needs according to plans.
- Participate positively in evaluative or feedback sessions for improvement of their skills.
- Participate in training and coaching sessions to improve their skills associated with all duties and tasks assigned.
- Communicate with professionals about their work and students' progress on assigned tasks.
- Move or accompany students from one place to another, assisting students with mobility and transition.
- Contribute to the effectiveness of the special education team by using appropriate communication, problem solving, and conflict management strategies.

FROM THE RESEARCH

As the list suggests, paraprofessionals offer many valuable services to students and teachers in support of students. However, in a review of recent research, Giangreco and his colleagues found persistent issues in the roles and responsibilities of these school personnel, including practices for hiring and retaining them, their preparation for their jobs, specific job expectations, respect for the work paraprofessionals complete, problems related to supervision, and student perceptions of these support personnel.

Sources: "Managing Paraeducators in Your School: How to Hire, Train, and Supervise Non-Certified Staff," by N. K. French, 2003, Thousand Oaks, CA: Corwin; "Preparing and Managing Paraprofessionals," by M. L. Trautman, 2004, *Intervention in School and Clinic, 39*, pp. 131–138; "Paraprofessionals in Inclusive Schools: A Review of Recent Research," by M. Giangreco, J. Suter, & M. Doyle. (2010). *Journal of Educational & Psychological Consultation, 20*, pp. 41–57.

Regardless, these service providers generally complete their work under the direction of teachers and other professional staff members. Paraprofessionals also might be called *paraeducators, instructional assistants, teaching assistants, aides,* or other titles, depending on local practices.

School districts use paraprofessionals in many different ways (Carter, O'Rourke, Sisco, & Pelsue, 2009), but two roles are especially common. Some paraprofessionals are assigned to specific students who need ongoing individual assistance. For example, a student with no ability to move his arms may have a paraprofessional who takes notes for him and completes other tasks such as feeding. A few students have medical conditions requiring that a specially trained paraprofessional be present to monitor their status. Paraprofessionals in this role may be referred to as *personal assistants* or *one-to-one assistants.*

A second and more common role for paraprofessionals is to assist in the delivery of special services for many students. These paraprofessionals often work in both inclusive classrooms and special education classrooms as well as on the playground, at assemblies, and during bus duty. These paraprofessionals' primary responsibility is to work with students with disabilities, but they sometimes also help other students and the teacher as the need arises and time permits. The Professional Edge on page 37 contains more information about working with paraprofessionals.

Other Specialists   Depending on student needs and state and local practices, other professionals also may participate in the education of students with disabilities. Here is a list of these individuals and a brief description of their roles:

- *Physical therapist.* Assesses and intervenes related to gross motor skills, that is, large muscle activity.
- *Occupational therapist.* Assesses and intervenes related to fine motor skills, that is, small muscle activity.
- *Adaptive physical educator.* Designs physical education activities for students with physical, health, or other special needs that affect participation in traditional programs.
- *Nurse.* Key person for gathering needed medical information about students with disabilities and interpreting such information from physicians and other medical personnel.
- *Bilingual special educator.* Professional trained in both special education and bilingual education who specializes in serving students from diverse cultural and linguistic backgrounds.
- *Mobility specialist.* Helps students with visual impairments learn how to become familiar with their environments and how to travel from place to place safely.
- *Sign language interpreter.* Listens to classroom instruction and relays it to students who are deaf or hard of hearing using sign language.
- *Professional from outside agencies.* Provides services away from school (for example, private school, hospital, juvenile justice system) and serves as the liaison between such services and school personnel, especially during transitions from such services back to school.
- *Advocate.* Serves as an advisor and sometimes represents parents at meetings related to their children with disabilities, especially when parents believe they are not knowledgeable enough about the legal and educational requirements of special education.

Parents and Students

When decisions are being made concerning a student with a suspected or documented disability, the best interests of the student and her family must be represented. The parents—or a person serving in the role of a parent, such as a guardian or foster parent—have the right to participate in virtually all aspects of their child's educational program (Olivos, Gallagher, & Aguilar, 2010; Trainor, 2010), a topic addressed in more detail later in this chapter.

Often parents are strong allies for general education teachers. They can assist teachers by reviewing at home what is taught in school, rewarding their child for school accomplishments, and working with school professionals to resolve behavior and academic problems.

Whenever appropriate, students with disabilities also should be active participants in decision making about their own education. Increasingly, educators are involving students so they can directly state their needs and goals and learn to advocate for themselves, a concept referred to as **self-determination** (Branding, Bates, & Miner, 2009; Chambers, Wehmeyer, Saito, Lida, Lee, & Singh, 2007). The extent of student participation on the team depends on the age of the student, the type and impact of the

Some professionals, like sign-language interpreters, provide highly specialized services to specific groups of students.

PROFESSIONAL EDGE
Self-Determination for Students with Disabilities

Think how you would react if other people constantly controlled your life, deciding what you should wear, where you should go, what career you should pursue, and what type of housing and roommates you should have. Beginning at a very young age, children typically begin to express their wishes, and they learn that they have a right to act on those wishes. (For example, have you ever tried to convince a 3-year-old that the two articles of clothing she selected to wear do not match?) But despite good intentions by professionals and parents, many students and adults with disabilities have been denied opportunities to make their own life decisions. Reversing this situation has become a goal for the field (for example, Martin, Van Dycke, Christensen, Greene, Gardner, & Lovett, 2006; Wehmeyer, 2007).

STUDENT-LED IEPS

When students lead their IEP meetings, they learn to think and advocate for themselves (Danneker & Bottge, 2009). They can learn to do this beginning at a very early age. For example, elementary students might have the role of introducing their parents to the team and describing to team members what they have been learning in school. Students in middle school might explain their disabilities and the impact of those disabilities, share their strengths, and discuss accommodations needed. In high school, students might lead the entire conference, working to ensure that the IEP and transition plan reflect their preferences and plans for the future.

General education teachers find that students who actively participate in their IEP meetings have better skills for interacting with adults, better understanding of their special needs, greater awareness of resources available to help them, and more willingness to accept responsibility for themselves (Test et al., 2004).

PERSON-CENTERED PLANNING

Another method of self-determination called *person-centered planning* was developed by professionals from both the United States and Canada and usually is related to IEP planning. It emphasizes these dimensions:

- *Community presence.* Identify the community settings that the student uses and the ones that would benefit him. The intent is to incorporate these settings into the educational planning process.
- *Choice.* Identify decisions made *by* the student and decisions made *for* the student. The goal of person-centered planning is to transfer as many choices to the student as possible.
- *Competence.* Identify the skills that will best assist the student to participate fully in the school and community and the strategies that will be most effective for teaching those skills.
- *Respect.* Clarify roles the student has in the school and local community. The goal is to strengthen and expand those roles and decrease or eliminate personal characteristics that might cause the student to be perceived by others in a stereotypical way.
- *Community participation.* Specify people with whom the student spends time at school and in other settings. The goal is to identify individuals who can advocate for the student and to foster friendships with age-appropriate peers.

A number of person-centered planning approaches have been developed, and you may find that one of these is used in your school district. They include Making Action Plans (MAPs), Planning Alternative Tomorrows with Hope (PATH), and Circle of Friends.

Sources: Adapted from "Benefits of and Barriers to Elementary Student-Led Individualized Education Programs," by J. Danneker and B. Bottge, 2009, *Remedial and Special Education, 30,* pp. 225–233; and *Person-Centered Practices: Building Personalized Supports That Respect the Dreams of People with Disabilities,* by REACH of Louisville, n.d., retrieved September 15, 2004, from http://www.reachoflouisville.com/person-centered/Default.htm. Reprinted with permission.

---

disability, and the professionals' and parents' commitment. In general, the older the student, the greater her ability to contribute, and the higher the value placed on her contribution, the greater the participation. Thus, first-grade students with disabilities usually are not expected to participate in making most decisions about their education. However, high school students with disabilities usually attend and participate in their team meetings, and their priorities and preferences are central to decision making (Arndt, Konrad, & Test, 2006). These students often have strong opinions about what they would like to do after high school, and they also take on more responsibility for monitoring their progress in reaching their goals (Hartman, 2009). You can learn more about student participation on teams in the Professional Edge.

How Can You Decide Whether a Student Need Might Be a Disability?

You will play a key role in deciding whether a student in your class should be evaluated for the presence of a disability. Although youngsters with obvious intellectual, sensory, and physical impairments usually are identified when they are infants or toddlers, learning, language, attentional, and behavioral disabilities—such as those displayed by Christopher, introduced at the beginning of the chapter—often are not diagnosed until children experience difficulty in school. Because you are the professional in daily contact with the student, you are the person most likely to notice an unmet need. It is your judgment that usually initiates the process of increasingly intensive interventions and, potentially, the special education decision-making process.

Analyze Unmet Needs

As you teach, you sometimes will discover that you have a nagging concern about a student. This concern might begin early in the school year, or it might take several months to emerge. For example, when you review a student's records of academic progress and consider your own impressions and evaluation of student work, you may decide that the student's achievement is not within the typical range, given the standards of your school district, community expectations, and state achievement standards. Should you ask other professionals to assess the student for interventions and eventually, if needed, for eligibility for special education? Perhaps. But first, you need to ask yourself some questions.

What Are Specific Examples of Unmet Needs?   Having a vague worry about a student is far different from specifically stating a concern. For example, sensing that a student is unmotivated is not a clear concern. What does the student do that leads you to conclude that motivation is a problem? Is it that the student doesn't make eye contact when speaking to you or that the rewards and consequences that other students enjoy seem to have no effect, positive or negative, on this student? If you are thinking that the student is not making enough academic progress, what does that mean? Is it that classmates have mastered letters, sounds, and blends, but this student knows only about half the letters? Is it that other students easily use basic math procedures in solving multiple-step equations, but this student makes computational errors in eight out of ten problems? Vague concerns and hunches must be supported by specific information. Phrases such as "slow in learning," "poor attitude toward school," "doesn't pay attention," and "never gets work completed" might have very different meanings to different professionals. To prepare to share your concern with others, your first step is to ask yourself "When I say the student . . . , what examples, supported with data, clarify what I mean?"

Is There a Chronic Pattern Negatively Affecting Learning?   Nearly all students go through periods when they struggle to learn, behave inappropriately, or otherwise cause you concern. Sometimes a situation outside school affects a student. For example, parents divorcing, the family being evicted from its apartment, elderly grandparents moving in with the family, or a family member being injured or arrested might negatively affect student learning or behavior. However, the impact of these traumatic events should not be permanent, and the student should gradually return to previous levels of functioning.

Students with disabilities also may be affected by specific situations and events, but their learning and behavior needs form a chronic pattern. In other words, they struggle over a long period of time regardless of the circumstances. For example, Betsy, who has a learning disability, has difficulty remembering sight words no matter what level they are or how creatively they are introduced. Jared, a high school student with an emotional disability, is withdrawn whether sitting in a large class or interacting in a small group. Julianna, an eighth grader who had a severe head injury last year, usually seems to grasp abstract concepts as they are taught, but she struggles to describe or apply them after instruction.

Are the Unmet Needs Becoming More Serious as Time Passes?   Sometimes a student's needs appear to become greater over time. For example, Ben, who seemed to see well at the beginning of the school year, now holds books closer and closer to his face, squints when he tries to read, and complains about headaches. Karen, who began the school year reluctant but willing to complete assignments, refuses to do any work during class by November. Indications that a student's needs are increasing are a signal to ask for input from others.

Is the Student's Learning or Behavior Significantly Different from That of Classmates?   As you think about your concerns about a student, ask yourself how he compares to other students. For example, it has been demonstrated that students at risk for special education referral achieve at a significantly lower level than other students and are more likely to have serious behavior problems (Hosp & Reschly, 2003). However, if you have eight students who are all struggling, the reason might be that the information or skills are beyond the reach of the entire group or that your teaching approach is not accomplishing what you had planned. Even though self-reflection is sometimes difficult, when many students are experiencing problems, it is important to analyze how the curriculum or teaching might be contributing to the situation. In such instances, you should make changes in those two areas before seeking other assistance.

Keep in mind that many students have needs that *do* signal the presence of disabilities. Perhaps you are an elementary teacher who cannot seem to find enough books at the right level for one student in your fourth-grade class who is almost a nonreader. Perhaps you are an eighth-grade social studies teacher who is worried about two students' apparent inability to read the textbook or understand the themes of history integral to your curriculum. Maybe you are an algebra teacher who finds that one student seems to lack many prerequisite skills for succeeding in the course. Students with disabilities have needs that are significantly different from those of most other students.

Do You Discover That You Cannot Find a Pattern?   In some instances, the absence of a pattern in students' learning or behavior is as much an indicator that you should request assistance as is a distinct pattern. Perhaps Curtis has tremendous mood swings, and you arrive at school each day wondering whether he will have a good day or a bad day. However, you cannot find a way to predict which it will be. Or consider Becka, who learns science with ease but is failing English, according to a colleague on your seventh-grade team. You are not sure why her learning is so different in the two subjects. In a third example, in physical education, Tyrone seems to have average motor skills on some days but on other days frequently stumbles and cannot participate fully in the learning stations you have created.

Communicate Your Observations and Try Your Own Interventions

Your analysis of your students' unmet needs is the basis for further action. Although you eventually may decide to formally seek assistance for one of your students, part of your responsibility in attempting to help the student is gathering other information and trying to resolve the problem first.

Contact the Parents   One of your first strategies should be to contact the student's family (O'Connor, 2010). Parents or other family members often can inform you about changes in the student's life that could be affecting school performance. Family members also can help you understand how the student's activities outside school might influence schoolwork, including clubs, gang involvement, employment, and responsibilities at home. Further, by contacting the family, you might learn that what you perceive as a problem is mostly a reflection of a cultural difference. For example, a student whose family emigrated from Thailand is extremely quiet because silence signals respect in her native culture, not because she is unable to participate.

Parents also are your partners in working to resolve some student learning problems (for example, Benner & Mistry, 2007; Hughes & Kwok, 2007). They can assist you in monitoring whether homework is completed and returned to school, whether behavior problems are occurring on the walk home, or whether a physician is concerned about a child's medical condition. If you have students whose homes do not have a telephone or e-mail access and whose parents do not have transportation to come to school, your social worker or principal often can help you make needed contact.

www.resources

http://www.rtinetwork.org
The RTI Action Network, part of the National Center for Learning Disabilities, includes many resources to help you understand and implement RtI procedures. Included are separate sections with ideas and links for elementary, middle school, and high school teachers.

Contact Colleagues   Especially as a new teacher, you will want to informally discuss your concerns with other professionals to gain additional perspectives on the student's needs. In many schools, a special education teacher, assistant principal, department chairperson, literacy coach, or another professional can arrange to observe the student in your class and then discuss the observation. If your school psychologist is available, you might ask for consultation assistance. In schools where grade-level teams or other types of teams or departments meet, you can raise your concerns in that context. One hallmark of today's schools is an array of professionals with expertise in many areas. With a little exploration, you will likely find that your school has an in-house resource you can access to check your perceptions against a broader perspective.

Try Simple Interventions   Part of your responsibility as a teacher is to create a classroom where students can succeed. To cultivate such a setting, you can make simple changes as part of your efforts to address a student's unmet needs. Here are some examples:

- Have you tried moving the student's seat?
- Have you incorporated teaching strategies that help the student actively participate in lessons (for example, using choral responding, in which all students together repeat answers aloud)?
- Have you thought about ways to make your tests easier for the student to follow (for example, using more white space between items or sections)?
- Have you given the student only part of an assignment at one time to prevent him from becoming overwhelmed?
- Have you observed the student closely to determine whether helping her work one problem is enough to get her to work on the rest?

These are just a few instructional adjustments that many teachers make; many others are presented throughout this textbook. Sometimes these small accommodations are sufficient to help a student learn. In any case, you should try common interventions before deciding a student might need the far more intensive service of formal interventions or special education.

Document the Unmet Need   If you anticipate requesting assistance for a student, you need to demonstrate the seriousness of your concern and your systematic attempts to help meet the student's needs. If you have implemented a plan to improve student behavior, keep a record of how effective it has been. If you have contacted parents several times, keep a log of your conversations. If you have tried strategies to improve student learning, be prepared to describe those strategies and share the data you have gathered related to their impact. Documenting student needs serves two main purposes. First, it helps you do a reality check on whether the problem is as serious as you think it is. If you gather data from other students as a comparison, you can judge whether the unmet needs of one student are significantly different from those of typical students. Second, the information you collect will help you communicate with other professionals. Special service providers cannot possibly meet every need in every classroom. Their work is reserved in large part for extraordinary student needs, and your documentation will help in decision making about the amount and intensity of support a student may require.

How Do Students Obtain Special Services?

The majority of students who receive special education have high-incidence disabilities (such as learning disabilities) that you may be the first to recognize. If you teach at the elementary level, you probably will have students nearly every year who you refer for possible special services. If you teach in middle school, junior high, or high school, you will find that many students with disabilities already have been identified before they reach your classes. However, there are exceptions; students may be found eligible for special education at any time during their school years. As a teacher, you always have the option of asking a team of professionals to consider whether one of your students should be considered for special education services.

Having a serious and documented concern about a student is only the first step in considering whether a disability may be present. Your concern brings the student to the attention of other school professionals so that further information can be gathered and decisions made. The specific, formal procedures that must be followed to determine student eligibility for special education services are designed to ensure that only students who truly need these services receive them. These procedures are described in the following sections and summarized in Figure 2.2, which illustrates the flow of the procedures from beginning to end.

Initial Consideration of Student Problems

General education teachers, principals, special services personnel, parents, physicians, and social service agency personnel all may initiate the process of determining whether a student's needs constitute a disability. Most often, however, a general education teacher notices a pattern of academic underachievement, inconsistent learning, serious behavior problems, difficulties in social skills, or a persistent physical or sensory problem. When such problems occur, the teacher brings the student to the attention of others who help decide whether special education services are warranted.

Depending on the policies of your state and local district, there are two ways that the process of formally addressing student learning and behavior concerns can begin: (1) accessing an intervention assistance team or (2) using response-to-intervention procedures, an option available since implementation of the 2004 reauthorization of the Individuals with Disabilities Education Improvement Act (IDEA).

Intervention Assistance Team   One way to begin the process of helping a student suspected of having a disability is to bring the problem to the attention of a team (Friend & Cook, 2010). This team, often called an **intervention assistance team,** usually includes general education teachers, special services personnel, and an administrator. Teachers who want to "bring a student to the team" complete a referral form, on which they describe the student's strengths and problems and describe efforts they have made to assist the student. The teacher then meets with the team to discuss the written information, consider alternative strategies for assisting the student, and determine whether the student should have a detailed assessment for potential special education services (Lane et al., 2003). The unifying characteristic of this type of team is an emphasis on problem solving among all members.

Response to Intervention   A more clearly data-driven and structured procedure for analyzing students' learning problems is called **response to intervention (RtI).** Currently authorized in federal law just for students who may have learning disabilities but increasingly used to address a wide variety of student academic and behavior needs across all school levels, response to intervention calls for the systematic use of increasingly intensive, research-based interventions as a means for deciding whether a disability exists (Colvin, Flannery, Sugai, & Monegan, 2009; Lembke, McMaster, & Stecker, 2010). It is based on the assumption that approximately 75 to 80 percent of students will be able to learn if they receive high-quality instruction, that approximately 15 to 20 percent will benefit from moderately intensive instruction, and that the remaining 5 to 10 percent will need highly intensive instruction and possibly special education services. The Instructional Edge provides examples of interventions and how they vary by intensity.

Here is an example of an RtI procedure. Ms. Petersen is a first-grade teacher. She uses a district-adopted reading program in her class that has been demonstrated through research to be effective with students. This is called a *Tier 1 intervention*. The most recent screening assessment showed that one of Ms. Petersen's students, Jorgé, has not made much progress in reading; his skills are still at a kindergarten level. A team agreed that Jorgé's problems are significant and decided that he should

FIGURE 2.2   The Decision–Making Process for Special Education

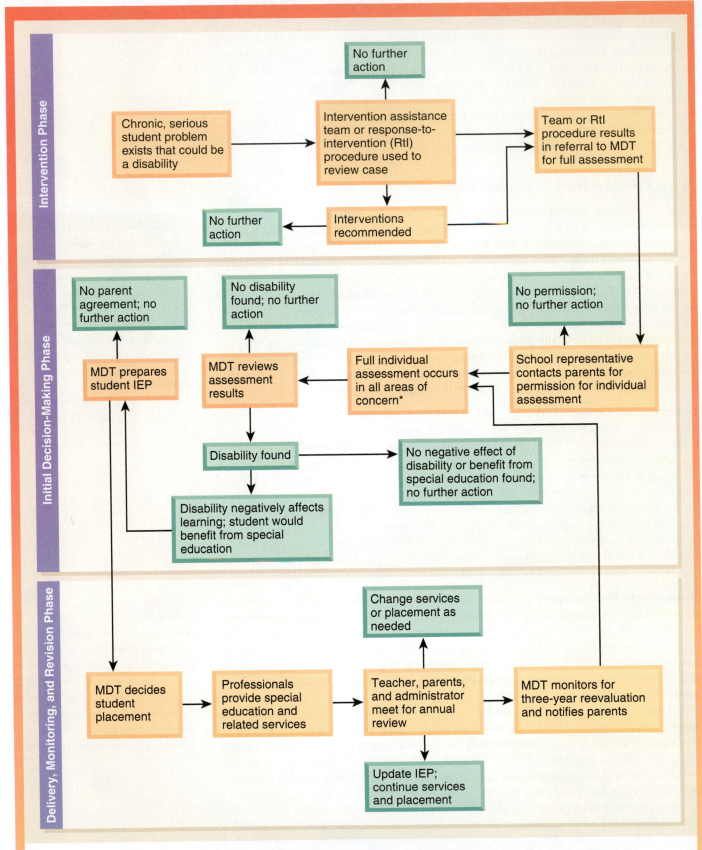

*Federal law permits the identification of students as having learning disabilities on the basis of RtI procedures. When this option is used, the full assessment activities may be significantly reduced.

INSTRUCTIONAL **EDGE**

RtI and Intensity

Response to intervention is based on increasingly intensive interventions designed to avoid, if at all possible, the need for special education. Here are several dimensions that are used to determine intensity:

- *Frequency of intervention* In Tier 2 (sometimes called targeted intervention), an intervention may be offered three or four times each week. In Tier 3 (sometimes called intensive intervention), interventions typically occur five times per week.
- *Duration of intervention sessions* In Tier 2, the intervention might be implemented for 30 minutes per session. In Tier 3, the intervention might be implemented for 45 minutes per session.
- *Location of the intervention* In Tier 2, the intervention may be implemented in the general education setting. For example, three fourth-grade teachers skill group all their students and provide interventions in homogeneous groups to students in need while other students complete practice or enrichment activities. In Tier 3, intervention typically occurs in a setting away from the general education classroom.
- *Group size* Although specific group guidelines do not exist, Tier 2 interventions tend to be delivered in larger groups in middle or high school (for example, 6–10 students) and smaller groups in elementary school (for example, 3–4 students). Tier 3 interventions often require a small group size—usually fewer than four— and sometimes comprise one-to-one instruction.

- *Individual implementing the intervention* In Tier 2, the general education teacher often is responsible for implementing the intervention, and in some cases paraprofessionals may assist with this instruction. At Tier 3, a reading specialist, psychologist, special educator, or other specialist may be assigned to instruct the targeted students.
- *Type of intervention* Tier 2 includes research-based programs and strategies that supplement, enhance, and support Tier 1 instruction (Vaughn, 2003). Tier 2 instruction is systematic and explicit, and it provides students with multiple opportunities to practice skills essential for success in Tier 1. Two examples in reading at the elementary level are peer-mediated instruction (such as peer tutoring) and repeated readings (reading the same story or material several times to improve reading fluency and comprehension). In Tier 3, students receive highly concentrated interventions that are more tailored to their individual needs. Examples of these interventions include teaching specific strategies to improve vocabulary, comprehension, or pre-algebraic math skills.

As you might imagine, several of these dimensions can be changed at one time. Further, students may move up and down through the tiers, depending on what data indicate about their learning.

---

participate in a supplemental reading program in a small group led by the school's reading specialist. This service occurred four times each week for 30 minutes and was considered a Tier 2 intervention. After 12 weeks, the team reviewed the data gathered weekly about Jorgé's progress and noted that he still was not making adequate progress to catch up to his peers. The team enrolled Jorgé in an even more intensive skills-based reading program delivered five days a week for 50 minutes. If data indicate that the Tier 3 intervention does not work, the team may review the data, gather additional assessment information, and make a decision about Jorgé's eligibility for special education.

Although RtI is most likely to be implemented at the elementary level, it can occur whenever professionals determine a student is experiencing learning problems that are significant and interfering with achievement (National High School Center, National Center on Response to Intervention, and Center on Instruction, 2010). For example, Dana is a ninth-grade student whose assessed skills in written language are far below those of her peers. As a Tier 2 intervention she is enrolled in a composition class with 11 other students; in this one-semester class the teacher focuses on key elements of written language. The goal is for Dana to complete the course and improve her skills so that she can take a more traditional elective next semester. If her skills do not improve, she will probably be enrolled in a Tier 3 elective with a smaller group of students with a teacher as well as a literacy coach.

IDEA permits RtI but does not mandate it, and so although it is becoming common practice you should check locally to see whether an RtI procedure is in place. Further, the specific number of tiers of intervention, the length of time that interventions are implemented, and the exact nature of the interventions vary depending on state and local policies (Dexter, Hughes, & Farmer, 2008; Zirkel & Krohn,

The concept of response to intervention (RtI) arose from recognition that the traditional approach for identifying students with LD was a "wait-to-fail" model, in which students had to fall far enough behind in achievement to show a large discrepancy with their potential. RtI calls for intervention as soon as a problem is documented.

CASE IN PRACTICE

Response to Intervention: Looking at the Data

Mr. Thomas is a fourth-grade teacher attending a meeting to discuss Samuel, one of his students who is a struggling reader. Here is a brief segment of the conversation among Mr. Thomas, the school psychologist, and the reading specialist:

Mr. Thomas: With assistance from Ms. Jefferson (a paraprofessional), I completed the reading fluency measure for all my students last week. Overall, the students are just a little below average for this point in the school year, reading at 85 words per minute with fewer than five errors. But Sam is reading at only 50 words per minute, making an average of eight errors.

School psychologist: With these data and the other information you've provided, we should discuss whether Sam should start receiving more intensive instruction.

Reading specialist: Looking at his data, I can add that I already have a group that he could join, if we can work out the schedule. There are four other students with similar levels of skills, and I'm using the supplemental fluency materials from our reading program. But I would need you to do a quick curriculum-based check twice each week to see if his fluency is improving.

Mr. Thomas: We can work on the schedule. It's important to do something so we can see that Sam is making progress. And we just need to talk a little bit about the data collection.

School psychologist: I'd also like to suggest that Sam participate in the peer tutoring program with the sixth graders. I think he would benefit from repeated reading with one of the older students.

Mr. Thomas: That's a good idea. I do have some questions, though. For how long will we try these two interventions? What will happen if Sam's reading fluency does not improve? I'm a little concerned that we should refer him for an assessment for special education. I spoke with his mother on Monday, and she commented that Sam is talking about hating school and being embarrassed about his problems with reading. She is very worried about keeping his attitude positive.

School psychologist: The guideline is to intervene for 12 weeks, but if we don't see any change in six weeks, we can meet to decide if we should make a different decision. Will Sam's mother agree to assist by reading with him at home each evening? That would provide both her and us with an ongoing basis for communicating.

REFLECTIONS

Why are you, as an elementary, middle school, or high school teacher, responsible for implementing increasingly intensive interventions for your students who struggle to learn? Why do professionals consider data-based decision making so important in planning interventions for students? If you were Mr. Thomas, what additional questions would you have about the planned intervention?

RESEARCH NOTE

Response to intervention is being used to address behavior concerns as well as academic concerns. Fairbanks, Sugai, Guardino, and Lathrop (2007) found that an intervention more intensive than overall classroom management strategies (that is, Tier 2) was effective in addressing the behavior problems of half the students studied; the other half responded to an even more intensive intervention (that is, Tier 3).

2008). The Case in Practice illustrates what might occur at a team meeting when RtI is being implemented.

Regardless of variations among RtI models, one element of RtI is consistent: Even though it is included in federal special education law, it is largely the responsibility of general educators to carry it out (Mellard, McKnight, & Woods, 2009; Walker-Dalhouse et al., 2009). That is, as a general education teacher, you may be asked to work with a small group of students in your grade level during scheduled reading and language arts time, or you may be asked to assist in gathering data concerning student skill acquisition. Ultimately, the goal of RtI is to prevent some students from ever needing special education. At the same time, following RtI procedures will help ensure that students who need specialized instruction will receive it as soon as a problem is noticed.

Note that whether an intervention assistance team or RtI procedure is initiated, a parent is not legally required to be involved in the process. However, educators should notify parents of their concerns and enlist parental assistance in trying to solve the problem. In some schools, parents are routinely invited to team meetings. Parents should never be surprised when the possibility of providing special education is raised. They should be made aware of the existence of any serious problem as soon as it is noticed.

The Special Education Referral, Assessment, Eligibility, Planning, and Placement Process

If a student does not respond to increasingly intensive interventions or the intervention assistance team believes the student's needs are serious enough to consider special education as an option, the student's parents are formally contacted and the assessment process begins. At this point, a **multidisciplinary team (MDT)**—consisting of parents, educators, and others as appropriate—assumes responsibility for making educational decisions regarding the student. No student may receive special education unless the steps discussed in the upcoming sections are followed.

Parents' Rights   Before any discussion of how a student comes to receive special education services can proceed, it is essential that you understand how central parents are in all aspects of the referral, assessment, eligibility, planning, and placement process (Yell, Ryan, Rozalski, & Katsiyannis, 2009). As summarized in Figure 2.3, parents are key participants in all decision making related to their child's suspected or documented disability. They must be informed of their rights in their own language

www.resources

http://www.speakingofspeech.com/IEP_Goal_Bank.html
The Speaking of Speech website includes a bank of IEP goals appropriate for students with different types of needs. Do these examples meet the criteria for high quality goals as outlined in this chapter?

FIGURE 2.3 Parents' Rights in Special Education

IDEA stipulates procedural safeguards to ensure protection of parents' rights to be active participants in their child's education. The following are some of the major safeguards provided to parents:

1. Parents are entitled to be members of any group that makes decisions about the educational placement of their child.

2. Parents are to be given written notice before the school initiates, changes, or refuses to initiate or change the identification or educational placement of their child.

3. Parents can participate directly in the determination of their child's eligibility for special education and the development of the individualized education program (IEP) and its periodic review, generally at least annually (but in some cases, every three years).

4. The school must obtain written, informed parental consent before conducting an initial formal evaluation and assessment and before initially placing a student in a program providing special education and related services.

5. Parents can inspect and review any educational records maintained by the school district or other agency providing services under IDEA. Access to educational records will be granted to parents without unnecessary delay and before any meeting regarding an IEP or before any hearing relating to identification, evaluation, or placement of the child. In no case should access be delayed more than 45 days after the request has been made.

6. Parents may request and the school district must provide information on where an independent educational evaluation may be obtained. In some instances, parents may have the right to an independent educational evaluation at public expense. The results of an independent evaluation obtained by the parents at private expense will be considered by the local school district in any decision about provision of a free appropriate public education to the child. Such results also may be presented as evidence at a due process hearing.

7. Parents have the right to request mediation as a means to resolving conflict with the school district concerning their child with a disability. Mediation must be available to parents prior to a due process hearing, but it may not delay a hearing. The district, not the parents, bears the cost of mediation.

8. Parents have the right to request a hearing before an impartial hearing officer in cases in which they disagree with school district decisions regarding their child's education. The hearing may relate to any aspect of special education. If the parents fail to win a due process hearing at the local level, they may appeal the results at the state department of education. After this step, if parents still are dissatisfied with the outcome of the hearing, they may initiate court action. Note, though, that if parents' legal actions are judged to be frivolous, the school district may seek to recover the funds spent in defending the district.

9. Parents must be fully informed of their rights and the procedural safeguards related to special education. These rights must be communicated in writing and in a form parents readily can understand.

Sources: Adapted from "Questions and Answers about IDEA," *NICHCY NewsDigest, 21* (2nd ed.), January 2000, Washington, DC: National Information Center for Handicapped Children and Youth, retrieved September 15, 2004, from http://nichcy.org/pubs/newsdig/nd21txt.htm; and "Parental Rights in Special Education," April 2004, Trenton: New Jersey Department of Education, retrieved September 15, 2004, from http://www.state.nj.us.njded/parights/prise.pdf.

Before a team can make a decision about a student's eligibility to receive special education, a comprehensive and individual assessment of strengths and needs must be completed.

and in a manner they can understand (Fitzgerald & Watkins, 2006). If you teach older students, you also should know that beginning at least one year before reaching 18 years of age, students also must be informed directly of their rights, and at age 18, most students assume the rights that parents have held for them (National Center on Secondary Education Transition, 2002).

The very first application of parents' rights comes before any assessment process begins. That is, parents must give written permission for their child to be individually assessed. Although it is not common for parents to deny permission, if they do, the process must stop unless the school district asks for a hearing to compel parents to comply. As you read about the rest of the procedures related to special education, you will notice many references to the rights parents have.

Components of Assessment Although the specific requirements regarding the types of data gathered vary somewhat by state and by the type of initial intervention processes used, assessment generally involves gathering information about a student's strengths and needs in all areas of concern. Typically, if the student has not had a vision and hearing screening and you have reason to suspect a sensory impairment, these tests precede other assessments. If sensory screening raises concerns, the parents are notified of the need for a more complete assessment by a physician or appropriate specialist.

Assessments completed by school professionals may address any aspect of a student's educational functioning (Yell, 2006). Often, for example, the student's intellectual ability is assessed. An individual intelligence test (often referred to as an *IQ test*) is administered and scored by a school psychologist or another qualified school professional. Academic achievement usually is assessed, too. The student completes an individual achievement test administered by a psychologist, special education teacher, educational diagnostician, or other professional. A third area often evaluated is social and behavior skills. This evaluation might involve a checklist that you and parents complete concerning a student's behavior, a test given by the school psychologist, or a series of questions asked of the student.

Another domain for assessment is the student's social and developmental history. A school social worker may meet with the parents to learn about the student's family life and major events in her development that could be affecting education. For example, parents might be asked about their child's friends and favorite out-of-school activities, their expectations for their child as an adult, and their child's strengths. Parents also might be asked whether their child has had any serious physical injuries, medical problems, or recurring social or behavior problems.

As another assessment component, a psychologist, counselor, or special education teacher often observes the student in the classroom and other settings to learn how he responds to teachers and peers in various school situations. For example, a psychologist may observe Scott, who usually plays with younger students during recess and gets confused when playground games are too complex. Scott also watches other students carefully and often seems to take cues for how to act from how they are acting. Similarly, a special educator may observe D. J., a sixth-grade student, in the cafeteria to try to understand what is triggering his many behavior incidents there. Such observations are helpful for understanding students' social strengths and needs.

If a potential need exists for speech, occupational, or physical therapy, another component is added to the assessment. The professionals in those areas complete assessments in their respective areas of expertise. A speech/language therapist might use a screening instrument that includes having the student use certain words, tell stories, and identify objects. The therapist also might check for atypical use of the muscles of the mouth, tongue, and throat that permit speech and for unusual speech

RESEARCH NOTE

According to IDEA, parents must receive a statement of their rights, written at a level they can easily understand (that is, seventh– or eighth–grade reading level). Fitzgerald and Watkins (2006) found that 92 percent or more of the parents' rights statements found on state department of education websites were written above this level.

habits such as breathiness in speaking or noticeable voice strain. Similarly, an occupational or physical therapist might assess a student's gait, strength and agility, range of motion, or ability to perform fine motor tasks such as buttoning and lacing.

Throughout the entire assessment process, IDEA specifically gives parents the right to provide information to be used as part of the evaluation. In addition, as the general education teacher, you typically provide details on the student's performance in class, patterns of behavior, and discrepancies between expectations and achievement. Your informal and formal observations play an important role in assessment.

Assessment Procedures   The exact procedures for assessing a student's needs vary according to the areas of concern that initiated the assessment process. The assessment must be completed by individuals trained to administer the tests and other assessment tools used; the instruments must be free of cultural bias; the student's performance must be evaluated in a way that takes into account the potential disability; and the assessment must provide data that are useful for designing an appropriate education for the student. School professionals are responsible for ensuring that these obligations are met.

RtI and Assessment   It should be noted that, at least for students being assessed to determine whether a learning disability exists, the data gathered as part of RtI procedures may be the basis for making that decision. Based on state and local policies, RtI data may be used in lieu of other assessments of ability and achievement, or, as is more common, these data may be used in addition to other assessment data.

Decision Making for Special Services

After a comprehensive assessment of the student has been completed, the multidisciplinary team (MDT) meets to discuss its results and make several decisions. The first decision the MDT must make is whether the student is eligible under the law to be categorized as having a disability. If team members decide that a disability exists, they then determine whether the disability is affecting the student's education and from that they decide whether the student is eligible to receive services through special education. In most school districts, these decisions are made at a single meeting, and parents must agree with the decisions being made or the student cannot receive special education services. Most school districts have specific guidelines to direct team decision making about the presence of a disability and the need for special education services. However, the decisions ultimately belong to the team. For example, most states specify that students identified as having a mild intellectual disability should have an IQ less than 70 as measured on an individual intelligence test and should have serious limitations in adaptive behaviors. However, if a student's score is slightly above 70 and her adaptive skills are particularly limited, a team can still decide that she has a mild intellectual disability. Likewise, if a student has a measured IQ lower than 70 but seems to have many adaptive skills, the team might decide that she does not have an intellectual disability.

If the MDT determines the student has a disability affecting her education and is eligible for services according to federal, state, and local guidelines, the stage is set for detailed planning of the student's education and related services. This planning is recorded in the student's **individualized education program,** or **IEP,** the document that outlines all the special education services the student is to receive. More details about IEPs and their preparation are provided later in this chapter.

The final decision made by the MDT concerns the student's placement. *Placement* refers to the location of the student's education. For most students (but not all), the placement is the general education classroom, often with some type of support offered, either there or part-time in a special education setting such as a resource room. According to IDEA, when a placement is a location other than general education, justification must be provided for that decision. Later in this chapter, special education services are discussed and placement options are outlined in more detail.

dimensions of DIVERSITY

In IDEA 2004, the federal government for the first time required states (and thus local school districts) to take steps to correct the disproportionate representation of students from minority groups, a problem that is particularly serious in the areas of learning disabilities, intellectual disabilities, and emotional disabilities.

In your school district, the essentials of the procedures described in the preceding sections must be followed, but the specific steps, paperwork required, and names for the different parts of the process may vary. Nonetheless, all school district procedures are designed to ensure that students with disabilities are systematically assessed and that a deliberate and careful process is followed to provide for their education needs, and you are a critical participant throughout that process.

Monitoring Special Education Services

In addition to specifying the procedures that must be followed to identify a student as needing special education services, federal and state laws also establish guidelines for monitoring student progress. The monitoring process ensures that a student's educational program remains appropriate and that procedures exist for resolving disputes between school district personnel and parents.

Annual Reviews   The first strategy for monitoring special services is the **annual review.** At least once each year, a student's progress toward his annual goals must be reviewed and the IEP changed or updated as needed. Not all multidisciplinary team members who participated in the initial decisions about the student's disability and educational needs are required to play a part in the annual review. However, a teacher instructing the student and an administrator or other professional representing the school district must meet with the student's parents to discuss whether goals and objectives (as required) have been met and what the next steps in the student's education should be. In practical terms, if your school district completes all annual reviews during a given month, you will find that the special educators with whom you work are unavailable because of their other responsibilities, such as meeting with parents. Depending on local practices, you will likely be asked to attend annual reviews for some students. For many students, a general education teacher is most knowledgeable about their day-to-day functioning. This concept was highlighted with the mandate in IDEA that a general education teacher participate in the development of most students' IEPs, not necessarily by writing them but by contributing a classroom perspective.

The most recent reauthorization of IDEA included a new provision related to reviewing a student's educational program. In some cases, an IEP may be reviewed once every three years instead of every year. If a state has this option, the IEP must be reviewed at natural transition points for the student (for example, moving from middle school to high school), and parents have the right to request that an annual review be completed.

Three-Year Reevaluations   A second monitoring procedure required by law is the **three-year reevaluation.** At least every three years, and more often if deemed necessary by the MDT, students receiving special education services must be reassessed to determine whether their needs have changed. This safeguard is designed to prevent students with disabilities from remaining in services or programs that may no longer be appropriate for them, and parents are informed of this reevaluation but do not have to give permission for it to occur. In some cases, the reevaluation includes administering all the tests and other instruments that were used initially to identify the student as needing special education. However, in some cases IDEA permits existing information to be used for reevaluation instead of requiring new assessments. In fact, with parent and team agreement, the reevaluation may not involve any new assessment at all (Yell, 2006). On the basis of the three-year reevaluation, the MDT meets again to develop an appropriate IEP.

Additional Reviews   In addition to annual reviews and three-year reevaluations, IDEA stipulates that an IEP must be revised whenever a lack of expected progress toward achieving goals is noted, reevaluation information is gathered, or parents bring to the attention of the MDT information that affects the IEP. This suggests that an IEP may need to be revised more frequently than the once per year mandated by the basic requirements of the law. In some cases, necessary changes can be made with parent approval and without reconvening the team.

Parents have one more formal mechanism for obtaining information about their child's learning. IDEA specifies that the parents of students with disabilities have the right to receive progress reports about their children as often as do parents of typical learners. In many school districts, this means that formal communication about student learning progress now occurs every six or nine weeks during the school year, that is, at the end of each grading period.

Due Process   Yet another strategy for monitoring students receiving special education services is **due process,** the set of procedures outlined in the law for resolving disagreements between school district personnel and parents regarding students with disabilities (Bateman, 2009). Due process rights begin when a student is first brought to the attention of a team as potentially having a disability. Both the school district and parents are entitled to protection through due process, but parents typically exercise their due process rights when they fear the school district is not acting in the best interests of their child (Wright & Wright, 2006). For example, if parents have their child independently evaluated because they believe the assessment for special education did not accurately portray his needs and if the school district does not agree with the findings of the independent evaluator, the parents may request a due process hearing. Parents also may request a hearing if they disagree with the goals and objectives listed on the IEP and with the way services are being provided to meet those goals and objectives.

Due process hearings seldom address blatant errors on the part of the school or parents regarding special education; most often, they reflect the fact that many decisions made about students with disabilities are judgment calls in which a best course of action is not always clear. For example, Mr. and Mrs. Dotson filed a due process complaint in a dispute about the services their son Jeremiah would receive when he transitioned from middle school to high school. They wanted him to spend much of the day in general education classes with assistance from a paraprofessional and other supports. School district personnel maintained that Jeremiah's behavior outbursts when faced with frustrating tasks as well as his tendency to become overwhelmed in unfamiliar situations indicated the need for most of his education to occur in a separate setting. When discussion reached an impasse, a hearing officer was assigned by the State Department of Education to hear the case and issue a decision.

In practice, most school districts and parents want to avoid due process hearings, which tend to be adversarial and can damage the parent–school working relationship to the detriment of the student. To foster a positive working relationship, IDEA requires that all states have a system in place to offer **mediation** to parents at no cost as an initial means for resolving conflicts with schools (Wright & Wright, 2006). In mediation, a neutral professional skilled in conflict resolution meets with both parties to help them resolve their differences informally. Mediation, however, is not allowed to cause delay in the parents' right to a due process hearing. A hearing is preceded by mediation—a less formal dispute resolution strategy—unless parents decline this option.

Whether or not mediation occurs, IDEA also mandates a dispute resolution session, a sort of last chance for reaching agreement (Hazelkorn, Packard, & Douvanis, 2008; Mueller, 2009). If neither mediation nor a dispute resolution session is successful, a hearing is conducted by an independent and objective third party selected from a list provided by the state, but the school district bears the expense (D'Angelo, Lutz, & Zirkel, 2004). If either party disagrees with the outcome of a due process hearing, the decision can be appealed to a state-level review hearing officer. If disagreement still exists, either party can then take the matter to court.

If a due process hearing occurs concerning a student you teach, you may be called to testify. In such a case, you would be asked to describe the student's level of functioning in your classroom, the supports you provided, and your efforts with

RESEARCH NOTE

Although nearly all students with disabilities participate in their school's music classes, a survey of 200 music educators indicated that they seldom participated in IEP meetings and believed they had inadequate preparation to work with these students (McCord & Watts, 2010).

fyi

When students who have IEPs transfer from district to district or even from state to state, IDEA requires the new school district to provide services similar to those provided by the previous school district until records can be reviewed and the previously received services adopted, amended, or dropped.

other special service providers to ensure the student was successful. An administrator and an attorney might help you prepare for the hearing, and they would answer any questions you might have about your role.

What Is an Individualized Education Program?

As mentioned earlier, the document that the multidisciplinary team uses to decide the best placement for a student with an identified disability and that serves as a blueprint for a student's education is called an *individualized education program* (IEP). The IEP addresses all areas of student need, including accommodations to be made in the general education setting and the services and supports to be provided there. The IEP also is the means through which student progress is documented (Etscheidt, 2006). General education teachers generally are involved as team participants in preparing an IEP if a student has any participation in the general education setting (Hackett, 2009; Turnbull, Huerta, & Stowe, 2006). Whether or not you are the teacher who serves in this role for particular students, if you have students with disabilities in your classroom, you will have opportunities to examine their IEPs or to meet with special educators to review highlights of these important plans, just as Ms. Lee, introduced at the beginning of the chapter, learned.

Accessing IEPs and learning about your state's requirements for them has been made more efficient with the increasing use of technology. The Technology Notes explains some of the electronic options related to IEPs and the procedures for developing them.

Required Components of an IEP

The essential components of the IEP were established by P.L. 94-142 in 1975, and they have been updated through the years. Although specific state requirements for IEPs vary somewhat, the federally required elements of IEPs are described in the following sections.

Present Level of Performance   Information about a student's current level of academic achievement, social skills, behavior, communication skills, and other areas of concern must be included on an IEP. This information serves as a baseline and makes it possible to judge student progress from year to year. Often, highlights of the information collected from the individual assessment of the student or response to intervention data are recorded on the IEP to partially meet this requirement. Individual achievement test scores, teacher ratings, and summary assessments by specialists such as speech therapists and occupational therapists also can be used to report the present level of performance. Another component of this assessment is information about how the student's disabilities affect involvement in the general education curriculum.

Annual Goals and Short-Term Objectives   *Annual goals* are the MDT's estimate of what a student should be able to accomplish within a year, related to meeting his measured needs resulting from the disability. For some students, annual goals may refer primarily to academic areas and may include growth in reading, math problem solving, and other curricular areas. Specifically, a student with a learning disability might have an annual goal to read and comprehend books at a particular grade level or demonstrate skills for finding and keeping a job. For other students, annual goals address desired changes in classroom behavior, social skills, or other adaptive skills. An annual goal for a student with a moderate intellectual disability, for example, may be to order a meal at a fast-food restaurant. A student with autism might have participating in conversation as a goal. Annual goals also may encompass speech therapy, occupational and physical therapy, and other areas in which a student has specialized needs. There is no right number of annual goals. Some students have as few as two or three, and others as many as eight or ten. However, IDEA specifies

TECHNOLOGY NOTES

Implementing Response to Intervention Using Technology

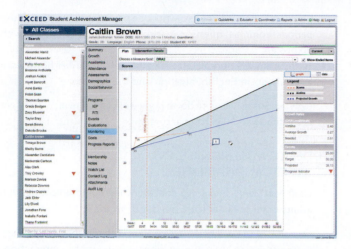

Effectively implementing response to intervention requires familiarity with research-based interventions, frequent and valid monitoring to student learning progress, and analysis of the gathered data so that next steps can be identified. Fortunately, many websites are providing free materials to teachers so that they can implement RtI without having to develop interventions, assessments, and graphing tools on their own. Here are two of the most comprehensive sites to help you with RtI.

INTERVENTION CENTRAL (http://interventioncentral.org)

This website has so many ideas and options for RtI that you may need several visits to explore all the information available. Here are highlights:

- Under "Academic Resources" you will find research-based interventions for reading comprehension, reading fluency, math, writing, and other skill areas.
- Under "Behavior Resources" you will find many positive ideas for addressing behavior problems, including bullying

and unmotivated students. Strategies include the use of behavior contracts and "mystery motivators."

- In the "tools" section, you will find a variety of templates for graphing data. Other tools include random item generators so that you can easily create assessments on skills such as reading comprehension, writing, and math computation.
- The RtI blog includes issues and topics, including the importance of principal leadership in implementing RtI and the dilemma of sustaining RtI when budget cuts limit staff members available to assist in implementing intensive interventions.

RTI WIRE (http://www.jimwrightonline.com/php/rti/rti_wire.php)

This website boasts being the most complete, free set of RtI resources available to teachers. Examples of the materials and information you can find at the site include these:

- In "understand the model" you will find descriptions of various approaches to RtI as implemented across the United States.
- In "use teams to problem solve," you will find descriptions of the various team models being used across the states to make RtI a reality.
- In "select the right intervention" are links to many sites with academic interventions that span topics and skills areas as well as grade levels.
- In "monitor student progress" are links to sites with data templates using a variety of recording strategies, from simple tallies of behaviors to more complex approaches such as time sampling.
- In "graph data for visual analysis," the tools include several Excel® spreadsheets preformatted so that you can easily enter and graph your student data.

---

that annual goals must be measurable, and increased emphasis is placed on annual goals that enable a student to progress in the general education curriculum.

Short-term objectives are descriptions of the steps needed to achieve an annual goal, and they may or may not be required for all students, depending on state policies. Federal law requires that short-term objectives be written only for the IEPs of students with significant intellectual disabilities. For example, for a student with multiple disabilities whose annual goal is to feed herself, short-term objectives might include grasping a spoon, picking up food with the spoon, and using the spoon to transport food from plate to mouth. The number of short-term objectives for each annual goal relates to the type and severity of the disability, its impact on student learning, and the complexity of the goal. Examples of IEP goals and objectives are included in the Professional Edge on the next page.

Extent of Participation in General Education   In keeping with the trend toward inclusive practices, the IEP must include a clear statement of justification for placing

dimensions of DIVERSITY

Although most researchers express concern at the overrepresentation of boys in special education (particularly those who are African American), others are concerned that girls, who are underrepresented, are being denied services that they need in order to succeed later in life (Arms, Bickett, & Graf, 2008).

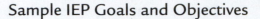

PROFESSIONAL EDGE

Sample IEP Goals and Objectives

The goals and objectives on IEPs are related to assessed student needs, and they are written in specific ways (Bateman & Linden, 2006). They must

- be aligned with the curriculum for the grade level of the student, regardless of the severity of the student's disability.
- be measurable and specify the conditions under which the student should be able to carry out an activity (such as the reading level of print material or the people with whom a student should communicate).
- indicate the level of mastery needed (such as a level of accuracy in an assignment).

Goals usually outline progress expected for approximately one school year. For all students with significant intellectual disabilities who take alternate assessments and, in some states, for all students with disabilities, goals are supplemented by short-term objectives or benchmarks that measure progress toward achieving the annual goal. The following are sample IEP goals and objectives:

STUDENTS WITH MILD/MODERATE DISABILITIES

- *Goal:* When assigned to write an essay of three paragraphs, Jerome will use complete sentences, capital letters, and punctuation with 80 percent accuracy.

Objective: When assigned to write one paragraph, Jerome will use periods, commas, question marks, and exclamation points with 90 percent accuracy.
- *Goal:* Susan will complete at least 80 percent of her homework assignments in English, algebra, and U.S. history.

Objective: Susan will write down homework assignments 90 percent of the time with 90 percent accuracy.

STUDENTS WITH SIGNIFICANT INTELLECTUAL DISABILITIES

- *Goal:* Maria will make eye contact when communicating with adults in school in at least five out of six trials.

Objective: Maria will make eye contact with the speech/language therapist during individual sessions in five out of six interactions initiated by the therapist.
Objective: Maria will make eye contact when the special education teacher calls her name and looks at her in at least five out of six interactions.
Objective: Maria will make eye contact when a classroom teacher calls her name and looks at her in at least five out of six interactions.

---

a student anywhere but in a general education classroom for all or part of the school day. Even for extracurricular and other nonacademic activities, if the team excludes the student from the setting for typical peers, a specific, evidence-based explanation of why that student cannot participate in such activities must be part of the IEP.

Services and Modifications Needed   The IEP contains a complete outline of the specialized services the student needs; that is, the document includes all the special education instruction to be provided and any other related services needed. Thus, a student receiving adaptive physical education has an IEP indicating that such a service is needed. A student's need for special transportation is noted on the IEP, too. A student who is entitled to transition or vocational assistance has an IEP that clarifies these services. Perhaps most important, the statement of services must include information about the supplementary aids and services, described in Chapter 1, to be provided so that the student can access and progress in the general education curriculum.

One additional element of this IEP component concerns assessment. IDEA stipulates that if a student needs accommodations (for example, extended time) on district or state assessments, including high-stakes assessments, these should be specified on the IEP and implemented throughout the school year, not just for high-stakes tests. If a student is to be exempt from such assessments, the team must ensure the student will complete an alternate assessment that takes into account her functioning levels and needs. The Elementary and Secondary Education Act set specific limits on which students are exempt from high-stakes testing and eligible for alternate assessments, and these limits were confirmed and clarified in IDEA. Most of the students with disabilities you teach will be required to complete mandated assessments, and their scores must be considered for measuring adequate yearly progress (AYP).

Part of identifying services is indicating who is responsible for providing them. Any of the professionals introduced earlier in this chapter could be listed on the IEP to deliver special services. As a general education teacher, you may be included, too. For some students, you will be the teacher who completes most of the required instruction; for others, you will assist but not be primarily responsible. For example, a student with a mild intellectual or learning disability probably will be able to complete many class tasks with minor accommodations that you can make. However, if your student has significant intellectual and physical disabilities, other professionals undoubtedly will help develop the materials and activities you will use when the student is in your classroom.

Behavior Intervention Plan   Every student with significant behavior problems, not just those students labeled as having emotional disabilities, must have as part of the IEP an intervention plan based on a functional assessment of the student's behavior. This requirement reflects the increasing pressure for students to be supported in general education settings and the acknowledged difficulty of accomplishing that goal without fostering appropriate student behavior.

Date of Initiation and Frequency and Duration of Service and Anticipated Modifications   Each IEP must include specific dates when services begin, the frequency of the services, the types of accommodations and modifications that are part of the services, and the period of time during which services are offered. Because the law generally requires that student progress in special education be monitored at least once each year (or alternatively, three years), the most typical duration for a service is a maximum of one year. If during the year an MDT member sees a need to reconsider the student's educational plan, additional IEP meetings can be convened or amendments made by phone with parent approval.

Strategies for Evaluation   When a team develops an IEP, the members must clarify how to measure student progress toward achieving the annual goals and how to regularly inform parents about this progress (Etscheidt, 2006). For example, when short-term objectives are written, the team indicates the criteria and procedures to be used to judge whether each objective has been met. For the student learning to move around the school without assistance, the criteria might include specific point-to-point independent movement, and a checklist might be used to judge student progress toward reaching the goal.

Transition Plan   For each student who is 16 years of age or older, part of the IEP is an outcomes-oriented description of strategies and services for ensuring that the student will be prepared to leave school for adult life. This part of the IEP is called a **transition plan.** Students with disabilities who are college bound might have a transition plan that includes improvement of study skills, exploration of different universities and their services for students with disabilities, and completion of high school course requirements necessary to obtain admission to a university. For students who plan to work immediately after graduation, the transition plan might include developing skills such as reading employment ads and filling out job applications, as well as developing important job skills such as punctuality and respect toward people in authority and customers. This plan must be tailored to match the assessed strengths and needs of the particular student. It is updated annually, with participation by professionals from agencies outside the school typically increasing as the student nears graduation or school departure at age 21 or 22.

In addition to the basic components, IEPs have several other requirements. For example, they are signed by the individuals who participate in their development, including the student's parent or guardian. In addition, if a student has highly specialized needs, they must be addressed in the IEP. Examples of such needs are behavior, communication, braille (unless specifically excluded on the IEP), and assistive technology. In such cases, appropriate supports, services, and strategies must be specified (Yell, 2006).

Working TOGETHER

Understanding the Intervention, Assessment, and Decision-Making Process

Even experienced teachers sometimes have questions about their roles and responsibilities related to intervention assistance teams, response to intervention procedures, the eligibility process, and the design of special education services. Here are a few common questions and their answers:

- I work in a high school, and most students already have been identified by the time they get to this level. Do high schools still need to have intervention assistance teams and procedures in place for response to intervention?

    Federal law requires that across all levels of schools, including high schools, a system must be in place to identify students who are not making expected academic progress. However, recent research indicates that RtI in high school must take into account significant context factors, including impact on graduation requirements, student choice in selecting interventions, involvement of parents, and staff members' perceptions of their roles (National High School Center et al., 2010).

- Do all the teachers on the middle school team need to attend the intervention assistance, response to intervention, and/or IEP team meetings for their students who have been referred or assessed?

    In most cases, it is not reasonable to expect all the teachers on the middle school team to attend a meeting about a student with a suspected or identified disability. The composition of the prereferral team is a school's decision. In some cases, the middle school team might actually serve as the intervention assistance team. In others, a representative from the team might work with the team monitoring a student's response to intervention. When an initial IEP is written, in nearly all cases one general education teacher can provide a representative perspective for the team.

- Are general education teachers responsible for writing parts of the IEP?

    Federal law requires participation of general education teachers in most IEP meetings because they bring an important viewpoint to them. However, those teachers generally do not write sections of the IEP. No matter what your role (for example, elementary, middle school, or high school teacher; related arts teacher; technology specialist), you are obligated to carry out any IEP provisions that pertain to you, including participating in services offered in the general education classroom and making adjustments to assignments and strategies as noted in the IEP.

The Value of IEPs

Although technical and potentially time consuming, IEPs guide the education of students with disabilities. An IEP helps you clarify your expectations for a student and provides a means for you to understand the student's educational needs. The document also informs you about the types of services the student receives and when the student's educational plan will next be reviewed.

Your job is to make a good-faith effort to accomplish the goals and/or short-term objectives on the IEP as they relate to your instruction. If you do that, you will have carried out your responsibility; if you do not do that, you could be held accountable. For example, suppose an IEP indicates that a student should learn the concept of freedom of speech. You can demonstrate that you are helping the student learn this by providing class discussion, role-play activities, and access to appropriate resources on the Internet, even if the student does not master this concept. If you state that the student is expected merely to read about the concept in the textbook chapter and you refuse to create opportunities for supported learning in this area, you may be violating the IEP.

Do you have questions about your role in the prereferral, referral, or IEP process? Additional considerations related to your role are presented in the Working Together.

Students with disabilities who are enrolled in faith-based private schools are entitled to some benefits from IDEA. Although these students must be identified by the public school district in that locale, they may receive only limited services that do not have to be available at the private school, only at the public school (Eigenbrood, 2004).

What Services Do Students with Disabilities Receive?

The services that a student with disabilities can receive are comprehensive, limited only by the stipulation that they must be necessary as part of that student's education. These services are provided in a variety of placements. Both the services and placements are determined by the multidisciplinary team.

Special Education and Related Services

As noted in Chapter 1, the types of services students receive can be grouped into three categories: special education, related services, and supplementary aids and services. *Special education* refers to the specially designed instructional services students receive. These services may include a curriculum aligned with the standard curriculum but significantly simplified, access to a special education teacher qualified to teach students with a particular disability, and individualized instruction using specialized approaches. When a student's special education teacher comes to the classroom and teaches with the general education teacher, that is special education. When a student leaves a classroom for 30 minutes three times each week for intensive tutoring, that is special education. When a middle school or high school offers a life skills class for students with disabilities, that is special education, too.

Related services refer to all the supports students may need in order to benefit from special education. Examples of related services are speech therapy, transportation, physical and occupational therapy, adapted physical education, counseling, psychological services, and social work. A student's need to ride a special bus equipped with a wheelchair lift is a related service, as is a student's need for assistance with personal care such as toileting.

Supplementary aids and services are all means used to enable students to succeed in a general education setting. They include materials that are written at a different level or reformatted to make them easier for students to read, peer or paraprofessional support, assistive and other technology, and even special professional development for general education teachers so they know how to address students' instructional needs.

As you might guess, the range of possibilities for special education, related services, and supplementary aids and services is immense. Some students, particularly those with high-incidence disabilities, receive a limited number of special education services and perhaps no related services at all. For example, Lucas, a high school student with a learning disability in math, attends a geometry class in which a special education teacher teams with a math teacher. Lucas's assignments are sometimes shortened, and he is allowed extra time to complete tests. He already is looking into colleges that are recognized for their support of students with his special needs. Students with more complex or severe disabilities may have a more highly specialized special education as well as numerous related services. For example, Charmon, a student with physical and intellectual disabilities, receives the services of a physical and occupational therapist, and speech/language therapist, as well as a special education teacher.

Student Placement and Educational Environments

Where students receive their educational services is guided by the principle of least restrictive environment (LRE), that is, the setting in which they can succeed that is most like the setting for other students. In today's schools, the LRE for most students is general education for more than 80 percent of the school day. Nearly all school districts still have some separate special education classrooms, but the requirement that teachers delivering core academic instruction be highly qualified and the increasing recognition that students with disabilities can, with supports, succeed when educated with typical peers has caused educators to rethink such classrooms for all except students with extraordinary needs. As in Ms. Turner's school, which you read about at the beginning of the chapter, emphasis now is on designing systems of support in general education settings. Figure 2.4 shows the IDEA continuum of placements, now referred to as *educational environments,* that must exist for students with disabilities; it also provides recent data on the percentage of students with disabilities in each of those placements.

As discussed earlier, the decision about placement is made by the MDT and reviewed along with the IEP at least annually (or in some states and for some students, every three years). Placement can be changed as often as appropriate, with parental

FIGURE 2.4 **IDEA Educational Environments for Students with Disabilities**

Percentage of time
outside general education

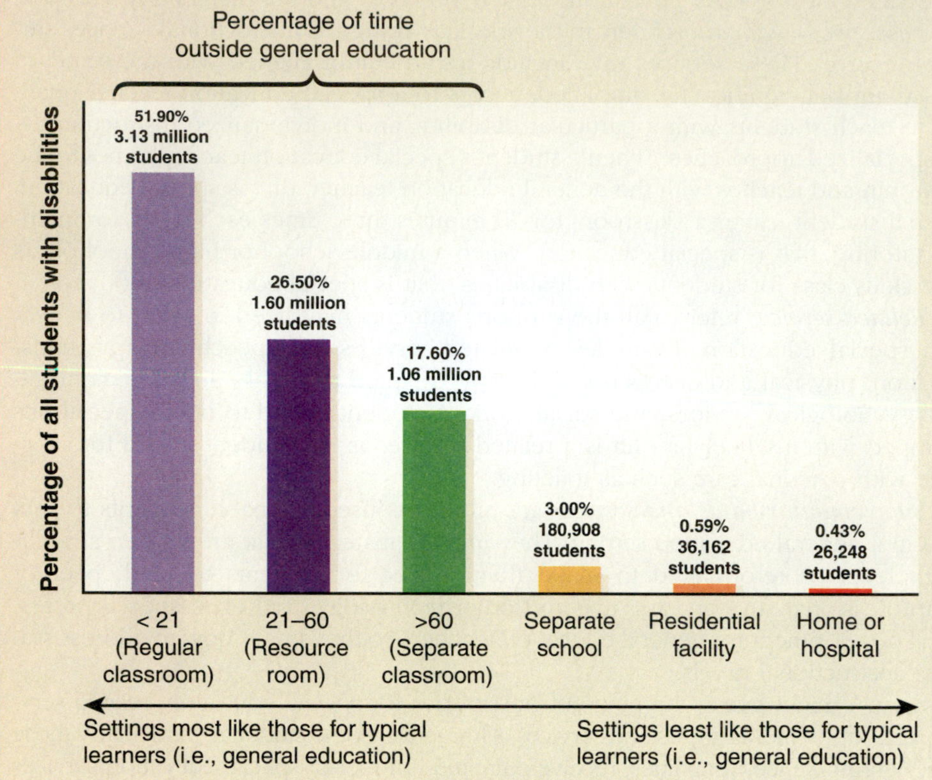

Source: U.S. Department of Education. (2009). *Twenty-eighth annual report to Congress on the implementation of the Individuals with Disabilities Education Act.* Washington, DC: Author.

permission. Generally, if the parents and school district representatives disagree about placement, the student remains in the current placement until the disagreement is resolved. Exceptions to this occur when discipline issues arise. Administrators may unilaterally change a student's placement (for example, through suspension) for up to 10 days in a school year, provided such methods are used with other students, too. If students with disabilities bring a weapon or drugs to school, they can be placed in an alternative educational setting for up to 45 school days while a decision is made concerning long-term placement (Yell, 2006).

Regular (General Education) Classes   More than half of students with disabilities spend more than 80 percent of the school day in a general education setting (U.S. Department of Education, 2009). A kindergartener with a communication disorder might be served by a speech/language therapist who comes to the classroom and teaches language lessons with the general education teacher. For a middle school student with intellectual and physical disabilities, an inclusion specialist might adjust a lesson on fractions by helping the student learn how to cut simple shapes into halves. For a high school student with a learning disability, a paraprofessional might provide assistance in biology class in carrying out lab directions and recording and completing assignments. This student also might have one special education class for instruction in study skills and learning strategies.

Resource Programs   Another group of students with disabilities attends school mostly in general education settings but also receives assistance in a special education classroom, often called a **resource room,** for 21 to 60 percent of the day (U.S. Department of Education, 2009). In elementary schools, resource programs sometimes are organized by the skills being taught. For instance, from 10:00 AM until 10:45 AM, basic math skills may be taught, and all the second- and third-grade students needing math assistance may come to the resource room at that time. Alternatively, some resource rooms are arranged by same-age groups. For example, all fifth graders with disabilities needing some separate service may go to the resource room together.

In middle schools and high schools, students are scheduled to have resource classes in the same way the rest of their classes are scheduled. For example, a student may attend a resource class that provides study strategies or reviews the curriculum being taught in general education classes. In some instances, core academic instruction is taught in the resource room by a special educator highly qualified in the academic area; this class might be called, for example, resource English or resource Algebra.

Separate Classes   Some students with disabilities attend *separate classes* for more than 60 percent of the school day (U.S. Department of Education, 2009). In this placement, a special education teacher has the primary instructional responsibility for the students who receive grades from the highly qualified special educator for the subjects taught there. However, a separate class placement does not mean that students remain in a single classroom or that they do not interact with typical peers. They may receive instruction in different classrooms from several special educators, particularly in high school. They may attend a general education class for part of the day or a certain class period, and they also may participate with peers in related arts, assemblies, and other school activities.

Although Kurt is in a separate class most of the day at his high school, he takes a horticulture class with students without disabilities. A paraprofessional accompanies him because he has limited ability to understand directions and needs close guidance from an adult to participate appropriately. At Kyle's elementary school, 30 minutes each day is called *community time,* during which students read and write together, share important events from their lives, and learn about their neighborhood and community. For community time, Kyle goes to Mr. Ballinger's fifth-grade class. The students are about Kyle's age and assist him with the community activities and learning. Kyle's special education teacher helps Mr. Ballinger plan appropriate activities for him during that time.

Separate Schools   A small number of students with disabilities attend public or private *separate schools* (U.S. Department of Education, 2009). Some separate schools exist for students with moderate or severe intellectual and physical disabilities, although such schools are, for the most part, becoming obsolete. Other separate schools serve students with multiple disabilities who need high levels of specialized services. For example, in a small community near Chicago, approximately 25 students are educated at a separate school. These students all need the services of a physical and occupational therapist; most have complex medical problems that must be closely monitored; and most cannot move unless someone assists them. These students have opportunities for contact with typical peers who are brought to the school through a special program to function as "learning buddies." Some students with serious emotional disabilities also attend separate schools. These students might harm themselves or others. They are not able to cope with the complexity and social stress of a typical school, and so the least restrictive environment for them is a school where their highly specialized needs, including therapeutic supports, can be addressed.

Residential Facilities   A few students have needs that cannot be met at a school that is in session only during the day. If students in separate settings have even greater needs, they might attend school as well as live in a public or private *residential facility.* Few students with disabilities are educated in this manner (U.S. Department of Education, 2009). The students for whom this placement is the LRE often are those with severe emotional problems or severe and multiple intellectual,

www.resources

http://www.ed.gov/about/reports/annual/osep/index.html
Many statistics about students with disabilities and how they receive education services come from the federally compiled annual reports to Congress on the implementation of IDEA. You can find copies of the reports from the past several years at this website.

sensory, and physical disabilities. In some states, students who are blind or deaf also might receive their instruction in a residential facility, an approach that is supported by some professionals and parents and opposed by others.

A somewhat different group of students also can be considered under the residential placement option. According to IDEA, children and young adults with disabilities who are incarcerated in the juvenile justice system must receive special education services. Further, children and young adults who are convicted of crimes and incarcerated as adults also may be entitled to special education services, unless the IEP team determines there is a compelling reason to discontinue services.

Home and Hospital Settings   A very small number of students with disabilities receive their education in a home or hospital setting (U.S. Department of Education, 2009). This placement often is used for students who are medically fragile, who are undergoing surgery or another medical treatment, or who have experienced an emotional crisis. For a few students with limited stamina, school comes to their homes because they do not have the strength to come to school. That is, a special education teacher comes to the home for a specified amount of time each week to deliver instruction. Home instruction also might be used for a student with serious behavior problems or for a student for whom there is disagreement about the appropriate school placement, pending resolution of the dispute.

One more point should be made about placement. For some students, the team may decide that their learning will suffer significantly if schooling stops during the summer. For these students, any of the services in any of the placements just described can be extended into school breaks and summer vacations through extended school year (ESY) programs.

Placements in separate classes and schools are far less preferred than those that support the education of students with disabilities in general education classrooms and schools. When placement includes a specialized setting, it often is appropriate for a specific skill or service and for a specific and limited period of time. The appropriate and required educational setting for most students with disabilities is the same classroom they would attend if they did not have a disability. This means that you, as a general education teacher, will play a central major role in the education of students with disabilities. Thus, it is important for you to understand the kinds of special services your students receive and your role in assisting to deliver them.

WRAPPING IT UP

BACK TO THE CASES

This section provides opportunities for you to apply the knowledge gained in this chapter to the cases described at the beginning of this chapter. The questions and activities that follow connect to the everyday activities of all teachers.

MS. KUCHTA will report information about the Tier 1 interventions she has used with Christopher at the meeting with the SIT. While some school districts have selected research-based Tier 1 interventions, other school districts may not have adopted specific strategies.

To help you understand RtI and the tiers of intervention, conduct a Google search using the key words "Response to intervention for reading disabilities" (or search for mathematics, writing, or another core academic area). Review at least three of the websites listed, noting the primary features of interventions described, and decide which you would consider for your own teaching. Share this information with two peers from your class and, as a group, determine which intervention you would recommend to the entire class.

MS. LEE is looking forward to working with the special educator and the speech/language therapist, but she is unsure of what to expect. Will this mean lots of meetings? Should she be keeping records of Jennifer's academic and language difficulties? Using information from the chapter, the Council for Exceptional Children (http://www.cec.sped.org/Content/NavigationMenu/SpecialEdCareers/Job_Profiles_Speci.htm), and the American Speech-Language-Hearing Association website (http://www.asha.org), outline how a special educator and speech/language therapist work with teachers and IEP teams. Then, explain what Ms. Lee should expect to happen in her classroom.

MS. TURNER, as you may remember, works with her school's inclusive practices leadership team. As time passes, she becomes concerned that students' right to an inclusive education may create unrealistic expectations for a general educator's ability to work with those who have exceptional learning needs. She has other concerns about the amount of paperwork and time required to meet the IDEA requirement that general education teachers participate in IEP meetings. How would you assure Ms. Turner that she is a necessary participant in the process and address her concerns? In your answer, specifically address both Ms. Turner's responsibilities and personal concerns. What resources might you access to supplement the information you found in this chapter?

SUMMARY

- The individuals who work to ensure that students with disabilities receive an appropriate education include general education teachers; special education teachers; related service providers such as school psychologists, counselors, speech/language therapists, social workers, administrators, paraprofessionals, and other specialists as well as parents and students.

- To determine whether special services are needed, general education teachers usually begin a process of deciding whether to request that a student be assessed for the presence of a disability by analyzing the nature and extent of the student's unmet needs; clarifying those needs by describing them through examples; determining that the needs are chronic and possibly worsening over time; comparing the student's needs to those of others in the class; possibly recognizing that no pattern seems to exist for the student's performance; and intervening to address the unmet needs and documenting those efforts.

- If concerns persist, the student's needs may be assessed by an intervention assistance team (IAT) or response to intervention (RtI) procedures.

- If increasingly intensive interventions do not resolve the concerns, a multidisciplinary team (MDT) follows federally established special education referral and assessment steps, including completing an individualized assessment with parental permission, making decisions about the need for special education, developing an individualized education program (IEP), and monitoring special education services.

- If parents and school district personnel disagree on any aspect of a student's special education program or services and if the disagreement cannot be resolved informally, due process procedures, including mediation and dispute resolution sessions, are used to ensure that the student receives an appropriate education.

- When an IEP is developed, it includes the student's present level of functioning, goals (and sometimes objectives), justification for any placement outside general education, needed services, the person(s) responsible for the services, beginning and ending dates for service delivery, and criteria for evaluation. The IEP also may include a behavior intervention plan and a transition plan and generally must be reviewed at least annually (in a few states, every three years).

- The services a student may receive, as outlined by the IEP, include special education, related services, supplementary aids and services, and a designation of placement: a general education classroom, resource program, or separate special education setting.

- General education teachers play an integral role in the education of students with disabilities, from the early identification of students who appear to have special needs, through assessment and identification, to IEP implementation.

APPLICATIONS IN TEACHING PRACTICE

A VISIT TO AN MDT MEETING

Ms. Richards teaches science to sixth graders. Beginning in the fall, she and her team members will be working with Natasha, a student newly identified as having a learning disability. Natasha enjoys many friends and extracurricular activities, but she has extraordinary difficulties with reading fluency, comprehension, and written expression. She also has significant problems organizing her work and remembering to complete and turn in assignments. To help set appropriate goals for the coming year, Ms. Richards is participating in an MDT meeting to create an IEP for Natasha. Although it would be ideal for all the sixth-grade team members to attend the meeting, that is not feasible, and so Ms. Richards is representing her colleagues as well.

General education (sixth-grade) science teacher: Ms. Richards
General education (fifth-grade) teacher: Mr. Tucker
Special education middle school teacher: Ms. Hill

(Continued)

APPLICATIONS IN TEACHING PRACTICE
A VISIT TO AN MDT MEETING   (*Continued*)

Principal: Ms. Hubbert
Psychologist: Ms. Freund
Speech/language therapist: Mr. Colt
Parent: Ms. Wright

Ms. Hubbert: Our next task is to develop goals for Natasha. I'd like to suggest that we discuss academics first, then social areas, and wrap up with related services needed. Let's look at Natasha's strengths first—in all those areas.

Mr. Colt: Natasha has a very strong speaking vocabulary. She is considerably above average in that realm.

Ms. Freund: Along with that, according to the assessment data, Natasha's general knowledge is very good. She also is near grade level in basic math skills.

Mr. Tucker: It's not really academics, but one strength I see that Natasha has is her willingness to help classmates. She really wants to assist everyone in class to learn even when she herself is struggling. She also was very active in extracurricular activities this year. She participated in the service learning program, volunteered to read to the kindergarten class, and competed in the after-school sports program.

Ms. Hill: As we write academic goals, then, we need to remember that Natasha has strong vocabulary skills and general knowledge and that she does not need services in math. Perhaps we can use her social skills and other interests to help in the academic arena. Ms. Wright, what strengths do you see in Natasha?

Ms. Wright: Hmmm. She minds me, that's for sure. And she helps out around the house with chores. She likes to help me watch her baby brother.

Ms. Hill: Helping really seems to be Natasha's thing—let's keep that in mind.

Ms. Hubbert: Let's focus for a minute on academic areas of need.

Ms. Freund: Reading comprehension and written expression are by far the areas that need the most work. Natasha's comprehension is just at a beginning third-grade level, and her written expression is about a year below that.

Ms. Wright: She says she doesn't like reading because the other kids make fun of her when she can't read the words, and they tease her when Mr. Tucker gives her a "baby book."

Ms. Richards: In middle school, that could be even more of a problem. We need to be sure that she uses the same textbooks as the other students next year. I'm sure we can also arrange to get some supplemental materials for her to use at home. Before we finish today, let's be sure that we talk about that some more.

Ms. Freund: Ms. Richards and Ms. Hill, given what you know and have heard about Natasha, what might be priorities for next year?

Ms. Hill: I agree that comprehension is the key. Given the data and the other information we're discussing, I think a goal should be for her to improve her comprehension to a fourth-grade level on reading tasks that include stories, textbooks, and other materials such as children's magazines.

Ms. Hubbert: Ms. Wright, how does that sound to you? [*Ms. Wright nods.*]

The conversation continues.

Before the meeting ends, the MDT has generated the following additional goals in reading comprehension using materials at her instructional level:

- Natasha will identify with 90 percent accuracy the main characters and the problem and solution in literature that she reads at a third-grade level.
- Natasha will comprehend 80 percent of both narrative and expository material she reads aloud (third- to fourth-grade level) and 80 percent on material she reads to herself.

QUESTIONS

1. What are the responsibilities of the professionals represented at the MDT meeting? Which of the professionals are required to attend? How would your responses be different if this were an annual review?
2. What role does Ms. Richards take at the meeting? Why is her presence helpful in creating an educational program for Natasha? How else might she contribute during this meeting? Now apply what you said about Ms. Richards to your own teaching role. What contributions should you make when plans are being made for the educational services for a student with a disability?
3. What is the purpose of having both the fifth-grade teacher and a sixth-grade teacher attend the meeting? How might this improve the quality of the IEP? What problems might it cause?
4. What steps likely were completed prior to this meeting? How did the general education teacher prepare? What other team responsibilities were met?
5. What part of the IEP is the team addressing? What other parts have to be completed before the meeting ends? What must occur for the IEP to be valid?
6. How might this meeting be different if Natasha was a kindergartener going to first grade? A tenth-grader going to eleventh grade?

Go to Topic 6: Response to Intervention and Topic 7: IEP Process, in the My EducationLab (http://www.myeducationlab.com) for your course, where you can:

- Find learning outcomes for Reponse to Intervention and IEP Process along with the national standards that connect to these outcomes.
- Complete Assignments and Activities that can help you more deeply understand the chapter content.
- Apply and practice your understanding of the core teaching skills identified in the chapter with the Building Teaching Skills and Dispositions learning units.
- Examine challenging situations and cases presented in the IRIS Center Resources. (optional)
- Access video clips of CCSSO National Teachers of the Year award winners responding to the question, "Why Do I Teach?" in the Teacher Talk section. (optional)
- Check your comprehension on the content covered in the chapter by going to the Study Plan in the Book Resources for your text. Here you will be able to take a chapter quiz, receive feedback on your answers, and then access Review, Practice, and Enrichment activities to enhance your understanding of chapter content. (optional)

chapter 3

Building Partnerships Through Collaboration

LEARNING Objectives

After you read this chapter, you will be able to

1. Explain what the term *collaboration* means, and describe how collaboration is part of providing services to students with disabilities.

2. Clarify how an emphasis on collaboration in schools shapes the roles and responsibilities that you have as a general education teacher.

3. Describe collaboration-based services for students with disabilities and other special needs, including shared problem solving, co-teaching, teaming, and consulting.

4. Identify ways you can work effectively with parents to successfully educate students with special needs.

5. Outline your responsibilities in working with paraprofessionals, and describe ways you can enhance collaboration with them.

MS. RANDELMAN and Ms. Pickett have four students in their co-taught biology class of 36 who have individualized education programs (IEPs). Natalie, who has a mild learning disability related to math, does not need assistance in the course. James receives services for emotional disabilities; he is fully capable of completing the work, but he has an extensive plan for addressing his behavior needs. Monika has autism, and the teachers have created comic strip-like stories with pictures to help her understand classroom expectations and to deal with social situations in the classroom. Janet, who has a physical disability and limited vision, comes to class on a motorized scooter but moves about using a walker. She is an average student, and most of her accommodations concern making sure she has large-print materials and assistance with handling lab equipment. During class periods, Ms. Randelman and Ms. Pickett share teaching responsibilities and group the students for instruction in a variety of ways—by skill needs, interest, and random assignment, among others. Their goal is to have every student pass the high stakes biology test at the end of the semester, a requirement for graduation.

What happens when two teachers share instructional responsibilities in a classroom? What topics might Ms. Randelman and Ms. Pickett need to discuss to ensure that their shared teaching is effective?

MS. SWANSON, a fourth-grade teacher, is meeting with Ms. O'Brien, a consultant on autism with whom the school district contracts for assistance when a challenging situation arises and a different and knowledgeable perspective might help to address it. They are discussing Brittany, a student who is spending more and more time in general education. Last year, the maximum amount of time was about an hour, and that occurred during the highly structured math time, a subject in which Brittany excels. This year, one of the goals on Brittany's IEP is for her also to receive reading and writing instruction in the general education classroom. Ms. Swanson comments on the strides Brittany has made in managing the bustling atmosphere of the class, but she is concerned that Brittany is having more and more difficulty transitioning from one activity to another, even though she has a picture schedule that shows her, with times and drawings of activities, each segment of the day. In fact, this meeting was convened when Brittany refused to come with her class to the media center, where the students were to meet a local children's author. Ms. O'Brien listens to the details of what happened, asks Ms. Swanson for her analysis of the situation, offers to observe in the classroom later that day, and plans to meet to decide what strategies might alleviate the behavior challenges.

What options do general education teachers have when one of their students with disabilities is experiencing extraordinary challenges? Why is it important to find solutions to such challenges, instead of deciding prematurely that the student should be placed in a separate special education setting? What is the place of consultation in services for students with disabilities?

MS. MACDOUGAL, the middle school inclusion facilitator, and Mr. Saunders, the seventh-grade team leader, are meeting with Chris's parents, Mr. and Mrs. Werner, for an after-school meeting. Mrs. Werner begins by declaring that the school is discriminating against Chris because of her learning disability. Mr. Werner asserts that Chris should not be singled out in any way because of her special needs and that he was unhappy to learn that she has been receiving tutoring during a lunch period study hall. He stresses that the family already provides tutoring for Chris so this type of discrimination will not occur at school. Further, Mr. and Mrs. Werner show the teachers Chris's modified assignment sheets, another example, they note, of discrimination. When Mr. Saunders starts to explain that he is modifying Chris's work so she can learn more in his class, Mr. Werner cuts him off, stating that a teacher's poor instructional practice is no excuse to destroy a child's self-concept through public humiliation.

If you were Mr. Saunders, what type of assistance would you want from Ms. MacDougal during this difficult interaction? How can you prevent miscommunication in your work with parents of students with disabilities? What should you do if a conflict occurs?

In the past, becoming a teacher—whether in general education or in special education— meant entering a profession frequently characterized by isolation and sometimes loneliness (Little, 1993; Lortie, 1975). Teachers typically spent most of the day alone in a classroom with students. They learned that they were expected to have all the skills to manage student learning and discipline issues, and they rarely had opportunities to discuss their questions, concerns, and misgivings with anyone, especially their colleagues at school.

Over the past several years, that atmosphere of isolation has changed (Troen & Boles, 2010; Waldron & McLeskey, 2010). Elementary school teachers are meeting on grade-level teams to share ideas and problem solve, and middle school and high school teachers are creating interdisciplinary teams to redesign curriculum and share instructional responsibility for smaller groups of students. Response to intervention, the data-based approach to remediating students' skills when they are struggling, is premised on a collaborative problem-solving process. School reform efforts also are characterized by partnerships. For example, entire schools are stressing the need to build collaborative professional learning communities to meet the current expectations of accountability for student learning and address the challenges of twenty-first-century schooling (Maher, Burroughs, Dietz, & Karnbach, 2010).

As the scenes that open this chapter illustrate, these emerging partnerships extend to special educators and other support staff as well. Particularly as schools increase inclusive practices, the working relationships among all the adults involved in the education of students with disabilities become critical (for example, Meadan & Monda-Amaya, 2008; Paulsen, 2008). For example, as a general education teacher, you may find that your grade level or department team periodically meets to discuss the progress of students with disabilities. The goal is to share ideas and concerns in order to collectively ensure that these students are reaching their academic potential. Similarly, you might find that some of your students cannot complete the grade-level work you are accustomed to assigning. To assist you, a special education teacher might meet with you to design the necessary accommodations.

At first glance, these interactions seem like logical, straightforward approaches to optimizing education. And often they are. However, because of the strong education tradition of professionals working alone and the still-limited opportunities many teachers have had in preparing to work effectively with other adults, problems sometimes occur (Friend & Cook, 2010). In some instances, support personnel are reluctant to make suggestions for fear they will sound as if they are interfering with a general education teacher's instruction. In other cases, a general education teacher insists that no change in classroom activities is possible, even though a special educator is available for co-teaching. And when professionals in schools disagree, they may be uncomfortable discussing the issues directly and struggle to find shared solutions.

Professionals in inclusive schools usually assert that collaboration is the key to their success in meeting the needs of all students (Conderman & Johnston-Rodriguez, 2009; Friend & Cook, 2010; Kozik, Cooney, Vinciguerra, Gradel, & Black, 2009; Leach & Duffy, 2009). The purpose of this chapter is to introduce you to the principles of collaboration and the school situations in which professionals are most likely to collaborate to meet the needs of students with disabilities. You also will learn how to develop strong working relationships with parents, an essential part of every teacher's responsibilities and an especially important one when educating students with special needs. The special partnerships that are formed when teachers work with paraprofessionals also are considered. Finally, you will find out how to respond when disagreements arise during collaboration.

What Are the Basics of Collaboration?

As a teacher, you will hear colleagues refer to many of their activities as **collaboration.** Sometimes they are referring to a team meeting to propose ideas to help a student; sometimes they mean sharing a classroom to teach a particular

PROFESSIONAL EDGE

Thinking About Roles and Responsibilities in Collaboration

This activity is designed to help you think about collaborating with special educators. Complete the activity by yourself, and then compare responses with classmates. If possible, ask individuals preparing to be special educators to complete the task as well. Then discuss areas of agreement and disagreement and the implications for working together, whether in the classroom or at other times.

First, review the list of responsibilities for general and special educators. Then decide which professional is responsible for each of them. List each responsibility in the appropriate section of the Venn diagram.

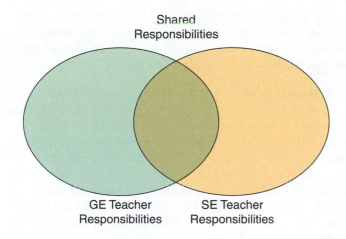

Shared
Responsibilities

GE Teacher
Responsibilities

SE Teacher
Responsibilities

TEACHER RESPONSIBILITIES RELATED TO STUDENTS WITH DISABILITIES

1. Plan for instruction
2. Write the IEP
3. Complete student assessments
4. Communicate with parents
5. Provide report card grades
6. Evaluate student work (for example, assignments, tests)
7. Provide supervision for work of paraprofessionals
8. Implement the classroom supports needed by student (for example, provide calculators, allow students to work on a computer)
9. Provide specially designed instructions to students, that is, learning options not usually found in the general education setting
10. Reteach instruction that students do not understand
11. Gather data about student learning and behavior
12. Prepare materials that take student needs into account (for example, create a word bank; rearrange test items to be clearer)
13. Respond to student behavior issues
14. Raise concerns about student achievement or behavior
15. Place the student's achievement in the context of the curriculum standards
16. Facilitate social interactions between students with and without disabilities
17. Assist students to identify postschool goals and arrange instruction to help them achieve those goals.

---

subject; and sometimes they even use the term as a synonym for inclusive practices. How can all these things be collaboration? Actually, they are not. Collaboration is how people work together, not what they do. As Friend and Cook (2010) have stated, collaboration is a *style* professionals choose to accomplish a goal they share. Professionals often use the term *collaboration* to describe any activity in which they work with someone else. But the mere fact of working in the same room with another person does not ensure that collaboration occurs. For example, in some team meetings, one or two members tend to monopolize the conversation and subtly insist that others agree with their points of view. The team is seated together at a table, but being together is not sufficient to ensure collaboration.

True collaboration exists only when all participants in a team or another shared activity feel their contributions are valued and the goal is clear, when they share decision making, and when they sense they are respected (Conoley & Conoley, 2010). It is how individuals work with each other that defines whether collaboration is occurring. In the Professional Edge, you can complete an activity designed to help you reflect on your thinking about the responsibilities of special education teachers and general education teachers when they collaborate.

Characteristics of Collaboration

Collaboration in schools has a number of defining characteristics that clarify its requirements. Friend and Cook (2010) have outlined these key attributes.

fyi

Along with teachers, you will collaborate with related services professionals such as speech/language therapists, counselors, and social workers. These professionals sometimes work in more than one school, and so challenges can include scheduling meetings and being sure communication is clear.

Collaboration Is Voluntary   Teachers may be assigned to work in close proximity, but they cannot be forced to collaborate. They must make a personal choice to use this style. For example, your principal may tell you and another teacher that you are expected to be part of a response to intervention team. You could choose to keep your ideas to yourself instead of readily participating. Or you could conclude that even though you did not plan on volunteering for this activity, as long as you are a team member, you will contribute. Your principal assigned the activity; you decided to collaborate. Because collaboration is voluntary, teachers often form close but informal collaborative partnerships with colleagues regardless of whether collaboration is a schoolwide ethic.

Collaboration Is Based on Parity   Teachers who collaborate must believe that all individual contributions are equally valued. The number and nature of particular professionals' contributions may vary greatly, but all participants need to recognize that what they offer is integral to the collaborative effort. If you are at a meeting concerning a student's highly complex needs, you might feel you have nothing to offer. However, you have important information about how the student responds in your class and the progress he has made in developing peer relationships. The technical discussion of the student's disabilities is not your area of expertise, nor should it be; your ideas are valued because of your knowledge and skills related to teaching in your classroom. This is an illustration of the collaboration concept of *parity*.

Collaboration Requires a Shared Goal   Teachers truly collaborate only when they share a goal. For example, if a fifth-grade teacher and a special educator want to design a behavior intervention to help support a student with an emotional disability, their goal is clear. They can pool their knowledge and resources and jointly plan the intervention. However, if one teacher wants the student to spend more time in a special education setting and the other opposes that solution, they are unlikely to work collaboratively on this issue. The teachers might even think at the outset that they share a goal—assisting the student—but that broad statement does not capture their differing views of how the student can best be assisted. They need to resolve this difference for collaboration to proceed.

Collaboration Includes Shared Responsibility for Key Decisions   Although teachers may divide the work necessary to complete a collaborative teaching or teaming project, they should share as equal partners the fundamental decision making about the activities they are undertaking. This shared responsibility reinforces the sense of parity that exists among the teachers. In the behavior intervention example, the teachers together decide what the key problems are, what strategies might work, how long to try an intervention, and how the intervention may affect the student. However, if they assign many tasks to just one person, they are not collaborating. Instead, one may ask the school psychologists for ideas, review a book of behavior intervention ideas, and talk to last year's teacher. The other may call the parents to seek their input, interview the student, and prepare any needed materials, such as a behavior chart.

Collaboration Includes Shared Accountability for Outcomes   This characteristic of collaboration follows directly from shared responsibility: That is, if teachers share key decisions, they also must share accountability for the results of the decisions, whether those results are positive or negative. If both teachers carry out their assigned tasks, the behavior intervention they design will have a high probability of success. If one teacher fails to carry out a responsibility, valuable time will be lost and their shared effort will be less successful. If something happens that is wonderful (for example, the student's behavior changes dramatically in a positive direction), the teachers will share the success. If something happens that is not so wonderful (for example, the intervention appears to have no impact on the behaviors of concern), they will share the need to change their plans.

Collaboration Is Based on Shared Resources   Each teacher participating in a collaborative effort contributes some type of resource. This contribution increases commitment

RESEARCH NOTE

Using teacher perception and student achievement data from a southeastern urban school district and applying a specific statistical method, Supovitz, Sirinides, and May (2010) found that principal leadership significantly affects teacher instructional practices and student learning in English/language arts.

and reinforces each professional's sense of parity. Resources may include time, expertise, space, equipment, and other assets. The teachers working on the behavior intervention contribute the time needed to make necessary plans, but they also pool their knowledge of working with students with behavior difficulties, share information about other professionals who might assist them, and contribute student access to the computer and other rewards they design.

Collaboration Is Emergent   Collaboration is based on a belief in the value of shared decision making, trust, and respect among participants. Yet, although these qualities are needed to some degree at the outset of collaborative activities, they are not well developed in a new collaborative relationship. As teachers become more experienced at collaboration, their interactions become characterized by the trust and respect that grow within successful professional relationships. If the teachers described throughout this section have worked together for several years, they may share freely, including offering constructive criticism to each other. If this is their first collaborative effort, they are much more likely to be a bit guarded and polite, because each is unsure how the other person will respond.

Some groups are collaborative while others are not. What would you say it takes to create and sustain collaboration?

Prerequisites for Collaboration

Creating collaborative relationships requires effort on everyone's part. Most professionals who have close collaborative working relationships note that it is hard work to collaborate—but worth every minute of the effort. They also emphasize that collaboration gets better with experience. When colleagues are novices at co-teaching or working on teams, their work seems to take longer and everyone has to be especially careful to respect others' points of view. However, with additional collaboration, everyone's comfort level increases, honesty and trust grow, and a sense of community develops. The following sections discuss some essential ingredients that foster the growth of collaboration.

Reflecting on Your Personal Belief System   The first ingredient for collaboration is your personal beliefs. How much do you value sharing ideas with others? Would you prefer to work with someone to complete a project, even if it takes more time that way, or do you prefer to work alone? If your professor in this course offered the option of a small-group exam, would you be willing to receive a shared grade with your classmates? If your responses to these questions suggest that you prefer working with others, you probably will find professional collaboration exciting and rewarding. If your responses are just the opposite, you might find collaboration somewhat frustrating. For collaboration to occur, all the people participating need to feel that their shared effort will result in an outcome that is better than could be accomplished by any one participant, even if the outcome is somewhat different from what each person envisioned at the outset (Friend, 2000; Sayeski, 2009).

Part of examining your belief system also concerns your understanding of and respect for others' belief systems. This tolerance is especially important for your collaborative efforts with special educators in inclusive programs. For example, what are your beliefs about changing your teaching practices so that a student with disabilities can achieve the standards for your curriculum? At first, you might say that changing your teaching practices is no problem, but when you reflect on the consequences of that belief, you might have second thoughts. For example, changing your practices may mean that you must give alternative assignments to students who need them, that you must deliberately change the way you present information and the way you expect students to learn that information, and that, if needed, you must grade students with disabilities differently from other students.

The special educators with whom you work are likely to believe strongly not only that alternative teaching practices are helpful in inclusive settings but that they are a requirement. How will you respond when you meet a colleague with this belief? If some general education teachers at your school oppose making accommodations for students with disabilities, will you feel pressured to compromise your beliefs and agree with them? As collaboration becomes more integral to public schools, in part because of inclusive practices, it becomes more and more essential to learn to value others' opinions and respectfully disagree while maintaining a positive working relationship.

Refining Your Interaction Skills   The second ingredient you can contribute to school collaboration is effective skills for interacting (for example, Ploessl, Rock, Schoenfeld, & Blanks, 2010). In many ways, interaction skills are the fundamental building blocks on which collaboration is based, because collaboration occurs through interactions with others (Friend & Cook, 2004). There are two major types of interaction skills: communication skills, and steps to productive interactions. You already may have learned about the first type, communication skills, in a public speaking or communication course. These skills include listening, attending to nonverbal signals, and

dimensions of DIVERSITY

Remember that nonverbal communication varies among cultures. The meaning of eye contact (or lack of eye contact) and appropriate distance during interactions are just two examples of nonverbal factors to consider in working with parents from cultures other than your own.

PROFESSIONAL EDGE

Barriers to Effective Communication

Effective communication is essential for professional collaboration. Here are some barriers to communication that teachers and administrators must overcome (Mostert, 1998). Which might apply to you?

- *Advice:* When you offer unsolicited advice to a colleague or parent, that person may be confused by your intent, may reject the advice and form an unfavorable opinion of you, or may feel obligated to follow the advice even if it seems inappropriate. In general, you should offer advice only when it is sought.
- *False reassurances:* If you offer parents or colleagues false reassurances about student achievement, behavior issues, or social skills, you may damage your own credibility and set the stage for future issues. Being truthful—but constructive—is the best strategy, even if you are concerned that a difficult situation may result.
- *Wandering interactions:* When another person communicates with you, it is sometimes easy to drift to peripheral topics that waste valuable time. For example, discussing a student's participation in varsity athletics when the concern is academic performance is a distraction that may reflect avoidance of the key issues.
- *Interruptions:* When you interact with others, they are entitled to your full attention. Responding to a colleague who comes to your classroom door or asking another person to wait while you make a phone call harms the interaction. During an interaction, it also is important to avoid interrupting others. If the person speaking has a language pattern that is slower than yours, you may have to make an especially concerted effort to wait until the person finishes speaking before responding.

- *Being judgmental:* If you tend to speak in absolute (for example, "The only way to resolve this is to . . ." or "I don't see any way for him to complete the work . . ."), you may be perceived as a professional who sees only one right answer. This may lead others to conclude that attempting to collaborate with you is futile.
- *One-way communication:* Communication is most effective when it involves all participants. If one person monopolizes the interaction, the others' points of view are not represented and any decisions made will likely be questioned later.
- *Fatigue:* If you are so tired that you cannot accurately follow the thread of a conversation, your communication may be impaired and you may misspeak or misunderstand others' messages. In such a case, it may be best to request rescheduling the interaction.
- *"Hot" words and phrases:* In some communities and in some schools, certain words are "hot" and prompt emotional responses. For example, even the words *inclusion* sometimes is considered controversial as is *response to intervention*. To facilitate productive interactions, such words (or even suspected words and phrases) are best avoided.

Do any of these barriers sound familiar? What examples of each can you and your classmates provide relating to your own communication experiences in internships or field experiences? What can you do to decrease the likelihood that these barriers will occur in your interactions with colleagues and parents?

asking questions and making statements in clear and nonthreatening ways (DeVito, 2009). They also include paralanguage, such as your tone of voice and your use of comments like "uh-huh" and "ok." Additional information about communication skills is included in the Professional Edge.

The other type of interaction skill comprises the steps that make interactions productive. Have you ever been in a meeting and thought the same topic was being discussed repeatedly? Perhaps you wished someone would say, "I think we've covered this; let's move on." Or have you ever tried to problem solve with classmates or friends, only to realize that every time someone generated an idea, someone else began explaining why the idea could not work? In both instances, the frustration occurred because of a problem in the interaction process, that is, the steps that characterize an interaction. The most needed interaction process for you as a teacher is shared problem solving (Knotek, 2003; Santangelo, 2009), a topic addressed later in this chapter. Other interaction process skills include conducting effective meetings, responding to resistance, resolving conflict, and persuading others.

You need both types of interaction skills to collaborate. If you are highly skilled in communicating effectively but cannot contribute to get an interaction from its beginning to its end, others may be frustrated. Likewise, even though you may know the steps in shared problem solving, if you speak to others carelessly or ineffectively, they may withdraw from the interaction.

Contributing to a Supportive Environment   The third ingredient for successful collaboration is a supportive environment (Waldron & McLeskey, 2010). As a teacher, you will contribute to this atmosphere through your personal belief system and interaction skills, but this environment includes other items as well. For example, most professionals working in schools that value collaboration comment on the importance of administrative support. Principals play an important role in fostering collaboration (Hines, 2008; Supovitz, Sirinides, & May, 2010). They can raise staff awareness of collaboration by making it a school goal and distributing information about it to staff. They can reward teachers for their collaborative efforts. They can urge teachers who are uncomfortable with collaboration to learn more about it and experiment in small-scale collaborative projects, and they can include collaboration as part of staff evaluation procedures. When principals do not actively nurture collaboration among staff, collaborative activities are more limited, more informal, and less a part of the school culture.

Another component of a supportive environment is having time available for collaboration (Johnston, Knight, & Miller, 2007; Sever & Bowgren, 2007). It is not enough that each teacher has a preparation period; shared planning time also needs to be arranged. In many middle schools, shared planning occurs as part of the middle school team planning period. In other schools, substitute teachers are employed periodically so that general education teachers and special services staff can meet. In yet other schools, quarterly workdays are scheduled for teachers and part of this time is for collaborative planning.

As a teacher, you will find that time is an important issue (Khorsheed, 2007). The number of tasks you need to complete during available preparation time will be greater than the number of minutes available. The time before and after school will be filled with faculty meetings, conferences with parents, preparation, bus duty, and other assignments. You can help yourself maximize time for collaboration if you keep several things in mind. First, it may be tempting to spend the beginning of a shared planning time discussing the day's events or comparing notes on some school activity. But if you engage in lengthy social conversation, you will be taking time away from your planning. A trick discovered by teachers in collaborative schools is to finish the business at hand first and then to chat about personal and school events if time is left. Second, because you never truly have enough time to accomplish all that you would like to as a teacher, you must learn to prioritize. You have to choose whether collaborating about a certain student or teaching a certain lesson is justified based on the needs of students and the time available. Not everything can be collaborative, but when collaboration seems appropriate, time should be allocated for it.

fyi

In our field work with thousands of experienced teachers each year, lack of time is consistently noted as the most serious obstacle to collaboration. Other professionals' work supports this observation (for example, Ploessl, Rock, Schoenfeld, & Blanks, 2010).

Collaboration traditionally has been thought of as the way in which professionals interact when they are face to face or perhaps on the phone. However, more and more collaboration is occurring through electronic means. It cannot always adequately replace face-to-face interactions, but it can enhance your other collaborative efforts and provide opportunities for you to learn from and about other professionals you might never have met. Here are examples of electronic collaboration options:

- Would you like to get ideas for lessons for students with disabilities? At oercommons.org you can search for lessons across grade levels and subject matter. You can specifically search for ideas related to "special education" and "inclusion." As you develop your own lessons, you can post them here to share with colleagues.
- Are you interested in finding out what your colleagues around the United States are saying about working with students with disabilities? At A to Z Teacher Stuff (http://forums.atozteacherstuff.com), you can join any of several discussion

forums concerning students with special needs or issues related to them. For example, recent postings include advice on managing time, working with special educators and co-teaching, and responding to the needs of students with autism. This website also includes a discussion forum for classroom discipline problems.

- Would you like to plan electronically with special educators or other colleagues? Wikis are webpages that you easily set up, which you can ask others to join and use to post lesson plans, assignments, or other materials. This enables you to work on shared items without waiting for them to be passed around through e-mail. You can establish a wiki in Google Groups (http://groups.google.com), or at Wikispaces (http://www.wikispaces.com).
- Are you thinking of blogging as a way of sharing with others with similar interests? This tool is being used to facilitate reflective teaching and as a means of sharing thoughts about teaching dilemmas. You can set up your own blog at blogger.com or http://www.edublogs.org.
- Do you sometimes wish that you could see how other teachers co-teach? How they conduct team meetings? How they find innovative ways to work with students with disabilities? Many examples are available at Teacher Tube (http://teachertube.com). This video site is searchable, and its content changes frequently.

If you explore the Internet, you undoubtedly will find other sites that focus on electronic collaboration. These sites can give you fresh ideas, basic knowledge, and a broader understanding of how you and others can make a profound difference in the lives of students with disabilities. These sites also can help you connect with colleagues from across the country and around the world who have similar interests and questions.

Technology offers new ways to enhance collaboration with colleagues and parents.

What Collaborative Services in Schools Foster Inclusion?

The basic principles of collaboration should be your guide to many types of partnerships in schools. These partnerships may involve other general education teachers, special education teachers, support staff such as speech therapists and counselors, paraprofessionals, parents, and others. Four of the most common collaborative activities concerning students with disabilities are shared problem solving, co-teaching, teaming, and consultation. As you read about these activities, keep in mind that the face-to-face interactions that characterize them can be extended with electronic collaboration using technology now readily available. This is the topic of the Technology Notes.

Shared Problem Solving

Shared problem solving is the basis for many of the collaborative activities that school professionals undertake on behalf of students with disabilities (Bahr & Kovaleski, 2006; Rubinson, 2002). Although shared problem solving sometimes occurs informally when a general education teacher and a special education teacher meet to decide on appropriate accommodations or other interventions for a student, it also occurs in many other contexts. For example, as you read the applications that follow, you will find that some variation of shared problem solving exists in each. This happens because one way of thinking about co-teaching, teaming, and consultation is as specialized problem-solving approaches.

You might be wondering why problem solving is such a critical topic for professional partnerships. In fact, you may consider yourself already adept at problem solving, because it is an ongoing responsibility of educators. However, as many authors have noted (for example, Friend & Cook, 2010), when professionals share a problem-solving process, it is much more complex than when educators problem solve alone, because the needs, expectations, and ideas of all the participants must be blended into shared understandings and mutually agreed-on solutions. Successful shared problem solving requires skilled participants.

Discover a Shared Need   The starting point for problem solving is discovering a shared need, which demonstrates the complexity of shared problem solving. If you face a problem that concerns only you, you try to resolve it by yourself. When you problem solve with colleagues and parents, all the participants need to perceive that a problem exists. Further, it is important that all participants believe they can have an impact on the problem, that they feel accountable for the results of problem solving, and that they can contribute constructively to resolving the problem. When these conditions exist, shared problem solving results in a high level of commitment. When these conditions do not exist, shared problem solving is not shared at all and may appear one sided, with some participants trying to convince others to contribute. For example, many teachers report they have been unable to enlist parents' help in resolving discipline problems. They then go on to describe meetings with parents in which school personnel describe the problem and the parents respond that they do not see such behavior occurring at home. Too often, instead of all parties working to come to a shared understanding of the problem behavior, this type of meeting ends with the parents superficially agreeing to assist in solving a problem they do not believe exists and the school professionals perceiving the parents as only marginally supportive. This dilemma can be avoided if more effort is made to identify a shared need to problem solve (Olivos, Gallagher, & Aguilar, 2010).

Identify the Problem   The most critical step in the problem-solving process is problem identification. However, when educators meet to share problem solving, they often feel pressured because of time constraints, and they may rush through this essential stage. Problem identification includes gathering information, compiling it, analyzing it, and reaching consensus about the nature of a student's problem.

In a shared problem-solving situation, you can help emphasize the importance of problem identification by asking whether everyone has agreed on the problem, by asking someone else to restate the problem to check your understanding of it, and by encouraging participants who have not spoken to share their opinions.

Consider the following situation, which shows what can happen when problem identification is not done correctly: A teacher in a shared problem-solving session says to the parent of a student whose attendance is irregular and who consistently comes to school without assignments or basic supplies, "We really need your help in making sure Demitrious gets up when his alarm goes off so he can catch the bus. And we'd like to establish a system in which you sign off on his written assignments." The parent replies, "It's so hard. I work until midnight, and I don't get up when it's time for the kids to go to school. I don't think he sees any point in the homework he's getting—that's why he doesn't bring it back." In this situation, the educator has identified the problem before the meeting has even started: Demitrious needs to assume responsibility, and his parents need to provide more guidance for school activities. Further, the teacher is proposing a solution to the

www.resources

http://cecp.air.org
The Center for Effective Collaboration and Practice is a federally funded organization designed to promote effective educational practices for students with emotional and behavior problems. This site includes links for parents, teachers, and other professionals on topics related to working together on behalf of these students.

problem and not exploring the problem itself. The parent's response suggests that she does not see the same problem; in fact, the parent is implying that perhaps the problem is not with Demitrious at all but with the school staff.

Consider how this interaction could have been handled differently: The teacher says to the parent, "Ms. Trenton, thanks so much for taking time off work to meet with us. We appreciate your concern for Demitrious. Lately, we've seen a problem with his attendance. We asked you to come to school so we can learn about your perspective on this situation and to let Demitrious know that we're working together to help him." When the parent replies with the comment about her working hours and Demitrious's perception of the homework, the teacher replies, "That's important information for us. We're hoping we can find ways to motivate Demitrious to come to school—and that includes assigning homework that he sees as valuable." In this situation, the school professionals are working with the parent to identify the problem, not presenting the problem to her.

RESEARCH NOTE

A study of parents' perceptions found that parents valued both the quantity and quality of communication from educators; a sense of educators' commitment to the welfare of their children as students; and a feeling of equality in power, trust, and respect (Blue-Banning et al., 2004).

Propose Solutions   Once a problem has been clearly identified, the next step is to create a wide range of options for solving the problem. One of the most common ways to come up with solutions is to brainstorm.

Brainstorming is based on two important principles. First, judgment is deferred; that is, to free the mind to be creative, people must suspend their predisposition to judge ideas. Second, quantity leads to quality; the more ideas that are generated for solving a problem, the more likely it is that novel and effective solutions can be found. Brainstorming requires openness and creativity. When implemented effectively, it often leads to several ideas that are highly likely to resolve the problem being addressed.

Evaluate Ideas   With a list of ideas, the next step in shared problem solving is to evaluate the ideas by considering whether they seem likely to resolve the problem and are feasible. One way to evaluate ideas is to use a decision sheet like that illustrated in Figure 3.1. On this decision sheet, the participants stated the problem—to find ways of encouraging Angela to work independently on classroom tasks—and generated ideas for achieving this goal. They then selected criteria by which to judge the merits of each idea. They considered the following:

- how well the idea would work for increasing the amount of time Angela spends on her independent assignments
- the extent to which the idea has a reasonable time cost
- the extent to which the idea preserves classroom routines

Ideas that were not seriously considered were crossed out, and the criteria for decision making were applied to those remaining, with each idea being rated against each criterion. In Figure 3.1, the two ideas with the highest ratings were assigning a study buddy and using picture directions.

Plan Specifics   Once one or two ideas have been chosen using a process such as the one just described, more detailed planning needs to occur. For example, suppose you and others have decided you would like to try having a high school service club provide volunteer tutoring in an after-school program. Some of the tasks to assign include asking club members about their interest in the project, arranging a place for the program, ensuring that needed supplies are available, obtaining permission to operate the program, establishing a schedule for students, determining who will provide adult supervision and scheduling it, advertising the program, and creating and conducting training sessions for the tutors.

Typically, at this step of shared problem solving, not only do participants list the major tasks that need to be completed to implement the solution, but they also decide who will take responsibility for each task. In addition, they specify a timeline for completing all the tasks and usually decide how long to implement the solution before meeting to evaluate its effectiveness.

FIGURE 3.1 A Sample Decision-Making Sheet for Problem Solving

Problem Statement: How can we encourage Angela to work independently on assigned classroom tasks?

Ideas:

Digitally record instructions	~~Don't give independent work~~
Have an assigned "study buddy"	Let her choose the assignment
Make the work easier	~~Make her stay in from recess to complete work~~
Use pictures for directions	Give her frequent breaks
Ask a parent volunteer to help	

Decision Making: (3 = high, 2 = medium, 3 = low)

Idea	Criteria			Total	Rank
	Time commitment is reasonable for teacher	Idea does not disrupt class routine	Angela will work for at least 5 minutes		
1. Recorded instructions	3	1	2	6	
2. Study buddy	3	3	3	9	1
3. Easier work	2	2	2	6	
4. Picture directions	3	2	3	8	2
5. Parent volunteer1	3	2	6		
6. Choose assignment	1	2	1	4	
7. Frequent breaks	2	2	2	6	

Implement the Solution   If all the steps in the shared problem-solving process have been carefully followed, then implementing the selected idea(s) may be the most straightforward part of the process. When problem solving occurs concerning a student with a disability in an inclusive school, each team member may have some responsibility for implementing the solution. Occasionally, you will have much of the immediate responsibility. In other cases, parents will have a major role to play. Each person involved must do his part for the solution to have a high probability of success. During implementation, it is helpful to keep some type of record documenting your efforts and how the intervention affects the student.

Evaluate Outcomes   After a period of time—anywhere from just a few days to two or more weeks—the professionals who are implementing the solution meet to evaluate its effectiveness. At this time, three possibilities exist:

1. If the solution has been especially effective, it may be judged a success. It then will be continued to maintain the results, discontinued if no longer needed, or gradually phased out.
2. If the solution seems to be having a positive effect but is not ideal for some other reason, it may be modified. For example, suppose a behavior management plan is helping a student attend class rather than skip it, but the general education teacher notes that the system is too time consuming. The problem-solving group may then try to streamline the plan to make it more feasible.

dimensions of DIVERSITY

At least some evidence indicates that gender differences exist among school psychologists in terms of the strategies they use in consulting with teachers (Getty & Erchul, 2009), with men relying more than women on expert power to influence teachers.

3. Even when the steps in problem solving are carefully completed, a solution occasionally is judged ineffective. The team then must decide what to do next: select a different solution, find additional solutions, or possibly reconsider whether the problem has been accurately identified. The team needs to consider all these possibilities before proceeding with additional problem solving.

Professionals who regularly employ the strategies of shared problem solving are quick to acknowledge that the steps do not automatically lead to a simple solution that always works. However, they report that when they problem solve in this fashion, they perceive that their professional time is well spent and that the problem-solving process is truly a collaborative endeavor.

Co-Teaching

Co-teaching occurs when two or more educators—a general education teacher and a special education teacher or other specialist—share the instruction for a single group of students, typically in a single classroom setting (Friend, 2008; McDuffie, Mastropieri, & Scruggs, 2009). Although any two teachers can teach together (and this sometimes occurs at elementary, middle, and high schools), we focus here on the unique arrangement of two professionals with potentially very different points of view and areas of expertise working together on behalf of all the students in a class, the type of arrangement that Ms. Randelman and Ms. Pickett, introduced at the beginning of the chapter, have in their classroom.

Co-teaching is becoming a very popular service delivery option in inclusive schools (Friend, 2008; Friend, Cook, Hurley-Chamberlain, & Shamberger, 2010). In a classroom with several students with disabilities, combining the strengths of the general education teacher and a special educator can create options for all students (Friend & Cook, 2010; Stivers, 2008). Co-teaching typically occurs for a set period of time either every day (for example, every morning from 9:30 until 10:15 or during second period seventh-grade math) or on certain days of the week (for example, on Mondays, Tuesdays, and Wednesdays during third period or second block). Other options for scheduling may be used, depending on student needs and the availability of special education teachers.

As effective as co-teaching is when carefully implemented, it is not the answer for every student with a disability or for every classroom in an inclusive school. Co-teaching is only one option for meeting the needs of students. It should be implemented when the number of students with disabilities in a class and the nature of their needs justify the presence of two teachers, or the class is one in which all students with disabilities must enroll (for example, a high school U.S. history class).

Many approaches are available to teachers who decide to co-teach. Friend (2008) has outlined some of the common ones, and they are depicted in Figure 3.2.

One Teach, One Observe In this approach, one teacher, leads the lesson and the other gathers data on students to understand them better and make instructional decisions. For example, while Ms. Tran, the general education teacher, leads a lesson in which students work in cooperative groups to answer questions about a map, Ms. Firestone, the special education teacher, systematically observes three students who are known to struggle with social skills. Ms. Firestone notes on a chart the number of times those students initiate interactions with peers, as well as how often other students direct comments

www.resources

http://coteach.com
At this website, you can find resources related to co-teaching and answers to common questions concerning this increasingly popular service delivery option for students with disabilities and other special needs.

Co-teaching, when two teachers share instruction in the general education setting, provides true curriculum access for students with disabilities.

FIGURE 3.2 Co-Teaching Approaches

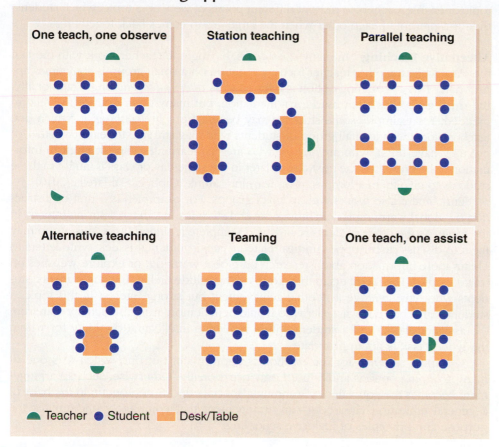

or questions to them. How can this information be helpful to the teachers? Teachers can observe students' ability to pay attention, work independently, participate during instruction, and seek assistance when they have questions. However this approach is used, it is essential that each educator sometimes take the primary teaching role in the class while the other observes. In this way, both teachers have the opportunity to watch the class in action, and both have credibility with students as a result of leading instruction.

Station Teaching In *station teaching,* three groups of students are arranged. Two stations include teacher-facilitated instruction; in the third station, students, alone or with a partner, complete a review activity or a project. If students cannot work independently, the last group can be eliminated. During the lesson, students move to each station. In an elementary school, an entire lesson based on stations may be completed in a single day; in a secondary school, a single station may take an entire class period or more. For example, in a ninth-grade math class, some of the students are working with the general education teacher to learn one method for solving quadratic equations. A second group is meeting with the special education teacher to learn an alternative method. A third group of students is working in pairs on an assignment. Each station lasts an entire class period.

Parallel Teaching Sometimes when two teachers are present, they find it advantageous simply to divide a heterogeneous class group and have each teacher instruct half the class. In this format, called *parallel teaching,* every student has twice as many opportunities to participate in a discussion or respond to teacher questions. A teacher particularly skilled in presenting information through pictures can use this approach while the other teacher emphasizes learning through listening. Students who prefer one method to the other can be placed with the appropriate teacher. In an elementary classroom, this approach may be used to enable students to read different books based on their interests or skill levels. In a secondary classroom, this approach may

RESEARCH NOTE

Co-teaching has been found to contribute significantly to raising the achievement scores of students with disabilities on mandated high-stakes achievement tests (Samuels, 2007).

give students more opportunities to respond during a discussion of a current events topic or enable teachers to present different points of view on a topic, which students then can present to each other when the large group comes back together.

Alternative Teaching   In many classrooms, having one teacher work with most of the class while the other teacher focuses attention on a small group is sometimes appropriate. This co-teaching option is referred to as *alternative teaching.* Traditionally, the small group has been used for remediation, but many other options are recommended. For example, some students may benefit from *preteaching,* in which one teacher works with a small group of students who may struggle to learn (whether or not they have IEPs), who are shy, or who are just learning to speak English. Information to be presented the next day or later in the same day or class is taught to these students to give them a jump start on learning (Munk, Gibb, & Caldarella, 2010).

Enrichment also works well in small groups. For example, as a unit of instruction on global warming is concluding, several students may have a strong interest in the topic. As the other students review and complete assigned tasks, this group may meet to discuss career opportunities related to environmental issues, write letters to obtain more information about research on global warming, or explore websites on related topics. The members in this group could include high-achieving students, students who have average academic achievement but strong interest in this topic, a student with a behavior disorder who would benefit more from this activity than from the assigned work, and a student with a moderate intellectual disability for whom the written task is not appropriate.

Grouping students for remediation is appropriate, but only when it is one of many grouping options and is used only occasionally. Otherwise, such an arrangement becomes the equivalent of running a special education program in the back of a general education classroom—an arrangement that completely undermines the purpose and principles of inclusive schooling.

Teaming   In the co-teaching option of *teaming,* the teachers share leadership in the classroom; both are equally engaged in the instructional activities. For example, one teacher may begin a lesson by introducing vocabulary while the other provides examples as a way to place the words in context. Two teachers may role-play an important event from history or demonstrate how to complete a lab activity. Two teachers may model how to address conflict by staging a debate about a current event. You reach the limits of teaming only when you run out of exciting ideas for creating instruction with two teachers instead of one. Co-teachers who use this approach find it the most energizing of all the co-teaching options, but you should also be aware that you and a co-teacher might not be compatible enough in terms of teaching style to use it. If that is the case, using several of the other approaches might be more effective.

One Teach, One Assist   Occasionally during instruction, one teacher is appropriately leading the lesson while the other is quietly assisting individual students. For example, while the special education teacher leads a lesson on a test review, the general education teacher helps students individually as they have questions about the vocabulary. Alternatively, while the general education teacher leads a lesson on the causes of World War II, the special education teacher helps keep students on task and responds quietly to student questions. The key to implementing this approach successfully is to use it sparingly. With overuse, one of the teachers, often the special educator, may perceive that she has no legitimate role in the class and is mostly like a teaching assistant (Scruggs, Mastropieri, & McDuffie, 2007). In addition, if this approach to co-teaching is used too frequently, students may become overly dependent on the extra help that always seems to be available.

Co-Teaching Pragmatics   As you consider these co-teaching approaches, you might notice that several other factors need to be taken into account in addition to how the teachers arrange themselves and the students (Damore & Murray, 2009;

Friend, 2008; Tannock, 2009). First, in a co-taught class, students are grouped so that those with disabilities are integrated appropriately with their peers without disabilities. Thus, in a station teaching arrangement, students with special needs are likely to be in each of the three groups although at times they may be placed together to meet a specific instructional need. When alternative teaching occurs, the smaller group may or may not contain students with disabilities. Second, both teachers take on teaching and supportive roles. Otherwise, the special education teacher may end up being seen as a helper who does not have teacher status. Third, the best approaches to use depend on student needs, the subject being taught, the teachers' experience, and practical considerations such as space and time for planning. Novice co-teachers may prefer station teaching or parallel teaching over teaming, especially in a class that includes several students with attention problems who would benefit from a smaller group structure. We make this recommendation because the former approaches require less minute-to-minute coordination with another teacher. Finally, the type of curriculum sometimes dictates the approach. For example, a topic that is sequential obviously cannot be taught in stations; it may be presented best through teaming followed by parallel-taught study groups.

Team effectiveness often can be demonstrated when members together are able to do more together than any single member could do alone.

Working on a Team

In Chapter 2, you learned that you have responsibility as a member of an intervention assistance team or response to intervention (RtI) team to problem solve about students before they are considered for special education (Bahr & Kovaleski, 2006; Duhon, Mesmer, Gregerson, & Witt, 2009; Lee-Tarver, 2006). You also learned you may be a member of the multidisciplinary team (MDT) that determines whether a student is eligible to receive special education services and then writes the student's IEP (Lytle & Bordin, 2001). These teams rely on collaboration among members, and it is important that you understand the concepts and procedures they and other school teams have that make them effective. The Case in Practice captures a few moments of a response to intervention team meeting illustrating this point.

When you think about highly successful teams, what comes to mind? Your favorite athletic team? A surgical team? An orchestra? What is it about these teams that makes them successful? **Teams** are formal work groups that have certain characteristics. They have clear goals, active and committed members, and leaders; they practice to achieve their results; and they do not let personal issues interfere with accomplishment of their goals. What are other characteristics of effective teams?

The teams you will be part of at school have many of the same characteristics as other kinds of teams (Fleming & Monda-Amaya, 2001). Their success depends on the commitment of every member and the clarity of their goals (Etscheidt & Knesting, 2007; Fratture & Capper, 2007). On effective school teams, members keep in mind why they are a team, setting aside personal differences to reach a goal that often is to design the best educational strategies possible for students with disabilities or other special needs.

Team Participant Roles   As a team member, you must assume multiple roles. First, in your professional role as a general education teacher, you bring a particular perspective to a team interaction, as do the special education teacher, counselor, adaptive physical educator, principal, and other team members (Shapiro & Sayers, 2003). You contribute an understanding of what students without disabilities are accomplishing in your grade or course, knowledge of the curriculum and its pace, and a sense of the prerequisites of what you are teaching and the expectations for students likely to follow the next segment of instruction.

CASE IN PRACTICE

An RtI Problem-Solving Meeting

At Triton Middle School, response to intervention is the responsibility of each team. Today, a sixth-grade team is meeting to review data on student progress. Present are the four core content area teachers (Mr. Land, science; Mr. Graf, math; Ms. Buchanan, English; Ms. Lincoln, social studies); Mr. Lashley, the assistant principal who helps the team analyze their data; Ms. Gardner, the reading specialist; and Ms. Dunn, the special educator assigned to the team. One student the team is discussing is Scott.

Ms Gardner: Scott has been participating in the Tigers Reading Club during intervention time for the past twelve weeks. His attendance is nearly perfect, and he is completing all the reading activities. I think our Tier 2 intervention is really working well for many students, but Scott still is not making enough progress in comprehension—it's still right at a mid-fourth-grade level, and our criteria indicate he should be approaching an early fifth-grade-level by now.

Ms. Dunn: I did some checking with Scott's fifth-grade teacher. She told me that Scott had gone back and forth between Tier 2 and Tier 3 interventions last year, but that their team decided he was making adequate progress. His records do not indicate he has ever been referred for special education services.

Ms. Buchanan: I see the comprehension problems in English. Scott tries, and he's a nice kid, but he misses a lot because he hasn't understood what he has read.

Mr. Land: I can say that exact thing about science. I try to discuss almost everything—not have the students just read in their books—partly because I know Scott has difficulty with the reading, even with a highlighted text and shortened assignments.

Ms. Lincoln: Same thing happens in social studies. I brought several samples of his work and his weekly quiz scores since the beginning of the year.

Mr. Graf: In math, he's doing well—his average on tests and assignments is slightly above the class average.

[Additional data on Scott's comprehension skills are discussed by team members.]

Mr. Lashley: Based on the data we have from progress monitoring and the information all of you have contributed, it seems like we're saying he needs a more intensive intervention. Does everyone agree?

[Head nods from everyone.]

Ms. Gardner: I think our best option is to have him enroll in the reading class for the next grading quarter. That would give him a daily computer-based, highly structured reading program with me as the teacher, and it would provide twice as much intervention time as he receives now.

The meeting continues...

REFLECTION

What collaborative roles do general education teachers play during response to intervention meetings? Why is it important that each teacher bring data to such a meeting and share it with colleagues? What parts of a problem-solving process did this meeting include? What role do you think parents should have in such a process? How is this type of collaboration an improvement over past practices for addressing student learning problems?

The second contribution you make is through your personal role, that is, the characteristics that define you as a person. For example, are you a person who sees the positive aspects of almost any situation? If so, you will probably be the person who keeps up the team's morale. Are you a detail-oriented person who is skilled at organizing? If so, you will probably be the team member who ensures that all the tasks get completed and all the paperwork is filed.

Third, you have a team role to fulfill as well. You may be the individual who makes sure the agenda is being followed or who watches the time so team meetings do not last too long. Or you may have the role of summarizing and clarifying others' comments or suggesting ways to combine what seem to be contradictory points of view into integrated solutions to student problems. As an effective member, you will recognize your strengths and use them to enhance the team; you also will be vigilant so your weaknesses do not interfere with the team's accomplishing its tasks. Common formal team roles include team facilitator, recorder, and timekeeper. These roles might rotate so that every team member has the opportunity to experience each one. Informal team roles include being a compromiser, information seeker, and reality checker. These informal roles are not usually assigned, but team members ensure that they are fulfilled as the need arises.

Team Goals   One of the keys to effective teams is attention to goals (Friend & Cook, 2010). Being clear and explicit about goals is particularly important in educational settings because team goals often are assumed or too limited. For example, on some response to intervention teams, teachers perceive the team goal to be to document interventions so that the special education identification procedures can begin. Others believe the team functions to help teachers address student learning problems so that any consideration of special education can be avoided, if at all possible. Note how crucial this difference in perception of team purpose is. Without clear and specific goals, teams often flounder.

Another aspect of team goals is especially important. The goals just discussed are commonly referred to as *task goals;* that is, they are the business of the team. But teams have another set of goals as well called *maintenance goals.* Maintenance goals refer to the team's status and functioning as a team. Maintenance goals may include beginning and ending meetings on time, finishing all agenda items during a single meeting, taking time to check on team members' perceptions of team effectiveness, and improving team communication both during meetings and outside them. These and other maintenance goals enable effective teams to accomplish the task goals they set.

Consultation

In some cases, you may not have direct support for a student in your classroom. Perhaps the student does not have an identified disability, or perhaps the student's needs can be met with occasional supports. For example, you might have an outgoing student who suddenly begins acting very withdrawn. Or you may learn that for the next school year, you will have a student who has a significant physical disability; you would like to know how to assist the student and whether you should seek special training. As illustrated in the chapter-opening story about Brittany, if you have a student with autism in your class, you might find that both you and the special education teacher need assistance from someone else to help the student learn the best ways to transition from activity to activity. These are examples of situations in which you might seek support through consultation.

Consultation is a specialized problem-solving process in which one professional who has particular expertise assists another professional (or parent) who needs the benefit of that expertise (Erchul & Martens, 2010). For example, you may contact a behavior consultant for assistance when a student in your class is aggressive. You might meet with a vision or hearing consultant when a student with one of those disabilities is included in your class. If you have a student who has received medical or other services outside school, you may consult with someone from the agency that has been providing those services.

Consultation is most effective when it is based on the principles of collaboration already presented, but its purpose is not reciprocal. That is, in consultation, the goal is for someone with specific expertise to assist you (or another professional); the other person may learn from you, but that is not the goal. The process of consulting generally begins when you as the teacher complete a request form or otherwise indicate you have a concern about a student (Dettmer, Thurston, Knackendoffel, & Dyck, 2009). The consultant then contacts you to arrange an initial meeting. At that meeting, the problem is further clarified, your expectations are discussed, and often arrangements are made for the consultant to observe in your room. Once the observation phase has been completed, the consultant and you meet again to finalize your understanding of

Working TOGETHER

Consultation with a Behavior Specialist

When teachers cannot find solutions for student issues, they sometimes call on the expertise of a consultant. Consultants usually have specialized knowledge and skills in a particular area (e.g., autism, behavior, reading), and they are employed to help teachers and other professionals find strategies to help students. Here is an example of what might occur in a consultation session regarding a student with increasingly serious behavior problems.

Mr. Davidson is meeting with Ms. Marks, the district behavior specialist, concerning Luis, a student identified as having an emotional/behavioral disability. Ms. Risik, the special educator, also is present. Mr. Davidson asked for assistance because of his concern that Luis is becoming increasingly aggressive when he is frustrated. The parent of another third-grader called Mr. Davidson to report that Luis is pushing students on the bus and bullying them with threats that he'll have his older brother beat them up.

Mr. Davidson: Thanks for meeting with me. I've been trying to do everything Ms. Risik has suggested to address Luis's behavior, but I'm not seeing any improvement. If anything, things are worse. Ms. Risik, you asked me to keep some data about what's occurring, and I did that. In the past week, I've intervened when Luis was threatening another student or trying to hit someone an average of three times each day. I've had two reports from playground supervisors of other incidents. What worries me most is that yesterday, Luis made a fist at me, used a word that is not allowed in our classroom, and would not apologize when I escorted him from the room. This is getting too serious for me to address.

Ms. Marks: Ms. Risik, what are you seeing?

Ms. Risik: Mr. Davidson really has implemented the behavior plan for Luis very carefully, and I really appreciate that, Mr. Davidson.

I'm also observing increasing frustration and aggression. When Luis was working with me in the resource room, he was struggling with work I have seen him do easily before, and he suddenly tore the paper in half, wadded it up, and threw it across the room. There have been several other incidents as well.

Ms. Marks: Listening to both of you, I agree that is sounds like Luis's aggression is increasing. Our first step is to figure out what might be triggering his behavior. Mr. Davidson, I know we need to do something fairly quickly, but would you be comfortable if I came to your room a couple of times this week to observe Luis? Sometimes an outside observer can pick up on patterns of what is happening. I'll also arrange to observe him in the lunchroom and on the playground and will check with the art and music teachers to see if they have noticed behavior changes. Then, if you're willing, we could meet next Monday to see if we can identify what is occurring and design a new plan to address the problem. If we decide a change is needed in the behavior plan that is part of Luis's IEP, we'll need to ask for a team meeting.

Mr. Davidson: That sounds fine with me. I'd prefer you observe during language arts—that seems to be a time of day that is particularly difficult for Luis.

Ms. Risik: If you'd like to observe Luis working in the resource room, please do. We really need some new solutions. I would not like to see the behaviors escalate any further—he had been having such a great year until recently.

Ms. Marks: I'm confident we'll come up with some new ideas. I just want to be sure that we address the real problem and not just a symptom of it—the behavior you're observing.

After a few minutes, the meeting breaks up, to be continued the following Monday.

the problem, generate and select options for addressing it, and plan how to implement whatever strategies seem needed. A timeline for putting the strategies into effect is also established. Typically, you then carry out the strategies. Following this phase, the consultant and you meet once again to determine whether the problem has been resolved. If it has, the strategy is either continued to maintain the success or eliminated as no longer needed. If the problem continues to exist, the consultant may suggest that you begin a new consulting process, or together you may decide that some other action is needed. When appropriate, the consultant closes the case. In the Working Together, you can learn more about what it's like to work with a consultant.

For consulting to be effective, both the consultant and the consultee (that is, you as the teacher) need to participate responsibly. Your role includes preparing for meetings, being open to the consultant's suggestions, using the agreed upon strategies systematically, and documenting the effectiveness of ideas you try. The consultant's role includes listening carefully to your concerns; analyzing data that can inform decision making; and working with you to design, implement, and evaluate feasible strategy. Together, your partnership can provide supports for many students whose needs do not require direct specialized services.

The Complexity of Professional Collaboration

As you have read the information about collaborative services for students with disabilities, you probably have realized that they are based on caring and committed professionals who believe in the power of shared efforts and are open to the ideas of colleagues. However, even when all the conditions essential for collaboration are in place, disagreements can occur. And occasionally, you may find yourself working with a colleague or group of colleagues with whom you have deep disagreements. What happens then? Is collaboration possible?

Although most professionals would prefer that all interactions be pleasant and based on agreements, that, of course, is not a real-world expectation. You may find that you believe that the special educator who reads tests to the students with disabilities in your class is providing so much assistance that they are getting higher scores than you think accurately represent their learning. Perhaps your principal has said that she expects you to co-teach next year, and you are not sure you want to participate—but you have not been given a choice. Or perhaps you and one team member tend to have different points of view on everything from making changes in grading policies for students with disabilities to classroom behavior expectations for them.

Disagreement is an inevitable by-product of collaboration. Disagreements can be minor or major, and the people involved can be committed to resolving them or maintaining their own viewpoints. Regardless, here are a few ideas for responding to disagreements:

- Try to view the situation from the perspective of the other person, using the concept of **frame of reference**—that is, the totality of the other person's viewpoint that is based on her background, experiences, education, and even work history in schools. Using a frame of reference can help you see things as the other individual sees them, a valuable first step in resolving a disagreement.
- See if you can get agreement by trying a solution that can be reevaluated at a later time. For example, if you think the special educator is providing too much assistance to students, perhaps the test could be read by a paraprofessional, or perhaps you could read the test while the special educator supervised the other students taking it. After trying one of these (or other) options two or three times, you and your colleague should review them for effectiveness. Sometimes a solution can be reached if everyone knows it can be changed later as needed.
- Examine your own part in the disagreement. If you tend to be a person for whom every issue is a big issue, a straightforward way to address disagreement is to work diligently to reflect on your behavior. If you tend to insist on your solution, you might want to deliberately work to sometimes acquiesce to others' preferences. For honest input on this difficult possibility, you might want to seek input from a colleague, mentor, or administrator.

In the Instructional Edge you will find examples of topics that sometimes are sources of disagreements between general and special educators. How could you use the strategies just outlined to find ways to resolve differences regarding them?

Perhaps the most important message related to disagreements with colleagues is this: Disagreements provide opportunities to create new and better options for students. Disagreements may be stressful, but you can turn them into solutions by thinking carefully about your views and the basis for them, engaging in constructive conversations with other professionals, and keeping in mind that any resolution ultimately has as its goal helping students with disabilities.

www.resources

http://www.newconversations.net/ New Conversations is a website dedicated to fostering collaboration by providing free materials to those interested. If you'd like to enhance your communication skills, the posted *Seven Challenges Workbook* has many practical ideas.

INSTRUCTIONAL EDGE

Co-Teaching Instructional Dilemmas

Co-teachers sometimes disagree on instructional and other classroom practices. Although you might consider this a negative, it really is not. Instead, disagreements on such matters create opportunities to create new solutions beneficial to students and satisfactory to teachers. Here are several common dilemmas that may require considerable discussion to generate solutions:

- The special educator believes that students need her support during instruction, and she often assists student with their assignments, quickly answers their questions, and provides structured guidance as they work. The general educator believes students need support, but that they also need to be challenged. She thinks students should attempt their work, try to find answers to their questions, and learn to follow directions independently.
- The general educator has a policy that students who are late turning in assignments should receive a grade penalty. The special educator argues that if the work was submitted, it should be given full value, even if the student's IEP did not specify extended timelines as an accommodation.

- The special educator believes that his students work very hard and that the grading scale should be adjusted for them. The general educator is very supportive of students with disabilities, but he believes that if many changes are made as supports, the highest grade that can be earned should be a B.
- The general educator has, in her opinion, appropriate classroom management. However, she perceives that some students with disabilities misbehave a great deal. The special educator finds the classroom expectations unclear, and she observes that students (not just those with disabilities) sometimes misbehave because they are often told what they do that is wrong but seldom told what they do that is right. She believes there should be a clearer system of rewards for appropriate behavior.

What is your role in resolving disagreements on topics such as these? What would you do if you and your co-teachers could not agree at all?

How Can You Work Effectively with Parents?

The partnerships presented thus far in this chapter have focused primarily on your interactions with special education teachers and other professionals who will support you in meeting the needs of students with disabilities in your classroom. In this section, we emphasize your working relationship with parents.

Having quality interactions with the parents of all your students is important, but it is vital with the parents of students with disabilities (McNaughton & Vostal, 2010). Parents may be able to help you better understand the strengths and needs of their child in your classroom. They also act as advocates for their child, so they can help you ensure that adequate supports are provided for the child's needs. Parents often see their child's experiences in your classroom in a way that you cannot; when they share this information, it helps both you and the student achieve more success. Finally, parents are your allies in educating students (Whitbread, Bruder, Fleming, & Park, 2007). When you enlist their assistance to practice skills at home, to reward their child for accomplishments at school, and to communicate to their child messages consistent with yours, then you and the parents can multiply the student's educational opportunities and provide a consistency that is essential to maximize student learning.

dimensions of DIVERSITY

Immigrant parents not only have to learn the language, culture, and expectations of living in the United States, but they also have to understand the U.S. education system and the complex workings of the special education system (Ramirez, 2005).

Understanding the Perspective of Family Members

You might be tempted to assume that because you work with a student with a disability in your classroom on a daily basis, you understand what it would be like to be the student's parent. This assumption could not be further from the truth. The parent of a high school student with a moderate intellectual disability as well as multiple physical disorders made this comment at a meeting of parents and teachers:

> You see my child in a wheelchair and worry about getting her around the building and keeping her changed. But remember, before you ever see her in the morning, I have gotten her out of bed, bathed her, brushed her teeth, washed her hair and

fixed it, fed her, and dressed her. I have made sure that extra clothes are packed in case she has an accident, and I have written notes to teachers about her upcoming surgery. When she's at school, I worry about whether she is safe, about whether kids fighting in the hall will care for her or injure her, and whether they are kind. And when she comes home, I clean up the soiled clothes, work with her on all the skills she is still learning, make sure that she has companionship and things to do, and then help her get ready for bed. And I wonder what will be the best option for her when she graduates in three years. You can't possibly know what it's like to be the parent of a child like my daughter.

What this parent so eloquently demonstrated is that you do not understand what it is like to be the parent of a child with a disability unless you too are the parent of such a child. This means you should strive to recognize that the range of interactions you have with parents is influenced in part by the stresses they are experiencing, their prior dealings with school personnel, and their own beliefs about their child and her future. How should this idea apply to teachers and other professionals as they work with Chris's parents, Mr. and Mrs. Werner, who were introduced at the beginning of the chapter?

Parents' Reactions to Their Child's Disability

Parents of children with disabilities have many reactions to their children's special needs, and these reactions may focus on positive or negative factors (Schuengel et al., 2009). Some parents go through several emotions roughly in a sequence; others may experience only one or several discrete reactions. For some, the reactions may be minor and their approach pragmatic. For others, their child's disability might affect their entire family structure and life. Part of your work with parents includes recognizing that the way they respond to you may be influenced by any of the following reactions to their children's disabilities (Ferguson, 2002):

1. *Grief:* Some parents feel grief about their child's disability. Sometimes this is a sorrow for the pain or discomfort their child may have to experience; sometimes it is sadness for themselves because of the added stress on the family when a child has a disability; and sometimes it is a sense of loss for what the child may not become. Grief may be temporary or it may be chronic (Ray, Pewitt-Kinder, & George, 2009), a realization nearly every day of how their lives are different from those of families with children who do not have disabilities. Parents have a right to grieve about their child—a right that educators should respect.

2. *Ambivalence:* Another reaction parents may have toward their child is ambivalence. This feeling may occur as parents attempt to confirm that the child's disability is not temporary or fixable, as they try to determine what the best educational options are for their child, and as they ponder how their child will live as an adult. The decisions that parents of children with disabilities have to make are often difficult, and they continue throughout childhood and adolescence and sometimes through adulthood. Parents often attend meetings with school personnel at which tremendous amounts of information are shared with little time for explanation, and they often meet with representatives from many different disciplines. It is no wonder they may feel ambivalent.

3. *Optimism:* A college student was once interviewing the parent of a student with a mild intellectual disability. When asked what it was like having a child with an intellectual disability in the family, the parent replied, "Mary is my child. Just like any other child, I love her as my child. She is sometimes funny and sometimes clever and sometimes naughty. She can really get into trouble. She's just like my other children, except she's Mary." For this parent, her child's special needs are just part of the configuration of needs that any child in any family might have; the emphasis is on the person, not the disability. There are many families like this one, in which the special needs of the child are met without an extraordinary reaction. Parents may work diligently to optimize their child's education,

dimensions of DIVERSITY

Many parents, especially those from minority groups, can find school an intimidating place. You can promote participation by encouraging parents to come to school meetings with a friend or another family member and by asking them positive questions early during meetings (for example, "What does your child say about school at home?").

and they are hopeful about their child's future. They work closely with educators and others to ensure that the child's life, whatever it may be, is the best one possible.

How parents respond when they have a child with a disability depends on many factors. One is the intensity and complexity of the disability. The reaction of parents whose child is diagnosed with a learning disability in third grade will likely be somewhat different from that of parents who learned two months after their child was born that she could not see.

Another factor affecting the way parents respond is how the information about the disability is shared with them. When such information is presented in a coldly clinical manner, without adequate sensitivity to the parents' emotions, their response can be quite negative. This is true even for mild disabilities. When one parent was told about her son's learning disability, she said, "Wait a minute. Stop and let me think. Do you realize what you've just said? You've just unraveled my whole way of thinking about my son. What do you mean a *learning disability?* What does that mean? Will it ever change? How can you sit there and keep talking as though it's no big thing?" A father related how he learned about his daughter's moderate intellectual disability. A physician simply said, "She's retarded. There's nothing we can do." The father left the office crying, partly because of the information and partly because of the insensitive way it had been communicated.

Yet another factor influencing a family's response to having a child with a disability is culture (Harry, 2008; Obiakor, 2007; Olivos, Gallagher, & Aguilar, 2010). In some cultures, disability is a spiritual phenomenon that may reflect a loss of the soul or evidence of transgressions in a previous life. In other families, a child with a disability is considered a reflection on the entire family. In some families, a disability is accepted as just part of who the child is. In others, it is believed that a cure should be sought. It is important to listen to family members as they discuss their child to better understand their perspective on him as well as their response to ideas and suggestions that you and the rest of the team make (Olivos, 2009).

One other factor that affects the parents' response concerns resources, including financial support (Lott, 2003). When parents have the resources necessary to provide what they believe is the best set of support services for their child, they are less likely to experience negative emotions. However, when parents know that their child

It is especially important when working with family members of your students with disabilities to respect and try to understand their perspectives and to learn from them about their child's strengths and needs.

would benefit from some intervention, such as surgery, a piece of computer equipment, or tutoring, they are invariably frustrated if they cannot provide that needed support and have difficulty accessing it from school and community resources. Another important resource is people. In large families, families with many supportive relatives living in the same community, or families with a strong network of neighbors and friends, the stresses of having a child with a disability are greatly reduced. When parents are isolated or when friends and family are uncomfortable with the child, the parents are likely to experience far more difficulties.

Family-Centered Practices   The recommended approach for working with families of students with disabilities is referred to as family-centered practices (Dunst, 2002; Hansuvadha, 2009). **Family-centered practices** are based on the notion that outcomes are best for students when their families' perspectives are respected, their families' input is sincerely sought, and school professionals view their job as helping families get the information they need to make the best decisions for their children. Do you agree with this approach? Most professionals do, but implementing it means setting aside preconceived notions about parents and families and sometimes respecting the fact that a family's goals for their child may not be the ones you would choose.

Your understanding of parents' and families' point of view is critical (Olivos et al., 2010; Starr, Foy, Cramer, & Singh, 2006). For example, some parents find school an unpleasant or intimidating place. They may have had negative experiences when they were students, or if they are from another country, they may be unfamiliar with the expectations for parental involvement in U.S. public schools. If the parents' primary language is not English, they may be uncomfortable because of the need for an interpreter, or they may misunderstand information communicated by school personnel, whether in face-to-face interactions or in writing. If parents are from a culture that views teachers as experts, they may wonder why you keep asking for their input. Some ideas for reflecting on and responding to parents from diverse cultures are included in the Professional Edge.

Some parents may not be visibly involved in their children's education because of pragmatic barriers. Parents who work at jobs that are far from school may not be able to take time off to participate in activities at school and may not be able to afford the lost work time. For some parents, involvement is largely a matter of economics: The costs of child care and transportation may prevent them from being able to work with you. These parents, however, may be involved through their work with their child at home.

In general, your attitude toward parents and their perceptions of their children greatly affect how you interact with them. If you telegraph through your choice of words, your question-asking skills, and your body posture that parents should see their children as you do and accept your input without question, then you are violating the principles of family-centered practice, and you probably will find that parents will not communicate with you readily. However, if you make parents feel welcome in your classroom or by phone or e-mail, listen carefully to their perceptions and concerns, treat them as important, and work with them to address student needs, then many benefits will ensue for the student, the family, and you (Olivos et al., 2010).

Collaborating with Parents

As a school professional, you can make family-centered practices a reality when you find ways to effectively collaborate with parents. Some examples of positive ways to partner with parents include home–school communication, parent conferences, parent education, and direct parent involvement in volunteer programs and similar activities.

Home–School Communication   One simple way to build a positive working relationship with parents is by using informal and formal home–school communication

---

RESEARCH NOTE

Families from traditional American Indian culture sometimes define disability in terms of a relationship between individuals with unequal abilities, not a status assigned based on medical diagnosis (Pewewardy & Fitzpatrick, 2009). This is an example of why cultural competence is so important in your work with families.

PROFESSIONAL **EDGE**

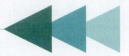

Involving Immigrant Parents of Students with Disabilities

Nearly all teachers and parents believe that they should form productive partnerships to best educate children. However, they also find that collaboration can be a challenge, especially if parents have only recently come to the United States and speak a language other than English. Here are some suggestions for fostering a positive working relationship:

- Try to understand the language needs of the family. If parents need information in a language other than English, they are entitled to receive it. If a translator is needed in meetings, this service should be provided. The translator often can be chosen by the parents or can be another parent of a child with a disability.
- Check to see whether English classes are offered to parents by your school district. In a large district, a welcome center or parent center also may operate. If so, share this information with parents.
- Use icons (for example, happy faces and sad faces) to convey information. If you need to send essential information to the family, ask about having it translated.
- Avoid jargon. Provide specific examples to illustrate the information you are communicating.
- Verify with parents that your communication has been understood. Be aware that some parents may consider it rude to ask you to repeat information, so you should be alert to the possible need to restate what you have said.

- Develop your own key vocabulary list in the parents' language (for example, special education terms, greeting words, and action words) so you can participate directly in some small way in communicating with them.
- Read about the family's culture. Ask parents who are bilingual to describe the education system in their native country.
- Welcome parents to your classroom and be respectful of cultural differences in the willingness to share information.
- Include cultural and religious holidays on school calendars.
- Visit families at home, if this practice is customary in your school district. However, remember that some families will prefer to meet you at a neutral location such as a library rather than in their home.
- Encourage family members to become involved in their child's education. Try to connect immigrant families with other families from their native country.
- Remember that confusion and misunderstanding are common when language and cultural differences exist. Be quick to seek further understanding and slow to lay blame. The dilemma may be related to language or culture.

Source: Adapted from "Involving Immigrant Parents of Students with Disabilities in the Educational Process," by S. Al-Ahssan and R. Gardner, *Teaching Exceptional Children, 34*(5), 2002, pp. 52–58. Copyright 2002 by The Council for Exceptional Children. Reprinted with permission.

strategies. For example, at the beginning of the school year, you can send home a letter to parents that introduces you and explains your classroom goals for the year. You can follow this up with a positive phone call to parents sometime during the first weeks of the school year. A positive call is particularly important for parents of students with disabilities because they often hear from educators only when a problem occurs.

You can continue a system of communication with parents throughout the school year. For example, some teachers send home weekly updates or newsletters to the parents of all their students (for example, Dardig, 2005); others send progress reports midway through a grading period. For a student who is struggling, you might exchange a notebook in which you briefly list accomplishments of the day and a parent writes back with information from home (Turnbull, Erwin, Soodak, & Shogren, 2011). A time-saving alternative is to have a checklist that describes the positive behaviors expected of your student (for example, "Raises hand to ask a question"; "Comes to class with all needed materials"). You can then check the items that were successfully completed for that day. For a student with severe disabilities in your class, a paraprofessional might assist by preparing under your direction daily communication to parents (Chopra, Sandoval-Lucero, Aragon, Bernal, De Balderas, & Carroll, 2004). Whenever you use a daily communication system, you should encourage parents to respond so you are aware of their perspectives and concerns.

Some teachers are finding that electronic communication can be a useful tool. If the families of your students have access to e-mail, you can send a group communication or electronic newsletter on a weekly basis, and you can send information about a specific student more frequently as needed. Some teachers also use e-mail to ensure that communication about homework is clear (Mitchell, Foulger, & Wetzel, 2009). Remember, though, that some families cannot readily access a computer, so you need to use an alternative means of communication with them.

Finally, your strategies for home–school communication may be influenced by culture (Harry, 2008). With some families, indirect communication through print or electronic media will not be effective. In such cases, your responsibility is to ensure that you reach out to parents through a phone call or an invitation to come to school to meet. Depending on local policy and parent preference, you might even suggest meeting the parents at a local library or another setting that might be perceived as more parent-friendly than school. In general, you should remember that if your goal is to enhance collaboration with parents, the communication approaches you select should clearly help you achieve that purpose.

Parent Conferences   In addition to the informal, day-to-day communication in which you engage with parents, you also can collaborate with them through conferences. Preparing for, conducting, and following up on parent conferences helps ensure that this communication vehicle is valuable for the parents of all your students, including those with disabilities.

Before a conference, you should clarify the purpose of the meeting. Is it to speak to a group of parents about your overall goals for the year? Is it to meet individually with parents to discuss their child's progress? You can help parents prepare for the latter type of meeting by sending a list of questions and suggestions home in advance of the conference. A sample of such a conference-preparation flyer is presented in Figure 3.3. As you prepare questions for parents, you also should think about the questions you wish to address with them and make a list. Finally, you will communicate more effectively if you have samples of student work, your grade and plan books, and other pertinent student records easily available.

During the conference, your goal is to create a two-way exchange of information. Whether meeting with parents by yourself or with a special educator, you can accomplish this goal when you greet parents positively, arrange to meet with them at a table instead of at your desk, set a purpose for the conference, and actively involve them in discussion. In addition, you should use language respectful of the parents, their child, and their culture. Avoid using jargon (for example, acronyms such as RtI and MDT). In addition, you should work to understand that parents might interpret the meaning of disability and educators' response to it in ways that differ from educators. For example, some African-American parents may distrust school professionals and the decisions made about their children because of past segregation and discriminatory special education practices (Salend & Duhaney, 2005).

FIGURE 3.3 **Sample Set of Questions to Help Parents Prepare for Conferences**

1. What are your priorities for your child's education this year?
2. What information would you like me to know that would help me better understand and instruct your child? What are your child's learning strengths? Unique needs?
3. What are the best ways to communicate with you? Phone or voice mail? E-mail or text message? Face to face? Written notes?
4. What questions do you have about your child's education?
5. How could we at school help make this the most successful year ever for your child?
6. Are there any topics you want to discuss at the conference for which I might need to prepare? If so, please let me know.
7. Would you like other individuals to participate in the conference? If so, please give me a list of their names so I can invite them.
8. Would you like me to have particular school information available? If so, please let me know.

What other questions would you add to this list? Remember to let parents know how to contact you prior to a conference. Also keep in mind that special educators usually participate with you in conferences regarding students with disabilities. They are invaluable in helping to respond to parent questions and concerns.

After a parent conference, you should complete several tasks. First, you should write a few notes to remind yourself of the important points discussed. These notes will help you improve the accuracy of your recollections. Second, if you made any major decisions regarding strategies that you and the parents will implement, you should write a brief note to the parents to confirm those decisions. Third, if you agreed to any action (for example, sending information to parents or asking a counselor to call parents), it is best to carry it out as soon as possible. Finally, if the special education teacher did not attend the conference, he may appreciate receiving a brief note from you with an update on the conference outcomes.

Parent Education   Another type of communication with parents can be accomplished through a variety of parent education activities (for example, Gyamfi, Walrath, Burns, Stephens, Geng, & Stambaugh, 2010). Although you probably would not undertake this type of activity without your colleagues, you may find parent programs helpful for informing parents and giving them an opportunity to discuss important matters concerning their children. For example, if your school decides to emphasize inclusive practices, an information session for the parents of all students might be very helpful. One school invited the parent of a student with disabilities to present on this topic to other parents at the beginning of the school year; the result was increased understanding and a positive start. Some schools offer parent programs related to understanding children's behavior, preparing for transitions from one school level to the next, and other topics of common interest, including ADHD and autism.

Parent Involvement   One additional type of collaboration with parents occurs through their involvement in their children's schools (Turnbull et al., 2011). Some parents, especially at the elementary level, make time to volunteer at school, tutoring students, assisting with clerical chores, and helping to supervise students on field trips. Other parents cannot make such commitments, but they might be willing to help design a newsletter by working at their convenience or to come to school on a Saturday to help set up for a special event. Alternatively, some schools help parents get involved by making school facilities more available. For example, some schools regularly hold evening sessions during which parents can bring their children to school to work on computers, read, or participate in discussion groups. Some schools find space in the building to set up a parent center, a comfortable gathering place designed for and operated by parents where books can be borrowed and important school district and community information is available.

The Complexity of Parent Collaboration   Just as with your interactions with colleagues, your interactions with parents sometimes will be successful and satisfying and sometimes will be challenging and perplexing. The notion of frame of reference applies as well. The more you can understand what is behind a parent's thinking, the better prepared you will be to try to work for a solution. Keep in mind that some parents of students with disabilities feel they have had to fight to get for their children the services to which they are entitled, and so they may come across as aggressive, even if you approach an interaction with the intent of collaboration. Occasionally, a parent will ask you for something that truly is not reasonable, and in such a case, you should enlist the assistance of the special education teacher and possibly an administrator in responding. If a disagreement with a parent occurs, avoid making unilateral statements such as "We don't offer any services in a special education classroom" or "I won't permit that type of assistance in my classroom." Remember that because students with disabilities have special rights, you run the risk of speaking in error and causing further difficulties. One strategy usually recommended is to let the parent know that you will be back in touch after checking on options. This provides you with the time needed to seek additional information, enlist assistance, and formulate options for resolving the matter. You can read about an example of a meeting in which a parent and professionals disagree in the Case in Practice.

CASE IN PRACTICE

Addressing Conflict with a Parent

Mitchell has been experiencing a variety of difficulties in his eighth-grade classes. The greatest concern expressed by his teachers is that he refuses to use any of the materials that have been specially prepared for him by the special educator, Ms. Antovich. This definitely is affecting his grades. His teachers believe he is quite capable of learning the material and have asked Mitchell's parents to come to school to discuss what to do. Along with Ms. Cox, Mitchell's mother, the meeting is being attended by Ms. Antovich; Mr. Roscoe, the team's math teacher; and Mr. Crain, the assistant principal. The school professionals have explained their concerns, and they are ready to seek Ms. Cox's assistance.

Mr. Crain: Given what we've described, Ms. Cox, I'm wondering what your reaction is.

Ms. Cox: I didn't realize letting Mitchell receive special education meant he was going to be singled out in class. No wonder he won't use the things Ms. Antovich is preparing. I'm sure he's embarrassed. He said something at home about that the other day, and I wasn't sure what he was referring to. Now I know. Just stop singling him out!

Ms. Antovich: I should clarify the types of adapted materials I've been providing, Ms. Cox. My goal is to make anything that is used in class as much like the other kids' materials as possible. Most of the time, several students are using them. I'm not sure it's the materials themselves that are the issue. I think Mitchell has decided that he doesn't want any type of assistance in class.

Mr. Roscoe: That is the impression I have. For example, it really helps Mitchell to use a calculator for computation, and calculators are available for all the students who want to use them. But Mitchell refuses. As a result, he makes avoidable errors and hurts his scores.

Ms. Cox: How many other kids use calculators?

Mr. Roscoe: Several do. It's just an accepted part of my class.

Ms. Cox: All I know is that he feels stupid in his classes. He's proud, just like his father. He doesn't want anyone to know that school is so hard for him, and I know he doesn't want people helping him.

Mr. Crain: You've added the information that Mitchell is embarrassed by any assistance received in the classroom, and that's helpful. We still have to address two key issues. First, Mitchell is unlikely to succeed in his classes without supports. With supports, he seems to do well, and so there is no justification for even thinking about pulling him out of his classes to a special education setting. Second, he sees supports as embarrassing. Perhaps we should focus on how to integrate supports better into the instruction so they are not seen by Mitchell as embarrassing.

Mr. Roscoe: I'm open to any ideas we can come up with. This is such a critical year in math instruction, and I know the other teachers feel the same way about their subjects.

Ms. Antovich: Ms. Cox, how would it be if I had a private conversation with Mitchell to raise the issue of embarrassment with him? I could then give you a call to discuss options we might try. But I'll really need your assistance in convincing Mitchell to do whatever we plan.

The meeting continued for another few minutes while details of the plan were outlined.

REFLECTION

What parts of a problem-solving process did this meeting include? How effective were the professionals in exploring Ms. Cox's perspective on her son's problem? What was the role of each professional attending the meeting? Could any of them have been excused? Should others have been invited? What did the professionals say that might have lessened Ms. Cox's concern? That could have increased it? Mitchell was not present at this particular meeting. Why not? How could Mitchell's input be included anyway? How might the meeting have been different with him present? What are your responsibilities as a professional educator when parents disagree with your perceptions of their child with a disability? What types of assistance might you seek to help address the matter?

How Can You Work Effectively with Paraprofessionals?

Throughout this chapter, the assumption has been made that all the individuals involved in forming school partnerships have equal status; that is, a general education teacher has approximately the same level of authority and equivalent responsibilities as a special education teacher, speech/language therapist, school psychologist, reading teacher, and so on. In many school districts, individuals in these types of positions are referred to as *certified staff* or *professional staff*.

One other partnership you may form involves another type of staff. As mentioned in Chapter 2, **paraprofessionals,** or paraeducators, are school personnel employed to assist certified staff in carrying out educational programs and otherwise helping in the instruction of students with disabilities. Although some school districts also employ other types of paraprofessionals, for this discussion, we refer only to paraprofessionals who are part of special education services. Paraprofessionals usually have completed two years of college or have passed an examination related to their responsibilities, but they generally are not required to have a four-year college degree. When students with disabilities are members of your class, a special educator may not have adequate time or opportunity to assist them frequently, or the students might not need the direct services of that professional. Instead, a paraprofessional might be assigned to you for a class period or subject or, depending on the intensity of student needs, for much of the school day (Giangreco, Suter, & Doyle, 2010; Devlin, 2008).

Understanding Your Working Relationship with Paraprofessionals

The partnerships you form with paraprofessionals are slightly different from those you form with certified staff because you have some supervisory responsibility for a paraprofessional's work, a situation that would not exist in your work with other colleagues (Carnahan, Williamson, Clarke, & Sorensen, 2009). For example, you may be expected to prepare materials for the paraprofessional to use in working with a group of students, you may have the responsibility of assigning tasks to this person on a daily basis, and you may need to provide informal training to the paraprofessional regarding your classroom expectations.

Many classroom teachers have never been supervisors, and they worry about what types of tasks to assign to a paraprofessional and how to set expectations (Devlin, 2008). Adding to the complexity of the situation is the fact that some paraprofessionals have extensive professional preparation, a teaching license, and years of classroom experience, which makes them prepared to do nearly everything you do; others meet only the minimum requirements and have little experience working with students. In Chapter 2 you learned about the types of responsibilities paraprofessionals may have in your classroom. If you will be working with a paraprofessional, you should receive a written description of that person's job responsibilities, specifying the types of activities that individual is to complete. Also you can arrange to meet with the special education teacher or another professional who has overall responsibility for the paraprofessional's job performance.

Two general guidelines for working effectively with paraprofessionals are these: First, paraprofessionals generally enjoy working with students and want to participate actively in that process, and they should have the opportunity to do so. However, they also are expected to help teachers accomplish some of the chores of teaching, such as record keeping and instructional preparation tasks. Second, paraprofessionals complete their instructional assignments under the direction of a teacher who either has already taught the information or has decided what basic work needs to be completed; that is, paraprofessionals should not engage in initial teaching, nor should they make instructional decisions without input from a certified staff member.

---

dimensions of DIVERSITY

Rueda and Genzuk (2007) found that in both general education and special education classrooms, Latino paraprofessionals often were given low-level tasks to complete. They proposed that these valuable school employees instead should be considered "cultural brokers."

---

www.resources

http://www.nrcpara.org
The National Resource Center for Paraprofessionals (NRCP) was founded in 1979 to support paraprofessionals who work in schools. This site includes several discussion boards, including one for teachers and administrators who have questions about working with paraprofessionals.

You have a key role in setting expectations for a paraprofessional who may work in your classroom, for ensuring that you and the paraprofessional are satisfied with your working relationship, and for resolving any problems that arise. At the beginning of the school year, you can orient the paraprofessional to your classroom by providing a place for him to keep personal belongings and instructional materials, explaining essential rules and policies for your classroom, clarifying where in the classroom you want him to work, and asking him to voice questions and concerns (French, 2003). It is particularly important to touch base with the paraprofessional frequently early in the school year to be certain that expectations are clear. The paraprofessional may be working in several classrooms and trying to remember several sets of directions from different teachers, all with their own styles. You might even find that discussing these topics is best accomplished in a meeting that includes the special education teacher, you, any other general education teachers involved, and the paraprofessional. Figure 3.4 outlines some questions you might want to ask concerning your work with paraprofessionals to ensure your experience is positive for you and your students as well as the paraprofessional.

To continue nurturing the working relationship you have with a paraprofessional, you should communicate clearly and directly all activities you would like him to complete. Some paraprofessionals report that they enter a classroom only to find that the teacher is already working with students and expects the paraprofessional to know what to do with the students with special needs, assuming that the special education teacher has provided this direction. Meanwhile, the special educator is assuming that the general education teacher is guiding the paraprofessional. Unfortunately, in this situation the paraprofessional may be left frustrated and wondering how to proceed.

Collaborating with Paraprofessionals

An often-asked teacher question regarding paraprofessionals is this: Given the supervisory nature of teacher–paraprofessional work, is it possible to collaborate with this group of staff members? The answer is yes. Paraprofessionals can collaboratively participate in shared problem solving about student needs, planning field trip and class activity details, and making decisions regarding how best to adapt information for a specific student (Giangreco et al., 2010). Your responsibility as a teacher is to encourage this type of collaboration. At the same time, you should clearly inform the paraprofessional when a matter being discussed is not one in which the principles

FIGURE 3.4 **General Educator's Questions for Working with Paraprofessionals**

- Is the paraprofessional in my class provided as a general support for students with disabilities, or is she assigned on behalf of a particular student?
- What range of activities should I expect the paraprofessional to complete related to academic instruction? Behavior? Student social interactions? Physical assistance?
- Are there specific activities the paraprofessional must carry out? Should not carry out?
- To what extent am I responsible for assigning the paraprofessional specific tasks and activities in the classroom?
- What strategies will be used to ensure that communication among the special education teacher, paraprofessional, and me is clear and consistent? How will we meet on a regular basis to discuss student progress, problems, and paraprofessional responsibilities in the classroom?
- Should the paraprofessional communicate directly with the parents?
- Should we discuss any issues related to confidentiality?
- What training has the paraprofessional had for working in my classroom? For working with students with disabilities? What preparation has the paraprofessional had related to the curriculum for which I am responsible?
- What should I do if I am uncomfortable with something the paraprofessional is doing or reporting or if other problems occur?
- What should I do on days on which I don't have anything in particular for the paraprofessional to do?

of collaboration are appropriate. It also is important that you tell paraprofessionals when they are meeting your expectations and that you promptly address any issues of concern as soon as you become aware of them. For example, Ms. Fulton is a paraprofessional in the seventh-grade math class. At a recent brief meeting, the math teacher thanked her for quietly answering students' questions about directions and providing assistance in reading items in the textbook. However, he also directed Ms. Fulton to avoid assisting students in answering the problems being worked. His judgment is that her help is approaching the level of providing students with answers. He illustrated his point by talking through with her an example of how to respond to a student who asks for assistance. His directions to Ms. Fulton were direct and clear but also respectful of her many years of experience in working with students with disabilities.

The Complexity of Collaborating with Paraprofessionals

Most of your interactions with paraprofessionals will be positive, and you will realize how valuable these school personnel are in inclusive classrooms. Although most paraprofessionals work diligently, have a tremendous commitment to working with students with disabilities, and manage their roles superbly, problems occasionally arise. If you teach older students, you might find that the paraprofessional does not have enough knowledge of the content being presented to reinforce student learning. A few paraprofessionals violate principles of confidentiality by discussing classroom or student matters away from school. Some paraprofessionals are disruptive in classrooms—for example, their speech is too loud or their interactions with students are too casual. If problems such as these occur and cannot be resolved directly between you and the paraprofessional, you should ask the special educator with whom you work to meet with you and the paraprofessional to problem solve. If further action is needed, an administrator such as a principal or special education coordinator can assist. Ultimately, you are directing the day-to-day work of the paraprofessionals in your class. If problems arise, it is your responsibility to follow up until they are resolved and students' support is being provided appropriately.

An entirely different type of problem can occur, but it is equally serious. Some paraprofessionals tend to hover over students with disabilities, preventing them from establishing social relationships with peers and fostering dependence instead of independence (Giangreco & Doyle, 2002). You should discuss this well-intentioned but inappropriate activity with such paraprofessionals and give clear, alternative directions for their interactions with students. By offering encouragement and addressing concerns, you can establish an environment that will make your collaboration with paraprofessionals invaluable.

WRAPPING IT UP

BACK TO THE CASES

This section provides opportunities for you to apply the knowledge gained in this chapter to the cases described at the beginning of this chapter. The questions and activities that follow demonstrate how the concepts that you have learned about in this chapter connect to the everyday activities of all teachers.

MS. RANDELMAN and Ms. Pickett ask for your advice on co-teaching. Briefly outline or describe two styles of co-teaching you might recommend to them. Assume that you have chosen to teach this grade level and subject area. For each of these two co-teaching styles, answer the following questions:

- Why would you select this style to teach this particular content?
- How does this style meet the needs of each student with special needs in the class?

MS. SWANSON and Ms. O'Brien began their professional relationship to consult about Brittany's difficulty transitioning to the media center. However, they discovered other areas where they wanted to work together to improve Brittany's learning experiences as well. They agreed to become more collaborative in their working arrangement. Where do you think they might encounter some difficulty as they make a shift in the relationship? What suggestions would you give them so that in the end their partnership is successful?

MS. MACDOUGAL listens to the exchange between the Werners and Mr. Sanders. As they discuss concerns, she determines that the meeting is not going to come to a productive end. She quickly decides to suggest that the participants enter into a shared problem-solving activity. Is this an appropriate strategy for this meeting? Provide reasons for your thinking. What type of problem solving activity might be beneficial in this type of situation? As a general education teacher, how can you help to resolve situations such as this one?

SUMMARY

- Collaboration has become an important job responsibility for all educators and is especially important in educating students with special needs.

- Collaboration is a style professionals use in interacting with others, and it involves key characteristics such as voluntary participation, parity, shared goals, shared responsibility for key decisions, shared accountability for outcomes, shared resources, and the emergence of trust, respect, and a collaborative belief system.

- You can help make your school's collaborative efforts more successful by identifying and clarifying your personal beliefs about collaboration, refining your interaction skills, and contributing to a supportive environment.

- Collaboration can occur in many programs and services, including shared problem solving, co-teaching, working in teams, and consulting.

- When working with parents, you should use *family-centered practices*, including striving to understand parents' perspectives on having a child with a disability; collaborating with them based on your respect for their perspective; communicating effectively with them in conferences and in other ways; and responding professionally to them in team meetings, annual reviews, and other interactions at which you and they are present.

- You may occasionally experience difficult interactions with parents; in these instances, using principles for effective communication and asking for assistance are essential.

- Understanding your roles and responsibilities as well as those of a paraprofessional is essential. Basing your collaboration on this understanding leads to positive working relationships, particularly if you directly and respectfully address problems that occur as paraprofessionals work with you on behalf of the students with disabilities.

APPLICATIONS IN TEACHING PRACTICE
COLLABORATION IN THE WASHINGTON SCHOOL DISTRICT

Although the administrators in the Washington School District would tell you that staff members have always worked together well, when increasing inclusive practices was made part of the district's strategic plan, it became clear that collaboration also needed to be a priority. Each principal was asked to work with staff members to incorporate collaboration into the school's improvement plan. Each school created a committee to study collaboration and its application in inclusive schools, set priorities, and plan staff development. Committee members also created a plan for evaluating the impact of increased collaboration on student outcomes.

In every elementary, middle, and high school, the teachers reviewed their school mission statement as a starting point for discussions of their beliefs about how students learn, how teachers teach, and how schools can be learning communities. In most of the schools, the teachers quickly realized that their mission statement did not explicitly say that teachers in the school were expected to work together to meet the needs of all their students. During after-school meetings, the mission statements were revised.

Next, teachers began to discuss various forms their collaboration might take. In one elementary school, Carole, a first-grade teacher anticipating a class group with many special needs, argued strongly for co-teaching. She stated that she needed someone to help her for at least a couple of hours each day. Peggy, another teacher, reminded her that with only two special education teachers and one paraprofessional available for everyone from kindergarten through fifth grade, she was asking for far too much, especially because these professionals also had other responsibilities. Jim, the special education teacher who works with students with moderate and severe disabilities, agreed. He noted that he had to reserve time to work individually with some of his students in a special education setting.

Co-teaching was a popular topic in other schools too. In the middle school, one special education teacher was assigned to each team, and the teachers learned that they had the responsibility for deciding how to co-teach while making sure that students' IEP goals were addressed. Most teams decided that co-teaching should occur mostly in English and math classes. In the high school, the teachers approached their investigations with caution. First, they decided that special education teachers should be assigned to academic departments. Then they decided that co-teaching would occur only in English and math for the upcoming year; other services would remain the same while everyone became accustomed to working together, even though teachers in science and social studies objected because of their need to improve student outcomes, especially for students with disabilities. These teachers also decided that they wanted to learn more about collaboration skills as they applied to their RtI process, and they arranged with a local consultant for professional development as well as for observations of and feedback related to their interactions during RtI meetings.

Principals made planning time a priority. They ensured that co-teaching teams could meet every week or so, but they also required that lesson plans be submitted after those meetings. Principals also decided to survey teachers, paraprofessionals, and parents at the halfway point of the school year and again at the end of the year in order to gauge perceptions of these efforts to enhance collaboration. They also worked with the district's data manager to develop several strategies to measure impact on student learning and behavior.

With much excitement and some anxiety, the district's administrators and teachers finished their detailed planning. They were a little concerned about new teachers who might be hired during the summer and how to help them become oriented quickly to the collaborative initiative. They also were concerned about whether they could demonstrate that working more closely improved student achievement, the ultimate goal. However, they felt they had worked closely to develop the plan and were eager to implement it.

QUESTIONS

1. Which characteristics of collaboration can you identify in the teachers' interactions and plans? Which are not evident?
2. How were the teachers working to ensure their collaborative efforts would be successful? What is the role of the principal in fostering collaboration?
3. How would you respond to Carole? What do you recommend she do? What do you recommend that her colleagues do in their interactions with her?
4. Why would it be important to incorporate a statement about collaboration into a school mission statement? Check the websites of your local schools. If their mission statements are posted, do they address collaboration, either directly or indirectly?
5. How could the teachers communicate with parents about their plans? What reactions might they expect from parents? Why? How could they involve parents in their programs?
6. How might collaboration among professionals be similar and different in the elementary schools, middle schools, and high schools? What opportunities and constraints might exist for each group?

Go to Topic 3: Collaboration, Consultation, and Co-Teaching in the MyEducationLab
(http://www.myeducationlab.com) for your course, where you can:

- Find learning outcomes for Collaboration, Consultation, and Co-Teaching along with the
  national standards that connect to these outcomes.
- Complete Assignments and Activities that can help you more deeply understand the chapter
  content.
- Apply and practice your understanding of the core teaching skills identified in the chapter
  with the Building Teaching Skills and Dispositions learning units.
- Examine challenging situations and cases presented in the IRIS Center Resources. (optional)
- Access video clips of CCSSO National Teachers of the Year award winners responding to the
  question, "Why Do I Teach?" in the Teacher Talk section. (optional)
- Check your comprehension on the content covered in the chapter by going to the Study
  Plan in the Book Resources for your text. Here you will be able to take a chapter quiz, re-
  ceive feedback on your answers, and then access Review, Practice, and Enrichment activities
  to enhance your understanding of chapter content. (optional)

chapter

4

Assessing Student Needs

LEARNING Objectives

After you read this chapter, you will be able to

1. Explain how general education teachers can contribute significantly to the assessment process.

2. Describe the uses of high-stakes, standardized achievement, and psychological tests in making educational decisions for students with special needs.

3. Describe how alternate assessments for students with significant intellectual disabilities can be developed and scored.

4. Define curriculum-based assessment and explain how it can help general education teachers.

5. Construct and use probes of basic academic skills, prerequisite skills and knowledge in content areas, and independent learning skills.

6. Use curriculum-based assessment to make special education decisions.

MS. LYONS is concerned that Rob, a student in her second-grade class, is not keeping up with the rest of the class in math. She knows that he will be taking the state math test in third grade, and she is afraid that if he continues to fall behind, he won't meet state standards. Mr. Blair, the special education teacher, suggests that Ms. Lyons do some informal assessment herself before referring Rob for special education or other services.

What kinds of assessments can Ms. Lyons use to clarify Rob's problems in math? How might these assessments help her make changes in Rob's math instruction? Under what circumstances should she refer Rob for special education or other services?

MR. BLOUNT teaches a high school U.S. history class. He has learned that three students with disabilities will be in his class this fall. Mr. Blount was told that these students have some reading problems and may have trouble reading the textbook. He decides to make up a test to give at the beginning of the year to see how well all of his students are able to use the textbook. Using a section of a chapter from the text, he writes questions to test how well students can figure out the meanings of key vocabulary words, use parts of the book (for example, the table of contents, glossary, and index), read maps, and read for information (for example, note main ideas and draw conclusions). When Mr. Blount gives the test, he finds that the three identified students have trouble reading the text, but many other students also have difficulty.

How might Mr. Blount use the information from this assessment to differentiate instruction for his students?

ROBERTO is a student with moderate to severe intellectual disabilities who is in Ms. Benis's sixth-grade social studies class. As a result of Roberto's cerebral palsy, he has significant cognitive, language, and motor deficits. Roberto can read his name, as well as some high-frequency sight words. He uses a wheelchair, and he has trouble with fine motor movements such as cutting and handwriting. Roberto speaks with the aid of a communication board.

How can Roberto meet state standards for sixth grade in social studies? What kinds of assessments can Ms. Benis use to determine whether Roberto is meeting standards in social studies?

As more and more students with disabilities are being served in general education classes, teachers need to make many important decisions that can greatly affect these students' success. This is particularly important in view of federal requirements in the Individuals with Disabilities Education Act (IDEA) that students with disabilities participate in district testing programs, have access to the general education curriculum, and make meaningful progress toward meeting general curriculum goals. For example, in the preceding vignettes, Ms. Lyons wanted to help Rob before he failed the state math test in grade 3. Mr. Blount wanted to find out whether his students could read the textbook for his history class to help him decide which students would benefit from adapting the book. Ms. Benis needed to include Roberto, who had significant disabilities, in her social studies class but had to figure out how he would meet state standards. To respond effectively in situations such as these, teachers need accurate, relevant information. Thus, they need to develop informal measures to help them make instructional decisions as well as participate in special education decision making. This chapter explores assessment strategies that help general education teachers contribute to the process of decision making for students with special needs. This process involves determining whether a student needs special education services; when a student is ready to learn in inclusive settings; when an alternative to state testing is required; and what classroom accommodations and modifications to try, continue to use, or change. The assessment strategies described are also helpful if your school is implementing RtI.

How Do Your Student Assessments Contribute to Special Education Decisions?

As a general education teacher, you make an important contribution to the process of identifying and meeting the needs of students with special needs. A major part of that contribution involves assessing student needs. **Assessment** has been defined as the process of gathering information to monitor progress and to make educational decisions when necessary (Overton, 2009). The most common ways of collecting information are through standardized, commercially produced tests, high-stakes state accountability tests, and informal tests devised by the teacher. Much of the information in this chapter is about ways in which these measures can be used to make decisions about students with special needs. General education teachers contribute assessment information in six important decision-making areas for students with special needs: screening, diagnosis, program placement, curriculum placement, instructional evaluation, and program evaluation.

Screening

In Chapter 2 you learned that **screening** involves the decision about whether a student's performance differs enough from that of his or her peers to merit further, more in-depth assessments to determine the presence of a disability. For example, to clarify Rob's problems in math, Ms. Lyons from the chapter-opening vignette examined the most recent group achievement test scores for her class in math and found that Rob was performing two years below grade

Students' needs can be identified, addressed, and monitored through assessment based on observation, screening, diagnostic testing, program placement and evaluation, curriculum placement, and instructional evaluation. What role do general education teachers play in assessing students' special needs?

level. Ms. Lyons then gave Rob some minitests on various math computation skills she had taught to see whether Rob was behind his peers on these skills. Using this information, Ms. Lyons found that a number of students were performing similarly to Rob. She therefore decided not to refer Rob for a more comprehensive evaluation until she first tried making some changes in the classroom with Rob and several other students. Screening assessments are at the heart of prevention-based systems such as RtI where they are referred to as universal screening measures. An explanation of universal screening including how to select and use universal screening measures is presented in the Instructional Edge.

Diagnosis

The major decision related to **diagnosis** concerns eligibility for special education services, a decision you first learned about in Chapter 2. Does a student meet established federal guidelines for being classified as having a disability? If so, what are the nature and extent of the student's disability? For example, Paula was a student in Ms. Clark's class. In September, when Paula appeared to be struggling to keep up with the class in reading, Ms. Clark paired her up with a classmate for 15 minutes before reading each day to go over key words and vocabulary. When Paula's reading accuracy and fluency problems persisted even after four weeks of this extra help, Ms. Clark arranged for her to have 30 minutes more practice later in the day with the reading teacher. After a month of this extra help, Paula still showed no improvement. Ms. Clark suspected she had a learning disability and referred her for a case study evaluation. The school psychologist gave Paula a test on cognitive functioning—including a test of memory, attention, and organization—and an individual achievement test. She found that Paula was slow in processing visual information (that is, letters, numbers, and shapes) and that her achievement in reading was significantly lower than that of other students her age. However, her achievement in math was at grade level. Ms. Clark evaluated Paula's classroom reading performance by having her read orally and answer questions from a grade-level trade book that was part of the classroom literature program. Paula's oral reading fluency was well below norms for her grade level, and she was able to answer only 40 percent of the comprehension questions correctly. In the end, Paula was declared eligible to receive services for learning disabilities, because she did not respond favorably to two levels of extra classroom help, she showed problems processing visual information quickly enough, and her achievement was significantly below grade level as measured by both a standardized achievement test and informal classroom reading tests. Working Together highlights effective ways to communicate to parents the results of diagnostic tests, as well as resulting decisions about placement.

Program Placement

The major **program placement** decision involves the setting in which a student's special education services take place (for example, in a general education classroom, resource room, or separate special education classroom). The individualized education program (IEP) team must make this decision carefully. In the past, the tendency was to pull students out of general education classrooms without considering whether they could be supported within the general education program instead. In today's schools, the emphasis is on doing all that can be done within the general education class first. This approach is consistent with guidelines for accessing the general education curriculum outlined in IDEA and RtI, in which students with learning disabilities are identified by monitoring how they respond to evidence-based instruction of varying intensity. Still, students have different needs, and some may require instruction in a specific area at a level of intensity that cannot be delivered in the general education classroom. That is why it is important to make placement decisions based on measures that accurately reflect student performance in class. For example, Carlos was eligible to receive services for learning disabilities in math. His IEP team needed to decide whether his learning needs could be accommodated by

fyi

Program placement decisions for students with moderate to severe intellectual disabilities should be based on the supports needed to meet the curricular goals outlined in their IEPs.

INSTRUCTIONAL **EDGE**

Using Universal Screening in RtI to Identify Students at Risk

What is universal screening?

The problem with identifying children who are experiencing academic difficulties is that by the time they are identified, they are already so far behind that catching up is often a losing proposition. A key feature of RtI is identifying and intervening with students at risk for academic problems early to prevent problems before they become insurmountable. The RtI process of assessing all students to identify those who are having difficulty learning despite an evidence-based Tier 1 program is called universal screening.

What are the qualities of effective universal screening measures?

Effective universal screening measures are accurate and practical, and they should not have negative or unintended consequences for students (for example, be biased) (Hughes & Dexter, 2010; Jenkins, 2009). Universal screening measures must accurately classify students who are at-risk or not at risk for academic failure. This means that only students who need extra support get it, and that students who need support are not overlooked. Overidentifying children who are at-risk (false positives) is costly to schools and can cause unneeded worry. Overlooking students (false negatives) needlessly delays support, creating more serious problems that may be more difficult to remediate later on. Universal screening measures must also be brief and easy to give. Last, effective universal screening measures should do no harm to the student. This means they should avoid leading to inequitable treatment and be linked to effective interventions.

How should a universal screening measure be chosen?

Jenkins (2009) suggests considering these ideas when choosing universal screening measures:

- A screening battery that measures multiple aspects of an academic area is more accurate than a test that measures only one. For example, if you are doing universal screening in reading, you would want to measure phonemic awareness, phonics, fluency, and comprehension. In math you would want to assess both math computation and math problem solving.
- Screening should be conducted more than once per year to detect students who may no longer be at risk or have become at risk.
- There is a research base that shows which universal screening measures are the most accurate. Consult that research base before you select a universal screening measure for your school. Not all universal screening measures are created equal.

How are at-risk students identified?

Currently there is no agreement as to what criteria should be used to identify students who are at-risk in Tier 1 (Hughes & Dexter, 2010). Some programs use a percentile approach whereby students performing below a certain percentile are considered at-risk (Hintze, 2007). For example, all children scoring below the 25th percentile may be considered at-risk.

What measures are commonly used for universal screening?

Most research-based universal screening measures are in the area of reading. Four assessment batteries are most commonly used for universal screening in reading within RtI programs. These include Dynamic Indicators of Basic Skills (DIBELS; http://dibels.uoregon.edu/measures/psf.php), AIMSWEB (http://www.aimsweb.com); Phonological Awareness Literacy Screening (PALS; http://pals.virginia.edu), and Texas Primary Reading Inventory (TPRI; http://www.tpri.org). There are a number of curriculum-based measures (CBM) available for screening in writing and math. Note that many universal screening measures can also be used for progress monitoring, a key part of RtI. For example, AIMSWEB also has universal screening assessments in math including math computation and math concepts and applications.

As you can see, universal screening measures are not as highly developed at the secondary level, largely because of the emphasis on the acquisition of subject matter knowledge rather than basic academic skills. A likely source is student performance on high stakes assessments and/or end-of-grade/class tests.

Internet resources for information about assessment within RtI gathered by Ysseldyke et al. (2010) are shown below.

- Florida Assessment for Instruction in Reading (FAIR)
  http://www.fcrr.org/FAIR_Search_Tool/FAIR_Search_Tool.aspx

- Intervention Central
  http://www.interventioncentral.com

- National Association of State Directors of Special Education
  http://www.nasde.org/Projects/ResponsetoInterventionRtIProject/tabid/411/Default.aspx

- National Research Center on Learning Disabilities
  http://www.nrcld.org/

- Renaissance Learning-Advanced Technology for Data Driven Schools
  http://www.renlearn.com/

- Research Institute on Progress Monitoring
  http://www.progressmonitoring.net/

- RTI Classification Tool and Resource Locator
  http://www.rtictrl.org/resources/

- RTI Action Network
  http://rtinetwork.org/

- System to Enhance Educational Performance (STEEP) and RTI
  http://www.joewitt.org/steep.html

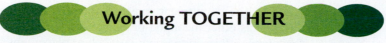

Working TOGETHER

Communicating Effectively with Parents

Mrs. Perez has just attended a multidisciplinary committee meeting for her son Jorge and is distraught. First, being in the same room with all those professionals made Mrs. Perez nervous; she felt like an outsider who was there because she had done something wrong. Second, she was embarrassed that her English wasn't very good, so she was afraid to say anything. She had hoped the meeting would result in Jorge's getting extra help, but that was not what happened at all.

The school psychologist, Mr. Tanner, talked too fast and used a lot of technical language Mrs. Perez didn't understand, such as "performance-based," "verbal IQ," and "age and grade-level expectations." He said Jorge was in the slow-learner range. Mrs. Perez was afraid that he meant her Jorge was stupid. She thought that Jorge was unable to understand tests because his English skills weren't very good, but she was afraid to say so.

When the special education teacher said that Jorge was two to three years below grade level in reading and writing and about one year below level in math, Mrs. Perez wondered whether that meant there was no hope for Jorge. His teacher said that Jorge was having trouble keeping up in class and that last year he had failed to pass the state tests in reading and writing. Mrs. Perez wanted to hear more about what the class was doing and how Jorge was coping with the material, but she was afraid she would offend Jorge's teacher. Mr. Tanner finished by saying that Jorge

was behind in his skills but achieving as expected given his ability. He said that Jorge wasn't eligible for special education services and asked Mrs. Perez if she had any questions.

Mrs. Perez knew that Jorge's English skills were holding him back, but now the committee members were telling her he couldn't get any extra help. Having a million questions but not knowing how to ask them, she nodded her head and left the meeting, afraid that there was no hope for her Jorge in school.

ADDRESSING THE DILEMMA

Chapter 3 presented communication barriers that can exist between parents and teachers, and this interaction illustrates many of those barriers. How could you address each of the following issues?

- Few attempts were made to make Mrs. Perez feel comfortable.
- Mrs. Perez has difficulty expressing herself in English.
- The team explained the testing and eligibility process using highly technical language that Mrs. Perez did not understand.
- The standardized tests were hastily explained.
- The team did not clearly ensure that Mrs. Perez agreed with its decisions.
- The team did not address Mrs. Perez's primary concern: Getting help for her son.

---

adapting the math methods and materials in the general education classroom or whether he should be provided more intensive math instruction in a resource room setting. Carlos's general education teacher gave Carlos and his classmates a series of informal math tests. She found that Carlos was significantly behind his peers on some but not all of the tests; his math problem solving was very deficient compared to that of his classmates, but his math computational skills were fine. The IEP team decided to keep Carlos in his general education class and to support his instruction in problem solving by providing him extra teacher-guided practice whenever a new problem-solving skill was introduced. The team also decided to carefully monitor Carlos's problem-solving skills; if those skills showed little improvement, they would consider other options.

Curriculum Placement

Curriculum placement involves deciding at what level to begin instruction for students. For an elementary school teacher, such a decision may mean choosing which reading or math book a student should use. For example, Ms. Tolhurst has her students read orally and answer questions to find the appropriate trade books for them to read. That is, she determines the level of difficulty at which the books in her classroom reading program are neither too easy nor too hard for them. At the secondary level, curriculum placement decisions are likely to determine which class in a sequence of classes a student should take. For example, Mr. Nowicki, the guidance counselor, was trying to decide whether to place Scott in Algebra 1. He asked the math department to identify basic math skills that all students entering algebra should have. The department constructed a test based on those skills and gave it to Scott as well as other incoming ninth graders.

Of course, information about curriculum placement also provides teachers with a good measure of the extent to which students with disabilities are accessing the general education curriculum, an explicit goal of IDEA. In the examples just mentioned, a student with a disability in Ms. Tolhurst's class who can read only books that are two levels below grade level could be seen as having difficulty accessing the general education reading curriculum. In contrast, a student who enters Mr. Nowicki's algebra class with all of the necessary prerequisite skills is fully accessing the district math curriculum.

Instructional Evaluation

Decisions in **instructional evaluation** involve whether to continue or change instructional procedures that have been initiated with students. These decisions are made by carefully monitoring student progress. For example, Ms. Bridgewater is starting a peer tutoring program to help Cecily, a student with severe intellectual disabilities, read her name and the names of her family members. Each week, Ms. Bridgewater tests Cecily to see how many of the names she has learned. She uses the results of the tests to find out whether the peer-tutoring program is helping Cecily make progress. In another example, Mr. Jackson decides to accompany each of his history lectures with a graphic organizer of the material. He gives weekly quizzes to find out whether the graphic organizer is helping his students better learn the material. Schools implementing RtI use information collected from progress monitoring assessments to assign students to instructional tiers.

Program Evaluation

Program evaluation decisions involve whether a student's special education program should be terminated, continued as is, or modified. One consideration is whether or not the student is accessing the general education curriculum by meeting standards, as evidenced by reaching goals or attaining benchmark levels on assessments. For example, when Addie, a student with a reading disability, attained benchmark levels in reading fluency and comprehension for her grade level, her program was changed. She was integrated into general education for the entire reading block, and her progress was carefully monitored to ensure that her gains were maintained.

Another way to evaluate the success of special education programming is by monitoring the attainment of IEP goals. For example, Amanda is receiving social work services twice per week. Her IEP goal is to decrease the number of times she has a verbal confrontation with Mr. Alvarez, her English teacher. Mr. Alvarez is keeping track of the number of times daily that Amanda refuses to comply with his requests to see whether sessions with the social worker are improving Amanda's behavior.

What Information Sources Are Used in Programming for Students with Special Needs?

A number of information sources are used in programming for students with special needs. The use of multiple assessment sources is consistent with the principle of nondiscriminatory testing, discussed in Chapter 2, which says that no single measure should be used to establish eligibility for special education services. The measures described in this section include high-stakes achievement tests, standardized achievement tests, psychological tests, alternate assessments, and curriculum-based assessments.

High-Stakes Achievement Tests

A key requirement of IDEA is that students with disabilities have maximum access to the general education curriculum. Unlike in the past, however, access today is defined not as spending a certain amount of time in general education but as making meaningful progress toward meeting general curriculum goals (Nolet & McLaughlin, 2005). In general education today, that means meeting educational standards. Standards, which are set by individual states, comprise what students should be able to know or do as a result of their public education. For the past three decades, general dissatisfaction with public education has dramatically raised learning standards and has led to increased accountability for schools as they teach students to attain those standards.

As you learned in Chapter 1, **high-stakes tests** are assessments designed to measure whether students have attained learning standards. These tests are a type of assessment referred to as *criterion referenced* because they involve comparing student performance to a specific level of performance, or benchmark, rather than to a norm, or average, as with traditional standardized achievement tests. Most states have created their own high-stakes tests based on an agreed-on set of learning outcomes. For each identified outcome, standards or benchmarks are set that represent an acceptable level of knowledge or competence. Schools are then evaluated on the basis of the percentage of students meeting standards on each of the learning outcomes identified. For example, State A wanted all its fifth graders to be able to comprehend the key elements of short stories, such as character, setting, problem identification, problem resolution, and moral. Reading experts were chosen by the state to create an item that would test student competence in comprehending short stories. The experts chose a short story written at the fifth-grade level and developed a series of multiple-choice questions about the story elements. They then tried out the test on a diverse sample of students and through careful analysis determined that students who could answer at least 90 percent of the story-element questions were competent at identifying story elements. State A then tested all its fifth-grade students on this item to determine the percentage that could identify key elements in short stories.

IDEA requires that most students with disabilities take their states' high-stakes tests. This is how districts can show the degree of access to the general education curriculum attained by students with disabilities. These IDEA requirements were reinforced by the reauthorization of the Elementary and Secondary Education Act of 2002 (ESEA), which requires that all children in each of grades 3 through 8 and at least once in grades 10 through 12 take high-stakes tests to show whether they are meeting state standards or making adequate progress toward them. ESEA requires that at least 95 percent of students with disabilities take high-stakes tests. Both IDEA and ESEA require that the results for students with disabilities be aggregated with the results of the other students and reported publicly. Results for students with disabilities must also be disaggregated and reported separately; students with disabilities who are tested are held to the same standards and levels of adequate yearly progress as their classmates without disabilities.

To ensure that the scores obtained are accurate, students with disabilities are entitled to a range of accommodations while taking high-stakes tests. Common accommodations include changing the setting of the test (for example, allowing students to take tests in special education classrooms), changing the timing of the test (for example, providing extended time or more frequent breaks), changing the response format (for example, allowing students to mark responses in test books rather than on Scantron sheets), and changing the presentation format (for example, using a braille edition of a test or giving directions in sign language) (Roeber, 2002; Thurlow,

RESEARCH NOTE

Solorzano (2008) reviewed the research on the use of high-stakes tests with English language learners. He concluded that high-stakes tests as currently constructed are inappropriate because they fail to take students' cultural and language differences into account. Caution is advised when interpreting them.

www.resources

Common Core Standards in English-language arts and mathematics have been developed for eventual use nation-wide. For more information, go to http://www.corestandards.org.

How do high-stakes tests relate to students meeting educational standards? What are the implications for students with special needs?

PROFESSIONAL EDGE

Accommodations for Students with Disabilities on Standardized Tests

Under guidelines from IDEA and NCLB, most students with disabilities are required to take district and state standardized tests, including state high-stakes tests. A list of standard accommodations provided is shown here. Keep in mind that research on effective strategies for determining which students get which accommodations is still being done. Given the range of abilities within all disability groups, it is recommended that teachers avoid using students' labels to make these decisions and instead base them on individual student characteristics.

UNIVERSAL DESIGN

As applied to assessment, universal design is the idea that tests designed with built-in supports minimize the need for accommodations (Lazarus, Thurlow, Lail, & Christensen, 2009). Lazarus et al. (2009) assert that universally designed assessments should have the following qualities:

- accessible, nonbiased items
- simple, clear, and intuitive instructions and procedures
- maximum readability and comprehensibility
- maximum legibility
- precise definition of what is being measured (p. 78)

TYPES OF TESTING ACCOMMODATIONS

Setting

- Provide special lighting.
- Provide adaptive or special furniture.
- Provide special acoustics.
- Administer the test to a small group in a separate location.
- Administer the test individually in a separate location.
- Administer the test in a location with minimal distractions.

Timing

- Allow a flexible schedule.
- Extend the time allotted to complete the test.
- Allow frequent breaks during testing.
- Provide frequent breaks on one subtest but not another.

Scheduling

- Administer the test in several sessions, specifying the duration of each session.
- Administer the test over several days, specifying the duration of each day's session.
- Allow subtests to be taken in a different order.
- Administer the test at a different time of the day.

Presentation

- Provide the test on audiotape.
- Increase spacing between items or reduce number of items per page or line.
- Increase size of answer spaces.
- Provide reading passages with one complete sentence per line.
- Highlight key words or phrases in directions.
- Provide cues (for example, arrows and stop signs) on answer forms.
- Secure papers to work area with tape or magnets.

Responding

- Allow marking of answers in booklet.
- Tape-record responses for later verbatim transcription.
- Allow the use of a scribe.
- Provide copying assistance between drafts.

Other

- Make special test preparations.
- Provide on-task/focusing prompts.
- Make any accommodation that a student needs that does not fit under the existing categories.
- Conduct an alternate assessment.

Source: Testing Students with Disabilities: Practical Strategies for Complying with District and State Requirements (2nd ed.), by M. L . Thurlow, J. L. Elliott, and J. F. Ysseldyke, 2003. Thousand Oaks, CA: Corwin. Reprinted with permission.

---

fyi

Rose (2000) has proposed a system of *universally designed assessments* that, through the use of the latest technology, allow for greater testing accuracy through multiple means of engagement, expression, and representation of information. For more information, go to the Center for Applied Special Technology (CAST) website at http://www.cast.org.

Elliott, & Ysseldyke, 2003). A more complete description of the accommodations available and a process for finding the right accommodations for individual students is provided in the Professional Edge. Up to 3 percent of students with disabilities are entitled to take alternate assessments geared to their individual needs as specified on their IEPs. Alternate assessments are described in more detail later in the chapter.

Why is the issue of high-stakes testing and students with disabilities important for you? The answer is that students with disabilities who are included in your classroom (except for those with significant intellectual disabilities) are expected to meet the same standards as everyone else. Furthermore, in 24 states, students need to pass an exam to receive a high school diploma (Johnson, Stout, & Thurlow, 2009), and at least six states require that students pass a test to be promoted to a certain grade (Thompson & Thurlow, 2003). Therefore, it is critical for you to carefully monitor the progress of your students with disabilities and, if needed, to provide extra supports or resources to ensure that the standards are met. Effective monitoring requires paying close attention to the results of high-stakes tests. More important, it requires you to keep track of student performance on a daily basis using assessments such as the ones described in this chapter.

Standardized Achievement Tests

Another common source of information for making educational decisions is **standardized achievement tests.** These tests are designed to measure academic progress, or what students have retained from the curriculum. Unlike the high-stakes tests just described, standardized achievement tests are *norm referenced*. In a norm-referenced test, the performance of one student is compared to the average performance of other students in the country who are the same age or grade level. Student performance is often summarized using grade equivalents and/or percentile ranks.

Group-Administered Tests   Two major types of standardized achievement tests are group-administered and individually administered diagnostic tests. As the name implies, group-administered standardized achievement tests are completed by large groups of students at one time; this usually means that the general education teacher gives the test to the entire class. These tests assess skills across many areas of the curriculum, none in much depth. For this reason, they are intended to be used solely as screening measures. Nonetheless, caution is advised in using these scores, even if only for screening. As with any test, the general education teacher should be sure that students with disabilities receive appropriate accommodations when taking the test. Otherwise, the resulting score may be a measure more of the disability than of the ability. For example, Alicia has a learning disability in reading and has problems comprehending written directions. When Alicia obtained a low score on a social studies test, it was hard to determine whether her low score was due to a lack of knowledge or her inability to follow the directions.

Another potential problem with group-administered standardized achievement tests is that the norms used to interpret scores are of little use when evaluating students with disabilities; these students are often excluded from the norming group because they have taken the test with accommodations. Also, all students may be affected by the fact that the content of the test might not match what is taught in a particular classroom (Ysseldyke, Burns, Scholin, & Parker, 2010). For example, one teacher stressed problem solving in his science class, whereas the standardized achievement test given in his district stressed the memorization of facts. Therefore, the teacher had to give his own tests to determine whether students were learning the material.

Finally, standardized achievement tests might be culturally biased and historically have led to the overrepresentation of minorities in special education classes (Skiba et al., 2008; deValenzuela et al., 2006). For example, Bill comes from a single-parent home in the city. When he read a story on a standardized achievement test about an affluent two-parent family in the suburbs, he had difficulty predicting the outcome.

Whereas in the past, group-administered standardized achievement tests were used to make administrative and policy decisions on a school district or even national level, it appears that today, high-stakes tests are being used more often for these purposes. Given the time and effort it takes to test an entire school, as well as the value of instructional time to children's learning, many schools have found it more prudent to use only their state's high-stakes accountability test.

Individually Administered Tests   A special education teacher or the school psychologist usually gives **individually administered diagnostic tests** as part of a student's case study evaluation. Although these tests may screen student performance in several curricular areas, they tend to be more diagnostic in nature. For example, an individually administered diagnostic reading test may include test components in

www.resources

For more information on the topic of state and national testing policies, access the website of the National Center on Educational Outcomes (NCEO) at http://education.umn.edu/nceo.

dimensions of DIVERSITY

Poverty often is mentioned as a key factor underlying the overrepresentation of ethnic minorities in special education. Skiba et al. (2005) studied the impact of poverty on representation in special education and found that its contribution was weaker than previously thought, and inconsistent. While poverty in U.S. society needs to be addressed, discriminatory practices within schools also need to be addressed.

the areas of letter identification, word recognition, oral reading, comprehension, and phonetic skills; a diagnostic test in math might include math computation, fractions, geometry, word problems, measurement, and time. Because individually administered diagnostic tests provide information on a range of specific skills, they can be useful as an information source in making educational decisions. For example, Tamara scored two years below grade level on the vocabulary subtest of an individually administered diagnostic test in reading. On the basis of this finding, the teacher of her Tier 2 RtI group added instruction in vocabulary taken from her American History text.

Although individually administered diagnostic tests may be more helpful than group-administered achievement tests, they are still subject to many of the same problems. Again, you should always verify findings from these tests using more informal measures based on the content you teach.

Psychological Tests

Psychological tests are used as part of the process of evaluating students with special needs, particularly to determine whether a student has intellectual or learning disabilities. Reports of the results of these tests are often written by school psychologists and consist of a summary of the findings and the implications for instruction. **Psychological tests** can include intelligence tests and tests related to learning disabilities (Overton, 2009; Salvia, Ysseldyke, & Bolt 2010).

The overall purpose of psychological tests is to measure abilities that affect how efficiently students learn in an instructional situation. These abilities are inferred based on student responses to items that the test author believes represent that particular ability. For example, comprehension, an important learning ability, is often assessed on psychological tests (Salvia et al., 2010). To test comprehension, students may be asked to read and answer questions about a series of directions or other tasks described in printed material. Student scores are then compared to a norm group of other same-age students, with an average score being 100. Other abilities commonly assessed by psychological tests include generalization (the ability to recognize similarities across objects, events, or vocabulary), general or background information, vocabulary, induction (the ability to figure out a rule or principle based on a series of situations), abstract reasoning, and memory (Salvia et al., 2010).

Psychological tests can be helpful if they clarify why students may not be learning in class and lead to effective changes in instruction. For example, the results of Tiffany's test showed that she had difficulty with visual memory. Her biology teacher, Ms. Fasbacher, felt that this was related to her poor performance in labeling parts of the human body on her tests. As a result, Ms. Fasbacher provided Tiffany with extra tutoring prior to each test. Interpreting the results of psychological reports seems less daunting if you follow these five general guidelines:

1. Do not be intimidated by the sometimes generous quantity of technical terms and jargon. You have the right to expect that reports be translated into instructionally relevant language.
2. In the event of discrepancies between psychological reports and your experience, do not automatically discount your experience. The results of psychological tests are most valid when corroborated by classroom experience. Keep in mind that your impressions are the result of many more hours of classroom observation than are psychological evaluations, which are based on fewer samples of student behavior and on samples that represent behavior that takes place outside the classroom.
3. Be sure to check the technical adequacy of the psychological tests included in your report. You may be surprised to find that many of these tests are not acceptable. The recent emphasis in RtI of using students' responses to instruction to identify learning disabilities further reinforces the importance of not relying solely on standardized tests.

fyi

Psychological tests may be better measures of expressive language skill, memory, fine motor abilities, and factual knowledge than of potential or reasoning ability (Marston et al., 2003). They also are time consuming to give and only indirectly related to daily classroom instruction.

INSTRUCTIONAL **EDGE**

Strategies for Fair Assessment of Diverse Students

Although today's teachers are much more aware of the possibility of bias in assessing poor students and students from culturally diverse backgrounds (Grossman, 1995), bias and discrimination continue to exist. The following two lists identify areas that can be problematic when assessing diverse students and provide strategies for assessing and interpreting their performance more accurately, respectively.

PROBLEM

1. Students may exhibit test anxiety due to lack of familiarity with the assessment process.
2. Students may lack motivation to perform well on tests because of differing cultural expectations.
3. Students may not respond to traditional motivators.
4. Students' test scores may be depressed because the assessor is unfamiliar or speaks a different language.
5. Students may have different communication styles; for example, they may not feel comfortable asking for help with directions or may respond using fewer words.
6. Students may be unwilling to take risks; for example, they may be reluctant to guess on a test even though it is to their benefit.
7. Students may be accustomed to working at a slower pace.
8. Students may lack exposure to test content.
9. Students may not be proficient in the language used for a test.
10. Students may speak with a dialect that differs from that of the assessor.

RECOMMENDATION

1. Give students practice tests.
2. Qualify test performance with class performance.

3. Individualize reinforcers; use individualistic, competitive, and cooperative goal structures.
4. Allow more time to establish rapport and gain trust.
5. Check for understanding of directions; avoid automatically penalizing students for not saying enough or not giving details.
6. Teach test-taking skills. For example, teach students strategies for when and how to make a best guess on a test.
7. Extend test-taking time to accommodate students' pace.
8. Eliminate unfamiliar content or do not give the test.
9. Assess students using both English and students' native language.
10. Do not count dialectical differences as errors; examine your attitudes about nonstandard dialects for potential bias.

RESEARCH NOTE

Abedi, Hofstetter, and Lord (2004) reviewed the research literature on the effectiveness of testing accommodations for English-language learners in the content areas of math, science, and social studies. The accommodations studied included assessing in the students' native language, modifying the level of English in questions, providing extra time, providing dictionaries and glossaries, and oral administration. In general, the researchers found evidence for the effectiveness of only two accommodations: (1) modifying the language (but not the content) of the test items by reducing low-frequency vocabulary and complex language structures and (2) providing students with definitions or simple paraphrases of potentially unfamiliar or difficult words on the test. Not surprisingly, the authors found that these accommodations helped all students, not just English-language learners. Research shows that curriculum-based assessment also works well with English-language learners, whether the assessment is in their native language or not (Deno, 2003).

---

4. Be sure to check for possible cultural bias. Psychological tests may discriminate against students from culturally diverse or disadvantaged backgrounds. The various ways in which psychological and other tests can be biased, along with suggestions for making them more fair, are presented in the Instructional Edge.
5. Keep in mind that the primary purpose of psychological tests is to establish possible explanations for particular learning, behavioral, or social and emotional problems. Such explanations should be springboards for helping students overcome these problems, not excuses for students' lack of achievement.

Alternate Assessments

As you have learned, IDEA and NCLB require states to include students with disabilities in statewide and districtwide educational assessments. Although most students with disabilities are able to participate when given appropriate accommodations, a small percentage of students are entitled to alternate assessments. The most common group of students taking **alternate assessments** are the 1% of all students with disabilities who typically work on a more individualized curriculum and do not have to meet the

dimensions of **DIVERSITY**

Psychological tests can be biased against students from diverse backgrounds. Use them only in conjunction with other formal and informal measures.

www.**resources**

The home page for the National Council on Measurement in Education (NCME), http://www.ncme.org, provides information on the organization and links to other relevant measurement-related websites.

Students with more severe disabilities participate in alternate assessments that stress authentic skills and experiences in real-life environments. What skills do you think are being assessed here?

same requirements as those students graduating with a standard diploma. In other words, they are required to meet the same broad standards as your other students, but they meet them in different, more basic ways. For example, one of the standards in Ms. Barber's state is that students develop an appreciation for literature. One of the ways that Darrell, a student with a significant intellectual disability, meets that standard is by watching a video of *Oliver Twist* and answering questions using his communication board. School districts may provide this option to up to 1 percent of their students.

While most school districts began using alternate assessments in 2002, the year required for implementation by IDEA, recent research has revealed that guidelines for conducting alternate assessments are still evolving (Towles-Reeves, Kleinert, & Muhomba, 2009). Alternate assessment information can be collected in a number of ways including (1) a portfolio or collection of student work gathered to demonstrate student performance on specific skills and knowledge; (2) an IEP-linked body of evidence or collection of work, similar to a portfolio, demonstrating student performance on standards-based IEP goals and objectives; (3) a performance assessment or direct measures of a student's skill, usually in a one-on-one assessment; (4) a checklist of skills reviewed by persons familiar with the student; and (5) a traditional test requiring student responses, typically with a correct and incorrect forced-choice answer format (Browder, Wakeman, & Flowers, 2006; Towles-Reeves et al., 2009).

The system of alternate assessment used by the state of Kentucky is a good example of a portfolio system (Kleinert & Kearns, 2004). In Kentucky, all students, regardless of disability, are required to meet standards in a range of areas, including using patterns to understand past and present events and to predict future events; using technology effectively; demonstrating knowledge, skills, and values that have lifetime implications for involvement in physical activity; and completing a postsecondary opportunities search (Kearns, Kleinert, Clayton, Burdge, & Williams, 1998). Although the portfolios reflect the same set of outcomes for all students, students with significant intellectual disabilities meet them in different ways. For example, Damon met the standard of completing a search for postsecondary opportunities by compiling a list of his work preferences and specific jobs aligned with his preferences. Sibilie demonstrated her effective use of technology by using an augmentative communication device across a range of school and community settings. Carolyn, a student with multiple disabilities, demonstrated achievement in skills and values related to physical activity by participating in a volleyball game in physical education class. Linus demonstrated his ability to use patterns to understand events by recognizing that on days when his paraprofessional wasn't in school he had less time to get ready for recess. A sample electronic portfolio used for an alternate assessment is shown in the Technology Notes box in Chapter 11.

Here are three questions considered when using alternate assessments with students with severe disabilities:

1. *What are the district's eligibility requirements for alternate assessments?* Keep in mind that only a small number of students have disabilities so severe that they are eligible. The decision to give an alternate assessment should not be based on whether the student is expected to do poorly on the general education assessment.
2. *Is the focus of the assessment on authentic skills and on assessing experiences in community or real-life environments?* For a younger child the community might mean the school, playground, or home; for a high school senior the community might mean the store, bank, or other commercial or public sites.
3. *Is the assessment aligned with state standards?* The skills assessed should have a meaningful relationship to content areas covered by the standards, such as reading and math. For example, one of Clifford's IEP goals in language is to communicate by pointing to pictures on a communication board. Chatrice is learning to give correct coins to the bus driver as a way to meet the math standards. As the general education teacher who is responsible for students' meeting the regular state standards, you may be in the best position to answer this question of standards alignment.

Up to 2 percent of students with disabilities can take alternate assessments based on modified academic achievement standards (U.S. Department of Education, 2007). This alternate assessment option is intended for students whose disabilities have prevented them from achieving grade-level proficiency and who are not likely to reach grade-level achievement within the same timeframe as their classmates without disabilities. Before this provision was added, these students either had to take the grade-level assessment, which often was too difficult, or an alternate assessment intended for students with severe intellectual disabilities, which was too easy.

When the modified academic achievement standards option is used, curricular goals are aligned with grade-level content standards, but the level of achievement expected may be simplified. For example, Josh needs to demonstrate meeting the seventh-grade language arts standard of analyzing how literary elements affect the meaning of text, such as the influence of setting on the conflict and its resolution. Josh does so by reading an easier version of *Swiss Family Robinson* and answering comprehension questions that have lower cognitive demand. It is the responsibility of the IEP team to determine eligibility for this alternate assessment option.

Curriculum-Based Assessments

Because of the limited utility of standardized achievement tests and psychological reports for making day-to-day instructional decisions, you need other tools in order to be a partner in the evaluation process. **Curriculum-based assessment (CBA) is an effective option that in many instances can be an alternative to standardized tests.** CBA has been defined as a method of measuring students' level of achievement in terms of what they are taught in the classroom (for example, Deno, 2003; Hosp, 2008; Tucker, 1985). In CBA, student performance also is measured repeatedly over time, and the results are used to guide instruction (Hosp & Hosp, 2003; Tucker, 1985). CBA has a number of attractive features. When using CBA, you select the skills that are assessed based on what you teach in class, thus ensuring a match between what is taught and what is tested. This match makes CBA measures accurate indicators of student access to the general education curriculum and ideal for use in pre-referral or response to intervention (RtI) systems. **Curriculum-based measurement (CBM)** is a particular kind of curriculum-based assessment. CBM is characterized by

www.resources

Learn about the National Assessment of Educational Progress (NAEP), the only ongoing national test of academic progress, at http://www.nagb.org.

fyi

Some states allow students who do not have significant intellectual disabilities but who are reading below grade level to take high-stakes tests at their reading level rather than their grade level. This use of out-of-level testing is not allowed in federal ESEA regulations. The government recommends using alternate assessments with modified standards instead.

a research base establishing its technical adequacy, as well as standardized measurement tasks and scoring procedures that are fluency based (Deno, 2003).

In the chapter-opening vignette, before referring Rob for special education eligibility determination, Ms. Lyons gave him some curriculum-based assessments in math to determine the specific kinds of problems he was having. She then implemented a peer-tutoring program and used these same tests to measure its effectiveness. Mr. Blount used an informal reading assessment based on his U.S. history textbook to see how well his students were able to read the text. Research shows that when teachers use CBA to evaluate student progress and adjust their instruction accordingly, student achievement increases significantly (Deno, 2003; Fuchs, Fuchs, Hamlett, & Stecker, 1991; Shinn, Collins, & Gallagher, 1998).

What Kinds of Curriculum-Based Assessments Can You Create for Your Students?

Two major kinds of CBAs are commonly used: probes of basic academic skills (for example, reading, math, and writing) and probes of content-area knowledge and learning strategies (for example, vocabulary knowledge, prerequisite skills, textbook reading, and note taking). Although probes of basic academic skills relate more directly to elementary school teachers and probes of content-area knowledge and learning strategies to middle and high school teachers, each of these measures is relevant for both groups. For example, high school students need to perform basic skills fluently if they are to have ready access to curriculum content; elementary school students need early training in learning strategies to make the difficult transition to middle and high school instruction easier.

Probes of Basic Academic Skills

Probes are quick and easy measures of student performance in the basic skill areas of reading, math, and written expression. They consist of timed samples of academic behaviors and are designed to assess skill accuracy and fluency. Probes can sample a range of skills in a particular area, as in a mixed probe of fifth-grade math computation

These teachers are using information from assessment probes to make decisions about their students with special needs. How can you use assessment probes to make decisions in your area of teaching?

problems in addition, subtraction, multiplication, and division; or they can sample one skill area, such as letter identification or writing lowercase manuscript letters.

Typically, students work on probe sheets for one minute. The teacher then records the rate of correct and incorrect responses as well as any error patterns. Student performance rates have been shown to be useful for making many of the important evaluation decisions described earlier in the chapter: screening, diagnosis, program placement, curriculum placement, instructional evaluation, and program evaluation (Deno, 2003; Hosp, 2008). The Professional Edge describes the importance of considering both student accuracy and student fluency when assessing basic academic skills.

Probes are classified according to how students take in task information (for example, seeing or hearing) and how they respond (for example, writing or speaking). They include four major types: see-say, see-write, hear-write, and think-write. For example, when reading orally from a textbook, students *see* the text and *say* the words. Hence, oral reading is referred to as a see-say probe. Similarly, in a spelling probe, students *hear* the teacher dictate words and *write* the words as they are dictated. This is a hear-write probe. As you develop CBAs, keep in mind the following three suggestions:

1. Identify academic skills that are essential in your particular course or grade. In the elementary grades, include skills in handwriting, spelling, written expression, reading (for example, letter identification, letter sounds, oral reading accuracy, and comprehension), and math (for example, number identification, computation, problem solving, time, and money). In secondary courses these could include key vocabulary, prerequisite skills, and independent learning skills.

2. Select skills representing a *sample* of skills that are taught, not necessarily every skill. Performance on these skills then acts as a checkpoint for identifying students in trouble or measuring student progress. For example, in assessing reading performance, having students read a passage aloud from their reading or literature book and then answer comprehension questions may not represent all the reading skills you have taught (such as words in isolation), but it will include a representative sample of many of these skills.

3. Even though CBA is considered informal assessment, its utility in helping to make instructional decisions depends on the teacher's keeping the difficulty level of the assessment items, as well as the administration and scoring procedures, consistent over time (Deno, 2003; Deno et al., 2009). For example, Ms. Solomon was concerned because her students were using the same words over and over in their writing. After showing them various strategies for increasing their variety of words used, she monitored their progress by taking a writing sample every month and measuring the percentage of different words they used.

4. Remember, curriculum-based assessment has been used successfully by teachers for many years. Therefore, assessments as well as norms or benchmarks may already exist for many of the skills you are teaching. See the WWW Resources margin note on page 121 for potential sources.

Probes of Reading Skills   The critical reading skills in the elementary years include phonemic awareness, letter sounds, word recognition, vocabulary, and comprehension. Phonemic awareness can be measured using a hear-say probe. Student ability to identify letter names and sounds can be assessed using a see-say probe. Word recognition and comprehension can be assessed using a see-say oral passage reading probe, such as the one in Figure 4.1.

Maze assessments (Shinn, Deno, & Espin, 2000) are curriculum-based measures for assessing reading comprehension that can be given either in groups or using a computer. Maze assessments are graded passages in which every seventh word is deleted; in place of each deleted word are three choices. One of the choices is the correct choice and the other two are distracters. Students read the passage silently and circle the answers they think are correct. Unlike most curriculum-based measures,

RESEARCH NOTE

Tindal et al. (2003) developed a series of curriculum-based measures in reading and math for use in alternate assessment programs. Their research showed that effective measures were brief and easy to give and provided information of potential use to teachers.

RESEARCH NOTE

Good (2002) studied the relationship between the oral reading performance of third-grade students and their performance on Oregon's high-stakes test. He found that of 91 students who met benchmark levels in oral reading fluency in May of grade 3, 90 met standards on the state test. Of the 23 students scoring below benchmark, only four met state standards.

PROFESSIONAL EDGE

Assessing Student Fluency on Basic Academic Skills

When basic skills or other academic content is assessed informally in the classroom, *student accuracy* is usually stressed. For example, we say that Jill formed 85 percent of her cursive letters correctly, John was 90 percent accurate on his addition facts, or Al identified key pieces of lab equipment with 100 percent accuracy. Although accuracy is important because it tells us whether a student has acquired a skill or section of content, accuracy is not the only useful index of pupil performance. *Student fluency,* or how quickly a student is able to perform a skill or recall academic material, is also relevant. Before you consider the reasons for assessing student fluency provided here, consider this: If your car needed service and you had your choice between two mechanics, both of whom did accurate work and charged $85 an hour but one of whom worked twice as fast as the other, which mechanic would you choose?

THE RATE RATIONALE

1. Students who are proficient in a skill are more likely to remember the skill, even if they do not need to use it very often. If they forget the skill, they need less time to relearn it.

2. Students who are proficient in a basic skill are better able to master more advanced skills. For example, students who can perform addition problems fluently often acquire advanced multiplication skills more easily.

3. Performance of basic skills at an automatic level frees students to perform higher level skills more readily. For example, students who can read fluently with understanding are more likely to be successful in high school classes that require reading lengthy textbook assignments in little time. Students who know their math facts without counting on their fingers can solve word problems more efficiently.

4. Students with special needs are often so labeled because they work more slowly than their peers. Fluency scores allow teachers to compare these students directly with their classmates on this important dimension of speed; they also provide a useful index of student progress, including, for some students, the extent to which supports are needed to access the general education curriculum.

USING THE RESEARCH

If you are interested in learning how your students' oral reading rates compare to national norms, Hasbrouck and Tindal (2006) have compiled national norms based on student oral reading fluency scores from multiple school districts across the country. These norms are shown in the accompanying table. Notice that separate norms

are presented for fall, winter, and spring to account for student growth during the year. So if Simone is reading 80 words correct per minute in February of second grade, she is reading above the 50th percentile for winter of grade 2.

Oral Reading Fluency Norms, Grades 1–8

Grade	Percentile	Fall WCPM	Winter WCPM	Spring WCPM
1	75		47	82
	50		23	53
	25		12	28
2	75	79	100	117
	50	51	72	89
	25	25	42	61
3	75	99	120	137
	50	71	92	107
	25	44	62	78
4	75	119	139	152
	50	94	112	123
	25	68	87	98
5	75	139	156	168
	50	110	127	139
	25	85	99	109
6	75	153	167	177
	50	127	140	150
	25	98	111	122
7	75	156	165	177
	50	128	136	150
	25	102	109	123
8	75	161	173	177
	50	133	146	151
	25	106	115	124

WCPM: Words correct per minute
SD: Standard deviation
Count: Number of student scores

maze assessments are not timed. The number or percentage of correct responses is scored. Research has shown that maze assessments are an effective, time-saving way of monitoring student progress in reading comprehension (Deno et al., 2009; Shinn et al., 2000).

If you are having your students read trade books, you may need to design your own questions, which can be a difficult task. Carnine, Silbert, Kame'enui, and Tarver (2010) have suggested one practical model for designing comprehension questions,

FIGURE 4.1 See-Say Probe: Oral Passage Reading

Time	1 minute
Materials	*Student*—Stimulus passage *Examiner*—Duplicate copy of stimulus passage, pencil, timer
Directions to Student	"When I say 'Please begin,' read this story out loud to me. Start here [examiner points] and read as quickly and carefully as you can. Try to say each word. Ready? Please begin."
Scoring	As the student reads, place a mark (/) on your copy over any errors (mispronunciations, words skipped, and words given). (If student hesitates for three seconds, give him the word and mark it as an error.) If student inserts words, self-corrects, sounds out, or re-peats, do not count as errors. When the student has read for one minute, place a bracket ( ]) on your copy to indicate how far the student read in one minute. (It is usually good practice to let students finish the paragraph or page they are reading rather than stopping them immediately when one minute is over.) Count the total number of words read during the one-minute sample. Tally the total number of errors (words mispronounced, words skipped, and words given) made during the sample. Subtract the total number of errors from the total words covered to get number correct (total words – errors = correct words per minute). If students complete the passage before the minute is up, compute student rate using this formula: $$\frac{\#correct\ words}{seconds} \times \frac{60}{1} = correct\ words\ per\ minute$$
Note	Probe is administered individually. If you use the optional comprehension questions, be sure to have students finish the passage first.

Billy decided to go down by the river and	(9)
demonstrate his fishing ability. He always could deceive	(17)
the fish with his special secret lure. He had his best	(28)
luck in his own place, a wooded shady spot downstream	(38)
that no one knew about. Today he was going to try	(49)
to catch a catfish all the boys called Old Gray. Old Gray	(61)
was a legend in this town, because even though many boys	(72)
had hooked him, he always managed to get away.	(81)
This time Billy knew that if he sat long enough, he could	(93)
catch his dream fish!	(97)

1. Who is the main character in this story?

2. Where does the story take place?

3. What problem is Billy trying to solve?

4. How is Billy going to try to solve the problem?

5. What do you think is going to happen?

Source: From *Curriculum-Based Assessment and Instructional Design,* by E. Lessen, M. Sommers, and W. D. Bursuck, 1987, DeKalb, IL: DeKalb County Special Education Association. Used with permission.

Using Story Grammars

Ms. Padilla's second-grade students have just read the story *The Funny Farola,* by Ann Miranda and Maria Guerrero. The story is about a girl and her family participating in an ethnic festival in their city. The girl, Dora, makes a *farola,* which is a type of lantern people carry while marching in a parade. Dora's family laughs at her farola, because it is in the shape of a frog. However, her unusual farola saves the day when it helps Dora and her parents find Dora's lost brother and sister. Ms. Padilla is assessing Chantille's comprehension of the story using the story grammar retelling format.

Ms. Padilla: Chantille, you have just read *The Funny Farola.* Would you tell me in your own words what the story is about?

Chantille: The story is about a girl named Dora who made this funny frog that she carried in a parade. You see, her brother and sister got lost at the parade 'cause they were having such a good time, but they got found again 'cause they could see Dora's frog.

Ms. Padilla: Chantille, where does this story take place?

Chantille: It took place in a city and the people were having a big festival. That's why they were having the parade.

Ms. Padilla: Chantille, what was the problem with Dora's frog?

Chantille: Well, it was called a *farola,* which is a kind of lantern. Everyone was making them for the parade. Dora's family laughed at her farola 'cause they had never seen a frog farola before.

Ms. Padilla: You said that Dora's sister and brother got lost. What did they do to solve that problem?

Chantille: Well, they saw Dora's frog, so they knew where to find them.

Ms. Padilla: How did you feel at the end of the story?

Chantille: I felt happy.

Ms. Padilla: Why did you feel happy?

Chantille: Well, 'cause Dora's brother and sister found their mom and dad.

Ms. Padilla: Chantille, what lesson do you think this story teaches us?

Chantille: Not to get lost from your mom and dad.

A score sheet that Ms. Padilla completed for Chantille is shown in the accompanying figure. A plus (+) means that Chantille responded accurately to that element without any prompting or questioning; a check mark (✓) means that Chantille mentioned the element after she was questioned or prompted; a minus (–) means that she failed to refer to the element even after questioning or prompts. Look at Chantille's scores. As you can see, she had a good idea of who the main characters were and received a + for this component (Characters). Chantille named two problems in the story: Dora making a farola that her family laughed at, and Dora's brother and sister getting lost. Chantille identified the problem of the lost kids without being prompted, and the problem of the funny farola with prompts; thus, a + and a ✓ were scored for Goal/Problem.

Story Grammar Retelling Checklist

Student Name   **Story Elements Evaluated**

	Theme		Setting		Characters		Goal/Problem		Attempts		Resolution		Reactions	
Chantille	–		✓		+		+	✓	–		+		+	

+ Responded correctly without prompting
✓ Responded correctly after prompting
– Did not identify relevant story component

It was unclear from Chantille's response exactly how the characters tried to solve their problem, so she received a – for Attempts. Chantille did say the problem was solved when Dora's brother and sister saw the frog; she received a + for this element of Resolution. However, she did not say how this resolved the problem of her family laughing at the farola, so she received a –. Chantille's reaction to the story was appropriate, so a + was scored. For Setting, Chantille received a ✓; she identified the setting after Ms. Padilla prompted her. Finally, Chantille received a – for Theme. This response was lacking, even after prompting.

Notice that Ms. Padilla's prompts included explicit references to the various story grammar components. For example,

she asked, "You said that Dora's sister and brother got lost. What did they do to solve that problem?" as opposed to asking a more general question, such as "What happened to Dora's sister and brother?" This use of specific language makes the story grammar components more clear, a necessary structure for younger, more naïve learners.

REFLECTION

How could story retellings be incorporated into a classroom literature-based program? How do you think these results will be helpful to Ms. Padilla?

based on story grammar. *Story grammar* is simply the description of the typical elements found frequently in stories. These include theme, setting, character, initiating events, conflict, attempts at resolution, resolution, and reactions. These elements can be used to create comprehension questions that may be more appropriate than traditional main idea and detail questions, because story grammar describes the organization of most stories that elementary school students are likely to read. The Case in Practice shows how a teacher uses story grammar with one of her second-grade students.

At times, you might not wish to ask questions about a story. Specific questions can give students clues to the answers, and they especially help students identify the information you think is important to remember or the way you organize this information. One way to solve this problem is to have students retell stories after they read them. Students themselves then must organize the information they think is important, and you can evaluate the completeness of their recall. Such a situation has two requirements for effective evaluation to occur: a standard set of criteria to evaluate the completeness of the retelling, and the opportunity to evaluate each student's retelling individually.

Probes of Written Expression   Written expression can be assessed using a think-write probe. In this probe, the teacher reads the students a story starter. The students then have one minute to plan a story and three minutes to write it. This probe can be scored in a number of different ways depending on the decisions you will be making. If you are merely interested in screening students for serious writing difficulty, use the number of intelligible words the student is able to write per minute (total words written, or TWW; Powell-Smith & Shinn, 2004). Intelligible words are those that make sense in the story. Norms for this written expression probe are available at this website: http://www.aimsweb.com/measures/written/norms.php. You can modify this measure to make it more appropriate for students in kindergarten and first grade by having them write only two sentences in response to the story starter (Coker & Ritchey, 2010). For students in high school, extending the length of time for writing to 7–10 minutes improves the accuracy and usefulness of the results (Espin, Wallace, Campbell, Lembke, Long, & Ticha, 2008). If you are interested in measuring the overall quality of the writing as well as collecting other diagnostic information, such as grammar usage, spelling, handwriting, punctuation, vocabulary, organization, or ideas, you can score this probe differently or give another probe designed to measure these areas specifically (see Hessler, Conrad, & Alber-Morgan, 2009; Howell & Morehead, 1993; Mercer, Mercer, & Pullen, 2011; and Vaughn & Bos, 2009 for sample informal assessments in these areas).

Probes of Math Skills   Teachers need to measure student math skills in two general areas: computation and concepts. Math computation includes operations in addition, subtraction, multiplication, and division, including math facts in each of these areas. Essential math concepts include money, measurement, word problems, graphs/charts, and geometry. See-write probes for both computation and problem solving have been developed and can be used for making the key special education decisions you have been learning about in this chapter (see Fuchs, Hamlett, & Fuchs, 1998; Fuchs, Hamlett, & Fuchs, 1999; and Howell & Morehead, 1993, as well as the WWW Resources on page 121). Of course, other types of probes might be needed such as think-write probes to measure number-writing skills, and see-say probes for skills such as the identification of numbers, coins, and geometric figures. For those teaching middle and high school math, Foegen (2008) has developed see-write probes to monitor progress in algebra.

Curriculum-Based Assessments in Content Areas

Although content-area teachers can use CBA probes to test student knowledge of subject matter (see Figure 4.2), they may need to take a somewhat different approach to student assessment. Content-area classrooms are characterized by high curricular demands with fewer opportunities for individualization; students are also expected

RESEARCH NOTE

Allinder, Bolling, Oats, and Gagnon (2000) found that students of teachers who regularly asked themselves the following questions when giving curriculum-based measures made more academic progress in math computation: On what skills has the student done well during the last two weeks? What skills should be targeted for the next two weeks? How will I attempt to improve student performance on the targeted skills?

RESEARCH NOTE

Clarke, Baker, Smolkowski, & Chard (2008) developed and tested four curriculum-based measures in math that can be used for universal screening and progress monitoring in RtI: oral counting, number identification, quantity discrimination, and missing number.

FIGURE 4.2 Using Curriculum-Based Assessment (CBA) Probes in Content Areas

Content Area	CBA Examples
Geography	Identify each state's location on a map by writing the correct state abbreviation.
	Match the terrain of an area to corresponding industries and products.
	Compare and contrast regions so that two similarities and two differences are provided.
Science	Given science terms to define, write the correct definitions.
	Identify steps in the scientific process, and describe how to apply each step to a given hypothesis.
	Describe the human body systems so that each system's function and relationship to other systems is stated.

Source: From "Applying Curriculum-Based Assessment in Inclusive Settings," by M. King-Sears, M. Burgess, and T. Lawson, *Teaching Exceptional Children, 32*(1), 1999, pp. 30–38. Copyright 1999 by The Council for Exceptional Children. Reprinted with permission.

to take responsibility for learning much of the material on their own. While IDEA and ESEA clearly state that the curricular expectations for most students with disabilities are the same as for their classmates without disabilities, students who enter a class significantly behind their classmates in either background knowledge or independent learning skills are likely to struggle. Thus, it is important to identify these students early so that they can be better prepared when they enter a content-area class. For example, at the beginning of this chapter, Mr. Blount assessed his U.S. history students' ability to read the class textbook independently because students in his class were expected to read much of the material on their own.

Assessments of Prerequisite Skills   Teachers can find out whether their students possess the knowledge and skills needed to be successful in their classes by using assessments of prerequisite skills. For example, the English department at a high school developed a test of prerequisite skills for ninth-grade English. All students were given this test at the beginning of the year to see what material needed to be reviewed in the first month of school.

The process of developing assessments of prerequisite skills is similar to the process of developing curriculum-based probes described previously in this chapter. This process consists of the following four steps:

1. Identify critical content learning or skills for your class.
2. Identify entry-level content or skills needed. Be certain these are not skills for which a bypass strategy is possible.
3. Develop a measure to assess the identified skills.
4. Administer the measure to your current class. If most of the class is unable to pass the test, you will need to teach and/or review the prerequisite skills or knowledge to the entire class prior to introducing new course material. If only a few students lack the prerequisites, then you will need to arrange for extra tutoring for them. If your school is doing RtI, this extra help could take place in a Tier 2 or Tier 3 instructional group.

Measures of Independent Learning Skills   When students enter high school, they find an environment often not as supportive as the smaller elementary and junior high or middle school environments they left. The student body is often larger and more diverse. Daily routines change and curriculum is more difficult

(Sabornie & deBettencourt, 2009). High schools also demand a much higher level of student independence through the application of a range of independent learning skills. These skills, often referred to as *learning strategies,* include note taking, textbook reading, test taking, written expression, and time management. A student's ability to perform these various skills independently can make the difference between passing or failing a class. For example, at the beginning of the chapter, Mr. Blount decided to assess textbook-reading skills because these were important for success in his class. A sample instrument to measure textbook-reading skills, which was originally developed by Voix (1968) and later adapted by Lessen, Sommers, and Bursuck (1987), is shown in Figure 4.3. Notice that the reading tasks for this measure are taken directly from the students' history and science textbooks. Doing this ensures that the results will be relevant for the particular classroom situation. Note also that this textbook-reading assessment can be given to the entire classroom at once, enabling the assessment of many students who have trouble reading their textbooks, not just students with special needs.

When students enter high school, they are likely to face demands for a higher level of independence and responsibility for their own learning.

As with the basic and prerequisite skills mentioned previously, probes can be developed to assess independent learning. A key consideration is that the tasks used for assessment should parallel the tasks students are faced with in your classroom: If you are evaluating textbook reading, the reading task should come from the textbook you are using in class; if you are measuring a student's ability to take lecture notes, the task should involve elements similar to a typical lecture delivered in your class.

Once the task has been selected, next decide what kind of measure to use. Three possible choices are direct observation checklists, analysis of student products, and student self-evaluation. With *direct observation checklists,* the teacher develops a list of observable steps necessary to perform a given strategy. Next, the teacher has a student perform a classroom task that requires her to use the strategy and records which behaviors the student performed on the checklist.

Although direct observation of student behavior can provide much more useful information, it is time consuming, particularly when you are a high school teacher who teaches many students each day. For most students, you can use analysis of student products or student self-evaluations. Nonetheless, if you have the luxury of a free moment with an individual student, such as before or after school or during a study hall, the time spent directly observing a student perform a task is very worthwhile.

Analysis of student products involves looking at student notebooks, tests, papers, and other assignments or written activities to find evidence of effective or ineffective strategy performance. In most cases, you can evaluate your whole classroom at once, and you do not have to score the products while you are teaching.

In *student self-evaluations,* students perform a task such as taking a test, are given a checklist of strategy steps, and are then asked to tell which of these steps they used (Mercer, Mercer, & Pullen, 2011; Miller, 1996). Student self-reports are useful for several reasons. They can provide information about strategy behaviors that cannot be directly observed. Student evaluations also stimulate student self-monitoring, a behavior critical for independent learning. Self-report measures can also include interview questions that further clarify strategy usage. For example, one teacher asked, "What was the first thing you did when you received your test?" As with all measures, student self-evaluations need to be corroborated by information from other sources (for example, direct observation checklists and student products). Such corroboration may be particularly important for students with special needs, many of whom have difficulty evaluating their own behavior.

FIGURE 4.3 Evaluating Content-Area Textbook-Reading Skills

Suggestions for specific types of questions are included here. The text in parentheses explains or offers additional information about a particular item.

Using Parts of the Book

1. On what page would you find the chapter called _____? (Tests ability to use table of contents.)

2. Of what value to you are the questions listed at the end of each chapter? (Tests understanding of a specific study aid.)

3. How are the chapters arranged or grouped? (Tests knowledge of text organization.)

4. What part of the book would you use to find the page reference for the topic _____? (Tests knowledge of index.)

5. On what page would you find the answer to each of the following questions? (Tests ability to use index.)

Using Source Materials

1. What library aid tells you the library number of a book so that you are able to find the book on the shelves? (Tests knowledge of functions of cataloging systems.)

2. What is a biography? (Tests knowledge of a type of reference book.)

3. Explain the difference between science fiction and factual science materials. (Tests knowledge of important types of science materials.)

Comprehension

These questions would be based on a three- or four-page selection from the textbook.

Vocabulary

1. Turn to page _____. How does the author define the word _____? (Tests ability to use context clues and the aids the author uses to convey the meaning of a word.)

2. Define _____.

3. What is a _____?

4. *Vocabulary in context:* From the paragraph on page 584 beginning "In Poland, the Soviet Union . . . ," write an appropriate and brief definition of each of the following words: _____, _____, and _____.

Noting Main Ideas

These questions would ask for main points of information, such as the main ideas of longer, important paragraphs of a chapter or the summary of an experiment. (*Examples:* What are atoms composed of? What reason was given for the conservation of human resources? What is the result of the photosynthetic process?)

Noting Details

These questions should ask for specific bits of information, such as an aspect of a process, the application of a law, the principal steps in an experiment, a life cycle, or incidents in the life of a scientist. (*Examples:* Describe the photosynthetic process. What are the different stages in the cycle of precipitation and evaporation? List the major incidents in the life of Marie Curie.)

Drawing Conclusions

Ask questions about the significance or value of a finding, the implication of a description of some species or natural phenomenon, causes and effects, or a comparison of two or more types of organisms. The questions should call for answers that are not stated in the text. (*Examples:* Illustrate the term *balance of life.* What conclusion can you draw from the importance of the photosynthetic process? What is the principal difference between mitosis and meiosis?)

Applying Theoretical Information

These questions would ask for examples of practical uses of scientific law and principles. (*Examples:* Explain the relationship of photosynthesis to the conservation of plant life. Explain the idea that air confined in a small area exerts pressure in all directions in relation to the action of air in a football.)

Following Directions

These questions would ask learners to show the sequence of steps or ideas for solving a problem or performing an experiment or the sequence of a chain of events. (*Examples:* What is the second step of the experiment? What should you do after you have placed the flask over the burner?)

FIGURE 4.3 **Evaluating Content-Area Textbook-Reading Skills**   *(Continued)*

Understanding Formulas and Symbols

These questions test student understanding of how symbols and formulas are used with scientific data. (*Examples:* What does the H refer to in the symbol H_2O? What does 40# mean?)

Maps and Graphs

Use questions that require knowledge of map and graph symbols and how to use them. (*Examples:* Use the graph on page 602 to answer these questions: By 1925, how many millions of people inhabited Earth? How many times over will the world population have increased from 2000 to 2050? Use the map on page 174 to answer these questions: Who ruled Gascony in the 12th century? Who governed the major portion of Flanders after 1550?)

Study Reading

Directions: Read pages 584–586. Take notes. Then, close your book and keep it closed. However, you may use the notes you made to help you answer the following questions. (Have questions on a separate sheet for distribution after notes have been made.) *Note:* Ask detail, main idea, and inference questions.

Sources: Adapted from *Evaluating Reading and Study Skills in the Secondary Classroom: A Guide for Content Teachers*, by R. G. Voix, 1968, Newark, DE: International Reading Association. Copyright 1968 by the International Reading Association. Reprinted with permission.

How Are Curriculum-Based Probes Used to Make Special Education Decisions?

Academic probes can help teachers make many of the assessment decisions discussed previously in this chapter. Several examples are discussed in the following sections.

Peer Comparison in Screening

The key question involved in screening is whether a student is different enough from his peers on important skills in a given academic area (or areas) to indicate that some form of accommodation is necessary. In an RtI school this may mean providing more intensive instruction for a student in a small Tier 2 group. If the difference between a student and his peers continues or worsens despite repeated attempts in the classroom to remediate, placement in a more intensive tier or referral to special education and a more comprehensive assessment may be necessary.

When screening, first select probes in the area(s) of suspected difficulty. Next, give the assessment to the student in question and compare his or her performance to benchmark or norm levels to find out the extent of the achievement gap. Benchmarks or norms are available for probes in most basic skill areas (see WWW Resources on this page). You might also want to assess your entire class to identify other students at risk and obtain valuable feedback about the overall effectiveness of your teaching.

Note the results of an oral reading fluency probe given by a third-grade teacher to his entire class in April, shown in Figure 4.4. Each score represents the number of correct words read orally per minute from a grade-level passage in the classroom reading program. The teacher was particularly interested in the performance of the student who ended up scoring 50 words correct per minute. According to the norms shown on page 114, this student is well below the 25th percentile score for this time of year of 78 words correct per minute, a definite sign of being at risk. Although this student may need extra support from the general education teacher or even a referral for special education eligibility determination, other factors should also be

www.resources

For CBM norms in reading, early literacy, spelling, early numeracy, written expression, and math, go to http://www.aimsweb.com/com/measures. For benchmarks in early literacy skills, go to http://dibels.uoregon.edu/measures.

FIGURE 4.4 Classroom Performance on Academic Skill Probe in Reading

Grade 3, Reading Orally in Context, April 2006

Number of correct words per minute read orally

190	136	103
189	128	99
172	125	97
160	123	86
159	120	84
151	119	80
139	119	50[*]
136	117	

Median 123
Median/2 61.5
[*]Denotes score of median/2 or lower

www.resources

The Center for Innovations at the University of Missouri (http://www .cise.missouri.edu/links/research-cbm-links.html) provides teachers with a wealth of resources to help implement research-based practices related to curriculum-based measurement.

considered, including how he performs across other academic skills assessed and whether other students in the class are having similar problems. This low score did prompt the teacher to seek prereferral consultation to get ideas for improving the student's reading performance. The teacher also planned to regularly monitor the student's progress in oral reading fluency to help guide future decision making about his program.

Note that three other students in the class scored 10 or more words below 97, the 50th percentile. According to Hasbrouck and Tindal (2006), this puts them at some risk in reading. The teacher decided to monitor the progress of these students more regularly while also providing them with a peer-tutoring program to give them extra practice in reading fluency. Finally, the teacher learned from this experience that 19 of his 23 students were achieving at acceptable levels on an important indicator of reading ability.

If benchmarks do not exist for the assessment selected, compare the performance of the student in question to half the median of the entire class or a subsample of the class (for example, five average performers). The median, or middlemost score, is used to summarize the scores because it is affected less by extreme scores than is the mean, or average, which could over- or underestimate the performance of the group as a whole. The teacher in Figure 4.4 used a score equal to one-half the median as a cutoff for identifying students who are having trouble with that particular skill (Shinn & Hubbard, 1992). Such a cutoff point typically identifies 6 to 12 percent of a class or grade level that may be experiencing difficulty with a particular skill (Bursuck & Lessen, 1987; Marston, Tindal, & Deno, 1984). As shown, the class scores range from a high of 190 words read correctly per minute to a low of 50 words read correctly per minute. The median, or middlemost, score for the class is 123 words read correctly per minute. A score of 61.5 words read correctly per minute is half the median. Our student in question was the only student scoring below this point. Deno et al. (2002) have shown that using the bottom 20 percent of a class can also be helpful in identifying students who are at risk. Finally, if this teacher were in an RtI school, the students at risk would have been identified earlier as part of schoolwide universal screening. The teacher would have also had the option of placing students into more intensive instructional tiers if needed. The Technology Notes illustrates a way to use software to evaluate the performance of your students.

Computerized Curriculum-Based Measurement

You may be wondering how you are going to assess your students systematically and still have time to prepare and teach your lessons. Researchers have developed a product that may help you (Fuchs, Hamlett, & Fuchs, 1998). They have developed software that makes scoring and interpreting curriculum-based measures in math much easier. In the system of Fuchs et al., students take a weekly probe test that measures required math operations for a given grade level. Students then are taught to enter their own data into a computer program that scores their test and summarizes the results.

The software program summarizes student performance using a display like the one shown in the accompanying figure. The graph shows the student's rate and accuracy on weekly math tests over time. This student (Sheila Hemmer) went from a score of 10 digits correct per minute at the beginning of October to a score of more than 30 digits correct per minute in March. The skills profile chart shows which skills (A1 = first skill in addition; S2 = second skill in subtraction) have been mastered and which may require more instruction.

INDIVIDUAL STUDENT PERFORMANCE

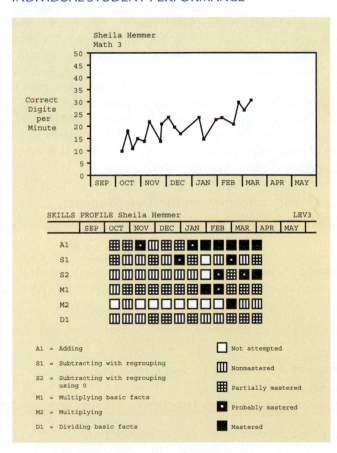

SUMMARY OF CLASS PERFORMANCE

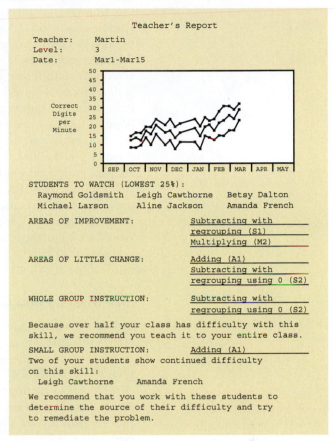

Teachers also receive a display like the one shown above. The graph shows the teacher, Mr. Martin, how his students progressed from October through March. The top line indicates scores at the 75th percentile; the middle line, scores at the 50th percentile; and the bottom line, scores at the 25th percentile. The lists below the graph provide information about which students should be monitored; areas in which the class has improved or not changed; and recommendations for skills that could be covered in whole-group instruction (most of the class needs instruction) or small-group instruction (only one or two students). These data could also be used for screening and progress monitoring in high school since students enrolled in higher-level math courses are often lacking more foundational math skills.

Similar software programs for math concepts and problem solving (Fuchs, Hamlett, & Fuchs, 1999) and reading (Fuchs, Hamlett, & Fuchs, 1997) are also available.

Sources: Figures from "Classwide Curriculum-Based Measurement: Helping General Educators Meet the Challenge of Student Diversity," by Fuchs, Fuchs, Hamlett, Philips, and Bentz, 1994, *Exceptional Children 60*(6), 518–537. Reprinted with permission.

Fluency and Accuracy in Diagnosis

CBA probes also can help teachers diagnose specific skills deficits. For example, a student who performs poorly on a math facts probe may not know the math facts or may simply be unable to write numbers fast enough. You can figure out which situation exists by examining the student's rate, or *fluency,* of think-write number writing. Likewise, keeping track of the number of errors per minute, or *accuracy,* in oral reading can help you detect a particular student's reading problem. Figure 4.5 shows the results of an oral reading probe for two seventh-grade students. The correct rate for both students is 75 words correct per minute. However, Student 1 seems to have a problem with reading fluency. When she reads, she reads accurately; the problem is that 75 words correct per minute is slow for a seventh-grade student. She will need help in fluency building, maybe as part of a Tier 2 RtI group. Student 2, on the other hand, is less accurate in her reading than Student 1; she is making many word identification errors and needs to be assessed further to ascertain whether these errors are a pattern or due to carelessness. If they are part of a pattern, she may require extra support in decoding skills in a resource room or as part of a Tier 3 RtI group.

The fact that CBA probes measure fluency as well as accuracy adds an important diagnostic dimension. For example, if the reading performance of the two students in Figure 4.5 were reported solely as a percentage of accuracy, the results would look like those shown in Figure 4.6. Using percentages alone, Student 1 does not appear to have a problem at all. However, as previously shown, she is reading much more slowly than Student 2.

Skill Mastery and Curriculum Placement

Inclusive education involves the use of a variety of instructional grouping arrangements. Sometimes students are grouped based on their skill levels; at other times a broader range of student skills is desired in a group. Students with special needs benefit from both types of instructional arrangements. You can use CBA probes to group your students by rank ordering and then visually inspecting your students' probe scores. For example, Mr. Glass wanted to form cooperative groups in math. He used scores on a problem-solving task probe, picking one lower performer, two middle performers, and one higher performer for each group. Ms. Robins, in contrast, found that three of her students were having difficulty with capitalization but the rest of the students were not. She formed a small group of those having difficulty to review capitalization rules. The small groups used in RtI are formed based on students' skill levels.

FIGURE 4.5 Reading Fluency Information for Two Students

Student 1		Student 2	
Number of words correct per minute	Number of words incorrect per minute	Number of words correct per minute	Number of words incorrect per minute
75	2	75	16

FIGURE 4.6 Percentage of Accuracy in Passage Reading for Two Students

Student 1	Student 2
Percentage of accuracy	Percentage of accuracy
96	70

Monitoring Student Progress and Instructional Evaluation

Although education has come a long way in terms of establishing a profession based on evidence-based practices, predicting whether a given practice will work for a given student in a particular situation is still difficult. Thus it is important that you carefully monitor the results of your teaching. This monitoring is particularly relevant for students with special needs who by definition are less likely to respond favorably to commonly used instructional methods.

CBA probes, because they are time efficient, easy to give, and match what is taught in the classroom, are ideal for monitoring student progress in class. For example, Mr. Harris was interested in whether Maria, a student with learning disabilities, was retaining any of the words featured on weekly spelling lists. She had scored 90 and above on her weekly tests, but Mr. Harris was unsure whether she was remembering the words from week to week. He developed a spelling probe using words from previous spelling lists. He gave the probe to his entire class and found that Maria and 10 other students were retaining only 20 percent of the words. As a result, he started a peer-tutoring program to help students review their words. Mr. Harris also set up group competitions and awards for groups scoring the highest on the review probes. Implementing these two activities improved Maria's and the other students' retention significantly.

A final example of a CBA probe is worthy of mention. Mr. Rock's school recently adopted a new algebra text. Mr. Rock wanted to make sure that the new text was meeting the needs of both his higher- and lower-performing students. He gave the class a see-write math probe containing a sample of representative problems taken from the new text and based on the state standards. Mr. Rock found that one of his students scored significantly below the rest of the class on the probe. Mr. Rock decided to provide him with extra math help as part of a Tier 2 after-school program. Mr. Rock also found that two other students got every problem correct, including several that hadn't been covered yet. He decided to place them in a more advanced algebra class.

Teaching approaches, no matter how well they are carried out, can affect students differently. By monitoring the progress of all of his students using CBA probes, Mr. Rock was able to meet their individual needs.

www.resources

For the latest research on student testing, curriculum, and achievement, go to the website of the National Institute on Student Achievement, Curriculum, and Assessment at http://www.ed.gov/offices/OERI/SAI/index.html.

WRAPPING IT UP
BACK TO THE CASES

This section provides opportunities for you to apply the knowledge gained in this chapter to the cases described at the beginning of this chapter. The questions and activities that follow demonstrate how the principles, concepts, and strategies you have learned about in this chapter connect to the everyday activities of general education teachers.

MS. LYONS has determined that Rob's needs should be discussed with the school's instructional assistance team. In addition to presenting information outlining Rob's specific problem areas in mathematics, Ms. Lyons will need to describe what teaching methods, strategies, and/or accommodations she has used to support his learning and how he has responded to them. How might Ms. Lyons document the instructional strategies she has tried with Rob and the results they have provided? Provide a rationale for your choices.

MR. BLOUNT has been proactive in assessing how well his students can use the assigned text in his class and has used the information gathered from those assessments to teach the prerequisite skills needed to learn from the text. However, he is aware that if his students with disabilities have difficulty reading textbooks, they may also have difficulty reading the texts of high-stakes, end-of-grade tests required in his school system. He wants to use appropriate accommodations during these tests. How should Mr. Blount determine which accommodations to use? Further, how might he prepare his students to use these accommodations?

ROBERTO will most likely have difficulty participating in the standardized assessments given in his state. Ms. Benis and Roberto's special education teacher met after school yesterday to discuss what assessment methods they will use to demonstrate Roberto's progress toward meeting state standards. At this meeting, the two teachers reviewed the full range of options available and prepared a list of pros and cons for each option. What would be on your list of options? As you prepare your list, include the pros and cons of each option based on what you know about Roberto.

SUMMARY

- General education teachers can make assessments that contribute to six decision-making areas of special education: screening, diagnosis, program placement, curriculum placement, instructional evaluation, and program evaluation.

- A number of information sources are used in programming for students with special needs including high-stakes tests, group-administered standardized achievement tests, individually administered diagnostic tests, psychological tests, and alternate assessments. All of these assessments are helpful in making instructional decisions for students with special needs, but there is no substitute for observing and measuring how students respond to instruction in class, a key component of RtI.

- A small percentage of students who are typically working on a more individualized curriculum do not have to meet the same requirements as those students graduating with a standard diploma. These students are eligible for alternate assessments whereby they are required to meet the same broad standards as your other students, but they meet them in different, more basic ways.

- Curriculum-based assessment (CBA) measures student achievement in terms of what they are taught in the classroom. There are two major kinds of CBA: probes of basic academic skills and measures of content-area knowledge and strategies.

- CBA is helpful in making a range of special education decisions, particularly those involving day-to-day instruction. CBA norms and peer comparison methods can help screen students in academic difficulty. Probes can also be used to help teachers diagnose specific skill deficits to help form instructional groups and allow teachers to monitor the progress of students in class by measuring student performance over time.

APPLICATIONS IN TEACHING PRACTICE
COLLECTING AND USING ASSESSMENT INFORMATION

Yolanda is a student with a learning disability in your class who has been receiving indirect support or consultation in one area. You are interested in knowing how she is doing relative to the rest of the class. Select the subject area in which Yolanda has been receiving indirect support (reading, math, or written expression). Then select a particular skill in that subject matter that you have been working on in your class (for example, in reading: word identification, passage reading, comprehension, letter or letter–sound identification; in math: any math computation skill, word problems, money, geometry; in written expression: writing mechanics, writing productivity, quality of ideas). Next, describe a curriculum-based assessment strategy you would use to judge how well Yolanda is doing on that skill as compared with her classmates. Respond to the following questions in your description.

QUESTIONS

1. How will you use curriculum-based norms to measure the extent of Yolanda's problem?

2. What additional information will you collect to clarify Yolanda's problem?
3. How will you use probe information to measure the effectiveness of classroom supports for Yolanda?
4. How will you use probe information to help you instruct the rest of the class?

If you are teaching a class for which the ability to read the textbook is an important skill, select a sample textbook from your content area. Then develop a curriculum-based assessment of content-area reading skills using the model shown in Figure 4.3.

QUESTIONS

1. How did you select the skills to be included on your probe?
2. How could you use the information collected to determine the nature and extent of classroom support needed for students with disabilities? For the rest of the class?

Go to Topic 8: Assessment in the My Education Lab (http://www.myeducationlab.com) for your course, where you can:

- Find learning outcomes for Assessment along with the national standards that connect to these outcomes.
- Complete Assignments and Activities that can help you more deeply understand the chapter content.
- Apply and practice your understanding of the core teaching skills identified in the chapter with the Building Teaching Skills and Dispositions learning units.
- Examine challenging situations and cases presented in the IRIS Center Resources. (optional)
- Access video clips of CCSSO National Teachers of the Year award winners responding to the question, "Why Do I Teach?" in the Teacher Talk section. (optional)
- Check your comprehension on the content covered in the chapter by going to the Study Plan in the Book Resources for your text. Here you will be able to take a chapter quiz, receive feedback on your answers, and then access Review, Practice, and Enrichment activities to enhance your understanding of chapter content. (optional)

chapter 5

Planning Instruction by Analyzing Classroom and Student Needs

LEARNING Objectives

After you read this chapter, you will be able to

1. Explain what it means to make instructional accommodations and modifications for students with disabilities and other special needs.

2. Describe the steps of the INCLUDE decision-making process for accommodating students with disabilities and other special needs in your classroom.

3. Identify and describe the key elements of a classroom environment.

4. Describe the major components of classroom organization, and explain how they can be adapted for students with disabilities and other special needs.

5. Explain various ways students can be grouped for instruction in an inclusive classroom.

6. Explain how the use of effective classroom materials and instructional methods can benefit students with disabilities and other special needs.

MR. RODRIGUEZ teaches world history at a large urban high school. When he introduces new content to his students, he teaches to the whole class. First, he reviews material that has already been covered, pointing out how that material relates to the new content being presented. Next, he provides any additional background information that he thinks will help students understand the new material better. Before Mr. Rodriguez actually presents new material, he hands out a partially completed outline of the major points he will make. This outline helps students identify the most important information. Every 10 minutes or so, he stops his lecture and allows students to discuss and modify the outline and ask questions. When Mr. Rodriguez completes his lecture, he organizes students into cooperative learning groups of four to answer a series of questions on the lecture. Manuel is a student with a learning disability in Mr. Rodriguez's class. He has a history of difficulty staying on task during lectures and figuring out what information to write down. He also has trouble remembering information from one day to the next. Mr. Rodriguez has noticed that Manuel has a particular interest in soccer and loves to perform for his classmates.

How well do you think Manuel will perform in Mr. Rodriguez's class? What changes in the classroom environment might help Manuel succeed? How might Mr. Rodriguez capitalize on Manuel's interests and strengths?

JOSH has cerebral palsy. He is in the normal range in ability; in fact, he excels in math. However, he has a lot of trouble with muscle movements, has little use of his lower body and legs, and also has problems with fine muscle coordination. As a result, Josh uses a wheelchair, has trouble with his speech (he speaks haltingly and is difficult to understand), and struggles to write letters and numbers correctly. Josh is included in Ms. Stewart's second-grade class.

How can Ms. Stewart set up her classroom to make it easier for Josh to fully participate? What aspects of the classroom environment will Ms. Stewart need to adapt for Josh? How can she use technology to facilitate Josh's inclusion? Why will math be an important subject for Josh in Ms. Stewart's class?

RESEARCH NOTE

The connection between effective instruction and positive student behavior is well established (Scott et al., 2001). Students who are successful have little incentive to disrupt the class or to act in ways that get them excluded from activities.

Disabilities and other special needs arise when characteristics of individual students and various features of students' home and school environments interact. Effective teachers analyze the classroom environment in relation to students' academic and social needs and make accommodations and modifications to ensure students' success in the classroom. For example, Manuel has difficulty staying on task and retaining new information. However, features of Mr. Rodriguez's class make it easier for Manuel to function. The partially completed lecture outlines help Manuel focus his attention on specific information as he tries to listen and stay on task; the pauses help him catch any lecture information he might have missed. The review sessions are intended to help Manuel retain information by giving him a mechanism for rehearsing newly learned material. In another case, Josh has some serious motor problems, but he may be able to function quite independently if Ms. Stewart makes her classroom accessible to a wheelchair and works with special educators to use assistive technology to meet Josh's needs in handwriting and oral communication.

This chapter introduces you to a systematic approach for helping all students with special needs gain access to the general education curriculum, a requirement of the Individuals with Disabilities Education Act (IDEA). Part of that approach is for you to be the best teacher you can be so that fewer of your students require individualized instruction in the first place. Despite your best efforts, however, there will always be students who require a more individualized approach. The **INCLUDE** strategy is provided for these students. Although there are other ways to differentiate instruction for students with disabilities, INCLUDE gives teachers a systematic process for accommodating students based on their individual needs and the classroom demands on, or expectations of the teacher.

The rest of this textbook expands and elaborates on this approach. Later chapters also present a more in-depth look at the relationship between your classroom environment and the diverse needs of learners. An important assumption throughout this text is that the more effective your classroom structure is, the greater the diversity you will be able to accommodate and the fewer individualized classroom changes you will need to make. This idea is incorporated into current RtI models, which focus on problem prevention by establishing a strong base of research-based practices in Tier 1.

How Can the INCLUDE Strategy Help You Make Instructional Accommodations and Modifications for Students with Special Needs?

At a recent conference presentation that included both general education teachers and special education teachers, one of the authors of this text asked the audience how many of those present worked with students with disabilities. A music teacher at the back of the room called out, "Everyone in schools works with students with disabilities!" He is right. As you have learned in the previous chapters, IDEA entitles students with disabilities to "access," "participation," and "progress" in the general education curriculum. These entitlements were reinforced by the Elementary and Secondary Education Act (ESEA; formerly No Child Left Behind), which requires that most students with disabilities meet the same standards as their classmates without disabilities. Therefore, although the professionals who specialize in meeting the needs of students with disabilities are valuable and provide critical instructional and support systems for students, ultimately you and your peers will be the primary teachers for many students with disabilities and other special needs, and you will form partnerships with special educators to meet the needs of others. That makes it critical for you to feel comfortable making accommodations and modifications for students in order for them to have fair access to your curriculum.

The INCLUDE strategy is based on two key assumptions. First, student performance in school is the result of an interaction between the student and the instructional environment (Broderick, Mehta-Parekh, & Reid, 2005; Pisha & Coyne, 2001; Smith, 2004). Consequently, what happens in a classroom can either minimize the impact of students' special needs on their learning or magnify it, making accommodations necessary. In the first chapter-opening example, Mr. Rodriguez engaged in a number of teaching practices that minimized the impact of Manuel's learning disability, such as starting each class with a review of material covered the day before, providing the students with lecture outlines to help them identify important ideas, and engaging his students in regular discussions of the material presented. Nevertheless, if part of Manuel's learning disability is in reading and the classroom text used in Mr. Rodriguez's class is too difficult for Manuel to read independently, Mr. Rodriguez will need to accommodate Manuel's problems in reading. This aspect of the INCLUDE approach is consistent with the idea behind RtI. If all students receive effectively delivered, evidence-based instruction, then fewer will be identified as needing more supports. Further, those eventually identified for special education—the most intensive level of support—will be only those truly in need.

The second key assumption of INCLUDE is that by carefully analyzing students' learning needs and the specific demands of the classroom environment, teachers can reasonably accommodate most students with special needs in their classrooms. You can maximize student success without taking a disproportionate amount of teacher time or diminishing the education of the other students in the class. For example, with the help of the special education teacher, Mr. Rodriguez provided Manuel with a digital text with a built-in speech-to-print component and study guide. Soon Mr. Rodriguez discovered that other students in the class could also benefit from using the digital text and made it available to them. In this way, reasonable accommodations often assist many students in the class.

The INCLUDE strategy contains elements of both universal design and differentiated instruction, two widely recognized approaches to addressing classroom diversity in general and inclusion in particular. The idea of **universal design** originated in the field of architecture, where it was learned that designing buildings for persons with diverse needs from the beginning makes them more accessible and saves money spent on costly retrofits of ramps and automatic doors. As applied to

How does the concept of universal design relate from architecture to teaching? How does this concept simplify the job of a general education teacher?

www.resources

For more information on universal design, go to the Teaching Every Student page of the Center for Applied Special Technology (CAST) website: http://www.cast.org/tes.

classrooms, the idea is that instructional materials, methods, and assessments designed with built-in supports are more likely to be compatible with learners with special needs than those without such supports (Curry, 2003; Hitchcock, Meyer, Rose, & Jackson, 2002; Pisha & Stahl, 2005), and they minimize the need for labor-intensive accommodations later on. For example, print alternatives such as graphics, video, and digital text allow students with reading problems to more readily access subject content. The use of templates with partially filled-in sections and links to more information can help students construct a better essay. Universal design is consistent with RtI's prevention emphasis; when effective practices are in place, many learning problems can be prevented.

The idea behind **differentiated instruction** is that a variety of teaching and learning strategies are necessary to meet the range of needs evident in any given classroom. Students' diverse needs are met by differentiating the content being taught, the process by which it is taught, and the ways students demonstrate what they have learned and their level of knowledge through varied products (Anderson, 2007; Broderick, Mehta-Parekh, & Reid, 2005). Differentiation is achieved by providing materials and tasks at varied levels of difficulty and with varying levels of instructional support, through the use of multiple grouping arrangements, student choice, and varied evaluation strategies (Tomlinson, 2000).

Differentiated instruction is consistent with the approach taken in this text for accommodating students with disabilities and other special needs. In fact, the INCLUDE process of determining student supports based on student needs and classroom demands is an ideal vehicle for implementing differentiated instruction in your classroom. The way differentiated instruction is addressed in INCLUDE also is consistent with the RtI principle that when it comes to providing effective instruction, one size does not fit all.

The INCLUDE strategy for differentiating instruction for students with special needs in the general education classroom follows seven steps:

INCLUDE

Step 1   **I**dentify classroom demands.
Step 2   **N**ote student learning strengths and needs.
Step 3   **C**heck for potential areas of student success.
Step 4   **L**ook for potential problem areas.
Step 5   **U**se information to brainstorm ways to differentiate instruction.
Step 6   **D**ifferentiate instruction.
Step 7   **E**valuate student progress.

These steps are designed to apply to a broad range of student needs and classroom environments. Throughout this text, this icon will denote suggestions for differentiating instruction according to this strategy, with an emphasis on the appropriate step.

INCLUDE

Step 1: Identify Classroom Demands

Because the classroom environment significantly influences what students learn, identifying and analyzing classroom requirements allows teachers to anticipate or explain problems that a given student might experience. Then, by modifying the environment, teachers can solve or reduce the impact of these learning problems. Common classroom demands relate to classroom management, classroom grouping, instructional materials, and instructional methods.

Classroom Management   The ways in which a teacher promotes order and engages students in learning in a classroom are referred to as *classroom management* (Doyle, 1986; Miller & Hall, 2005). Classroom management includes a number of factors:

- *Physical organization,* such as the use of wall and floor space and lighting
- *Classroom routines* for academic and nonacademic activities
- *Classroom climate,* or attitudes toward individual differences

- *Behavior management,* such as classroom rules and monitoring
- *The use of time* for instructional and noninstructional activities

Classroom management strategies can have real benefits for students with disabilities. For example, LaVerna is a student who needs accommodations in physical organization; she uses a wheelchair and requires wide aisles in the classroom and a ramp for the step leading to her classroom. Shawn has behavioral difficulties and thus would benefit from a behavior management system: He might go to his next class prior to the end of each period to eliminate potential opportunities to fight with classmates. He would also benefit from an efficient use of time: Minimizing transition times or the amount of time between activities would eliminate further opportunities for inappropriate interactions with his classmates.

Classroom Grouping   Teachers use a variety of *classroom grouping* arrangements. Sometimes they teach the whole class at once, as when they lecture in a content area such as social studies. At other times teachers may employ small-group or one-to-one instruction. For example, they may teach a small group of students who have similar instructional needs, such as a group of students who all require extra help on multiplication facts or an individual student who needs extra help with an English assignment. Teachers also may group students of differing interests and abilities in an effort to foster cooperative problem solving and/or peer tutoring. Students respond differently to these types of groupings. For example, Mike needs accommodations in classroom grouping in order to succeed; he might do better in a small group in which other students read assignments aloud so that he can participate in responding to them. Using a variety of grouping strategies based on student need is sometimes referred to as *flexible grouping,* an essential part of differentiated instruction (Anderson, 2007).

Instructional Materials   The types of *instructional materials* teachers use can have a major impact on the academic success of students with special needs. Although many teachers choose to develop or collect their own materials, published textbooks are most commonly used. Published textbooks include basic skills texts called *basals,* often used in reading and mathematics, and texts that stress subject-matter content in areas such as history and biology. Other materials commonly used by teachers include concrete representational items such as manipulatives and technological devices, including audiovisual aids, telecommunication systems, and computers. Roberta's use of large-print materials to assist her in seeing her work and Carmen's use of a study guide to help her identify important information in her world history text are both examples of differentiating instruction by making changes in instructional materials.

Instructional Methods   The ways in which teachers present content or skills to students and evaluate whether learning has occurred are the essence of teaching and are crucial for accommodating students with special needs. These are their *instructional methods.* Teachers use a number of different approaches to teach content and skills. Sometimes they teach skills directly, whereas at other times they assume the role of a facilitator and encourage students to learn on their own, providing support only as needed. Instructional methods also involve student practice that occurs either in class, through independent seatwork activities or learning centers, or out of class through homework. Ms. Correli's decision to use a PowerPoint presentation in class and then give Lon a copy of the slides to help his learning is an example of an accommodation in presenting subject matter. Using a paraprofessional to write a student's words is an example of an accommodation in student practice.

Student evaluation, or determining the extent to which students have mastered academic skills or instructional content, is an important aspect of instructional methods. Grades frequently are used to communicate student evaluation. For some students, grading is an appropriate evaluation strategy. But for others, such as Anita, a fifth-grade student who has a moderate intellectual disability and is learning to recognize her name, a narrative report might be a better evaluation tool. When evaluating students with disabilities, teachers must focus on measuring what a student knows rather than the extent of his disability. For example, Alex, who has a severe learning disability in writing, may need to answer test questions orally to convey all he knows; if he gives written answers, only his writing disability may be measured.

INCLUDE

Step 2: Note Student Learning Strengths and Needs

Once instructional demands are specified, the *N* step of INCLUDE calls for noting student strengths and needs. Remember that students with disabilities are a very heterogeneous group; a disability label cannot communicate a student's complete learning profile. For example, some students with intellectual disabilities can learn many life skills and live independently, whereas others will continually need daily assistance. Also keep in mind that students with disabilities are more like their peers without disabilities than different from them. Like their nondisabled peers, they have patterns of learning strengths and weaknesses. Focusing on strengths is essential (Epstein, 2004; Farmer, Farmer, & Brooks, 2010; Shaywitz, 2003). Teachers who see the strengths in students teach positively, helping students to see themselves and others positively, to see learning positively, and to overcome their weaknesses (Tomlinson & Jarvis, 2006). Three areas describe student learning strengths and needs: academics, social-emotional development, and physical development. Problems in any one of these areas may prevent students from meeting classroom requirements, resulting in a need for differentiated instruction. Strengths in any of these areas can help students overcome these problems. For example, a student with good listening skills may be able to compensate for her reading problem by using a digital recording of her civics and government textbook.

Academics   The first part of academics is *basic skills,* including reading, math, and oral and written language. Although these skills might sometimes be bypassed (for example, through the use of a calculator in math), their importance in both elementary and secondary education suggests teachers should consider them carefully. For example, a student with a severe reading problem is likely to have trouble in any subject area that requires reading, including math, social studies, and science and on any assignment with written directions.

Cognitive and learning strategies make up the second part of academics. These strategies involve "learning how to learn" skills, such as memorization, textbook reading, note taking, test taking, and general problem solving. Such skills give students independence that helps them in adult life. Students with problems in these areas experience increasing difficulty as they proceed through the grades. For example, students who have difficulty memorizing basic math facts likely will have trouble learning to multiply fractions, and students who cannot take notes may fall behind in a civics course based on a lecture format.

Survival skills, the third area of academics, are skills practiced by successful students, such as attending school regularly, being organized, completing tasks in and out of school, being independent, taking an interest in school, and displaying positive interpersonal skills (Brown, Kerr, Zigmond, & Harris, 1984; Kerr & Nelson, 2009). Students lacking in these areas usually have difficulty at school. For example, disorganized students are not likely to have work done on time, nor are they likely to deliver parent permission forms for field trips to their parents or return them to school. Survival skills also help some students compensate for their other problems. For example, given two students with identical reading problems, teachers sometimes offer more help to the student who has good attendance and tries hard.

Social-Emotional Development   Students' social-emotional development involves classroom conduct, interpersonal skills, and personal-psychological adjustment. Classroom conduct problems include a number of aggressive and disruptive behaviors, such as hitting, fighting, teasing, hyperactivity, yelling, refusing to comply with requests, crying, and destructiveness. Although most of these behaviors may be exhibited by all children at one time or another, students with special needs may engage in them more frequently and with greater intensity.

Conduct problems seriously interfere with student learning and can lead to problems in interpersonal relations and personal-psychological adjustment. For example, students who are disruptive in class are less likely to learn academic skills and content. Their outbursts also may be resented by their peers and may lead to peer rejection, social isolation, and a poor self-image. Interpersonal skills include but are not limited to initiating and carrying on conversations, coping with conflict, and establishing and maintaining friendships. Although these skills are not ordinarily part of the explicit school curriculum, their overall impact on school adjustment makes them important. For example, students lacking in peer support may have difficulty completing group projects (an example of student practice) or finding someone to help with a difficult assignment (an example of homework).

Personal-psychological adjustment involves the key motivational areas of self-image, frustration tolerance, and proactive learning. For example, students with a poor self-image and low tolerance for frustration may do poorly on tests (an example of student evaluation); students who are inactive learners may have difficulty pursuing an independent science project (an example of student practice).

Physical Development   Physical development includes vision and hearing levels, motor skills, and neurological functioning. Students with vision problems need adapted educational materials. Students with poor fine motor skills may need a computer to do their homework, an accommodation in student practice. Finally, students with attentional deficits may need a wider range of approaches for instruction, including lecture, discussion, small-group work, and independent work.

Step 3: Check for Potential Areas of Student Success

INCLUDE

The next INCLUDE step is *C,* analyzing student strengths in view of the instructional demands identified in Step 1 and checking for activities or tasks students can do successfully. Success enhances student self-image and motivation. Look for strengths in both academic and social-emotional areas. Reading the "Current Levels of Performance" section of the IEP is a good way to begin identifying a student's strengths. For example, Jerry does not read but can draw skillfully. In social studies, his teacher asks him to be the class cartographer, drawing maps for each region of the world as it is studied. Kareem has a moderate intellectual disability and learns very slowly, but he always comes to school on time. His second-grade teacher appoints him attendance monitor. Dwayne has attention deficit–hyperactivity disorder (ADHD), is failing all his classes in school, and is beginning to become difficult to handle at home. His parents and teachers have noticed, however, that he is able to identify personal strengths, has a good sense of humor, and can enjoy a hobby. They support Dwayne's positive interests by enrolling him in the school band.

Step 4: Look for Potential Problem Areas

INCLUDE

In the *L* step of the INCLUDE strategy, student learning needs are reviewed within a particular instructional context, and potential mismatches are identified. For example, Susan has a learning need in the area of expressive writing; she is unable to identify spelling errors in her work. This is an academic learning need. When evaluating students' work, her world cultures teacher, who believes that writing skills should be reinforced in every class, deducts one letter grade from papers that contain one or more spelling errors. Susan also cannot read the history text accurately and fluently enough to understand it. For Susan to succeed in history class, these mismatches need to be addressed. Similarly, Sam has a severe problem that prevents him from speaking fluently. This physical problem creates a learning need. His fourth-grade teacher requires that students present book reports to the class. Again, a potential mismatch exists that could prevent Sam from succeeding. Mismatches such as those experienced by Susan and Sam are resolved by differentiating instruction, the topic of the next two INCLUDE steps.

INCLUDE

Step 5: Use Information to Brainstorm Ways to Differentiate Instruction

Once potential mismatches have been identified, the *U* step of INCLUDE is to use this information to identify possible ways to eliminate or minimize their effects. IDEA stipulates two ways to differentiate for students with disabilities: accommodations and modifications.

Accommodations   Instructional accommodations typically are defined as supports provided to help students gain full access to class content and instruction, and to demonstrate accurately what they know (Byrnes, 2008; Nolet & McLaughlin, 2005). It is important to remember that with accommodations, school expectations that students meet learning standards remain unchanged. This means that students with disabilities receiving accommodations are expected to learn everything their classmates without disabilities are supposed to learn (Nolet & McLaughlin, 2005). Examples of accommodations include bypassing students' learning needs by allowing them to employ compensatory learning strategies, making an adjustment in classroom teaching materials, using group organization, and teaching students basic or independent learning skills.

Bypass or *compensatory strategies* allow students to gain access to or demonstrate mastery of the school curriculum in alternative ways. For example, Susan, the student with problems in spelling and reading, could benefit from several bypass strategies. For spelling, having a computerized spell checker could help. Alternatively, she could enlist the help of a peer to proofread her work. To help Susan access content in her government text, she could use an electronic reader. She also could be allowed to have her exams read to her so she could demonstrate her knowledge without her reading disability being an obstacle. Bypassing cannot be used in a primary area of instruction, however. For instance, Susan cannot spell check her spelling test, but she can spell check her science homework. Similarly, she cannot have a reading test read to her, but it would be appropriate to have a history test read to her. Also, bypassing a skill does not necessarily mean that the skill should not be remediated. Susan may need both spelling and reading instruction, either as part of her English class or in a more intensive pullout type of setting. Finally, bypass strategies should encourage student independence. For example, Susan might be better off learning to use a spell checker rather than relying on a peer proofreader.

Teachers can also provide accommodations in their *instructional methods, materials, grouping,* and *classroom management* to help students succeed. For example, if Ramos has attention problems, he might be seated near the front of the room, and he might benefit from a special system of rewards and consequences as well as a classroom from which "busy" bulletin board displays are removed. All these are classroom management accommodations. A change in classroom instruction would be to call on Ramos frequently during class discussions and to allow him to earn points toward his grade for appropriate participation. Ramos might pay better attention in a small group—a grouping change—and he might be better able to comprehend his textbooks if the key ideas are highlighted—a materials accommodation. These types of accommodations can be provided as supports in Tiers 1 and 2 in schools implementing RtI.

A third option for accommodating students with special needs is to provide *intensive instruction on basic skills and learning strategies*. Often a special education teacher carries out this instruction in a resource setting. This approach

What classroom demands might this student have difficulty meeting? What bypass strategies or accommodations might help him demonstrate that he has learned his assignment as well as his classmates have?

assumes that basic skills and learning strategies are prerequisites for successful general education experiences. It also assumes that some students require instruction delivered with a greater degree of intensity than can reasonably be provided by a general educator responsible for 20–30 or more students (Bursuck, Smith, Munk, Damer, Mehlig, & Perry, 2004).

Unfortunately, the results of research on whether skills taught in pullout programs transfer to the general education class are mixed (Kavale & Forness, 2000). Some studies show positive results (Freeman & Alkin, 2000; Marston, 1996; Snider, 1997), whereas others show minimal effects (Baker & Zigmond, 1995; Wang, Reynolds, & Walberg, 1988). Studies do suggest that teachers play an important role in determining whether skills taught in a separate setting transfer to their classrooms (Ellis & Lenz, 1996; Sabornie & deBettencourt, 2009). For example, Ms. Henry had Jamie in her English literature class; Jamie was receiving Tier 2 support on taking effective lecture notes. First, Ms. Henry found out what strategy for note taking Jamie was learning. Then she reminded Jamie to perform the strategy before she delivered a lecture and sometimes even during a lecture. Finally, Ms. Henry collected Jamie's notes on a weekly basis to see whether she was performing the strategy correctly, giving specific feedback to her as needed and reporting her progress to the special education teacher.

Of course the general education teacher also can provide this type of instruction. This option is feasible when many students have similar instructional needs and when the teacher can easily monitor skill development. For example, Mr. Higgins, a seventh-grade science teacher, lectures frequently. As a result, students need to be proficient note takers. At the beginning of the school year, Mr. Higgins noticed during a routine check of student notebooks that many students were not taking adequate notes. With assistance from the special education teacher, he taught note taking as part of science. Three students for whom note taking was especially difficult handed in their notes each day so Mr. Higgins could monitor their progress. The Working Together discusses a co-teaching situation in which the general education teacher is developing a strategy to provide accommodations in her classroom with the help of the special educator.

Working TOGETHER

The Reluctant Co-Teacher

Juanita Kirk, a math teacher, initially was excited about co-teaching with Susan Harris, the special educator assigned to the seventh-grade team. Now, though, she is disillusioned. Although Susan was offered paid planning time during the summer, she declined to participate, explaining that she had made her family the focus of her summers and that she would not make professional commitments during that time. Juanita could understand that, but then, at their first meeting in the fall, Susan explained to Juanita that she had always disliked math and had not studied it since she was in high school. She said that she would be most comfortable adjusting to co-teaching by spending the first semester taking notes for students, learning the curriculum, and then helping individual students after instruction had occurred. She stated clearly that she did not have much time for preparing outside class given all her other responsibilities, and she also made it clear that she did not consider it her responsibility to grade student work.

Juanita was surprised. This was not at all what she expected co-teaching to be. She envisioned a partnership in which she and her colleague not only could make instruction more intensive but also could energize math instruction by using various grouping arrangements and brainstorming new ways to reach their students. Now six weeks into the school year, she is beginning to think that co-teaching is more like having an assistant in the classroom—an assistant who is highly paid for not doing very much work. She wonders if this is how co-teaching looks in English, the other seventh-grade course to which Susan is assigned.

ADDRESSING THE DILEMMA

If you were Juanita, how might you address this situation by using ideas in this chapter and in chapter 3?

Modifications   **Instructional** or curricular **modifications** are made when the content expectations are altered and the performance outcomes expected of students change (Giangreco, 2007; Nolet & McLaughlin, 2005). Typically, students who receive modifications have behavioral and/or intellectual disabilities that are so significant that the curricular expectations in general education are inappropriate. These are usually the same students described in chapter 4 as being eligible for alternate assessments. Instructional modifications are generally of two types: teaching less content and teaching different content (Nolet & McLaughlin, 2005). For example, in order to meet district grade-level science standards, Ms. Lamb's class was learning to label the parts of the human digestive system and state the purpose for each. Manny, a student with a significant intellectual disability included in Ms. Lamb's class, met the same learning standard by pointing to his stomach when asked where food goes when it is eaten. This is an example of teaching less content. In contrast, teaching different content means that the curricular outcomes are different from those of the rest of the class. For example, an instructional goal for Tony, a student with autism, is to remain calm when there is a change in the classroom schedule.

It is important to reserve instructional modifications for students with only the most significant disabilities. Otherwise, instructional modifications reduce a student's opportunity to learn critical knowledge, skills, and concepts in a given subject, leaving gaps in learning that can interfere with meeting school standards and that can be a disadvantage in later school years and beyond. For example, when one class was learning four reasons for the worldwide spread of AIDS, Steven, a student with a learning disability, was required to learn only two reasons, because he had difficulty remembering information. However, when Steven was required to take the state high-stakes science test, he was held responsible for learning the same information about AIDS as everyone else. It would have been more effective for the school to help Steven better remember science content by using a memory-enhancing device rather than reducing the amount of information. In short, reducing or simplifying content inappropriately can lead to watering down the curriculum.

INCLUDE

RESEARCH NOTE

Byrnes (2008) found that written descriptions of accommodations on student IEPs were often ambiguous and led to considerable confusion on the part of teachers as to how to implement them. For suggestions on how to write and interpret IEP descriptions of accommodations, see Byrnes (2010).

Step 6: Differentiate Instruction

After you have brainstormed possible accommodations or modifications, you can implement the *D* step in INCLUDE, which involves selecting strategies to try. A number of guidelines are suggested here to help you decide which strategies to select.

- *Select Age-Appropriate Strategies:* Students' accommodations and modifications should match their age. For example, using a third-grade book as a supplement for an eighth-grade science student who reads at the third-grade level would embarrass the student. In such a situation, a bypass strategy such as a digitally-recorded textbook would be preferable if the student has the necessary background and intellectual skills to listen to the book with understanding. A good rule of thumb is to remember that no students, whether in first or twelfth grade and regardless of their special needs, want to use what they perceive as "baby" books or materials.
- *Select the Easiest Approach First:* Accommodations need to be feasible for the general education teacher. Although making accommodations and modifications often means some additional work for you, it should not require so much time and effort that it interferes with teaching the entire class. For instance, it is easier to circle the 6 out of 12 math problems you want Maria to complete than to create a separate worksheet just for her.
- *Select Accommodations and Modifications You Agree with:* You are more likely to implement an approach successfully if you believe in it (Polloway, Bursuck, Jayanthi, Epstein, & Nelson, 1996), especially in the area of behavior management. For example, in selecting rewards for good behavior, if you are uncomfortable with giving candy, try giving time for desirable activities such as time on the computer.

However, accommodations and modifications should not be considered only in light of teacher beliefs. IDEA is clear that the unique needs of students take precedence over the convenience of schools and professionals. With imagination and some input from special educators, you will undoubtedly find strategies that match your teaching approach while maximizing your students' learning.

- *Determine Whether You Are Dealing with a "Can't" or a "Won't" Problem:* Blankenship and Lilly (1981) describe a "can't" problem as one in which the student, no matter how highly motivated, is unable to do what is expected. A "won't" problem is one in which the student could do what is expected but is not motivated to do so. Each type of problem may require a different accommodation. A student unable to do what is expected might need a bypass strategy; a student unwilling to do the work might need a behavior management strategy. Making this distinction can also save you time. For example, if a student fails a test because she does not feel like working on the day of the test, then a teacher's attempt to provide extra tutorial assistance will likely be wasted effort. "Can't" and "won't" problems are particularly relevant for adolescents, who are often less likely than younger students to work to please their teachers.

- *Give Students Choices:* Adding the element of choice challenges students to make decisions, encourages them to be more responsible for their own learning, and allows them to more readily demonstrate what they know by tapping into their strengths and interests (Anderson, 2007; Carolan & Guinn, 2007).

- *Select Strategies with Demonstrated Effectiveness:* Over the past 30 years, a massive body of professional literature on effective teaching practices has accumulated. Being familiar with this research can help you avoid fads and other unvalidated practices. The strategies suggested throughout this text are based on research and form a starting point for your understanding of validated practices. Such an understanding has always been important, but it is particularly important in view of the recent emphasis placed on evidence-based practices in IDEA and ESEA legislation, as well as in RtI, which requires the use of evidence-based practices in all of its instructional tiers. Ways to select evidence-based practices are described in the Professional Edge.

Step 7: Evaluate Student Progress

Although there are many effective teaching practices, it is difficult to predict which will be effective for a given student. As a result, once an accommodation or modification is implemented, the *E* step of INCLUDE is essential: Evaluate strategy effectiveness. You can track effectiveness through grades; observations; analysis of student work; portfolios; performance assessments; and teacher, parent, and student ratings. Monitoring student progress in this way will help you decide whether to continue, change, or discontinue an intervention. In RtI, information obtained through progress monitoring is used to assign students to more intensive instructional tiers, including special education.

In the next section, the relationship between how you run your classroom and the diverse needs of learners is examined. As you have read, the use of effective practices allows teachers to accommodate more diversity in their classrooms while at the same time reducing the need for making more individualized adaptations. The key features that contribute to a successful classroom are shown in Figure 5.1. These features include classroom management, classroom grouping, instructional materials, and instructional methods.

How Is an Inclusive Classroom Managed?

Classroom management comprises all of the things teachers do to organize students, space, time, and materials to maximize effective teaching and student learning (Wong & Wong, 1998). As described here, classroom management involves physical organization, routines for classroom business, classroom climate, behavior management,

fyi

To learn more about how to critically read single subject and group experimental research articles see Tankersley et al. (2008) and Cook et al. (2006).

INCLUDE

INSTRUCTIONAL EDGE

Selecting Evidence-Based Practices for RtI

As you have already learned, evidence-based practices are a key part of RtI. Evidence-based practices are those instructional techniques that have been shown by research to be most likely to improve student outcomes in a meaningful way (Cook, Tankersley, Cook, & Landrum, 2008a). While the primary benefit of using evidence-based practices is boosting student achievement, evidence-based teaching, when implemented with integrity, also can help schools determine when students have learning disabilities and when they fail to learn because of ineffective instruction. That is why using RtI is an accepted alternative for identifying students with learning disabilities in IDEA 2004.

Are evidence-based practices the same as best practices?

Evidence-based practices should not be confused with what are often referred to as best practices. While best practices can be evidence-based, they often include practices that are recommended based on personal experience, opinion, and preference (Cook et al., 2008a). In fact, so many teaching techniques have been referred to as best practices it is not at all clear which ones are based on research and which are not. This situation makes the selection of evidence-based practices for RtI a difficult one.

How do I decide whether a given practice is evidence-based?

Cook et al. (2008a) suggest using two guidelines when deciding whether a given practice is evidence-based, one based on the quality of the research and the other on the quantity. The quality of research means that the research clearly shows that the practice leads to increased student achievement, and that no other explanations are likely. This level of quality, sometimes referred to as experimental control, can be accomplished in two ways: (1) systematically comparing the outcomes of two randomly selected groups, one that uses the practice versus a comparison or control group that does not, or (2) systematically comparing a student's performance when the practice is in place versus when it is not in place (Cook et al., 2008a). The first type of research is called group experimental research and the second type is called single-subject research. Single-subject and group experimental research are not the only valuable kinds of research, but they are the only kinds of research that establish a causal relationship between a teaching practice and student achievement. For example, qualitative research involving interviews, focus groups and/or in-depth observations of individuals or small groups, and quantitative studies that don't involve random assignment or control groups are useful in exploring new techniques that can eventually be put to the causality test using experimental research.

It is not enough, no matter how high the quality of the study, to simply show that an instructional practice worked once. It is also important to show that the technique worked again, with more and/or different students under varied classroom conditions. So the quantity of research, as well as the quality, is important to consider in selecting a practice.

How important is it that I carry out evidence-based practices the same way they are done in the research?

Carrying out the teaching practice the same way it was done in the research is called **treatment fidelity** and it is a critical part of RtI.

When teaching practices are not carried out as designed, students may be unnecessarily placed in more intensive tiers, or even special education. While changes to evidence-based practices can eventually be made, be sure to first give them every chance to work as intended in the research.

If a practice is evidence-based, is it guaranteed to work in my classroom?

Group research, as the term implies, is based on the average performance of groups of students. While a given study may clearly show that the group as a whole performed better, individual students within the group may not have performed as well. Teaching strategies validated by single-subject research may not apply to other students who may differ in some way or may be in classrooms that also differ. There are no guarantees that a teaching strategy will work, even one based on research of high quality and quantity. That is why the progress monitoring component of RtI is so important. When assessments show progress isn't being made, and you are sure that the teaching practice was used as designed, you can make necessary instructional changes before the student falls further behind.

Can I use practices that are not evidence-based?

Some teaching practices may not be evidence-based simply because researchers have not conducted enough studies or have not systematically reviewed the findings from studies that have been done (Cook et al., 2008a). For example, we know a lot more about evidence-based practices in reading than in math and written expression. This means that you can select reading practices with greater certainty that they will work. Whether or not a practice is evidence-based is rarely a yes-no decision; all teaching practices range along a continuum from ineffective to evidence-based, with plenty of gray areas in between. Still, selecting evidence-based practices should not be left to chance; we know enough to improve the chances of a given child considerably, and practices for which we have the most evidence should always be used before selecting practices for which we have less evidence.

Are there sources that can help me select evidence-based practices?

Teachers often don't have time to read and digest research articles, and there are sources that can help. However, be sure to select sources that evaluate research objectively and according to the highest scientific standards. The U.S. Department of Education's What Works Clearinghouse (http://www.whatworks.ed.gov) is a good source of evidence-based practices in many instructional areas. For evidence-based practices in reading, go to the Florida Center for Reading (http://www.FCRR.org) and also consult The Report of The National Reading Panel (http://www.nationalreadingpanel.org). For evidence-based practices in math go to http://ies.ed.gov/ncee/wwc/pdf/practiceguides/rti_math_pg_042109.pdf and the Final Report of the National Math Panel (http://www.ed.gov/about/bdscomm/list/mathpanel/report/final-report.pdf). RtI websites listed in the Instructional Edge in Chapter 2 are also good sources for evidence-based practices.

FIGURE 5.1 **Overview of Classroom Environments**

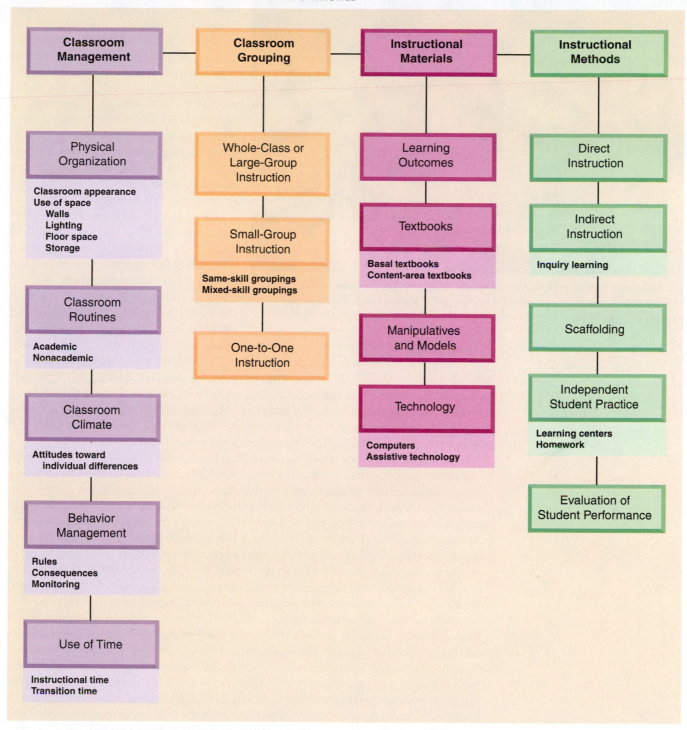

and use of time. The classroom management strategies described in the following sections are part of a larger body of strategies for promoting positive student behavior called *positive behavior supports (PBS)* (Sugai & Horner, 2008). PBS is described in greater depth in Chapter 12. You also may need to use the INCLUDE strategy to make accommodations for students with special needs in all of these areas.

Physical Organization

The way a classroom is physically organized can affect student learning and behavior in a number of areas (Kerr & Nelson, 2009). Carefully arranged classrooms can decrease noise and disruption, improve the level and quality of student interactions, and

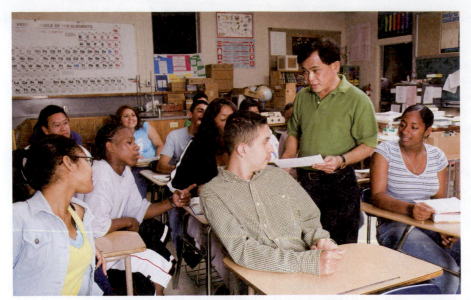

This is a teacher-centered grouping arrangement for large-group instruction. What are some advantages and disadvantages of this strategy for students with special needs? What other ways of grouping students should be part of a teacher's instructional repertoire?

increase the percentage of time that students spend on academic tasks (Paine, Radicchi, Rosellini, Deutchman, & Darch, 1983; Sutherland, Lewis-Palmer, Stichter, & Morgan, 2008). The physical organization of a classroom influences learning conditions for all students, as well as the accessibility of instructional presentations and materials for students with sensory and physical disabilities. Physical organization includes the appearance of the classroom and the use of space, including wall areas, lighting, floor space, and storage.

Wall areas can be used for decorating, posting rules, displaying student work, and reinforcing class content, sometimes through the use of bulletin boards. For example, one teacher taught a note-taking strategy and posted the steps on a bulletin board to help her students remember them. In using wall space, keep in mind two possible problems. First, wall displays may divert students with attention problems from concentrating on instruction. These students should be placed where they are least likely to be distracted by displays. Second, students may not notice that important information appears on a display, and teachers may need to direct their attention to it. For example, Ms. Huerta posted a display showing graphic representations of the basic fractions. She reminded her students to look at these fractions while they were doing their independent math work.

Lighting, either from windows or ceiling lights, also can affect students with disabilities. Students with hearing loss might need adequate light to speech-read; they also are likely to have problems with glare in areas where the light source comes from behind the speaker. Students with visual impairments also have difficulty working in areas that are not glare free and well lighted. Occasionally, students with learning or emotional disabilities may be sensitive to and respond negatively to certain types of light. In most cases, problems with lighting can be remedied easily by seating students away from the glare caused by sunshine coming through the classroom windows.

The organization of floor space and the kinds and placement of furniture used also need to be considered. For example, floors that do not have a nonslip surface can make wheelchair and other travel difficult for some students. Furniture that is placed in lanes can block access to the chalkboard or equipment such as computers and make mobility difficult for students in wheelchairs or students with visual impairments. Tables, pencil sharpeners, and chalkboards that are too high may prove inaccessible to students who use wheelchairs. Desks that are too low can interfere with students who have prostheses (artificial limbs). Placement and configuration of special equipment in science labs, computer centers, and vocational areas also can present difficulties in accessibility for students with special needs. For example, the lathe in the woodworking room might be positioned too high for a person in a wheelchair to operate; the space between work areas in the science lab might not be wide enough for a wheelchair to pass. Many of these physical features of classrooms may be beyond your control. If they become a problem, seek assistance from a special education teacher.

The arrangement of your class should be predictable. This means that you should not make major changes without first considering their impact on students with disabilities and then informing these students so they have time to adapt. For example, Mr. Tate decided to move one of the bookshelves in his classroom. He noticed, however, that the new location blocked the passageway from the door to the desk of a student in his class who was blind. Mr. Tate informed the student of the move in advance, and together they worked out an alternative route to the student's desk.

The arrangement of student desks, whether in rows, circles, or small groups, can have considerable impact on students with disabilities and other special needs. For example, traditional row configurations, which provide students with an immediate, unobstructed view of the teacher, have been shown to help students with attention disorders focus better when the teacher is instructing the whole group at one time. However, the placement of desks into clusters of four works better when using mixed-ability, cooperative learning groups to help integrate a student who is socially withdrawn. Another important consideration about floor space concerns student monitoring: Teachers should be able to see all parts of the classroom at all times, whether they are teaching large or small groups or are working at their desks. Designing such visual access means that all specially designated areas in the classroom, such as learning/interest centers, computer stations, small-group instructional areas, and study carrels, need to be positioned so they can be monitored.

An additional area of physical organization is storage. For example, students with visual disabilities may need to store equipment such as audio recorders, large-print books, braille books, and magnifying devices. For students with severe disabilities, space might be needed to store book holders, paper holders, page turners, braces, crutches, and communication boards.

Routines for Classroom Business

Establishing clear routines in both academic and nonacademic areas is important for two reasons. First, routines that are carefully structured (that is, clear to students and used consistently) reduce nonacademic time and increase learning time. Second, you can prevent many discipline problems by having predictable classroom routines.

Most students, especially those with special needs, find stability in knowing that classroom activities will be similar each day. In the absence of this stability, misbehavior often follows. Many examples of misbehavior can be related to breaks in school routines. On the day of a field trip, elementary school students are more likely to hit or push, to delay beginning assignments, and to do poor work. In middle schools and high schools, teachers often dread shortened schedules for assemblies and other school programs because of increased student behavior problems.

You can create daily classroom routines that help students learn. For example, you might expect fourth graders to enter your classroom each morning, begin their morning work, and read quietly if they finish before instruction begins. Having routines for sharing time, setting up science experiments, preparing to go to physical education, moving to the computer lab, and so on helps students meet your expectations. Routines are especially helpful to students who need a strong sense of structure in classroom life. In secondary schools, routines might include having specific lab procedures, starting each class with a five-minute review, or scheduling a particular activity on the same day every week. For example, in a geometry class, students who complete their assignments might choose to begin the day's homework, complete a Math Challenger worksheet from the activity file, or work on research papers or other long-term projects.

Classroom Climate

A number of authors have noted that classroom climate contributes significantly to the number and seriousness of classroom behavior problems (Marzano & Marzano, 2003) as well as student achievement (Hattie, 2009). Classroom climate concerns the overall atmosphere in the classroom—whether it is friendly or unfriendly, pleasant or unpleasant, and so on. Climate is influenced by the attitudes of the teacher and students toward individual differences. For instance, is the classroom characterized by a cooperative or a competitive atmosphere? Is the classroom a safe place for all students to take risks? Are skills for interacting positively with students and adults actively supported in the classroom?

dimensions of
DIVERSITY

Kleinfeld (cited in Gay, 2002), in her 1974/1975 research on Athabascan Inuit and American Indian children, found that the most effective teachers demonstrated personal caring and concern for students while at the same time demanding and facilitating high academic performance. Foster (1995, 1997) and Ladson-Billings (1994) observed similar traits among effective teachers of African-American students.

Teachers who communicate respect and trust to their students are more successful in creating a positive classroom environment in which fewer behavior problems occur (Arends, 2004; Marzano, 2003). For example, Mr. Elliott reprimanded a student who talked out of turn by saying, "I know you have a question about your work, and I'm glad you care enough to ask for help; but I need to have you raise your hand because I can only help people one at a time." Mr. Elliott showed respect for the student and built the student's trust by not putting her down. Yet Mr. Elliott stuck to his rule about not speaking before being called on and explained why it was important. Similarly, Ms. Belson asked Harriet to define the word *diffident*. Harriet gave an incorrect definition, saying it meant "being bored." Ms. Belson said, "Harriet, I can see how you might think the meaning is 'bored' because *diffident* looks a lot like *indifferent*. The word actually means 'lacking in confidence.'"

You can build the overall quality of your communication with your students in many small ways. For example, finding the time each week to speak privately with students lets them know that you care about them as individuals. Asking older students sincere questions about their friends, out-of-school activities, or part-time jobs also conveys your interest in them. Taking the time to write positive comments on papers lets students know that you appreciate their strengths and do not focus only on their special needs. When you encourage each student to achieve his or her own potential without continually comparing students to one another, you are communicating the idea that each class member has a valuable contribution to make. Teachers who fail to take these small steps toward positive communication with students or who publicly embarrass a student or punish a group because of the behavior of a few soon may create a negative classroom climate that thwarts appropriate and effective learning.

A final dimension of teacher–student communication concerns language differences. When students struggle to understand English, their behaviors may at first appear to be challenging. For example, a first grader is asked to complete several directions at one time and has a tantrum as a result of the frustration of not understanding. Similarly, a high school student apparently ignores a teacher's direction to put away project supplies and spend any remaining time beginning the homework assignment. When the teacher addresses this behavior, the student pushes everything off his desk. Is this a behavior problem or an example of misunderstanding and frustration? Teachers working with students who are not proficient English speakers should take care to distinguish problems that result from language differences from misbehavior.

Behavior Management

Behavior management refers to teacher activities that directly promote positive student behavior. It includes establishing classroom rules, providing consistent consequences, and monitoring student behavior.

Rules help create a sense of order and expectations for a classroom, and they form a significant first step in setting up a learning environment based on preventive classroom management. Teachers who are effective classroom managers have well-defined rules for their classrooms (Marzano, 2003; Olson, Platt, & Dieker, 2007; Ornstein & Lasley, 2004).

Effective classroom rules share three key characteristics: They are brief and specific, positively worded and clearly understood by students (Alberto & Trautman, 2008; Doyle, 1990), and accommodate students from different cultures (Grossman, 1995).

Be sure to explain rules carefully to your students so that they are understood. Post rules during the first weeks of school, explain and discuss them, and model them for students. Early attention to setting your classroom expectations has a yearlong payoff. By rehearsing and focusing student attention on rules, you make them part of students' understanding of their classroom interactions. If you do not take this time to teach the rules, too often they become merely a bulletin board display, ignored by teachers and students alike.

Also, be sure that your rules accommodate students from different cultures. For example, rules about respecting other students' property may be puzzling for Latino students, for whom sharing one's belongings is a highly valued activity. Similarly, rules related to aggressive behavior may need to be enforced with care for students whose parents expect them to stand up for themselves, especially when someone says something derogatory about a student's family (Grossman, 1995). It is important to note that taking cultural differences into account does not necessarily mean that the rules need to be changed, only that the rules may need to be more carefully explained and enforced.

In addition to having clear expectations, teachers also need to tie their expectations to a set of consistent *consequences*. This means demonstrating that the same consequences apply to everyone and on a consistent basis. For example, Ms. DuBois has a rule that students are to raise their hands before speaking in class. She has also established the consequence that students receive one point for each class period they go without a single talk-out. Points earned figure into each student's grades for the class. Ms. DuBois is careful only to give points to students who meet the criterion of no talk-outs per day, regardless of who is involved or what the circumstances are, because she knows that enforcing rules arbitrarily greatly diminishes their effectiveness. Ms. DuBois also is sure to provide specific verbal praise along with the points to increase students' future chances of behaving appropriately without receiving points. Of course, Ms. DuBois realizes that sometimes rules need to be individualized, as in the case of Justin, a student with Tourette's syndrome, who is allowed one talk-out per class as specified on the behavior intervention plan (BIP) included in his individualized education program (IEP).

Finally, teachers need to *monitor* student classroom behaviors frequently. For example, you should scan the room to check that students are following the rules. To do this, you always need to have a clear view of the entire class, regardless of the activity in which you or the class are engaged. When student behavior is not carefully monitored, students choose not to follow the rules consistently. For example, Charmaine was a student in Ms. Patrick's fifth-grade class who had behavior problems. Ms. Patrick had a rule that students needed to complete all their independent work before they could go to the computer station to play a problem-solving game. Ms. Patrick did not have time to monitor Charmaine's behavior. One day, she saw Charmaine at the computer station and asked her whether she had completed her assignments. Not only had Charmaine not completed her assignments on that day, but she hadn't done any work for the past three days. Thereafter, Ms. Patrick was careful to monitor the work progress of all her students.

Use of Time

The way teachers use time in the classroom is one of the most important aspects of classroom organization. Effectively using instructional time and managing transition time constitute two particularly important tasks.

Using Instructional Time   The amount of time that students are meaningfully and successfully engaged in academic activities in school is referred to as **academic learning time** (Arends, 2004). Research has shown that more academic learning time in a classroom results in increased student learning (Berliner, 1990). Time usage is particularly important for students with special needs, who may need more time to learn than their peers.

Paine et al. (1983) suggest several ways in which teachers can maximize academic learning time. One way is to minimize the time spent on organizational activities such as taking the lunch counts, completing opening activities, getting drinks, sharpening pencils, cleaning out desks, and going to the bathroom. For example, teach students how to perform organizational tasks efficiently and how to observe a firm time schedule when carrying them out. Another way is to select activities that have the greatest teaching potential and that contribute most to students' achieving the core school curriculum. Although learning activities can be fun, they should ultimately be selected for the purpose of teaching students something important. Finally, the research-based

RESEARCH NOTE

Stichter, Stormont, and Lewis (2008) studied the use of time in high and low-poverty schools. They found that teachers in high-poverty schools engaged in more noninstructional talk, had more instructional down time, and had higher numbers of students exiting during instruction. Why do you think this is so?

PROFESSIONAL EDGE

Using "Sponges" to Increase Academic Learning Time

You almost always have times during the day when you have a minute or two before a scheduled academic activity or before the class goes to lunch, an assembly, or recess. You can fill that extra time with productive activities by using "sponges." Sponges are activities that fit into brief periods of time and give students practice or review on skills and content you have already covered in class. The following lists of sponges can help you "soak up" that extra classroom time.

EARLY ELEMENTARY SPONGES

1. Tell students to be ready to state one playground rule.
2. Tell students to be ready to list the names of classmates that begin with *J* or *M* and so on.
3. Tell students to be ready to draw something that is drawn only with circles.
4. Tell students to be ready to think of a good health habit.
5. Flash fingers—have students tell how many fingers you hold up.
6. Say numbers, days of the week, and months and have students tell what comes next.
7. Ask what number comes between two numbers: for example, 31 and 33, 45 and 47.
8. Ask students what number comes before or after 46, 52, 13, and so on.
9. Write a word on the board. Have students make a list of words that rhyme with it.
10. Count to 100 by 2s, 5s, 10s, and so on, either orally or in writing.
11. Think of animals that live on a farm, in the jungle, in water, and so forth.
12. Name fruits, vegetables, meats, and the like.
13. List things you can touch, things you can smell, and so on.

DISMISSAL SPONGES

1. "I Spy"—ask students to find something in the room that starts with *M, P,* and so on.
2. Ask students to find something in the room that has the sound of short *a,* long *a,* and so forth.
3. Number rows or tables. Signal the number of the table with fingers, and allow students to leave accordingly.
4. Count in order or by 2s, 5s, and so on.
5. Say the days of the week, the months of the year, and so on.
6. Ask what day it is, what month it is, what date it is, or what year it is. Ask how many months are in a year, how many days are in a week, and so on.

7. Use reward activities:

"We have had a good day! Who helped it to be a good day for all of us? Betty, you brought flowers to brighten our room. You may leave. John, you remembered to rinse your hands, good for you. You may leave. Ellen showed us that she could be quiet coming into the room today. You may leave, Ellen. Bob remembered his library book all by himself. Dawn walked all the way to the playground—she remembered our safety rules. Lori brought things to share with us. Tom surprised us with a perfect paper—he must have practiced. . . ." Students' good deeds can be grouped together to speed up dismissal. The teacher can finish with, "You're all learning to be very thoughtful. I'm very proud of all of you and you should be very proud of yourselves."

8. Use flashcards. The first correct answer earns dismissal.
9. Review the four basic shapes. Each student names an object in the room in the shape of a triangle, circle, square, or rectangle.

UPPER ELEMENTARY AND MIDDLE SCHOOL SPONGES

1. List the continents.
2. Name as many gems or precious stones as you can.
3. List as many states as you can.
4. Write an abbreviation, a roman numeral, a trademark, a proper name (biological), or a proper name (geographical).
5. Name as many countries and their capitals as you can.
6. List the names of five parts of the body above the neck that are spelled with three letters.
7. List one manufactured item for each letter of the alphabet.
8. List as many nouns in the room as you can.
9. List one proper noun for each letter of the alphabet.
10. Name as many parts of a car as you can.
11. List as many kinds of trees as you can.
12. List as many personal pronouns as you can.
13. Name as many politicians as you can.

How many sponges can you think of for your grade or subject area? Additional ideas for sponges can be found at the Busy Teachers' Web Site K–12: http://www.ceismc.gatech.edu/busyt.

Sources: From "Effective Teaching for Higher Achievement," by D. Sparks and G. M. Sparks, 1984, *Educational Leadership, 49*(7).

---

strategies described in this chapter and throughout this book for managing your classroom, grouping your students, and adapting your methods and materials also help ensure the productive use of your students' time. One specific technique to increase the academic learning time of your students is described in the Professional Edge.

Managing Transition Time   Just as important as the amount of time spent in activities is the management of transition time. **Transition time** is the time it takes to change from one activity to another. Transition time occurs when students remain at their seats and change from one subject to another, move from their seats to an activity in another part of the classroom, move from somewhere else in the classroom back to their seats, leave the classroom to go outside or to another part of the school building, or come back into the classroom from outside or from another part of the building (Paine et al., 1983).

Research studies show that teachers sometimes waste academic learning time by not managing transitions carefully (Ornstein & Lasley, 2004). Paine et al. (1983) suggest that you have rules devoted specifically to transitions and that you teach these rules directly to students. As with all rules, those for transitions need to be consistently monitored and reinforced.

The way you organize classroom materials also can affect the management of transitions. For example, you need to have all materials ready for each subject and activity. In addition, materials should be organized so that they are easily accessible. No matter how well organized your transitions are, you still may need to adapt them for some students with disabilities. Students with physical disabilities may need more time to take out or put away their books. Students with physical and visual disabilities may have mobility problems that cause them to take more time with such transitional activities as getting into instructional groups or moving from room to room. Furthermore, you may need an individualized system of rewards or other consequences to guide students with ADHD or behavior disorders through transition times.

**dimensions of
DIVERSITY**
For ideas about designing lesson plans for English-language learners, go to http://coe.sdsu.edu/people/imora/MoraModules/ELDInstruction.htm.

How Can You Group All Your Students for Instruction in Inclusive Classrooms?

Students with special needs benefit from a variety of classroom grouping arrangements, including large- and small-group instruction, one-to-one instruction, and mixed- and same-skill groupings. The flexible use of classroom grouping arrangements is an important part of differentiated instruction (Broderick, Mehta-Parekh, & Reid, 2005). Remember that the particular arrangement you choose depends on your instructional objectives as well as your students' particular needs.

Whole-Class or Large-Group Instruction

Students with special needs benefit from both whole-class (or large-group) and small-group instruction. Tier 1 in RtI is whole-class instruction. One advantage of whole-class instruction is that students spend the entire time with the teacher. In small-group instruction, students spend part of the time with the teacher and also spend time working independently while the teacher works with other small groups. Research shows that the more time students spend with the teacher, the more likely they are to be engaged (Rimm-Kaufman, La Paro, Downer, & Pianta, 2005) and the more they learn (Rosenshine, 1997; Rosenshine & Stevens, 1986). This increase in learning may be because students are more likely to go off task when they are working on their own, particularly when they have learning or behavior problems. Whatever grouping arrangements you use, try to make sure that students spend as much time as possible working with you.

Another advantage of whole-group instruction is that it does not single out students with special needs as being different from their peers. However, you may need to make accommodations within whole-group instruction for students with disabilities. For example, students in Mr. Nichols's fourth-grade class were reading *Charlotte's Web* as a large-group instructional activity. Simone read more slowly than the rest of the class. To help her keep up, Mr. Nichols provided a digital version of the book. He also gave Simone more time to answer comprehension questions about the story in class because it took her longer to look up some of the answers. In another example, before his lectures, a high school science teacher identified technical words he was going to use and then worked before school with a small group of students with vocabulary problems to help them learn the words.

Small-Group Instruction

You may encounter situations in which small-group instruction is more appropriate for students with special needs. You can use same-skill groupings and mixed-skill groupings in setting up your groups.

Same-skill groupings, often referred to as *homogeneous groupings,* are helpful when some but not all students are having trouble mastering a particular skill and need more instruction and practice. For example, Ms. Rodgers was showing her students how to divide fractions that have a common denominator. She gave her class a quiz to see who had learned how to do the problems. She found that all but five students had mastered the skill. The next day, Ms. Rodgers worked with these five students while the rest of the class did an application activity. Small-group instruction is not only for students with disabilities; most students benefit from extra help in a small group at one time or another. In fact, many times students with special needs do not need extra instruction.

Small same-skill groups have also proven effective in basic skill areas when students are performing well below most of the class (Bursuck et al., 2004; Mosteller, Light, & Sachs, 1996). For example, Lori is in Ms. Hubbard's fourth-grade class and is reading at the second-grade level. Lori is learning decoding and vocabulary skills in a small group with other students who read at her level. Because the group is small and homogeneous, Ms. Hubbard is able to proceed in small steps, present many examples, and allow students to master skills before they move on. Lori is making progress and feels good about herself because she is becoming a better reader. Tier 2 and Tier 3 instruction in RtI is usually carried out in small same-skill groups.

Clearly, some students do require instruction that is more individualized and intensive than can be provided in the large group (Bursuck et al., 2004). However, small same-skill groups should be used only when attempts to make accommodations in the large group have been unsuccessful. Same-skill groups tend to become permanent and take on a life of their own. Thus, the ultimate goal of any small group should be its eventual dissolution. Also, on many days students can benefit from instruction with the rest of the class. For example, Lori's group participates in large-group reading when the teacher is reading a story and the class is working on listening comprehension. Another potential problem in using same-skill groupings is the danger that students in a low-achieving group in one area will be placed in low-achieving groups in other areas even though their skill levels do not justify it. For example, just because Lori is in the lowest-level reading group does not automatically mean she needs to be in a low-achieving group in math.

The major advantage of **mixed-skill groupings,** or *heterogeneous groupings,* is that they provide students with special needs a range of positive models for both academic and social behavior. In mixed-skill groupings, students often help each other so such groups can also be a vehicle for providing direct instruction to individual students, something for which classroom teachers often do not have the time. In addition, mixed-skill groups, like large groups, may be less likely to single out students with special needs.

One-to-One Instruction

Providing **one-to-one instruction** for students with special needs can be very effective under some circumstances. In this grouping arrangement, students work with a teacher, a paraprofessional, or a computer on well-sequenced, self-paced materials that are geared to their specific level. For example, Waldo is having trouble with addition and subtraction facts. For 15 minutes each day, he works at the classroom computer station on an individualized drill-and-practice program. Right now he is working on addition facts through 10. When he masters these, the software will automatically provide more difficult problems. Shamika, a student with a moderate intellectual disability, works with a paraprofessional on selecting food items for a balanced lunch while the rest of the class listens to a presentation on the process of performing a nutritional analysis. One-to-one instruction is sometimes an option in the more intensive tiers in RtI.

Although one-to-one instruction may be appropriate in some circumstances, it is not necessarily the grouping arrangement of choice in either general or special education. First, it is inefficient; when it is carried out by the classroom teacher the extensive use of one-to-one instruction will result in less instructional time for everyone. Second, the logistics of one-to-one instruction sometimes require that students complete much independent work while the teacher moves from student to student. This can lead to high levels of off-task behavior, a problem many students with special needs experience (Mercer & Pullen, 2009). Third, the lack of peer models in one-to-one instruction makes it more difficult to motivate students, a problem particularly relevant at the high school level (Ellis & Sabornie, 1990). Sometimes, habitual use of one-to-one instruction can exclude students from critical social interactions. Fourth, there is evidence to suggest that groups as large as three are equally effective (Vaughn et al., 2003). Finally, when a student requires this type of instruction for extended periods of time, further analysis is required of her needs and instructional setting.

The teaching materials you use have a great impact on whether your students meet the standards expected of them (Coyne, Kame'enui, & Carnine, 2007). In evaluating your materials, consider the learning outcomes targeted and the quality with which the materials are designed.

How Can You Evaluate Instructional Materials for Inclusive Classrooms?

Learning Outcomes

Instructional materials are designed to cover a range of *learning outcomes*. These outcomes reflect Bloom's revised taxonomy related to levels of thought. The six levels of thought, from lowest to highest, include remembering, understanding, applying, analyzing, evaluating, and creating (Anderson & Krathwohl, 2001, pp. 67–68):

1. *Remembering* involves retrieving, recognizing, and recalling relevant knowledge from long-term memory. For example, Ms. Lopez's American history class was studying the Revolutionary War. One of her remembering outcomes was for students to recall two major colonial leaders.
2. *Understanding* involves constructing meaning from oral, written, and graphic messages through interpreting, giving examples, classifying, summarizing, inferring, comparing, and explaining. For understanding, Ms. Lopez's students compared the family backgrounds of two colonial leaders.
3. *Applying* involves using information to solve a problem or produce some result. For this level of outcome, Ms. Lopez's students constructed a theory as to why colonial leaders refused to abolish slavery.
4. *Analyzing* is breaking up material into its parts and determining how the parts relate to one another and to an overall structure or purpose through differentiating, organizing, and attributing. For analyzing, Ms. Lopez's students differentiated how the colonists reacted to each British provocation leading up to the start of the Revolutionary War.
5. *Evaluating* involves making judgments based on criteria and standards through checking and critiquing. For this level of thought, students critiqued the colonial leaders as to their qualifications to lead the country as president.
6. *Creating,* the highest level of thought, involves putting together elements to form a coherent whole or reorganizing elements into a new pattern or structure through generating, planning, and producing. For creating, some of Ms. Lopez's students composed a song about the colonial leaders.

Keep in mind several important points when selecting the levels of thought required by your students' learning outcomes. First, in general, select outcomes reflecting a range of levels of thought, even if a range is not represented in the textbooks you are using. Textbooks and teachers tend to stress remembering at the expense of other levels of thought. Second, base your selection of outcomes on your

PROFESSIONAL EDGE

Guidelines for Evaluating Basals and Other Basic Skills Curricula

Before evaluating any material, read the evaluative questions below and place an asterisk next to each that is critical for the type of material you are examining. Answer each question with yes or no. Examine all your responses in a single area, paying special attention to the questions you designated as critical. Rate each area inadequate (1), adequate (2), or excellent (3). If the area is inadequate, designate whether the features can be easily modified (M).

Rating Scale:	Inadequate	Adequate	Excellent	Easily modified
	1	2	3	M

1 2 3 M   Effectiveness of Material

Yes	No	Is information provided that indicates successful field testing or class testing of the material?
Yes	No	Has the material been successfully field tested with students similar to the target population?
Yes	No	Are testimonials and publisher claims clearly differentiated from research findings?

1 2 3 M   Prerequisite Skills

Yes	No	Are the prerequisite student skills and abilities needed to work with ease in the material specified?
Yes	No	Are the prerequisite student skills and abilities compatible with the objectives of the material?
Yes	No	Are the prerequisite student skills and abilities compatible with the target population?

1 2 3 M   Content

Yes	No	Are students provided with specific strategies rather than a series of isolated skills?
Yes	No	Does the selection of subject matter, facts, and skills adequately represent the content area?
Yes	No	Is the content consistent with the stated objectives?
Yes	No	Is the information presented in the material accurate?
Yes	No	Is the information presented in the material current?
Yes	No	Are various points of view—including treatment of cultural diversity, individuals with disabilities, ideologies, social values, gender roles, and socioeconomic status—represented objectively?
Yes	No	Are the content and the topic of the material relevant to the needs of students with disabilities?

1 2 3 M   Sequence of Instruction

Yes	No	Is the scope and sequence of the material clearly specified?
Yes	No	Are facts, concepts, and skills ordered logically?
Yes	No	Does the sequence of instruction proceed from simple to complex?
Yes	No	Does the sequence proceed in small, easily attainable steps?

---

students' strengths and needs, not their labels. Teachers tend to choose outcomes requiring lower levels of thought for students with disabilities and other special needs, regardless of their learning profiles. Use the INCLUDE strategy to choose the appropriate level of learning for all of your students.

The nature of the instructional materials you use is another very important consideration in accommodating students with special needs in your classroom. Consider the learning outcomes you desire as you select instructional materials that include textbooks, manipulatives and models, and technology.

Textbooks

Basal textbooks (often called *basals*) are books used for instruction in any subject area that contain all the key components of the curriculum being taught for that subject. The careful evaluation of basals is vital. Well-designed textbooks require fewer accommodations for students with special needs, thereby saving you much time and energy. For example, a math basal that contains plenty of practice activities does not need to be adapted for students who require lots of practice to master a skill. Similarly, a science textbook that highlights critical vocabulary and includes clear context cues to help students figure out the words on their own may make it unnecessary for

Rating Scale:	Inadequate	Adequate	Excellent	Easily modified
	1	2	3	M

1 2 3 M   **Behavioral Objectives**

Yes   No   Are objectives or outcomes for the material clearly stated?

Yes   No   Are the objectives or outcomes consistent with the goals for the target population?

Yes   No   Are the objectives or outcomes stated in behavioral terms, including the desired behavior, the conditions for measurement of the behavior, and the desired standard of performance?

1 2 3 M   **Initial Assessment and Placement**

Yes   No   Does the material provide a method to determine initial student placement in the curriculum?

Yes   No   Does the initial assessment for placement contain enough items to place the learner accurately?

1 2 3 M   **Ongoing Assessment and Evaluation**

Yes   No   Does the material provide evaluation procedures for measuring progress and mastery of objectives?

Yes   No   Are there enough evaluative items to measure learner progress accurately?

Yes   No   Are procedures and/or materials for ongoing record keeping provided?

1 2 3 M   **Instructional Input (Teaching Procedures)**

Yes   No   Are instructional procedures for each lesson either clearly specified or self-evident?

Yes   No   Does the instruction provide for active student involvement and responses?

Yes   No   Are the lessons adaptable to small-group and individualized instruction?

Yes   No   Are a variety of cueing and prompting techniques used to gain correct student responses?

Yes   No   When using verbal instruction, does the instruction proceed clearly and logically?

Yes   No   Does the material use teacher modeling and demonstration when appropriate to the skills being taught?

Yes   No   Does the material specify correction and feedback procedures for use during instruction?

1 2 3 M   **Practice and Review**

Yes   No   Does the material contain appropriate practice activities that contribute to mastery of the skills and concepts?

Yes   No   Do practice activities relate directly to the desired outcome behaviors?

Yes   No   Does the material provide enough practice for students with learning problems?

Yes   No   Are skills systematically and cumulatively reviewed throughout the curriculum?

Source: From *Instructional Materials for the Mildly Handicapped: Selection, Utilization, and Modification*, by A. Archer, 1977, Eugene: University of Oregon, Northwest Learning Resources System. Used by permission of the author.

---

teachers to prepare extensive vocabulary study guides. A set of questions to help you evaluate basals and other basic skills materials is included in the Professional Edge.

Carefully evaluating basals helps alert you to any accommodations you may need to make. For example, a spelling basal with little provision for review can be troublesome for students who have problems retaining information; you may want to develop review activities for every three lessons rather than every five, as is done in a given book. Many teachers choose to develop or collect their own materials rather than depend on published basal series. For example, some teachers have their students read trade books instead of traditional reading books; others have their students engage in the actual writing process rather than, or in addition to, answering questions in a book. Still others involve their students in real-life math-problem solving rather than use basal math books. Even if your school does not use basals, the guidelines discussed here for teaching basic skills apply. Of course, the selection of materials is also critical in RtI schools where evidence-based practices are required within all of the instructional tiers. For example, having a research-based reading basal as part of a core curriculum in reading in Tier 1 makes the use of proven practices more likely, provides continuity for children and adults, supplies most necessary teaching tools, and ensures a systematic progression of skills or content, not leaving instruction to chance (Bursuck & Damer, 2011).

RESEARCH NOTE

Harniss, Caros, and Gersten (2007) found that students with special needs learned more when using a text that linked content information into "big ideas," helped students organize information, and provided extensive practice and review.

Content-area textbooks, which are books used for instruction in subject areas such as science and social studies, also need to be evaluated. In secondary schools, students often are expected to read their textbooks to access curriculum content (Sabornie & deBettencourt, 2009; Mercer & Pullen, 2009). Because students are required to read and understand their texts, often without previous instruction, the texts should be written at a level at which students can easily understand them. Armbruster and Anderson (1988) refer to readable textbooks as "considerate." Considerate textbooks are easier for students to use independently and require fewer teacher adaptations. The following guidelines refer to aspects of considerate textbooks involving content, organization, and quality of writing.

Check the Content Covered in the Text to See Whether It Stresses "Big Ideas" Rather Than Facts in Isolation   "Big ideas" are important principles that enable learners to understand the connections among facts and concepts they learn (Coyne et al., 2007). For example, in a text that stressed facts in isolation, students learned that Rosa Parks was an important figure because she led the Montgomery bus boycott in 1955. In a text that stressed big ideas, students learned that the bus boycott, led by Rosa Parks in 1955, was carried out in response to the problem of segregation in the South in the early 1950s and that the boycott was the first in a series of civil rights protests eventually leading to the Civil Rights Act of 1965.

Check to See Whether Support Is Provided for Student Comprehension
Support for student comprehension can be detected in the following three ways:

1. *Check the organization of the headings and subheadings:* Make an outline of the headings and subheadings in a few chapters. How reasonable is the structure revealed? Is it consistent with your knowledge of the subject matter?
2. *Check the consistency of organization in discussions of similar topics:* For example, in a science chapter on vertebrates, information about the different groups of vertebrates should be similarly organized; that is, if the section on amphibians discusses structure, body covering, subgroups, and reproduction, the section on reptiles should discuss the same topics, in the same order.
3. *Look for clear signaling of the structure:* A well-designed text includes information headings and subheadings. The most helpful headings are those that are the most specific about the content in the upcoming section. For example, the heading "Chemical Weathering" is a more helpful content clue than the heading "Another Kind of Weathering." A well-signaled text also includes format clues to organization. Page layouts, paragraphing, marginal notations, graphic aids, and the use of boldface, italics, and/or underlining can all serve to highlight or reinforce the structure. For example, a discussion of the four stages in the life cycle of butterflies could be signaled by using a separate, numbered paragraph for each state (that is, 1. Egg; 2. Larva; 3. Pupa; 4. Adult) and by including a picture for each stage. Finally, look for signal words and phrases that designate particular patterns of organization. For example, the phrases *in contrast* and *on the other hand* signal a compare-and-contrast organization, whereas the words *first, second,* and *third* indicate an enumeration or list pattern.

Check to See That Important Background Knowledge Is Activated   Despite the importance of background knowledge for comprehension (Beck & Mc-Keown, 2002; Marzano, 2004), many textbooks assume unrealistic levels of students' background knowledge (Gersten, Fuchs, Williams, & Baker, 2001). A failure to activate important background knowledge may be especially problematic for students with special needs, who are more likely to lack this information (Hallahan et al., 2005; Lerner & Johns, 2008). A number of textbook features indicate adequate attention to background knowledge. For example, social studies texts often activate background knowledge by providing definitions for important vocabulary content, displaying geographical information on maps, and featuring timelines delineating when key events took place (Coyne et al., 2007). As with all of the dimensions of effective materials we have discussed, using a text that fails to adequately take background knowledge into account means that you will have to provide it.

Check for Quality of Writing   The quality and clarity of writing can also affect student comprehension. Quality of writing can be evaluated in five ways:

1. *Look for explicit or obvious connectives, or conjunctions:* The absence of connectives can be particularly troublesome when the connective is a causal one (for example, *because, since, therefore*), which is frequently the case in content-area textbooks. Therefore, look especially for causal connectives. For example, the sentence *Because the guard cells relax, the openings close* is a better explanation than the sentences *The guard cells relax. The openings close.*

2. *Check for clear references:* Another problem to watch for is confusing pronoun references when more than one noun is used. For example, consider the following: *Both the stem of the plant and the leaf produce chloroform, but in different ways. For one, the sun hits it, and then . . .* Here, the pronouns *one* and *it* could be referring to either the stem or the leaf. Also, look out for vague quantifiers, those that do not modify the noun being quantified (for example, *some, many, few*). For example, the sentence *Some whales have become extinct* is clearer than *Some have become extinct.* In addition, check for definite pronouns without a clear referent (for example, *She saw him,* where the identity of *him* is not specified).

3. *Look for transition statements:* Transitions help the reader move easily from idea to idea. Given that a text covers many topics, make sure that the topic shifts are smooth. For example, in a biology chapter on the respiratory system, the text signals the transition from naming the parts of the respiratory system to describing the actual respiratory process by stating *Next, the role each of these parts of the body plays in the respiratory process will be described.*

4. *Make sure chronological sequences are easy to follow:* In a discussion of a sequence of events, the order of presentation in the text should generally proceed from first to last; any alteration of the order could cause confusion if not clearly signaled.

5. *Make sure graphic aids are clearly related to the text:* Graphic aids should contribute to understanding the material rather than simply provide decoration or fill space, should be easy to read and interpret, and should be clearly titled and labeled and referenced in the text so the reader knows when to look at them.

No matter how well designed conventional basal and content-area texts may be, they are still largely print based and fixed and uniform in format. As a result, conventional materials are likely to present barriers for students with disabilities (Pisha, 2003). For example, students who are blind will need a print alternative, such as braille; students with physical challenges may be unable to turn the pages in a text; students with attention and organizational problems may be unable to identify main ideas; and students with reading disabilities may not be able to read material accurately and quickly enough to comprehend it. Unfortunately, teachers may lack both the time and expertise to adapt these materials.

Modern digital texts can present the same content as conventional printed books but in a format that is more flexible and accessible (Pisha & Stahl, 2005). Digital versions of texts can be easily converted to braille, virtual pages can be turned with the slight press of a switch, and any words in the text can be read aloud. An example of a textbook made more accessible through technology is described in the Technology Notes in Chapter 10.

Manipulatives and Models

Manipulatives and models can help students make connections between the abstractions often presented in school and the real-life products and situations these abstractions represent. *Manipulatives* are concrete objects or representational items, such as blocks and counters (for example, base-10 blocks for math), used as part of instruction. *Models* are also tangible objects; they provide a physical representation of an abstraction (for example, a scale model of the solar system). Strategies to help

dimensions of DIVERSITY

Duke (2000) studied the use of informational texts in first-grade classrooms. She found few informational texts present, and that only 3.6 minutes of class time per day involved activities with information texts. The use of informational texts was even lower in high-poverty schools. Why is it important to spend time using informational text?

www.resources

Acquiring digital texts can be difficult. Bookshare offers free for all students with disabilities access to thousands of digital books, textbooks, teacher-recommended reading, periodicals, and assistive technology tools. For more information go to http://www.Bookshare.org.

The use of manipulatives and models in this biology class makes learning more concrete. What are ways manipulatives and models can be used to make subject matter content in other areas more concrete?

students make these connections have great potential benefit for students with special needs, who may lack the background knowledge and reasoning skills to understand abstractions (Cass, Cates, Smith, & Jackson, 2003; Smith, 2004). Still, manipulatives and models should be used carefully, because their use with students with special needs has not been heavily researched (Cass et al., 2003; Stein, Kinder, Silbert, & Carnine, 2005). When using these tools, consider the following seven guidelines (Marzola, 1987; Ross & Kurtz, 1993):

1. *Select materials that suit the concept and developmental stage of the students:* When you are first introducing a concept, materials should be easy to comprehend. Generally, the order in which you introduce materials should follow the same order as students' understanding: from the concrete to the representational to the abstract. However, not all students need to start at the same level. For example, in a biology lesson on the heart, many students benefit from viewing a three-dimensional model of a human heart, whereas other students are able to understand how a heart works just by seeing a picture of one.

2. *Use a variety of materials:* Students with disabilities may have trouble transferring their understanding of a concept from one form to another. For example, Curtis's teacher always demonstrated place value using base-10 blocks. When Curtis was given a place-value problem using coffee stirrers, he was unable to do it. Curtis's teacher could have prevented this problem in the first place by demonstrating place value using a range of manipulative materials, such as coffee stirrers, paper clips, and so on.

3. *Use verbal explanations whenever possible to accompany object manipulation:* Models and manipulative demonstrations should be preceded and accompanied by verbal explanations of the concept or skill being demonstrated. Verbal explanations are valuable because students may not be able to identify the important features of the model on their own. For example, Ms. Balou put a model of a two-digit-by-two-digit multiplication problem on the board. She verbally explained to her students all the steps in computing the problem and wrote each step on the whiteboard as it was completed.

4. *Encourage active interaction:* It is not enough just to have the teacher demonstrate with manipulatives or models as students observe. Students need to interact actively with models and manipulatives. Hands-on experience helps them construct their own meaning from the materials.

5. *Elicit student explanations of their manipulations or use of models:* Encourage your students to verbalize what they are doing as they work with models and manipulatives. This is a good way for you to assess whether they really understand the concept or skill. For example, Ms. Conway had her students name the main parts of the human heart using a model. Mr. Abeles had his students explain out loud how they would subtract 43 from 52 using base-10 blocks. Although explanations can help you evaluate how your students process information, students with special needs may not be able to articulate concepts right away because of language problems or a lack of reasoning skills. These students may require frequent demonstrations of how to articulate what they are doing.

6. *Present clear guidelines for handling manipulatives to prevent management problems:* Although manipulatives can be helpful instructional tools, they also can create management problems, particularly in larger groups when your physical access to students is limited. For example, Ms. Leifheit wanted her students to manipulate blocks to show the sounds in words. Each child received three blocks. When the children heard a word such as *man,* they were to move a block as they said each sound: *m-a-n.* Ms. Leifheit had trouble getting students' attention at the beginning of the lesson because they were busy handling the blocks. She also found that students were not listening to her say the words, again because they were playing with the blocks. Ms. Leifheit decided to break the class into smaller groups so she could more carefully monitor student use of the blocks. She also established a simple rule: When the teacher is talking, students are not to touch their blocks.

7. *Move your students beyond the concrete level when they are ready:* Some students with special needs may have trouble moving from one learning stage to another. One effective way to help students make the transition from the concrete to the abstract is to pair concrete tasks with paper-and-pencil tasks. For example, Ms. Conway had her students label a picture of a human heart (representational stage) after they had observed and discussed a physical model (concrete stage). Mr. Abeles had his second-graders solve subtraction problems using manipulatives and then record their answers on a traditional worksheet without the presence of any pictures (abstract stage).

Technology

Teachers today have available to them a broad array of technologies to enhance the presentation of material to their students. As mentioned in Chapter 1, technologies range from low- to high-tech options. One common use of computers in inclusive classrooms is to provide instruction to students through drill-and-practice programs, tutorials, and simulations. In general, *drill-and-practice programs* are used often with students with special needs. Such programs have been shown to be effective for these students largely because they allow students to learn in small steps, provide systematic feedback, and allow for lots of practice to mastery. Still, not all drill-and-practice programs are created equal (Bursuck & Damer, 2011; Okolo, 2000). Look for programs that

- Directly relate student responding to the instructional objective
- Have animation or graphics that support the skill being practiced
- Provide feedback that helps students locate and correct their mistakes
- Store information about student performance or progress that can be accessed later by the teacher
- Have options for controlling features such as speed of problem presentation, type of feedback, problem difficulty, and amount of practice

Computers also can provide initial, sequenced instruction for students, using tutorials in problem solving, decision making, and risk taking and using simulations. Each of these forms of computer-assisted instruction has potential advantages and disadvantages (Roblyer, Edwards, & Havriluk, 2004). For example, *tutorials* can present instruction to mastery in small, sequential steps, an instructional approach shown to be effective with students with special needs. Tutorials also can provide one-to-one instruction at varying levels of difficulty, something teachers usually do not have time to do. Still, you need to check to be sure that students have the necessary prerequisite skills to benefit from the tutorials. In addition, tutorials may not provide sufficient review for students, and students may not be motivated enough to work through them independently (Roblyer et al., 2004). *Simulations* are of great potential benefit in teaching students to be active learners by confronting real-life situations. However, simulations may be difficult

www.resources

The National Center to Improve Practice in Special Education through Technology, Media and Materials has gathered and synthesized information about technology, disabilities, and instructional practices through a broad range of resources. This site also provides opportunities for teachers to exchange information, build knowledge, and practice through collaborative dialogue: http://www2.edc.org/ncip.

to integrate with academic curriculum, may require much teacher assistance, and can be time consuming (Roblyer et al., 2004).

Assistive technology (AT) is an important part of an inclusive classroom. An assistive-technology device is any piece of equipment that is used to increase, maintain, or improve the functional capabilities of a child with a disability. An assistive-technology service is any service that directly assists a child in the selection, acquisition, or use of an assistive-technology device, according to the Technology-Related Assistance for Individuals with Disabilities Act of 1998. As you have already learned, a range of high- to low-tech AT is available to enable students with disabilities to communicate or to access information by allowing them to bypass their disability. Ways to use INCLUDE to determine the AT needs of students with disabilities are described in the Technology Notes.

TECHNOLOGY NOTES

Using INCLUDE to Determine Assistive-Technology Needs

According to IDEA, the IEP team must consider whether a child needs assistive-technology (AT) devices and services as part of his or her plan for an appropriate education. This decision is further complicated by the fact that more than 29,000 AT devices exist for individuals with disabilities and aging adults (Baush & Hasselbring, 2004). The INCLUDE strategy can assist greatly in helping the team make this decision. What follows is a series of questions related to AT that teams may want to incorporate into the INCLUDE process. These questions were adapted from ones originally suggested by Beigel (2000); Marino, Marino, and Shaw (2006); and Pedrotty-Bryant, Bryant, and Raskind (1998).

IDENTIFY CLASSROOM DEMANDS

1. How do you present information? For example, teachers who use a lot of classroom discussions place a particular demand on students' speaking abilities; teachers who lecture frequently place a strain on students' writing and organizational skills.

2. What types of grouping arrangements do you use? An emphasis on cooperative learning places a burden on student communication skills.

3. What types of assignments do you make? For example, a project-driven class requires students to find and organize resource materials and then present them to the class in a clear, orderly way.

4. What are the primary ways you assess and evaluate your students? Oral assessments can place a strain on student verbal communication skills; written assessments place demands on written language skills such as handwriting, spelling, and sentence and paragraph construction.

5. How comfortable are you with having a learner who uses AT in the classroom? Your role in this process is very important. Without your support for learning to use AT and then continuing its use, a student may abandon her device.

6. What is the physical structure of your classroom and school? Issues such as whether there are adequate electrical outlets or tables large enough to accommodate a computer and various peripherals need to be considered.

NOTE LEARNER STRENGTHS AND NEEDS AND CHECK FOR POTENTIAL SUCCESS AND PROBLEM AREAS

1. What purposeful motoric movement does the student have? A purposeful movement is one that the learner controls in a conscious, consistent manner (Beigel, 2000, p. 240). Examples of purposeful motoric movement include raising an eyebrow, moving the fingers of one hand in a motion similar to that of typing, and using a pen or pencil to write or draw.

2. How willing is the student to try new activities or tasks? Using AT requires a willingness to change on the part of the student. Your knowledge of the student in this area can help determine the nature of the equipment selected (for example, easy to use or hard to use) as well as the amount of time needed to achieve independent usage.

3. What does the student desire from the use of AT? The personal goals of the learner can greatly influence AT usage. Relevance of the material is an important factor in learning to perform any skill. For example, Tamra had an expressed desire to write poetry and was quite receptive to learning to use a laptop with a large keyboard especially designed for her.

4. What emotional and psychological supports does the student need when learning to use the device? Some students may require considerable emotional and psychological support as they learn to use an AT device. You or other staff working with the student should provide such support when it is needed, as students who become frustrated or disinterested will not likely use the device. It is important to remember that

students cannot be forced to use AT; they can only be encouraged and supported whenever using the device.

5. What level of training do the student and others who interact with the student need? You, the student, and other staff working with the student need to be given the opportunity to see how the various devices work and to see who needs training and in what areas.

6. What impact, if any, do the student's socioeconomic status and cultural background have on the use of AT? Students who live in poverty, as well as their parents, are less likely to have previous experience with technology and may need more extensive training. There is also the question of the impact of culture on the acceptance of AT by students and their families.

BRAINSTORM AND DIFFERENTIATE INSTRUCTION

You need to consider the features of the technical devices as well as the extent to which they help students meet identified IEP goals:

1. How durable is the device? All devices that are used in schools should be able to withstand bumps and jars common in schools.

2. What setup and maintenance issues must be addressed? How easy is the device to update and repair? Do compatibility issues with other technology already in the classroom need to be addressed? Devices that are difficult to maintain, take a long time to repair, are not easily upgraded, or are incompatible with other technology should be avoided because eventually they will be abandoned.

3. How willing is the vendor of the device to provide a trial or loaner period of use for the student? You often need to try several devices in the school environment before a final AT decision can be made.

4. What is the reputation of the company in terms of construction, service, training, and reliability? These questions can be answered by consulting publications that deal with AT (*Team Rehab, TAM Connector*), contacting organizations (Council for Exceptional Children, Center for Applied Special Technology), and asking others who use AT.

5. Does the student have the psychomotor skills needed to use the device in a functional manner? This question should be answered during student assessment. Many devices can be adapted for students with limited motoric control; if a device cannot be adapted, then it is unrealistic to expect that it will be used.

6. Is the device aesthetically acceptable to the student? Some students may prefer a certain color or type of mouse; others may prefer a brightly colored exterior as opposed to the typical colors of blue, black, and beige; still others may want to decorate their equipment (as long as this doesn't interfere with its function). If students' aesthetic needs are not addressed, they may feel the device does not fit into their social milieu and will not likely use it.

7. Does the device meet the student's needs in a way that is easily understood by others? Students should be able to use their devices without causing a distraction. In addition, the device should not be so complex that only the vendor is able to program the device or explain how it can be used.

8. How portable is the device? For AT to be useful, the student or support person must be able to move the device from one class to another—from an elementary classroom to a special class such as art or physical education or between various academic classes in a middle or high school environment.

EVALUATE STUDENT PROGRESS

The ultimate goal of AT is to enable students to more readily meet their IEP goals. Pedrotty-Bryant et al. (1998, p. 55) suggest that teachers ask the following questions when determining whether the assistive technology selected is an appropriate match for the student.

- To what extent does the AT assist the student in compensating for the disability?
- To what degree does the technology promote student independence?
- What is the student's opinion of the technology adaptation?
- What is the family's opinion of the AT?
- Is the AT efficient and easy for the student to use?
- Does the device promote meeting IEP goals and objectives in the least restrictive environment?

How Can You Analyze Instructional Methods in Relation to Student Needs?

Teachers use a number of instructional methods in class, including direct instruction, indirect methods of instruction, scaffolding, independent student practice, and evaluation of student performance. Each of these methods should be analyzed in relation to student needs and then used and/or adapted as needed.

Elements of Direct Instruction

Several decades of research in teaching effectiveness have shown that many students learn skills and subject matter more readily when it is presented systematically and

www.resources

For more information about direct instruction, consult the Association for Direct Instruction at http://www.adihome.org.

www.resources

Another way to engage students through unison responding is by using computerized classroom response systems. For more information go to http://cft.vanderbilt.edu/docs/classroom-response-system-clickers-bibliography/

explicitly in what is often referred to as **direct instruction** (Rosenshine & Stevens, 1986; Stronge, 2002). Direct instruction consists of six key elements:

1. *Review and check the previous day's work (and reteach if necessary):* This aspect of direct instruction may include establishing routines for checking homework and reviewing relevant past learning and prerequisite skills. These procedures are important because students with special needs might not retain past learning and/or know how to apply it to new material. For example, on Thursday Ms. Guzik taught her students how to round to the nearest whole number. On Friday she gave her class a word problem to solve that required rounding. Before the students solved the problem, she pointed to a chart in the front of the room that displayed a model of how to round numbers and suggested that they refer to this chart as they solved the problem.

2. *Present new content or skills:* When content or skills are presented, teachers begin the lesson with a short statement of the objectives and a brief overview of what they are going to present and why. Material is presented in small steps, using careful demonstrations that incorporate illustrations and concrete examples to highlight key points. Included within the demonstrations are periodic questions to check for understanding.

3. *Provide guided student practice (and check for understanding):* At first, student practice takes place under the direct guidance of the teacher, who frequently questions all students on material directly related to the new content or skill. You can involve all students in questioning by using unison oral responses or by having students answer questions by holding up answer cards, raising their hands when they think an answer is correct, or holding up a number to show which answer they think is right. For example, when asking a yes-or-no question, tell your students to hold up a 1 when they think the answer is yes and a 2 when they think the answer is no.

   This approach can be used with spelling too. Have your students spell words on an index card and then hold up their answers. Unison responses not only give students more practice but also allow you to monitor student learning more readily. Prompts and additional explanations or demonstrations are provided during guided practice when appropriate. Effective guided practice continues until students meet the lesson objective. For example, Mr. Hayes was teaching his students how to add *es* to words that end in *y*. After modeling two examples at the board, he did several more examples with the students, guiding them as they applied the rule to change the *y* to *i* before they added *es*. Next, Mr. Hayes had students do a word on their own. Students wrote their answers on individual whiteboards and held up the boards when directed by Mr. Hayes. Mr. Hayes noticed that five students did not apply the rule correctly. He called these students up to his desk for additional instruction and had the rest of the students work independently, adding *es* to a list of words on a worksheet.

4. *Provide feedback and correction (and reteach when necessary):* When students answer quickly and confidently, the teacher asks another question or provides a short acknowledgment of correctness (for example, "That's right"). Hesitant but correct responses might be followed by process feedback (for example, "Yes, Yolanda, that's right because . . ."). When students respond incorrectly, the teacher uses corrections to draw out an improved student response. Corrections can include sustaining feedback (that is, simplifying the question, giving clues), explaining or reviewing steps, giving process feedback ("The reason we need to regroup in this subtraction problem is that the top number is smaller than the bottom number"), or reteaching last steps ("Remember, at the end of this experiment you need to tell whether the hypothesis was accepted or rejected. Let me show you what I mean"). Corrections continue until students have met the lesson objective, with praise used in moderation. Specific praise ("I'm impressed by how you drew a picture of that story problem!") is more effective than general praise ("Good job, Leon").

5. *Provide independent student practice:* Students practice independently on tasks directly related to the skills taught until they achieve a high correct rate. Practice activities are actively supervised and students are held accountable for their work.

6. *Review frequently:* Systematic review of previously learned material is provided, including the incorporation of review into homework and tests. Material missed in homework or tests is retaught (Rosenshine & Stevens, 1986).

It is important to note that for older students or for those who have more subject-matter knowledge or skills, these six steps can be modified, such as by presenting more material at one time or spending less time on guided practice. For example, when a second-grade teacher presented a unit on nutrition, she spent a whole week defining and showing examples of complex carbohydrates, fats, sugar, and protein. In an eighth-grade health class, this material was covered in one day, largely because students already had much background information on this topic. Moreover, each of the direct instruction steps is not required for every lesson you teach, although they are particularly helpful to students with learning and behavior problems, who have been shown to benefit greatly from a high level of classroom structure (Hallahan et al., 2005; Mercer & Pullen, 2009; Swanson & Deshler, 2003). The Case in Practice presents an example of a direct instruction lesson. The Instructional Edge describes how direct instruction techniques can be used to enhance Tier 1 instruction in RtI.

> ### RESEARCH NOTE
>
> Students are usually more attentive during fast-paced presentations (Darch & Gersten, 1985). The key to providing a fast-paced presentation is to begin the directions for the next question (or for correction of the current question) immediately after the students respond to the first question. It also helps to limit your own talk.

CASE IN PRACTICE

A Direct Instruction Lesson

This direct instruction lesson is designed to help students use pronouns clearly. Notice that Mr. Francisco first reviews the preskill of what a pronoun is. Then he guides students through the skill of substituting pronouns for nouns.

Mr. Francisco: Remember, yesterday we said that for every noun, there's a more general word called a *pronoun.* So, for the word *boys,* the pronoun is *they.* For the word *car,* the pronoun is *it.* What's the pronoun for the word *James?*

Students: He.

Mr. Francisco: Right. You're going to rewrite sentences so they have no nouns, only pronouns. Here's the first sentence: *Elephants eat grass.* What's the noun in the subject?

Students: Elephants.

Mr. Francisco: What's the pronoun that replaces *elephants?*

Students: They.

Mr. Francisco: What's the noun in the predicate?

Students: Grass.

Mr. Francisco: What's the pronoun that replaces *grass?*

Students: It.

Mr. Francisco: What is the entire sentence with pronouns?

Students: They eat it.

Mr. Francisco: Right. Look at the pronouns written on the board: *he, she, it, they, him, her, them.* You're going to use these words to rewrite sentences so they won't have any nouns, just pronouns. Here's Sentence 1: *George is watching birds.* What noun is the subject?

Students: George.

Mr. Francisco: What's the noun in the predicate?

Students: Birds.

Mr. Francisco: What's the sentence with pronouns in place?

Students: He is watching them.

Mr. Francisco: Good. Look at the next sentence: *Fred and Carlos build houses.* You are going to write it with pronouns in place of the nouns. [Teacher observes students and gives feedback.]

Mr. Francisco: Here's the sentence you should have: *They build them.*

[Teacher repeats with two more examples.]

REFLECTION

What direct instruction steps did Mr. Francisco use here?

Why is direct instruction particularly effective for students with learning and behavior challenges? In what situations would you *not* want to use direct instruction? Why?

Sources: Adapted from *Reasoning and Writing: A Direct Instruction Program,* by S. Engelmann and B. Grossen, 2001, Columbus, OH: SRA/McGraw-Hill.

INSTRUCTIONAL **EDGE**

Enhancing the Effectiveness of Tier 1 Instruction in RtI

You learned earlier in this chapter that the more effective your instruction is in the first place, the fewer the students who will require individualized accommodations. RtI's prevention-based, multitiered system is based on the similar idea that fewer students require instruction in more intensive tiers when evidence-based practices are effectively used in the less-intensive tiers. That is why the quality of instruction in Tier 1, the place where students are first taught, is so important. A successful experience in Tier 1 bodes well for future student success. An unsuccessful experience can lead to the need for "catch-up" in more-intensive tiers, and the process of catching students up is never quick or easy (Francis, Shaywitz, Stuebing, Fletcher & Shaywitz, 1996; Juel, 1988).

You can enhance the effectiveness of Tier 1 instruction by using the following evidence-based teaching techniques validated by Bursuck & Damer (2011). While all students benefit from these enhancements, students who are at risk or who have disabilities derive particular benefit from them.

- Establish a comfortable level of predictability at the beginning of lessons by telling students what they are learning, why they are learning it, and what the behavioral expectations are during the lesson.

- Actively engage students by providing them with many opportunities to respond, frequently through using unison responding.
- Present material to students in concise statements using language they understand.
- Maximize student attention and learning by employing a perky pace throughout every lesson.
- Provide support or scaffolding when students are learning new skills or content by clearly modeling new skills and providing the right amount of guided and independent practice.
- Facilitate retention by adding examples of previously learned material to examples of newly learned material.
- Correct students immediately after an error by modeling the correct answer/skill, guiding students to correct the error, and then asking the same question again so students have another opportunity to answer it.
- Continue instruction until the skill or concept presented is learned to mastery.
- Motivate students by employing a 3:1 ratio of positive to corrective teacher comment.

Indirect Methods of Instruction

Indirect instruction is based on the belief that children are naturally active learners and that given the appropriate instructional environment, they actively construct knowledge and solve problems in developmentally appropriate ways (Knight, 2002). This type of teaching is often referred to as *constructivistic* because of the belief that students are capable of constructing meaning on their own, in most cases without explicit instruction from the teacher (Hallahan et al., 2005; Knight, 2002). Indirect instruction is used by classroom teachers for both basic skills and content areas.

A common indirect method is called **inquiry learning,** or *discovery learning* (Jarolimek, Foster, & Kellough, 2004; Maroney, Finson, Beaver, & Jensen, 2003; National Research Council, 1999). Unlike direct instruction, which is very teacher centered, in the inquiry approach the teacher's role is that of a facilitator who guides learners' inquiry by helping them identify questions and problems (Jarolimek et al., 2004; Knight, 2002). The learners therefore are placed in situations that require considerable initiative and background knowledge in finding things out for themselves. In this way, students are actively involved in their own learning (Jarolimek et al., 2004).

You can see these elements of inquiry learning in a social studies lesson on Inuit or native Alaskan people developed by Lindquist (1995). The goal of the lesson was for students to "realize that there are many different groups of Inuit people, each having unique customs and traditions, but whose culture has been shaped by the Far North" (Lindquist, 1995, p. 54). First, the teacher gave the students five minutes to list everything they knew about the Inuit people. The teacher then had some students share their lists with the class.

Student sharing of their background knowledge was followed by a short film on the Inuit people. After the film, the students were asked to cross out anything on their lists that the film caused them to change their minds about. When the children had revised their lists, the teacher divided the class into pairs; each pair was asked to research a different Inuit tribe. They were to gather information about food, shelter, clothing, and language. Each pair of students recorded information about their particular tribe on a data sheet and reported their information to the class. As each group reported, the teacher synthesized the information on an overhead chart, creating a graphic display for comparing and contrasting similarities and differences among the various tribes.

Scaffolding

Scaffolding is an approach that has been used successfully to support students as they develop problem-solving skills (Larkin, 2001; Olson et al., 2007). Scaffolds are "forms of support provided by the teacher (or another student) to help students bridge the gap between their current abilities and the intended goal" (Rosenshine & Meister, 1992, p. 26).

www.resources

Find information on how to scaffold instruction for students at this link: http://iris.peabody.vanderbilt.edu/sca/chalcycle.htm.

Before using scaffolding, you need to find out whether students have the necessary background ability to learn a cognitive strategy (Rosenshine & Meister, 1992). For example, a strategy for helping a student read a physics textbook is not useful if the student lacks basic knowledge of mathematics and physical properties. Similarly, teaching a strategy for solving math word problems cannot succeed if the student does not have basic math computation skills. Using scaffolding to teach higher-order cognitive strategies consists of six stages:

1. *Present the new cognitive strategy:* In this stage, the teacher introduces the strategy concretely, using a list of strategy steps. The teacher then models the strategy, including all "thinking" and "doing" steps. For example, Mr. Bridges is teaching his history class how geographic features and natural resources affect the growth and location of cities. First, he introduces the problem-solving strategy to his students: (a) define the problem, (b) propose hypotheses to explain the problem, (c) collect data to evaluate your hypotheses, (d) evaluate the evidence, and (e) make a conclusion. These steps are posted on the chalkboard for easy reference. Mr. Bridges then models the strategy by showing students a map of the state of Illinois and thinking out loud as he applies the steps. For example, he explains how he would sort through many pieces of information in determining which factors led to the development of Chicago (for example, being on Lake Michigan) and which did not (for example, cold climate).

2. *Regulate difficulty during guided practice:* At this stage, students begin practicing the new strategy using simplified materials so they can concentrate on learning

With appropriate support, nondirect instruction can be effective for students with special needs. What steps should this teacher take to ensure effective instruction using scaffolding?

the strategy. First, the strategy is introduced one step at a time. Students are guided carefully through the steps, with the teacher anticipating particularly difficult steps and completing these difficult parts of the task as necessary. Before tackling difficult problems, such as the geography of Chicago, Mr. Bridges has his students use the problem-solving steps to solve simpler problems on topics familiar to them. For example, he has them solve problems such as why the cookies someone made were dry, why a hypothetical student is late for school every day, or why the school lunches taste awful. He also helps students brainstorm ideas for how to collect data, a step that can be difficult. Mr. Bridges does this by compiling an initial list of data collection procedures for each problem. For the problem of why the cookies were dry, Mr. Bridges gives his students a list of possible data collection procedures, such as identifying the ingredients, finding out how long the cookies were baked, and figuring out how old the cookies were.

3. *Provide varying contexts for student practice:* Students practice the strategy on actual classroom tasks under the teacher's direction. The teacher starts out leading the practice, but the students eventually carry out the practice sessions in small cooperative groups. In Mr. Bridges's class, students practice the problem-solving strategy using examples from their history textbooks.

4. *Provide feedback:* The teacher provides corrective feedback to students using evaluative checklists based on models of expert problem solving carefully explained to the students. Students are encouraged to evaluate their performance using these checklists. For example, each time Mr. Bridges's students use the problem-solving strategy, they evaluate their performance by asking themselves questions such as these: Did we clearly state the problem? Did we state a complete list of hypotheses? How thorough were our data collection procedures? Were we able to evaluate all the hypotheses using the information collected? Did we interpret the results accurately? Were our conclusions consistent with our results?

5. *Increase student responsibility:* Next the teacher begins to require students to practice putting all the steps together on their own. Student independence is encouraged by removing elements of the scaffold. For example, prompts and models are diminished, the complexity and difficulty of the materials are increased, and peer support is decreased. The teacher checks for student mastery before going to the last step, independent practice.

6. *Provide independent practice:* Finally, the teacher provides the students with extensive practice and helps them apply what they have learned to new situations. For example, Mr. Bridges shows his students how problem solving can be used in other subjects, such as science.

Independent Student Practice

The major purpose of practice is to help students refine or strengthen their skills in various areas. Consider the following seven guidelines for using practice activities effectively in your classroom:

1. *Students should practice only skills or content they have already learned:* This guideline is particularly important in order for students to be able to perform practice activities independently. Tasks that are too difficult can lead to high levels of off-task behavior.

2. *Practice is more effective when students have a desire to learn what they are practicing:* Whenever possible, point out to students situations in which they can use the skill in other phases of learning. For example, you may explain to your students that if they learn to read more quickly, they will be able to finish their homework in less time.

3. *Practice should be individualized:* Exercises should be organized so that each student can work independently.

4. *Practice should be specific and systematic:* Practice should be directly related to skills and objectives you are working on in class. This guideline is particularly

important for students with special needs, who require more practice to master academic skills.

5. *Students should have much practice on a few skills rather than little practice on many skills:* Focusing on one or two skills at a time is less confusing and gives students more practice on each skill.

6. *Practice should be organized so that students achieve high levels of success:* Correct answers reinforce students and encourage them to do more. Most students need at least 90 percent accuracy when doing practice activities, though higher-achieving students can tolerate a 70 percent rate as long as the teacher is present to assist them (Good & Brophy, 1986).

7. *Practice should be organized so that the students and teacher have immediate feedback:* You need to know how students are progressing so you can decide whether to move to the next skill. Students need to know how they are doing so they can make meaningful corrections to their work (Ornstein & Lasley, 2004).

For students with special needs, consider these additional questions: What are the response demands of the activity? Do students have to answer orally or in writing? How extensive a response is required? Do the students have enough time to finish the activity? Response demands are important because students who are unable to meet them will not be able to do the practice activity independently. For example, Mr. Edwards is having his class practice weekly vocabulary words by orally stating their definitions. Ross stutters and is unable to answer out loud. Mr. Edwards allows Ross to submit a written list of definitions. Ms. Osborne is having her students complete short-answer questions in their chemistry books. Clarice has a physical disability and is unable to write her answers independently. She uses an adapted classroom computer to prepare her answers. Mr. Nusbaum has asked his students to write a paragraph summarizing the reasons for the stock market crash of 1929. Maurice cannot write a coherent paragraph but can answer orally into an audio recorder. Amanda writes very slowly, so Mr. Nusbaum gives her more time to complete the activity.

Learning Centers One common way of providing practice for students is through *learning centers,* classroom areas where students work alone or in groups as they engage in a variety of activities, often without the assistance of the classroom teacher (Opitz, 2007). Learning centers are called by a variety of names, including "interest centers, learning stations, activity areas, free choice areas, booths, and enrichment centers" (Patillo & Vaughn, 1992, p. 12). Well-designed learning centers can provide students with disabilities opportunities to be more actively engaged in learning, practice new skills, increase proficiency in skills acquired, and apply knowledge and skills to novel situations (King-Sears, 2007, p. 138). Learning centers can provide teachers with ways to provide differentiated instruction.

The key to effective use of learning centers is to design activities that are meaningful and can be accomplished independently. To do that, you must have a clear idea of what you want your students to learn ("Where are we going?"), how your students can practice information taught ("Who needs to practice what?"), and what your students' learning levels are ("What kinds of activities allow students to meaningfully practice and/or apply information learned?") (King-Sears, 2007, p. 138). Use the INCLUDE strategy to make accommodations for individual students as necessary. You can also employ a special type of teacher-led learning center by using the station-teaching option for co-teaching that you read about in Chapter 3.

Homework Another common form of practice used by teachers is *homework.* Research shows that homework has a positive effect on student achievement, when it is properly assigned and monitored (Cooper, 1989). Effects are greatest at upper grade levels and for lower-level tasks (Hattie, 2009).

Homework is often a challenge for students with special needs. For example, most teachers expect homework to be completed independently, and students must have the sensory, academic, and organizational skills to do so. A student with a severe reading disability might be unable to read a chapter in a geometry book and answer the questions without some form of accommodation such as a peer reader or recorded text. Similarly, a student with fine motor difficulties might be unable to answer the questions unless allowed to do so orally or with an adapted word processor. In addition, you may need to provide this same student more time or to assign fewer questions. Therefore, it is important that you carefully examine your own particular homework requirements and modify them to ensure full participation by all your students.

Evaluation of Student Performance

The major purpose of student evaluation is to determine the extent to which students have mastered academic skills or instructional content. Chapter 4 discussed formal and informal assessments that can be used to evaluate student progress. Student evaluations are also communicated through grades, which are determined in a number of ways, including classroom tests and assignments. Because student evaluation is so important, you need to consider how classroom tests and assignments may interact with student learning needs. Most critical is that the method of evaluation measures skill or content mastery, not a student's disability. For example, Carson, a student who has ADHD, should be given tests in small segments to ensure that the tests measure his knowledge, not his attention span. Similarly, Riesa, a student with a severe learning disability in writing, needs to take an oral essay test in physics if the test is to be a valid measure of her knowledge of physics rather than her writing disability. The type of report-card grade used, as well as the system used to arrive at that grade, might also need to be modified for some students. For example, Hal was discouraged about always getting a C in English, no matter how hard he tried. His teacher decided to supplement his grade with an A for effort to encourage Hal to keep trying. Mr. Henning encouraged his students to come to class on time by giving them credit for punctuality.

WRAPPING IT UP

BACK TO THE CASES

This section provides opportunities for you to apply the knowledge gained in this chapter to the cases described at the beginning of this chapter. The questions and activities that follow demonstrate how the principles and concepts you have learned about in this chapter connect to the everyday activities of all teachers.

MR. RODRIGUEZ has provided a digital copy of the text and a daily review of previously presented content, outlines of lectures, and small-group discussions to support Manuel's learning of content. Step 7 of the INCLUDE strategy asks teachers to evaluate student

progress. Using information in this chapter and Chapter 4, suggest two assessment methods that Mr. Rodriguez might use to monitor Manuel's progress. Explain why you selected these two methods.

JOSH may face peers who have difficulty adjusting to his speech. As a result, they may shy away from interactions with him. Based on information provided in this chapter, describe two ways Ms. Stewart can use classroom management, grouping, instructional materials, or specific teaching methods to support Josh's interactions with peers. Explain why you think these methods would be helpful for Josh.

SUMMARY

- Instructional accommodations are support provided to help students gain full access to class content and instruction, and to demonstrate accurately what they know. Instructional or curricular modifications are made when the content expectations are altered and the performance outcomes expected of students change.

- The INCLUDE strategy is a decision-making process to help teachers make accommodations and modifications for stu-

dents with special needs. The steps in INCLUDE are identify classroom demands; note student learning strengths and needs; check for potential areas of student success; look for potential problem areas; use information to brainstorm ways to differentiate instruction; differentiate instruction; and evaluate student progress.

- An important part of the INCLUDE strategy is analyzing classroom demands. Demands covering four major areas should be analyzed: classroom management, classroom grouping, instructional materials, and instructional methods.

- Classroom organization includes physical organization, classroom routines, classroom climate, behavior management (including classroom rules, consequences, and monitoring), and use of time.

- Key aspects of classroom grouping involve the use of whole-class and small instructional groups, same-skill and mixed-skill groups, and one-to-one instruction.

- Instructional materials that need to be evaluated are basal textbooks, content-area textbooks, manipulatives and models, and instructional and assistive technology.

- Instructional methods should be analyzed in terms of student needs. Common methods to consider are direct and indirect instruction, independent student practice, and student evaluation. Sometimes students with disabilities or other special needs require extra support in order to be successful. These supports are called scaffolds.

APPLICATIONS IN TEACHING PRACTICE

PLANNING ACCOMMODATIONS IN THE INSTRUCTIONAL ENVIRONMENT

Consider the following two scenarios:

- Verna is a student with a learning disability in Ms. Chang's fourth-grade class. Ms. Chang uses whole-group instruction in math. This method is sometimes hard for Verna, who is behind her peers in math. Verna is slow to remember math facts, has trouble keeping numbers straight in columns, and sometimes forgets a step or two when she is computing a problem that requires several steps.

- Mr. Howard teaches U.S. history. About half of his fourth-hour class struggle in reading; four students receive special education services for learning disabilities. Mr. Howard has been assigned a special education teacher, Ms. Riley, to co-teach the class with him. Mr. Howard and Ms. Riley think the class can benefit from learning the following textbook-reading strategy (Bartelt, Marchio, & Reynolds, 1994):

R   *Review* headings and subheadings.

E   *Examine* boldface words.

A   *Ask* "What do I expect to learn?"

D   *Do* it: Read!

S   *Summarize* in your own words.

QUESTIONS

1. Identify the demands in Ms. Chang's class that are likely to be challenging for Verna.

2. How can Ms. Chang use the remaining steps in the INCLUDE strategy to help Verna succeed in the large group?

3. How can Ms. Chang use direct instruction to teach students to round numbers to the nearest 10? Design such a lesson.

4. How can Mr. Howard and Ms. Riley use the approaches for co-teaching you learned about in Chapter 3 to teach the reading strategy and still cover the history content required by the state?

5. How can they use scaffolding to teach the READS strategy?

6. Find a drill-and-practice computer program for elementary or high school students and evaluate it. Does it meet the criteria discussed in this chapter?

PEARSON
myeducationlab

Go to Topic 10: Instructional Practices and Learning Strategies in the MyEducationLab (http://www.myeducationlab.com) for your course, where you can:

- Find learning outcomes for Instructional Practices and Learning Strategies along with the national standards that connect to these outcomes.

- Complete Assignments and Activities that can help you more deeply understand the chapter content.

- Apply and practice your understanding of the core teaching skills identified in the chapter with the Building Teaching Skills and Dispositions learning units.

- Examine challenging situations and cases presented in the IRIS Center Resources. (optional)

- Access video clips of CCSSO National Teachers of the Year award winners responding to the question, "Why Do I Teach?" in the Teacher Talk section. (optional)

- Check your comprehension on the content covered in the chapter by going to the Study Plan in the Book Resources for your text. Here you will be able to take a chapter quiz, receive feedback on your answers, and then access Review, Practice, and Enrichment activities to enhance your understanding of chapter content. (optional)

chapter

6

Students with Low-Incidence Disabilities

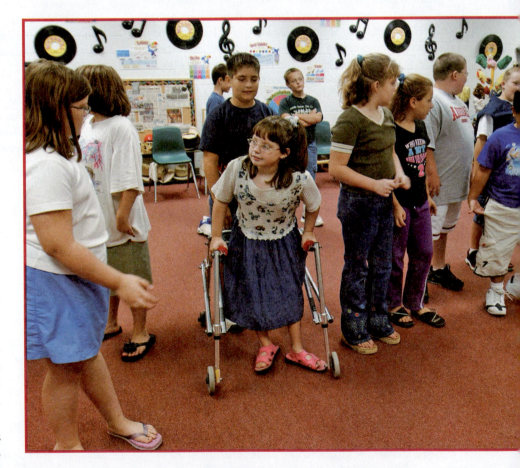

LEARNING Objectives

After you read this chapter, you will be able to

1. Describe what it means to say that a student has a low-incidence disability, and apply the INCLUDE strategy to effectively instruct these students in your classroom.

2. Outline the characteristics of students with autism spectrum disorders and the accommodations general educators can make for them.

3. Describe the characteristics of students with moderate, severe, and multiple disabilities, including intellectual disabilities and deaf-blindness and the accommodations general educators can make for them.

4. Explain the characteristics of students with sensory impairments (that is, vision or hearing loss) and the accommodations general educators can make for them.

5. Explain the characteristics of students with physical, medical, and health impairments and the accommodations general educators can make for them.

6. Critically analyze your own beliefs about and skills for implementing inclusive practices for students with low-incidence disabilities.

KYLIE is a first-grade student with a moderate intellectual disability. She is described by her teachers and her mother as a "bundle of energy," and she is enthusiastic about school and all the activities that occur in her classroom. Although Kylie is just learning to recognize colors and identify shapes and is a prereader, she receives nearly all her instruction in the first-grade classroom. Because Ms. Wilson often uses cutouts, puppets, and other concrete strategies to illustrate the literature being read, Kylie follows along without much difficulty. When other students work on writing or editing, Kylie works with a computer program, either practicing shapes and colors or learning to recognize her name.

What are the learning characteristics and needs of students like Kylie? What are appropriate expectations for Kylie's teacher to have for her this year? What accommodations does Kylie need to succeed in first grade? If Ms. Wilson has a question about Kylie, how can she find an answer?

SEAN is a twelfth-grade student identified as having Asperger syndrome, a type of autism spectrum disorder (ASD). Although he spent much of the day in a special education classroom when he was in elementary school, he now receives all his core academic instruction in general education classes. His special education teacher, Ms. Morrow, is working with him one period a day to ensure that he understands assignments, completes the school's learning and study skills curriculum, and prepares to attend community college next year. Sean generally has done very well in high school. One of his greatest supports has been his friend Jonas, who explains when Sean does not understand a classmate's joke and inconspicuously guides Sean when he seems unsure of himself in social situations. As Sean looks forward to college, he is not worried about the academic requirements; he is a very bright young man who grasps most concepts easily. His greatest concerns are dealing with large classes, being surrounded by strangers who may not understand his special needs, and advocating for himself by going to the Office of Disability Services.

What are autism spectrum disorders? What should Sean's teachers do to help him learn? What accommodations might Sean need now, in high school, and later in the community college?

More than anything, **CYNTHIA** wishes she could be like everyone else. Now in seventh grade, Cynthia has missed nearly two years of school because of illness. She was diagnosed as a toddler with a rare disorder that makes her highly susceptible to catching diseases such as those common in children. Her disorder also makes her tire very easily, and her health is further compromised by her severe asthma. When she becomes ill, she often needs to be hospitalized, and her pediatrician ordered that she be educated at home for nearly her entire sixth-grade school year. Cynthia really liked the teacher who brought her books and assignments from her middle school, but what she really wanted was to be at school. This year, she feels like she is not accepted because she missed making friends with the other students last year. Cynthia wants to be a pediatrician when she grows up, but for now she is struggling to keep up with middle school academic expectations. She is very capable, but there are many gaps in her learning because of her necessary absences.

What are the responsibilities of general education teachers for students who have chronic and serious illnesses that cause them to miss school? How could teachers help students be part of their class groups when they cannot attend school? How could teachers help Cynthia catch up on learning, given all the school she has missed?

PEARSON
myeducationlab

To check your comprehension on the content covered in chapter 6, go to the Book Resources in the My EducationLab for your course, select your text, and complete the Study Plan. Here you will be able to take a chapter quiz, receive feedback on your answers, and then access review, practice, and enrichment activities to enhance your understanding of chapter content.

Students like Kylie, Sean, and Cynthia have the same right as other students to be part of a classroom community with nondisabled peers. For Kylie, attending first grade with her classmates prepares her for the demands of school and also creates the expectation that she can be a valued and contributing member of her community during and after her school years. For Sean, being successful in college depends on receiving the strong academic background available in general education classes. For Cynthia, the issue is not her ability to learn but rather the opportunity to meet academic expectations while dealing with chronic and serious health problems. To be successful, though, all these students may need specialized instruction, equipment, and other assistance.

In this chapter, you will learn about the characteristics and needs of students with **low-incidence disabilities,** which include autism; moderate, severe, and multiple disabilities; sensory impairments; and physical, medical, and health disabilities. The federal terms for these disabilities and the number of students with these disabilities served through the Individuals with Disabilities Education Act (IDEA) are summarized in Table 6.1. You also will explore accommodations specific to the unique needs of these students that general education teachers and other professionals can make to enable them to learn.

TABLE 6.1 **School-Age Students with Low-Incidence Disabilities Receiving Special Education Services in 2004–2005[a]**

Federal Disability Category	Defining Characteristics	Total Number of Students	Percentage of All Students Receiving IDEA Services	Percentage of All Students Ages 6–21
Mental retardation	• Significant below-average general intellectual functioning with deficits in adaptive behavior • Identified between birth and 18 years of age • Adversely affects educational performance	555,524	9.21[b]	.84
Multiple disabilities	• Two or more disabilities so interwoven that none can be identified as the primary disability • Adversely affect educational performance	132,033	2.19	.20
Hearing impairments	• Hearing loss is permanent or fluctuating, mild to profound in nature, in one or both ears • Loss may be referred to as *hard of hearing* or *deaf* • Adversely affect educational performance	71,712	1.19	.11
Orthopedic impairments	• Physically disabling conditions that affect locomotion or motor functions • May be the result of a congenital anomaly, disease, accident, or other cause • Adversely affect educational performance	69,910	1.08	.10
Other health impairments	• Conditions resulting in limited strength, vitality, or alertness and caused by chronic or acute health problems • Adversely affect educational performance	508,085	8.42	.77
Visual impairments	• Vision loss in which the student cannot successfully use vision as a primary channel for learning or has such reduced acuity or visual field that processing	25,504	.42	.04

TABLE 6.1 (*Continued*)

Federal Disability Category	Defining Characteristics	Total Number of Students	Percentage of All Students Receiving IDEA Services	Percentage of All Students Ages 6–21
	information visually is significantly inhibited and specialized materials or modifications are needed • Adversely affect educational performance			
Autism	• Developmental disability characterized by impairments in communication, learning, and reciprocal social interactions • Usually identified in infancy or early childhood • Adversely affects educational performance	165,552	2.74	.25
Deaf-blindness	• Presence of both a vision loss and hearing disability that causes severe communication and related problems • Adversely affects educational performance	1,659	0.00	.00
Traumatic brain injury	• Impairment manifested by limited strength, vitality, alertness, or other impaired development resulting from a traumatic brain injury • Adversely affects educational performance	23,189	.38	.04
Developmental delay	• Significant delay in one or more of these areas: Physical development, cognitive development, communication development, social or emotional development, or adaptive development • Needs special education and related services • Applicable for children ages 3–9	74,255	1.23	.11

[a]Students ages 6–21 receiving services through IDEA, Part B (U.S. Department of Education, 2009). Note that the disability category development delay does not distinguish among children with mild versus significant disabilities; not all children in this category may have low-incidence disabilities.

[b]Because federal categories of disability do not distinguish among students with various degrees of mental retardation, it is difficult to provide a precise estimate of the number of students with moderate or severe intellectual disabilities. However, approximately one-third of the students in this category have moderate or severe intellectual disabilities.

Source: From *Twenty-Eighth Annual Report to Congress on the Implementation of the Individuals with Disabilities Education Act* (2009). Washington, DC: Author.

What Are Low-Incidence Disabilities?

When you work with students with low-incidence disabilities, you will notice immediately the diversity of their abilities and needs, the range of educational services they access, and the variety of specialists who ensure they receive an appropriate education. The following points can help you keep in perspective these students' uniqueness and your role in their education:

1. Students with low-incidence disabilities together make up less than 20 percent of all the students with disabilities in schools. That means that you are unlikely to teach these students every year unless your school has a program that brings together students with such disabilities from across your school district, sometimes referred to as a *cluster program* or *district class*. Otherwise, you may encounter students with low-incidence disabilities only a few times in your career.

fyi

According to IDEA, children ages 3 through 9 may be identified as having a **developmental delay,** a label indicating the presence of a significant physical, intellectual, communication, or social or emotional delay without naming a specific disability category.

2. Students with low-incidence disabilities often have received some type of special education service since birth or shortly thereafter. They might come to kindergarten already having attended an infant program and preschool program in a daycare, inclusive preschool, or special education setting where their special needs were addressed. You also may find that many supports and extensive technical assistance are available for your students with low-incidence disabilities.

3. Students with low-incidence disabilities need the same type of attention from you that other students do. If you are unsure about a student's needs, it is nearly always best to rely on the same professional judgment you use in working with other students. If you encounter difficulty, you can access the technical support that special education professionals offer. Students with certain disabilities, especially significant or complex ones, often are accompanied by paraprofessionals or personal assistants, who might work with them for several years. Such an individual may be able to offer insight about responding to a given student, but the responsibility for ensuring the student's educational success is yours.

You may have some concerns about meeting the needs of a student with a low-incidence disability in your classroom. The Professional Edge suggests questions you can ask to prepare for teaching a student with a low-incidence disability. The questions address the student's strengths and potential, learning and social needs, and physical or health needs. They also cover domains in which accommodations might be needed, including the physical arrangement of the classroom. What other questions would you add?

PROFESSIONAL EDGE

Questions to Ask When Working with Students with Low-Incidence Disabilities

When you teach a student with a low-incidence disability, you probably will have concerns about the student's needs and your responsibilities for helping her succeed. In your conversations with special educators, related services personnel, and administrators, you might ask questions such as these:

STUDENT STRENGTHS AND NEEDS

1. What are the student's greatest strengths?
2. What activities and rewards does the student most enjoy?
3. What are the student's needs in these domains: academic? social? emotional? behavioral? other?
4. Does the student have physical or health needs that require my attention? For example, does the student need to take medication? Is the student likely to have a reaction to medication? Does the student tire easily? Does the student need assistance in moving from place to place?
5. What else should I know about this student's strengths and needs?

STUDENT GOALS

1. What are the three or four most important instructional goals for this student in my class? What are the academic, social, behavioral, emotional, and other goals?
2. What are the goals for this student in each subject (for elementary teachers)? How do the goals for this student interface with the instructional goals of this course (for secondary teachers)? Overall, how do the goals for this student align with the general curriculum?

3. What are the goals that this student is working on throughout the day? Which goals are emphasized during different periods of the day?

STUDENT SUPPORTS AND ACCOMMODATIONS

1. If I have a question about the student, whom should I talk to? What other professionals may be in contact with me about this student or come to my classroom?
2. Does the student have a paraprofessional or interpreter? If a paraprofessional is assigned, what responsibilities should that person carry out? For what activities should the student, not the paraprofessional, be responsible? To what extent can the paraprofessional help other students in the class?
3. What other services (for example, speech/language services) will the student access? How often? Who will be in touch to help arrange these services? Will they be delivered in the classroom or in another location?
4. Do I need to adjust the physical environment for this student? If so, how?
5. Do I need to adjust my expectations for this student because of physical or health needs? If so, how? Are there restrictions on this student's participation in any class activities? If so, what?
6. How can I best adjust my teaching to accommodate the student's needs?

What Accommodations Can You Make for Students with Autism Spectrum Disorders?

www.resources

The website of the Autism Society of America, at http://www.autism-society.org/site/PageServer, provides a variety of information about ASD and links to resources helpful for teachers.

Autism was first identified as a disorder in 1943 by Dr. Leo Kanner. Since then, it has been the source of much research and ongoing professional debate about its causes and characteristics. Professionals now recognize that autism is a unique disorder that occurs in many forms, and they usually refer to this group of disabilities as **autism spectrum disorders (ASD)** to convey its diverse nature. The prevalence of autism spectrum disorders has been rising steadily over the past decade, partly due to better diagnosis (Fighting Autism, 2010; National Institute of Mental Health, 2007). ASD is believed to occur in some form, on average, in 1 in 110 children (Centers for Disease Control and Prevention, 2010) and soon may be considered a high-incidence disability. This disability affects boys more than girls in a ratio of approximately 3:1 to 4:1, and in approximately half the cases it is accompanied by an intellectual or other disability. Thus, many individuals with autism spectrum disorders are of average ability and some are gifted or talented (Adcock & Cuvo, 2009).

Characteristics of Students with Autism Spectrum Disorders

Although autism is like most of the other low-incidence disabilities in that it can exist in many variations, from mild to severe, and cannot be treated as a single disorder with a single set of adaptations, it does have specific characteristics.

Social Relationships   Significant difficulty with social relationships is a defining characteristic of individuals with autism. Many students with autism resist human contact and social interactions from a very early age and have difficulty learning the subtleties of social interaction (Denning, 2007; Wang & Spillane, 2009). These students often do not make eye contact with others, and they can seem uninterested in developing social relationships. For example, typical young children often ask the teacher to watch them do something ("Look at me!"), and they bring interesting items to share with their teacher and classmates. A young child with autism, however, may not seek out such opportunities for social interactions. Arturo, a 15-year-old with autism, was frustrated that he had no friends. However, in his conversations with peers he was observed to repeatedly list all the species of birds found in his geographic area and to never ask others about their interests. Because he could not take on the perspectives of others, he was socially isolated.

Communication   A key reason students with autism spectrum disorders experience difficulty in social relationships is the challenges they face in using and responding to traditional verbal and non-verbal communication (for example, Frea, 2010; Murray, Ruble, & Willis, 2009). These students often have significantly delayed language development, and if they have language skills, they struggle to maintain conversation with another person. In writing about her experiences of being autistic, Temple Grandin, one of the most famous individuals with ASD and a university professor who has designed livestock facilities, provides clear examples of her communication problems (Grandin, 2002). She explains that when she was young she simply did not have the words to communicate and so frequently resorted to screaming. She also comments that as she grew up, she observed others but did not understand how to fit in.

General educators can make a huge difference in the lives of students with autism when they help them learn social skills for interacting with their peers and other adults.

Unlike Grandin, many students with autism spectrum disorders cannot write or otherwise easily communicate about their experiences, and they may use behaviors instead of words to convey many needs. Unless they are taught alternative behaviors, they might hit a peer as a way of saying hello or run from the classroom instead of saying they do not like the assignment just given. Some students with autism have *echolalic speech;* they repeat what others have said instead of producing original communication. Working to ensure productive communication is a central part of working with students with ASD.

Student Interests   Another characteristic of students with autism is a narrow range of interests. For example, one student may be fascinated with radios to the exclusion of nearly everything else; another might focus on a single period in history and have an expert's understanding of that era. When students with autism have such interests, they can spend countless hours absorbed in a private world of exploration. They might act bored with every topic and every activity unless it relates to their special interest. This behavior sometimes has a negative impact on social relationships with peers and adults, because individuals with ASD may not discern that others are not as interested in their preferred topic as they are, a point illustrated in the example of Arturo earlier in this section. However, researchers now are exploring how students' focused interests can be used as a tool for fostering the development of social and communication skills (Winter-Messiers et al., 2007).

Student Stress   Students with autism have a low threshold for and difficulty in dealing with stress (Carnahan, Hume, & Clarke, 2009; Myles & Adreon, 2001). A change in classroom seating assignments could be difficult for a student with autism, as could the introduction of a new route from the classroom to the bus or the need to persist on a task with several steps. Particular noises or odors or a noisy environment also can be stressful. Many students with autism respond to stress with stereotypic behaviors. They complete the same action or motion again and again. For example, they may rock rapidly in the chair, spin an object repeatedly, or twirl their arms. In other situations, students might develop a ritual to complete a task. They might need 10 minutes to prepare to complete an assignment because they need to arrange paper and pencil on the desk in a precise pattern, check that all the books in the desk are also stored in a specific order, and make sure the desk is aligned precisely at the intersection of tiles on the classroom floor. In your classroom, you should be aware of potentially stressful situations for a student with autism. You can allow time for the student to prepare for the situation, talk about the situation well in advance, assign a peer partner to assist the student, and enlist the assistance of a special educator or paraprofessional. If a student's response to stress is demonstrated with aggressive or disruptive behavior, you should work closely with a special educator, behavior consultant, or other specialist to address the problem.

Students with Asperger Syndrome

One group of students with autism spectrum disorders that should be highlighted comprises those with Asperger syndrome (Ivey & Ward, 2010). Students with **Asperger syndrome** have extraordinary difficulty in social interactions, such as making eye contact, using facial expressions appropriately and understanding those of others, and seeking out peers and other people, even though their language and intellectual development are typical (Laushey, Hefflin, Shippen, Alberto, & Fredrick, 2009). They also may have difficulty in using language correctly, confusing whether to use first-person (*I*), second-person (*you*), or third-person (*she* or *he*) pronouns. These students also may insist on specific routines in the classroom and at home, and as noted earlier, they may have extraordinary interest in a specific topic (for example, models of aircraft, countries in Asia) and fail to realize that others may not share their focused enthusiasm. Many students with Asperger syndrome have very high intellectual ability, and they appropriately spend the school day with peers in

RESEARCH NOTE

In 2010, *The Lancet*, the prestigious medical journal that published in 1998 the study that led many parents and professionals to believe that the measles-mumps-rubella (MMR) vaccine causes autism, retracted the study. Its author was found to have acted unethically.

general education classrooms and continue on to college (Adreon & Durocher, 2007; Chen, Planche, & Lemonnier, 2010). However, because of their difficulty with social interaction, they may struggle to make friends. Sean, the student you met at the beginning of this chapter, has Asperger syndrome.

Accommodations for Students with Autism Spectrum Disorders

Although it is impossible to provide a comprehensive list of strategies for helping students with ASD to succeed in your classroom, the following suggestions illustrate how your efforts can make a significant difference in these students' lives.

Responding to Behavior   Students with autism spectrum disorders often have behaviors that are unusual and can be disturbing to teachers and students who do not understand them. These behaviors also can interfere with learning. However, many of the behaviors can be corrected with highly structured behavior support programs. Others have relatively simple solutions, and some can be ignored. For example, if a student with autism withdraws from classroom activities and begins rocking every day at about 11:00 AM, it could be a signal that he is too hungry to work until an 11:45 AM lunchtime. Providing a snack in a quiet corner of the classroom could reduce the problem. Many students with autism spectrum disorders can receive some or all of their education in a general education classroom, provided that needed supports are in place (Lytle & Todd, 2009; Myles, 2005).

Generally, the accommodations that help to reduce behavior problems involve creating a structured and predictable environment, which will reduce student stress and encourage appropriate social interactions (for example, Banda, Grimmit, & Hart, 2009; Kluth, 2003). To create a positive learning environment, establish clear procedures and routines for classroom tasks and follow them consistently. For example, in an elementary classroom, you can create procedures for students to retrieve their coats at lunchtime or begin each day with the same activities in the same order. For secondary students, you can set a clear pattern in your instruction by beginning each class with a 3-minute review followed by a 20-minute lecture followed by a 15-minute individual or small-group work session. Instead of relying on words to prompt students about these procedures, work with a special educator to create picture cards that depict the procedures. Students with ASD often respond better to pictures than words. Several specific strategies for working with students with autism spectrum disorders are summarized in the Instructional Edge.

In addition to structure, students with ASD may need opportunities during the day to work alone and be alone (Myles & Adreon, 2001). This time serves as a break from the stresses of the classroom and the social and communication demands of that setting. A special education teacher probably can advise you about whether this is necessary for a particular student and can assist in making arrangements for a quiet place, sometimes referred to as *home base,* for the student to work.

Fostering Social Interactions   To help a student with social interactions with peers and adults, you can observe the student's behavior to understand its purpose from her perspective (Denning, 2007). If a student has been working in a small group but suddenly leaves the group and runs out the door, it could be a signal that she has misunderstood a comment made by another student. Other social areas in which general education teachers can work with special educators to accommodate students with autism spectrum disorders include teaching them to wait, to take turns, to stop an activity before it is complete, to negotiate, to change topics, to finish an activity, to be more flexible, to be quiet, and to monitor their own behavior.

Communicating with Students   Communication with students with autism is accomplished through a wide variety of strategies (Grandin, 2007; Toth et al., 2006). Some students with autism can communicate adequately with speech, especially when they do not feel pressured. Other students learn to communicate through sign

fyi

Discrete trial training (DTT) is a highly structured approach to working with young students with autism. Based on applied behavior analysis (ABA), this one-to-one teaching approach presents information in very small amounts. The approach is intensive, often implemented for 30 to 40 hours per week. This is not an approach you as a teacher would use in the classroom, but the students with autism you teach may have learned many skills using it.

INSTRUCTIONAL EDGE

Teaching Students with Autism Spectrum Disorders

Specialized techniques can be used to teach students with autism spectrum disorders (ASD). These approaches are designed to draw on students' strengths, focus their attention, and address their unique needs. Three examples of approaches demonstrated to be effective with these students are social stories, the picture exchange communication system (PECS), and visual schedules.

SOCIAL STORIES

Students with ASD often experience difficulty understanding social expectations, especially when those expectations vary across situations. An example situation concerns when it is OK to run at school. This social story might assist a student with autism:

Running

I like to run. It is fun to go fast.
It's OK to run when I am playing outside.
I can run when I am on the playground.
I can run during P.E.
It is not OK to run when I am inside, especially at school.
Running in the hallways is not safe.
Teachers worry that someone may get hurt if I run into them.
When people are inside, they walk.
I will try to walk in the hallways and run only when
I am outside on the playground.

After preparing this type of story, the teacher reads it several times with the student, preferably just before the situation in which running is an issue. As the student learns to follow the advice in the story, the teacher gradually reduces repetition of the story until it is no longer needed. Social stories can be used in many situations. Try writing a social story for each of these situations:

- a high school student who is using profanity when speaking with adults at school

FIGURE 6.1 PECS Uses Pictures of Objects, Similar to Those Depicted, to Foster Communication

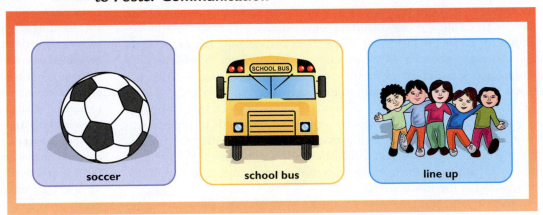

soccer   school bus   line up

language, just as many students who are deaf or hard of hearing do. For these students, the motor activity of signing seems to help them successfully convey their needs and preferences. For yet other students, communication boards are useful tools. By simply touching pictures, students can communicate with others even when they cannot speak the appropriate words. When communication involves following directions or mastering certain skills, video modeling, as explained in the Technology Notes on page 176, can be helpful. Yet other communication devices that help students who have limited speech, including those with autism, are described later in this chapter.

In general, when you learn that you will teach a student with autism, you should ask to meet with a special educator who can share with you the student's strengths and needs and help you plan for the school year. Few single descriptors are adequate to describe these students, and their diversity and complexity will sometimes frustrate you and at other times make you proud to be a professional educator.

FIGURE 6.2 Examples of Visual Schedules

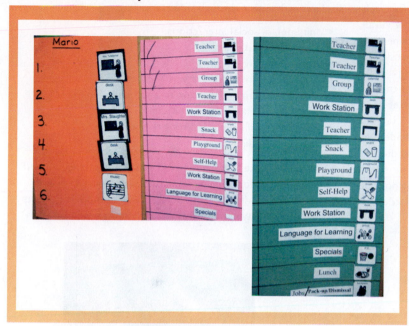

- a middle school student who talks only about one topic
- an elementary student who takes her shoes off when in the cafeteria

PICTURE EXCHANGE COMMUNICATION SYSTEM

The picture exchange communication system (PECS) is a strategy for teaching individuals with ASD to initiate communication with peers and others. PECS is taught to students in a highly structured series of steps. Initially, the teacher or another person working with the student exchanges a picture of a desired item (for example, a crayon, a basketball) for the actual item when the student points to it or picks it up (see Figure 6.1). No words are used.

As students learn the system, they begin to initiate communication by bringing a picture to another individual to obtain the pictured item or make a need known. Eventually, students use this system to form sentences and answer questions. Research has demonstrated the effectiveness of this system (Yoder & Lieberman, 2010). If you teach students with autism, you might interact with them using PECS.

VISUAL SCHEDULES

Most students with ASD benefit when they have a clear and consistent schedule that is explained ahead of time. Working with a special educator, you can develop visual schedules that use pictures only, pictures and words, or words only (see Figure 6.2). Visual schedules can be displayed in the classroom, placed on the student's desk, or kept in an assignment notebook.

Sources: From *Social Stories*, by the Center for Autism and Related Disabilities, University of Florida, n.d., retrieved November 23, 2004, from http://card .ufl.edu/handouts/socialstories.html; *Visual Schedule Systems*, by L. Kamp and T. McElean, 2000, Vancouver, BC: Special Education Technology—British Columbia, retrieved November 23, 2004, and from http://www.setbc.org/ projects/vss/default.html; *Beyond Autism PECS Pictures/Icon Pages* (p. 15), n.d., retrieved November 23, 2004, from the Beyond Autism website, http://trainland.tripod.com/pecs15.htm.

What Accommodations Can You Make for Students with Moderate, Severe, or Multiple Disabilities?

Students with moderate, severe, or multiple disabilities include those whose intellectual impairments and adaptive behavior deficits are so significant and pervasive that considerable support is needed for them to learn. This group also includes students with multiple disabilities, that is, students who have two or more disabilities that significantly affect their learning. Both groups of students typically have activities and assignments that differ somewhat from those of other students in your class, but their work still should be aligned with the general curriculum for which you are responsible. These students also can benefit from social interactions with classmates who do not have disabilities.

Teaching Skills to Students with Autism Through Video Modeling

Because students with autism often respond better to pictures and other nonverbal signals than to words, one option for teaching them a wide variety of skills is *video modeling* (Gul & Vuran, 2010). In video modeling, professionals either use a commercially available video or prepare a video that demonstrates the skill for the student. In the latter option, the individual modeling the skill could be a teacher or another professional familiar to the student, a peer, a sibling, or even the student (if the student occasionally is successful in completing the targeted skill). The video may be in a standard format, much like an instructional video you might watch. Some videos, though, are done "over the shoulder," so that it looks the way it would if the student was performing it (for example, facing someone tying shoes versus looking down as though tying your own shoes). The student watches the video, often on a PDA or similar device, in order to learn the skill.

These are examples of behaviors that have been taught to students with autism through video modeling:

- Initiation of social interactions
- Conversational skills
- Reciprocal play
- Transition from one activity to another
- Transition from one location to another within the school
- Life skills such as making a purchase
- Functional skills such as setting the table
- Perspective taking

Would you like to learn more? If you visit youtube.com and search for "video modeling," you will find examples of an over-the-shoulder video model for tying shoes, as well as modeling videos for taking turns, playing games, and participating in conversation.

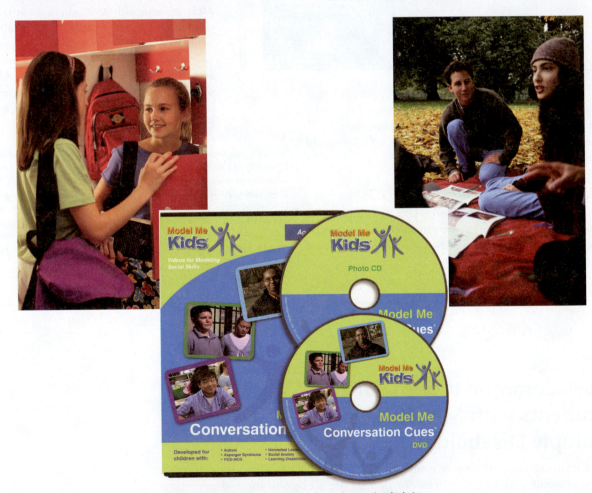

Video modeling is an evidence-based practice helping many students with autism to learn important skills.

Characteristics of Students with Moderate to Severe Intellectual Disabilities

Students with moderate to severe intellectual disabilities have ongoing needs for support during their school years and into adult life. Some students are able to learn academic, social, and vocational skills that enable them to live independently or semi-independently as productive adults. Others' learning will be more limited, and they may need intensive services throughout their lives. In many school districts, students with moderate or severe disabilities are integrated for at least a small part of the day into general education classrooms, most often at the elementary school level but sometimes at the middle school and high school levels as well, sometimes for related arts such as art, music, or physical education and less often for core academic subjects.

Most states use scores on intelligence tests and adaptive behavior scales to determine the presence of an intellectual disability. Although intelligence tests must be interpreted carefully and are not helpful in designing instruction for students, an overall IQ score of less than 70 with significant difficulty in the area of adaptive behaviors (for example, ordering a meal in a restaurant) leads to eligibility for special education in the category of mental retardation. Students with moderate or severe intellectual disabilities generally have IQ scores of approximately 55 or below. Kylie, whom you learned about at the beginning of the chapter, is a student with a moderate intellectual disability. As you read the following sections, think about how she might learn in your classroom.

Learning Needs and Rate   Generally, students with moderate or severe intellectual disabilities have several noticeable characteristics. First, the amount of information they can learn may be limited, and second, the rate at which they learn may be slow. For example, Destiny, a middle school student with a severe intellectual disability, is learning to communicate her needs to others. She has a communication device that enables her to indicate that she needs a drink of water, that she needs to use the bathroom, and that she is hungry. Her paraprofessional sometimes works with her on this skill, but her classmates also ask her questions related to these needs. Jordan, an elementary student with a moderate intellectual disability, is learning how to tell a story from a picture book and recognize his name and address. He practices these skills as opportunities arise during general instruction and when other students are completing individual assignments that are beyond his capability.

Students with moderate or severe intellectual disabilities usually also need to learn many other essential skills that go beyond academics. One example is social skills. Several IEP goals and objectives may relate to participating in one-to-one or small-group interactions with peers; responding to questions asked by others; and sharing toys, games, or materials. Without direct assistance from teachers implementing inclusive practices, these students may have difficulty making friends throughout their school careers (Doré, Dion, Wagner, & Brunet, 2002; Solish, Perry, & Minnes, 2010).

Maintenance of Learned Skills   A second characteristic of individuals with moderate or severe intellectual disabilities is that they may have difficulty maintaining their skills; without ongoing practice, they are likely to forget what they have learned. In the classroom, you may find this means that it is not necessary to provide new activities each day. For example, Jordan, the student mentioned previously who is learning to recognize his name and address, will need computer practice on that skill for many days. In addition, once he has identified the information, he should practice printing it on cards, writing it on the chalkboard, and saying it aloud.

dimensions of DIVERSITY
Kim, Lee, and Morningstar (2007) interviewed 10 Korean-American parents of children with severe disabilities. They relied heavily on their community networks, and they noted that teachers of their children needed "special hearts."

For students with intellectual disabilities, the goal of education is similar to that for other students: to learn essential skills and to be prepared for a rich and rewarding adult life.

Generalization of Learning   A third characteristic of students in this group is that they may have difficulty generalizing skills learned in one setting or situation to another. It is thus critical that they learn as many skills as possible in context. For example, rather than have these students practice buttoning and unbuttoning out of context, as part of a segregated classroom exercise, they can apply this skill in the morning and afternoon as they enter and leave school wearing coats or sweaters. Older students need to learn how to greet classmates and teachers appropriately, for example, with a handshake or by just saying hello instead of shouting or tightly hugging them. This skill is most easily taught as students meet and greet people throughout the school, not in a special education classroom.

Crystal is a young woman with **Down syndrome,** a genetic disorder that often includes a moderate intellectual disability. Her story is typical for such a student in a school district committed to inclusive education. She attended elementary school with her peers even though she did not always learn the same things they were learning. Her teachers expected her to behave appropriately, and her peers helped her when she got confused by the teacher's directions or otherwise needed support in the classroom. As Crystal moved to middle school, she participated with peers in co-taught science and social studies classes and exploratory classes such as nutrition and computers, and she received some of her reading and math instruction in a special education classroom. In high school, she took several classes, including choir, U.S. history, home economics, career exploration, and family living. She also entered a vocational preparation program so she would be ready to get a job after high school. At 21, Crystal graduated from high school. She now works in a local medical office. Her job includes duplicating medical records, doing simple filing, completing errands, and helping get mail ready to send. Crystal's success as an adult is in large part a result of learning many skills while in inclusive schools.

Accommodations for Students with Moderate to Severe Intellectual Disabilities

Are you a bit surprised at the implication in this chapter that students with significant intellectual disabilities should participate in general education? Had you assumed that they would receive specialized instruction in a special education classroom? Unfortunately, the latter perception is still common (Bentley, 2008), but research indicates that students with moderate or severe intellectual disabilities benefit from attending school as members of general education classrooms (for example, Browder, Wakeman, Spooner, Ahlgrin-Delzell, & Algozzine, 2006).

INCLUDE

Match Expectations to Instruction   Although students with significant disabilities are not expected to learn all the same information as other students, the goals and objectives on their IEPs should be related to the grade-level or course competencies. In this regard, the INCLUDE strategy and collaborating with colleagues can help you effectively teach students with moderate or severe intellectual disabilities. For example, in a social studies class, the goal for most students might be to understand detailed topographical maps. At the same time, a student with a moderate intellectual disability might work to locate on a map states where relatives live, and a student with a severe intellectual disability might work to identify photos of businesses in the community. Table 6.2 provides additional examples of how the skills that might appear on a student's IEP can be mapped onto the general curriculum.

Students with multiple disabilities often have medical, intellectual, social, and behavioral needs, and several professionals, including a special educator, a speech-language therapist, and a physical therapist, may come to your classroom to support them.

TABLE 6.2 Sample Skills from an IEP Mapped onto Fifth-Grade School Subjects

IEP Objectives	Activities/Subjects				
	Social Studies	Math	Reading	Physical Education	Lunch
To recognize pictures for expressive communication purposes	Use daily schedule to get out book Match pictures related to social studies	Determine story problem for peers by matching same pictures	Answer questions by pointing to pictures Sequence three pictures in order to retell story	Choose equipment using photographs Choose partner using school photographs	Use pictures to request type of milk from cafeteria person Point to pictures to converse with peers
To follow directions quickly	Watch peers get out materials and follow their lead Sequence pictorial cards in order Put away materials and get ready for next subject	Watch peers get out materials and follow their lead Work on math skills as instructed Change activity when directed	Watch peers get out materials and follow their lead Find appropriate page in book Answer questions by pointing Put away materials and get ready for next subject	Line up for PE Move to area on floor by PE teacher Follow teacher and group	Line up for lunch with class Go to lunch room Stay at table until dismissed
To interact with peers in a positive way	Sit with classmates Do not destroy peers' work Pass out materials	Sit with classmates Do not destroy peers' work Pass out materials Respond to three offers of help	Sit with classmates Choose book to read from Respond to peers' questions	Respond to peers when they initiate Share equipment Clap for peers when they do well	Respond to peers when they initiate Initiate topics using schedule and magazine Respond to peers' questions
To make decisions	Decide who will read to her Request help when needed Pick appropriate pictures from three pictures based on question	Decide which math activities to do Decide which manipulatives to use: first, second, third	Choose book to read Choose peer to read with Choose place to read	Decide which two of three exercises to do and in what order	Choose milk Choose person to sit next to Choose where to go when finished eating and with whom
To work independently	Stay on task without adult nearby for 10 minutes Raise hand to get help	Stay on task without adult nearby for 10 minutes Raise hand to get help	Stay on task without adult nearby for 10 minutes Raise hand to get help	Stay on task without adult nearby for 10 minutes Start each exercise/activity on own Raise hand to get help	Stay on task without adult nearby for 10 minutes Obtain milk with peer support Eat meal with no prompts

Source: Adapted from "First Steps: Determining Individual Abilities and How Best to Support Students" (pp. 46–47), by J. E. Downing, 2008, in *Including Students with Severe and Multiple Disabilities in Typical Classrooms: Practical Strategies for Teachers* (3rd ed.), Baltimore: Paul H. Brookes Publishing Co. Reprinted with permission.

Working TOGETHER

Collaborating to Support Students with Significant Disabilities

Collaboration is essential for students with low-incidence disabilities to have opportunities to participate in general education settings. One approach that has been useful for students, parents, and school professionals is called the McGill Action Planning System (MAPS). Developed in Canada by experts in inclusive practices for students with significant disabilities, MAPS is based on a set of questions focusing on strengths that parents, other family members, professionals, students, and peers answer in one or more meetings intended to ensure that a student has positive learning experiences. Here are the questions that guide this process:

- *What is this student's history?* This question is answered by family members so that others have a better understanding of the student.
- *What is your dream for the child?* As participants answer this question, they think about what they want for the student and what they think the student wants. This is a question of vision, not present-day realities.
- *What is your nightmare?* Parents sometimes find this question particularly hard to answer because it requires thinking of their child facing difficulties. But if participants can verbalize their fears, they will have taken an important step in making sure the worst never occurs.
- *Who is the student?* Participants take turns describing the student until no one has anything else to add. When the list is completed, particular people in the group, such as family

members, identify what they believe are three especially important descriptors.

- *What are the student's gifts?* The answer to this question may be based on responses to the other questions. Team members focus on what they believe the student can do, instead of what the student cannot do.
- *What are the student's needs?* The parents' answers to this question might vary considerably from those of the student's peers or teachers. When the list has been completed, the group decides which needs demand immediate attention.
- *What would an ideal day at school be like for the student?* Some MAPS groups answer this question by outlining a typical school day for students without disabilities who are the student's age. The team might think about how the needs outlined in answering the previous questions could be met at school and the supports that would be required.

Consider the various people involved in the MAPS process. Why is it critical to include general education teachers? What unique contribution might a student's peers make? How does MAPS represent a model for collaboration that also could be useful in thinking about working together on behalf of other students? How is the MAPS process similar to INCLUDE?

Source: From *The MAPS Process: Seven Questions,* by the Circle of Inclusion Project, University of Kansas, 2002. Retrieved November 22, 2004, from http://www.circleofinclusion.org/english/guidelines/modulesix/a.html.

Enlist Natural Support Systems Peers, older students, parent volunteers, student teachers, interns, and other individuals at school all can assist a student with a moderate or severe disability (Carter & Kennedy, 2006; Carter & Pesko, 2008). Peers often can answer questions or respond to basic requests without adult intervention. They sometimes also can make needed adjustments in equipment, retrieve dropped articles, and get needed instructional materials for the student. Older students can serve as peer tutors or special buddies, both for instruction and for the development of appropriate social skills. Parents, student teachers, interns, and others all can assume part of the responsibility for supporting students. For example, a student teacher can work with a small instructional group that includes both typical learners and a student with an intellectual disability.

Collaborate with Families As with your other students, when you teach a student with a moderate or severe disability, you should communicate regularly with the student's parents. Families know their children better than school professionals do, and parents can provide valuable information about teaching them. Parents also might have questions about how to reinforce at home the skills learned at school (Snell, Chen, Allaire, & Park, 2008). One strategy for drawing on parent, family, and peer knowledge about a student with a low-incidence disability to plan an effective education is included in the Working Together.

Like all parents, the parents of students with moderate or severe disabilities respond to their children based on many factors, including their culture. For example, in some Puerto Rican, Mexican, and Colombian families, the mother or both parents are blamed for having a child with significant disabilities, and raising this child is seen as penance for past sins (Olivos, Gallagher, & Aguilar, 2010; Rogers-Adkinson, Ochoa, & Delgado, 2003). These parents' degree of acceptance of a child at a low level of functioning may frustrate teachers trying to help the student to learn skills and relying on parents to practice the skills at home. For students who are bilingual, issues may arise as educators try to teach English survival words (for example, *stop, danger*) at school when only the native language is spoken in the home.

Access Assistive Technology Both high- and low-technology options help students learn. For example, digital cameras create infinite opportunities to take photos of signs, locations, people, and other items that can be used as tools for contextual learning. Many students who cannot use language to communicate use various forms of **augmentative and alternative communication (AAC)**, that is, various communication forms—unaided (for example, gestures) or aided (for example, computer software)—that enable students to convey their messages. These are addressed in the Technology Notes. Other students use technology to aid movement.

Students with Multiple Disabilities

Because students with multiple disabilities often have extraordinary needs, they are considered a distinct group in IDEA. Most students with multiple disabilities have an intellectual disability and a physical or sensory impairment. The needs of these students and the accommodations that help them succeed can be similar to those for students with moderate and severe intellectual disabilities, the differences being mostly a matter of degree and complexity. However, a few issues that particularly concern these students may arise more often. You may find that the number of special service providers who come to the classroom to work with students with multiple special needs (for example, a special educator, a paraprofessional, a speech/language therapist, or an occupational therapist) is high and occasionally a distraction in the classroom. Also, care must be taken that a wheelchair, computer equipment, other therapeutic equipment, and specialized materials (for example, large books in three-ring binders made with many pictures) for a student with multiple disabilities are seamlessly integrated into classroom practices so as not to interfere with traffic patterns, safety, and storage.

Because many students with multiple disabilities have limited speech and do not easily convey their preferences and needs, communicating with them can be a challenge. One strategy for communication is using alternative and augmentative communication (AAC) systems, which are sometimes used by students with moderate or severe intellectual disabilities (and other disabilities affecting communication), as described in the previous section.

Deaf-Blindness

Although students with dual sensory impairments, or *deaf-blindness,* typically are not totally blind or deaf, they do have extraordinary needs related to navigating the environment, making sense of events that most teachers and students take for granted, and learning with a limited ability to see and hear (Byrnes & Majors, 2004). These students sometimes have average or above-average intelligence (as did Helen Keller), but they often have intellectual or other disabilities. They typically need a wide array of special services throughout their school careers and into adulthood (Nelson, 2005).

How a student with deaf-blindness is educated in any particular school varies considerably. The student may spend most of the day in a separate class, part of the day in general education, or much of the day in that setting. Regardless of placement, a student who is deaf-blind will need extensive supports (Correa-Torres, 2008; Bruce, 2007). Should you be informed that you will have a student with this disability, you

Augmentative and Alternative Communication

Augmentative and alternative communication (AAC) is the term for an individual's use of ways other than speech to send a message to another individual, and it may substitute for speech or be an addition to speech. AAC includes

- nonaided communication, such as sign language and gestures and facial expressions
- aided communication, such as using computers and other simple or complex devices as tools

You might be familiar with a children's story about AAC: E. B. White's *The Trumpet of the Swan,* in which Louis, a swan who cannot make the same sounds as other swans, learns to use a trumpet as his voice.

Many students with low-incidence disabilities use AAC devices either as their primary means of communication or as supplements to traditional speech. These are some examples of AAC devices that your students might use:

- *Communication boards.* Many students with significant disabilities use communication boards. These boards may be as simple as a set of pictures that depict common tasks or needs. The student points to the appropriate picture using a finger, fist, elbow, eyes, or alternative means such as a head pointer. More complex communication boards are electronic. Pointing at pictures may activate prerecorded messages, such as "I need to be excused to the restroom" and "Hello. My name is Jorge. What is your name?" For middle and high school students, communication boards can be designed to include necessary key vocabulary terms.

- *Switches and scanning devices.* Some students cannot push a button or point at a picture. However, they might be able to indicate a choice using a switch. Thus, when a scanning device is used, a series of options is presented (for example, "I am hungry," "I am thirsty," or "I am tired"), and the student chooses the one that communicates the intended message. The switch is the means for making the choice. The student may have the motor control to slap a large button switch to stop items being shown on a computer screen, or she may make a slight head movement that activates a switch with an electronic voice that responds.

Information about augmentative and alternative communication is available on many websites and from many organizations, including these:

- Augmentative and Alternative Communication Connecting Young Kids (YAACK), a website with basic information and links to many other resources (http://aac.unl.edu)
- International Society for Augmentative and Alternative Communication (ISAAC) (http://www.isaac-online.org)

Source: Adapted from *AAC: More than three decades of growth and development,* by R. A. Sevcik & M. A. Romski, 2010, Rockville, MD: American Speech-Language-Hearing Association. Retrieved June 16, 2010, from http://www.asha.org/public/speech/disorders/AACThreeDecades.htm.

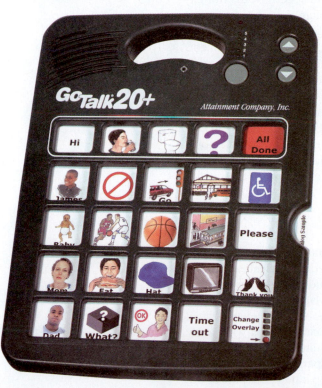

Communication boards can be simple or complex and tailored to meet the needs of the student and the learning situation.

Students with physical limitations sometimes use switches to operate their computers, activate their communication boards, and participate in other activities (e.g., activating a spinner used in an instructional game).

should meet with a special educator to learn about expectations for the student, your role in the student's education, and answers to the many questions you may have (for example, how can you assist the student to communicate with peers?).

What Accommodations Can You Make for Students with Sensory Impairments?

Students with *sensory impairments* have either vision loss or hearing loss so significant that their education is affected. Their specialized needs can range from minimal to complex. Because school learning relies heavily on seeing and hearing, students with these disabilities often experience academic problems and need both teacher accommodations and adaptive equipment.

In some cases, a vision or hearing problem is identified by professionals in the school setting. If you notice any of the symptoms described in the Professional Edge, you should alert your school nurse or health technician as well as the student's parents.

Students with Visual Impairments

Students with **visual impairments** cannot see well enough to use vision as a primary channel for learning without significant assistance. Generally, the term *blind* is reserved to describe the few students who have little or no useful vision. They use touch and hearing for most learning. Most students with visual impairments are *partially sighted,* meaning that they have some useful vision.

fyi

You may have heard the term **legal blindness.** This means the vision in the best eye, with correction, is 20/200 or lower (what a person with normal vision can see at 200 feet can only be seen at 20 feet), or the visual field is 20 degrees or less (the person sees a small slice of what others can see).

PROFESSIONAL EDGE

Warning Signs That Students May Have Vision or Hearing Loss

As a school professional, you sometimes will be in a unique position to judge whether a student may be experiencing a vision or hearing loss. If you observe any of these warning signs, you should alert your school nurse and follow district guidelines for seeking other assistance for the student.

SIGNS OF POSSIBLE VISION LOSS

- Frequent rubbing or blinking of the eyes
- Short attention span or daydreaming
- Poor reading
- Avoiding close work
- Frequent headaches
- A drop in scholastic or sports performance
- Covering one eye
- Tilting the head when reading
- Squinting one or both eyes
- Placing head close to book or desk when reading or writing
- Difficulty remembering, identifying, and reproducing basic geometric forms
- Poor eye–hand coordination skills

SIGNS OF POSSIBLE HEARING LOSS

- Failure to pay attention to casual conversation
- Giving wrong, inappropriate, or strange responses to simple questions

- Apparently functioning below intellectual potential
- Frequent and recurring ear infections
- Complaints of ringing in the ears, "head noises," and/or dizziness
- Complaints of pain in the ears or discharge
- Withdrawing from interactions with peers
- Frustration or other unexplained behavior problems
- Limited speech or vocabulary
- Frequent mispronunciation of words
- Placing head close to book or desk when reading or writing
- Watching a speaker intently to hear
- Failure to hear someone who is speaking from behind
- Turning up the volume on the television or when using the computer
- Difficulty hearing when using the phone

Sources: Adapted from *Warning Signs of Vision Problems,* by Eye Care Council, 1998, retrieved November 22, 2004, from http://www.seetolearn.com/warning.html; *An Educator's Guide to Hearing Impairment,* by N. Crowe, November 2002, retrieved November 22, 2004, from http://www.nsac.ns.ca/envsci/staff/ncr/hearing.pdf; and *Teaching Students Who Are Hard of Hearing,* by Northeast Technical Assistance Center, n.d., Rochester, NY: Author, retrieved November 22, 2004, from http://www.netac.rit.edu/publication/tipsheet/teaching.html.

Characteristics of Students with Visual Impairments

Students with visual impairments have the same range of intellectual ability as other students, but they typically have had fewer opportunities to acquire information usually learned visually (Pogrund & Fazzi, 2002). For example, students generally learn about maps by looking at them. Although students who are blind can learn by feeling a raised map, this method is not as efficient as seeing it. The same problem can occur with academics. Students with visual impairments often experience learning difficulties simply because they cannot easily use vision to process information. Think about how you read this text: You probably scan the pages, focus on words and phrases in boldface print, and visually jump between reading the type and looking at figures, features, and photos. If you could read this book only by magnifying it 15 times, by listening to it on digital recording, or by reading it in braille, you would find it much more tedious to scan, select important words and phrases, and go back and forth between components. If you multiply this dilemma across all the visual learning tasks students face, then you can begin to understand the challenges of learning with a visual impairment.

As is true for all individuals, students with visual impairments vary in their social and emotional development. Some students encounter little difficulty making friends, interacting appropriately with peers and adults, and developing a positive self-concept. Other students need support in these areas (Ayers, 2009; Correa-Torres, 2008). For example, it is important to teach some students who cannot see to adhere to social norms, such as facing a person when talking, taking turns, and keeping an appropriate social distance. Conversely, teachers should keep in mind that some students might miss another student's or a teacher's puzzled expression about something they had said and continue to interact as if they were understood. Teachers also should help other students to understand that a student with a visual impairment cannot help a wiggling eye or that such a student stands a little too close during interactions because she has difficulty judging distance.

INCLUDE

Accommodations for Students with Visual Impairments

Accommodations needed by students with visual impairments depend on many factors, and the INCLUDE strategy can guide your planning. First, take into account the student's overall ability level, use of learning strategies and other learning skills, and attentional and motivational levels, just as you would for any other student. Then, working with a special educator, make accommodations relative to your classroom demands, the amount of the student's residual vision, and the nature of her vision problems. Be sure to keep in mind that these students have many essential life skills to master that other students take for granted (for example, proper eating manners, maintaining appropriate social distance during interactions, keyboarding, signature writing, and proficiency in using assistive technology). These skills sometimes are referred to as the *expanded core curriculum,* because they are as essential to these students as are the skills of the traditional curriculum (Lohmeier, Blankenship, & Hatlen, 2009), and time must be made in their school careers to teach these skills. Some specific accommodations you can make and unique needs you must consider for students with visual impairments are covered in the following sections.

Orientation and Mobility   One important area of need for students with visual impairments is orientation and mobility, that is, the sense of where they are in relation to other objects and people in the environment and the ability to move about within a space. For example, students with visual impairments need to understand where furniture, doorways, bookshelves, and the teacher's desk are in the classroom in relation to their own location. In addition, they need to be able to move from the classroom to the auditorium to the cafeteria and out to the bus in a timely manner. Your first task in preparing for a student with a visual impairment might be to arrange your classroom carefully, leaving adequate space for all students to move about. Depending on the amount of sight the student has, you might need to keep furniture and supplies in consistent places and make sure the student has an opportunity to learn where everything is. If you decide to rearrange the room or move your supplies, alert the student with a visual impairment to the changes and allow opportunities to adapt to them.

Teaching Students with Visual Impairments
You might be asked to modify your teaching slightly to accommodate a student with a visual impairment. For example, you might need to use a whiteboard with a black felt-tipped marker instead of a traditional chalkboard, or you might need to provide the student with paper that has

Especially with advances in technology, students with sensory impairments often can pursue the same occupations as others.

heavy black lines instead of the traditional light blue ones. In addition, you should be sure to recite what is written on the board; call students by name so the student with a visual impairment can learn the sounds of classmate's voices and where they are seated; allow the student to move close to demonstrations and displays; give specific directions instead of using general words such as *here* and *there;* seat the student to optimize visual learning (for example, away from bright light or near the front of the room); and possibly assign a peer buddy. Usually, an itinerant vision specialist or another special educator will alert you to accommodations needed.

Some students with visual impairments need additional time to complete assignments, whether during class or as homework. Other may need a change-of-pace activity. A student who is fidgeting or refusing to work might be fatigued; this is a common problem for students who have to make extraordinary efforts to learn using residual vision. Letting the student take a break or substituting an alternative activity both helps the student and prevents discipline problems. Also keep in mind how to plan alternative learning opportunities for students. If you are talking about history and using a timeline, for example, use white glue or some other means of marking points on the timeline so a student with a visual impairment can participate meaningfully in the discussion by touching the points and feeling the distance between them. A vision specialist can help you develop such alternative learning opportunities.

Learning Tools for Students with Visual Impairments   Students with visual impairments use a wide variety of devices or equipment to facilitate their learning. If they have some residual vision, they can use devices to help them acquire information visually. Some use simple devices such as magnifying lenses and bright lights to read or do other schoolwork. Others hold their books close to their eyes or at a specific angle to see the print. Many students with visual impairments use computers with speech synthesizers or text enlargers. For students who read braille, assignments can be printed on a braille printer as well as a standard printer so both teacher and student can read them. Examples of the learning tools available for students with visual impairments are included in the Technology Notes.

Students with Hearing Loss

Students who are deaf or hard of hearing, referred to in IDEA as having **hearing impairments,** cannot hear well enough to use hearing as a primary channel for learning without significant assistance. Because a huge proportion of both formal

Assistive Technology for Students with Visual Impairments

The electronic braillewriter has six keys that the student simultaneously presses down in various combinations to produce the special system of raised dots that can be read through touch. Some braillewriters come with a speech synthesizer.

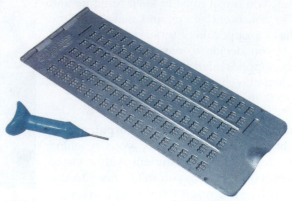

Although used less frequently with the increased availability of electronic braillewriters, the slate and stylus is an inexpensive and simple device for producing Braille.

Large-print books are low-tech options for students with visual impairments.

Specially designed magnifying glasses sometimes are a low-tech aid for students with visual impairments.

Specialized computer software for people with visual impairments includes tools such as screen-reading software and a speech synthesizer, braille translation software and a braille printer, and screen enlargement software.

and incidental learning occurs through understanding language in casual conversations, presentations by teachers and others, and overheard information, many professionals consider deafness and other hearing loss to be primarily language or communication impairments (for example, Luckner & Muir, 2001). A small number of students with hearing impairments are *deaf;* they cannot process linguistic information through hearing, either with or without hearing aids. Most students with hearing loss, however, are *hard of hearing,* meaning that they have some residual hearing that lets them process linguistic information, usually by using hearing aids or other assistive devices.

One key factor professionals consider in judging the seriousness of a student's hearing loss is the age when the loss occurred. Students who have been deaf or hard of hearing since birth are often at a disadvantage for language learning because they did not go through the natural process of acquiring it. These students can speak, but because they learned to talk without hearing how they sounded, their speech may be difficult to understand. They might prefer sign language and an interpreter for communicating with you and others. Students who lose their hearing after they learn language, that is, after about age 5, sometimes experience fewer language and speech difficulties.

Characteristics of Students Who Are Deaf or Hard of Hearing

Students with hearing loss have the same range of intellectual ability as other students. However, if intelligence is assessed using a test based on language, students with hearing loss might have lower scores. Academically, many of these students struggle because their hearing loss affects their ability to understand language, which in turn affects their learning (Antia, Jones, Reed, & Kreimeyer, 2009; Donne & Zigmond, 2008). For example, they might have difficulty learning vocabulary and as a result understanding the materials they read and the lessons you present (Marschark, Convertino, & LaRock, 2006). They may miss subtle meanings of words, which can affect both their learning and their social interactions. One simple example can illustrate the complexity of learning language. Think of all the meanings you know for the word *can.* As a noun, it refers to a container made of metal for storing food— for example, *a can of peas.* But it also means a container with a lid, as in the type of can that tennis balls are packaged in. *Can* also has slang meanings as a synonym for both *bathroom* and *prison.* As a verb, it means "to be physically able," as in *I can lift that box.* It also refers to preserving produce from the garden, as in *I plan to can green beans this year;* to losing a job, as in *I just got canned;* and to the state of being likely, as in *Can that be true?* If you think about all the words in the English language that have multiple and sometimes contradictory meanings, it becomes easier to understand the difficulties faced by students who are deaf or hard of hearing, who may not informally learn these meanings.

Socially and emotionally, students who are deaf or hard of hearing are sometimes immature (Stevenson, McCann, Watkin, Worsfold, & Kennedy, 2010). This lack of maturity occurs for two reasons. First, much of the etiquette children acquire comes from listening to others and imitating what they say and do. This learning is not available to many students who are deaf or hard of hearing. Second, these students can become confused in interactions that involve many people and multiple conversations. Because these types of situations often are uncomfortable for them, students with hearing impairments sometimes avoid them and fail to develop the social skills needed in group interactions. For example, Jim is a seventh-grade student with a moderate hearing loss. When students work in lab groups in Mr. George's science class, Jim tends to withdraw because he cannot follow what everyone is saying. Sometimes he tries to participate in the activity, but he often does so by making an exaggerated face or drawing a cartoon to show others. He does this even when the other students are working intently, and they become annoyed with his antics. When Jim realizes his attempts to participate are not being successful, he pulls away from the group and becomes passive. Mr. George and the special education teacher

www.resources

The National Association of the Deaf, at http://www.nad.org, has the goals of advocating for people who are deaf or hard of hearing, providing information on topics related to hearing loss, and serving individuals with these special needs.

are working to address this problem. Mr. George makes sure that he monitors the groups' work, and he sometimes intervenes by asking Jim a question that helps him interact appropriately with his peers.

Accommodations for Students Who are Deaf or Hard of Hearing

Accommodations for students who are deaf or hard of hearing emphasize helping them use whatever residual hearing they may have and accessing language to promote formal and informal learning. Although the specific types of accommodations needed by a student you teach will be determined by the multidisciplinary team that writes the student's IEP, the following are some common ones.

Teaching Students Who Are Deaf or Hard of Hearing Many students who are deaf or hard of hearing get some information through *speech reading,* or watching others' lips, mouth, and expressions. Given this, the teacher should always face the class when presenting information and stand where no glare or shadow makes it difficult for students to see. Using an overhead projector or Smartboard™ instead of writing on the chalkboard also is a good idea. A teacher also should stand in one location instead of moving around the room, and the student should sit near the teacher. These adjustments facilitate speech reading but also are necessary if an interpreter is present. Teachers should avoid exaggerating sounds or words; doing this makes it more difficult for the student, not easier. Teachers also should use as many visual aids as possible. Important directions can be written on the whiteboard, using either words or, for younger students, pictures. For older students, major points in a lecture can be written on an overhead projector or on the whiteboard.

As with students who have visual impairments, safety also must be kept in mind for students with hearing loss. Assigning a buddy to assist such a student during a fire, tornado, or earthquake drill is a simple strategy for addressing this issue. For other specific considerations regarding safety, a special educator with expertise in working with these students can assist you.

If a student who is deaf or hard of hearing uses sign language, you might consider enrolling in a sign class yourself and, especially in elementary and middle school, inviting a deaf education teacher to your class to teach some signs to the entire group. High school students may have an option for learning sign language as a course. Students generally enjoy learning some signs, and both you and they will be better able to communicate with the student who cannot hear. For example, you might use the sign for "line up" instead of asking students to do this. When you use the sign, everyone, including the student with hearing loss, will understand. An example of how to include students who are deaf or hard of hearing in the general education classroom is described in the Case in Practice.

Learning Tools for Students Who Are Deaf or Hard of Hearing Students with some residual hearing often use amplification devices such as hearing aids. If you have a student who wears hearing aids, you should be alert for signs of inattention that signal the hearing aid is not turned on or the battery needs to be replaced. Another type of amplification device is an FM system consisting of a microphone worn by the teacher and a receiver worn by the student. When the teacher talks, the sound is converted into electrical energy and carried on a specific radio frequency through the air. The receiver converts the electrical energy back to sound, amplifies it, and sends it to the student's ear.

Keep in mind that hearing aids and FM systems both amplify sounds, but they do not discriminate the teacher's voice from other sounds. Thus, a student wearing hearing aids can be distracted by background sounds such as the amplified noise of someone typing on the computer keyboard, a door slamming, or chairs scraping on the floor. A student using an FM device also hears the amplified sound of a teacher's jewelry hitting the microphone or the static from a teacher fingering the microphone. Any of these extraneous noises can interfere with a student's understanding of

CASE IN PRACTICE

Including Students Who Are Deaf or Hard of Hearing

Ms. Skinner is a fifth-grade teacher at Lunar Elementary School. This year in her class of 31, she has two students with hearing loss. The girls, who are twins, have profound hearing loss that has been present since birth. Because they use sign language as their primary means of communication, they are accompanied by Ms. Mohammed, an interpreter.

Ms. Skinner discusses what it is like to teach in this class:

When I first heard I was going to get Jenna and Janice this year, I was worried. I knew they'd been in fourth grade and done well, but there's so much more curriculum at this level. I didn't know how I was going to teach everything and also do all the work necessary for Jenna and Janice and at the same time deal with end-of-grade testing and all that pressure. As it turns out, it hasn't been much of an adjustment at all. Ms. Mohammed interprets for the girls, and she adds explanations if they need it. The hardest part for me was learning to stay in one place when I talk. For a teacher like me, who is constantly moving around the room, that has been difficult. Ms. Mohammed has taught all of us some basic signs—that puts us all in touch. Jenna

and Janice have some serious academic problems, mostly related to vocabulary, but the other kids just think of them as classmates. I've learned a lot this year. I'm a lot more confident that I really can teach any student who comes through my door!

REFLECTION

Why might teachers worry about having students like Jenna and Janice in their classrooms? What is the best way to get over this worry? How would having these students in a middle school social studies class or high school civics class differ in terms of expectations and accommodations compared to those in an elementary class? What aspects of teaching might be particularly challenging for you if you had students like Jenna and Janice in your classroom? How would you help these students compensate for their difficulty in vocabulary? What do you imagine is the impact of having an interpreter in the classroom most of the time? What type of assistance might you ask from the twins' parents to help them master the subjects you will be teaching?

---

spoken information and distract from learning. Amplification clearly assists some students who have hearing impairments, but it has limits.

A third type of device also is becoming common. Cochlear implants are sophisticated electronic hearing devices that are most helpful to individuals with severe or profound hearing loss. They are being used with children even under the age of two, and it is likely that you will teach a student who uses this technology. A cochlear implant has external and internal components. First, there is a receiver and stimulator system implanted under the skin in the bone behind the ear. In addition, there is an externally worn microphone, sound processor, and transmitter system that is held with a magnet, typically behind the ear. The microphone picks up sound from the environment, and the processor filters that sound and transmits it to the internal receiver; there it is turned into electric impulses, which are transmitted through the cochlea, part of the inner ear, to the brain. Cochlear implants enable students to perceive sound, but they are not a cure for a hearing loss. Students using them usually continue to need speech-language therapy and other supports commonly used by students who are deaf and hard of hearing (Fagan & Pisoni, 2010).

Students who have a severe or profound hearing loss often use sign language. Sometimes they use *American Sign Language (ASL)*, a distinct language that is not based on standard English grammar and structures. Learning ASL is like learning any other second language. Other students use a manually coded English (MCE) system, such as *signed exact English (SEE)*, that is, spoken English converted to a set of signs. With either method, students sometimes also use *finger spelling*, in which every letter of a word is spelled out. Finger spelling may be needed for names or technical terms for which no signs exist. Especially in secondary schools, students who use sign language sometimes are accompanied by interpreters who translate your words and those of classmates (Stinson, Elliot, Kelly, & Yufang, 2009). Some high school students may use another communication option called *C-print.* Using a computer, the captionist types what is being said in class using a standard set of abbreviations. The student, usually using a second computer connected wirelessly to the computer of the captionist, reads what is being said with only a three-second delay. You can learn about other examples of technologies that support students with hearing loss in the Technology Notes feature.

What Accommodations Can You Make for Students with Physical, Medical, or Health Disabilities?

Some students receive special education and related services because they have physical disorders, chronic or acute medical problems, or health impairments that interfere with their learning. In IDEA, three categories of disabilities can be loosely grouped in this area: orthopedic impairments, other health impairments, and traumatic brain injury. **Orthopedic impairments (OI)** are diseases or disorders related to the bones, joints, and muscles. **Other health impairments (OHI)** include medical and health conditions such as AIDS, seizure disorders, cancer, juvenile diabetes, asthma, and combinations of disorders such as those Cynthia, whom you met at the beginning of the chapter, is experiencing. **Traumatic brain injury (TBI)** is any insult to the brain caused by an external force, including injuries sustained in auto accidents and during play. Students with these kinds of disabilities, which are caused by a wide variety of physical and health problems, differ greatly in their levels of ability and academic achievement and in their needs, which can range from modest to extensive. The following sections provide just a few of the most common examples of the specific conditions that fall into these disability categories.

Orthopedic Impairments

Students with orthopedic impairments, often referred to as *physical disabilities*, are those with significant physical needs. The types of special needs these students may have include the following.

Students with Cerebral Palsy   In public schools, the largest group of students with orthopedic impairments comprises those who have *cerebral palsy (CP)*. Some 8,000 infants and preschoolers are diagnosed each year as having this condition (United Cerebral Palsy, 2001). Cerebral palsy occurs because of injury to the brain before, during, or after birth and results in poor motor coordination and unusual motor patterns. These problems can occur in just the arms or legs, in both the arms and legs, or in a combination of limbs and with varying degrees of severity. For some students, CP also affects other muscle groups, such as those controlling the head and neck. Thus, some students with cerebral palsy walk on their toes with their knees close together. Their arms may be positioned with their elbows bent and their hands positioned near shoulder height. Other students with CP need braces or a walker to move about. Yet others use wheelchairs. For some students, head supports prevent the head from lolling side to side. Intellectually and academically, students with CP can be gifted, average, or below average, or they might have intellectual disabilities.

Don is a student with cerebral palsy. His arms and hands are drawn up close to his body, and he does not control their movement. He moves around school in a motorized wheelchair, and Mike, his personal assistant, helps with personal care (for example, going to the bathroom, eating) and tasks such as writing. Don's intellectual ability is average but his physical disabilities sometimes cause others to think he has an intellectual disability as well, especially because his speech is difficult to understand. Don's teachers have learned to engage him in class activities by asking

www.resources

Information about the causes, classification, prognosis, treatment, and psychological aspects of cerebral palsy can be found at the website for United Cerebral Palsy, at http://www.ucp.org.

yes-or-no questions to which he can respond fairly easily. If they ask a question requiring a longer answer, they give Don time to form the words needed and do not let other students speak for him.

Students with Spinal Cord Injuries   A second orthopedic impairment is *spinal cord injury*. As the term implies, this injury occurs when the spinal cord is severely damaged or severed, usually resulting in partial or extensive paralysis (National Spinal Cord Injury Statistical Center, 2009). Spinal cord injuries most often are the result of an automobile or other vehicle accident. The characteristics and needs of students with this type of injury often are similar to those of students with cerebral palsy. Judy suffered a spinal cord injury in a car accident. She was hospitalized for nearly half the school year, and at the time she returned to school, she could not walk and had the use of only one arm. She is as bright and articulate as ever and still gets in trouble when she challenges teachers' authority. What has changed is how she moves from place to place.

Cerebral palsy and spinal cord injuries are just two of many types of orthopedic impairments students can have. You also may teach students who have physical disabilities caused by amputations or birth defects that result in the absence of all or part of a limb. Likewise, you might have a student with juvenile rheumatoid arthritis, a chronic swelling of the joints usually accompanied by soreness and limited mobility. Whatever orthopedic impairment a student has, your responsibility is to learn about the student's needs and work with special education professionals to ensure those needs are met through various accommodations.

Muscular dystrophy is a group of diseases that weakens the muscles. Students with this disorder have increasing difficulty walking and eventually require a wheelchair. Some students with this disorder have a normal lifespan, but others die as children or young adults.

Accommodations for Students with Orthopedic Impairments

The accommodations you make for students with physical disabilities will depend on the nature and severity of the disabilities and on the students' physical status. For example, you need to be alert to changes you might need to make in the physical environment so that students can comfortably move into, out of, and around the classroom. Examples include rearranging classroom furniture and asking for a work-table for the student. Of course, students with orthopedic impairments also may use assistive technology, a topic you have learned about earlier in this chapter and in other chapters. Ideas to help you think about the best uses of such technology are presented in the Technology Notes.

A second area of accommodation to consider for students with orthopedic impairments involves their personal needs (Friend, 2011). Many students become fatigued and might have difficulty attending to learning activities late in the school day. A few take naps or otherwise rest. Other students need to stop during the school day to take medication. Some students need assistance with personal care, such as using the bathroom and eating. Students who use wheelchairs might need to reposition themselves or be repositioned by an adult because of circulation problems. Paraprofessionals typically assume personal-care responsibilities and those related to moving students.

It is not possible to generalize about students' academic and social needs. Some students with orthopedic impairments enjoy school and excel in traditional academic areas. Some students with cerebral palsy are gifted. Other students with these disabilities experience problems in learning. Some are charming and gregarious students who are class leaders; others have a low self-concept and have problems interacting with peers. If you think about a student like Judy, the student introduced previously who has a spinal cord injury, you can imagine that her reaction to her accident and need to use a wheelchair are influenced by many factors, including her family support system, her self-concept, and her peers' reactions. The suggestions throughout this text for working with students to help them learn and succeed socially are as applicable to this group of students as to any other.

dimensions of
DIVERSITY

In choosing assistive technology, professionals should base decisions on a family's priorities, resources, and concerns, including stressors and cultural values, in order to avoid the possibility of assistive technology abandonment (Parette, Hourcade, & Huer, 2003). What adjustments might you need to make in your classroom arrangement and procedures to accommodate the needs of a student with a physical disability?

Assistive Technology for Students Who Are Deaf or Hard of Hearing

Cochlear implants are devices that electronically transmit sound to the brain, bypassing the ear itself.

Some students with hearing loss benefit from an FM system in which the teacher wears a microphone that transmits her voice to a receiver worn by a student.

C-print is a system in which a typist enters words the teacher and classmates say into a laptop computer. The words are almost instantaneously displayed on a second computer used by the student with the hearing loss.

Closed captioning, words printed on the screen that correspond to what is being said, enables students with hearing loss to watch television and videos.

PROFESSIONAL **EDGE**

What to Do When a Student Has a Seizure

As an educator in an inclusive school and as a responsible citizen, you should know how to respond when someone has a seizure. The Epilepsy Foundation recommends these steps for responding to seizures:

- Stay calm
- Prevent injury

  During the seizure, you can exercise common sense by ensuring there is nothing within reach that could harm the person if she struck it.
- Pay attention to the length of the seizure
- Make the person as comfortable as possible
- Keep onlookers away
- Do not hold the person down

  If the person having a seizure thrashes around there is no need for you to restrain them. Remember to consider your safety as well.
- Do not put anything in the person's mouth

  Contrary to popular belief, a person having a seizure is incapable of swallowing her tongue, so you can breathe easy in the knowledge that you do not have to stick your fingers into the mouth of someone in this condition.
- Do not give the person water, pills, or food until fully alert
- If the seizure continues for longer than five minutes, call 911
- Be sensitive and supportive, and ask others to do the same

After the seizure, the person should be placed on her left side with the head turned. Stay with the person until she recovers, usually 5 to 20 minutes.

Further information about what to do in the case of seizures and more information about this disorder are available from the Epilepsy Foundation at http://www.epilepsyfoundation.org/.

Source: From *Seizure First Aid*, by the Epilepsy Foundation, 2004. Retrieved June 16, 2010, from http://www.epilepsyfoundation.org/epilepsy/firstaid/. Reprinted with permission.

Other Health Impairments

Students with health impairments often are not immediately recognizable to a casual observer. However, their disabilities may be significant.

Students with Seizure Disorders   One group of health impairments is seizure disorders, or *epilepsy*, a physical condition in which the brain experiences sudden but brief changes in functioning. The result often is a lapse of attention or consciousness and uncontrolled motor movements. A single seizure is not considered a symptom of epilepsy, but if several seizures occur, the disorder is diagnosed. About 300,000 children and adolescents have a seizure disorder, but the availability of effective medications means that most of these students rarely have a seizure (Epilepsy Foundation, n.d.).

Epilepsy can produce different types of seizures. *Generalized tonic-clonic seizures* (previously called *grand mal seizures*) involve the entire body. The steps you should take when a student has a generalized tonic-clonic seizure are summarized in the Professional Edge. Other seizures do not involve the entire body. *Absence seizures* (previously called *petit mal seizures*) occur when students appear to blank out for just a few seconds. If they are walking or running, they might stumble because of their momentary lapse of awareness. If you observe a student with these symptoms, alert the school nurse or another professional who can further assess the student.

Although no relationship exists between seizure disorders and academic performance, you may find that a student with this disability is reluctant to engage in interactions with peers out of fear of their reaction to the seizures (Mittan, 2005). Students also may experience low self-esteem. If a student will likely have recurring seizures, you may want (with student and parent support) to explain epilepsy to your class or ask a specialist to do that. What is important is that typical learners understand that, although somewhat frightening, epilepsy is not dangerous, is not controlled by the student who has the disorder, and is not contagious.

Students with Sickle-Cell Disease   Another health impairment is *sickle-cell disease*. This disorder is inherited and occurs most often in African-American individuals, with an incidence of 1 in 500. Out of every 12 African Americans, one carries the gene for the disorder. The disease also is occasionally found in other groups,

Keep in mind that many students have more than one of the disabilities described in this chapter. For example a student may have autism and a hearing loss, or he may have a chronic health condition and an orthopedic impairment.

www.resources

At the website for the Sickle Cell Disease Association of America (http://www.sicklecelldisease.org), you can find news, research updates, discussion boards, and resources related to this genetic disorder.

including Greeks and Italians (Operation Sickle Cell, 2007). Sickle-cell disease occurs when normally round blood cells are shaped liked sickles. This makes the blood thicker and prevents it from efficiently carrying oxygen to tissues. The effects on individuals who have this disorder are fatigue and reduced stamina, as well as mild to severe chronic pain in the chest, joints, back, or abdomen; swollen hands and feet; jaundice; repeated infections, particularly pneumonia; and sometimes kidney failure (National Institutes of Health, 2010). No reliable treatments currently are available for individuals who have this disease. In children, sickle-cell disease can affect growth. Students with this disorder experience crises in which their symptoms are acute and include high fevers, joint swelling, and extreme fatigue; they are likely to miss school during these times. A student with this health impairment sometimes experiences cognitive impairment and often needs assistance in making up for missed instruction and encouragement for dealing with the pain and discomfort (Daly, Kral, & Brown, 2008).

Students with Asthma or Allergies   A fourth group of health impairments includes *asthma* and *allergies*. Children with asthma comprise the largest group of chronically ill children in the United States. Approximately 5 million youngsters have this illness, and at any single time, most educators have two students in their classrooms who have asthma (Asthma and Allergy Foundation of America, 2010). This disease can be triggered by allergens such as pollen, dust, and animal dander, but often it can be controlled with medication.

Allergies are the third most common chronic illness among children and adolescents. For example, approximately one in four children and adolescents have a food or digestive allergy (for example, milk, wheat, peanuts, shellfish) (Centers for Disease Control and Prevention, 2008). Other common causes of allergies are cat dander, insects (for example, bee stings, ant bites), pollen and mold, and plants (for example, poison ivy).

RESEARCH NOTE

Acquired immune deficiency syndrome (AIDS) results when an individual is infected with the human immune-deficiency virus (HIV) and can no longer fight off infection. In 2007, approximately 3800 children under the age of 13 were living with AIDS (Hall et al., 2008).

Only students with moderate or severe asthma or allergies may be eligible for special education services. Those with milder needs are likely to be assisted through a Section 504 plan, introduced in Chapter 2 and discussed further in Chapter 8. However, any student with these health issues may need special consideration in your classroom. For example, these students probably are absent more than other students and need assistance in mastering missed concepts. When in school, they sometimes feel tired or generally unwell, and they may need to be excused from some activities (Madden, 2000). Some students use an inhaler to treat their condition; for others, emergency medication must be kept nearby.

Additional Disorders and Conditions That May Affect Students   Students may have many other health impairments. For example, you may have a student who has been badly burned and is undergoing medical treatment and physical or occupational therapy to restore range of movement in affected limbs. You may have a student who has cancer and misses many days of school for treatments. Other health impairments your students might have include hemophilia, a genetically transmitted disease in which blood does not coagulate properly; juvenile diabetes, a condition in which the body does not produce enough insulin to process the carbohydrates eaten; AIDS; or cystic fibrosis, a genetically transmitted disease in which the body produces excessive mucus that eventually damages the lungs and causes heart failure. As noted for students with asthma or allergies, keep in mind that some students with these health impairments are not eligible for special education because their conditions do not negatively affect their educational performance. They are likely to receive support through Section 504 plans.

dimensions of DIVERSITY

Approximately 11,000 new cases of cancer were diagnosed in children ages birth–14 in 2009 (National Cancer Institute, 2009). The most common types of childhood cancer are leukemia (blood cell cancers) and brain and other central nervous system tumors, and Caucasian children are the most likely racial group to develop them.

Accommodations for Students with Health Impairments

As noted throughout this discussion, the accommodations you make for students with health impairments often relate to helping them make up work missed because of absence or hospitalization and to recognizing and responding to their social and emotional needs; however, you may find that you also have questions about their

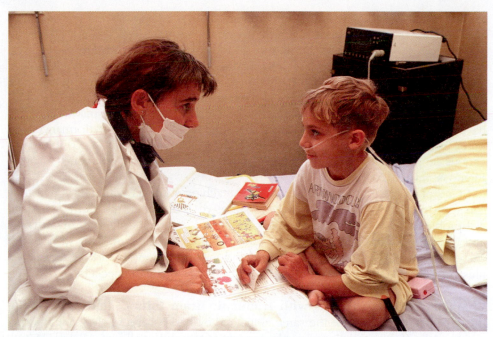

When students are hospitalized for serious illnesses, a special education teacher is likely to obtain schoolwork from you and help the student keep up academically.

academic and health needs (Wodrich & Spencer, 2007). General strategies for working with students with health impairments include these:

1. Find out the students' most difficult problems, and help them work through them. Strategies include having students write or draw about their concerns and referring students to the school counselor or social worker as you see a need.
2. Provide materials for the students about others who have a similar disease or disorder. Books, videotapes, websites, movies, and other informational materials can help students with health impairments understand how others have successfully coped with their illnesses. These materials also can be useful for explaining the needs of these students to peers without disabilities.
3. Consider including death education in your curriculum if you have a student with a life-threatening condition, such as cancer. A special educator, counselor, or social worker probably can prepare a unit and help you present it. Alternatively, prepare yourself for responding to the potential death of a student and helping classmates cope with this loss.
4. Work closely with families. Parents often can be the most valuable source of information concerning their children's status and needs. In addition, they can alert you to upcoming changes in medications and emotional problems occurring at home, and they can help their children work on missed school assignments (Shepard & Mahon, 2002).

In terms of academic and curricular adaptations, you should respond to students who have health impairments as you would to students with disabilities. Using the INCLUDE strategy, you can identify their needs. If modifications in the environment, curriculum, or instruction are needed, you can carry them out using the suggestions made throughout the remainder of this text.

Traumatic Brain Injury

Traumatic brain injury (TBI), sometimes called *acquired brain injury*, occurs when a student experiences a trauma to the head from an external physical force that results in an injury to the brain, often including a temporary loss of consciousness. TBI is the

INCLUDE

 fyi

Tourette syndrome (TS), a tic disorder that includes involuntary body movements (mild or severe), occurs in about 10 out of every 10,000 school-age children. The symptom most commonly associated with TS is uncontrolled shouted obscenities, but this actually occurs in only about 15 percent of cases (Centers for Disease Control and Prevention, 2004).

leading cause of disability and death among children, and it has many causes, including falls, bicycle and motor vehicle accidents, sporting accidents, accidents on playground equipment, child abuse, and gunshot wounds (Brain Injury Association of America, 2009). More than 1 million children and adolescents sustain a TBI each year. Although most of these injuries are mild, some 30,000 of these youngsters have a lifelong disability as a result of TBI (National Dissemination Center for Children with Disabilities, 2010). Whether TBI is the result of a severe injury or a mild one, it can have a pervasive and significant impact on a student's educational performance, and predicting the point at which they will reach their best outcomes is impossible given various lengths of recovery time and alternative patterns for treatment (Arroyos-Jurado & Savage, 2008).

One of the most perplexing aspects of teaching students with TBI is that they can appear just as they did prior to their injuries yet have significant learning and social problems. They also can seem back to normal one day, only to seem lethargic and incapable of learning the next. Because of the extreme variability in needs of students with TBI, the information presented in this section should be considered illustrative. If you teach a student with TBI, seek input from a specialist.

Characteristics of Students with Traumatic Brain Injury   Intellectually, students with TBI might have the same abilities they had before, or they might experience a loss of capacity. For example, after an automobile accident, Michael, a high school honor student who used to be a class leader, was left struggling to remaster basic math facts. His injury profoundly affected his learning. Students might experience difficulty initiating and organizing their learning tasks, remembering what they have learned, and reasoning or problem solving. They also might have difficulty processing verbal information and producing spoken and written language.

Students with TBI also may have other needs. Depending on the severity of the injury and extent of recovery, some students have limited use of their arms and legs. Others have problems in fine motor movements, such as those needed to grasp a pencil or turn the pages of a book. Yet others have limited strength and stamina. Socially and emotionally, students with TBI may have changes in their personalities; they are not who they used to be. Many of these students remember what they were able to do prior to their injuries and sometimes become depressed as they recognize their limitations (National Dissemination Center for Children with Disabilities, 2010). They also may display behavior problems when a sudden disruption in schedule occurs, as when an assembly interrupts an accustomed routine. Some of the most common challenges for students with TBI, along with potential responses teachers can make, are described in Table 6.3.

Families and Traumatic Brain Injury   It is especially important to mention families when discussing TBI (Wade, Carey, & Wolfe, 2006). Often parents and siblings have witnessed a student in a totally unresponsive state. They might be tremendously relieved that the student survived but at the same time traumatized by the amount of physical care he needs and the drain the injury has had on the family's financial and psychological resources. Families dealing with a child with TBI may experience a range of emotions, including shock, denial, sorrow, and anger (Carnes & Quinn, 2005). Eventually, many families adapt. Regardless, you need to be sensitive to the family's stress and their changing capacity to follow up on homework as well as schoolwork to support your efforts.

Accommodations for Students with Traumatic Brain Injury

If you teach a student with TBI, you might attend at least one planning meeting to discuss the details of the student's abilities and needs and to prepare for helping the student in the classroom. This transition planning typically occurs when a student is moving from a hospital or rehabilitation center back to school and usually involves personnel from both settings.

TABLE 6.3 Classroom Accommodations for Students with Traumatic Brain Injury

Post-TBI Cognitive Challenges	Macroenvironment	Microenvironment	Structure and Pacing	Teaching Style
Attention/ Concentration	Seat student near teacher. Minimize distractions. Use FM unit and earplugs to minimize external noise. Provide out-of-classroom activities in low-stimulation environments.	Use peer note takers. Use tape recorders. Provide assignments and activities in writing. Use large-print books with low density on the page.	Use small groups for teaching. Alternate instruction, activity, and rest. Schedule classes to capitalize on periods of highest attention.	Refocus student with verbal and/or nonverbal cues. Plan frequent breaks.
Information-processing speed		Use peer note takers and tape recorders. Review taped materials/ peer notes to identify missed critical information.	Slow the pace of classroom instruction. Allow extra time for completion of in-class tests/assignments/ homework. Reduce homework load. Allow more time for student to respond.	Do not rush or challenge the student. Provide anticipatory cuing to prepare responses in advance. Frequently repeat information to enhance processing abilities.
Memory	Provide written materials to back up classroom instruction.	Use tape recorder to review critical information. Use an organizer as an external memory aid. Test using multiple-choice format. Use fact cards and cue sheets to aid recall. Use highlighters to focus attention to information.	Utilize the student's best learning modality (for example, visual, auditory). Encourage tape-recording new class content. Encourage writing down class assignments in daily organizer.	Provide adequate repetition for mastery. Encourage student to repeat information to ensure comprehension.
Executing functioning	Designate a specific location to return homework. Display classroom schedule.	Develop a system to indicate that homework has been handed in. Use a binder with subject sections and pockets for homework. Color-code sections of binder and book covers by subject. Create maps to aid between-class travel; do in-school travel training.	Review daily routines to reorient student. Cue student to record homework assignments. Encourage outlining oral and written assignments.	Encourage student to use organizer daily. Break large projects or tasks into component parts or steps. Prepare student before the topic shifts.

Source: Adapted from *Students with Traumatic Brain Injury: Identification, Assessment, and Classroom Accommodations*, by M. Hibbard, W. A. Gordon, T. Martin, B. Raskin, and M. Brown, 2001, New York: Research and Training Center on Community Integration of Individuals with Traumatic Brain Injury, Mount Sinai School of Medicine. Retrieved November 22, 2004, from http://mssm.edu/tbinet/alt/pubs/tbikids.pdf.

In your classroom, accommodations relate to physical needs, instructional and organizational routines, academic content, and the social environment (Arroyos-Jurado & Savage, 2008). For example, because students with TBI need structure and routine, you should follow a consistent pattern in classroom activities, expect consistent types of student responses, and keep supplies and materials in consistent places in the classroom. If a break in routine is necessary, you can prepare the student by alerting him, assigning a buddy, and staying in close proximity.

You may need to make changes in the academic expectations for a student with TBI. Because students might know information one day but forget it the next or learn with ease sometimes but struggle to learn at other times, the need for flexibility is ongoing. Students also are likely to become frustrated with their inability to learn the way they did in the past, so your patience in reteaching information, providing additional examples and exercises, and using strategies to help them focus attention is essential.

Socially, emotionally, and behaviorally, students with TBI rely on you to set clear expectations but also to be supportive of and responsive to their changing needs. One student, Gary, had been in a coma but gradually regained enough ability to function that he returned to his middle school—at first for only an hour or two each day and eventually for the entire day. However, he continued to forget common words and grew increasingly frustrated when he could not convey messages. His teachers began providing the words he needed. Because many students with TBI seem unable to form a realistic picture of how they are functioning, you might need to confront them gently about socially inappropriate behavior. Frustrated with his language skills, Gary yelled at friends, yet his sentences remained unclear. Teachers intervened to help him learn to manage his anger and to assist friends to understand him.

In general, many of the accommodations needed by students with TBI are largely the same as those needed by students with physical or health disabilities, learning disabilities, and emotional disabilities. The uniqueness of students with TBI and the reason they are grouped as a separate category in IDEA is that their needs are difficult to predict, change either slowly or rapidly, and vary in intensity. Teachers who are patient and willing to meet students wherever they are and work forward from there can help students with TBI achieve school success.

fyi

Because of the complex behavioral challenges often experienced by students with TBI, an RtI procedure may provide a valuable means of assessing their needs, designing appropriate strategies, and monitoring their effectiveness (Dykeman, 2009).

WRAPPING IT UP

BACK TO THE CASES

This section provides opportunities for you to apply the knowledge gained in this chapter to the cases described at the beginning of this chapter: Kylie, Sean, and Cynthia.

KYLIE appears to be learning successfully in her first-grade year. Her teachers have made the necessary accommodations and modifications to support her learning needs. However, Kylie's mother is beginning to question whether Kylie should continue to be fully integrated into the general education classroom as she progresses into upper-elementary grades. She has requested a meeting with several of the upper-grade teachers. You have been invited to this meeting, which will be held tomorrow afternoon. In preparation for the meeting, the principal has given each of you a list of questions to answer:

1. Why is it important for Kylie to continue her education with same-age peers in the general education classroom?
2. What can you do to support Kylie's learning needs?

3. What life skills are essential for Kylie to learn that can best be taught in the general education classroom?

Prepare your response to each question. Then discuss your responses with classmates.

SEAN, as you may recall, has an autism spectrum disorder. Given what you know about him and this disorder, explain how you would establish and maintain your classroom to provide a supportive environment for a student like him. Remember what you learned in Chapter 5 about using the INCLUDE strategy to guide your teaching of students with exceptional learning needs. Step 1 of the strategy requires teachers to consider their classroom demands. Your answer should include topics such as physical classroom organization, routines, and learning groups, as well as any other areas that you consider important for Sean's welfare.

CYNTHIA does not have difficulty learning, but she has missed so much school that she is behind her peers and she also feels isolated. Using the INCLUDE strategy, complete an analysis of her needs and generate ideas about how you might help her to grow both academically and socially. What questions would you like to ask the special educator regarding working with Cynthia? How would you coordinate your efforts with other members of your middle school team?

SUMMARY

- Students with low-incidence disabilities comprise less than 20 percent of all students with disabilities, but they account for eight of the federal categories of disability (that is, orthopedic impairments, other health impairments, traumatic brain injury, hearing impairments, visual impairments, deaf-blind, multiple disabilities, and autism) and part of the mental retardation category.

- Students with low-incidence disabilities have tremendously diverse abilities, challenges, and needs. Although you will probably teach only a few such students during your career, you will find that many of the strategies you already have learned are effective in teaching them, and other professionals and parents are available to assist you in creating successful learning experiences for them.

- Students with autism spectrum disorders (ASD), referred to as *autism* in federal special education law, have a wide range of intellectual and other abilities, and they have impairments in social relationships, communication, range of interests, and capacity to respond to stressful events. They need a highly structured learning environment with clear procedures and routines. Recently, considerable attention has been paid to students with one type of ASD, Asperger syndrome.

- Students with moderate or severe intellectual disabilities or multiple disabilities learn slowly, and they usually need assistance to maintain and generalize their skills. They may not learn as much as other students or in the same ways, but their goals and objectives are aligned with the general curriculum, and they benefit from teachers who use a variety of instructional strategies and develop partnerships with parents. Students who are deaf-blind have particularly unique needs. They may or may not have additional disabilities, and they often require highly specialized instruction.

- Students with sensory impairments (i.e., those who are blind or low vision, or deaf or hard of hearing) often have needs related to academic learning, social and emotional skills, and skills for living in their environments. They may use adaptive equipment or materials to help them learn.

- Some students have orthopedic impairments (that is, physical disabilities), other health impairments (that is, serious medical or health conditions), or traumatic brain injury (that is, trauma to the head from an accident or other injury). Students in these groups often have medical problems that directly or indirectly affect their learning, varying intellectual levels, and social and emotional challenges, and they are likely to need a range of instructional and behavioral accommodations.

APPLICATIONS IN TEACHING PRACTICE
PLANNING FOR STUDENTS WITH LOW-INCIDENCE DISABILITIES

Mr. Walker teaches English to ninth graders. This year he will have several students with learning disabilities and emotional disabilities in his class, but his primary concern is Terrell, a young man who has cerebral palsy and limited vision. Mr. Walker has been told that Terrell has average intelligence and is quite capable of following the standard course of study for English but that he needs several accommodations. Mr. Walker is meeting with Ms. Bickel from the special education department to ask questions about Terrell.

Mr. Walker: I need more information about Terrell. Can he really do the work? How much can he see? How is he going to take tests? What is his assistant supposed to be doing? Am I accountable if Terrell has a medical problem during class? Is it likely that will happen? I hear that Terrell has all sorts of computer equipment and a motorized wheelchair. I have 34 other students in that class period, and I'm concerned about just fitting everyone in the door!

Ms. Bickel: It sounds like you haven't gotten the information I thought you had. Let me try to clarify. Terrell is a very good student. He usually gets As and Bs in his core academic classes, and he is highly motivated to learn. He has every intention of going to college, and right now he hopes to be an editor. Because he can't use his voice, he talks using his communication board. I'll be working with you to be sure the board includes all the key words you want it to contain. All Terrell has to do is point his head toward the answer he wants and the laser pointer will activate the board, which says the answer out loud. One accommodation Terrell probably will need is extra time to answer; he really wants to participate but might need a moment to get the laser beam focused on the answer he wants to give. His equipment is all adapted to take into account his limited vision.

Mr. Walker: I'll have to see how that works. What does his assistant do?

Ms. Bickel: Mr. Owen is responsible for Terrell's personal care and making sure he gets from class to class. He also takes notes for Terrell and records answers Terrell gives on his communication board. He can help you out in class if there's a chance, but Terrell needs his attention much of the time.

Mr. Walker: Oh, I wasn't trying to get more help. I just need an idea of what this will be like. I need an extra place for Mr. Owen in class, don't I?

Ms. Bickel: Yes, he'll need to sit next to Terrell most of the time.

The teachers continue talking for another 45 minutes, problem solving about the space issue and trying to ensure that Terrell will experience success and that Mr. Walker understands Terrell's needs. In the first week of school, Ms. Bickel asks Mr. Walker how it is going with Terrell. Mr. Walker comments that he is surprised how smoothly things are going. Terrell spoke via the communication board in class on the first day, and the other students asked a few questions about the equipment. Most of them already knew Terrell, however, and were accustomed to interacting with him. Mr. Walker asks whether Ms. Bickel can help him deal with two other students who already seem to have behavior problems.

QUESTIONS

1. What type of disability does Terrell have? Why is he included in Mr. Walker's English class?
2. What accommodations should Mr. Walker make in his classroom and his instruction to address Terrell's special needs? If Terrell was an elementary school student or a middle school student, which accommodations would be the same? Which accommodations might be different? How? Why?
3. If you were meeting with Ms. Bickel, what additional questions would you ask about Terrell? About needed accommodations?
4. What assistance would you need from Ms. Bickel to feel comfortable teaching Terrell?
5. What would your expectation be for working with Terrell's parents? What might you learn from them that would help you be more effective in teaching Terrell? How would your expectations for working with Terrell's parents be different if he was a younger student?
6. Review the entire chapter and all the information about students with low-incidence disabilities presented in it. What are the benefits of inclusive practices related to students in this group? What concerns and questions do you have for working with students with low-incidence disabilities? Which of your personal and professional beliefs will be most challenged when you work with students with low-incidence disabilities? Why?

PEARSON
myeducationlab

Go to Topics 15: Intellectual Disabilities, 18: Autism, 19: Physical Disabilities and Health Impairments, and 20: Sensory Impairments in the MyEducationLab (http://www.myeducationlab.com) for your course, where you can:

- Find learning outcomes for Intellectual Disabilities, Autism, Physical Disabilities and Health Impairments, and Sensory Impairments along with the national standards that connect to these outcomes.
- Complete Assignments and Activities that can help you more deeply understand the chapter content.
- Apply and practice your understanding of the core teaching skills identified in the chapter with the Building Teaching Skills and Dispositions learning units.
- Examine challenging situations and cases presented in the IRIS Center Resources. (optional)
- Access video clips of CCSSO National Teachers of the Year award winners responding to the question, "Why Do I Teach?" in the Teacher Talk section. (optional)
- Check your comprehension on the content covered in the chapter by going to the Study Plan in the Book Resources for your text. Here you will be able to take a chapter quiz, receive feedback on your answers, and then access Review, Practice, and Enrichment activities to enhance your understanding of chapter content. (optional)

chapter

7

Students with High-Incidence Disabilities

LEARNING Objectives

After you read this chapter, you will be able to

1. Explain what is meant by *high-incidence disabilities,* and describe their prevalence and the key elements of the federal definitions for each of the high-incidence categories.

2. Describe the characteristics and needs of students with communication disorders, and explain how you can differentiate classroom instruction for them using the INCLUDE strategy.

3. Describe the academic characteristics and needs of students with learning and behavioral disabilities and how you can differentiate instruction for them using the INCLUDE strategy.

4. Describe the social and emotional characteristics and needs of students with learning and behavioral disabilities and how you can meet these needs in the classroom.

WILL is a fourth-grade student at LaForb Elementary School. Most people who know him outside school would never guess that he has a learning disability. He converses easily with children and adults, has a great sense of humor, and is renowned among his peers for his "street smarts." Unfortunately, things don't go as well for Will in school. While he passed his third-grade end-of-grade test in math, the tests in reading and written language were another story altogether. Will reads slowly, struggling with each word, and as a result he often cannot tell his teacher what he has read. His written language is also a problem. When he does attempt a written assignment, it takes him an extremely long time to write even a few sentences. The sentences contain many misspelled words, are poorly constructed and illegible, and convey little meaning. As a fourth-grader, Will has been more disengaged from his classes. He is spending longer periods of time in the hall or the principal's office, usually for refusing to do his classwork and homework. Recently, Will's frustration has been growing as the pressure mounts to get ready for his end-of-grade tests and middle school.

What disability does Will seem to have? What factors may be contributing to his academic problems? What kinds of differentiated instruction should Will's teacher provide to help him progress in the general education curriculum? What other kinds of support do Will and his teacher need? Why do students like Will often become discipline problems?

RENAYE is nearly 15 and is usually in some kind of trouble in school and out. According to her grandmother, she has always been a strong-willed child, but she seems to have become more aggressive after losing her mother in a car wreck when she was in the third grade. ReNaye's grades have been going down consistently since then. She does well in English, but her math grades have been getting lower each year. Last year, she scored "not proficient" on the end-of-grade test in math for the first time. She also frequently refuses to work in her history and science classes. In class, ReNaye gets upset easily and resorts to bullying and teasing her classmates. She has had several discipline referrals, and the principal keeps threatening to suspend her for her actions but has yet to follow through. Her attendance has been sporadic at best, and her teachers and grandmother don't know what to do to help her.

What is ReNaye's likely disability? How can her general education teachers accommodate her behavior? What kinds of support do ReNaye and her teachers need?

fyi

Students with mild intellectual disabilities comprise two-thirds of the federal category of mental retardation. The federal definition for mental retardation is in Table 6.1.

Students like Will and ReNaye have high-incidence disabilities. These students' disabilities affect their language, learning, and behavior. You probably will teach students with high-incidence disabilities in your classroom. The expectation in the Individuals with Disabilities Education Act (IDEA) is that these students will spend most of their time in general education, while meeting the same curricular standards as their classmates without disabilities. In order to meet the goals set forth in IDEA, students with high-incidence disabilities require support from general and special education professionals. Usually this support is in the form of instructional accommodations rather than modifications. For instance, Will is learning word-processing skills to help him overcome his problems with spelling and handwriting. He is also using texts on a text-to-speech hand-held device in his science and social studies classes, which are sometimes co-taught. ReNaye and her teachers have developed a behavior intervention plan in which she is allowed extra access to the computer lab for attending class and complying with teachers' requests. This chapter covers characteristics and needs of students with high-incidence disabilities and differentiated instruction that enable these students to gain better access to the general education curriculum.

What Are High-Incidence Disabilities?

Students with **high-incidence disabilities** have speech or language disabilities, learning disabilities, emotional disturbance, or mild intellectual disabilities. These students make up approximately 80 percent of all students who have disabilities (U.S. Department of Education, 2006a). The federal terms for high-incidence disabilities and the proportion of students with these disabilities served through IDEA are summarized in Table 7.1. Students with high-incidence disabilities share three important characteristics:

1. They are often hard to distinguish from peers without disabilities, particularly in nonschool settings.
2. They often exhibit a combination of behavioral, social, and academic problems.
3. They benefit from systematic, explicit, highly structured instructional interventions such as those discussed in Chapter 5, this chapter, and throughout the remainder of this book. Having these interventions in place will help them meet the same standards as their classmates without disabilities.

In the sections that follow we will cover the characteristics and needs of students with high-incidence disabilities, including how to accommodate them in your classroom. Students with communication disorders will be discussed first, followed by students with learning and behavioral disabilities.

What Accommodations Can You Make for Students with Communication Disorders?

Communication is the exchange of ideas, opinions, or facts between people. Effective communication requires a sender to send a message that a receiver can decipher and understand. Students with communication disorders have problems with speech and/or language that interfere with communication. They need accommodations that help them better understand and express oral language.

Understanding Speech Problems

Speech is the behavior of forming and sequencing the sounds of oral language (Friend, 2011). One common speech problem is with **speech articulation,** resulting in the inability to pronounce sounds correctly at and after the developmentally appropriate age. For example, Stacey is in second grade but cannot pronounce the *s* sound, a sound most students master by age 5. Other speech difficulties involve voice and fluency. Examples of these speech problems are shown in Figure 7.1.

TABLE 7.1   **Proportion of Students with High-Incidence Disabilities Receiving Special Education Services in 2002–2003[a]**

Federal Disability Category	Defining Characteristics	Total Number of Students	Percentage of All Students Receiving IDEA Services	Percentage of All Students Ages 6–21
Learning disabilities[b]	A heterogeneous group of disorders resulting in significant difficulties in the acquisition and use of listening, speaking, reading, writing, reasoning, and mathematical skills. Disorders are intrinsic to individuals and presumed to be due to central nervous system dysfunction. Disorders are *not* primarily due to (a) sensory or motor disorders; (b) intellectual or developmental disabilities; (c) emotional disturbance; or (d) environmental, cultural, or economic disadvantage.	2,789,895	46.4%	4.2%
Emotional disturbance[c]	Behavioral or emotional responses in school programs that are so different from appropriate age, cultural, and ethnic norms that they adversely affect academic performance. More than a temporary, expected response to stressful events in the environment. Consistently exhibited in two different settings, at least one of which is school related. Persists despite individualized interventions within the educational program.	483,415	7.9%	0.7%
Speech[d] or language[e] impairments	Speech is disordered when it deviates so far from the speech of other people that it calls attention to itself, interferes with communication, or causes the speaker or listeners distress. Three kinds of speech disorders are articulation (abnormal production of speech sounds), voice (absence of or abnormal production of voice quality, pitch, loudness, resonance, and/or duration), and fluency (impaired rate and rhythm of speech, for example, stuttering). Language is disordered when comprehension and/or use of a spoken, written, and/or other symbol system is impaired or does not develop normally. Language disorders may involve form (word order, word parts, word usage), content (word meaning), or function (words that communicate meaningfully).	1,137,692	18.7%	1.7%

[a]Students ages 6–21 receiving services through IDEA, Part B (U.S. Department of Education, 2006). Additional students receive services under Part H of the same law, and under Chapter 1.
[b]Adapted from National Joint Committee on Learning Disabilities, definition of learning disabilities as cited in Hammill, 1990, p. 77.
[c]Adapted from Forness and Knitzer (1992).
[d]From definitions developed by Van Riper and Emerick (1996).
[e]From definitions developed by the American Speech-Language-Hearing Association (1993).
Source: From *Twenty-Eighth Annual Report to Congress on the Implementation of the Individuals with Disabilities Education Act,* 2006, Washington, DC: U.S. Department of Education.

FIGURE 7.1 Speech Problems

Articulation

1. Has difficulty pronouncing sounds correctly (at and after the developmentally appropriate age). Frequent articulation errors include *f, v, k, g, r, l, s, z, sh, ch,* and *j.* Sounds may be distorted or omitted, or one sound may be inappropriately substituted for another.
2. Speech may be slurred.

Voice

1. Speech is excessively hoarse.
2. May use excessive volume or too little volume.
3. Speech has too much nasality.
4. Speech lacks inflection.

Fluency

1. Stutters when speaking.
2. May have excessively slow rate of speech.
3. May exhibit uneven, jerky rate of speech.

Sources: Adapting Instruction in General Education for Students with Communication Disorders, by D. Barad, 1985, unpublished manuscript, De Kalb: Northern Illinois University; and *Introduction to Communication Disorders* (3rd ed.), by R. Owens, D. Metz, and A. Haas, 2007, Boston: Allyn & Bacon.

Because communication is social, students with speech disorders, such as **stuttering,** often experience social problems. Students who can clearly communicate draw positive attention from peer relationships, but students who cannot are often avoided by their peers and sometimes ridiculed. The experience of peer rejection can be devastating, leading to a lack of confidence, a poor self-image, social withdrawal, and emotional problems later in life (Cowen, Pederson, Babijian, Izzo, & Trost, 1973). For example, after years of being ridiculed by peers, Jeffrey, a high school ninth grader who stutters, speaks infrequently and has no friends. He would like to ask a girl in his math class out but is petrified he will not be able to do so without stuttering.

Understanding Language Problems

Language is a system of symbols that we use to communicate feelings, thoughts, desires, and actions. Language is the message contained in speech. Language can exist without speech, such as sign language for people who are deaf, and speech without language, such as birds that are trained to talk (Hardman, Drew, & Egan, 2005). Students who have language problems have trouble with either or both of two key parts of language: receptive language and expressive language. **Receptive language** involves understanding what people mean when they speak to you. **Expressive language** concerns speaking in such a way that others understand you. Receptive language problems occur when students are unable to understand what their teachers and peers are saying. For example, students with receptive language difficulties may not understand questions, may have trouble following directions, and may not be able to retain information presented verbally. Students with expressive language problems are unable to communicate clearly; their spoken language may include incorrect grammar, a limited use of vocabulary, and frequent hesitations. Some common receptive and expressive language problems are listed in Figure 7.2.

Students with language problems also may have difficulty using language in social situations. For example, they may be unable to vary their conversation to match the person with whom they are talking or the context in which it is occurring. Students with language problems also may experience problems taking turns while speaking during a conversation, recognizing when a listener is not understanding the message and taking action to clarify, and in general being a considerate speaker and listener (Vaughn & Bos, 2009). As with problems in communicating clearly, challenges in using language appropriately can seriously impede students' social development and peer relationships. General education teachers can intervene in the classroom to help such students socially.

FIGURE 7.2 Language Problems

Receptive Language Problems

1. Does not respond to questions appropriately
2. Cannot think abstractly or comprehend abstractions as idioms ("mind sharp as a tack"; "eyes dancing in the dark")
3. Cannot retain information presented verbally
4. Has difficulty following oral directions
5. Cannot detect breakdowns in communication
6. Misses parts of material presented verbally, particularly less concrete words such as articles (*the* book; *a* book) and auxiliary verbs and tense markers ("He *was* going"; "She *is* going")
7. Cannot recall sequences of ideas presented orally
8. May confuse the sounds of letters that are similar (*b, d; m, n*) or reverse the order of sounds and syllables in words (*was, saw*)
9. Has difficulty understanding humor or figurative language
10. Has difficulty comprehending concepts showing quantity, function, comparative size, and temporal and spatial relationships
11. Has difficulty comprehending compound and complex sentences

Expressive Language Problems

1. Uses incorrect grammar or syntax ("They walk down together the hill"; "I go not to school")
2. Lacks specificity ("It's over there by the place over there")
3. Frequently hesitates ("You know, um, I would, um, well, er, like a, er, soda")
4. Jumps from topic to topic ("What are feathers? Well, I like to go hunting with my uncle")
5. Has limited use of vocabulary
6. Has trouble finding the right word to communicate meaning (word finding)
7. Uses social language poorly (inability to change communication style to fit specific situations, to repair communication breakdowns, and to maintain the topic during a conversation)
8. Is afraid to ask questions, does not know what questions to ask, or does not know how to ask a question
9. Repeats same information again and again in a conversation
10. Has difficulty discussing abstract, temporal, or spatial concepts
11. Often does not provide enough information to the listener (saying, "*We* had a big fight with *them*," when *we* and *them* are not explained)

Sources: Adapting Instruction in General Education for Students with Communication Disorders, by D. Barad, 1985, unpublished manuscript, De Kalb: Northern Illinois University; and *Strategies for Teaching Students with Learning and Behavior Problems* (7th ed.), by S. Vaughn and C. S. Bos, 2009. Copyright © 2009 by Pearson Education, Inc. Reprinted by permission.

Early language development forms the underpinning for much of the academic learning that comes when students go to school. It is not surprising then that students with speech and language disorders are likely to have trouble with academics as well (Catts & Kamhi, 2005). Problems with sounds can result in students' having difficulties acquiring word analysis and spelling skills. Receptive language problems can make comprehension very difficult and can result in trouble understanding mathematical terms such as *minus, regroup,* and *addend* and confusion in sorting out words with multiple meanings, such as *carry* and *times* (Mercer & Pullen, 2009). Further, language disabilities can seriously impede the content-area learning stressed in middle, junior high, and high school. In these settings, much information is provided orally using lecture formats, the vocabulary and concepts covered are much more abstract, and students are expected to learn with less support from the teacher. These demands are difficult for students with language disorders.

Another part of learning independently is solving problems. Students with language disorders may have difficulty verbalizing the steps to solve a problem. For example, when Veronica, a language-proficient student, solves word problems, she talks to herself as follows: "First I need to read the whole problem. Then I need to decide what the problem is asking for and whether I need to add, subtract, multiply, or divide. Okay, the problem is asking how much Alex weighs. It says that Alex is 3 pounds heavier than Dominique and that Dominique weighs 125 pounds. So if Alex weighs 3 pounds more, his weight will be a bigger number than Dominique's, so I need to add." A student with language problems cannot talk herself through such problems.

dimensions of DIVERSITY

It is incorrect to view students as having communication disorders when they use ethnic or regional dialects, speak a form of nonstandard English learned at home, or are native speakers of languages other than English and have limited English proficiency.

INCLUDE

Accommodations for Students with Communication Disorders

As discussed in Chapter 5, the INCLUDE strategy suggests that before you differentiate instruction, you should carefully consider potential student problems in view of your instructional demands. For students with speech and language problems, note especially any areas in which students are required to understand oral language (for example, listening to a lecture or a set of verbal directions) or to communicate orally (for example, responding to teacher questions or interacting with classmates when working in cooperative groups). The following discussion highlights specific suggestions for working with students with speech and language disorders.

Create an Atmosphere of Acceptance Help students who have difficulty expressing themselves believe they can communicate without worrying about making mistakes. You can foster this nonjudgmental atmosphere in several ways. First, when a student makes an error, model the correct form instead of correcting the student's mistakes directly:

Teacher: Kareem, what did Jules do with the frog?
Kareem: Put pocket.
Teacher: Oh. He put it in his pocket?
Kareem: Yes.

Second, try to allow students who stutter or have other fluency problems more time to speak, and do not interrupt them or supply words that are difficult for them to pronounce. Offering praise or other reinforcement for successful efforts to communicate, as you would for your other students, is also helpful. Sometimes, you should praise even an attempt:

Teacher: Anthony, what did you do when you went home yesterday?
Anthony: Television.
Teacher: Great, you told me one thing you did. You watched television.

Finally, try to minimize peer pressure. One effective way to do this is to model and reinforce tolerance of individual differences in your classroom.

Encourage Listening and Teach Listening Skills Even though students spend more time listening than doing any other school activity, very little time is devoted to teaching listening skills (Lerner & Johns, 2008). Stressing listening is particularly important for students with receptive language disorders. Take the following four steps to stress listening:

1. Listen carefully yourself and praise listening among your students. For example, when Ms. Hernandez listens to a student speak, she leans forward and nods. Many of her students copy these listening behaviors.
2. Be sure to engage your students' attention before you begin speaking by increasing your proximity to the listeners, by giving direct instruction (such as, "Listen to what I'm going to say"), and by reducing competing stimuli (have only one activity going on at one time, or have only one person speak at a time). You also can use verbal, pictorial, and written advance organizers to cue students when to listen (for example, "When we get to number 3 on this list, I want you to listen extra carefully for an error I am going to make") (Sabornie & deBettencourt, 2009).
3. Make oral material easier to understand and remember by simplifying vocabulary, simplifying sentence structure using high-frequency words, repeating important information, giving information in short segments using visual aids for emphasis, having students rehearse and summarize information, and using cues that signal when you are going to say something important (Mandlebaum & Wilson, 1989).
4. Teach listening skills directly. Provide practice on skills such as predicting what might be heard, following directions, appreciating language, identifying main ideas and supporting details, drawing inferences, differentiating fact from fiction, and analyzing information critically.

RESEARCH NOTE

Saunders, Foorman, and Carlson (2006) observed 85 kindergarten classrooms and found that English language learners in classrooms with separate English language development blocks had significantly higher English oral language and literacy scores than students who were part of the regular language arts block. Why do you think this is so?

When you speak, you also can enhance your students' listening skills by stressing words that are important to meaning. For example, say "He *hit* the *ball*" or "*He* hit the ball," depending on what you want to emphasize. Stressing inflectional patterns, such as using an upward inflection when asking a question, also helps students better understand what you are saying (Moats, 2007).

Use Modeling to Expand Students' Language   You can expand the language of students with expressive language problems by adding relevant information to student statements:

Student: John is nice.
Teacher: Yes, he is very nice, polite, and considerate of other people's feelings.

You can also expand language by broadening a minimal statement:

Student: My weekend was fun.
Teacher: You had a great time last weekend on your trip to the mountains.

Modeling to expand students' language is most effective when it is done as an ongoing part of your everyday communications. Students also can learn to model behavior for each other.

Provide Many Meaningful Contexts for Practicing Speech and Language Skills   The goal of successful language programs is to teach students to use appropriate language in a variety of social and academic situations, both in and out of school. You can help students with all types of speech and language problems meet that goal by providing as many opportunities as possible to practice language skills within meaningful contexts (Hardman et al., 2005). Practice helps students refine language skills and make them more natural and automatic. When students practice in many different contexts, they can apply what they learn more readily. For example, Ms. Crum just taught her class the meaning of the word *ironic*. During health class, the students discussed the irony of the government's warning people against fat consumption and then funding school lunches that are high in fat. During a trip to the museum, Ms. Crum pointed out the irony of the guard's telling them to be quiet when he was wearing shoes that squeaked loudly when he walked.

It is also helpful to encourage students with communication disorders to talk about events and experiences in their environment, describing them in as much detail as possible (Hardman et al., 2005). For example, Ms. Cusak, a first-grade teacher, starts every Monday by having two students tell about something they did over the weekend. Mr. Drake, a sixth-grade teacher, uses a *Saturday Night Live* format whereby students in his class act out something funny that happened to them over the weekend.

Finally, whenever possible, instruction should be embedded in the context of functional areas. For example, in Ms. Taylor's consumer math class, she has students go out to appliance stores, talk to salespeople about service contracts, and then describe and compare the various service contracts that are available. In Ms. Ellen's second-grade class, students invite and converse with classroom visitors.

Who Are Students with Learning and Behavioral Disabilities and What Are Their Academic Needs?

Students with learning and behavioral disabilities have learning disabilities, mild intellectual disabilities, and emotional disturbance. These are the students who are most likely to be included in your classroom. Students with **learning disabilities** are students who achieve less than typical students academically because they have trouble with processing, organizing, and applying academic information. Students with learning disabilities are of normal intelligence, have presumably received adequate instruction, and have not been shown to be sensory impaired, emotionally disturbed, or environmentally disadvantaged. Students with **mild intellectual disabilities** are

INCLUDE

students who have some difficulty meeting the academic and social demands of general education classrooms, in large part because of below-average intellectual functioning (that is, scoring 55–70 on an IQ test). Students with mild intellectual disabilities can meet at least some of the academic and social demands of general education classrooms. Students with **emotional disturbance** are of average intelligence but have problems learning primarily because of external (acting out, poor interpersonal skills) and/or internal (anxiety, depression) behavioral adjustment problems. The process of identifying students with learning disabilities using RtI is described in the Case in Practice.

Students with learning disabilities, mild intellectual disabilities, and emotional disturbance differ in a number of ways (Hallahan et al., 2009; Sabornie, Evans, & Cullinan, 2006). The behavior problems of students with emotional disturbance are more severe, and students with mild intellectual disabilities have lower levels of measured intelligence. Students with learning disabilities may have more pronounced learning strengths and weaknesses than students with mild intellectual disabilities, who are likely to show lower performance in all areas. Still, the academic and social characteristics of students with these disabilities overlap considerably. All three groups may experience significant problems in academic achievement, classroom behavior, and peer relations (Stichter, Conroy, & Kauffman, 2007).

dimensions of DIVERSITY

African–American students, especially those in urban middle schools, are at risk of being overidentified for behavior disorders; children from Latino or Asian–American families are at risk of underidentification (Coutinho & Oswald, 2000). What are factors that may account for this?

CASE IN PRACTICE

Identifying Students with Learning Disabilities Using RtI

IDEA 2004 allowed school districts to use RtI to identify students with learning disabilities as an alternative to using discrepancy formulas. When using a discrepancy formula approach, students are declared learning disabled if their intelligence is within the normal range, but their level of achievement is not. Typically, a standard of difference is declared, beyond which a student can be identified as having a learning disability.

The process of using the discrepancy between student ability and achievement to identify students with learning disabilities has come under attack, in large part because by the time the discrepancy is large enough to qualify for special education, they are already so far behind that catching up is difficult.

The RtI approach to identifying learning disabilities can be clearly seen in the accompanying progress-monitoring graph for Marni. Marni is new to the school, and her progress in reading is being monitored weekly in terms of words read correctly per minute from fourth-grade reading passages using a curriculum-based measure of oral reading fluency. Marni's progress graph is divided into four parts: Tier 1, Tier 2, Tier 3, and Tier 4. In Tier 1, Marni received correctly delivered evidence-based instruction for four weeks from her general education teacher, yet she failed to make adequate progress. The RtI team decided to differentiate her instruction by moving her into Tier 2. Note that an aimline was drawn from her median performance in Tier 1 of 40 words correct per minute to benchmark performance in

May, which in grade 4 is 120 words correct per minute. Use of an aimline was a quick way to judge Marni's progress; if she was at or above the line, her progress would be considered adequate. If she was below the line four consecutive times, her program would need to be changed.

For Tier 2, the team suggested that Marni's teacher provide her with paired reading five times each week using books at her instructional level. Paired reading is an evidence-based practice whereby students practice reading orally with a classmate (Bursuck & Damer, 2011). During this time, Marni's teacher continued to monitor her progress in oral reading weekly. After the paired reading was introduced, Marni's performance improved some, but wasn't sustained; she performed below her aimline for four consecutive weeks, a warning signal that she was falling further behind her classmates. Therefore, the team proposed a Tier 3 intervention, which, in Marni's school, was not special education, but an alternative reading curriculum where she would receive small-group, intensive instruction in all reading areas for 60 minutes a day. The team continued to monitor her progress.

For the first four weeks Marni was still below the aimline, but was making progress. Therefore the team elected to keep her in Tier 3. However, after the next four weeks it was clear that her rate of progress had slowed, and rather than allowing her to fall further behind her classmates, Marni was referred to special education, which was Tier 4. At that point, with written approval from her family, additional assessments were given to Marni by the school psychologist to see if she had processing deficits associated with a learning disability. The results showed definite problems in a number of information processing areas including working memory, oral language, attention, and phonological processing. After ruling out emotional, cultural, medical, and environmental factors, Marni was declared eligible for special education as a student with a learning disability. Marni remained in the same reading curriculum, but was moved to a small group of three taught by the special education teacher for 90 minutes per day. The small group accommodated her attention problems and allowed the teacher to provide more intensive support for Marni's skill acquisition. Increased time for reading was done in hopes of eventually catching Marni up to her classmates. The team continued to monitor Marni's oral reading fluency weekly.

Response to Intervention (RtI), Classroom-Based Progress Graph: Marni

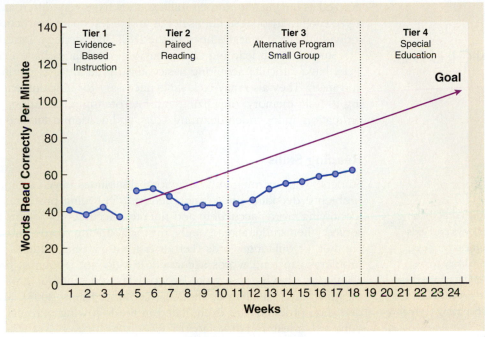

Although scientists have developed sophisticated computerized imaging techniques to detect neurological differences in children with learning and behavioral disabilities, the precise causes of these disabilities in individual children are largely unknown because learning and behavior result from a complex interaction between students' individual characteristics, the various settings in which they learn, and the tasks or other demands they face in those settings (Hallahan et al., 2005; Smith, 2004). It is often difficult to identify the primary cause of a learning or behavior problem. For example, Thomas is lagging behind his classmates in acquiring a sight-word vocabulary in reading. Learning disabilities tend to run in his family, but Thomas's school district also changed reading series last year. In addition, Thomas's parents separated in the middle of the school year and divorced several months later. Why is Thomas behind in reading? Is it heredity? Is it the new reading program? Is it his parents' marital problems? All these factors may have contributed to Thomas's problem.

The most important reason students with high-incidence disabilities are grouped for discussion is that whatever behaviors they exhibit and whatever the possible causes of these behaviors, these students benefit from the same instructional practices (Algozzine, Ysseldyke, & Campbell, 1994; Bateman, 2004; Coyne, Kame' enui, & Carnine, 2007). These practices are introduced in this chapter and covered in considerable depth throughout the rest of this book. For example, Raeanna has a mild intellectual disability. She has difficulty reading her classmates' social cues. As a result, she does not recognize when she is acting too aggressively with her classmates and often is rejected. Del is a student with learning disabilities. He also has trouble reading the social cues of his peers. Although Raeanna and Del may learn new social skills at different rates, both can benefit from social skills training that provides considerable guided practice and feedback on how to read social cues. The point to remember is that categorical labels are not particularly useful in describing specific students or developing instructional programs for them (Hardman et al., 2005). For example, both Damon and Aretha have learning disabilities, yet their areas of difficulty differ. Damon has a severe reading problem but excels in mathematics and various computer applications. Aretha, on the other hand, is reading at grade level but has significant problems with math. Though both students are categorized as having learning disabilities, they have very different needs. You must analyze each individual student's needs and differentiate instruction, as necessary. This individualization is at the heart of the INCLUDE strategy, introduced in Chapter 5.

Students with learning and behavioral disabilities have many academic needs. They have difficulty acquiring basic skills in the areas of reading, written language, and math. They also may lack skills necessary for efficient learning, such as attending to task, memory, organizing and interpreting information, reasoning, motor coordination, independent learning skills, and academic survival skills.

Reading Skills

Students with learning and behavioral disabilities have two major types of reading problems: decoding and comprehension. Decoding problems involve the skills of identifying words accurately and fluently. Accuracy problems are most readily observed when students read orally, mispronouncing words, substituting one word for another, or omitting words (Lerner & Johns, 2008). Students with reading fluency problems can read words accurately but do not recognize them quickly enough. They read slowly, in a word-by-word fashion, without grouping words together meaningfully (Hallahan et al., 2005; Lerner & Johns, 2008). Many of these reading decoding problems are exemplified in the following oral reading sample by a student with a learning disability:

> Then Ford had, uh, other i . . . a better idea. Take the worrrk to the men. He deee. . . . A long rope was hooked onto the car . . . wheels. . . . There's no rope on there. The rope pulled the car . . . auto . . . the white wheels along . . . pulled the car all along the way. Men stood still. Putting on car parts. Everybody man . . . put on, on, a few parts. Down the assembly line went the car. The assembly line saved . . . time. Cars costed still less to buh . . . bull . . . d . . . build. Ford cuts their prices on the Model T again. (Hallahan et al., 2005, p. 370)

Here is the passage the student tried to read:

> Then Ford had another idea. Take the work to the men, he decided. A long rope was hooked onto a car axle and wheels. The rope pulled the axle and wheels along. All along the way, men stood still putting on car parts. Down the assembly line went the car. The assembly line saved more time. Cars cost still less to build. Ford cut the price on the Model T again. (Hallahan et al., 2005, p. 370)

Students who have serious difficulties decoding written words are sometimes referred to as having *dyslexia*. The Professional Edge discusses the meaning of this term and suggests instructional approaches for students with this disorder.

Students with learning and behavioral disabilities often have problems comprehending stories in the elementary grades and content-area textbooks and advanced literature in the upper grades (Bursuck & Damer, 2011). Although these difficulties result in part from poor decoding skills, they may also occur because they lack background and vocabulary knowledge as well as strategies for identifying the key elements of stories and content-area texts. For example, after Connor's grandmother talked to him about her homeland of Vietnam, he was able to

INCLUDE

PROFESSIONAL **EDGE**
Understanding Dyslexia

The term *dyslexia* is used a lot. You hear that a friend's child has dyslexia, or you see a person who is dyslexic on television, or you read that Albert Einstein and Thomas Edison had dyslexia. The word *dyslexia,* which means "developmental word blindness," has a medical sound to it, but until recently there was little convincing evidence to show that it was medically based. Thanks to the development of computerized imaging techniques, such as functional magnetic resonance imaging (fMRI) and positron-emission tomography (PET scan), as well as recent studies of twins (Olson, 2006), evidence of an organic, genetic basis for dyslexia is beginning to accumulate.

Recent studies using computerized imaging show that the brain activity of students with dyslexia differs from that of students who are good readers (Shaywitz, 2003; Shaywitz & Shaywitz, 2007; Simos et al., 2007). For example, from an early age and often into adulthood, dyslexics show a pattern of underactivation in a region in the back of the brain that enables first accurate and then automatic reading. This pattern of underactivity appears to be present in dyslexics regardless of their age, sex, or culture (Shaywitz, 2003). That is why dyslexics have problems initially "cracking the code" and then problems later on developing reading fluency.

Studies of twins, sibling analysis, and family pedigree analysis have confirmed a genetic basis for learning disabilities (Fiedorowicz, 2005; Olson, 2006). Twin studies have shown that if one twin has a reading disability, the probability of the other twin having a reading disability is 68 percent for identical twins and 40 percent for fraternal twins. Studies also have shown that if there is a family history of dyslexia, the probability of an offspring having a reading disability is significantly increased (Fiedorowicz, 2005). While specific chromosomal links have been hypothesized, no definite conclusions about the genetic transmission of reading disabilities have been reached.

Knowing the cause of severe reading problems is one thing; knowing what to do to help students who have these problems is another altogether. Put very simply, students with dyslexia have serious problems learning to read despite normal intelligence, normal opportunities to learn to read, and an adequate home environment. Although the precise organic cause of dyslexia continues to be researched, considerable evidence suggests that reading problems associated with dyslexia are phonologically based (Blachman, 1997; Foorman, 2003; Stanovich & Siegel, 1994). Students with dyslexia have difficulty developing *phonemic awareness,* the understanding that spoken words are made up of sounds. Phonemic awareness problems make it hard for these students to link speech sounds to letters, ultimately leading to slow, labored reading characterized by frequent starts and stops and multiple mispronunciations. Students with dyslexia also have comprehension problems largely because their struggle to identify words leaves little energy for understanding what they read.

Students with dyslexia also have trouble with the basic elements of written language, such as spelling and sentence and paragraph construction. Finally, students with dyslexia may have difficulty understanding representational systems, such as telling time, directions, and seasons (Bryan & Bryan, 1986). Dyslexia commonly is considered a type of learning disability, and students with dyslexia are served under the learning disability classification of IDEA.

It is important to identify students with dyslexia and other severe reading disabilities early, before they fall far behind their peers in word-recognition reading skills. Early identification is particularly urgent given recent studies showing that effective language instruction appears to generate repair in underactivated sections of the brain (Odegard, Ring, Smith, Biggan, & Black, 2008; Shaywitz, 2003; Shaywitz, Morris, & Shaywitz, 2008; Simos et al., 2007). The use of RtI to identify reading disabilities will likely help schools to identify children earlier than the traditional approach of establishing a discrepancy between children's ability and reading achievement. This is because schools using a discrepancy model often have to wait for children to get older to have a large enough discrepancy between achievement and ability to be eligible for special education services. In this way, students who appear to be learning letter names, sounds, and sight words at a significantly slower rate than their classmates can receive intensive support as early as kindergarten. See the Instructional Edge in Chapter 4 on page 102 for universal screening measures used to identify children at risk for reading failure early.

FROM THE RESEARCH

A large body of research (Blachman, 2000; Foorman, 2003; McCardle & Chhabra, 2004; Moats, 2007; National Early Literacy Panel, 2008; National Reading Panel, 2000; Oakland, Black, Stanford, Nussbaum, & Balise, 1998; Shaywitz et al., 2008; Snow, Burns, & Griffin, 1998; Swanson, 2000) shows that many students with severe reading disabilities benefit from a beginning reading program that includes the following five elements:

1. *Direct instruction in language analysis.* For example, students need to be taught skills in phonemic segmentation by orally breaking down words into their component sounds.
2. *A highly structured phonics program.* This program should teach the alphabetic code directly and systematically by using a simple-to-complex sequence of skills, teaching regularity before irregularity, and discouraging guessing.
3. *Writing and reading instruction in combination.* Students need to be writing the words they are reading.
4. *Intensive instruction.* Reading instruction should take place in groups of four or fewer and include large amounts of practice in materials that contain words they are able to decode.
5. *Teaching for automaticity.* Students must be given enough practice that they are able to read both accurately and fluently.

For students who are dyslexic, visit the website Dyslexia: The Gift at http://www.dyslexia.com. Curriculum aids, a bookstore, discussion board, and links to further information are provided.

Using Assistive Technology (AT) in Reading

Most students with learning and behavioral disabilities have reading problems, and unfortunately, the reading problems persist into their preteen and adolescent years. At the same time, these students are spending more time in general education classes where access to content depends on reading independently textbooks written at their frustration level. While attempts to remediate their reading skills need to continue, AT can help students with learning and behavioral disabilities access content independently by bypassing their reading disability. A text-to-speech screen reader can be helpful for students who are unable to read their content textbooks, but have good listening skills. The particular screen reading tool required depends on how it is used. The various uses for screen-reader programs, along with corresponding examples of AT tools are shown below (Bisagno & Haven, 2002; Bursuck & Damer, 2011).

Use	AT Tool
Read aloud large volumes of straight text from the computer screen	Simple text (Apple) ReadPlease (PC)
Navigate and search the Internet	eReader (CAST.org) Home Page Reader (IBM)
Provide real-time aural feedback on written text that student types	Co:Writer 4000 (Don Johnston) WordSmith (textHELP)
Provide customized visual presentation of text as well as read-aloud	Kurzweil 3000 (Kurzweil Educational Systems) Freedom Scientific
Read aloud large volumes of straight text from hand-held eReader	Kindle (Amazon) Sony 505 Digital Reader Apple IPAD

Here are some additional suggestions when using AT for print access (Bisagno & Haven, 2002; Bursuck & Damer, 2011):

- Using a screen writer requires having an electronic version of the text to be read. E-text can be obtained from other sources such as Bookshare.org.
- To convert course readers and text not available electronically to e-text, a scanner, OCR software, and adequate editing time are needed.
- For students who prefer a human to a computerized voice, prerecorded audiofiles, CDs, or MP3 downloads are available from organizations such as Recordings for the Blind and Dyslexic or public and college libraries.
- If a recorded version of a book is not available, have the book read by a volunteer or paid reader.
- For more technical texts such as science and math, using a human reader who has knowledge of the subject is preferable.
- Bypass strategies using AT are not a substitute for learning how to read. Be sure your students are receiving systematic explicit instruction in reading decoding and comprehension as needed.

●··●··●

---

www.resources

Learn why some students struggle to learn to read and what can be done about it at http://www.childrenofthecode.org.

understand a well-written expository text about the Vietnam War. Todd's teacher asked him questions about a book he had just read as part of his classroom literature program. Todd was unable to tell her where the story took place (setting) or the lesson of the story (moral) because the answers to these questions were not directly stated in the story and Todd lacked the necessary inference strategies to figure them out. In another instance, Patsy was unable to answer a study question comparing the causes of World Wars I and II because she could not locate key words, such as *differences* and *similarities*. In addition, students with these disabilities may not be able to adjust their reading rate to allow for skimming a section of text for key information or for reading more slowly and intensively to answer specific questions. For example, Dennis takes a lot of time to locate key theorems in his geometry book because he thinks he needs to read every word in the chapter while he is looking for them.

Written Language Skills

The written language difficulties of students with learning and behavioral disabilities include handwriting, spelling, and written expression. Handwriting problems can be caused by a lack of fine motor coordination, failure to attend to task, inability to perceive and/or remember visual images accurately, and inadequate handwriting instruction in the classroom (Mercer & Pullen, 2009). Students may have problems in the areas of letter formation (is the letter recognizable?), size, alignment, slant, line quality (heaviness or lightness of lines), straightness, and spacing (too little or too much between letters, words, and lines).

Students with learning and behavioral disabilities also have trouble with spelling (Moats, 2007; Wanzek et al., 2006). The English language consists largely of three types of words: those that can be spelled phonetically, those that can be spelled by following certain linguistic rules, and those that are irregular. For example, the words *cats, construction,* and *retell* can be spelled correctly by applying phonics generalizations related to consonants, consonant blends (*str*), vowels, root words (*tell*), prefixes (*re*), and suffixes (*ion, s*). The word *babies* can be spelled by applying the linguistic rule of changing *y* to *i* and adding *es*. Words such as *said, where,* and *through* are irregular and can be spelled only by remembering what they look like. Students with learning and behavioral disabilities may have trouble with all three types of words.

These students have two major types of written expression problems: product problems and process problems (Isaacson, 2001; Mercer & Pullen, 2009). Their written products are often verb–object sentences, characterized by few words, incomplete sentences, overuse of simple subject–verb constructions, repetitious use of high-frequency words, a disregard for audience, poor organization and structure, and many mechanical errors, such as misspellings, incorrect use of punctuation and capital letters, and faulty subject–verb agreements and choice of pronouns (Mercer & Pullen, 2009).

These students also have trouble with the overall process of written communication. Their approach to writing shows little systematic planning, great difficulty putting ideas on paper because of a preoccupation with mechanics, failure to monitor writing, and little useful revision (Mercer & Pullen, 2009). A writing sample from a student who has a disability is shown in Figure 7.3. What types of product problems do you see in this sample? What process problems do you think might have led to these problems?

fyi

Teachers often mistake natural stages of child and adolescent development for signs of the presence of learning disabilities or emotional problems. Reversing letters or confusing *b* and *d,* for example, is common among children first learning to write.

RESEARCH NOTE

In manuscript writing, five letters (*q, z, u, j,* and *k*) account for 43 percent of all illegible letters written. For cursive writing, the letters *a, e, r,* and *t* accounted for about 50 percent of all illegible letters written (Mercer & Pullen, 2009).

FIGURE 7.3 Written Expression Sample of a 14-Year-Old Student with a Learning Disability

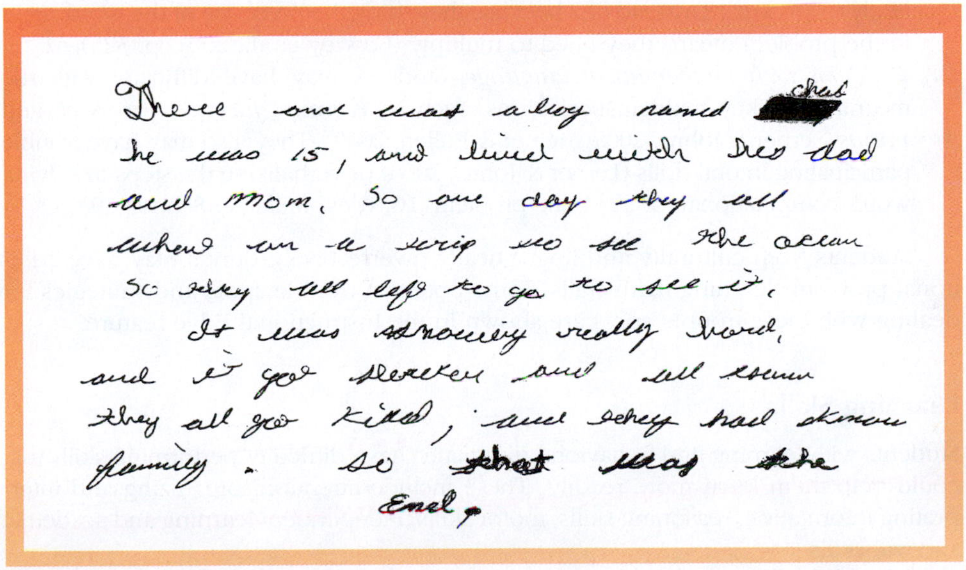

Math Skills

Math also can be problematic for students with learning and behavioral disabilities (Cawley, Miller, & Hudson, 2007; Strang & Rourke, 1985; Swanson & Jerman, 2006; Vukovic & Siegel, 2010). Common problems include the following:

1. *Problems with spatial organization.* Students may be unable to align numbers in columns, may reverse numbers (write a 9 backward, read 52 as 25), or may subtract the top number from the bottom number in a subtraction problem:

$$
\begin{array}{r}
75 \\
-39 \\
\hline
48
\end{array}
$$

2. *Lack of alertness to visual detail.* Students misread mathematical signs or forget to use dollar signs and decimals when necessary.

3. *Procedural errors.* Students miss a step in solving a problem. For example, they may forget to add a carried number in an addition problem or to subtract from the regrouped number in a subtraction problem:

$$
\begin{array}{r}
29 \\
+53 \\
\hline
72
\end{array}
\qquad
\begin{array}{r}
41 \\
-28 \\
\hline
23
\end{array}
$$

4. *Failure to shift mindset from one problem type to another.* Students solve problems of one type, but when required to solve problems of another type, they solve them in the way they did those of the first type. For example, Kristy has just completed several geometry problems that required finding area. The next problem asks for the perimeter, but she continues to compute area.

5. *Difficulty forming numbers correctly.* Students' numbers are too large or are poorly formed, which makes solving computational or algebraic problems awkward, particularly when the students are unable to read their own numbers.

6. *Difficulty with memory.* Students are frequently unable to recall basic math facts or use their working memory when solving problems involving multiple steps.

7. *Problems with mathematical judgment and reasoning.* Students are unaware when their responses are unreasonable. For example, they do not see the obvious errors in $9 - 6 = 15$ or $4 + 3 = 43$. They may also have trouble solving word problems. For example, they may be unable to decide whether to add or subtract in a word problem, focusing on cue words such as *less, more,* or *times* rather than comprehending accurately the situation described in the problem. This difficulty is shown in the following problem: "A boy has three times as many apples as a girl. The boy has 6. How many does the girl have?" Students with disabilities are likely to answer 18 instead of 2 because they think the presence of the word *times* in the problem means they need to multiply (Cawley et al., 2001, p. 325).

8. *Problems with mathematical language.* Students may have difficulty with the meanings of key mathematical terms, such as *regroup, formula, intersect,* and *minus* (Lerner & Johns, 2008; Mercer & Pullen, 2009). They also may have trouble participating in oral drills (Lerner & Johns, 2008) or verbalizing the steps in solving word, computational, or algebraic problems (Cawley, Miller, & School, 1987).

Students from culturally and linguistically diverse backgrounds may have additional problems learning math skills. Some potential trouble spots and strategies for dealing with these trouble spots are shown in the Instructional Edge feature.

Learning Skills

Students with learning and behavioral disabilities have difficulty performing skills that could help them learn more readily. These include attention, organizing and interpreting information, reasoning skills, motor skills, independent learning and academic survival skills.

INSTRUCTIONAL EDGE

Accommodating Learners in Math Who Are Linguistically and Culturally Diverse

Math can be a challenging subject for all students, including those with learning and behavioral difficulties. Students from linguistically and culturally diverse backgrounds may face additional challenges when learning math. In the following table, Scott and Raborn (1996) present some potential trouble spots and suggested strategies for teaching math to students from linguistically and culturally diverse backgrounds.

Trouble Spot	Recommendation
Learning a new language	• Determine the student's level of proficiency in both English and the native language. • Assess math abilities in both languages. • If a student is stronger in math than in English, provide math instruction in the primary language. • Listen to the words you most frequently use in teaching math. Work together with the ESL teacher to help the student learn these words or to help you learn them in the student's language. • Use a variety of ways to communicate such as gesturing, drawing sketches, writing basic vocabulary and procedures, rewording, and providing more details. • Provide time and activities that will allow students to practice the English language and the language of math.
Cultural differences	• Use word problem situations that are relevant to the student's personal cultural identity (e.g., ethnicity, gender, geographical region, age). • Share examples of the mathematical heritage of the student's culture (e.g., folk art, African and Native American probability games, measurement systems). • Involve family and community members in multicultural math.
Tricky vocabulary	• Use concrete activities to teach new vocabulary and the language of math. • Use only as many technical words as are necessary to ensure understanding. • Give more information in a variety of ways to help students understand new vocabulary. • Develop a picture file; purchase or have students make a picture dictionary of math terms and frequently used vocabulary.
Symbolic language	• Allow students to draw pictures, diagrams, or graphic organizers to represent story problems. • Make clear the meanings and function of symbols. • Point out the interchangeable nature of operations. • In algebra, teach students to translate phrases to mathematical expressions.
Level of abstraction and memory	• Allow students to develop mathematical relationships using concrete representations accompanied by verbal descriptions. • Develop mathematical understanding from concrete to abstract form. • Use visual and kinesthetic cues to strengthen memory. • Keep distractions to a minimum.

Source: From "Realizing the Gifts of Diversity among Students with Learning Disabilities," by P. Scott and D. Raborn, 1996, *LD Forum, 21*(2), pp. 10–18. Reprinted by permission of the Council of Learning Disabilities.

Attention Students may have difficulty coming to attention or understanding task requirements (Hallahan et al., 2005). For example, Janice frequently fails essay tests; she is unable to focus on key words in the questions to help her organize a response. As a result, she loses valuable writing time just staring at the question and not knowing how to begin. Benito misses important information at the beginning of science lectures because he takes five minutes to begin to attend to the teacher's presentation.

Students also may have trouble focusing on the important aspects of tasks. For example, Anita can tell you the color of her teacher's tie or the kind of belt he is wearing but nothing about the information he is presenting. When Arman tries to solve problems in math, he is unable to tell the difference between information that is needed and not needed to solve the problem.

Finally, students with learning and behavioral disabilities may have trouble sticking to a task once they have started it. This lack of task persistence is largely due to a lack of confidence resulting from a history of school failure. The emotional repercussions of school failure are covered later in this chapter in the discussion of the personal and psychological adjustment of students with learning and behavioral disabilities. Memory problems also may make learning difficult for students (Hallahan et al., 2005; Lerner & Johns, 2008). Some problems occur when information is first learned. For example, Carla cannot remember information when it is presented just once. Sal has practiced science vocabulary many times but still cannot remember some of them. Students may also have trouble with working memory (Mabbott & Bisanz, 2008; Swanson, Zheng, & Jerman, 2009). For example, Denise adds a column of numbers such as 6, 8, 4, and 5. When it is time to add in the 5, she forgets that the total up to that point was 18. Finally, students may also fail to retain what they learn. For example, Abby correctly identified the major parts of the human digestive system in Biology class Friday, but she failed to recall them accurately when asked by the teacher to do so the following week.

Organizing and Interpreting Information   Students with learning and behavioral disabilities may have trouble *organizing and interpreting* oral and visual information despite adequate hearing and visual skills (Lerner & Johns, 2008). For example, Rodney is a student with a learning disability who has trouble with visual tasks. He frequently loses his place while reading and copying; has trouble reading and copying from the chalkboard; does not notice details on pictures, maps, and photographs; is confused by worksheets containing a great deal of visual information; and often cannot remember what he has seen. LaTonya has trouble with auditory tasks. She has difficulty following oral directions, differentiating between fine differences in sounds (*e/i, bean/been*), taking notes during lectures, and remembering what she has heard.

Reasoning Skills   Students also may lack the *reasoning* skills necessary for success in school. Important reasoning skills include reading comprehension, generalization (the ability to recognize similarities across objects, events, or vocabulary), adequate background and vocabulary knowledge, induction (figuring out a rule or principle based on a series of situations), and sequencing (detecting relationships among stimuli) (Salvia et al., 2010). For example, Stu has difficulty understanding a lecture on the civil rights movement because he lacks necessary background information; he is unsure what a *civil right* is. Tamara has trouble recognizing a relationship on her own, even after repeated examples; her teacher presented five examples of how to add *s* to words that end in *y*, but Tamara still could not figure out the rule.

Motor Skills   Some students with learning and behavioral disabilities may have *motor coordination and fine motor impairments* (Lerner & Johns, 2008). For example, Denise is a first-grade student who has some fine motor and coordination problems. She has trouble using scissors, coloring within the lines, tying her shoes, and printing letters and numbers. Cal is in third grade. His handwriting is often illegible and messy. He is also uncoordinated at sports, which has limited his opportunities for social interaction on the playground because he is never selected to play on a team.

Independent Learning   Students with learning and behavioral disabilities have been referred to as *passive learners,* meaning that they do not believe in their own abilities; have limited knowledge of problem-solving strategies; and even when they know a strategy, cannot tell when it is supposed to be used (Hallahan et al., 2005; Lerner & Johns, 2008). Being a passive learner is particularly problematic in the upper grades, where more student independence is expected. For example, when Laverne reads her science textbook, she does not realize when she comes across information that she does not understand. So instead of employing a strategy to solve this problem, such as rereading, checking the chapter summary, or asking for help, she never learns the information. As a result, she is doing poorly in the class. When Darrell studies for tests, he reads quickly through his text and notes but does not use strategies for remembering information, such as asking himself questions, saying the information to himself, or grouping into meaningful pieces the information he needs to learn.

Academic Survival Skills   Students with learning and behavioral disabilities also may have problems in the area of **academic survival skills,** such as attending school regularly, being organized, completing tasks in and out of school, being independent, taking an interest in school, and displaying positive interpersonal skills with peers and adults (Brown et al., 1984; Kerr & Nelson, 2009). For example, Duane is failing in school because he rarely shows up for class; when he does attend class, he sits in the back of the room and displays an obvious lack of interest. Nicole is always late for class and never completes her homework; her teachers think she does not care about school at all.

Learning Styles

The idea of teaching to a child's learning style has been recommended as a way to meet the individual needs of students with learning and behavioral disabilities for at least 40 years (Landrum & McDuffie, 2010). In fact, in the experience of the authors, it is difficult to have a conversation with teachers about teaching students with special needs without the topic of learning styles coming up. The assumption behind a learning styles approach is that differing students have differing preferences for how to learn and that when the mode of teaching matches that preference, achievement is enhanced (Hattie, 2009). Dunn's model of learning styles (Dunn, 1983), the most common, has five dimensions: biological, which includes preferences for conditions such as room temperature or lighting; emotional, such as being persistent versus needing breaks when learning; sociological, such as having a preference for working in groups or alone; physiological, including preferences for time of day or needs for mobility; and psychological, such as being impulsive versus reflective, left brained versus right brained, or a global versus or analytic thinker (Hattie, 2009; Landrum & McDuffie, 2010). Examples of using a learning styles approach would include introducing content sequentially for analytic learners and using the "big picture" for global learners, teaching visual learners content using visual models rather than lecturing, and providing hands-on activities for tactile learners. Despite its broad intuitive appeal, the learning styles approach lacks a solid research base (Kavale, Hirshoren, & Forness, 1998; Landrum & McDuffie, 2010). Plus, the feasibility of being able to teach using one modality while excluding others is questionable at best. For example, try teaching reading visually while excluding anything auditory. For this reason, we suggest actively engaging students through all of their senses using universally designed instruction and then differentiating instruction as needed using INCLUDE.

Some parents and teachers have tried other unproven interventions in search of quick fixes for students with learning and behavioral disabilities. The issue of using unproven, controversial therapies is discussed in the Professional Edge.

What Are the Social and Emotional Needs of Students with Learning and Behavioral Disabilities?

Considering students' social needs is crucial, because students who have social adjustment problems in school are at risk for academic problems (Anderson, Kutash, & Duchnowski, 2001; Lane, Wehby, & Barton-Arwood, 2005; Morgan, Farkas, Tufis, & Sperling, 2008), as well as serious adjustment problems when they leave school (Carter & Wehby, 2003; Kauffman, 2005). Students with learning and behavioral disabilities may have needs in several social areas, including classroom conduct, interpersonal skills, and personal and psychological adjustment.

PROFESSIONAL EDGE

Controversial Therapies in Learning and Behavioral Disabilities: What Does the Research Say?

Being the parent or teacher of a student with learning disabilities is not easy. Students with learning and behavioral disabilities often do not respond favorably to the first approach tried—or for that matter, to the first several. Failure and frustration can lead to the search for miracle cures. This problem is compounded by the fact that journals that publish research about the effectiveness of various treatments are not normally read by parents and teachers. Unfortunately, this void is readily filled by a steady stream of information, much of it not substantiated by research, from popular books, lay magazines, television talk shows (Silver, 2006), and the Internet. Sinha and Efron (2005) recently surveyed Australian parents of children with ADHD and found that 68 percent of them had used or were currently using controversial therapies.

As a teacher, you need to be well informed about these therapies so you can give parents reliable, up-to-date information when they come to you for advice. The best way to get this information is to read professional journals. Any treatment may work for a few students, but this is not the same as demonstrating effectiveness in a controlled research study. If you or a student's parents decide to use a controversial therapy, you must monitor its effectiveness carefully and discontinue it if necessary. Several controversial therapies are summarized here, including the latest research findings for their effectiveness. Note that much of the material in the feature was taken from Silver (2006).

NEUROPHYSIOLOGICAL RETRAINING

In this group of approaches, learning difficulties are seen as the result of dysfunctions in the central nervous system that can be remediated by having students engage in specific sensory or motor activities. One common example of this approach is *patterning* (Doman & Delacato, 1968), in which students are taken back through earlier stages of development (creeping and crawling). Another approach is *optometric visual training*, in which students do eye exercises designed to improve their visual perception and hence their reading skills. A third approach, *vestibular training*, takes children through tasks involving spatial orientation, eye movements, and balance, with the goal of improving their academic performance, especially in reading. A fourth neurophysiological approach is *applied kinesiology*. According to this chiropractic theory, learning disabilities are caused when "two specific bones of the skull shift out of position and cause pressure on the brain" (Silver,

2006, p. 393). The treatment, which consists of manipulating the bones of the skull as well as other bones and muscles, can be quite painful for the child. A fifth approach is *auditory processing training*. This theory attributes learning disabilities to the failure of the body to organize incoming auditory stimuli into meaningful patterns, despite normal hearing. Training involves filtering out sounds believed to be interfering with the child's auditory perception, the eventual goal being to teach the ear to do this filtering on its own. Examples of auditory processing training include Bernard's auditory training integration and the Tomatis method.

A final neurophysiological approach is the so-called brain gym (Hyatt, 2007). The brain gym consists of a series of movements that are claimed to activate the brain, promote neurological repatterning, and facilitate whole-brain learning (Dennison & Dennison, 1994). The brain gym approach is based on the theory that learning problems are caused when sections of the brain and body don't work together, thereby blocking a child's ability to learn (Dennison & Dennison, 1994). The prescribed movements are intended to improve the integration of mind–body movements and in so doing enhance learning. No research provides evidence that any of these methods improves students' cognitive functioning or reading ability (American Academy of Pediatrics, 1999; Spaulding, Mostert, & Beam, 2010).

DIET CONTROL THERAPIES

A number of therapies involve using diet to control hyperactivity and other learning disorders. One of these (Feingold, 1975) claimed to decrease student hyperactivity by eliminating various artificial flavors, colors, and preservatives from the student's diet. Most research studies have shown that the Feingold diet is not effective in controlling hyperactivity (Bateman et al., 2004; Smith, 2004). Others have suggested that refined sugars in the diet lead to hyperactivity. Again, these claims have not been supported by research (Barkley, 1995; Rojas & Chan, 2005).

Another diet therapy for learning disorders involves using megavitamins to treat emotional or cognitive disorders (Cott, 1977, 1985). This therapy has not been verified by research (Smith, 2004). One theory purports that deficiencies in trace elements such as copper, zinc, magnesium, manganese, and chromium along with the more common elements of calcium, sodium, and iron cause learning disorders, but these claims remain unsubstantiated. Still another theory claims that hypoglycemia (low blood-sugar levels) causes learning disabilities. Clinical studies on this theory have been inconclusive (Rappaport, 1982/1983; Smith, 2004).

Finally, combinations of herbs, spices, and other ingredients have been recommended in recent years as a treatment for ADHD, as well as for learning disabilities. The effectiveness of these alternative medicines has yet to be validated by research.

SCOTOPIC SENSITIVITY SYNDROME

This syndrome has been defined as a difficulty in efficiently processing light, which causes a reading disorder (Irlen, 1991; Lerner & Johns, 2008). Symptoms include abnormal sensitivity to light, blinking and squinting, red and watery eyes, frequent headaches, word blurriness, print instability, slow reading, skipping and rereading lines, and difficulty reading at length because of general eye strain and fatigue (Irlen, 1991). Following a screening test, students identified as having scotopic sensitivity are treated with plastic overlays or colored lenses, which can be expensive. Although many people treated with tinted lenses claim that the lenses eliminate their symptoms and help them read better, research shows that the effects of the lenses are mixed (Silver, 2006). Caution is advised.

ALLERGIES

Although there seems to be a relationship between allergies and brain functioning, a clear cause-and-effect relationship has yet to be established (Silver, 2006). Two persons who have written a lot about the relationship between allergies and learning disabilities and ADHD are Dr. Doris Rapp and Dr. William Crook. Dr. Rapp suggests the elimination of certain foods from the diet, such as milk, chocolate, eggs, wheat, corn, peanuts, pork, and sugar. She performs an "under-the-tongue" test (not validated) that she claims determines whether a child is allergic to any or all of these foods. Dr. Crook's recent work has focused on child reactions to a specific yeast and the development of specific behaviors following a yeast infection. According to Silver (2006) and Smith (2004), neither Crook nor Rapp supports these findings with research. In addition, the established profession of pediatric allergies does not accept either of these treatments (Silver, 2006).

EMERGING THERAPIES

Rojas and Chan (2005) have reported on a number of therapies being recommended more often to treat learning and behavior difficulties often associated with ADHD. These therapies include fatty acid supplementation, homeopathy, yoga, massage, and green outdoor settings. Rojas and Chan conclude that the overall body of evidence does not support the use of any of these therapies either alone or in concert with treatments of established effectiveness, such as medication and behavior therapy.

CONTROVERSIAL THERAPIES AND THE INTERNET

As the number of Internet sites created for specific disabilities and related health issues increases, so too does information about controversial therapies. Because information on the Internet is not reviewed for quality, Ira (2000) suggests that you do the following to determine the credibility of the various websites you visit:

1. Click on the About Us or Contact Us links or buttons at a website. These links may inform you of who is on the team of people running a particular website. Many sites, particularly those that want to prove their credibility, feature a page describing their background, history, and affiliations (the About Us section) and mailing and e-mail addresses and phone numbers (the Contact Us section).
2. Try to establish links with other sites. Sites with reliably usable information may have endorsements from prominent special needs organizations or may have links to other websites with more information on the subject. Look for links to other associations or educational or even government-supported institutions related to the subject. The more independent sites that validate a recommendation, the more credible it is. The following are specific sites that may address doubts about the credibility of a particular controversial therapy:

http://www.interdys.org	International Dyslexia Society
http://www.ldanatl.org	Learning Disabilities Association of America
http://www.ncld.org	National Center for Learning Disabilities
http://www.cldinternational.org	Council for Learning Disabilities

3. Ask friends and special needs associations to recommend websites that are informative. You can also e-mail people you think can offer advice on the credibility of a particular site.
4. Examine the content of the site for typographical and grammatical errors. As with books, magazines, and journals, credibility is often reflected in editorial excellence.
5. Check to see how often the site is updated. A site that is updated regularly with new research findings is most likely to be run by people interested in learning the truth rather than perpetuating their own point of view.
6. Check to be sure that a given finding has been validated by a credible, refereed research publication. Many of these publications are available on the Web.

Students who are experiencing emotional problems might be withdrawn, anxious, or depressed. What can you do to help these students in your classroom?

Students with learning and behavioral disabilities may engage in a number of aggressive or disruptive behaviors in class, including hitting, fighting, teasing, hyperactivity, yelling, refusing to comply with requests, crying, destructiveness, vandalism, and extortion (Deitz & Ormsby, 1992; Friend, 2010; Hallahan et al., 2009). Although many of these behaviors may be exhibited by all children at one time or another, the classroom conduct of students with behavioral disorders is viewed by teachers as abnormal, and their behavior has a negative impact on the other students in class (Cullinan, 2007; Hallahan et al., 2009; Kauffman & Landrum, 2009).

For example, Kenneth is an adolescent with learning and behavior problems. His father died last year, and his mother has been working two jobs just to make ends meet. Kenneth has begun to hang out with a rough crowd and has been getting into fights in school. He has also been talking back to his teachers frequently and refusing to comply with their requests. Kenneth's behavior has gotten so bad that other students and their parents are complaining about it to the teacher. Guidelines for disciplining students like Kenneth are described in Chapter 12.

Interpersonal Skills

Students with learning and behavioral disabilities are likely to have difficulty in social relations with their peers. Evidence for these problems comes from more than 20 years of research showing that these students have fewer friends, are more likely to be rejected or neglected by their peers (Estell et al., 2008), and are frequently rated as socially troubled by their teachers and parents (Smith, 2004). Many of these problems can be traced to the failure of students to engage in socially appropriate behaviors or social skills in areas such as making friends, carrying on conversations, and dealing with conflict.

There are a number of explanations for why students have social skills problems. Some students may simply not know what to do in social situations. They may lack knowledge because they do not learn from naturally occurring models of social behavior at home or in school. Students also may have trouble reading social cues and may misinterpret the feelings of others (Bauminger & Kimhi-Kind, 2008; Bryan, 2005). For example, a story was told recently about five boys sitting on the floor of the principal's office, waiting to be disciplined. Four of the boys were discussing failing or near-failing grades and the trouble they were going to be in when the fifth boy, a student with a learning disability, chimed in to say that his grandparents were coming to visit the next week.

Other students may know what to do–but not do it. For example, some students with learning and behavioral disabilities are impulsive; they act before they think. In Del's sessions with the school social worker, he is able to explain how he would act in various social situations, but in an actual social setting, he gets nervous and acts without thinking.

Some students may choose not to act on their previous knowledge because their attempts at socially appropriate behavior may have gone unrecognized, and they would rather have negative recognition than no recognition at all. For example, James was rebuffed by one group of students so often that he began to say nasty things to them just to provoke them. He also began to hang out with other students who chronically misbehaved because, according to James, "At least they appreciate me!"

Finally, some students may know what to do socially but lack the confidence to act on their knowledge in social situations, particularly if they have a history of social rejection or lack opportunities for social interactions. Consider Holly, a student who is socially withdrawn. Holly worked for a year with her school counselor to learn how to initiate a social activity with a friend but is afraid to try it out for fear of being rejected.

Personal and Psychological Adjustment

Students with little success at academics and/or social relationships may have personal and psychological problems as well (Alexander & Cooray, 2003; Torgesen, 1991). One common personal problem is self-image. Students with learning and behavioral disabilities often have a poor self-concept; they have little confidence in their own abilities (Lerner & Johns, 2008; Licht, Kistner, Ozkaragoz, Shapiro, & Clausen, 1985; Silver, 2006). Poor self-image can in turn lead to **learned helplessness.** Students with learned helplessness see little relationship between their efforts and school or social success. When these students succeed, they attribute their success to luck; when they fail, they blame their failure on a lack of ability. When confronted with difficult situations, students who have learned helplessness are likely to say or think, "What's the use? I never do anything right anyway."

Not surprisingly, low self-esteem and learned helplessness often result in actions likely to be interpreted as a lack of motivation. For example, Denny is a 15-year-old sophomore in high school. He has been in special education since the second grade. He has never received a grade better than a C and has received quite a few Ds and Fs. Last quarter, Denny started to skip classes because he felt that even when he went to class, he did not do well. Denny is looking forward to dropping out of school on his sixteenth birthday and going to work for a fast-food chain, where, he reasons, at least he will be able to do the work. Of course, learning problems often coexist with motivational problems (Morgan, Fuchs, Compton, Cordray, & Fuchs, 2008) as many years of failure exact a toll on their confidence.

Students with learning and behavioral disabilities also may have severe anxiety or depression (Cullinan, 2007; Maag & Reid, 2006). Depressed or anxious students may refuse to speak up when in class, may be pessimistic or uninterested in key aspects of their lives, may be visibly nervous when given an assignment, may become ill when it is time to go to school, or may show a lack of self-confidence when performing common school and social tasks. For example, Barrett is a 9-year-old boy with a consistent history of school failure. He is sick just about every morning before he goes to school. At first his mother let him stay home, but now she makes him go anyway. When at school, Barrett is very withdrawn. He has few friends and rarely speaks in class. Barrett's teachers tend not to notice him because he is quiet and does not cause problems. If you have a student in your class who you think may be depressed, consult the Diagnostic Criteria for Major Depression (American Psychiatric Association, 2000).

www.resources

LD OnLine is an interactive guide to learning disabilities for parents, students, and teachers. This website offers newsletters, teaching tips, and more: http://www.ldonline.org.

Keep in mind that while students with learning and behavioral disabilities are at risk for having personal and psychological adjustment problems, not all of these students have these problems. In one study, Nunez et al. (2005) found that just under half of the students with learning disabilities did not differ in self-concept and learned helplessness from their classmates without disabilities. Using INCLUDE to find the individual needs and strengths of your students will help ensure that you will make accommodations for them based on their unique needs.

What Accommodations Can You Make for Students with Learning and Behavioral Disabilities?

As you have just read, students with learning and behavioral disabilities have a range of learning and social-emotional needs. Although these needs may make learning and socializing difficult for them, students with learning and behavioral disabilities can succeed in your classroom if given support. Some initial ideas about how you can accommodate students with learning and behavioral disabilities in your classroom are discussed next. A more in-depth treatment of such accommodations can be found in Chapters 8 through 12.

INCLUDE

Addressing Academic Needs

As you have already learned, you can discern whether students with learning and behavioral disabilities need differentiated instruction by using the INCLUDE strategy to analyze their academic needs and the particular demands of your classroom. In most cases, students with learning and behavioral disabilities are expected to meet the same curricular expectations as their classmates without disabilities. Therefore, when differentiating their instruction, provide them with instructional accommodations rather than modifications. Try the three types of

In what ways might students with cognitive, emotional, and behavioral disorders have difficulty learning? How can teachers address each of these areas of difficulty?

accommodations described in Chapter 5: bypassing a student's need by allowing the student to employ compensatory learning strategies; making an accommodation in classroom management, grouping, materials, and methods; and providing the student with direct instruction on basic or independent learning skills. For example, Jessica, who has learning disabilities, has enrolled in Mr. Gresh's high school general science class. Mr. Gresh uses a teaching format in which the students first read the text, then hear a lecture, and finally conduct and write up a lab activity (demands). Jessica has severe reading and writing problems. She is reading at about a sixth-grade level and has difficulty writing a legible, coherent paragraph (student learning needs). However, she does have good listening skills and is an adequate note taker (student strength). In Mr. Gresh's class, Jessica will have difficulty reading the textbook and meeting the lab-writing requirements independently (problem). She will be able to get the lecture information she needs because of her good listening skills (success). Mr. Gresh, with help from Jessica's special education teacher, brainstorms a number of possible accommodations for Jessica and then agrees to implement three of them. He develops a study guide to help Jessica identify key points in the text (materials and methods). He also sets up small groups in class to review the study guides (grouping) and assigns Jessica a buddy to help her with the writing demands of the lab activity (bypass). Finally, Mr. Gresh and the special education teacher set up a schedule to monitor Jessica's progress in writing lab reports and reading the textbook (evaluation). Several more examples of how the INCLUDE strategy can be used to differentiate instruction are provided in Table 7.2.

Addressing Social and Emotional Needs

One of the most important reasons given for inclusive education is the social benefit for students with and without disabilities (Freeman & Alkin, 2000; Stainback & Stainback, 1988). Unfortunately, experience shows that many students with learning and behavior problems do not acquire important social skills just from their physical presence in general education classes (Hallahan et al., 2005; Sale & Carey, 1995). Although much of the emphasis in your training as a teacher concerns academics, your responsibilities as a teacher also include helping all students develop socially, whether or not they have special needs. As with academics, the support students need depends largely on the specific social problems each student has. Students who have significant conduct problems benefit from a classroom with a clear, consistent behavior management system. In classrooms that are effectively managed, the rules are communicated clearly and the consequences for following or not following those rules are clearly stated and consistently applied. Conduct problems also can be minimized if students are engaged in meaningful academic tasks that can be completed successfully. Still, conduct problems may be so significant that they require a more intensive, individualized approach. For example, ReNaye, whom you read about at the beginning of this chapter, repeatedly talked out and loudly refused to carry out any requests her teachers made of her. Her school attendance was also spotty. ReNaye's general education teachers got together with her special education teacher to develop a **behavior contract.** The contract specified that for each class ReNaye attended without incident, she would receive points that her parents would allow her to trade for coupons to buy gasoline for her car.

Accommodations depend on the types of interpersonal problems your students have. You can use **social skills training** for students who do not know how to interact with peers and adults (Lane et al., 2005; McGinnis & Goldstein, 2005; Stichter et al., 2007; Walker & Rankin, 1983). For example, Tammy is very withdrawn and has few friends. One day her teacher took her aside and suggested that she ask one of the other girls in class home some day after school. Tammy told her that she would never do that because she just would not know what to say. Tammy's teacher decided to spend several social studies classes working with the class on that skill and other skills such as carrying on a conversation and using the correct words and

www.resources

The Center for Effective Collaboration and Practice promotes collaboration among federal agencies serving children who have, or are at risk of, developing emotional disabilities. Its website provides many links to resources on issues of emotional and behavioral problems in children and youth. Visit http://cecp.air.org.

TABLE 7.2 Differentiating Instruction for Students with Learning and Behavioral Disabilities Using Steps in the INCLUDE Strategy

Identify Classroom Demands	Note Student Strengths and Needs	Check for Potential Successes, Look for Potential Problems	Differentiate Instruction
Student desks in clusters of four	*Strengths* Good vocabulary skills *Needs* Difficulty attending to task	*Success* Student understands instruction if on task *Problem* Student off task—does not face instructor as she teaches	Change seating so student faces instructor
Small-group work with peers.	*Strengths* Good handwriting *Needs* Oral expressive language—problem with word finding	*Success* Student acts as secretary for cooperative group *Problem* Student has difficulty expressing self in peer-learning groups	Assign as secretary of group Place into compatible small group Develop social skills instruction for all students
Expectation for students to attend class and be on time	*Strengths* Good drawing skills *Needs* Poor time management	*Success* Student uses artistic talent in class *Problem* Student is late for class and frequently does not attend at all	Use individualized student contract for attendance and punctuality—if goals are met, give student artistic responsibility in class
Textbook difficult to read	*Strengths* Good oral communication skills *Needs* Poor reading accuracy Lacks systematic strategy for reading text	*Success* Student participates well in class Good candidate for class dramatizations *Problem* Student is unable to read text for information	Provide audiotaped textbook Highlight student text
Lecture on women's suffrage movement to whole class	*Strengths* Very motivated and interested in class *Needs* Lack of background knowledge	*Success* Student has near-perfect attendance and tries hard *Problem* Student lacks background knowledge to understand important information in lecture	Give student choice of video to view or leveled book to read before lecture Build points for attendance and working hard into grading system
Whole-class instruction on telling time to the quarter hour	*Strengths* Good coloring skills *Needs* Cannot identify numbers 7–12 Cannot count by 5s	*Success* Student is able to color clock faces used in instruction *Problem* Student is unable to acquire time-telling skills	Provide extra instruction on number identification and counting by 5s

TABLE 7.2 (*Continued*)

Identify Classroom Demands	Note Student Strengths and Needs	Check for Potential Successes, Look for Potential Problems	Differentiate Instruction
Math test involving solving word problems using addition	*Strengths* Good reasoning skills *Needs* Problems mastering math facts, sums of 10–18	*Success* Student is good at solving problems *Problem* Student misses problems due to math fact errors	Allow use of calculator
Multiple-choice and fill-in-the-blanks test	*Strengths* Good memory for details *Needs* Cannot identify key words in test questions Weak comprehension skills	*Success* Student does well on fill-in-the-blank questions that require memorization *Problem* Student is doing poorly on multiple-choice parts of history tests	Use bold type for key words in multiple-choice questions Teach strategy for taking multiple-choice tests Give student choice of alternatives to show knowledge other than multiple-choice items

demeanor when asking another student whether he or she would like to play a game. She felt that many of the students in class besides Tammy would benefit from these lessons. First, Tammy's teacher posted the steps involved in performing these skills on a chart in front of the classroom. Then she and several students in the class demonstrated the social skills for the class. She next divided the class into small groups, and each group role-played the various skills and was given feedback by classmates and peers. To make sure that Tammy felt comfortable, the teacher put her in a group of students who had a positive attitude and liked Tammy. An example of how to carry out social skills training is presented in the Case in Practice. Maag (2006) examined studies involving the use of social skills training with students with emotional and behavioral disorders. He found little evidence in these studies that social skills, once learned, either were maintained or generalized to other settings. Therefore, when using social skills training, be sure to remind your students to keep using them, carefully and continually monitor their usage using the Evaluate step in INCLUDE, and reteach if needed. You will learn more about the self-management of behavior in Chapters 10 and 12.

For students who know what to do in social situations but lack the self-control to behave appropriately, **self-control training** can be used (Henley, 2003; Kauffman & Landrum, 2009). Self-control training teaches students to redirect their actions by talking to themselves. For example, Dominic did not handle conflict very well. When his friends teased him, he was quick to lose his temper and to verbally lash out at them. His outbursts only encouraged the students, and they continued teasing and taunting him any chance they got. Dominic's teacher taught him a self-control strategy to help him ignore his friends' teasing. Whenever he was teased, Dominic first counted to 5 to himself to get beyond his initial anger. He then told himself that what they were saying wasn't true and that the best way to get them to stop was to ignore them and walk away. Whenever he walked away, Dominic told himself he did a good job and later reported his efforts to his teacher.

Some students may know what to do socially but lack opportunities for using their social skills. For example, students who are newly included in your classroom and/or new to the school need opportunities to interact with classmates to get to

fyi

Motivation is an important factor in the achievement of students with learning and behavior problems (Sideridis & Scanlon, 2006). Passive learning, learned helplessness, and a low self-image all play an important part in student motivation.

CASE IN PRACTICE

A Social Skills Training Session

Ms. Perez and her first-grade class are working on a unit on social skills in social studies. They are learning the skill of listening to someone who is talking by doing the following:

1. Look at the person who is talking.
2. Remember to sit quietly.
3. Think about what is being said.
4. Say yes or nod your head.
5. Ask a question about the topic to find out more.

Jeanine, a student in the class, has just practiced these listening skills in front of the class by role-playing the part of a student who is talking to her teacher about an assignment. In the role-play, Ms. Perez played herself. The class is now giving Jeanine feedback on her performance.

Ms. Perez: Let's start with the first step. Did Jeanine look at me when I was talking? Before you answer, can someone tell me why it's important to look at the person who is talking?

Lorna: You don't want the other person to think you're not listening. So you really have to *show* them you are listening.

Ms. Perez: That's right, Lorna. Well, how did Jeanine do on this one?

Charles: Well, she looked at you at first, but while you were talking she looked down at her feet. It looked like she wasn't listening.

Jeanine: I was listening, but I guess I should have looked at her all the way through.

Ms. Perez: Yes, Jeanine. To be honest, if I didn't know you better, I would have thought that you didn't care about what I was saying. You need to work on that step. The next step is to remember to sit quietly. How did Jeanine do with this one?

Milton: I think she did well. She remembered not to laugh or play around with anything while you were talking.

Ms. Perez: I agree, Milton. Nice work, Jeanine. Now, can someone tell me what the next listening step is?

Kyrie: It's to think about what the person is saying.

Ms. Perez: Right, Kyrie. Let's let Jeanine tell us herself how she did on this one.

Jeanine: Well, I tried to think about what you were saying. Once I started to think about something else, but I did what you told us and started thinking about a question I could ask you.

Ms. Perez: Good, Jeanine. Trying to think of a question to ask can be very helpful. How do you think you did on the next step? Did you nod your head or say yes to show you were following me?

Jeanine: I think I did.

Ms. Perez: What do the rest of you think? Did Jeanine say yes?

Tara: Well, I saw her nod a little, but it was hard to tell. Maybe she needs to talk louder.

Ms. Perez: Jeanine, you need to nod more strongly or the teacher won't realize you are doing it.

REFLECTIONS

What teaching procedures is Ms. Perez using to teach her students listening skills? Do you think they are effective? What could she do to make sure that her students use this skill at school? For what settings outside school would these and other social skills be important?

know them better. One way to create opportunities for social interaction is to allow students to work in small groups with a shared learning goal. For example, Thomas is a student with a mild intellectual disability who is part of Mr. Jeffreys' sixth-grade class. This is Thomas's first year in general education; until this year, he was in a self-contained special education classroom. Mr. Jeffreys has decided to use peer-learning groups in science because he thinks they will be a good way for Thomas to get to know his classmates and make some friends. Every two weeks, Thomas has the opportunity to complete various lab activities with a different group of his choice.

Students who exhibit learned helplessness can benefit from **attribution retraining** (Ellis, Lenz, & Sabornie, 1987b; Fulk, 1996; Mercer, Mercer, & Pullen, 2011). The idea behind attribution retraining is that if you can convince students that their failures are due to lack of effort rather than ability, they will be more persistent and improve their performance in the face of difficulty (Hallahan et al., 2005; Schunk, 1989). You can enhance student self-image by using the following strategies (Mercer & Pullen, 2009):

1. *Set reasonable goals.* When setting goals for students, make sure they are not too easy or too hard. Self-worth is improved when students reach their goals through

considerable effort. Goals that are too ambitious perpetuate failure. Goals that are too easy can give students the idea that you think they are not capable of doing anything difficult.

2. *Provide specific feedback contingent on student behavior.* Feedback should be largely positive, but it should also be contingent on completion of tasks. Otherwise, students are likely to perceive your feedback as patronizing and just another indication that you think they are unable to do real academic work. Do not be afraid to correct students when they are wrong. Providing corrective feedback communicates to students that you think they can succeed if they keep trying and that you care about them.

3. *Give students responsibility.* Assigning a responsibility demonstrates to students that you trust them and believe they can act maturely. Some examples for younger students include taking the class pet home over a holiday break, taking the lunch count, being a line leader, taking messages to the office, and taking attendance. For older students, try giving students input into classroom decisions such as selecting learning groups and developing their own assignments, including setting due dates.

4. *Teach students to reinforce themselves.* Students with a poor self-image say negative things about themselves. You can help students by reminding them of their strengths, encouraging them to make more positive statements about themselves, and then reinforcing them for making these statements.

5. *Give students a chance to show their strengths.* Part of the INCLUDE strategy is to identify student strengths and then help students achieve success by finding or creating classroom situations in which they can employ their strengths. For example, Cara cannot read very well but has an excellent speaking voice. After her group wrote a report on the 1960 presidential election, Cara was given the task of presenting the report to the whole class.

dimensions of DIVERSITY

A small proportion of high school students with disabilities are lesbian, gay, bisexual, or transgender (LGBT) persons. LGBT students with disabilities may need support to address socially appropriate behaviors and strategies for interpreting the messages they may receive, whether positive or negative (Harley et al., 2002).

INCLUDE

WRAPPING IT UP

BACK TO THE CASES

This section provides opportunities for you to apply the knowledge gained in this chapter to the cases described at the beginning of this chapter. The questions and activities that follow demonstrate how these standards and principles, along with other concepts that you have learned about in this chapter, connect to the everyday activities of all teachers.

WILL has difficulty with two important basic skills: reading and writing. His teachers need more information about methods for supporting Will's reading and writing so that he can learn the content needed to pass his end-of-grade tests and make a smooth transition to middle school. Two popular websites offer information specifically for and about persons with learning disabilities: Schwab Learning (http://schwablearning.org) and LD Online (http://ldonline.org). Your task is to visit those websites and find information that you think would help teachers meet the learning needs of students with problems similar to Will's. Complete an annotated list of articles, videos, and links

to additional information from those websites that you might share with Will's teacher and the peers in your class. How do you think Will would be supported if he were in an RtI school?

RENAYE, as you may remember, demonstrated aggressive and noncompliant behaviors. Her behavior was addressed with a behavior contract. However, over the years she has missed opportunities to learn due to her frequent absences and discipline referrals, resulting in lower grades and a failed end-of-grade test in ninth-grade mathematics. Most likely she lacks some basic skills and knowledge that she will need to successfully progress. Now her team is meeting to discuss how they can help her make up the missed work and successfully pass the math test. Using the information from the text, as well as from your search for solutions to Will's difficulties, describe two or three teaching strategies or accommodations that you think would help ReNaye's teachers support her. Provide a rationale for your answer.

SUMMARY

- Students with high-incidence disabilities are those who have speech and language disabilities, learning disabilities, emotional disturbance, or mild intellectual disabilities. These students make up approximately 80 percent of all students who have disabilities. They are often hard to distinguish from their peers; exhibit a combination of behavior, social, and academic problems; and benefit from systematic, highly structured interventions.

- Some students have communication disorders. Students with speech problems have trouble in the areas of articulation, voice, and fluency. Language problems involve receptive and/or expressive language. The academic and social performances of students with speech and language problems can be enhanced through a number of accommodations, including creating an atmosphere of acceptance, actively encouraging and teaching listening skills, using modeling to expand students' language, and teaching within contexts that are meaningful for students.

- Students with learning and behavioral disabilities have many academic needs. They may also lack skills necessary for efficient learning, such as attending to task, memory, organizing and interpreting information, reasoning, motor coordination, independent learning skills, and academic survival skills. Accommodations for students with learning and behavioral disabilities in academic areas include bypassing their disability; making an adjustment in classroom management, grouping, materials, and methods; and providing students with direct instruction on basic or independent learning skills.

- Students with learning and behavioral disabilities have social and emotional difficulties in classroom conduct, interpersonal skills, and personal and psychological adjustment. Accommodations for students with learning and behavioral disabilities in social areas include individualized behavior management, social skills training, self-control training, and attribution retraining.

APPLICATIONS IN TEACHING PRACTICE

USING THE INCLUDE STRATEGY WITH STUDENTS WITH HIGH-INCIDENCE DISABILITIES

Answer the following questions to show how you would apply the INCLUDE strategy to differentiate instruction for the students described in the vignettes at the beginning of this chapter. To help you with this application, refer to Table 7.2, to the section on the INCLUDE strategy in Chapter 5, and to information gathered for Back to the Cases.

QUESTIONS

1. What communication, academic, behavioral, and social and emotional needs does each student have?

2. Keeping in mind the major aspects of the classroom environment, including classroom management, classroom grouping, instructional materials, and instructional methods, what kinds of problems are these students likely to have?

3. How would you differentiate instruction for each of these students?

4. Are the accommodations you would make reasonable in terms of teacher time and ease of implementation? What support (if any) would you need to carry them out?

5. How can you monitor the effectiveness of your differentiated instruction? What can you do next if your first attempt is ineffective?

Go to Topics 14: Learning Disabilities/ADHD, 16: Communication Disorders, and 17: Emotional and Behavioral Disorders in the MyEducationLab (www.myeducationlab.com) for your course, where you can:

- Find learning outcomes for Learning Disabilities/ADHD, Communication Disorders, and Emotional and Behavioral Disorders along with the national standards that connect to these outcomes.
- Complete Assignments and Activities that can help you more deeply understand the chapter content.
- Apply and practice your understanding of the core teaching skills identified in the chapter with the Building Teaching Skills and Dispositions learning units.
- Examine challenging situations and cases presented in the IRIS Center Resources. (optional)
- Access video clips of CCSSO National Teachers of the Year award winners responding to the question, "Why Do I Teach?" in the Teacher Talk section. (optional)
- Check your comprehension on the content covered in the chapter by going to the Study Plan in the Book Resources for your text. Here you will be able to take a chapter quiz, receive feedback on your answers, and then access Review, Practice, and Enrichment activities to enhance your understanding of chapter content. (optional)

chapter 8

Students with Special Needs Other Than Disabilities

LEARNING Objectives

After you read this chapter, you will be able to

1. Describe students protected under Section 504 and the accommodations general education teachers can make for them.

2. Explain accommodations general education teachers can make to address the special needs of students with attention deficit–hyperactivity disorder (ADHD).

3. Outline how general education teachers meet the needs of their students who are gifted and talented.

4. Explain how cultural diversity influences education, critically analyzing your own response to students from cultures other than your own and your skills for addressing their needs.

5. Describe how general education teachers can accommodate students at risk for school failure, including students affected by poverty, abuse or neglect, substance abuse, and other factors.

MARIA is an eighth-grade student whose family immigrated to the United States from Mexico three years ago. At first, Maria attended a bilingual program in which she learned some core content in Spanish while working on her English skills. For the past year, though, she has not received any special educational support. Maria is bilingual—a speaker of both Spanish, the language spoken in her home, and English, the language she usually speaks at school. However, she still sometimes misunderstands what her teachers mean and struggles with some of the material being taught. Her language skills are not yet advanced enough to easily grasp abstract concepts. Maria likes school; she wants to go to college but is not sure this is a realistic goal. Her parents both work, but she has three sisters and a brother, and there is no extra money for higher education. Her oldest sister attends the community college, working in a full-time job to earn the money she needs to contribute to the family and pay tuition, and Maria is eager to be old enough to earn money too. Maria's teachers are already encouraging her to become an educator; they recommended her for a special summer program designed to recruit future teachers who will work in their communities. Maria is thrilled to have this opportunity.

What special needs might students like Maria have? What is your responsibility for finding ways to help all your diverse students succeed in school? How can you develop a better understanding of students and families from diverse cultures?

SETH is struggling in middle school. He still has difficulty remembering the combination to his locker, and he often forgets to bring to class his assignment notebook or his textbooks or his homework or his pen, or something else. He has been embarrassed several times when his teachers have reprimanded him after he didn't answer the question asked or seemed to ignore directions given in class. Seth hates it when he draws attention to himself, and yet that is happening all too often. Seth's parents, after a conversation with the pediatrician and with Seth, had decided that the transition to middle school was a good time to try to address Seth's ADHD without medication, but they are having second thoughts. Seth has a Section 504 plan that all his teachers are aware of, but the accommodations it includes—preferential seating, frequent change-of-pace activities, and others—are not adequately addressing the ADHD characteristics Seth has.

Does Seth have a disability? What are Seth's special needs? What is the responsibility of school personnel for meeting those needs?

LYDIA is a fourth-grade student who is gifted and talented. She has been reading since age three, and she frequently borrows her sister's high school literature anthology as a source of reading material. She knew most of the math concepts introduced in fourth grade before the school year began. She has a strong interest in learning French and playing flute and piano, and she volunteers to read to residents of a local nursing home. Lydia's idea of a perfect afternoon is to have a quiet place to hide, a couple of wonderful books, and no one to bother her. Lydia's teacher, Mr. Judd, enjoys having her in class because she is so enthusiastic about learning, but he admits that Lydia's abilities are a little intimidating. He also has noticed that Lydia doesn't seem to have much in common with other students in class. She is a class leader but does not appear to have any close friends, as other students do.

To what services is Lydia entitled because of her giftedness? Is Lydia typical of students who are gifted or talented? What can Mr. Judd do to help Lydia reach her full potential? What social problems are students like Lydia likely to encounter?

TAM is a junior in high school, but he doubts that he will finish the school year. He describes school as "pointless," and he continues to come only because he would hate to hurt his mother's feelings by dropping out. He is absent often, especially from his first-block U.S. history class, and he usually does not bother to do homework or read assignments. Tam does not belong to any clubs at school or participate in any athletics. After school, Tam hangs out with his friends, often congregating in the alley behind an electronics store and not returning home until well after midnight. He is considering an offer to run drugs that recently was made by Michael, a 21-year-old dropout who Tam admires. Tam has a juvenile record; he is on probation for stealing a car. Michael told him, though, that the risks of prison are minimal until he turns 18 and that his record will be expunged at that time even if he gets arrested again. Tam's rationale is that he knows many people who make money this way. Tam's teachers describe him as "unmotivated," a student who has vastly more potential than they see him using.

How many public school students are similar to Tam? What other characteristics and behaviors might Tam display in school? If Tam were your student, how would you try to reach him? What are your responsibilities to students like Tam?

PEARSON
myeducationlab

To check your comprehension on the content covered in chapter 8, go to the Book Resources in the MyEducationLab for your course, select your text, and complete the Study Plan. Here you will be able to take a chapter quiz, receive feedback on your answers, and then access review, practice, and enrichment activities to enhance your understanding of chapter content.

Most educators agree that many students who are not eligible to receive special education have needs as great as or greater than those of students protected by the Individuals with Disabilities Education Act (IDEA). For example, Maria has made great progress in learning English, but she still experiences difficulties with the technical language of academic content. Even though Seth has a significant attention problem, he does not qualify for special education. Lydia's teacher is concerned that he cannot possibly make time to provide the advanced instruction that would benefit her, but her school district does not offer any programs for students who are gifted or talented until middle school. Tam's teachers worry about his future and are frustrated that they cannot make his life better and help him reach his potential. They feel powerless to influence students like Tam, who have so many difficulties in their young lives, and they question how traditional academic standards and activities can be made relevant for those students.

This chapter is about students who are not necessarily eligible for special education but whose learning is at risk and whose success often depends on the quality of the instruction they receive and the care provided by general education teachers. The students considered in this chapter fall into one or more of these groups: Those who have functional disabilities protected by Section 504, the civil rights law introduced in Chapter 1, but who are not protected by IDEA; those with attention deficit-hyperactivity disorder (ADHD); those who are gifted and talented; those whose native language is not English and whose cultures differ significantly from those of most of their classmates; and those who are at risk because of life circumstances, including poverty, child abuse, drug abuse, transience (for example, migrant families), and other factors.

Even though the students discussed in this chapter generally are not eligible for special education services, there are four reasons they are included in this textbook:

1. Students with these types of needs often benefit greatly from the same strategies that are successful for students with disabilities. Thus, one purpose is to remind you that the techniques explained throughout this text are applicable to many of your students, not just those who have individualized education programs (IEPs).
2. You should recognize that you will teach students with a tremendous diversity of needs resulting from many different causes, disability being just one potential factor. Creating appropriate educational opportunities for all your students is your responsibility.
3. Students with special needs often are referred for special education services because caring teachers recognize that they need help. It is essential that you realize that special education is much more than help and is reserved for just the specific groups of students already described in Chapters 6 and 7.
4. Although many special educators are committed to helping you meet the needs of all your students, including those at risk, they cannot take primary responsibility for teaching students like Maria, José, Lydia, and Tam. These are not students who "should be" in special education. Rather, they represent the increasingly diverse range of students that all teachers now instruct. As such, they highlight the importance of creating classrooms that respect this diversity and foster learning regardless of students' unique needs, backgrounds, and experiences.

dimensions of
DIVERSITY

Equity pedagogy is the term that describes the use of instructional strategies that address the learning characteristics and cognitive styles of diverse populations. If you complete an Internet search using this term, you can find research and teaching resources for effectively working with all your students.

This chapter also highlights how complex student needs have become (Assouline, Nicpon, & Whiteman, 2010; Delgado, 2010; Frattura & Capper, 2006). For example, you probably realize that students with disabilities also can have the special needs described here. For example, a student with a physical disability also might be academically gifted. A student with an intellectual disability also might live in poverty. A student with a learning disability might speak a language other than English at home. You probably recognize, too, that the student groups emphasized in this chapter are not necessarily distinct, even though it is convenient to discuss them as if they were. Students who live in poverty can also be gifted and members of a cultural minority. An abused student can be at risk because of drug abuse.

Keep in mind as you read this chapter that your responsibility as a teacher for all students—regardless of their disabilities and other special needs—is to use the principles of the INCLUDE strategy to identify strengths and needs, arrange a supportive instructional environment, provide high-quality instruction, and foster student independence. When students have multiple needs, these tasks can be especially challenging, and you should seek assistance from colleagues, parents, and other professional resources.

INCLUDE

Which Students Are Protected by Section 504?

In Chapter 1, you learned that some students with special needs who do not meet the eligibility criteria for receiving services through IDEA are considered functionally disabled, as defined by **Section 504** of the Vocational Rehabilitation Act of 1973. The primary goal of this law is to prevent discrimination against these individuals. Students with functional disabilities are entitled to receive reasonable accommodations that help them benefit from school. These accommodations can include some of the same types of services and supports received by students eligible through IDEA, but there are crucial differences between the two statutes as well (Richards, Brown, & Forde, 2007).

Understanding Section 504

First, the definition of a disability in Section 504 is considerably broader than it is in IDEA. In Section 504, any condition that substantially limits a major life activity, such as the ability to learn in school, is defined as a *disability*. This definition means that students with a wide range of needs that do not fall within the 13 federal disability categories for education are eligible for assistance through Section 504, including students with significant attention problems, drug addiction, chronic health problems, communicable diseases, temporary disabilities resulting from accidents or injury, environmental illnesses, and alcoholism (Office for Civil Rights, 2009).

Second, unlike IDEA, Section 504 does not provide funds to school districts to carry out its requirements (Zirkel, 2009). The expectation is that schools should take whatever steps are necessary, even if additional funds are required, to eliminate discrimination as defined through this statute. Third, the responsibility for making accommodations for students who qualify as disabled through Section 504 belongs to general education personnel, not special education personnel. Special educators might provide some informal assistance, but their aid is not mandated as it is in IDEA. The types of accommodations required vary based on student needs but could include alterations in the physical environment, such as providing a quiet workspace or a room with specialized lighting; modifications in instruction, such as decreasing the number of items in an assignment, allotting additional time to complete it, or providing a note-taker; organizational assistance, such as checking a student's backpack to ensure that all materials for homework are there; and making changes in a student's schedule, such as allowing a rest period. Table 8.1 summarizes these and other differences between these important laws.

The regulations governing Section 504 are similar to those for IDEA. That is, for students to receive assistance through Section 504, their needs must be assessed and a decision made concerning their eligibility (Richards et al., 2007). School districts must screen students (typically using some type of response to intervention or pre-referral process), convene a team and obtain parent permission to evaluate student needs (although formal testing, as is typical for IDEA, is not necessarily required), determine eligibility for services, and create a plan to implement services in the general education classroom.

When students are determined eligible and have Section 504 plans, those plans cover their instructional programs as well as after-school programs, field trips, summer programs, and other extracurricular activities (T. E. C. Smith, 2002). The plans outline

fyi

Effective in 2009, the Americans with Disabilities Act Amendments (ADAA) expanded that law's list of major life functions to include reading and concentrating, provisions that also would apply to Section 504; the result may be an increase in the number of students eligible for a Section 504 plan (Zirkel, 2009).

TABLE 8.1 Examples of Differences between IDEA and Section 504

Component	IDEA	Section 504
Purpose	To provide federal financial assistance to state and local education agencies to assist them in educating children with disabilities	To eliminate discrimination on the basis of disability in all programs and activities receiving federal financial assistance
Individuals protected	All school-age children who fall within 1 or more of 13 specific categories of disability and who, because of such disability, need special education and related services	All school-age children who have a physical or mental impairment that substantially limits or may limit a major life activity, have a record of such an impairment, or are regarded as having such an impairment (major life activities include walking, seeing, hearing, speaking, breathing, learning, reading, concentrating, working, caring for oneself, performing manual tasks, and others)
Free and appropriate public education (FAPE)	Requires that FAPE be provided only to those protected students who, because of disability, need special education or related services Defines FAPE as special education and related services; a student can receive related services under IDEA if and only if the student is provided special education and needs related services to benefit from special education Requires a written IEP and a required number of specific participants at the IEP meeting.	Requires that FAPE be provided only to those protected students who, because of disability, need regular education accommodations, special education, or related services. Defines FAPE as regular or special education and related aids and services; a student can receive related services under Section 504 even if the student is in regular education full time and is not provided any special education Does not require an IEP but does require a plan prepared by a group of persons knowledgeable about the student
Funding	Provides additional funding for protected students	Does not provide additional funds; IDEA funds may not be used to serve students protected only under Section 504
Evaluation	Requires reevaluation to be conducted at least every three years Does not require a reevaluation before a change of placement but evaluation data, including progress toward goals and objectives, should be considered	Requires periodic reevaluation; the IDEA schedule for reevaluation can suffice Requires reevaluation before a significant change in placement
Placement procedures	An IEP meeting is required before any change in placement	A reevaluation meeting is required before any "significant change" in placement
Grievance procedures	Does not require a grievance procedure or a compliance officer	Requires districts with more than 15 employees to (1) designate an employee to be responsible for assuring district compliance with Section 504 and (2) provide a grievance procedure for parents, students, and employees
Due process	Contains detailed hearing rights and requirements	Requires notice, the right to inspect records, the right to participate in a hearing and to be represented by counsel, and a review procedure
Exhaustion	Requires the parent or guardian to pursue an administrative hearing before seeking redress in the courts	Does not require an administrative hearing prior to Office for Civil Rights involvement or court action; compensatory damages possible
Enforcement	Enforced by the U.S. Office of Special Education Programs (OSEP); compliance monitored by state department of education and OSEP	Enforced by the U.S. Office for Civil Rights

Source: From *Meeting the Needs of All Students,* by the Parent Advocacy Coalition for Educational Rights, 2004, Minneapolis, MN: Author. Retrieved July 26, 2007, from http://www.pacer.org/parent/504.html#IDEA504. Reprinted with permission from PACER Center, 952-838-9000.

P R O F E S S I O N A L **EDGE**

Section 504 Accommodations

Many types of accommodations can be written into a Section 504 plan. The only guidelines are that the adjustments should be (1) individualized to meet students' needs and (2) reasonable, or designed to "level the playing field" for these students. These accommodations should go beyond those typically offered to all students (for example, allowing students to choose from among several projects). Here are some examples of classroom accommodations you might find in a Section 504 plan:

- Seat the student nearest to where the teacher leads most instruction.
- Provide clues such as clock faces indicating beginning and ending times for instruction or assignments.
- Establish a home–school communication system for monitoring behavior.
- Fold assignments in half so the student is not overwhelmed by the quantity of work.
- Make directions telegraphic—that is, concise and clear.
- Record lessons so the student can listen to them again.

- Use multisensory presentation techniques, including peer tutors, experiments, games, and cooperative groups.
- Provide practice tests that are very similar in structure and appearance to actual tests.
- Mark right answers instead of wrong answers.
- Send a set of textbooks to be left at home so the student does not have to remember to bring books to and from school.
- Provide audio books so the student can listen to assignments instead of reading them.

Remember that Section 504 accommodations may vary greatly depending on a student's special needs, such as a medical condition or physical problem, drug or alcohol abuse, ADHD, or others.

Sources: Adapted from *Ideas for an IEP or Section 504 Plan*, by D. Simms, 2000, retrieved on September 13, 2000, from http://www.angelfire.com/ny/ Debsimms/education.html; and *Sevier County (TN) School System Section 504 Examples of Program Accommodations and Adjustments*, retrieved December 3, 2004, from http://www.slc.sevier.org/504ana.htm. Adapted by permission of the Sevier County Department of Special Education.

---

the accommodations needed, who is to implement them, and how they will be monitored. A sample of the types of accommodations that may be incorporated into a Section 504 plan is presented in the Professional Edge.

Students Eligible for Services under Section 504

Although many students can qualify for assistance through Section 504, three groups are addressed in this chapter: students with medical or health needs, students with learning problems, and students with attention deficit–hyperactivity disorder (ADHD). The first two groups are discussed here; students with ADHD are covered in more depth in the subsequent section.

Students with Chronic Health or Medical Problems   Students with chronic health or medical problems—for example, those with communicable or chronic diseases—who are not eligible for IDEA services according to established criteria and as determined by a multidisciplinary team, comprise one of the major groups that can qualify for assistance through Section 504. For example, a student who has asthma not serious enough to be considered a disability under IDEA might have a Section 504 plan. The plan could address accommodations related to the student's need for occasional rest periods, opportunities to take medication, exemption from certain physical activities, and provisions to make up assignments and tests after absences. Similarly, a student with severe allergies might have a Section 504 plan that specifies materials in school that cannot be used (for example, paints, chalk, peanut products), guidelines for participation in physical education, and requirements for providing assignments that can be completed at home if necessary.

The increasing rate of childhood obesity has led to yet another group who might receive accommodations: students who have diabetes. The student who is diabetic might have a plan that addresses

When students have functional disabilities that limit their access to education, they may be eligible for a Section 504 plan that specifies the supports they need.

permission to use the restroom whenever requested; permission to keep a bottle of water present during class; permission to test blood glucose as necessary, including in the classroom; and postponement of high-stakes testing without penalty if blood glucose is too high or too low.

Students with Learning Problems   A second group of students who may receive support under Section 504 comprises those who experience significant learning problems but who are not determined to have a learning disability (Brady, 2004) according to state criteria. For example, Carson is a student who experiences extraordinary difficulty in reading. Although his school district does not recognize the term *dyslexia,* a local clinic has diagnosed him with that disorder. A recent evaluation led to a conclusion that he is not eligible for special education services as learning disabled. However, he is showing signs of anxiety related to reading tasks (for example, crying when asked to read), and the team decided that he should have the protection of a Section 504 plan because the combination of problems is affecting his school success, a major life activity. Carson receives remedial reading instruction, but his Section 504 plan includes testing in a separate, quiet location with some tests read aloud and access to text-to-speech software for classwork.

As you can tell, some of the responsibility for implementing Section 504 plans belongs to administrators, who authorize physical modifications to classrooms and make arrangements for students, for example, to have rest periods or take medications. Your responsibility is to implement instructional accommodations outlined in the plan, such as providing assignments in advance and allowing extra time for work completion. Your interactions with students protected by Section 504 differ from your interactions with other students only in your responsibility to make the required accommodations.

How Can You Accommodate Students with Attention Deficit–Hyperactivity Disorder?

Students with attention problems have been a concern of teachers for many years. In fact, labels such as *hyperkinesis* and *minimal brain dysfunction* have been applied to these students since the 1940s (Barkley, 2006), and the first medication to help them was developed in the 1950s (Eli Lilly, 2003). The challenges that these students present for teachers, parents, and peers have raised awareness that they have a disorder, prompted research about their characteristics and needs, and fostered the development of new interventions for assisting them in school and everyday life. Some students with significant attention problems as described in this section are eligible for services through IDEA, but many receive assistance through Section 504 (Mattox & Harder, 2007).

The term for significant attention problems is **attention deficit–hyperactivity disorder (ADHD),** a condition defined in the *Diagnostic and Statistical Manual of Mental Disorders (DSM–IV–TR)* (American Psychiatric Association, 2000). ADHD is diagnosed when an individual has chronic and serious inattentiveness, hyperactivity, and/or impulsivity that is more severe and occurs more frequently than in peers.

Students with ADHD generally have symptoms that fall into one of these three categories (American Psychiatric Association, 2000):

1. *ADHD—predominantly inattentive type.* Students in this group often appear to daydream. They may not hear teacher directions, sometimes skip parts of an assignment they do not notice, and frequently lose things. However, they do not move around more than their peers.

2. *ADHD—predominantly hyperactive–impulsive type.* Students in this group move around far more than their peers, and they tend to be impulsive, acting before thinking. They squirm in their seats, tap pencils or fingers, and blurt out answers during instruction.

fyi

Attention deficit disorder (ADD) is an earlier term, no longer recommended, for describing attention problems. Some professionals still use the terms ADHD and ADD interchangeably.

3. *ADHD—combined type.* Students in this group display the characteristics of both of the other types of ADHD. They experience extraordinary difficulty both in focusing their attention and in restricting their movement.

Think about Seth, the student you met at the beginning of the chapter. Which type of ADHD seems to best characterize him?

Estimates of the prevalence of ADHD suggest that 3 to 7 percent of all children, some 4.7 million, have this disorder and that it occurs in boys as opposed to girls at a rate of approximately two to one (Bloom & Cohen, 2007; Centers for Disease Control and Prevention, 2010b). It is one of the most commonly diagnosed childhood psychiatric disorders, and it also occurs frequently with other disabilities, including learning disabilities and emotional disabilities (for example, Daviss, Diler, & Birmaher, 2009; Dietz & Montague, 2006).

The causes of ADHD are not clear. Researchers have found that one important factor is heredity (Levy, Hay, & Bennett, 2006). Students who have ADHD are likely to have a family pattern of this disorder. Researchers also have found that the brains of individuals with ADHD are different from those of others: The amount of electrical activity is unusually low in the parts of the brain regulating attention, and the chemicals in the brain that transmit information may not function properly (Barkley, 2006). Environmental factors, including cigarette smoking and alcohol use during pregnancy, also may contribute to the development of ADHD (NIMH, 2009a). A few authors have suggested that ADHD is caused by food additives or food allergies, inner ear problems, vitamin deficiencies, or bacterial infections, but none of these causes has been demonstrated to be valid (NIMH, 2009a).

Usually, a diagnosis of ADHD is the result of individualized testing for intellectual ability and achievement, a medical screening completed by a doctor, and behavior ratings completed by family members and school professionals (NIMH, 2009b). Based on that information, a school team decides whether the student's disorder meets the criteria of other health impairment under IDEA, whether a Section 504 plan is needed, or whether no specific intervention is warranted.

Characteristics and Needs of Students with Attention Deficit–Hyperactivity Disorder

The characteristics and needs of students with attention deficit–hyperactivity disorder can vary considerably. Although all students might occasionally demonstrate some symptoms of ADHD, students diagnosed with this disorder display many of them prior to 7 years of age. Further, their symptoms are chronic and extraordinary. Consider this account from Mr. Benjamin, a high school English teacher:

> Nick challenges my skills as a teacher. Sometimes he'll be looking out the window or doodling, and yet when I call on him he knows the answer. Other times, he doesn't seem to even have processed what I'm asking. Sometimes he fidgets . . . wiggles his knee or taps with his pen. He gets frustrated easily, and if I don't pay close attention to him in class, he will give up, especially on writing assignments, and just stare until someone calls his name. I'm trying to use strategies to hold his attention—more participation opportunities for him, more changes in activities during class—and they do help. I worry about whether he's really mastering the material.

Intellectually, students with ADHD can function at any level, although the disorder usually is diagnosed in students who do not have intellectual disabilities. These students' shared characteristics relate to how their brains function. That is, ADHD is not really about inattention; rather, it is the inability to *regulate* attention. The disorder develops when students fail to develop *executive functions,* that is, the ability to carry out the mental activities that help most people regulate their behavior (Barkley, 2006; Brown, 2007). Executive functions include these four activities:

1. *Working memory*—the ability to remember what tasks are supposed to be done and how much time there is to do them

fyi

Determining whether a student has ADHD is a decision that can be made only by a pediatrician or family physician. Educators should never offer a diagnosis to parents, but if a parent asks, they may encourage parents to contact their child's doctor to discuss their concerns.

www.resources

http://www.chadd.org
Children and Adults with Attention-Deficit/Hyperactivity Disorder (CHADD) is a nonprofit organization dedicated to bettering the lives of those with ADHD and their families.

2. *Self-directed speech*—the silent self-talk that most people use to manage complex tasks

3. *Control of emotions and motivation*—the ability to talk oneself into calming down when faced with a difficult or frustrating task

4. *Reconstitution*—the ability to combine skills learned across a variety of settings in order to carry out a new task, such as a student's knowledge that the rule for speaking in a low voice applies not only in the classroom but also in the hallways, lunchroom, and office.

Many academic problems can be related to executive functions. Students with ADHD may have difficulty in reading, especially long passages for which comprehension demands are high; in spelling, which requires careful attention to detail; in listening, especially when a large amount of highly detailed information is presented; and in math, which often requires faster computational skills than students with ADHD can handle (DuPaul et al., 2006; Reid, Trout, & Schartz, 2005).

Socially and emotionally, students with ADHD are at risk for a variety of problems (Kats-Gold & Priel, 2009). For example, they are more likely to be depressed or to have extremely low self-confidence or self-esteem. Likewise, they are likely to have conflicts with parents, teachers, and other authority figures. These students often are unpopular with peers, frequently are rejected by them, and have difficulty making friends. Students with ADHD may feel demoralized, but they also may be bossy and obstinate. Seth, introduced at the beginning of this chapter, displays both academic and social characteristics typical of a student with ADHD.

The frequency of behavior problems of students with ADHD varies (Duhaney, 2003). Students whose disorder is inattention might not act out in class, but they may be disruptive when they try to find a lost item or constantly ask classmates for assistance in finding their place in a book or carrying out directions. Students with hyperactive–impulsive disorder often come to teachers' attention immediately because they have so many behavior problems. Their constant motion, refusal to work, and other behaviors can be problematic even in the most tolerant environment. Examples of the behaviors displayed by students with ADHD are included in Figure 8.1.

dimensions of DIVERSITY

In a study with nearly 500 participants, Monuteaux, Mick, Faraone, and Biederman (2010) found that symptoms of ADHD declined for both boys and girls as they got older. Girls more than boys, however, retained co-occurring psychological disorders as they moved into adolescence.

FIGURE 8.1 Behavior Characteristics of Students with Attention Deficit–Hyperactivity Disorder

Inattention

- making careless mistakes
- having difficulty sustaining attention/easily distracted
- seeming not to listen
- failing to give close attention to details in schoolwork and related activities
- failing to finish tasks
- having difficulty organizing
- avoiding tasks that require sustained attention
- losing things
- being forgetful

Hyperactivity

- fidgeting
- being unable to stay seated
- moving excessively (restlessness), including climbing on furniture and other items
- having difficulty making and keeping friends
- talking excessively
- being prone to temper tantrums
- acting in a bossy way
- being defiant

Impulsivity

- blurting out answers before questions have been completely asked
- having difficulty awaiting a turn
- interrupting conversations/intruding upon others
- acting before thinking
- being viewed as immature by teenage peers
- failing to read directions

Sources: Adapted from "Arranging the Classroom with an Eye (and Ear) to Students with ADHD," 2001, *Teaching Exceptional Children, 34*(2), pp. 72-81; and "Psychiatric Disorders and Treatment: A Primer for Teachers," by S. R. Forness, H. M. Walker, and K. A. Kavale, 2003, *Teaching Exceptional Children, 36*(2), pp. 42-49.

Interventions for Students with Attention Deficit–Hyperactivity Disorder

As a result of a series of studies (Miranda, Jarque, & Tárraga, 2006; MTA Cooperative Group, 2004), professionals now recommend that five types of interventions be used for students with ADHD: environmental supports, academic interventions, behavior interventions, parent education, and medication.

How can you arrange your classroom to improve learning for students with ADHD? What are other interventions you could implement to foster student success?

Environmental Supports The way you arrange your classroom can either foster learning for students with ADHD or impede it. To help students, your classroom should be free from distracting items, such as mobiles hung from the ceiling that twirl in air currents and piles of extra books or art supplies. Some students might benefit if you let them work using a *desk carrel,* a three-sided cardboard divider that blocks visual distractions. You also can provide a classroom environment conducive to learning for these students by having very clear classroom rules and routines. Further, if a change in the normal pattern of classroom activities is necessary, you can alert all students and make sure to support those with ADHD by assigning peer partners to assist them or by quietly letting them know what activity is next. Finally, you can consciously pace your instruction to mix tedious or repetitive classroom activities with those that permit students more variety and activity.

Academic Interventions Students with ADHD typically struggle with academic achievement, although the extent of their learning problems can vary considerably (Volpe, DuPaul, Jitendra, & Tresco, 2009). To assist students with ADHD academically, use the INCLUDE model as a strategy to design lessons and effectively teach these students. As you implement the steps of INCLUDE, keep these ideas in mind for teaching students with ADHD:

INCLUDE

1. Try to emphasize only essential information. For example, keep oral instructions as brief as possible. Rather than giving directions by providing multiple examples and then recapping what you have said, instead list directions by number using very clear language—for example, "First, put your name on the paper. Second, write a one-sentence response for each question. Third, put your paper in the basket on the counter by the door."
2. When reading for comprehension, students with ADHD tend to perform better on short passages than on long ones. Thus, rather than have a student with ADHD read an entire story or chapter, have him read just a small part of a long story or expository passage and check comprehension at that point; then have him read another part and so on. Similarly, when older students have lengthy assignments, it is better to break them into smaller parts, assigning each component individually and checking progress.
3. In math, give students extended periods of time to complete computational work because their attentional problems interfere with their efficiency in this type of task.
4. In all large-group instruction, keep the pace perky and provide many opportunities for students to participate, such as trading answers to questions with a partner, working with manipulatives, and repeating answers as a class after one student has responded.

Additional suggestions for teaching students with ADHD are presented in the Instructional Edge. In addition to the types of interventions just outlined, most

INSTRUCTIONAL **EDGE**

Strategies for Teaching Students with ADHD

- Give clear and complete directions for all in-class assignments and homework, including the amount of time allotted and evaluation criteria.
- Provide a rationale to students for each assignment they are asked to complete.
- Check students' understanding of assignments by having them repeat back the directions.
- Break long assignments into several shorter assignments.
- Schedule time while students work in class for them to obtain teacher feedback about their progress.
- Motivate students by commenting on their strengths and accomplishments.
- Ensure that instruction is fast paced.

- Use high levels of student participation and movement during instruction.
- Tailor questions to students' knowledge and skill levels.
- Use visual organizers (for example, graphic organizers, semantic webs).
- Help students remember important instructional tasks by using learning strategies (see Chapter 10).
- Draw on students' interests during instruction (for example, their culture and experiences).
- Have students work with peer partners.

Source: Adapted from "Educational Interventions for Students with ADD," by S. J. Salend, H. Elhoweris, and D. vanGarderen, 2003, *Intervention in School and Clinic, 38,* pp. 280–288.

---

recommendations for helping students with ADHD academically are similar to those for students with learning and emotional disabilities and other students who need highly structured and especially clear instruction. Later chapters in this book feature many additional instructional approaches that meet the needs of students with ADHD.

Behavior Interventions   For responding to behavior of students with ADHD, professionals generally recommend interventions that emphasize structure and rewards, such as specific verbal praise ("Martin, you began your work as soon as I gave the assignment") or stickers and other symbols of appropriate behavior ("Tamatha, you will earn a sticker for each five math problems you complete"). Reprimands and consequences may be needed at times, but these should be mild and used less often than rewards.

As the INCLUDE strategy outlines, you should first consider environmental demands and address these as a means of preventing behavior problems. For example, students with ADHD exhibit less acting-out behavior when they sit near the front of the room in an area with few visual or auditory distractions (for example, away from posters and bulletin board displays and computers signaling with tones and music). Likewise, allowing a student to move from one desk to another in the classroom and permitting her to stand while working are examples of simple environmental support strategies that may help prevent serious behavior problems.

If a student needs to be corrected, provide a clear and direct but calm reprimand. If you say "Tamatha, I know you are trying hard, but please try to remember to raise your hand before speaking," Tamatha might not even realize that you are correcting her. A preferred response would be to say quietly to her "Tamatha, do not call out answers. Raise your hand." This message is much clearer.

Parent Education   Yet another dimension of working successfully with students with ADHD involves parent education and collaboration (Mattox & Harder, 2007; Young & Amarasinghe, 2010). Although offering parent education generally is not the sole responsibility of a new teacher, you can contribute in this area by suggesting that parents of students with ADHD be invited to sessions to learn strategies for responding to their children's behavior, ways to create a discipline system that includes both rewards and consequences, tips for helping these children to make friends, and skills for working with school professionals to ensure academic success. Parents of students in middle school and high school also benefit from learning about their children's rights and responsibilities as they graduate from school and

RESEARCH NOTE

Three high school students with ADHD improved their on-task behavior during a study hall by using self-monitoring or self-monitoring combined with a system of rewards (Graham-Day, Gardner, & Hsin, 2010).

INCLUDE

enter a college or work setting (Wolraich et al., 2005). Parents from some cultural groups may be less comfortable than other parents in seeking or participating in parent education programs, and you may be able to assist them by explaining the offered training and encouraging them to attend (Mattox & Harder, 2007). Parent education by itself is not sufficient to address the needs of students with ADHD, but it can help to maximize the benefits of other interventions.

Medication   The most common intervention for students with ADHD demonstrated by researchers to generally have significant benefit (Vaughan, Roberts, & Needelman, 2009) is medication. Prescribing medication is a decision that is made by parents with their physicians; educators may not tell parents that a child needs this intervention. Approximately 2.5 million students take medication for ADHD (Centers for Disease Control and Prevention, 2010b), and medication is most commonly taken by students ages 9 to 12. It is effective for 70 to 80 percent of the students for whom it is prescribed, especially if combined with other interventions (that is, environmental supports, academic and behavior interventions, and parent education) (MTA, 2004).

The most common type of medication prescribed for students with ADHD is a group of stimulants, including Ritalin, Cylert, Adderall, and Focalin. However, students may take other medications, including antidepressants such as Norpramin, Tofranil, and Zoloft; antihypertensives such as Clonidine and Tenex; and Strattera, a relatively new medication developed specifically for this disorder. More information about the medications prescribed for ADHD is presented in Table 8.2.

Despite the apparent effectiveness of medications in treating ADHD, their use remains somewhat controversial (Akram, Thomson, & Boyter, 2009). Teachers encounter the problem of students not consistently taking their medication or sharing their medication. This situation can result not only in a loss of learning, but it can potentially endanger other students. Another issue concerns the proper dosage. Some researchers contend that a dosage high enough to cause an improvement in behavior can negatively affect a student's academic learning and performance (Forness & Kavale, 2001). A third area of concern pertains to side effects. Some parents and professionals believe that medication may suppress weight and height gain, even though research indicates that this side effect is temporary (DuPaul et al., 2006; Kollins, Barkely, & DuPaul, 2001). Yet other parents are concerned that taking medication may predispose their children to future drug use and problems in adulthood, another perception that has not been supported by research (Golden, 2009).

As a teacher, your responsibilities related to medication are indirect. You should know about the medications commonly prescribed, alert your school nurse and parents if you suspect that a change in student learning or behavior might be related to medication, and be prepared to respond to parental and medical inquiries regarding the effects of medication on particular students.

Many students with ADHD continue their education after high school and access the supports they need through the Americans with Disabilities Act.

Families of Children with Attention Deficit–Hyperactivity Disorder

Just like families of other students with disabilities and special needs, families of students with ADHD cannot be described using a single set of characteristics. However, it is fair to say that for many families, having a child with ADHD affects every area of family functioning and adds significant stress for parents and siblings both at home and in interactions with school personnel (Harpin, 2005).

When working with families of students with ADHD, you have to be careful not to blame parents for their children's ADHD but at the same time not to condone

TABLE 8.2 Overview of Medications Commonly Used for ADHD

Brand Name [Generic Name]	Type of Medication	Advantages	Disadvantages	Comments
Concerta [Methylphenidate]	Psychostimulant	Works quickly Lasts up to 12 hours	Not recommended for children in families with a history of tic disorders	First true once-a-day ADHD medication approved by the FDA
Ritalin [Methylphenidate]	Psychostimulant	Excellent safety record Easy to use and evaluate Works in 15–20 minutes	Lasts only 4 hours Must be administered frequently	Most frequently prescribed medication Watch for tics or Tourette's syndrome
Ritalin SR (sustained release) [Methylphenidate]	Psychostimulant	Excellent safety record Easy to use and evaluate Long lasting (6–8 hours)	Does not work as well as regular Ritalin	Can be used along with regular Ritalin
Focalin [Dextromethylphenidate]	Psychostimulant	Works quickly Only half the dose of Ritalin is needed	Lasts only 4–5 hours Must be administered frequently	Refined form of Ritalin
Dexedrine [Dextroamphetamine]	Psychostimulant	Excellent safety record Rapid onset (20–30 minutes)	Lasts only 4 hours Must be administered frequently	Some students have fewer side effects than when on Ritalin
Dexedrine (sustained release) [Dextroamphetamine]	Psychostimulant	Excellent safety record Long lasting (6–8 hours)	Slower onset (1–2 hours)	Can be used along with standard Dexedrine, which permits once-daily dosing
Adderall [Single-entity amphetamine product]	Psychostimulant	Works quickly May last somewhat longer than other standard stimulants (3–6 hours)	High potential for abuse	May help students for whom Ritalin has not been effective
Adderall XR [Single-entity amphetamine product]	Psychostimulant	Works quickly Lasts about 12 hours	High potential for abuse	Not recommended for long-term use
Tofranil and Norpramin [Imipramine and desipramine]	Antidepressant	Long lasting (12–24 hours) Can be administered at night Often works when stimulants do not	Has possible side effects May take 1–3 weeks for full effects Should not be started and stopped abruptly	High doses may improve depression symptoms and mood swings
Catapress [Clonidine]	Antihypertensive	Can be used with students with Tourette's syndrome	Tablets are short lasting (4 hours) Patches are expensive	Often has positive effect on defiant behavior
Strattera [Atomoxetine hydrochloride]	Norepinephrine re-uptake inhibitor	Lasts about 8–10 hours Noncontrolled prescription medication	Relatively new medication Long-term effects on children are not known	First nonstimulant ADHD medication approved by the FDA

Sources: From *Special Education: Contemporary Perspectives for School Professionals* (3rd edition), by M. Friend, 2011, Upper Saddle River, NJ: Pearson; and "Medication Chart to Treat Attention Deficit Disorders," by H. C. Parker, 2003. Retrieved December 2, 2004, from http://www.ldonline.org/ld_indepth/add_adhd/add_medication_chart.html. Reprinted by permission of Harvey C. Parker.

inappropriate student behavior that a parent might excuse by saying that the child can't help it. For example, adolescents with ADHD may have more negative moods than other teens, and they may be prone to tobacco and alcohol abuse (Owens & Bergman, 2010). Parents and family members are faced with responding to these children's emotions and potentially harmful behaviors.

How Can You Accommodate Students Who Are Gifted and Talented?

In addition to students who cannot meet typical curricular expectations, you also will have in your classroom students who have extraordinary abilities and skills. The term used to describe these students is **gifted and talented**. The federal definition for this group of students is stated in the 1988 Jacob Javits Gifted and Talented Students Education Act (Javits Act, P.L. 100–297), which identifies children and youth who possess demonstrated or potential high-performance capability in intellectual, creative, specific academic and leadership areas or the performing and visual arts. The federal definition further clarifies that these students need services in school that other students do not. However, unlike the services offered through IDEA, federal legislation does not require specific services for gifted and talented students, and so the extent to which programs exist is determined largely by state and local policies (Council of State Directors of Programs for the Gifted, 2007). In fact, the Javits Act is not a funding mechanism for programs for students who are gifted and talented. Its purpose is to provide a means of coordinating efforts to enhance schools' ability to serve these students, and its emphasis is on identifying and educating students who are traditionally underrepresented in programs for students who are gifted and talented (for example, students with disabilities).

Because the provision of service to students who are gifted and talented varies across the United States, prevalence is difficult to determine. In today's schools, approximately 6 percent of students are served as gifted and talented (National Association for Gifted Children, 2008).

The reported prevalence of giftedness and talent is greatly affected by two factors. First, over the past several years, researchers and writers have offered alternative definitions of giftedness and questioned traditional criteria for identification that rely on intelligence measures (that is, IQ tests). For example, Gardner (1993, 2006) argues that measured IQ is far too narrow a concept of intelligence and that a person's ability to problem solve, especially in new situations, is a more useful way of thinking about intelligence. He has proposed that *multiple intelligences* describe the broad array of talents that students possess, and he describes these eight intelligences:

1. verbal/linguistic
2. visual/spatial
3. logical/mathematical
4. bodily/kinesthetic
5. musical
6. intrapersonal (that is, self-understanding)
7. interpersonal
8. naturalist
9. existentialist

Notice the wide range of abilities captured in this notion of intelligence. The impact of using these broader definitions is that 20 percent or more of students could be identified as being gifted or talented, according to some estimates (Callahan, 2005).

The second factor that affects the number of students identified as gifted and talented is the notion of potential. Although some students who are gifted and talented easily can be identified because they use their special abilities and are willing to be recognized for them, others go unnoticed. These students mask their skills from

www.resources

http://www.gifted.uconn.edu/ The University of Connecticut's Neag Center for Gifted Education and Talent Development highlights current trends in the field, programs for students who are gifted and talented, and resources to help teachers understand these students through its National Research Center on the Gifted and Talented (NRC/GT).

fyi

Giftedness traditionally has referred to students with extraordinary abilities across many academic areas and *talent* to students with extraordinary abilities in a specific area. Now, however, the terms often are used interchangeably.

peers and teachers because low expectations have been set for them or their unique needs have not been nurtured. Groups at risk for being underidentified include young boys, adolescent girls, students who are so highly gifted and talented as to be considered geniuses, students from racially and culturally diverse groups, and students with disabilities (Birdsall & Correa, 2007; Moore, Ford, & Milner, 2005). In many school districts, focused attention has been placed on these groups to ensure such students are identified.

RESEARCH NOTE

In a study of gifted students from low-income, minority, and twice exceptional groups, long-term participation in gifted programs was found to have a positive impact on both confidence and the development of thinking and communication skills (Baska, Feng, Swanson, Quek, & Chandler, 2009).

Characteristics and Needs of Students Who Are Gifted and Talented

Students who are gifted and talented have a wide range of characteristics, and any one student considered gifted and talented can have just a few or many of these characteristics. The following information about student characteristics is intended to provide an overview of students who are gifted and talented and should be viewed as a sample of what is known, not a comprehensive summary.

Intellectual Abilities and Academic Skills   The area of intellectual functioning and academic skills is the most delineated aspect of gifted education. Students who are gifted and talented generally have an extraordinary amount of knowledge because of their insatiable curiosity, keen memory, unusual ability to concentrate, wide variety of interests, high levels of language development and verbal ability, and ability to generate original ideas. They also have an advanced ability to comprehend information using accelerated and flexible thought processes, a heightened ability to recognize relationships between diverse ideas, and a strong capacity to form and use conceptual frameworks. These students tend to be skilled problem solvers because of their extraordinary ability to pick out relevant information and their tendency to monitor their problem-solving efforts (Reis & Sullivan, 2009).

The intellectual abilities of students who are gifted and talented sometimes lead them to high academic achievement, but not always. Consider these three students who are gifted and talented:

Students who are gifted and talented have many profiles. They may excel in all academic areas and be highly popular with peers, or they may have a specialized talents and experience feelings of isolation.

- Belinda was identified as gifted and talented in second grade. She has been reading since age 3, seems as comfortable interacting with adults as with peers, and invariably becomes the leader of the groups of children with whom she plays, even when they are older. She enjoys school immensely and wants to be a university professor when she grows up. Belinda is similar to Lydia, whom you read about at the beginning of this chapter.
- Tomas also is identified as gifted and talented. He has been taking violin and piano lessons since age 5, and now in the seventh grade he is an accomplished pianist. He already plans to major in music theory when he goes to college, and he offers his own interpretations of both classical and contemporary music. In his academic studies, however, Tomas is slightly below average in achievement. He also is somewhat shy; he appears more comfortable with his musical instruments than with his peers.
- Charles is a sophomore in high school. He lives in a neighborhood where education is not valued and getting high grades is viewed as showing off. As a result, the nearly straight As that used to define Charles's report cards have dropped over the past year, and now he is earning mostly Cs and Ds.

How might the needs of these students differ? How could you encourage each student to reach his or her potential?

Social and Emotional Needs   Socially and emotionally, students who are gifted and talented can be well liked and emotionally healthy, or they can be unpopular and at risk for serious emotional problems (Lopez & Sotillo, 2009; Van Tassel-Bask, Cross, & Olancho, 2009). Affectively, they tend to have unusual sensitivity to others' feelings as well as highly developed emotional depth and intensity, a keen sense of humor that can be either supportive or hostile, and a sense of justice. They often have a sense of obligation to help others and may become involved in community service activities. Teachers sometimes assign these students to help other students, an acceptable practice unless done so often that it interferes with advanced learning opportunities. These students often set high expectations for themselves and others. That sometimes is positive, but it also can lead to feelings of frustration, isolation, and alienation, especially when they cannot meet the expectations they have set (Peterson & Ray, 2006; Renzulli & Park, 2002).

Because some students who are gifted have a superior ability to recognize and respond to others' feelings, they can be extremely popular with classmates and often sought as helpmates. However, if they tend to show off their talents or repeatedly challenge adult authority, they may be perceived negatively by peers and teachers and have problems developing appropriate social relationships (Colangelo & Davis, 2003). For example, Ms. Ogden is concerned about eighth-grader Esteban. On some days, he seems to have just a four-word vocabulary: "I already know that." He says this to his teachers, his peers, and his parents about nearly any topic under discussion. Although it is often true that Esteban does know about the subject being discussed, Ms. Ogden finds herself becoming annoyed at his style of interacting, and she knows the other students do not want to be grouped with Esteban because of it.

Behavior Patterns   Students who are gifted and talented display the entire range of behaviors that other students do. They can be model students who participate and seldom cause problems, often serving as class leaders. In this capacity, students are sensitive to others' feelings and moderate their behavior based on others' needs (Colangelo, 2002). However, because students who are gifted and talented often have an above-average capacity to understand people and situations, their negative behavior can sometimes be magnified compared with that of other students. This behavior can be displayed through an intense interest in a topic and refusal to change topics when requested by a teacher. Other behavior problems displayed by some students who are gifted and talented include being bossy in group situations, purposefully failing, and valuing and participating in counterculture activities (Colangelo, 2002).

Interventions for Students Who Are Gifted and Talented

Although some school districts operate separate classes and programs for students who are gifted and talented, you likely will be responsible for teaching these students in your classroom. Four specific strategies often used to challenge students who are gifted and talented are curriculum compacting, acceleration and enrichment, specific differentiation strategies during instruction, and individualized interventions (VanTassel-Baska, 2003). As you read the following descriptions of these strategies and the examples of their implementation, think about how the INCLUDE strategy could guide you in implementing them. In the Case in Practice, you can see an application of instruction for a student who is gifted and has a learning disability.

Curriculum Compacting   Some students who are gifted and talented already have mastered much of the traditional curriculum content of the public schools, and they may be bored when asked to listen to a lecture or complete an assignment that does not challenge them (Reis & Renzulli, 2004). In *curriculum compacting*, teachers assess students' achievement of instructional goals and then eliminate instruction on goals already met. The time gained is used to pursue special interests, work with a mentor, or study the same topic at a more advanced level. How could you use curriculum compacting in your planned teaching?

With the recognized need to address giftedness and talent among the entire population, including students from diverse groups (Bonner, 2003), identification procedures now may comprise both traditional measures (for example, intelligence and achievement tests) and nontraditional measures (for example, nonverbal ability tests, creativity tests, student portfolios, performance-based measures) (Bracken & Brown, 2006).

INCLUDE

CASE IN PRACTICE

Meeting the Needs of a Twice-Exceptional Student

Ms. Davis is taking a few minutes to reflect on the meeting she and her seventh-grade team had yesterday with their school psychologist, the facilitator for their school's program for students who are gifted and talented, and the special education teacher. The meeting was called because of the teachers' concerns about Isaac, a student whom the teachers characterize as a student of "contradictions." Here are examples of what they mean:

- For a multimedia project in English, Isaac produced original music and directed several classmates to produce a performance he recorded expertly using video equipment he borrowed from a teacher at the high school. The day the project was due, however, he forgot to bring it to school and told his teacher that it wasn't very good anyway.
- In social studies, Isaac can explain in detail not just the events of world history but also the societal forces that influenced them. His mother attributes this knowledge to his love of the documentaries and other programming on history available on television.
- In math, Isaac struggles. He often disrupts class by making jokes ("I know what algebra is—it's underwear for a mermaid (algae-bra)." "Did you hear what happened in the other class? Mr. Somers asked John to solve the problem 'What is 2q + 8q?' When John said '10q,' Mr. Somers said, 'You're welcome!'").

The other professionals at the meeting spent some time explaining that Isaac is *twice exceptional;* that is, he is gifted and also has a learning disability. This is why he has a learning-strategies class as one of his electives and is in the co-taught English class.

In reviewing information about Isaac and discussing how to help him reach his potential (and reduce disruptions in class), the professionals talked about how to help him use his significant intellectual abilities in a constructive way. The psychologist advised the teachers that Isaac sometimes uses humor and inappropriate classroom remarks to distract his teachers so that he can avoid tasks he is afraid he may not do well. The special educator mentioned that she is concerned about Isaac's self-esteem; he told her privately that having the label *LD* means he's "retarded," and nothing she said seemed to change his opinion of his abilities. Suggestions for working with Isaac included giving him as many choices as possible regarding assignments, offering ways other than reading for him to acquire information, and arranging peer tutoring in math, the class in which Isaac struggles the most.

REFLECTION

What does it mean for a student to be *twice exceptional?* Besides LD, what do you think are other disabilities that might occur with giftedness? How would such students be similar to or different from Isaac? Why might students who are twice exceptional have low self-esteem? How can you help these students succeed? Should a student like Isaac be enrolled in a program for students who are gifted? Why or why not?

---

fyi

One form of acceleration often seen in high schools is the College Board's Advanced Placement (AP) program. Students have the option of completing college credit for advanced courses taken in high school.

Acceleration In some school districts, you may learn that *acceleration* is part of the programming available for students who are gifted and talented (Colangelo et al., 2010). That is, these students may skip a grade or complete the standards for two grades in a single year. In high school, acceleration may relate to a specific subject. For example, a student with extraordinary math skills might enroll in advanced coursework in that area while following the traditional curriculum for English and social studies.

Enrichment *Enrichment* is an instructional approach that provides students with information, materials, and assignments that enable them to elaborate on concepts being presented as part of the standard curriculum and that usually require high levels of thinking (Eckstein, 2009; Reis, 2007). This common classroom option requires you to find related information, prepare it for the students who need it, and create curriculum-relevant alternative activities for them. For enrichment to be effective, you need to ensure that students have opportunities to complete assignments designed to encourage advanced thinking and product development, that they do such assignments in lieu of other work instead of as additional work, and that many learning resources are available to them both in and out of the classroom.

Differentiation Perhaps one of the most practical approaches you can use for working with students in your class who are gifted and talented is to systematically plan lessons based on *differentiation,* the same approach introduced for your work with students who have disabilities (Hertberg-Davis, 2009; Tomlinson, 2005). Recall that differentiation is based on the understanding that students should have multiple ways to reach their potential. Just as you will analyze the strengths and needs of students with disabilities and design and evaluate effective ways to teach them, you should do the same for students who are gifted and talented. For example, Ms. Clinton's English class is reading *Romeo and Juliet.* Six students—four who have disabilities and two who are English language learners—are experiencing difficulty reading the play and have been provided a version with contemporary language. The questions they are assigned once they have read the first act include these: What is the Capulet family like? The Montagues? Why don't the two families like each other? However, the pretest data of two students indicate they are familiar with the play and know its detail. Their assignment after reading the first act is to stage that part of the play, setting it in modern times. They also are asked to explain how *Romeo and Juliet* is an example of classic tragic form, a topic they are expected to research independently.

Specialized Interventions   All of the previously described approaches may be effective for students who are gifted and talented, but students who have special circumstances—those who live in poverty, who are from nondominant cultures, or who also have disabilities—may need even further special attention. For example, some students may downplay their abilities because academic achievement is not valued in their immediate community and they fear being rejected (Van Tassel-Baska et al., 2009). For these students, you may want to find mentors from similar backgrounds so students see that drawing on their talents can lead to positive outcomes.

www.resources

http://nces.ed.gov/ccd
The National Center for Education Statistics' Common Core of Data, updated annually, can inform you about diversity in schools nationwide, in your state, or in a specific district. This website also has information designed to help students understand their schools.

PROFESSIONAL EDGE

Gifted Underachievers

Gifted underachievers may be students who do poorly on tests, do not turn in daily work, or achieve below grade level. At the same time, they learn quickly when interested, are highly creative, and value projects they choose themselves. The following strategies help you better match your instruction to the needs of these students.

Provide more flexibility to foster peer and social relationships among students

- Allow students to teach classmates and others.
- Organize multiage groups across grade levels.

Assist students with successful transitions

- Develop a mentor program for younger students by older students.
- Offer transition survival courses when students change grade levels/schools.
- Provide parent education programs about transitions.

Promote empowerment and autonomy for students

- Solicit student input for planning learning activities.
- Include some self-paced/mastery learning opportunities.
- Promote recognition and awards for achievement and effort.
- Provide leadership training and opportunities for students to demonstrate leadership skills.
- Involve students in evaluating school activities and providing and implementing ideas for improvement.

Improve the learning environment for students

- Expand learning beyond the classroom and into the community, including service learning.
- Create ways for students to participate in classroom and school governance.
- Use flexible instructional groups based on needs.
- Create alternative assignments that students do in lieu of traditional classwork.
- Make sure your classroom is culturally responsive, that is, respectful of students' diverse backgrounds and needs.
- Promote grading systems that encourage students to continue to try (for example, provide full credit for work, even if submitted late).
- Enlist the assistance of parents in encouraging their children and helping them manage the stresses of school.
- Encourage positive confrontation and conflict resolution.

Think about how each of these ideas applies to the grade level you plan to teach. Teachers sometimes refer to students such as gifted underachievers as "unmotivated," inferring that unless the students change, they will not learn. What is your role in motivating such students? How might your teaching strategies relate to student motivation?

Source: "Gifted and Talented Students at Risk," by K. Seeley, 2004, *Focus on Exceptional Children, 37* (4), pp. 1–9; and Center for Comprehensive School Reform and Improvement. (2008). *Gifted and talented students at risk for underachievement* [Issue Brief]. Washington, DC: Author.

For some students, interacting with peers from a similar background can be helpful, especially if they are given tasks that foster critical thinking skills. In addition, students in this group may benefit when technology is integral to instruction, either as a resource for learning or a tool for accessing learning, as might be the case for students with disabilities. The Professional Edge on page 249 provides a checklist that can be useful for recognizing students who might be gifted underachievers.

What Are the Needs of Students from Culturally Diverse Backgrounds?

The racial, cultural, and linguistic diversity of U.S. classrooms has been increasing for decades, and all indications are that it will continue to do so. For example, in 1972, just 22 percent of students enrolled in grades 1 through 12 were members of minority groups. In 1988 that number had grown to 32 percent, and in 2008, the most recent statistics available, it had increased to 45 percent of all students (National Center for Education Statistics, 2010). Approximately 10.3 percent of all U.S. public school students are English language learners; nearly 80 percent of these students speak Spanish as their first language. The largest 100 school districts in the United States—the districts that account for 22 percent of all the school-age students in the country—are educating approximately 36 percent of all the students in the country who belong to minority groups.

Evidence suggests that students from some racial/ethnic groups experience extraordinarily high failure rates in school. For example, in 2007–2008, dropout rates for census reporting groups were as follows: Asian/Pacific Islander, 2.2 percent; White, 2.8 percent; Hispanic, 6.0 percent; Black, 6.7 percent; and American Indian/Alaska Native, 7.3 percent (Stillwell, 2010). Although some of these students may later return to complete school in a GED program, many will not.

The reasons for these students' failure to complete school are complex and interrelated but involve several identifiable factors. First, students from racial and ethnic minority groups often lack role models because most teachers are from the majority Anglo-European culture (Wiggins, Folo, & Eberly, 2007). In addition, instructional practices can negatively affect students. In particular, teaching practices that do not allow opportunities for student-centered learning can put students from different cultures at a disadvantage because students' background and experience may lead them to learn more effectively from small-group peer interactions (Bennett, 2003; Nieto, 2002/2003). A mix of teaching approaches is needed. Finally, the lack of specialized school programs can penalize students. For example, few schools operate mentor programs specifically designed to connect students from diverse cultures with leaders in business, industry, and education. These contacts can be essential for helping students succeed, as is the case for Maria, whose story was part of this chapter's introduction.

Diversity and Special Education

The relationship among school failure, special education, and diverse student needs is not a comfortable one (Artiles, Kozleski, Trent, Osher, & Ortiz, 2010). Historically, students from racial and cultural minorities sometimes were inappropriately placed in special education programs based on discriminatory assessment practices. Evidence suggests that this unfortunate bias is still an issue today, particularly for African-American students and some English-language learners (Waitoller, Artiles, & Cheney, 2010). The reasons for this bias continue to be studied. Some researchers maintain that the issue concerns poverty more than race or ethnicity, a topic addressed later in this chapter. But it also involves bias in curriculum and instruction, teacher attitudes, and the special education referral process (Artiles et al., 2010; Skiba, Poloni-Staudinger, Simmons, Feggins-Assiz, & Chung, 2005).

The most promising way to address such biases occurs in a procedure that you have already learned about: response to intervention (Orosco & Klingner, 2010). In RtI,

---

dimensions of DIVERSITY

Students who are gay, lesbian, or bisexual report fewer instances of harassment when their schools offer support groups designed specifically for them (Goodenow, Szalacha, & Westheimer, 2006).

How are students from culturally diverse backgrounds at risk for school failure? How can you promote student acceptance of cultural differences in your classroom?

a team of professionals can carefully analyze several types of data and make decisions about the best ways to increase students' rates of learning so that consideration for special education can, if at all possible, be avoided. RtI is particularly important when students' language or culture may inadvertently lead teachers to think they have a disability. It helps teachers to systematically and consistently use a variety of increasingly intensive and evidence-based interventions, and the collaborative nature of the RtI process increases the likelihood that successful interventions can be found, and if not, that the student's learning problems are truly the result of a disability and not cultural or language difference (Greenfield, Rinaldi, Proctor, & Cardarelli, 2010).

Cultural Awareness

Understanding the characteristics of students who are members of racially and culturally diverse groups involves recognizing that learning and behavior problems can be created by the contradictions between some of these students' home and community experiences and the expectations placed on them at school (Banks, 2007). It also means acknowledging that teachers sometimes misunderstand students and their parents, which can lead to miscommunication, distrust, and negative school experiences.

If you live in an area where many different cultures are represented in a single classroom, the thought of learning about all of them can be intimidating. It is probably not possible, nor is it necessary, to learn many details about all the cultures of your students (Trumbull & Pacheco, 2005). However, it is your responsibility to learn the fundamental characteristics students might have because of their backgrounds. For example, some students might hesitate to ask questions because of concern about interacting with the teacher, who is perceived as an authority figure. If you understand this reticence, then you can make a special effort to initiate interactions with these students. Further, when a student displays troublesome behavior, you should determine whether a cultural reason may have prompted the behavior before responding to it or assuming that it represents misbehavior. Of course, you also should keep in mind that not all students from diverse backgrounds encounter these problems, nor do all families from racial or ethnic minority groups use discipline practices different from those schools use.

dimensions of
DIVERSITY

http://www.nmai.si.edu/
subpage.cfm?subpage
=collaboration&second=radio
The National Museum of the
American Indian includes many
resources, including educational
and entertaining audiotapes that
preserve the oral tradition of
Indian cultures.

INCLUDE

The INCLUDE strategy can be a valuable tool for making decisions about instruction for students from culturally and linguistically diverse groups. First, you should consider the demands of the classroom setting and identify the strengths and interests students bring to the learning environment. Next, you should look for potential problem areas throughout your entire instructional program. Use that information to brainstorm ideas for resolving the problems and select those with the most potential for success. As you go through this process, it is essential to monitor student progress and make adjustments as needed. An example of strategies related to teaching reading to students who are English-language learners is included in the Instructional Edge.

The impact of cultural and linguistic diversity in educational settings can be examined in more detail from three perspectives, each briefly considered in the following sections: how cultural factors affect student behavior, how teaching approaches can be tailored to culturally diverse groups, and how communication with nonnative English speakers can be enhanced.

Cultural Factors and Student Behavior   Various cultural values can affect students' behaviors and how educators interpret these behaviors. For example, for some Native American and immigrant students, time is a fluid concept not necessarily bound by clocks (Hodgkinson, 2000/2001). A student might come to school late by Anglo-European cultural standards that measure time precisely but on time according to events happening at the student's home. Another example of the differences between Anglo-European standards and some students' cultures concerns school participation. Hispanic students sometimes are more likely to participate when they have established close relationships with their teachers and peers (Banks, 2007). Contrast this fact with the common high school structure, in which one teacher sees as many as 180 students each day and often uses an instructional format that minimizes interaction. In such a setting, some Hispanic students—especially those who have only recently come to the United States—can be at a great disadvantage.

Informed Instructional Decision Making   Effective decisions about teaching strategies are made by matching the needs of students from culturally diverse backgrounds to instructional approaches (Richards et al., 2007). For example, many African-American students, as well as many Hispanic-American and Asian-American students, respond well to cooperative rather than competitive teaching and learning environments (Bennett, 2003). Likewise, because traditional Native American students sometimes dislike responding individually and out loud in a large-group situation, you may need to create opportunities for individual contact and quiet participation. Such instructional thinking and approaches, referred to as *equity pedagogy,* should become integral to your teaching (Zirkel, 2008).

Cross-Cultural Communication   For students who do not speak English as their native language, going to school can be a frustrating experience, resulting in some common problems. First, students who do not use English proficiently can easily be discriminated against when they are assessed, their scores reflecting their language skill more than their learning of curricular content. Second, students with limited English skills sometimes are perceived by teachers and classmates as deficient (Artiles et al., 2010). Teachers might have difficulty understanding students and assume they have limited ability, and peers may exclude them from social activities because of language differences. Third, language-related issues sometimes lead to the belief that when English is not students' primary language, these students must be segregated from other students to learn. If you understand your students' levels of language proficiency as summarized in the Professional Edge on page 254, you can ensure that your instruction takes language into account and avoid or reduce some of the challenges nonnative English speakers face.

For students from culturally and linguistically diverse backgrounds, home–school communication is critical. You might have difficulty even in basic communication,

INSTRUCTIONAL **EDGE**

English-Language Learners and Reading

Although English-language learners (ELLs) often have trouble learning to read (Vaughn et al., 2008), these are ways you can make your reading instruction more meaningful for them while also building their oral language skills.

TEACH SEGMENTING AND BLENDING

When students *segment* words, they break words apart into their individual phonemes (fish = /f/-/i/-/sh/). When they *blend,* they say a spoken word when the sounds are said slowly (/f/-/i/-/sh/ = fish).

- Give ELLs more opportunities to use new English vocabulary by having them blend or segment these new words before using them in complete sentences.
- Have ELLs segment and blend using words from their first language. For example, have them blend a name such as *Jorgé* or clap the sounds in holidays such as Navidad or Cinco de Mayo.
- During story time, while building student vocabulary and listening comprehension skills, ask students to segment and blend words taken from a picture book about their culture.

TEACH ASSOCIATIONS BETWEEN WRITTEN LETTERS AND SOUNDS

Home, school, and community interests can be used to teach ELLs the associations between written letters and sounds, or *phonics.*

- Have Spanish-speaking students sound out decodable Spanish words appearing on signs, community newspapers, and in books written in Spanish. Then have students use the English equivalents of these words in complete sentences orally, in writing, or both.
- Show students pictures of words after they have sounded them out. Doing this will ensure they are using phonics to figure out the words while also building their English vocabulary. Showing pictures also provides additional opportunities for the students and teacher to engage in dialogue about the word—and build oral language skills.
- Distinguish between errors and articulation differences. For example, José read the word *meet* as /mit/. In Spanish, a long *e* is often pronounced as a short *i;* therefore, *meet* could be identified correctly but pronounced as /mit/. José's teacher asked him to use the word in a sentence which allowed her to check José's word reading skills while also reinforcing his vocabulary and syntactical knowledge by having him use the word in a sentence.

BUILD STUDENTS' READING FLUENCY

Reading fluency is the ability to read connected text accurately, quickly, and with expression and is an important bridge between word recognition and comprehension. It also requires the reader to use intonation and stress to convey meaning. Understanding the importance of reading with expression is difficult for ELLs since languages such as Spanish convey differences in meaning by changing word order.

- Read a section of text related to cultural themes, mores, values, traditions, history, or customs to students, modeling appropriate stress and intonation. Then have students read the same section back to you, provide them with feedback, and have them repeat as needed.
- For independent practice, provide digitally recorded models of orally read text. Have students try to read like the recording, and then evaluate their performance.

TEACH VOCABULARY, INCLUDING IDIOMS

As you learned in Chapter 5, ELLs may learn basic vocabulary but struggle to learn the meaning of English-language idioms, such as "up the creek."

- Have students practice reading idioms with the appropriate rhythm and stress in connected speech (Celce-Murcia, 2000, p. 170): All talk and no action; Talk shop; Talk is cheap; Talk someone's head off.
- Say each phrase and then have students repeat it, imitating your tone and inflection; discuss the meaning of each idiom (Bursuck & Damer, 2011). Also have students use each idiom in a sentence and write stories or draw pictures of idioms they choose.

ENHANCE ORAL LANGUAGE

The key to reading comprehension for ELLs is knowledge of oral language (Yang, 2002). Oral language can be enhanced through student reading or by reading to students.

- Select material relevant to students' experiences and backgrounds.
- Encourage students to summarize passages using familiar words after reading or listening.
- Keep a balance between expository (informational) and narrative (storytelling) material. Schools with higher proportions of students at risk tend to stress stories despite the fact that these students have major gaps in background knowledge.
- Because ELLs may be reluctant to volunteer to answer questions, call on nonvolunteers to answer in class while helping students to elaborate as they respond using modeling and guided practice.
- When you read aloud, talk slowly to give students the time needed to process what you are saying.
- When reading a long section of text, ask questions periodically rather than just at the end. This approach provides more direct support for comprehension and holds students' attention while modeling a question-asking strategy students eventually should use themselves.
- Have students write about the text they are reading or listening to improve their reading comprehension skills.

PROFESSIONAL EDGE

Levels of Language Proficiency

When you teach students who are English-language learners, you should understand their level of language proficiency, keeping in mind that language proficiency for any single student could vary significantly depending on whether the task at hand involves speaking, listening, reading, writing, or a combination of them. This chart outlines a continuum of five levels of language proficiency, including the performance definition and some of the ways students function for each.

At the given level of English-language proficiency, English-language learners will process, understand, produce, or use:

5: Bridging
- The technical language of the content areas
- A variety of sentence lengths of varying linguistic complexity in extended oral or written discourse, including stories, essays, and reports
- ▶ Oral or written language approaching comparability to that of English-proficient peers when presented with grade-level material

4: Expanding
- Specific and some technical language of the content areas
- A variety of sentence lengths of varying linguistic complexity in oral discourse or multiple related paragraphs
- ▶ Oral or written language with minimal phonological, syntactic, or semantic errors that do not impede the overall meaning of the communication when presented with oral or written connected discourse with occasional visual and graphic support

3: Developing
- General and some specific language of the content areas
- Expanded sentences in oral interaction or written paragraphs
- ▶ Oral or written language with phonological, syntactic, or semantic errors that may impede the communication but retain much of its meaning when presented with oral or written narrative or expository descriptions with occasional visual and graphic support

2: Beginning
- General language related to the content area
- Phrases and short sentences
- ▶ Oral or written language with phonological, syntactic, or semantic errors that often impede the meaning of the communication when presented with one- to multiple-step commands, directions, or questions or a series of statements with visual and graphic support

1: Entering
- Pictorial or graphic representation of the language of the content areas
- Words, phrases, or chunks of language when presented with one-step commands or directions
- ▶ *WH*-questions (that is questions beginning with the words *who, what, where, when, why,* and *how*) or statements with visual and graphic support

Source: From *English Language Proficiency Standards for English Language Learners in Kindergarten through Grade 12: Frameworks for Large-Scale State and Classroom Assessment,* by M. Gottlieb, 2004, Madison, WI: WIDA Consortium. Retrieved December 1, 2004, from www.doe.state.de.us/DPIServices/Desk_Ref/ ELP_StandardsOV.pdf. Reprinted with permission.

however, because of language differences and the lack of availability of an interpreter. A second problem you may face concerns cultural values and parent responses to school personnel (Green, 2005; Obiakor, Utley, Smith, & Harris-Obiakor, 2002). For example, in a traditional Asian family, pride and shame often are emphasized and indirectness is valued. Imagine a parent conference in which an insensitive teacher describes in detail the academic and learning problems an Asian child is having and directly asks the parents whether they can assist in carrying out a home–school behavior change program. If the parents follow traditional Asian values, they might be humiliated by the public accounting of their child's failures and embarrassed at the teacher's direct and unnecessary request for their assistance.

A third example of the importance of communication relates to parents' perceptions of school and how they should interact with school personnel contrasted to school staff expectations for parent involvement. For example, the parents of some students may find school foreign and intimidating and believe that their role is to listen passively to what school personnel say. Other parents may not trust educators enough to share important information with them about their children (for example, Brandon, Higgins, Pierce, Tandy, & Sileo, 2010).

Families and Diversity

Many teachers find that not only do they have to put focused effort into understanding students and family members because of language barriers and cultural differences, but also that they simply do not grasp the day-to-day realities of their students' and students' families' lives. Probably the single best strategy for improving understanding is to set aside all the books, lesson plans, and ideas about diversity and multiculturalism and simply *listen* to families (Trumbull & Pacheco, 2005). In addition to making time to learn about families, Sánchez (1999, pp. 354–357) recommends that you be willing to do the following:

1. Step outside your comfort zone by going into the community to learn about your students' and similar families.
2. Adopt the unequivocal view that all families are involved in and significant to their children's education and that schooling is only one source of education.
3. Examine your own story more deeply.
4. Challenge stereotypes and reduce prejudice.
5. Explore the sociocultural context in the lives of families and teachers.
6. Examine your own teaching practices from a family perspective.
7. Distribute power.

You can respond with respect and sensitivity to your students, as well as their families, by being careful to recognize that the most important factor about working with others is that unless you have been in their situation, you cannot completely understand it. The Working Together provides some suggestions for fostering collaboration with families by focusing on making them feel welcomed and valuable in their children's education.

Multicultural and Bilingual Education

Creating a classroom in which students' cultures are acknowledged and valued is a fundamental characteristic of **multicultural education,** that is, curriculum and instruction that reflect the diversity of society. Multicultural education begins with such basics as examining how you decorate your classroom and how you select learning materials. Do your bulletin boards display the work of students from ethnic and cultural minority groups? When you portray historical events, do you include information about members of several cultural groups? Does your classroom contain stories or literature about successful individuals from a variety of cultures? Is respect for diversity infused throughout your curriculum?

If the school in which you teach has a very diverse student population, programs for supporting **English-language learners (ELLs)** are important. For example, **bilingual education programs** are based on the assumption that students need to learn English by being immersed in the language environment, but until a level of proficiency in English is achieved, many students do not learn concepts and skills from English-language instruction (Bennett, 2003). In bilingual programs, students spend part of the school day receiving instruction in core academic areas in their native language and the remainder of the day with English-speaking students. Yet other students learn through English as a second language (ESL) programs in which instruction occurs primarily in English, although separate from general education, and no specific attempt is made to preserve students' native language. In a few elementary schools, English-language learners participate in the typical classroom, with a bilingual teacher co-teaching the class for all or part of the day (Reeves, 2006; York-Barr, Ghere, & Sommerness, 2007).

www.resources

http://www.nabe.org
The National Association for Bilingual Education is an organization concerned with the quality of education received by students whose native language is not English. Its website includes articles, research reports, and other resources.

Working TOGETHER

Creating a School Environment for Collaborating with Parents

Collaboration between school professionals and parents and families is less about creating a set of activities than it is about forming a mindset based on "want to" rather than "ought to." This is especially important when working with families from diverse racial and cultural groups. To foster this positive approach toward working with parents and families, try these ideas:

- Survey the parents of your students to find out what information they need. Arrange to have your survey translated into the languages spoken in the homes of your students.
- Call to invite uninvolved parents to come to a school event or activity.
- Work with other professionals at your school to contact parents' places of worship for ideas on how to foster positive relationships with parents and the community.
- Let parents know a specific time and/or day of the week they can reach you by telephone or in person at school.
- Ask parents to volunteer in your classroom, either tutoring students or teaching mini-lessons about their hobbies, interests, or jobs.
- Provide your school e-mail address for parents who prefer this communication mode.

- Call parents to praise their child—and do this more than once.
- Develop home-learning activity packets that are related to your learning objectives. However, be sure they are family friendly—that is, that only basic supplies are needed to complete them.
- With parent permission, connect an uninvolved parent with a parent who is involved.
- Keep a list of community resources at your fingertips. Although your school social worker or other professionals also might have this information, you may be able to offer informal assistance in a way that is respectful and low key.
- Have your students create a newsletter to send home. In it, describe important activities. Have secondary students keep a journal for their parents, outlining what they are studying.
- Ask for parents' input regarding what works best with their child, especially regarding discipline and rewards.

Source: Adapted from *Home-School Collaboration: Building Effective Parent-School Partnerships,* by S. L. Christenson, 2002, Minneapolis: Children, Youth, and Family Consortium, University of Minnesota. Retrieved December 5, 2004, from http://www.cyfc.umn.edu/schoolage/resources/home.html. Reprinted by permission.

www.resources

http://www.nccp.org
The National Center for Children in Poverty, which is associated with Columbia University, provides a wealth of information about children living in poverty. The site includes information about immigrant children, children receiving welfare, children's health care, and many other related topics.

If you develop curiosity about your students' cultures and languages, you can be sensitive to their learning needs and responsive to them. If you consider yourself as much a learner as a teacher in interacting with these students, you will become culturally competent and help them effectively access the curriculum and succeed in school.

How Can You Meet the Needs of Students Who Are at Risk?

In addition to all the other special needs you find among students, you will likely encounter one that is found in virtually every public school classroom in the country. That special need is being at risk for school failure. Students who are *at risk* are those who have been exposed to some condition or situation that negatively affects their learning, like Tam, whom you met at the beginning of this chapter. Most teachers include in this description students who were prenatally exposed to drugs, including alcohol; students who use drugs or whose family members are drug users; students who are homeless; and students who have been neglected. Others include students who are bullies and those who are victims, as well as those who have recently experienced the death of someone close to them. Students who are school phobic are at risk, as are those who are considered suicidal, physically unattractive or obese, socially underdeveloped, and slow or marginal learners. For many educators, it is difficult to understand the range of problems students face and the tremendous impact these problems have on their lives.

You might be wondering why students who are at risk are discussed in a text about students with disabilities. Three reasons are central:

1. With a well-designed education, many students who are at risk for school failure succeed in school. The strategies for accommodating the needs of students with disabilities are usually effective for students at risk; these strategies are discussed throughout this text. By using the INCLUDE strategy, you can identify ways to help these students reach their potential.
2. Effective early school experiences for students who are at risk, increasingly based on response to intervention processes, can establish a pattern of success in school learning that carries through high school (Gersti-Pepin, 2006). Without such experiences, students at risk are more likely to be identified as having learning or emotional disabilities.
3. Many students with disabilities also are students at risk. Many students with disabilities have been abused, some live in poverty, and others use illegal drugs.

    Increasing your understanding of risk factors and approaches for working with students at risk benefits all students at risk for school failure, whether they have disabilities or not.

INCLUDE

Characteristics and Needs of Students at Risk

Intellectually, socially, emotionally, behaviorally, and physically, students considered at risk are as diverse as students in the general school population. What distinguishes them from other students is the high likelihood that they will drop out of school prior to earning a high school diploma and that they will experience difficulty throughout their lives. Some students at risk also share other characteristics and needs, including a tendency to be noncompliant, problems in monitoring their own learning and behavior, language delays, difficulties with social relationships, and problems understanding the consequences of their behaviors (Severson, Walker, & Hope-Doolittle, 2007). To illustrate further the needs these students have, three representative groups of students at risk are briefly discussed in the following sections: (1) students who live in poverty, including those who are homeless; (2) students who have been abused or neglected; and (3) students who live in homes in which substance abuse occurs or who themselves are substance abusers. Keep in mind that even though this discussion treats each group as distinct for the sake of clarity, any single student could be in all three groups.

fyi

Homeless children have to make many educational and personal adjustments as a result of four conditions in their lives: constant moving, frequent change of schools, overcrowded living quarters, and lack of basic resources such as clothing and transportation.

Students Who Live in Poverty   Approximately 41 percent (that is, 29.9 million) of U.S. children under 18 years of age live in low-income families, $22,050 for a family of four (National Center for Children in Poverty, 2010). A total of 19 percent of children live in poverty, that is, their family income is even lower, half or less of the level to be considered low income. Moreover, 56 percent of these children (that is, 16 million) have at least one parent who works full-time year-round; just 19 percent do not have an employed parent.

Students who live in poverty have many problems that affect their learning. These children score significantly lower on academic assessments than students who do not live in poverty, and they are more likely to have been retained at least once (Walker-Dalhouse & Risko, 2008). They also might not have nutritious meals to eat, a safe and warm place to play and sleep, or needed supplies to complete homework. These students are sometimes worried about their families' circumstances, and older students might be expected to work evenings and weekends to help support the family or to miss school to babysit younger siblings. Students living in poverty also are more likely than advantaged students to experience parental neglect, witness violence, and change schools and residences frequently.

Some poor families are homeless. It is now estimated that 39 percent of all homeless individuals are children under age 18, and they are likely to access the system of homeless shelters, on average, for up to a year (National Coalition for the Homeless, 2009). In addition to families who are homeless, many are in temporary living

**dimensions of
DIVERSITY**

Students who are mobile account for approximately 1 percent of all learners (Titus, 2007). Examples of mobile students include those displaced by catastrophes such as hurricanes and children of migrant workers.

arrangements with relatives or friends. Homelessness results in many educational problems. Students sometimes leave their neighborhood school or transfer from school to school when they move to a shelter or stay with family or friends. This can leave gaps in their learning. Some students are placed in foster care when the family is homeless, and this arrangement affects their social and emotional adjustment. In addition to learning problems, students who live in poverty or who are homeless sometimes (although not always) display acting-out, restless, or aggressive behaviors; anxiety; depression; and regressive behaviors (Popp, Stronge, & Hindman, 2003).

Students Who Are Abused or Neglected   A second group of students at risk includes those who are physically abused, sexually abused, psychologically abused, or neglected each year (U.S. Department of Health and Human Services, 2010). Did you know that in 2007, 1760 children died as a result of abuse or neglect? Although the precise meaning of the term **child abuse** varies from state to state, it generally refers to situations in which a parent or other caregiver inflicts or allows others to inflict injury on a child or permits a substantial risk of injury to exist. **Child neglect** is used to describe situations in which a parent or other caregiver fails to provide the necessary supports for a child's well-being, such as basic food and shelter, education, medical care, and other items. Figure 8.2 summarizes the demographic characteristics of students who are abused and the individuals who abuse them.

Some students who have been abused or neglected show visible signs, such as bruises, burns, and other untreated physical problems. They also might complain of hunger. Table 8.3 provides a list of student characteristics that might signal to school professionals the presence of abuse or neglect.

You should be aware that as a teacher, you have a legal and ethical obligation to report suspected child abuse of your students (for example, Hinkelman & Bruno, 2008). Although the specific reporting requirements for teachers vary from state to state, federal law requires that every state maintain a hotline and other systems for reporting abuse, and every state has statutes that define abuse and neglect and establish reporting procedures. If you suspect that one of your students is being abused, you should follow your school district's procedures for reporting it. If you are unsure about those procedures, you should notify your principal, school social worker, or school nurse.

www.resources

http://www.nlm.nih.gov/medline plus/childabuse.html
At the Child Abuse website of the National Institutes of Health, you can find information about the symptoms of child abuse and your responsibilities as an educator for reporting it.

Students Who Live with Substance Abuse or Are Substance Abusers   A third group of students at risk for school failure comprises those involved in substance abuse. Some students' parents have abused drugs and alcohol. The impact on students can begin before they are born and often affects them throughout their lives. Babies born to mothers who drink alcohol heavily during pregnancy may have a medical condition called **fetal alcohol syndrome (FAS)** or a milder form known as **fetal alcohol syndrome disorder (FASD).** Babies with FAS or FASD are smaller than expected, may have facial and other slight physical abnormalities, and often experience learning and behavior problems when they go to school. The prevalence estimate for these disorders is 0.3–1.5 in every 1000 live births. Some researchers estimate that as many as 1 in 8 children in the United States has some type of permanent brain damage related to the mother's alcohol use during pregnancy (National Organization on Fetal Alcohol Syndrome, 2004), and FAS and FASD together are considered the leading preventable cause of childhood intellectual impairment. Students with FAS or FASD tend to use poor judgment, leaving a situation when things do not go as planned or failing to predict the consequences of their behavior.

Another type of substance abuse concerns maternal drug abuse; babies born to mothers using drugs often are low in weight. They also are likely to become overstimulated, which leads to an array of behaviors associated with irritability. When these children reach school age, they are likely to experience a wide variety of learning and behavior problems. Some are low-achievers, and others may become eligible for special education services. These children may be inattentive, hyperactive, and impulsive (Conners et al., 2004).

FIGURE 8.2 Child Abuse: A National Profile

In 2008, more than 6.0 million children were reported to child protective services because of suspected abuse or neglect. Some 772,000 of these cases were substantiated. This was a decrease (12.1 cases per 1,000 children versus 10.3 cases per 1,000 children) from 2006.

Racial and Ethnic Backgrounds of Abused and Neglected Children
Cases per 1,000 children

Caucasian	8.6
African American	16.6
Hispanic	9.8
American Indian/Alaska Natives	13.9
Asian American	2.4
Pacific Islander	11.6

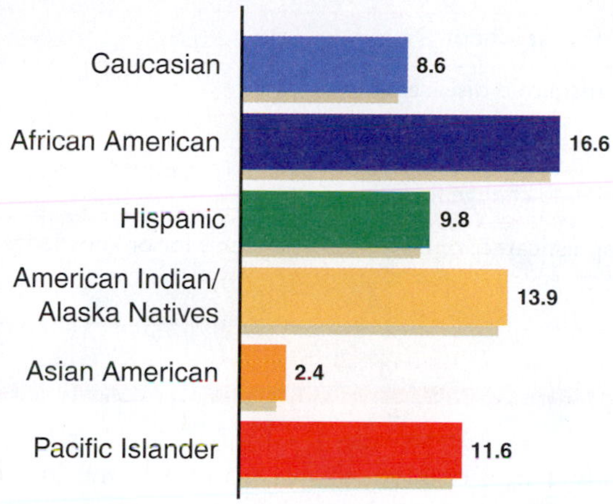

Breakdown by Type of Abuse*
Percent of substantiated cases: 2008

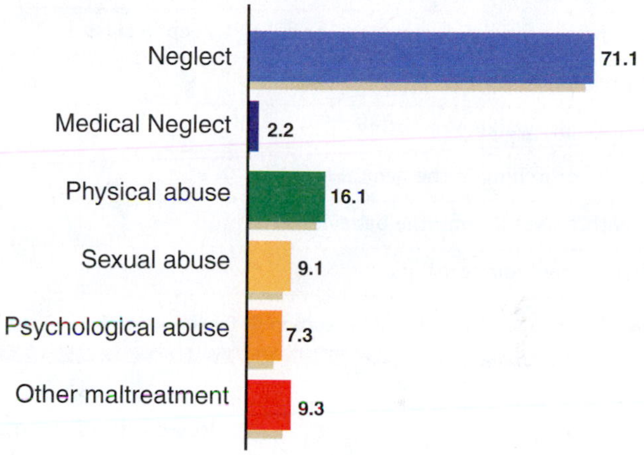

Neglect	71.1
Medical Neglect	2.2
Physical abuse	16.1
Sexual abuse	9.1
Psychological abuse	7.3
Other maltreatment	9.3

Characteristics of Fatalities (*n* = 1,740)

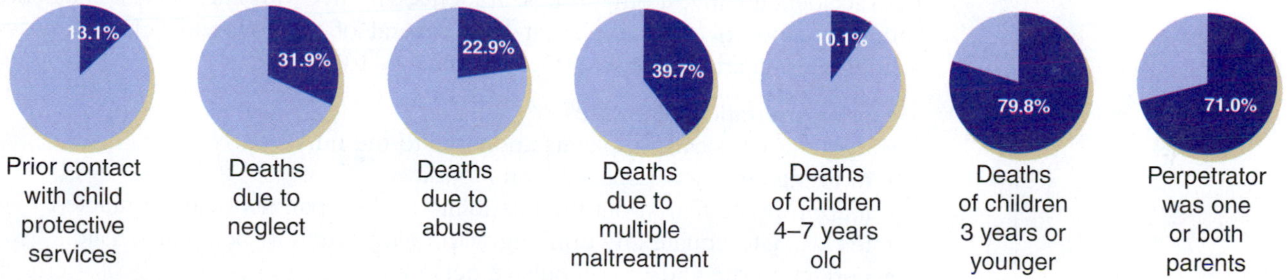

Prior contact with child protective services	Deaths due to neglect	Deaths due to abuse	Deaths due to multiple maltreatment	Deaths of children 4–7 years old	Deaths of children 3 years or younger	Perpetrator was one or both parents
13.1%	31.9%	22.9%	39.7%	10.1%	79.8%	71.0%

Perpetrator Profile

Neglected Child	61.1%
Physically Abused Child	10.0%
Sexually Abused Child	6.8%
Multiple Maltreatments	13.4%
Female	56.2%
Male	42.6%
Unknown Sex	1.1%
Parents	80.1%
Other Relatives	6.5%
Unmarried Partner of Parent	4.4%
Age 19 or Younger	4.8%
Age 20–29	35.9%
Age 30–39	34.5%
Age 40–49	16.1%
Age 50 or Older	8.8%

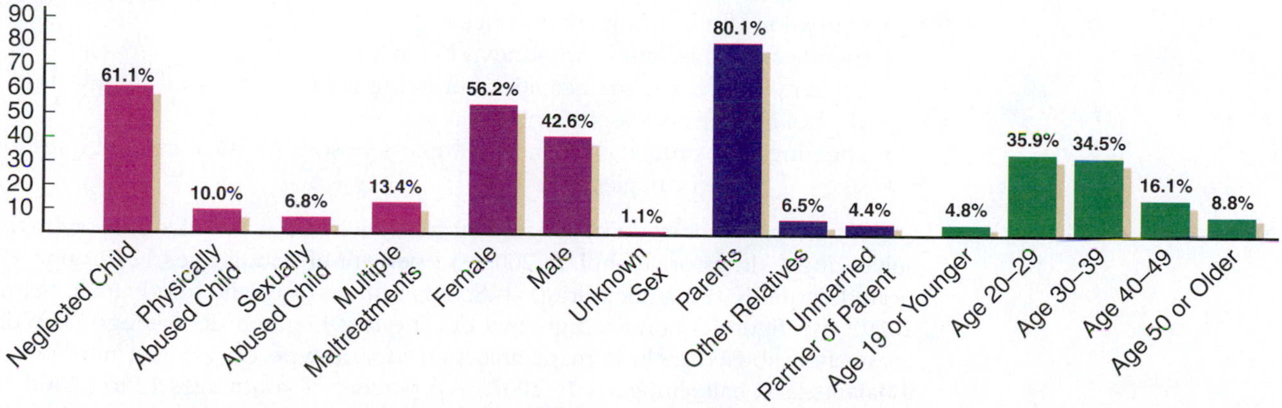

Source: Based on U.S. Department of Health and Human Services, Administration on Children, Youth and Families. (2010). *Child maltreatment 2008*. Washington, DC: Author. Retrieved June 26, 2010 from http://www.acf.hhs.gov/programs/cb/pubs/cm08/cm08.pdf.

*Total is more than 100 percent because some children were reported for multiple types of abuse.

TABLE 8.3   Characteristics of Students Who Are Abused or Neglected

• unexplained bruises and welts	• unexplained fractures
• unexplained lacerations or abrasions	• wariness of adult contacts
• apprehensiveness when other children cry	• fear of parents or going home
• unexplained absences	• behavioral extremes such as aggression and withdrawal
• unattended physical problems and medical needs	• constant lack of supervision
• hunger	• poor hygiene
• inappropriate dress	• begging or stealing food
• constant fatigue, listlessness, or falling asleep in class	• extended stays at school
• pregnancy	• sexually transmitted disease
• difficulty walking or sitting	• torn, stained, or bloody underclothing
• pain or itching in the genital area	• unwillingness to change for gym
• withdrawal to infantile behavior	• bizarre, sophisticated, or unusual sexual behavior or knowledge
• poor peer relationships	

Source: Information from United Federation of Teachers, 2007.

Researchers estimate that nearly 1 in 4 children grows up in a home in which alcohol or drugs are abused. These children are at risk because of a number of factors. For example, they are at risk for being neglected or abused. In homes in which drugs are abused, children may be passive recipients of drugs that can be inhaled, or they may accidentally ingest other drugs. Students who live in homes in which alcohol or drugs are abused often display at least several of the following characteristics at school (Germinario, Cervalli, & Ogden, 1992, p. 106):

- poor or erratic attendance
- frequent physical complaints and visits to the nurse
- morning tardiness, especially on Mondays
- inappropriate fear about the possibility of their parents being contacted
- tendency to equate any drinking with being drunk or being alcoholic
- perfectionistic and/or compulsive behavior
- difficulty concentrating, hyperactivity
- sudden emotional outbursts, crying, temper tantrums
- regression (for example, thumbsucking)
- friendlessness, isolation, withdrawn behavior
- passivity during routine activities but being active or focused during drug and alcohol awareness lessons
- lingering after drug and alcohol awareness lessons to ask unrelated questions
- signs of abuse or neglect

A third group of students affected by substance abuse includes those who themselves abuse drugs or alcohol. In 2008, 9.3 percent of youths ages 12 through 17 reported currently using illicit drugs (U.S. Department of Health and Human Services, 2009); this figure continues a gradual decline that began a decade ago. The drugs most often abused include marijuana, prescription-type drugs used nonmedically, inhalants, and hallucinogens. In 2007, 14.6 percent of youth ages 12 to 17 indicated they were current alcohol drinkers, with more than half of those classified as binge drinkers (Substance Abuse and Mental Health Services Administration, 2009). Among youths ages 12 through 17, 11.4 percent were current cigarette smokers. Students with emotional disabilities are at particularly high risk for alcohol and drug abuse. Students who are substance abusers often have poor diets and sleep disturbances, feel a great deal of stress, and are at risk for depression and suicide. In school, they typically recall only information taught while they are sober, interact poorly with peers and teachers, and display excessive risk-taking behaviors.

As you can see, students who live in poverty, who are abused or neglected, and who live with substance abuse, as well as other students at risk, collectively have many characteristics and needs that affect their learning. Although some of these students are resilient and do not suffer long-term consequences from their stressful lives (Jaffee, Caspi, & Moffit, 2007; Jones, 2007), the majority do not thrive without the support of an understanding school system and knowledgeable and committed teachers.

Interventions for Students at Risk

As a teacher, you sometimes will be faced with the frustrating situation of not being able to relieve your students of the stresses that often prevent them from learning to their potential. You can offer these students a safe environment by providing clear expectations and instructional support, making school an important place in their lives.

Generally, recommendations for intervening to teach students at risk include four goals, none of which is completely unique to these students: Set high but realistic expectations, establish peers as teaching partners, collaborate with other professionals, and support family and community involvement. Each recommendation is discussed briefly here.

In 2008, 19.6 percent of children from 6 to 11 years old were obese as were 18.1 percent of those ages 12–19 (Centers for Disease Control and Prevention, 2010a). These rates are triple what they were in 1980.

Set High but Realistic Expectations   When you are teaching students who are at risk, it is tempting to make assumptions about how much they are capable of learning. For example, you might think that a student who does not have books at home and whose parents are either unable or unwilling to read with her cannot be a successful learner. Having low expectations can lead to overusing teaching strategies that emphasize drilling students on lower-level academic skills. Although drill activities have a place in educating students at risk, they must be balanced with other approaches. Students need to learn thinking processes along with basic skills, and they need to learn to construct their own knowledge along with receiving it from you.

One other strategy for setting high expectations should be mentioned. Many professionals understand that *tracking*—that is, grouping students for instruction by perceived ability—can discriminate against students at risk (Nomi, 2010). For example, a recent longitudinal study of student achievement in mathematics found that when students were heterogeneously grouped in middle school math classes, they took more math classes in high school and did better in whatever classes they took than did students who had been homogeneously grouped for math in middle school (Burris, Heubert, & Levin, 2006).

Grouping students heterogeneously generally does not place high-achieving students at a disadvantage, and it may help raise the achievement of at-risk learners. Although teachers appropriately group students by their needs for instruction in specific skills as part of their overall instructional plan and some secondary schools offer advanced classes that result in a limited amount of tracking, you should be aware of the potential negative effects of tracking. As a teacher, you can ensure that you do not overuse this type of grouping in your classroom, and you can work with your colleagues to create a school in which students of many different abilities learn together.

Some of your students may live in difficult circumstances, and their lives out of school may have profound influences on their readiness for and focus on learning.

Mini-Me: A Little Technology with a Big Impact

The Mini-Me recorder is a small, round device that permits the teacher to record a 10- to 20-second message, which the student then can play back by pushing a button. This is the same technology used in musical and prerecorded greeting cards. This small device can provide support to many learners who struggle, enabling them to experience more independence and confidence. Some examples of its use include these:

- Flashcards of key sight words are prepared by the teacher using foamboard (because it is thick enough to insert the Mini-Me device). The teacher records one of the words on each Mini-Me and attaches it to the appropriate flashcard. The student first attempts to say the word and then pushes the button to check for the correct answer.
- Using cards similar to those just described, all students can participate in peer tutoring. For example, in a kindergarten or first-grade class, students can show each other their word cards and then check their answers by pushing the playback button on the Mini-Me.
- For a student with ADHD, a brief recorded message might be prepared each day with a reminder of the day's homework or items to bring to school the next day (library books, permission form for the field trip). The Mini-Me could be placed in a student's backpack.

What other uses can you think of for this recording device? For elementary age students? For middle school and high school students? How might such a device facilitate student learning in English or language arts? Math? Science? Social studies?

Mini-Me Recording Device

Source: Adapted from "Using Assistive Technology to Include Low-Performing Students in Peer Tutoring: A Little Help from Mini-Me," by R. R. Van Norman, 2007, *Journal of Special Education Technology, 22*(1), pp. 53–57.

One word of caution about setting standards is necessary: Some students who are at risk live in such high-stress situations outside school that they might not have much support from their parents and other family members for completing school assignments and homework. For example, one teacher described a high school student who always slept in class. In-school suspension did not help, nor did attempts to contact the student's parents. The teacher later learned that this student left school each day, cooked dinner for her younger siblings, and then worked at a fast-food restaurant until midnight. Having high expectations is important, but they need to be tempered with understanding of the circumstances in students' lives outside school.

Effective instruction for students at risk includes the same strategies you would use for other students, with particular attention to the physical and social-emotional challenges these students often face. Students at risk need a structured learning environment, systematic instruction in basic skill areas, and strategies for learning independence. The Technology Notes provides one example of a tool to enhance the learning of at-risk students.

Establish Peers as Teaching Partners   Peers learning from one another is a strategy that was recommended earlier for students from diverse cultural and linguistic backgrounds; it is also useful for at-risk students. For example, Peer-Assisted Learning Strategies (PALS) is a highly structured classwide peer tutoring program that has been used across all grade levels to improve outcomes in reading (McMaster, Fuchs, & Fuchs, 2006). In this program, higher achieving students are partnered with those who are struggling, and they learn specific ways to interact with each other and reinforce each other. Research has demonstrated that most students improve in fluency and comprehension in a PALS program.

Collaborate with Other Professionals   A third strategy for teaching students who are at risk involves increasing your problem-solving capability by adding the skills and resources of your colleagues. Problem solving with your colleagues about at-risk students allows you to check your own perspectives against theirs, gain access to their expertise, and coordinate your efforts. For example, if you are teaching Shaneal, a student whom you suspect has been abused, you can first ask the counselor or social worker whether there is any past documentation of abuse and you can request that one of these professionals speak with the student. For students at risk who are struggling academically, the response to intervention procedure now in place in most schools can help you in identifying and implementing effective instructional strategies.

Support Family and Community Involvement   It is essential that you maintain positive contact with parents and other caregivers of your at-risk students, just as you would with other students. However, the level of participation you can expect will vary considerably. Some parents will be anxious to ensure that their children have all the advantages an education can give them, and they will do all they can to assist you in teaching. Parents who are not functioning well themselves, however, probably cannot be expected to participate actively in their children's education. To involve families and communities in their children's education, you might try several ideas. Sometimes it might be more appropriate to require a student to bring to school something personally important from home and to base an assignment on that, rather than to assign more traditional homework. It also can be helpful to assist parents in connecting with community resources such as health clinics and social service agencies. One school district that was struggling because of the rapidly increasing number of at-risk students worked with local church leaders to connect families with resources and improve the communication between school personnel and families.

When you think about the diversity of students you may teach, it is easy to become overwhelmed by the challenge of meeting all students' instructional needs. Classrooms designed to celebrate diversity, rather than treat it as a deficiency or an exception, are classrooms that blend structure and flexibility and provide many options for learning.

WRAPPING IT UP
BACK TO THE CASES

This section provides opportunities for you to apply the knowledge gained in this chapter to the cases described at the beginning of this chapter. The questions and activities that follow demonstrate how these standards and principles, along with other concepts that you have learned about in this chapter, connect to the everyday activities of all teachers.

MARIA and her teachers have set a goal for Maria to become a teacher and are hopeful that she will be able to attend a summer program where she can learn more about teaching. You are concerned that her English-language skills may hamper her experience—particularly her difficulties with abstract concepts. Review what you have learned about teaching students who experience language processing difficulties and consult the Professional Edge on page 254. Suggest strategies, technologies, or instructional supports that will help Maria prepare for the new challenge and support her learning experience during the summer program. Explain why you believe your suggestions may benefit Maria.

SETH, as you may recall, is having a difficult time in middle school, struggling with the large and more complex setting and concerned about the attention he draws to himself. Take on the role of being one of Seth's teachers and assume that you have scheduled a meeting to talk with his parents. Who else would you like to have attend the meeting? What would the main focus of the meeting be? As you discuss Seth's needs (review the Professional Edge on p. 237 and the Instructional Edge on page 242), what additional accommodations might you recommend? List these and justify each. What is your role in discussing medication—what could you say and what should you definitely not say?

LYDIA, as you may remember, has special talents and academic ability. However, her family is very concerned that she is not getting appropriate opportunities to use her talents and academic ability. You have invited family members to a conference tomorrow afternoon in which you will address their concerns with a proposal for future accommodations. In preparation, you ask a peer to work with you to do the following:

- Develop a matrix of pros and cons for the instructional strategies commonly used with students who are gifted and talented
- Write a rationale for using or not using each strategy for Lydia

- Create a proposal to present to the family that includes a combination of strategies you believe will be most appropriate

TAM, as you may recall, is a student at risk and needs help. His first-block history teacher sat at your table during lunch today. During a general conversation about working with at-risk students, the teacher shared Tam's story. Based on the interventions you read about in this chapter for students who are at risk, what strategies might you suggest your colleague employ to help Tam?

SUMMARY

- Some students receive specialized services through Section 504, federal legislation requiring that accommodations be provided by general educators to students who have functional disabilities (for example, physical or medical conditions, significant learning needs) that limit their access to an education.

- One specific group of students who receive Section 504 assistance comprises those with attention deficit–hyperactivity disorder (ADHD), a medically diagnosed disorder characterized by chronic and severe inattention and/or hyperactivity–impulsivity. Students with ADHD may receive a variety of environmental, academic, and behavior interventions; training to assist their parents in understanding and responding to their needs; and medication.

- Students who are gifted and talented include those with generally high intellectual ability as well as those with talents in specific areas such as music. The interventions used most often to help them achieve school success are curriculum compacting,

enrichment and acceleration, differentiation, and individualized interventions.

- Students from culturally and linguistically diverse backgrounds and their families sometimes have values that differ from those of schools. Teachers need to learn about students' cultures, teach in a manner that is responsive to those cultures, and acknowledge and value diverse cultures in the classroom in order to teach students from these backgrounds effectively.

- Students at risk for school failure because of environmental influences such as poverty, child abuse, and drug addiction also have special needs. Because students at risk often live in unpredictable and stressful environments, strategies for teaching them include setting appropriate expectations, establishing peers as teaching partners, collaborating with other professionals, and working closely with families and community members.

APPLICATIONS IN TEACHING PRACTICE

DIVERSITY IN A HIGH SCHOOL CLASS

Ivan Robinson is a first-year teacher in a large urban school district. Although it is only the fourth week of school, he is concerned. Although he is confident of his knowledge of the curriculum, as well as his teaching skills, and he feels he has a strong commitment to teaching all the students assigned to him, he is worried that he won't be able to meet the vast and diverse array of needs represented among his students. For example, Thuan, who just immigrated to the United States from Vietnam, speaks very little English and seems overwhelmed by nearly everything at school. Mr. Robinson can't recall ever seeing Thuan smile. Whatever topic Mr. Robinson discusses, he knows that much of the information is beyond Thuan's understanding because of language differences and that Thuan does not have the context for grasping many of the topics that are central to the curriculum.

Then there is Sonny. Sonny is supposed to be taking medication for ADHD, but it doesn't seem to be having the intended effect on him. At an after-school meeting, Mr. Robinson, the school psychologist, the counselor, and the assistant principal discussed the matter

with Sonny, and it was noted that Sonny recently had decided he had outgrown the need for medication and sometimes was not taking it. Sonny did say, though, that a few times he decided to catch up by taking a double dose. The counselor is supposed to follow up on this unhealthy and potentially dangerous thinking about medication and keep Mr. Robinson informed. In the meantime, Sonny is in his class and, as Mr. Robinson puts it, is either "bouncing off the walls or zoned out."

Jenny is a concern as well. She and her twin sister, Jenna, are struggling academically despite receiving a lot of individual attention and having supportive parents. Neither girl's reading comprehension is strong. Both girls have been referred in the past for special education services, but neither is eligible to receive them. Mr. Robinson knows that the twins' father has been out of work for nearly a year, that the girls generally have little supervision after school, and that the family is barely getting by on donations from friends and their church. Mr. Robinson heard last week that one of the grandparents had also come to live with the family. He wonders how much of the twins' learning problems are related to their home situation.

Mr. Robinson also teaches Kimberly, who just moved into the district and is so far ahead of the other students that Mr. Robinson finds her just a bit intimidating. Two other students, Lisa and Paul, are from families that have very little; they come to school without supplies and seem reluctant to interact with the other students.

As he reflects on his class, Mr. Robinson realizes that more than a third of the students have a special need of one kind or another, and he suspects that he knows only a fraction of their life stories. He wants to reach them all and truly make a difference in their lives, but he is not sure he can accomplish his goal.

QUESTIONS

Before you answer the following questions, place Mr. Robinson and his students in a grade level that you might teach, whether elementary, middle, or high school. After responding, discuss with your classmates what is similar across the school levels and what is different.

1. How typical is the type of class Mr. Robinson has? What other types of diverse needs might you expect to be represented in a class you will teach?
2. What general strategies might Mr. Robinson use in his class that would benefit many students with special needs and harm none?
3. For each student with special needs Mr. Robinson has identified, consider how the INCLUDE strategy could be used. Fill in the following chart, perhaps working with a classmate to generate ideas for information not specifically outlined in the preceding student descriptions. Be sure to address academic, social-emotional, behavioral, and medical-physical needs.

	Thuan	Jenny and Jenna	Kimberly	Sonny	Lisa and Paul
Identify					
Note					
Check					
Look					
Use					
Decide					
Evaluate					

4. Mr. Settle is the special educator with whom Mr. Robinson works. What is Mr. Settle's role in assisting Mr. Robinson and other teachers in the school to meet the diverse needs of students, including those who do not have IEPs? Who else might assist Mr. Robinson as he designs instruction and plans how to help his students succeed?
5. How might Mr. Robinson work with the parents of his students to help ensure their needs are addressed? What barriers might he encounter and how might he address them? What inadvertent biases could he have toward his students' families? How could these biases relate to your own views as a novice educator?
6. What realistic expectations can Mr. Robinson set for himself as a teacher for this school year?

myeducationlab

Go to Topics 14: Learning Disabilities/ADHD and 5: Cultural and Linguistic Diversity in the MyEducationLab (www.myeducationlab.com) for your course, where you can:

- Find learning outcomes for Learning Disabilities/ADHD and Cultural and Linguistic Diversity along with the national standards that connect to these outcomes.
- Complete Assignments and Activities that can help you more deeply understand the chapter content.
- Apply and practice your understanding of the core teaching skills identified in the chapter with the Building Teaching Skills and Dispositions learning units.
- Examine challenging situations and cases presented in the IRIS Center Resources. (optional)
- Access video clips of CCSSO National Teachers of the Year award winners responding to the question, "Why Do I Teach?" in the Teacher Talk section. (optional)
- Check your comprehension on the content covered in the chapter by going to the Study Plan in the Book Resources for your text. Here you will be able to take a chapter quiz, receive feedback on your answers, and then access Review, Practice, and Enrichment activities to enhance your understanding of chapter content. (optional)

Differentiating Instruction

LEARNING Objectives

After you read this chapter, you will be able to

1. Describe ways you can differentiate instruction for students by teaching preskills; sequencing instructional examples; and providing additional instruction, practice, and review.

2. Describe accommodations you can make when activating background knowledge, organizing content, and teaching terms and concepts.

3. Make lessons accessible for students with special needs by improving the clarity of your written and oral communication.

4. Describe strategies for involving parents in teaching their children.

5. Adapt independent practice activities for students.

6. Describe how you can make modifications in your classroom materials and activities for students with moderate to severe intellectual disabilities.

MS. DIAZ was teaching her fourth-grade class how to write percentages for fractions using this example from her math book:

Write a percent for $\frac{7}{8}$.

$\frac{7}{8}$ means $7 \div 8$.

$$0.87\frac{4}{8} = 0.87\frac{1}{2} = 87\frac{1}{2}\%$$

$$8)\overline{7.00}$$
$$\underline{64}$$ Divide until the answer is
$$60$$ in hundredths. Give the
$$\underline{56}$$ remainder as a fraction.
$$4$$

$\frac{7}{8} = 87\frac{1}{2}\%$, or 87.5%

To show her students how to do this problem, Ms. Diaz wrote the example on the board, pointing out that the fraction 7/8 means 7 divided by 8. She then explained that they would have to divide until the answer was in hundredths and would have to give the remainder as a fraction. Following this instruction, Ms. Diaz assigned the students ten similar problems to do independently. Abdul, who is a student in this class, has a learning disability. Abdul has experienced some difficulties with math skills since he entered the second grade. He has difficulty learning new skills unless he is given many opportunities for instruction and practice. Abdul answered none of the ten problems correctly. He missed converting the fraction to a percentage because he forgot that it means 7 divided by 8; Abdul divided 8 by 7 instead.

How could this lesson have been taught to Abdul to prevent this misunderstanding? How can Ms. Diaz differentiate instruction for him if he continues to struggle with problems of this type?

CECILY is a student with a hearing loss who is in Ms. Boyd's U.S. history class. Cecily has failed every test so far, because the tests are based mainly on the textbook, which she has difficulty reading. Cecily can read most of the words in the text but is unable to pick out the main ideas. Cecily also has trouble figuring out the meanings of key vocabulary words in context, even though they are highlighted in the text, and she does not know how to use the glossary. Last week, Cecily was assigned a chapter to read for homework. She spent almost two hours trying to comprehend 15 pages of text, and when she was done, she cried in frustration because she could not remember anything she had read. Until recently, Cecily has enjoyed a small group of friends who teach her popular phrases while she teaches them sign language for their favorite topics—clothes, movies, and boys. However, her friends are doing much better in class than Cecily and she's embarrassed.

What can Ms. Boyd do to help Cecily read and remember key ideas in her textbook? What can she do to help Cecily understand new vocabulary words?

ALBERT has attention deficit–hyperactivity disorder (ADHD) and is included in Ms. Olivieri's second grade class. Ms. Olivieri uses learning centers as a way of giving her students extra practice on skills she has already taught in class. Sometimes she has her students read text and answer questions independently. For example, yesterday students reread a story covered in reading class and completed a graphic organizer requiring them to identify key story parts such as setting, main characters, problem, and problem resolution. Other days she has students work together playing learning games like vocabulary dominoes, or timing each other reciting math facts, word parts, or science vocabulary. Albert struggles with the independent activities. He complains that the work is too hard for him, and he has particular difficulty with assignments that have multistep directions and more than one part. As a result, he often wanders away from the centers, either getting help from other students in class or bothering them. Ms. Olivieri feels she is already spending too much time helping Albert.

What can Ms. Olivieri do to make centers a more successful experience for Albert and give herself more time to work with other students?

fyi

This chapter presents instructional accommodations and modifications for steps 5 and 6 of the INCLUDE strategy presented in Chapter 5:

Step 5   Use information from steps 1–4 to brainstorm ways to differentiate instruction.

Step 6   Differentiate instruction.

INCLUDE

INCLUDE

As you have already learned, the curriculum methods and materials teachers use have a strong influence on how readily students learn in the classroom. In fact, the better the materials and the teaching, the fewer the individual accommodations required for students with special needs. However, for a variety of reasons, you may not have control over the materials used in your school. Furthermore, despite your best teaching efforts, some students will still need individual accommodations or modifications to gain access to important skills and content. For example, in the cases just described, merely showing Abdul how to do one problem is not enough. He needs guidance through a number of examples before he is ready to do problems independently. In addition, you can help Cecily focus on important information in her textbook by giving her a study guide that has questions pertaining to the most important content in each chapter. You can also have Cecily identify vocabulary she does not know and ask a classmate to help her with the meanings before she reads. For Albert, you can make sure all directions are clearly written using words he can identify; you can also give directions for center activities orally, guide students through several practice examples before they are required to work independently, and break his assignments into several shorter activities. Of course, you also want to be sure that Albert has the academic skills necessary to complete center assignments independently.

The purpose of this chapter is to provide you with strategies for differentiating instruction by making accommodations and modifications in curriculum materials, teacher instruction, and student practice activities that are reasonable to carry out and increase the likelihood of success for students with disabilities. Remember, most students with disabilities included in your classroom are expected to meet the same curricular goals as their classmates without disabilities. Therefore, most of the strategies for differentiating instruction covered in this chapter fall into the category of accommodations, which, as you learned in Chapter 5, are supports that allow students to more readily access the general education curriculum. In addition, with RtI being used in many schools, differentiated instruction is often carried out using more intensive instructional tiers. For example, Cecily might be given extra instruction in vocabulary in a small Tier 2 group.

It is also important to note that the instructional accommodations described in this chapter can sometimes be carried out with your entire class. At other times, they might be presented with individual students or as a part of small groups. The way you choose to accommodate your students with special needs depends on classroom demands, the characteristics of individual students, and the overall level of functioning of your class. For example, in the case of Abdul, if he has many other classmates who are struggling to write percentages for fractions and if he can attend to a task in a large group, then Ms. Diaz can accommodate him by building more guided practice into her large-group instruction. If only Abdul and a few of his classmates are having trouble learning percents or if Abdul has trouble paying attention in a large group, then Ms. Diaz might better accommodate Abdul by instructing him either one-to-one or in a small group. You can use the INCLUDE strategy to help you make decisions about the best way to make accommodations for your students with special needs.

Instructional modifications, as you learned in Chapter 5, are used for students who have more significant disabilities and who have alternative curricula specified on their individualized education programs (IEPs). Strategies for making appropriate instructional modifications are covered at the end of this chapter, as well as in Chapter 6.

How Can You Make Accommodations for Students with Special Needs in Basic Skills Instruction?

Basic skills instruction means primarily instruction in the academic skills of reading, writing, and math. However, you may also apply effective principles for differentiating basic skills instruction to content areas such as science. Four aspects of basic skills instruction for which you may need to make accommodations for students with disabilities are preskills; the selection and sequencing of examples; the rate of introduction of new skills; and direct instruction, practice, and review.

Teaching Preskills

Darrell is in Ms. Rayburn's second-grade class. In language arts, he is experiencing a problem common to many students with special needs. On Tuesday, Darrell was at his desk reading a book on his favorite topic: magic. However, when Ms. Rayburn asked Darrell specific questions about the book, he was unable to answer them. It turned out that Darrell was unable to identify most of the words in the book and was just pretending to read. Another student, Tamika, is in Mr. Thomas's Algebra 1 class. She is having difficulty solving basic equations with one unknown because she has yet to master basic math computational skills.

Preskills are basic skills necessary for performing more complex skills. Prior to teaching a skill, you should assess students on the relevant preskills and, if necessary, teach these skills. Darrell was unable to comprehend the book about magic because he lacked the word identification skills needed to read the words. He may need instruction in word attack skills; he may also need to be encouraged to read trade books at his reading level. Tamika needs additional instruction and practice on her computational skills if she is going to be successful in Algebra 1. Because textbooks do not generally list preskills, you need to ask yourself continually what preskills are required, and you should be vigilant for students who lack them. Looking at the instructional demands in this way is a key part of applying the INCLUDE strategy. Determining the potential impact of student preskills on instruction may mean informally assessing such skills using curriculum-based assessments like those you learned about in Chapter 4.

If you are teaching a skill and find that most of your students lack the necessary preskills, teach these preskills directly before teaching the more complex skill. If only one or two students lack preskills, you can accommodate them with extra practice and instruction through a peer or parent volunteer or with the help of a special service provider or paraprofessional. For example, Ms. Cooper was preparing a lesson on how to find the area of a rectangle. Before beginning the lesson, she gave her students a multiplication probe and found that almost half the class was still having problems with their multiplication facts. Ms. Cooper set up a peer tutoring program in which students who knew their facts were paired with students who did not; the pairs practiced facts for 10 minutes each day for a week. Students who preferred to work alone practiced their math facts using a drill-and-practice computer-based program. Ms. Cooper still introduced finding the area of rectangles as scheduled, but she allowed students to use calculators, a bypass strategy, until they had mastered their facts.

Selecting and Sequencing Examples

The way you select and sequence instructional examples also can affect how easily your students learn. For example, Alex's practice activities for a week in Mr. Huang's third-grade math class are shown in Figure 9.1. Mr. Huang has been covering two-digit subtraction with regrouping. On Monday through Thursday, Alex was given five of these problems and got them all right. On Friday, he was asked to do a mixture of problems, some requiring regrouping and some not. Alex got only three of the problems correct because he was unable to discriminate between subtraction problems that required regrouping and those that did not. He was unable to differentiate these two types of problems in part because his daily practice pages had included only one problem type. Carefully preparing the **example selection** you use for instruction and student practice can help students learn to differentiate among problem types.

You can help students make key discriminations between current and previous problem types by using examples that at first require the application of only one particular skill (Carnine, Silbert, Kame'enui, & Tarver, 2010). When students can

fyi

Assessing student preskills does not always have to be done using paper-and-pencil tasks. Simply questioning your students orally takes less time and can give you relevant information immediately.

www.resources

High-interest, low-reading-level material is essential for teachers to have for older students with reading problems, but it is always at a premium. *The Key* New Readers Newspaper Project provides stories on all different topics at beginning, middle, and advanced reading levels. Go to http://www.keynews.org

INCLUDE

FIGURE 9.1 **Alex's Math Work**

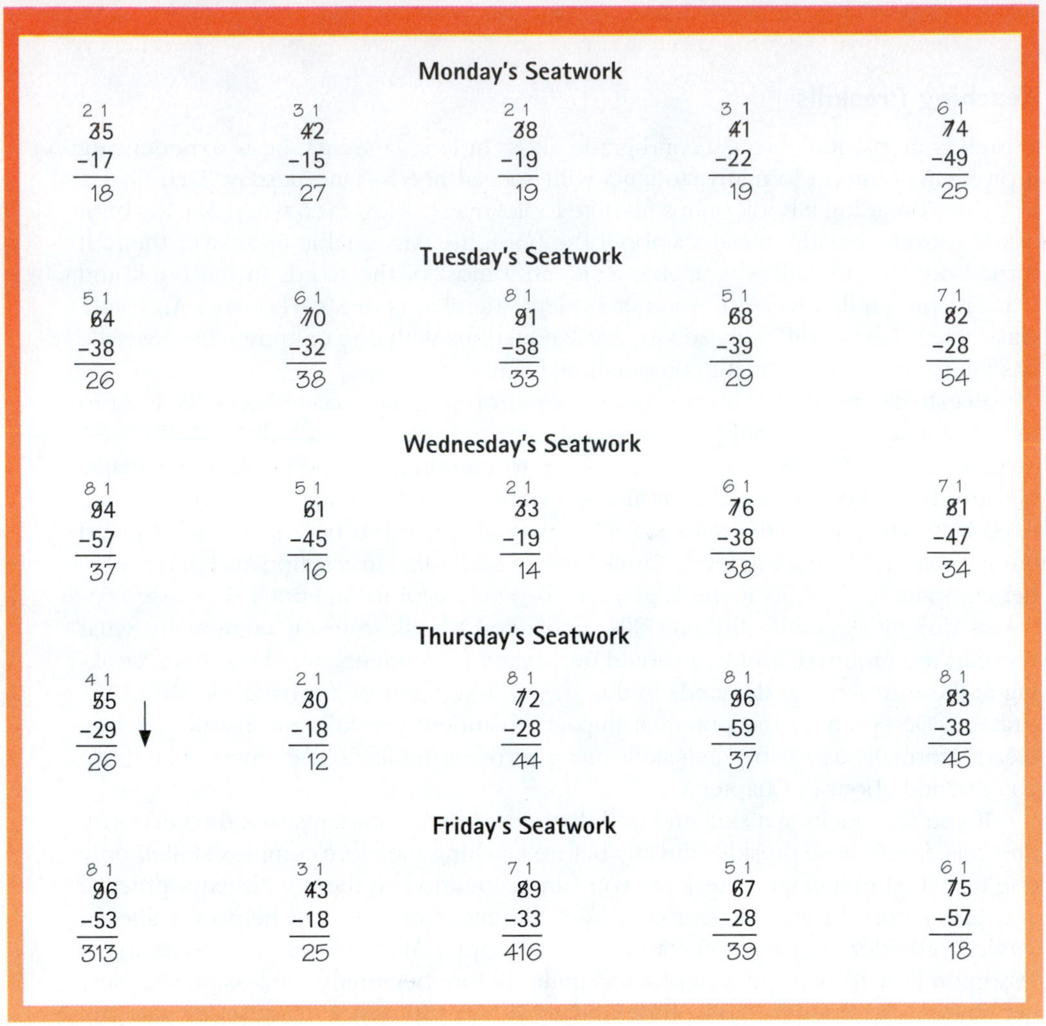

Monday's Seatwork

²¹ 3̷5	³¹ 4̷2	²¹ 3̷8	³¹ 4̷1	⁶¹ 7̷4
−17	−15	−19	−22	−49
18	27	19	19	25

Tuesday's Seatwork

⁵¹ 6̷4	⁶¹ 7̷0	⁸¹ 9̷1	⁵¹ 6̷8	⁷¹ 8̷2
−38	−32	−58	−39	−28
26	38	33	29	54

Wednesday's Seatwork

⁸¹ 9̷4	⁵¹ 6̷1	²¹ 3̷3	⁶¹ 7̷6	⁷¹ 8̷1
−57	−45	−19	−38	−47
37	16	14	38	34

Thursday's Seatwork

⁴¹ 5̷5 ↓	²¹ 3̷0	⁸¹ 7̷2	⁸¹ 9̷6	⁸¹ 9̷3
−29	−18	−28	−59	−38
26	12	44	37	45

Friday's Seatwork

⁸¹ 9̷6	³¹ 4̷3	⁷¹ 8̷9	⁵¹ 6̷7	⁶¹ 7̷5
−53	−18	−33	−28	−57
313	25	416	39	18

perform these problems without error, add examples of skills previously taught to help students discriminate between the different problem types. Doing this also provides students with needed review. An easy accommodation for Alex would have been to add several problems that did not require regrouping to each daily teaching and practice session once he had demonstrated that he could compute the regrouping problems accurately when they were presented alone.

Ms. Owens ran into a different example-related problem when teaching her students word problems in math. In her examples, when a word problem included the word *more,* getting the correct answer always involved subtracting, as in the following problem:

> Alicia had 22 pennies. Juanita had 13. How many more pennies does Alicia have than Juanita?

However, on her test, Ms. Owens included the following problem:

> Mark read 3 books in March. He read 4 more books in April. How many books did Mark read?

Several students with special needs in Ms. Owens's class subtracted 3 from 4 because they thought the presence of the word *more* signaled subtraction. Ms. Owens needed to include problems of this latter type in her teaching to prevent such misconceptions.

Consider this example: When Mr. Yoshida taught his students how to add *ed* to a word ending in *y*, he demonstrated on the board as follows:

carry + ed = carried hurry + ed = hurried

Next, Mr. Yoshida had his students add *ed* to five words ending in *y*. Finally, he assigned students ten practice problems in their English books that looked like this:

Write the past tense of *marry*.

A number of students were unable to answer the questions in the book, even though they knew how to add *ed* to words ending in *y*, because the practice examples in the book required students to know the meaning of "past tense" and how to form the past tense by adding *ed*. The book's practice activity was very different from the instructional examples Mr. Yoshida used, which only required students to add *ed* to words ending in *y*.

Both Ms. Owens's and Mr. Yoshida's examples demonstrate an important aspect of selecting instructional examples: The range of your instructional examples should match the range of the problem types used when you assess student learning. Ms. Owens could have prevented problems in her class by expanding her range of examples to include word problems that contained the word *more* but were not solved by subtracting. Mr. Yoshida could have better prepared his students for the practice activities in the English book by using examples that referred directly to forming the past tense by adding *ed*. Note that some students with special needs still may struggle even when appropriate instructional examples are used. These students may require an individual accommodation that could be as simple as a reminder that the word *more* can have more than one meaning or that the past tense is formed by adding *ed* to a verb. Or the accommodation could be as involved as providing additional instruction using concrete representations of the different meanings of *more* or verbs ending in *ed*.

The following shows a different example selection problem. Tawana's class was learning several high-frequency sight words that appeared in their classroom reading program. On Wednesday, Tawana learned the word *man*, but on Thursday, after the word *men* was presented, she was unable to read *man* correctly. Tawana's word identification problem illustrates another example selection problem, namely, **example sequencing**. The visual and auditory similarities of *man* and *men* make learning these words difficult for many students who are at risk and students with learning disabilities, who may have trouble differentiating words that look and/or sound the same. One way to prevent this problem is to separate the introduction of *man* and *men* by introducing other dissimilar high-frequency words, such as *dog, house,* and *cat*. Students with special needs also may need differentiated instruction such as more practice learning the words, color coding the vowels *a* and *e*, and spelling the two words using letter blocks.

This same sequencing idea can be applied to teaching letter sounds. For example, when deciding on the order in which to teach the sounds, consider separating letters that look and sound the same, such as *b* and *d, m* and *n,* and *p* and *b*. The careful sequencing of instruction can also be applied to teaching higher-level content. For example, when Mr. Roosevelt, a chemistry teacher, taught the chemical elements, he separated those symbols that look and/or sound similar, such as bromine (Br) and rubidium (Rb), and silicon (Si) and strontium (Sr). Knowledge of how sequencing can affect learning can help you recognize the need to differentiate instruction. For example, Ms. Mann, unlike Mr. Roosevelt, was unable to change the order in which she taught the chemical elements without drastically modifying her chemistry text. When she noticed that bromine and rubidium were taught closely together, she allowed more time for students to practice in their study groups before introducing another element.

fyi

Student errors and misconceptions also stem from the over- or under-generalization of concepts. Careful selection and sequencing of a range of examples can help prevent these kinds of errors.

dimensions of
DIVERSITY

Listening is the weakest skill for English-language learners. Khisty (2002) suggests: (1) displaying words as they are spoken or pointing to words in prepared text as they are delivered; (2) contextualizing instruction through models, real objects, drawings, and other visual aids; and (3) having students act out problems or concepts.

INCLUDE

www.resources

The ProQuest K–12 website, at http://www.proquestk12.com, provides lesson plans that include modifications for students with special needs.

Deciding the Rate of Introduction of New Skills

Students sometimes have difficulty learning skills that are introduced at too fast a rate. For example, Mr. Henry was teaching his ninth-grade English students how to proofread rough drafts of their writing for errors in using capital letters and punctuation marks. He reviewed the rules for using capital letters, periods, commas, question marks, and exclamation points. Next, he had students take out their most recent writing samples from their portfolios to look for capitalization and punctuation errors. Carmine found that he had left out capital letters at the beginning of two sentences, but he did not find any of the punctuation errors he had made. A number of other students in the class had the same problem. The dilemma was that Mr. Henry had taught his students to proofread their papers for capital letters and punctuation marks simultaneously. A better pace might have been first to work on proofreading for capitalization errors and then to add one punctuation mark at a time (first periods, then commas, followed by question marks, and then exclamation points).

In another example of the **rate of skill introduction,** Ms. Stevens was working on reading comprehension with her students. She introduced three new comprehension strategies at once: detecting the sequence, determining cause and effect, and making predictions. However, when applying the INCLUDE strategy using results from her universal screening measure, she recognized that Carlos, a student with a mild intellectual disability, learned best when he was taught one strategy at a time. Ms. Stevens accommodated Carlos by forming a Tier 2 group with three other students who, like Carlos, would benefit from learning these comprehension strategies one by one before being asked to carry them out simultaneously. Mr. Wallace, the special education co-teacher, taught the group, starting with instruction on detecting the sequence. You can learn more about working with special education teachers in the Working Together.

These examples demonstrate an important principle about introducing new skills to students with special needs: New skills should be introduced in small steps and at a rate slow enough to ensure mastery before teaching more new skills. Further, you may want to prioritize skills and even postpone some, as Ms. Stevens did. Many commercially produced materials introduce skills at a rate that is too fast for students with disabilities. As just illustrated, a common accommodation is to slow down the rate of skill introduction and provide more practice. Other students in the class, including those with no formally identified special needs, often benefit from

Working TOGETHER

Asking for Help

Ms. Gabriel is starting her first year as a high school history teacher. She just found out that she will have four students with learning disabilities included in her fifth-period U.S. history class. The special education teacher, Mr. Colbert, left the students' IEPs in her mailbox with a brief note asking her to look them over to see what kinds of accommodations she is required to make in her teaching. The IEPs state that she is supposed to modify their homework assignments and adapt the textbook.

Ms. Gabriel is confused. In the first place, she is unsure exactly what an *accommodation* is. Second, she doesn't know what the IEP means by *modifying* homework and *adapting* the text. She's particularly worried about homework because she knows students won't like it if they know that other students are doing less

homework. Ms. Gabriel feels that Mr. Colbert should have met with her to explain more clearly what she needed to do. Still, she is new to the school and is afraid to admit she doesn't know what to do. Mr. Colbert is also the wrestling coach, and Ms. Gabriel doesn't feel very comfortable communicating with him.

- How could Ms. Gabriel request a meeting with Mr. Colbert while at the same time setting a positive tone for working together?
- What communication strategies can Ms. Gabriel employ at the meeting to both get the information she needs and establish a good working relationship with Mr. Colbert in the future?

such accommodations as well. If a student happens to be the only one having a problem, you can seek additional support from special needs staff, paraprofessionals, peers, and/or parent volunteers.

Given the current atmosphere of accountability in U.S. schools, it is often hard for teachers to slow down the rate at which they introduce new information for fear they will be unable to cover all the material that will appear on high-stakes tests. Although covering content efficiently is an important consideration, learning is usually best served when teachers carefully construct a foundation of skills and concepts based on student performance rather than on the school calendar.

Slowing down the rate of skills introduced is an accommodation in the way curriculum is presented, but it is not the same thing as reducing the amount of curriculum to be learned. You need to be careful not to reduce the expectations for your students with special needs who are expected to meet the goals of the general education curriculum. Otherwise, they will have difficulty meeting state standards. However, for your students with moderate to severe intellectual disabilities, it may be appropriate to make an instructional modification by decreasing the amount of curriculum. For example, Ms. Evers modified Robin's curriculum by shortening her spelling lists from 15 to 3 words and selecting only high-frequency words as specified on her IEP.

Providing Direct Instruction and Opportunities for Practice and Review

Students who are at risk or have disabilities may require more direct instruction and review if they are to acquire basic academic skills. Consider the following example. Youn is in Ms. Howard's spelling class. On Monday, Ms. Howard gave students a pretest on the 15 new words for the week. On Tuesday, the students were required to use each word in a sentence. On Wednesday, the teacher scrambled up the letters in all the words and had the students put them in the correct order. On Thursday, students answered 15 fill-in-the-blank questions, each of which required one of the new spelling words. On Friday, Youn failed her spelling test even though she had successfully completed all the spelling activities for that week. Youn performed poorly because the daily spelling activities did not provide her with enough direct instruction and practice on the spelling words. Although activities such as using spelling words in sentences are valuable in the right context, they do not provide practice on the primary objective of this particular lesson, which is spelling all 15 words correctly from dictation. One way to differentiate Youn's instruction would be to have a peer tutor give her a daily dictation test on all 15 words; have Youn write each missed word three times, saying each letter in the word as she writes; and then retest her on all 15 words again.

This example demonstrates another problem that students with special needs have when learning basic skills: retention. Melissa had mastered addition facts with sums to 10 as measured by a probe test in October, but when she was given the same test in January, she got only half of the facts correct. Similarly, Thomas, in his civics class, could define the equal protection clause of the Constitution in November, but he could not remember what it was when asked to define it in February. A common way to differentiate instruction for such students is to schedule more review for them. This review should be more frequent following your initial presentation of the material and then can become less frequent as learning is established. For example, instead of waiting until January to review addition facts, Melissa's teacher could first provide review weekly, then every other week, and then every month. Thomas's civics teacher could periodically review key concepts and information that Thomas may need to apply later, either through homework, a learning center activity, an instructional game or contest, or an activity in a co-taught class. If Thomas and Melissa were the only ones in their classes in need of review, their teachers could accommodate them individually by giving them extra help before school while the rest of the class was working independently, or as part of a Tier 2 small group in RtI. You can learn more about Tier 2 groups in RtI in the Instructional Edge.

INSTRUCTIONAL **EDGE**

Providing Differentiated Instruction Using Tier 2 in RtI

While Tier 1 in RtI is evidence-based, it is also the least intensive tier, mainly employing large-group instruction with fewer supports for student learning. Some students need more intensive instruction in Tier 2, the subject of this feature. As you read about Tier 2, remember that much of the research on RtI has been done in the area of elementary school reading, so caution is advised when applying these recommendations to other subject matter areas and grade levels (Gersten et al., 2009).

WHAT IS TIER 2 INSTRUCTION?

Tier 2 consists of instruction provided in Tier 1, plus additional small group sessions that provide extra practice of targeted skills and content covered in Tier 1. As in Tier 1, all instruction in Tier 2 is evidence-based. In some schools, instruction in Tier 2 is carefully scripted using the same research-based intervention for all children having similar problems in a given area. This is called the standard protocol model. Other RtI schools use a more individualized approach whereby interventions are chosen based on graphed individual student data. Greater intensity is achieved in Tier 2 through more systematic and focused instruction, smaller instructional groups, and more frequent progress monitoring.

WHO IS ELIGIBLE FOR TIER 2 INSTRUCTION?

Students enter Tier 2 when their performance on universal screening measures dips below benchmark scores, a set percentile, or below standard on a high stakes or end-of-grade test. While the number of students eligible for Tier 2 varies, it is estimated as being around 15%. In a class of 25 students, this would amount to 3–4 students.

WHERE, WHEN, AND FOR HOW LONG DOES TIER 2 INSTRUCTION TAKE PLACE?

Tier 2 instruction usually takes place in small, same-skill groupings of 3–4 students. These groups meet 3–5 times per week, for 20 to 40 minutes in elementary school, up to 60 minutes per session in

high school (Bursuck & Damer, 2011). Tier 2 groups can take place either inside or outside the general education classroom, with some middle school groups taking place in literacy labs and even within after-school programs (Johnson & Smith, 2008).

WHO TEACHES TIER 2 GROUPS?

Tier 2 instruction can be carried out by a variety of staff including general education teachers, Title 1 teachers, special education teachers, and paraprofessionals, all carefully prepared to ensure instructional quality.

HOW LONG DO STUDENTS REMAIN IN TIER 2 GROUPS?

The amount of time students spend in Tier 2 varies, but in many systems time in Tier 2 is of a limited duration, ranging from 8–12 weeks. During that time student progress is regularly monitored. Students who progress to grade level exit Tier 2, although they continue to be monitored to ensure their performance is maintained. Students who fail to show progress despite receiving well-delivered Tier 2 instruction usually move to more intensive instruction in Tier 3, although students can remain in Tier 2 longer if they show significant improvement despite still performing below benchmark levels.

WHAT IS THE ROLE OF THE GENERAL EDUCATION TEACHER IN TIER 2?

The role of the general education teacher in Tier 2 varies. Perhaps your most important role is to teach Tier 1 so well that fewer students require Tier 2 instruction. Beyond that, general education teachers play an important role in progress monitoring by regularly measuring student performance and using the results to help the RtI team decide who exits Tier 2 and who remains. Last, while general education teachers can teach Tier 2 groups themselves, it can be difficult to do so with quality and consistency while still discharging your many other instructional responsibilities.

A related concern is that teaching approaches that are indirect and provide little practice may be appropriate for some students but may need to be supplemented for others. For example, Felix and Bill were learning to read in Ms. Farrell's class. Neither boy had learned the *ch* sound (as in *chin*). On Monday, Felix came across the word *chair* in a trade book he was reading. His teacher pronounced the word and said, "That sound at the beginning of *chair* is the same sound you hear at the beginning of *cherry*." The next day, Felix came to the word *chip* in his book, and he figured it out; he remembered what Ms. Farrell had told him the day before and was able to make the connection between the beginning sound in the orally presented word *cherry,* and the *ch* in *chair,* and then *chip*. For Felix, one example in his book and a brief teacher explanation were enough for learning to occur. On Monday, Bill also came across a *ch* word, and he too was told what the word was and that it began with the same sound as the word *cherry*. Unlike Felix, however, when Bill came across another *ch* word the next day, he could not remember the sound of these letters. Having the teacher tell him another word that *ch* began with was too

TABLE 9.1 **Direct Instruction of *ch* Sound**

Teacher	Student
I. Teach directly the ch sound in isolation. Teacher writes on the board: *ch, or, ee, ch, th, sh, ch,* and *ing.*	
1. Teacher models by saying the sound of the new letter combination and tests by having the students pronounce it. Teacher points to *ch.* "These letters usually say *ch.* What sound?"	"*ch*"
2. Teacher alternates between the new combination and other combinations. Teacher points to a letter combination, pauses 2 seconds, and asks, "What sound?"	Say the combination sound
3. Teacher calls on several individual students to identify one or more letter combinations.	
II. Teach directly the ch sound in words. Teacher writes on the board: *chin, chair, chip, boot, beam, chomp, stain, chum, moon,* and *chat.*	
1. a. Students identify the sound of the letter combination in *chin,* then read the word. Teacher points under the combination letters and asks, "What sound?"	"*ch*"
b. Teacher points to left of word. "What word?"	"*chin*"
c. Teacher repeats step 1(a–b) with remaining words.	
2. a. Students reread the list without first identifying the sound of the letter combination. Teacher points to *chin,* pauses 2 seconds, and asks, "What word?"	"*chin*"
b. Teacher repeats step 2(a) with remaining words.	
3. Teacher calls on individual students to read one or more words.	

Source: Adapted from *Direct Instruction Reading* (5th ed.), by D. Carnine, J. Silbert, E. J. Kame'enui, and S. G. Tarver, 2010, Upper Saddle River, NJ: Merrill/Pearson Education. Copyright © 2010. Reprinted with the permission of Pearson Education, Inc., Upper Saddle River, NJ.

indirect; he needed the teacher to say, "The sound of *ch* is /ch/. What's the sound of *ch?*" In addition, one practice example was not enough. Bill required more direct instruction and practice than did Felix, such as that provided in the activity shown in Table 9.1.

This discussion of Felix and Bill raises an important issue: General education teachers need to know more than one approach to meet the needs of individual students, an idea at the heart of differentiated instruction as well as of RtI. Felix can learn sounds with minimal instruction while reading books; Bill cannot. Bill's teacher may need to accommodate Bill and other students in the class by providing them with some direct instruction on letter–sound correspondence. This direct instruction can involve having students both say and write their sounds.

Another example reinforces the idea that some of your students may need more direct instruction and practice. Mr. Diaz was teaching his English students how to write a persuasive essay, including how to develop a thesis, add supporting details, reject counterarguments, and end with a conclusion. He described the steps in writing a persuasive essay while showing students an example of a well-written persuasive essay. He then asked the students to write a one-page persuasive essay for homework. Brenda handed in her essay the next day; although her paper showed some potential, her thesis lacked clarity, her details were sketchy, and she forgot to reject possible counterarguments. Brenda needed more instruction and guided practice on how to write a persuasive essay than Mr. Diaz had provided. Mr. Diaz could have applied the INCLUDE strategy, anticipated Brenda's problems, and provided guided practice by writing essays with the class until even lower performers such as Brenda seemed comfortable performing the task. He also could have had the students write a persuasive essay independently in class so that he could monitor their performance and accommodate individual students using corrective feedback and more instruction, if necessary.

dimensions of
DIVERSITY

In Native American cultures, children learn skills by first observing them and then doing them. Native American students benefit from direct teaching that first stresses modeling or demonstrations. You can enhance demonstrations for your Native American students by showing them the final product before the demonstration (Sparks, 2000).

INCLUDE

CASE IN PRACTICE

Applying INCLUDE to a Basic Skills Lesson

Ms. Dettman loves to look on the Internet for what she calls "teacher-tested" lesson plans. She found a lesson yesterday on the topic of math word problems (Bowen, n.d.), an area in which her students often struggle and in which she is always looking for something different to do. The teacher who used this technique claimed that it had had a positive impact on her class's performance last year on the state's high-stakes test in math. Ms. Dettman decided to try it.

In this lesson, the teacher posts a daily word problem on tagboard. The skill targeted (for example, division, fractions) varies from day to day. The problem is read aloud first thing in the morning and students have until lunchtime to solve it. The students keep a special file folder containing an answer sheet for the week's problems. Students are required to show their work. After lunch, three or four students go to the board to solve the problem. They talk aloud about how they solved the problem. Each child has an incentive chart posted in class. Every day, two students collect and score papers and points are awarded for correct answers. Students receive a prize when they reach a certain number of points, and then a new chart is posted.

Ms. Dettman has a group of four students in class who have trouble in math; three of these students have learning disabilities in both reading and math. Because the curricular goals for these students are the same as those for everyone else in the class, instructional modifications are not required. Ms. Dettman reviewed the demands of this activity to see whether any accommodations were needed. She identified the following seven demands:

1. Read the problem.
2. Identify the operation needed to solve the problem (for example, add, subtract).
3. Write a number sentence.
4. Convert the number sentence to a computation problem.
5. Solve the computation problem.
6. Label the answer.
7. Check work.

Next, Ms. Dettman thought about areas where she might need to make accommodations. She considered the students' preskills. Three of the students have reading problems, but the fact that the story problems would be read out loud eliminated the need for an accommodation such as a bypass strategy. However, Ms. Dettman thought the students would have trouble translating the story problems into a sentence; they all have reading comprehension problems and had previously struggled to pick the correct operation when they solved word problems in class. The four students also don't know their

math facts, and their computational accuracy is inconsistent, even though they understand the concepts behind the four basic operations. Computation could be a definite problem as well. None of the students struggles with handwriting, so the writing demands of solving the word problem would not be problematic. In addition, one student is artistically inclined, a strength that Ms. Dettman planned to build on.

Ms. Dettman was concerned about the fact that different types of story problems were selected for the activity each day in the lesson plan. She thought that this variety might confuse the four students who seem to work best when new problem types are added gradually as others are learned. Ms. Dettman was also concerned that student modeling of problem solving at the board by thinking out loud was a great idea, but she felt the students with problems in math might not benefit from it without more careful structuring.

Ms. Dettman decided to make the following accommodations for the four students. Although she would continue to work with them on improving the accuracy of their math computation skills, for this activity she would allow them to bypass their current difficulties in this area by letting them use calculators.

Ms. Dettman also decided to provide the students with a visual diagram to guide them through the problem-solving steps, along with small-group guided practice to ensure they used the strategy appropriately. Part of that small-group guided practice would include teacher and student think-alouds to make the problem-solving steps more conspicuous for the students. Also, when students came to the board to solve problems out loud in the large group, bonus points would be awarded to those students paying careful attention, particularly to the think-aloud part. Ms. Dettman would use only story problems that the students were capable of solving independently. That way, they would get needed independent practice as well as a realistic opportunity to earn points and cash them in for a prize at the end of the week.

Finally, Ms. Dettman would appoint the student with artistic talent to be the class artist. She would come to the board and draw a picture representing the problem.

REFLECTION

Why do you think Ms. Dettman made instructional *accommodations* for the four struggling students rather than instructional *modifications*? How did Ms. Dettman use the INCLUDE strategy to come up with instructional accommodations for those students? How effective and feasible are these accommodations? What would you do differently if you were the teacher?

Finally, it is important to remember that practice is most effective when it *follows* direct instruction; practice is never an adequate substitute for direct instruction. For example, Mr. Hanesworth designed a board game in which students get to move ahead if they can answer a division fact problem. The problem is that five students in his class still do not understand the concept of division. For them, the board game practice activity is likely to result in failure. Mr. Hanesworth can accommodate these learners in a small group by providing additional instruction on division for them while allowing the rest of the class to play the board game independently. Of course, later on, Mr. Hanesworth can reward the hard work of the small group by allowing them to practice a skill they know using a game-like format.

Clearly, you may need to differentiate instruction to enable students with special needs to acquire basic skills. An example of how to differentiate basic skills instruction using INCLUDE is presented in the Case in Practice. In addition, the Technology Notes on page 278 introduces ways to use technology to assist students with special needs with their writing. Students also may need accommodations when subject-area content is presented, the primary teaching focus as students move into the upper grades.

INCLUDE

How Can You Make Accommodations for Students with Special Needs When Teaching Subject-Area Content?

The instruction of academic content includes areas such as social studies and science. This instruction often involves the use of textbooks and lecture–discussion formats, but it also can include other activities, such as videos, films, hands-on activities, and cooperative learning. Although content-area instruction generally is associated with instruction in secondary schools, the information presented here is relevant for elementary teachers as well. Social studies and science have always been taught at the elementary level, and now there are even high-stakes science tests that may be administered as early as third grade. In this section, you learn how you can differentiate instruction to help students with special needs learn subject-area content. Strategies for making accommodations are stressed for activating background knowledge, organizing content, and teaching terms and concepts. As with basic skills, you can provide accommodations for students with disabilities by changing how you teach the entire class or by making individualized accommodations either one to one or in small groups. Strategies for teaching science to English-language learners (ELLs) are described in the Instructional Edge on page 279.

Activating Background Knowledge

The amount of background knowledge students have can greatly influence whether they can read subject matter with understanding. To illustrate, read this list of words:

are	making	between
only	consists	often
continuously	vary	corresponding
one	curve	points
draws	relation	variation
set	graph	table
if	values	isolated
variables	known	

dimensions of DIVERSITY

Relating content to students' background knowledge makes material more relevant. It also motivates students to draw on their own background knowledge when they encounter new information, helping them assume responsibility for learning (Gersten, Baker, & Marks, 1998).

Using Web-Based Programs to Improve Student Writing Performance

As you learned in Chapter 7, students with disabilities face many challenges with writing (Graham, 2006). Tele-Web (Technology-Enhanced Learning Environments on the Web) is an Internet-based software program that can help students with disabilities overcome these problems. Tele-Web helps students write expository text that is well organized; contains an introduction, body paragraphs, and a conclusion; and meets the knowledge demands of the reader (Englert, Zhao, Dunsmore, Collings, & Wolberg, 2007). Tele-Web uses two devices to support student writing. First, mapping tools are used to help students generate ideas and details for their papers. Students are taught to move their ideas, or supporting details, to their respective boxed categories using a click-and-drag feature that is also part of Tele-Web.

The second device is a template known as the *supported report*. First, a printed reminder of the teacher's oral instructions appears at the top of the screen. To help students stage their ideas, *Title* and *Introduction to Paper* boxes appear. Next, a *Topic Sentence Box* prompts students to generate a topic sentence for their first paragraph. Immediately following the topic sentence box is a *Supporting Details Box* used to cue students to choose details that support their topic sentence. Each time students click to add a paragraph, new topic sentence and paragraph boxes appear. Finally, a *Concluding Sentence Box* is provided near the bottom of the computer screen prompting students to conclude their papers.

In addition to these features, Tele-Web uses a pop-up window to prompt students to evaluate their writing through a series of self-questions. Example questions include: Did I tell what the pet looks like? Did I use a topic sentence? Did I use concluding sentences? The questions disappear when students return to composing their papers, fostering independence by providing only temporary support.

Tele-Web has three additional features that allow students to access online support: (1) a spell checker that matches words in the paper against an online dictionary; (2) a text-to-speech function that allows the computer to read back student text; and (3) an online submission feature through which teachers provide feedback and students revise and publish their papers.

Englert et al. (2007) tested Tele-Web against a paper-and-pencil approach to teaching writing that offered similar supports but without the use of computers. The papers of students with disabilities who used Tele-Web had a greater range of information about their writing topics and were better organized, showing a clear relationship among the introduction, body, and conclusion.

Shown below is a list of other Internet sources for software that can help students with writing assignments (Gillette, 2006):

SOFTWARE PROGRAMS THAT CAN READ DIGITIZED TEXT

- Write OutLoud (Don Johnston Incorporated)
  http://www.donjohnston.com

- Read OutLoud (Don Johnston Incorporated)
  http://www.donjohnston.com

- Kurzweil 3000 (Kurzweil Educational Systems)
  http://www.kurzweiledu.com

- Read & Write Gold
  http://www.texthelp.com

SOFTWARE PROGRAMS THAT ASSIST STUDENTS WITH PLANNING COMPOSITIONS

- Draft Builder (Don Johnston Incorporated)
  http://www.donjohnston.com

- Inspiration (Inspiration)
  http://www.inspiration.com/store/main/index.cfm

TALKING WORD PROCESSORS

- IntelliTalk III (IntelliTools) Intellitools
  http://www.intellitools.com

- Word 2010 (Microsoft)
  http://www.microsoft.com/office/word/produinfo/default.mspx

VOICE RECOGNITION SOFTWARE

- Scansoft Dragon Naturally Speaking
  http://www.nuance.com/naturallyspeaking/standard

- Word 2010 (Microsoft)
  http://www.microsoft.com/office/word/prodinfo/default.mspx

WORD PREDICTION SOFTWARE

- Co:Writer (Don Johnston Incorporated)
  http://www.donjohnston.com

- Read & Write Gold
  http://www.texthelp.com

How might speech-synthesis and word-prediction programs help this student with her journal entries? What other types of assistive technology might help her with her writing?

INSTRUCTIONAL **EDGE**

Strategies for Teaching Science to English-Language Learners

ELLs struggle in science, yet information about teaching science to ELLs can be hard to find (Watson, 2004). While ELLs share the characteristic of having limited English proficiency, it is important to realize that they are a diverse group. ELLs come to your science classroom with different levels of background knowledge, literacy in their native language, family involvement in their education, intellectual ability, and motivation to do well in school, to name a few areas. All of these factors, in addition to English proficiency, should be considered when differentiating ELLs' science instruction using these strategies (Short & Echevarria, 2004/2005; Watson, 2004):

- For students in your class who speak little or no English, label parts of your classroom and lab equipment with both English names and names from the students' native language. Using Spanish, for example, the labels would be *science book/ciencialibro*. Besides helping to initiate communication with your ELLs, labeling in English and another language also demonstrates to English-speaking students the difficulties students face when learning a new language. Requiring all of your students to learn both names effectively reinforces this idea.

- Place less emphasis on the traditional approach of having students read the textbook prior to engaging in a laboratory activity. Instead, start with the laboratory experience. The concreteness of laboratory experiences makes the text more comprehensible.

- Whenever possible, show objects, draw pictures, or act out the meanings of key terms. For example, when teaching the concept of *scientific classification,* one teacher demonstrated the concept by having students take off their left shoes and put them in a pile in the front of the room. The students classified the shoes in different ways, such as shoes that lace, slip on, and buckle.

- Repeat instructions, actions, and demonstrations as needed, speaking slowly and using simple sentence structure whenever possible.

- Demonstrate procedures and provide clarifying diagrams and illustrations before students begin lab work. For example, before students begin a lab exercise, provide them with a written procedural guide, go over key terms by placing them on the board, demonstrate the procedures, and actively monitor students' performance by circulating among them as they are completing the lab.

- Assign lab partners to ELLs. The lab partners should be strong in science and work well with other students. Placing two ELLs together in a group along with one English speaker is also effective, particularly if one of the ELLs is more advanced than the other in English skills. Encouraging ELLs to express their thoughts to a partner before reporting to the whole class promotes language learning and the confidence to speak out in class.

- If appropriate, enlist the support of parents in building students' background knowledge about topics before they are introduced in class. Background knowledge provided in students' native language allows them to better follow what is discussed, even if they don't know every word.

- Schedule time for review at the end of each lesson, pointing out key concepts and vocabulary while making connections to lesson objectives and state standards. This is essential, because ELLs may concentrate so intently on processing language during instruction that they are unable to identify the most important information expressed.

- Give feedback to your students on their language use in class. For example, model for your students how scientists talk about their experimental findings. Have students try to use the language of scientists when orally presenting their lab reports, and give them feedback on their performance.

Were you able to read all of them? Do you know the meanings of all these words? Now read the following passage:

> If the known relation between the variables consists of a table of corresponding values, the graph consists only of the corresponding set of isolated points. If the variables are known to vary continuously, one often draws a curve to show the variation. (From Michaelson, 1945, as cited in Lavoie, 1991)

Chances are, unless you are a math major, if you were asked to summarize what you just read, you would be unable to do so despite the fact that you probably answered yes when asked whether you could read and understand all the words individually. You may lack the background knowledge necessary to understand this very technical paragraph. The knowledge students bring to a content-area lesson is often as important for understanding as the quality of the textbook or instructional presentation (Marzano, 2004; Pressley, 2000). For students to understand content material, they need to relate it to information they already know.

Unfortunately, teachers often fail to consider background information. Students with disabilities and students who are at risk may have two problems related to background knowledge: They may simply lack the necessary knowledge, or they may know the information but be unable to recall it or relate it to the new information being presented.

Using the Prep Strategy   One teaching strategy for determining how much knowledge students already have about a topic so that you can decide how much background information to present in class prior to a reading assignment is called the **PReP (PreReading Plan) strategy** (Langer, 1984). The PReP strategy has three major steps:

1. *Preview the text or lesson, and choose two to three important concepts*. For example, for a science lesson, Mr. Amin chose the concept of photosynthesis and the keywords *cycle* and *oxygen*.
2. *Conduct a brainstorming session with students*. This process involves three phases. In Phase 1, students tell you what comes to mind when they hear the concept. This gives you a first glance at how much they already know about the topic. Student responses in Phase 1 can be written or oral. The advantage of written responses is that you can assess the background knowledge of your entire class at once. The disadvantage of written responses is that for students who struggle to write, it is difficult to gauge whether an unacceptable response is due to a lack of knowledge about the topic or simply the result of a writing problem. This is a good time to differentiate your instruction using INCLUDE. If students have a writing problem, modify your approach by questioning them orally. In Phase 2, students tell you what made them think of their responses in Phase 1. This information can help you judge the depth of, and/or basis for their responses, and it also provides a springboard for students to refine their responses in Phase 3. In Mr. Amin's class, he discovered in Phases 1 and 2 that two of the students mistakenly thought that photosynthesis had to do with photography because of the presence of *photo* in the word. This error provided an opportunity to build on students' knowledge. Mr. Amin explained that *photo* means light and that in photography, a camera takes in light to make pictures. He then said that plants take in light too, and when the light combines with chemicals in the plant, carbohydrates and oxygen are made. This process is called *photosynthesis*. In this way, Mr. Amin used what the students already knew to teach them a concept they did not know. In Phase 3, students can add to their responses based on the discussion in Phase 2.
3. *Evaluate student responses to determine the depth of their prior knowledge of the topic*. During this step, you can decide whether students are ready to read the text and/or listen to a lecture on photosynthesis or whether they first need more information. Determining the needs of your students with respect to the demands of your instruction is an important part of INCLUDE. In Mr. Amin's class, two students continued to have trouble understanding that photosynthesis was something plants did with light to make carbohydrates and oxygen. They needed more information before they were ready to read the chapter. Mr. Amin accommodated these students by showing them a video illustration of photosynthesis in the morning before school began. The video includes concrete examples that weren't necessary to use with the rest of the class.

INCLUDE

Preparing Anticipation Guides   Anticipation guides can help you activate student knowledge about a particular topic and construct bridges to new information by encouraging students to make predictions (Readence, Moore, & Rickelman, 2000; Vacca & Vacca, 2007). **Anticipation guides** consist of a series of statements, some of which may not be true, related to the material that students are about to read (Roe, Smith, & Burns, 2005). Before teaching, students read these statements that either challenge or support ideas they may already have about the subject. This process catches their interest and gives them a reason for listening and reading. Providing questions or statements prior to reading also aids comprehension for all students, including those with disabilities.

For example, Ms. Henry constructed an anticipation guide prior to teaching a unit on the nervous system. Her anticipation guide included the following statements:

- A person cannot function without the nervous system.
- The nervous system helps us study and learn about new things.
- There are gaps between the nerve cells in our bodies.
- Nerve cells do different jobs in the body.
- The central nervous system is only one part of the nervous system.
- Our brains do not control our reflexes.
- Persons cannot hold their breath until they die.
- Some people can swim without thinking about it.

When using the anticipation guide, Ms. Henry needed to differentiate her instruction for several of her students with reading problems. After distributing the guide, she met with these students in a small group and read each item out loud, clarifying terms such as *central nervous system, reflexes,* and *nerve cells.* Ms. Henry also accommodated students with reading problems by highlighting important ideas from the selection, dividing the text into smaller sections, having these students complete the anticipation guide with peer buddies, and giving students a chance to read the text at home before discussing it in school (Kozen, Murray, & Windell, 2006).

Providing Planning Think Sheets   Activating background information and building bridges to current knowledge are also of concern to teachers when asking students to write. Some researchers recommend **planning think sheets** to help writers focus on background information as well as on the audience and purpose of a paper (Englert et al., 1988). For audience, students are asked to consider who will read the paper. For purpose, students clarify why they are writing the paper (for example, to tell a story, to convey information, or to persuade someone). Finally, students activate background knowledge and organize that knowledge by asking themselves questions such as "What do I know about the topic?" and "How can I group or label my facts?" (Englert et al., 1988; Vaughn & Bos, 2009). A planning think sheet for a paper assignment might contain write-on lines for students to answer the following questions (Raphael, Kirschner, & Englert, 1986):

- What is my topic?
- Why do I want to write on this topic?
- What are two things I already know that will make it easy to write this paper?
- Who will read my paper?
- Why will the reader be interested in this topic?

Students may need more teacher modeling and guided practice before being able to complete think sheets independently. You can deliver these accommodations using a small teacher-led group. You can further differentiate instruction and motivate students by providing a range of paper topics that students can choose from. Students also can be permitted to respond orally to the questions.

Organizing Content

Research shows that many students, including students with special needs, have difficulty understanding important ideas and their interrelationships in content areas (Baker, Kame'enui, Simmons, & Simonsen, 2007). These students can benefit from the use of supports or scaffolds that help them identify and understand important information. As you learned in Chapter 5, one form of support is to organize the curriculum according to big ideas rather than facts in isolation. Another form of support is to make these big ideas more evident to students through the use of advance organizers, cue words for organizational patterns, study guides, and graphic organizers.

www.resources

For the latest research on using background knowledge to improve student comprehension go to: http://www.cast.org/publications/ncacbackknowledge.html.

www.resources

The TESOL (Teachers of English to Speakers of Other Languages) website, at http://www.tesol.org, provides news and links regarding the fastest-growing sector of school-age children: those who come from non-English-speaking backgrounds.

Using Advance Organizers   **Advance organizers** include information presented verbally and/or visually that makes content more understandable by putting it within a more general framework. They are particularly effective for students with special needs who may have limited background knowledge and reading and listening comprehension skills (Swanson & Deshler, 2003). Examples of advance organizers include the following (Lenz, 1983):

- identifying major topics and activities
- presenting an outline of content
- providing background information
- stating concepts and ideas to be learned in the lesson
- motivating students to learn by showing the relevance of the activity
- stating the objectives or outcomes of the lesson

While a well-constructed advance organizer presented to the entire class will meet the needs of most students, those with disabilities or other special needs may benefit from a more individualized approach. For example, Mr. Serano motivated Zak by tying an advance organizer for a lesson about weather to Zak's interest in aviation. Ms. Williams explained to Rinaldo that his lesson objective was to identify and write numbers from 10 to 100. The rest of the class was learning to add two-digit numbers. Ms. Hardy used an individualized advance organizer to communicate to Carlos, who struggles with writing, that he could demonstrate what he learned in the unit on explorers by designing a map showing the countries the major explorers came from. The rest of the class wrote two-page papers about the countries involved in exploration, including the major explorers from each country.

Employing Cue Words for Organizational Patterns   Big ideas are often the central focus of an **organizational pattern** of information. The most common patterns of information include the descriptive list including the sequence of events in time, comparison/contrast, cause/effect, and problem/solution (Baxendell, 2003; Ellis, 1996). Each of these patterns of information can be made more conspicuous for students through the use of cue words. For example, cue words for a list, description, or sequence might include *first, second,* and *third;* cue words for comparison/contrast would be *similar, different, on the one hand,* and *on the other hand;* cue words for cause/effect might be *causes, effects, because,* and *so that;* and cue words for problem/solution would be *problem, solution,* and *resolve.* Cue words are important for students with disabilities, many of whom have difficulty telling the difference between important and unimportant information (Hallahan et al., 2005; Kame'enui et al., 2007).

Text that does not contain clear cue words requires students to make a number of inferences, which may be difficult for students. Rewriting the book is obviously not a reasonable way to differentiate instruction. Instead, you can accommodate students by helping to make the key concepts more explicit using teaching strategies described in this text, such as study guides and graphic organizers. Or, you can use alternative means of presenting the same information, such as videos or books that are more clearly written.

Constructing Study Guides   The general term **study guide** refers to outlines, abstracts, or questions that emphasize important information in texts (Conderman & Bresnahan, 2010; Mercer, Mercer, & Pullen, 2011). Study guides are helpful in improving comprehension for students with special needs in content-area classrooms (Lovitt, Rudsit, Jenkins, Pious, & Benedetti, 1985). For example, at the beginning of this chapter, Cecily was having trouble picking out key ideas in her U.S. history text, a common problem for students at all educational levels. She might benefit from a study guide that cues students to important information by asking them questions about it. Procedures for constructing study guides are shown in the Professional Edge on page 284. A sample study guide for a section of a social studies text on Truman's Fair Deal is shown in Figure 9.2.

FIGURE 9.2 **Sample Study Guide for Truman's Fair Deal Vocabulary**

> **Consumables** are products that _____.
>
> Some positive examples of consumables are _____, _____, and _____.
> A negative example of a consumable is _____.
>
> **Big Ideas**
>
> The **problem** was that after World War II, price controls were lifted and the cost of _____,
> _____, and other consumer goods went _____.
>
> The **solution** was for workers to _____.
>
> The **effect** was that _____ and _____.

Study guides can be used with the entire class or as an accommodation for individuals or small groups of students. Horton (1987) suggests the following ways to differentiate instruction using study guides:

1. Allow 2 or 3 inches of margin space in the study guide in which students can take notes. Draw a vertical line to indicate the margin clearly. For example, in the study guide in Figure 9.2, the answer to the first vocabulary question is "*Consumables* are products that cannot be used over again." You may want to have students write this vocabulary word along with its complete definition in the margin. Some students find a new word easier to understand if you first use the overhead or PowerPoint to discuss the definition along with a series of positive and negative examples. Specific strategies for presenting new vocabulary are presented later in the chapter.

2. Print page numbers next to the sentences in the study guide to show where to find missing words in the textbook.

3. Print the missing words at the bottom of the page to serve as cues.

4. Leave out several words for more advanced students and fewer for students with special needs. For example, in Figure 9.2, the *effect* part of the big idea could be simplified as "The *effect* of strikes such as the railroad strike was that the stability of the American economy was threatened and ____."

5. Model how to use the study guides by completing a sample study guide in front of the class while thinking out loud (Conderman & Bresnahan, 2010).

6. Arrange for reciprocal peer-teaching situations; pair students and have them take turns being the teacher and the student.

7. Use the study guide for homework assignments. Assign students a passage in the text and give them accompanying study guides (either with or without the pages marked for easy reference). Have them complete the guides and study the material for homework.

8. Ask students to keep and organize their study guides from a number of passages and to study them as they review for unit or end-of-semester tests.

9. Place reading passages, study guides, and tests on a computer. Design the study guide using a hypertext format with highlighted questions or key words containing a link to the website that will help answer the question (Conderman & Bresnahan, 2010). Be sure to take into account your students' capabilities using computers, using INCLUDE to make accommodations as needed. Use print-to-speech software for students who have difficulty with word reading.

10. Whenever possible, write the study guide at a reading level that fits most of your students. Students with reading and writing problems may need to have the study guide read to them or respond to the questions orally.

11. To discourage students from only learning material on the study guide, supplement the study guide with other instructional methods and construct test questions that are not taken word-for-word from the study guide (Conderman & Bresnahan, 2010).

www.resources

The Education Development Center's webpage for the National Center to Improve Practice in Special Education through Technology, Media, and Materials, at http://www2.edc.org/ncip, provides many ideas on how to implement research-based teaching practices with students with special needs.

PROFESSIONAL EDGE

How to Develop Study Guides

Study guides help improve the comprehension of all students, especially those with special needs who are included in content-area classrooms. Follow these steps to develop a study guide from a content-area textbook:

1. Go through the entire book and mark the chapters you want to cover for the term and those you do not.
2. Indicate the sequence in which you will assign the chapters; that is, note the one that comes first, second, and so forth.
3. Read the material in the first chapter carefully. Mark the important vocabulary, facts, and concepts that you expect students to learn. Cross out any material you do not intend to cover.
4. Divide the chapter into logical sections of 1,000- to 1,500-word passages. (The length will depend, of course, on how detailed the material is and how much of it you deem important.)
5. Write brief sentences that explain the main ideas or emphasize the vocabulary, facts, or concepts in the passage. Write 15 sentences per passage.
6. Place these sentences in order so the material in one leads to the next and so forth.
7. To create questions, either leave out a few words in each sentence or change each sentence into a question. For example, the

following statement was identified as important in a chapter on natural disasters:

> A 2 percent sales tax was passed to pay for relief efforts after the massive floods of 2005.

This statement could be turned into a question by leaving out several words:

> _____ was passed to pay for relief efforts after the massive floods of 2005.

You could also change the statement into a question:

> How did the people pay for the relief efforts after the massive floods of 2005?

8. Project the sentences and/or questions using large type.
9. Prepare sheets for the students, using regular type.
10. Prepare an answer sheet for the teacher.
11. Develop a multiple-choice test to cover the material in the study guide. The test should have 10–15 items, with four possible choices for each question.

Source: From "How to Develop Study Guides," by Thomas C. Lovitt and Steven V. Horton, from *Reading and Writing Quarterly,* January 1987, Volume 3, Issue 4, pp. 333–343.

INCLUDE

12. Use INCLUDE to decide whether to put related but more basic information in the guide. For students with more significant challenges, make an instructional modification by changing the content load so it remains related to the topic at hand but is more basic. For example, Ms. Hall required that Al, a student with a mild intellectual disability in her fourth-grade class, identify fruits and vegetables that were high in fiber, while the rest of the class responded to questions about the biochemical processes involved when the body digests fiber. When the students were tested on the content covered in the guide, Al was held responsible for answering his more basic questions, which covered content that had been previously specified on his IEP.

Study guides are not a substitute for direct instruction. The amount of direct instruction necessary varies with the difficulty of the material. In general, students need more help completing study guides for texts that assume high levels of student background knowledge and in which key information needs to be inferred as opposed to being explicitly presented. The INCLUDE strategy can help you determine whether more direct instruction is needed and whether it needs to be delivered as part of large- or small-group instruction, or a Tier 1 or Tier 2 group.

Creating Graphic Organizers   Another way teachers can help students organize content is to use **graphic organizers.** This strategy gives students a visual format to organize their thoughts while looking for main ideas (Baxendell, 2003). Archer and Gleason (2010) suggest the following five guidelines for constructing graphic organizers:

1. Determine the critical content (for example, vocabulary, concepts, ideas, generalizations, events, details, facts) that you wish to teach your students. Helping students focus on the most critical information is important for several reasons. First, students with disabilities may have trouble identifying the most important information in an oral lesson or textbook chapter. In most cases this

FIGURE 9.3 **Comparison/Contrast Concept Map**

Attribute	Native Americans	Settlers
Land	Shared	Owned
	Lived close to it without changing it	Cleared it
	Respected it	Used it

Summary

Native Americans and settlers had different ideas about land. Native Americans shared the land whereas the settlers owned individual pieces of it. Native Americans lived close to the land; they respected it and did not change it. Settlers used the land for their own gain.

will be content stressed in your state's standards. Second, it is easier for students to remember several main ideas than to remember many isolated details. Third, putting too much information on a graphic organizer can make it so visually complex that students may have trouble interpreting it.

2. Organize concepts into a **concept map,** a type of graphic organizer or visual representation that reflects the structure of the content, such as stories, hierarchies (top-down and bottom-up), feature analysis, diagrams, compare/contrast, and timelines. Because the purpose of a graphic organizer is to clarify interrelationships among ideas and information, you should keep it as simple as possible. Figure 9.3 shows a completed comparison/contrast concept map.

3. Design a completed concept map. Completing the map before you teach with it will ensure that the information is clear and accurate and can be presented to your students in a timely manner.

4. Create a partially completed concept map to be completed by students during instruction. Having students fill out the map as you present your lesson is an excellent way to keep them on task. Also, many students with disabilities benefit from a multisensory approach; seeing the information on the graphic, hearing it from the teacher, and writing it on the map helps them better retain the information presented.

5. Create a blank concept map for students to use as a postreading or review exercise. This structure for review is easy for students to use.

Once you have constructed graphic organizers, you can use them as follows (Archer & Gleason, 2010):

1. Distribute partially completed concept maps to your students.

2. Project the map on a screen using PowerPoint or an overhead projector, displaying only those portions you wish students to attend to. Limiting the amount of information you present at one time will help students with attention problems who have trouble focusing on more than one piece of information at a time.

3. Introduce the information on the concept map proceeding in a logical order; stress the relationships among the vocabulary, concepts, events, details, facts, and so on.

4. At natural junctures, review the concepts you have introduced. You can do this by projecting the blank map and asking students questions about the content. This review is essential for students who have difficulty learning large amounts of information at one time.

5. At the end of the lesson, review the critical content again using the blank concept map. You can also have students complete the blank maps for homework. These maps will help students organize their studying and also help you find out what they have learned.

In most cases, using graphic organizers will be helpful for your entire class. Students with attention or listening problems may benefit from the additional accommodations of having a completed graphic explained to them prior to instruction for

www.resources

These two sites provide collections of many ready-to-use graphic organizers: http://www.teachervision.fen.com/graphic-organizers/printable/6293.html and http://www.graphic.org.

dimensions of DIVERSITY

You can make key concepts more explicit for English-language learners by using teaching strategies described in this text, such as study guides and graphic organizers.

use as an advance organizer and then completing a blank organizer after instruction with the teacher or a peer for extra practice and review. Students with gaps in background knowledge may benefit from additional work with graphic organizers that summarize background information. This can be provided as part of small-group or one-to-one instruction. For example, to prepare some of his students with special needs to complete the graphic organizer shown in Figure 9.3, Mr. Jackson read sections of two stories: one about the settlers in Ohio in the 1700s and another about the Delaware tribe, who also lived in Ohio at the time. He also differentiated instruction by providing additional ways for students to demonstrate their knowledge of this and other differences between settlers and Native Americans by having students write short stories or produce their own picture books.

Teaching Terms and Concepts

Content-area instruction is often characterized by a large number of new and/or technical vocabulary words and concepts. Students who have special needs or who are at risk are likely to have difficulty with the vocabulary and concept demands of many content-area texts and presentations. For example, consider the following passage from a general science text:

> Thousands of years ago, Scandinavia was covered by a thick ice sheet. The mass of the ice forced the crust deeper into the denser mantle. Then the ice melted. The mantle has been slowly pushing the land upward since then. This motion will continue until a state of balance between the crust and mantle is reached again. This state of balance is called *isostasy* (ie-sosstuh-see). (Ramsey, Gabriel, McGuirk, Phillips, & Watenpaugh, 1983)

Although the term *isostasy* is italicized for emphasis, other technical terms and concepts, such as *crust* and *mass,* also may pose a problem for students and require special attention. These words may be particularly difficult because students are likely to be familiar with their nonscientific meanings, which are quite different from their technical meanings (for example, *mass* as in church; *crust* as in bread). You need to check student understanding and teach vocabulary directly, if necessary, using one of the strategies covered in this section.

This teacher is modeling positive and negative examples to clarify the meaning of a new concept. How can using both examples and nonexamples help make the meaning of new terms and concepts clear?

Using Definitions   Carnine et al. (2010) propose an approach to teaching terms and concepts using definitions that employ positive and negative examples following three steps:

1. State your definitions clearly and simply. Your definitions should only contain words that students already know.

    Consider the following definition of consumables, a word from the study guide in Figure 9.2:

    consumables: a resource whose availability is permanently changed by its usage.

    This definition uses a number of words that younger or even at-risk middle or high school students might not know. Instead, consider the following more learner-friendly definition:

    consumables: products used by persons and businesses that must be replaced regularly because they wear out or are used up.

2. Ask students a series of questions to find out whether they can discriminate positive examples from negative examples. For examples, if you were teaching *consumables* using a definition, you might say the following:

    Consumables are products used by persons and businesses that must be replaced regularly because they wear out or are used up. What are consumables? ("Consumables are products used by persons and businesses that must be replaced regularly because they wear out or are used up.")

    Last month we had to replace three of our light bulbs. Are light bulbs consumables? ("Yes, light bulbs are consumables.") How do you know? ("They are products that wear out and need to be replaced.")

    In Ellen's neighborhood most people have lived in the same house for more than 20 years. Are houses consumables? ("No, houses aren't consumables") How do you know? ("Houses don't need to be replaced regularly because they don't wear out.")

    Sarah was out of skin cream and hand lotion and had to go to the store to get some more. Are Sarah's skin cream and hand lotion consumables? ("Yes, Sarah's skin cream and hand lotion are consumables.") Why do you say that? ("Because she used them up and they had to be replaced.")

    Randy went to the gas station to fill his tank and change his oil. Are gas and oil consumables? ("Yes, gas and oil are consumables.") How do you know? ("Because they can be used up and have to be refilled.")

    The class went to the park for a picnic and went swimming in the river. Is the river a consumable? ("No, the river is not a consumable.") Why do you say that? ("Because it is not a product and can't be replaced.")

    What are consumables? ("Consumables are products used by persons and businesses that must be replaced regularly because they wear out or are used up.")

3. Ask a series of open-ended questions to discover whether students can discriminate the new word from words they learned previously. For example, after teaching consumables, ask, "What are consumables?" Also ask for the definitions of words previously introduced: "What are durable goods? natural resources?"

Note that having students repeat the definition after it is first presented helps keep it in working memory and makes it easier for them to answer the questions that follow. Also, requiring students to answer in complete sentences using the new word rather than answer with only a yes or no forces them to use the word. The more times students use a new word, the greater the likelihood they will learn it. Responding in complete sentences reinforces important expressive language skills that are often problematic for students with special needs. If students have been taught a word using a definition or synonym, follow your question with "How do you know?" Their reasons for answering yes or no will reveal whether they are correctly using the definition or just guessing.

FIGURE 9.4 Concept Diagram

Concept Name:	Nonviolent resistance	
Definition:	Protesting in a peaceful way	

Always	Sometimes	Never
Peaceful	Done in a group	Violent
	Done individually	

	Positive Examples	Negative Examples
	Picketing	Shouting match
	Boycott	Physical attack
	Sit-in	Revolutionary war
	Hunger strike	Riot

English-language learners and other learners with special needs cannot rely solely on linguistic information to learn and retain vocabulary. For these students, accommodations can include bringing in real objects and visuals, such as photographs; matching your actions with your words by conducting demonstrations; allowing students to hear and see vocabulary by using films, DVDs, and books on tape; and having students engage in hands-on activities by performing pantomime and drawing pictures (Hill & Flynn, 2006). Students can also be motivated by personalizing the questions in your vocabulary instruction. For example, when Ms. Hendrix taught her students the meaning of *vehicle,* she included in her presentation photos of the family cars of her hard-to-motivate students. She further engaged Rohan by giving him the job of holding up the photos in front of the class during the presentation.

Making Concept Diagrams Constructing **concept diagrams** is a method that combines graphic organizers with the methods just described using definitions and positive and negative examples (Bulgren, Schumaker, & Deshler, 1988). A sample concept diagram for the concept of nonviolent resistance is shown in Figure 9.4. First, the teacher selects a keyword from a story or lecture. Next, she constructs a diagram that features the definition of the word; the characteristics that are always present, sometimes present, and never present; and positive and negative examples that can be used to model the word. Finally, the teacher presents the concept diagram to students as follows (Carnine et al., 2010):

1. Present the word and its definition.
2. Discuss which characteristics are always, sometimes, and never present.
3. Discuss one of the positive examples and one of the negative examples in relation to the characteristics.
4. Check other positive and negative examples to discover whether they match the characteristics.

How Can You Improve Clarity in Written and Oral Communication?

In effective instruction, ideas are clearly tied together, which enables students to understand them more easily. The need for instructional clarity applies to both your written communication and oral communication. Written communication, in many school situations, involves the use of textbooks and other printed materials, such as handouts, homework, and written tests. Oral communication can include instructional behaviors such as giving directions, asking questions, and delivering lectures.

When a textbook is not written clearly or a lecture is not presented clearly, students have to make critical connections between ideas on their own, a skill that many students who are at risk may not have. Students may not be able to recognize that

fyi

Stahl and Shiel estimate that teachers can realistically teach 300 words per year, which translates to about 8–10 per week (as cited in Armbruster, Lehr, & Osborn, 2001). Since there will never be enough time to teach all of the words students are unlikely to know, words taught need to be selected carefully.

they do not understand the material, or they may not be aware of strategies to try when instruction is difficult to understand. For example, when reading a text, they may not know how to use keywords and headings or how to look at the end-of-chapter questions to get main ideas. During oral presentations, students may not feel comfortable asking questions to clarify the information presented because often they are not sure what to ask and are afraid of looking stupid. Finally, students may lack the background knowledge necessary to construct meaning on their own. If you communicate clearly and use materials that do so as well, students with special needs can be more successful and the need for differentiated instruction will be reduced.

Clarity in Written Communication

The importance of clearly written communication is illustrated by these two textbook passages about western migration in the United States:

> Many of the farmers who moved in from New England were independent farmers. Land cost about a dollar an acre. Most men could afford to set up their own farms. Livestock farming was quite common on the frontier. Hogs could be fed in the forests. The cost of raising hogs was low. (Senesh, 1973, as cited in Armbruster, 1984)

> Most of the farmers who moved in from New England were independent farmers. Being an independent farmer means that the farmer can afford to own his own farm. Around 1815, most men could afford their own farms because lands were cheap—it cost only about a dollar an acre. Many of these independent farms were livestock farms. For example, many frontier farmers raised hogs. Hog farming was common because hogs were inexpensive to keep. The cost of raising hogs was low because the farmer did not have to buy special feed for the hogs. The hogs did not need special feed because they could eat plants that grew in the surrounding forests. (Armbruster, 1984)

The second passage is much easier to understand; it requires fewer inferences by the reader and fewer accommodations by the teacher. It also defines *independent farmer* for the reader. If students were reading the first passage, you might have to provide this definition—which you could do orally or in a study guide. The reason farmers turned to raising livestock can be inferred from the first paragraph, but it is stated directly in the second. For students reading the first paragraph, teachers may need to pose questions prior to reading to establish an understanding of this relationship: for example, "Why did the farmers turn to raising livestock?" Vocabulary not explained clearly in context may need to be covered more directly in large or small groups using strategies for teaching vocabulary covered in this and the next chapters.

Another aspect of written language that can make comprehension more difficult is the use of pronouns. A general rule of thumb is that the closer a pronoun is to its referent, the easier it is to translate. Consider the following section of text:

> Now life began to change. The Eskimo hunters could see that these tools were useful. So they became traders, too. They trapped more furs than their families needed. Then they brought the furs to the trading posts. There they could trade the furs for supplies they had never had before. Because the new tools helped Eskimo hunters get along better, they became part of the Eskimo environment. (Brandwein & Bauer, 1980)

Many readers may have trouble figuring out whom *they* refers to in this passage. Although the placement of most pronouns is not this problematic, understanding pronouns can be difficult for students with special needs. However, students can be taught to make sense of pronouns (Carnine et al., 2010). Before students read, identify unclear pronouns. Have students underline the pronouns in a passage. Then show them how to find the pronouns' referents by asking questions. Consider the following example:

Passage

Curtis and Dorva skipped school. They were grounded for a week. He was sorry. She got mad.

www.resources

The CAST (Center for Applied Special Technology) website, at http://www.cast.org, has many helpful suggestions for the universal design of learning materials and teaching practices. This site provides a link to the National Center on Accessing the General Curriculum webpage, which offers research, solutions, and resources for universal design.

Student Questioning

Teacher: "Curtis and Dorva skipped school." Who skipped school?
Students: Curtis and Dorva.
Teacher: "They were grounded for a week." Was Curtis grounded?
Students: Yes.
Teacher: Was Dorva grounded?
Students: Yes.
Teacher: "He was sorry." Was Curtis sorry?
Students: Yes.
Teacher: Was Dorva sorry?
Students: No.
Teacher: "She got mad." Did Dorva get mad?
Students: Yes.

Depending on the level of sophistication of your class, this instruction could be done with the entire class or performed as differentiated instruction for individual students who struggle to understand sentences containing pronouns. The accommodation could also be made as part of a Tier 2 group.

Clarity in Oral Communication

Just as the quality of textbook writing affects student learning, so too does the quality of teachers' oral language. Three particularly important areas of oral language are giving directions, asking questions, and presenting subject matter (such as in a lecture).

Giving Directions   Giving oral directions is the most common way that teachers tell their students what they want them to do. When directions are not clear and have to be repeated, valuable instructional time is wasted. Consider this set of directions given by a middle school teacher at the beginning of a social studies lesson:

Unclear Instruction

All right, everyone, let's settle down and get quiet. I want you all to get ready for social studies. Shh. . . . Let's get ready. Alice and Tim, I want you to put those worksheets away. We need our books and notebooks. (Evertson et al., 1983, p. 143)

How clear is the teacher about what she wants her students to do? Now read this alternative set of directions:

Clearer Instruction

All right, everyone, I want all of you in your seats facing me for social studies. [Teacher pauses.] Now, I want you to get out three things: your social studies book, your spiral notebook, and a pencil. Put everything else away so that you have just those three things—the social studies book, the spiral notebook, and the pencil—out on your desk. [As students get out their materials, the teacher writes "Social Studies, page 55, Chapter 7 on Italy" on the chalkboard. She waits until students have their supplies ready and are listening before she begins talking.] (Evertson et al., 1983, p. 143)

In the first example, the teacher does not get the students' attention before giving them directions. She is also unclear in communicating what she wants her students to do. For example, the words *settle down* and *get ready* are not defined for the students. In the second example, the teacher first gets her students' attention and then very specifically states all the things they need to do.

Lavoie (1989) has suggested four guidelines for giving directions that are helpful either for your entire class or as accommodations for individual students with special needs:

1. State commands specifically, using concrete terms. In the Clearer Instruction example, the teacher was very specific about what the students needed to do to get

ready for social studies. They had to get out three things: their books, notebooks, and pencils. The first teacher told them only to "get ready."

2. Give "bite-size" directions; avoid a long series of directions. The second teacher first had her students sit down and face her; then she had them take out their materials; finally, she had them turn to the chapter they were going to read that day.

3. Whenever possible, accompany explanations with a demonstration. For example, Mr. Gaswami asked his students to take out their science books, turn to the beginning of the chapter, identify five keywords, and define them using the glossary. Mr. Gaswami showed his students what he wanted them to do by opening his book to the chapter, pointing out that the keywords were italicized, and then defining several keywords to demonstrate how to find and paraphrase the meanings using the glossary in the back of the book. He also displayed pictorial images of these directions on the board to help students read and remember all the steps.

4. Use cuing words such as "Look up here" and "Listen, please" before giving directions. Gestures such as a raised hand are also effective in getting students' attention.

Asking Questions   Asking students questions is a vital part of instructional clarity. The way you question your students is important for several reasons. Questioning is a quick way of assessing what your students have learned. In addition, questioning through the use of follow-up probes can help you analyze your students' errors.

Wilen, Ishler, Hutchinson, and Kindsvatter (1999) suggest the following guidelines for using questions in your classroom:

1. *Phrase questions clearly to ensure that students know how to respond.* For example, a vague question such as "Why were bank failures and the stock market crash of 1929 important?" forces students to guess rather than to consider carefully a direct response to the question. Better wording would be "What were the two primary causes of the Great Depression?"

2. *Provide a balance between higher- and lower-level questions.* The important point to keep in mind is that both kinds of questions are important. Lower-level, or convergent, questions help you find out whether students have the basic understanding necessary for higher-level thought. Further, critical and creative thinking can be developed by using convergent and evaluative questions. Although incorporating more higher-level skills into the curriculum is positive, it is important to realize that lower-level knowledge is still important, particularly for students with special needs, who may not readily acquire lower-level knowledge. Failing to help these students acquire this understanding can prevent them from ever developing higher-level understanding. Also, lower-level questions can give students an opportunity to succeed in class. Finally, research suggests that lower-level questions may be most appropriate in teaching basic skills to students who are at risk (Berliner, 1984; Emmer, Evertson, Sanford, Clements, & Worsham, 1983).

3. *Adapt questions to the language and skill level of the class, including individual students in the class.* Your questions should accommodate a range of needs, from lower-performing students to gifted students. For example, a question for a lower-performing student might be, "From what you have just read, how does the demand for a product affect its supply?" For students with more skills, the question might become, "Going beyond the article a little, how does price affect supply and demand and at what point is market equilibrium reached?"

4. *Vary the wait time depending on the nature of the question asked.* If the question covers review material or material of little difficulty, the wait time—or time you allow your students to think about the answer—is brief. However, if a question covers material that is new and/or difficult for your students, give them more time to think before responding. In general, teachers tend to give their students too little think time (Cotton, 1989). Extending thinking time to just 3 seconds

fyi

Another use of cueing is to let a student know that he or she can expect to be called on to respond orally when you present a particular signal that only the student knows. This way the student can attend to a lesson with less anxiety about speaking in class.

between the end of a question and the start of an answer benefits students in a number of ways:

- Students give longer, more accurate answers.
- The number of times students don't respond decreases.
- Many more students volunteer answers.
- More students with special needs volunteer answers.
- More capable students are less likely to dominate class discussions. (Bursuck & Damer, 2011, pp. 283–284)

5. *Involve all students in classroom questioning by calling on nonvolunteers as well as volunteers.* Calling on all students also allows you to monitor student learning efficiently. In addition, calling on nonvolunteers (who frequently are students with disabilities or other special needs) demonstrates that you hold them accountable for listening and leads to higher levels of on-task behavior. However, as mentioned before, you should match questions with student ability to maximize the likelihood of student success. Finally, for lower-level questions, consider using choral responding, or having all students respond at once together. Unison responding allows more student opportunities for practice and recitation and can lead to higher levels of correct responses and on-task behavior (Carnine, 1981).

6. *Scaffold incorrect answers and "no responses."* Often students with disabilities will not attempt to answer questions because they are worried about making errors in front of their classmates or are unsure of their speech. Even when you increase your thinking time, some of these students will not volunteer answers and, when you call on them, will say, "*I don't know,*" or silently shrug their shoulders. Increase your support for these students using this four-step "cue-clueing procedure" suggested by Bursuck and Damer (2011). For example, Ms. Baroody asked the class, "*What is one detail in this section that led me to decide the main idea as 'Mae was fascinated by science?'*" She scaffolded her instruction for Lovelle, a student whose hand wasn't raised, as follows:

1. First Ms. Baroody provided a cue, "*Lovelle, what are some of the things that Mae was doing in this section that showed she was fascinated with learning science?*"
2. Next, Ms. Baroody gave Lovelle a 3-second thinking pause to formulate an answer. He still didn't respond so she moved to step 3.
3. Ms. Baroody increased her support and provided a cue so obvious she was certain it would lead Lovelle to the right answer. "*Lovelle, look at sentence 4 and read it.*" (Lovelle read: "Mae spent many hours at the library reading books about science and space.") Then Ms. Baroody asked, "*So where did she go to learn more about science?*" (Lovelle answered, "The library.")
4. Ms. Baroody then reinforced and expanded Lovelle's answer to bolster his confidence: "*Yes, that's absolutely right, Lovelle. The information in the book describing how Mae went to the library and spent all that time reading about science and space was a clue that she must really like science.*" (Bursuck & Damer, 2011, p. 284).

INCLUDE

Use the INCLUDE strategy to ensure that the questions you ask in class match the instructional levels of your students. For example, as part of a curriculum modification stated on her IEP, Melissa was learning to identify numbers from 100 to 999; the rest of the class was learning long division. During a class presentation on how to solve three-digit division problems, Mr. Henry called on Melissa to identify the hundreds-place number that was being divided. Sam, another student in the class, was expected to learn the same long division problems as everyone else, but he was clearly having trouble doing so, as judged by his homework and in-class performance. Mr. Henry questioned him in a different way by asking him to explain the first step in solving the problem after it had already been solved at the board.

Presenting Subject Matter   Communicating clearly to your students when you are presenting subject-area content orally, such as in a lecture, also is important. The following section of a lecture was delivered during a geography lesson on Italy:

RESEARCH NOTE

Okolo, Ferretti, and MacArthur (2007) analyzed discussions in four middle school history classes. They found that the teacher who had the most student participation and highest state test scores responded to students on an individual basis, used repetition, and personalized history by linking it to students' thoughts and experiences.

Teacher 1

Italy is in southern Europe, down by France and the Mediterranean Sea. It's a peninsula in the Mediterranean. There are a lot of beautiful islands in the Mediterranean off of Italy and Greece as well. Sardinia and Sicily are islands that are part of Italy. Corsica, Capri, and some other islands like Crete and Cyprus are in the same part of the world, but they don't belong to, although they may be close to, Italy. You could turn to the map of Europe that's in your text to see where Italy is. (Evertson et al., 1983, pp. 143–144)

The language used by this teacher lacks clarity. For example, he presents information about a number of islands but is unclear in explaining how these islands relate to the main topic, which seems to be the location of Italy. The teacher is also vague when he says, "[The islands] don't belong to, although they may be close to, Italy." In addition, the teacher uses the word *peninsula* but does not define it. Finally, this explanation needs the visual display of a map to bring clarity to it, but the teacher refers to a map only at the end of the explanation, almost as an afterthought. Then, rather than require students to refer to it, he leaves them with the impression that its use is voluntary. The only students who will know where Italy is after this lecture are those who already knew before the lecture. Many students with special needs will likely be left behind. An example of another lecture on the same topic is much clearer:

Teacher 2

Now, I want all eyes on me. [The teacher then gestures to the world map next to her. The continent of Europe is highlighted.] The continent we have been studying the past month is highlighted here on this map of the world. What continent is it? [The teacher calls on a nonvolunteer who is also a struggling student to identify the continent. The teacher then shows a map of Europe with the countries they have already studied highlighted: France, Switzerland, and Austria.] What are the names of these countries that we have already studied? [The teacher has the class respond in unison and then shows the map of Europe with Italy highlighted.] This is the new country we are studying today. It is called *Italy*. [The teacher writes the word *Italy* on the board as she says it.] What is this country called? [The teacher has the class respond in unison.] Italy is a large peninsula shaped like a boot that extends into the Mediterranean Sea. [The teacher writes *peninsula* on the board, sounding out the syllables as she writes.] What's the word everyone? [Because students have studied the word once before, the teacher calls on a nonvolunteer to define it.] Corrine, what is a *peninsula*?

While this teacher's presentation is much clearer, she may still need to differentiate instruction for her students. For example, Juan, a student with attention problems, may respond better to a video than to a teacher lecture. Carmen, who has a learning disability, has trouble organizing information presented orally and may benefit from using a graphic organizer of the key geographical features of Italy. Damon, a struggling student who has difficulty retaining information, may be assisted by completing a blank copy of the graphic organizer as part of a student study team. Of course other students in the class may benefit from these accommodations as well.

How Can You Involve Parents in Teaching Their Children?

Teachers are always looking for ways to find extra help for students who take more time to learn new content or skills. That is why we often hear teachers say, "If only his parents would work with him more at home." Although we know parents can promote learning by showing affection for their children, by displaying interest in their children's schoolwork, and by expecting academic success, the effectiveness of parents tutoring their children at home is less clear. The results of research on the effectiveness of parent teaching are mixed; some experts say it is effective whereas others question it (Erion, 2006; Mercer & Pullen, 2009). When determining whether to involve parents in tutoring their children, Mercer and Pullen (2009) suggest taking the following factors into account:

1. Are there reasons for deciding against tutoring (for example, mother–father disagreement over the necessity of tutoring, health problems, financial problems, marital problems, or a large family with extensive demands on parental time)?
2. Do parents have the resources of a professional (for example, a teacher) to answer their questions about the tutoring? The success of home tutoring may depend on cooperative efforts.
3. Can the sessions be arranged at a time when there is no interruption from siblings, callers, or other demands? Children need sustained attention in order to learn.
4. Will the child become overwhelmed with academic instruction and resent the home sessions or feel overly pressured?
5. Do the parents become frustrated, tense, disappointed, or impatient during the tutorial sessions? These parents may spend their time better with the child in activities that are mutually enjoyable.
6. Do the tutorial sessions create tensions among family members? For instance, do the siblings view the sessions as preferential treatment?
7. Does the parent resent tutoring the child or feel guilty every time a session is shortened or missed? Are the sessions usually enjoyable and rewarding?

Of course, if you decide to have parents tutor their child, the same strategies for teaching skills and content to students with special needs covered earlier in this chapter still apply. For example, only skills or content at a student's level should be presented, and the progression of skills or content should be gradual and based on student mastery. In addition, parents should be carefully trained to present new information or skills clearly and enthusiastically and to provide appropriate corrections and encouragement as needed. Parents should also limit the length of the tutoring sessions to 15 minutes for children up to grade 6 and 30 minutes for older students and should begin and end each session with an activity that the child enjoys and is successful at (Cummings & Maddux, 1985, as cited in Mercer & Pullen, 2009). Also, care must be taken to select the most appropriate time to tutor and to select a place that does not restrict the activities of other family members and is not too distracting. Finally, tutoring should be held at the same time and place to establish a clear routine (Mercer & Pullen, 2009, p. 125).

What Accommodations Can You Make for Students to Help Them Succeed in Independent Practice?

As discussed in Chapter 5, the main purpose of practice activities is to provide students with opportunities to refine skills or solidify content that they have already learned and to allow you to monitor their performance. To achieve these purposes, students should be able to complete independently practice activities such as seatwork, practice that is included as part of learning centers, and homework assignments.

Even under ideal circumstances and with the best intentions, it is difficult to design practice activities that meet the needs of all students in your class. Problems arise because of individual characteristics, and individual accommodations need to be made using INCLUDE. For example, students with severe reading problems may have difficulty reading directions that are clear to everyone else. Students with attention problems may have trouble answering questions that have multiple steps. Students with physical disabilities may be unable to perform the writing requirements of their

INCLUDE

assignments. In the case of students with severe intellectual disabilities, practice activities may need to be modified totally so they are consistent with the students' skill levels and the goals and objectives on their IEPs.

Differentiating Seatwork Assignments

Affleck, Lowenbraun, and Archer (1980) have suggested five accommodations you can make to directions to ensure that students with special needs know what to do before working independently. Use INCLUDE to figure out whether these accommodations need to be done with your entire class or with only one or a small group of students:

1. Verbally present the tasks. This strategy can be applied to the whole class, particularly when many students are having problems with the directions. You can accommodate the needs of individual students by pairing a worksheet with a digital recording that explains the directions.
2. Add practice examples that you can do with the whole class or a small group of students who are having particular difficulty.
3. Write alternative sets of directions. You can project these, or you can distribute individual copies to students.
4. Highlight the important words in the directions.
5. Have students help each other when the directions are difficult.

Differentiating Learning Center Activities

As you learned in Chapter 5, another way to provide extra practice for students is in classroom learning centers. Examples of how to differentiate activities in learning centers are shown in Figure 9.5.

INCLUDE

Before starting independent practice, complete sample items for the students. Talk through each step, modeling your thought process and decision making. Use questioning to check that students understand directions.

FIGURE 9.5 Examples of Differentiated Learning Center Activities

OUTCOME:
Students read or listen to information and then write or type responses to questions about the information.

MATERIALS:
Books, audio books, computer software for typing, worksheets with varied levels of questions about the information.

DIFFERENTIATION:
• Some students complete fill-in-the-blank responses.
• Some students respond to a prompt and write an essay response.
• Some students complete an outline as they are listening.

Source: Adapted from "Designing and Delivering Learning Center Instruction," by M. E. King-Sears, 2007, *Intervention in School and Clinic, 42*(3), pp. 137–147.

www.resources

For homework help, students can go to these two sites—http://www .infoplease.com/homework and http://www.highschoolhub.org/ hub/hub.cfm—and be linked instantly to information on the academic subject of their choice, including math, English, literature, social studies, and science. Students can also be linked to tutorials in a wide range of subject areas.

INCLUDE

Differentiating Homework Assignments

As they do with in-class practice activities, students with special needs may have difficulty completing traditional homework assignments. A major reason for student failure to complete homework assignments independently, successfully, and without undue stress is that the assignments are too difficult to begin with. Before you give your students an assignment, ask yourself the following questions:

1. What skill (for example, reading, written expression, or math) demands does the assignment make on the students? Are the students capable of meeting these skill demands?
2. What background knowledge (for example, vocabulary or concepts) does the assignment demand of the students? Are the students capable of meeting the demand for background knowledge?
3. Is the purpose of the assignment clear to students?
4. If the assignment involves skill practice, does it include a lot of practice on a few skills rather than a little practice on a lot of skills?
5. Are clear, written directions provided for how to complete the assignment?
6. Is enough time allotted to complete the assignment?

Even if you answered yes to all these questions, students with special needs may require additional accommodations. For example, students with reading problems may need extra assistance with homework directions. Students with physical disabilities may need assignments shortened, or they may need to respond orally rather than in writing. Remember to use the INCLUDE strategy to make accommodations that fit your assignments and the individual characteristics of your students with special needs. Finally, the success of homework also depends on the involvement of parents. Parent involvement is particularly important for students with disabilities because they are more likely to struggle with homework (Bursuck et al., 1999). Parents play two key roles: overseeing the homework process while their children are at home and communicating with the school regularly about homework. Parents can oversee the homework process by having daily discussions about homework with their children, creating an environment at home that is conducive to getting homework done, supervising homework activities periodically during the time set for homework, and providing support and encouragement for homework completion (Bursuck et al., 1999).

Despite the importance of homework, home–school communication about it sometimes is a problem (Harniss, Epstein, Bursuck, Nelson, & Jayanthi, 2001; Munk et al., 2001). Parents of students with special needs may want much more communication with teachers about homework and feel that teachers should make more of an effort to initiate such communication (Munk et al., 2001). Likewise, teachers may feel that parents do not initiate communication about homework often enough, take homework seriously enough, and follow through with commitments they make about helping their children with homework (Epstein et al., 1997).

Contacts with parents about homework can be increased by conducting parent–teacher meetings in the evening for working parents and by taking advantage of e-mail, a great potential time-saver (Harniss et al., 2001). Another strategy for increasing communication is to establish a homework hotline that can be accessed by phone or a website that provides certain types of homework assistance. You can also involve parents in the homework process at the beginning of the school year and on an ongoing basis thereafter using checklists, newsletters, informed notes, phone calls, and parent discussion groups (Margolis, 2005). For example, at the open house at the beginning of the school year, Ms. Ordonez gives parents information about course assignments for the semester, homework support available in the classroom, and policies on missed homework and extra-credit assignments. She then sends

All students can benefit from homework and other independent practice activities. What are some strategies you can use to make homework and other assignments more effective for students with special needs?

home school progress updates every four weeks; the progress reports include a section on homework completion.

Teachers also can ask parents whether they want to have homework information sent home daily, to sign that they reviewed their children's homework, and to note their children's efforts and describe their difficulties. By signing assignments and indicating their children's effort or difficulty in completing them, parents communicate to their children that they and the teacher are working together and care about homework being completed (Margolis, 2005). It is also important to understand that homework may be a lower priority for families when compared to other home issues. For example, Mr. Gentry knew that Dominique's family had recently been evicted from their apartment and were living in their car. Until Dominique's family was able to find another place to live, Mr. Gentry arranged for him to complete his homework before or after school. Ultimately, the most effective way of warming parents to the homework process is to only send home work that students can complete successfully and independently.

How Can You Make Instructional Modifications for Students with Moderate to Severe Intellectual Disabilities?

Students with moderate to severe intellectual disabilities often cannot perform some or all of the steps in tasks carried out every day by students without disabilities. In the past, this inability to perform tasks in the same way as other students was interpreted to mean that these students could not benefit from these activities. Today, the emphasis is on making modifications for students with moderate to severe disabilities so that they can meet the same curricular standards but in a more functional way, as guided by their IEPs (Lowell-York, Doyle, & Kronberg, 1995; Nolet & McLaughlin, 2005).

One way to modify materials and activities for students with moderate to severe disabilities is to conduct an **environmental inventory.** The purpose of an environmental inventory is to find out what modifications are needed to increase the participation of these students in the classroom as well as in community environments (Vandercook, York, & Forest, 1989) and to help them meet functional curricular objectives specified on their IEPs. The environmental inventory process involves asking yourself four questions:

1. What does a person who does not have a disability do in this environment?
2. What does a person who has a disability do in this environment? What is the discrepancy?
3. What types of supports and/or modifications can be put in place to increase the participation level or independence of the student with special needs?
4. What functional outcomes can the student meet as a result of this participation?

An example of how this process is used in a classroom environment is shown in Figure 9.6. This example involves Roberto, a student with moderate to severe intellectual disabilities whom you read about at the beginning of Chapter 4. Roberto is in Ms. Benis's sixth-grade social studies class. The class is working in small groups on depicting the steps in the recycling process for paper, metal, and plastic. Each group is studying a different recycled material. Roberto lacks the motor and cognitive skills necessary to participate like everyone else.

Ms. Benis decides to modify instruction for Roberto. She assigns him to the group that his friend Seth is in. She also decides to use different materials with Roberto. Ms. Benis has a paraprofessional help Roberto find pictures of recycled products; Seth helps Roberto paste these pictures onto the group's diagram. Mr. Howard, Roberto's special education teacher, helps Roberto identify recycled products in grocery stores and restaurants. Roberto's parents help him sort the recycling at home. All of these activities help Roberto meet his IEP goal of participating in community recycling efforts. Examples of making instructional modifications using INCLUDE are described in the Case in Practice.

FIGURE 9.6 Environmental Inventory Process

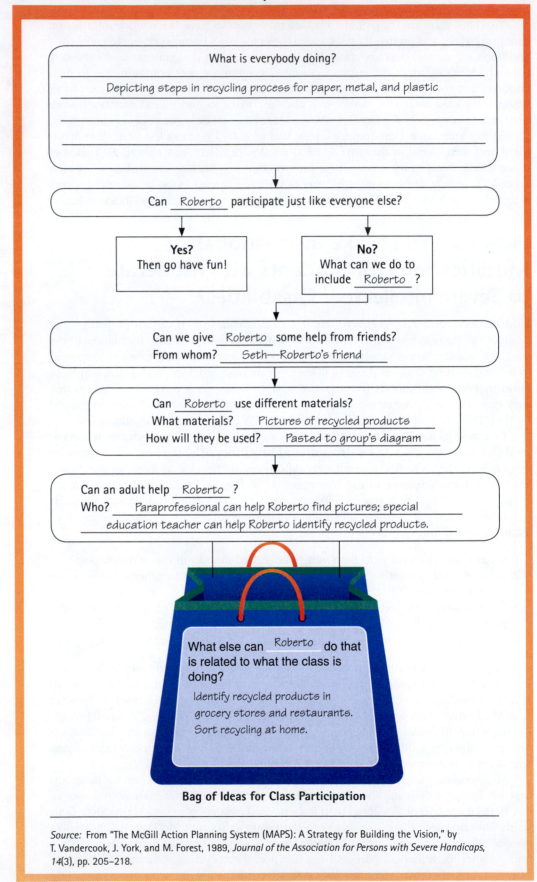

What is everybody doing?

Depicting steps in recycling process for paper, metal, and plastic

↓

Can **Roberto** participate just like everyone else?

Yes?
Then go have fun!

No?
What can we do to include **Roberto**?

↓

Can we give **Roberto** some help from friends?
From whom? **Seth—Roberto's friend**

↓

Can **Roberto** use different materials?
What materials? **Pictures of recycled products**
How will they be used? **Pasted to group's diagram**

↓

Can an adult help **Roberto**?
Who? **Paraprofessional can help Roberto find pictures; special education teacher can help Roberto identify recycled products.**

What else can **Roberto** do that is related to what the class is doing?

Identify recycled products in grocery stores and restaurants.
Sort recycling at home.

Bag of Ideas for Class Participation

Source: From "The McGill Action Planning System (MAPS): A Strategy for Building the Vision," by T. Vandercook, J. York, and M. Forest, 1989, *Journal of the Association for Persons with Severe Handicaps, 14*(3), pp. 205–218.

CASE IN PRACTICE

Making Instructional Modifications in a Middle School Consumer and Food Science Class

Mr. Gagliano teaches a middle school consumer and food science class. He recently taught a unit on cooking and nutrition, including how to shop for food. The targeted state standards for the unit were as follows:

1. Students demonstrate the knowledge and skills needed to remain physically healthy.
2. Students evaluate consumer products and services and make effective consumer decisions.

One part of the unit covered vegetarianism. The goal was for the students to plan, shop for, and cook a vegetarian meal. After defining *vegetarianism* and providing a brief history of vegetarianism in the United States, Mr. Gagliano planned to show a video on the Food and Drug Administration (FDA) nutritional guidelines, including how to decipher nutritional information on a food product label. Mr. Gagliano then planned to break the class into four groups and assign each group the task of designing a vegetarian meal meeting FDA nutritional guidelines.

Ramone is a student with moderate intellectual disabilities who is included in Mr. Gagliano's class. Ramone can do basic math at about the second-grade level and reads below the first-grade level. Although his oral language skills are adequate to carry on a conversation, his ability to interact with others in a small group is limited. Ramone's IEP objectives include the following:

1. Prepare three basic meals independently.
2. Use a calculator to budget money while shopping.
3. Make purchases with the "next-dollar" strategy (for example, paying $6.00 and "one more dollar for cents" for an item that costs $6.62).
4. Increase functional sight-word vocabulary to 200 words.
5. Work appropriately in small groups for up to 50 minutes.

Mr. Gagliano and Ms. Henning, Ramone's special education teacher, met to decide how Ramone's instruction during this unit could be modified. They agreed that the curricular demands for the rest of the class were not appropriate for Ramone, and they planned the following instructional modifications based on Ramone's IEP:

1. Ramone will record the possible choices for the menu (for example, main dishes, dessert, drink). He will actively participate in the making of the final choices. A classmate will help him with spelling as needed.
2. Ramone will record the choices for the grocery list. He will also be assigned the job of checking the kitchen to make sure that items on the list are not already there.
3. Ramone will practice reading the words from the grocery list with the help of his group.
4. Ramone will assist with the shopping, using his calculator to budget the group's money, making purchases using the "next-dollar" strategy, and reading his grocery words to find his items. Ramone will be assisted by his group as needed.
5. Ramone will assist the group in cooking the meal.

Following the activity, Ramone, with assistance from Mr. Gagliano and Ms. Henning, evaluated his performance using checklists based on his related IEP objectives. The evaluations were placed in Ramone's alternate assessment portfolio.

REFLECTION

Do you think it was appropriate for the teachers to plan instructional modifications for Ramone rather than instructional accommodations? How were the expectations for Ramone different from those for his classmates? How were they similar? Should students such as Ramone get credit for meeting state standards when their instruction is modified? How useful is the INCLUDE strategy in planning instructional modifications for students with moderate to severe disabilities?

Source: Adapted from "Creating and Using Meaningful Alternate Assessments," by H. Kleinert, P. Green, M. Hurte, J. Clayton, and C. Oetinger, 2002, *Teaching Exceptional Children, 34*(4), pp. 40–47. Copyright 2002 by the Council for Exceptional Children. Reprinted with permission.

WRAPPING IT UP

BACK TO THE CASES

This section provides opportunities for you to apply the knowledge gained in this chapter to the cases described at the beginning of this chapter. The questions and activities that follow demonstrate how these standards and principles, along with other concepts that you have learned about in this chapter, connect to the everyday activities of all teachers.

MS. DIAZ notes that lately Abdul has been showing signs of losing the motivation to try new math skills. She has increased the number of examples and practice opportunities each time she introduces a new skill and provides oral and written directions for all seatwork activities. Another teacher has suggested that she use an advance organizer whenever she introduces a new skill. Develop an advance organizer for the lesson in the case study for teaching conversion of fractions into percentages. After you have completed that task, explain why using advance organizers might help increase Abdul's motivation to learn new skills, especially math skills.

CECILY, as you may remember, struggles with reading comprehension. At the end of this case, we ask how Ms. Boyd might help her read and remember content in her history text. Later in the chapter, we suggest that a study guide might be a useful tool for Cecily. Developing effective study guides that move beyond the *remembering* level of Bloom's taxonomy (see the Learning Outcomes section in Chapter 5) is a skill that requires practice. Construct a study guide that would effectively support and extend Cecily's learning as she listens to the history text, using the following instructions.

Ask one to three classmates to form a work group. Select a portion of a chapter from this text and individually develop a study guide for that portion (see the Professional Edge "How to Develop Study Guides"). Once everyone in the group has completed a study guide, compare your guides using these questions:

- Do you and your peers agree on the important or key topics? Do you agree on the important vocabulary words to be included? Note and discuss differences.
- Do the study guides match the objectives listed at the beginning of the chapter?
- Are your questions written to help Cecily understand the material at the higher levels of Bloom's taxonomy (applying, analyzing, evaluating, and creating)? Are they also written to help her with knowledge and comprehension of specific facts?
- Collaborate with your peers to incorporate everyone's ideas into a single study guide that will meet Cecily's needs.

ALBERT, as you may remember, struggles to independently complete practice activities in learning centers. Ms. Olivieri has taken several steps to help him. First, before including an independent practice activity in a center, she makes sure all of her students, including Albert, are able to perform accurately the skill involved. She makes sure she reviews previously learned skills that apply to the skills being practiced too. Ms. Olivieri also offers numerous examples of work that she expects students to complete while working in the centers. Finally, she provides clear, step-by-step directions in both oral and written formats. She has noted that Albert's ability to do correct work has improved. However, he still has difficulty completing the same quantity of work that his peers are able to complete. Once he has completed some portion of the work, he is out of his seat to sharpen a pencil, throw away scrap paper, or chat with a friend. Since Ms. Olivieri has experienced some success with Albert, she is encouraged to continue working to help him become independent in completing his work in centers. What might she try next? Explain why you selected these strategies or interventions.

SUMMARY

- Teachers may need to differentiate basic skill instruction in the areas of preskills; selecting and sequencing examples; the rate of introduction of new skills; and the amount of direct instruction, practice, and review.

- In teaching subject-area content to students with special needs, teachers may need to differentiate instruction when activating background knowledge, organizing content, and teaching terms and concepts.

- Teachers can improve clarity in written communication by selecting printed materials that clearly tie ideas together, have clear pronoun referents, and require fewer student inferences.

- Teachers can improve oral communication by giving clear directions, asking questions appropriately, and presenting subject matter using direct, unambiguous language.

- Teachers may need to differentiate independent practice activities such as seatwork, those found in learning centers, and homework.

- Students with moderate to severe intellectual disabilities often cannot perform some or all of the steps in everyday tasks. These students require instructional modifications based on an alternative curriculum set forth on their IEPs. Teachers can use an environmental inventory as well as the INCLUDE strategy to modify classroom activities for these students.

APPLICATIONS IN TEACHING PRACTICE
DEVELOPING A REPERTOIRE OF INSTRUCTIONAL ACCOMMODATIONS

You want to teach a group of at-risk students to spell the following contractions: *can't, aren't, couldn't, shouldn't, wouldn't, don't, won't,* and *isn't.*

QUESTIONS

1. What preskills should you be concerned with, how can you assess them, and what can you do with students who do not know them?
2. How can you sequence instruction? Why did you choose this particular sequence?
3. How can you provide direct instruction, practice, and review for your students?
4. At what rate should you introduce the contractions?
5. How can you evaluate whether your students have learned the contractions?

Develop a graphic organizer for a major concept in Chapter 1 of this text.

QUESTIONS

1. How did you select the concept? Is it a big idea?
2. How would you use the graphic organizer to teach students who are at risk or other students with special needs?

Design a lesson to teach the concept of *differentiated instruction* using a definition.

QUESTIONS

1. Is your definition stated clearly, simply, and concisely?
2. What positive and negative examples did you use?
3. How can you find out whether your students know the meaning of the concept?
4. How can you find out whether your students can differentiate this concept from other concepts presented in the text?
5. How would you teach the concept using a concept diagram format?

You are teaching a lesson on the respiratory system. First you describe the respiratory process (for example, diaphragm contracts; air rushes into nose and/or mouth; air travels down trachea; air enters lungs through bronchial tubes; and so forth) using a chart showing the key parts of the respiratory system (for example, nose, throat and trachea, bronchial tubes, lungs). Next you plan to have students work in small, heterogeneous groups on labeling a model of the respiratory system and describing all the key steps in the respiratory process.

QUESTIONS

1. Based on this lesson, complete an environmental inventory for a student with a moderate to severe intellectual disability.
2. Using INCLUDE, what other modifications might you make for this student?

PEARSON myeducationlab

Go to Topics 10: Instructional Practices and Learning Strategies, 11: Reading Instruction, and 12: Content Area Teaching in the MyEducationLab (www.myeducationlab.com) for your course, where you can:

- Find learning outcomes for Instructional Practices and Learning Strategies, Reading Instruction, and Content Area Teaching along with the national standards that connect to these outcomes.
- Complete Assignments and Activities that can help you more deeply understand the chapter content.
- Apply and practice your understanding of the core teaching skills identified in the chapter with the Building Teaching Skills and Dispositions learning units.
- Examine challenging situations and cases presented in the IRIS Center Resources. (optional)
- Access video clips of CCSSO National Teachers of the Year award winners responding to the question, "Why Do I Teach?" in the Teacher Talk section. (optional)
- Check your comprehension on the content covered in the chapter by going to the Study Plan in the Book Resources for your text. Here you will be able to take a chapter quiz, receive feedback on your answers, and then access Review, Practice, and Enrichment activities to enhance your understanding of chapter content. (optional)

chapter

10

Strategies for Independent Learning

LEARNING Objectives

After you read this chapter, you will be able to

1. State ways that teachers can encourage student self-awareness, self-advocacy, and self-determination.

2. Explain how teachers can create their own learning strategies.

3. Describe the steps involved in teaching learning strategies. Analyze each step, discussing why it is important for building independent strategy usage.

4. List and describe research-based learning strategies in the areas of reading and reading comprehension, listening and note taking, written expression, math problem solving, and time and resource management. Discuss how they can be applied to the students you will be teaching.

5. Describe ways that teachers can help students perform learning strategies independently after they have learned how to do them.

GERALD is a student with learning disabilities in Mr. McCrae's ninth-grade English class. Gerald has had problems in the area of written expression throughout his school years, consistently failing to meet standards on the state high-stakes assessment. It is not that he does not have good ideas. When Gerald talks about what he is going to write, it sounds great. However, when he tries to get his ideas on paper, he becomes very frustrated. Writing is difficult for Gerald. One problem is that his papers lack organization. They rarely have a good introduction and conclusion, and the body is usually out of sequence. Gerald also makes a lot of mechanical errors; his papers are full of misspellings, and he frequently leaves out punctuation marks and capital letters. When asked by Mr. McCrae why he does not proofread his papers, Gerald responded that he does.

What can Mr. McCrae do to help Gerald learn to organize his papers better? How can he help Gerald proofread his papers better for mechanical errors?

TRACI is a student in Ms. Cord's fourth-grade class. Last year, Traci didn't meet standards on the state high-stakes assessment in math, but her scores were not low enough to make her eligible for special education services. Traci has trouble solving word problems in math because she does not have a systematic way of working on them. When she starts a problem, she looks for the numbers right away rather than first reading the problem carefully. For example, one day she saw the numbers 23 and 46 in a problem and automatically added them to get a sum of 69. The problem called for subtraction, but Traci did not know that, because she had not read the problem.

What can Ms. Cord do to help Traci solve math word problems more successfully? How can Ms. Cord help Traci become a more successful independent problem solver?

RON is a twelfth-grade student with a moderate intellectual disability who has problems with organization. He is often late for school, because, according to his parents, he rarely plans ahead and is always getting his materials ready for school at the last minute. Ron is usually late for class as well. He says that he cannot keep track of what he needs to bring to each class, so he is constantly going back to his locker, which makes him late. His locker is a complete mess. In the afternoons, Ron has a part-time job helping to clean copying and fax machines as part of a work-study program. His supervisor has expressed concern that Ron has been late for work several times and frequently misses his bus, causing his co-workers to have to drive him home.

What can Ron's teachers do to help him become better organized?

Gerald, Traci, and Ron share a common problem: They are unable to meet independently the academic and organizational demands of school. Being able to work and solve problems independently has become increasingly important as more and more students are expected to meet state and federal standards and as the demands of the twenty-first-century job market have become increasingly complex. Gerald needs to be able to organize his papers better, not just in English but in all areas, because teachers often judge quality on the basis of organization, neatness, and the number of spelling or punctuation errors. Traci needs to solve problems more systematically, not just in math but in other classes and outside school as well. Ron needs a strategy for managing his time: Being punctual and having the necessary supplies or materials are essential for success on his alternate assessments as well as eventually in the world of work. The fact is, as students move through the grades and on to careers or postsecondary education, more and more independence is expected and necessary for success.

Students need to perform independently in five key areas: gaining information, storing and retrieving information, expressing information, self-advocating, and managing time (Ellis & Lenz, 1996). Gaining information involves skills in listening to directions during lessons and on the job and in reading and interpreting textbooks, source books, and other media. Storing information consists of strategies for taking notes and preparing for tests or other evaluations. Students also need to retrieve information when needed. For example, they need to remember how to carry out a task such as cleaning and clearing a table or how to follow safety procedures during science lab. Expressing information includes the tasks of taking tests and writing papers. It also involves employment tasks such as developing a printed menu for a fast-food restaurant. Self-advocacy skills build student self-determination, helping students set realistic school or life goals and develop and carry out a plan to meet those goals. Finally, students need to have the time management skills to organize their time and efforts toward meeting their goals.

Although all these skills become more important as students progress through school, independence should be stressed at all levels of instruction. Unfortunately, many students, including those who are at risk or have other special needs, lack basic independent learning skills. Traditionally, when students needed learning-strategy instruction, they were referred to special education classes, remedial reading or math programs, or special study-skills courses. But in inclusive classrooms, learning strategies can be taught to students with disabilities or other special needs in several ways. Moreover, learning strategies often can be covered in class so that all students can benefit. For example, when Mr. Cooper discovered that many of his students in U.S. history were having trouble taking notes, he presented a note-taking strategy to his whole class. Similarly, Ms. Carpenter taught her biology class a strategy for taking multiple-choice tests because her students were scoring low as a group on these kinds of questions.

When students have more intensive skill needs, more individualized strategy instruction might take place outside the classroom, sometimes in a Tier 2 RtI group. For example, some students with special needs may need to have a strategy broken down into small steps, view multiple demonstrations of a strategy, and practice the strategy many times before they learn it. If the collaborative support of other education professionals is lacking, this level of instruction may be difficult to deliver within the time and curricular constraints of the general education classroom. Ron, from the chapter-opening case, has just such extraordinary needs. He needs a strategy designed specifically for his organizational problems; a plan for getting to his afternoon job on time would not be relevant for the rest of his classmates. In cases such as these—in which a special educator teaches a strategy to individual students—your job is to encourage and monitor student use of the strategy in your class and to provide students with feedback on their performance. However, in most cases, you can teach many of these skills in your class while still covering the required academic content. In fact, teaching learning strategies to students allows you to cover more material because your students become able to learn on their own.

You should do all you can to encourage the use of independent learning strategies and teach them to your students. This chapter focuses on ways you can build student independence in learning by encouraging student self-awareness and self-advocacy skills, developing and teaching independent learning strategies directly in class, and teaching students to use specific strategies on their own.

How Can You Encourage Student Self-Awareness, Self-Advocacy, and Self-Determination?

As students move through elementary, middle, and high school and on to postsecondary education or the world of work, the level of independence expected by those around them increases. Teachers expect students to come to class on time, master content through reading and lectures, keep track of assignments, organize study and homework time, set realistic career goals, and participate in curricular and extracurricular activities to meet these career goals. Students also must recognize when they have a problem and know where to go for help. Clearly, students need to look out for themselves, to become self-advocates. **Self-advocacy** is an important part of self-determination, or the ability to make decisions and direct behavior so that the desired goals are achieved (Holverstott, 2005). While the goal of becoming self-determined is important for all students, it is particularly important for students with special needs, who, as you learned in Chapter 7, are at risk for learned helplessness and low self-esteem.

Adjusting to changing expectations can be difficult for all students, but especially for those with disabilities. Many students with special needs are not aware of their strengths and weaknesses (Brinckerhoff, 1994; Scanlon & Mellard, 2002) and lack self-advocacy skills (Durlak, Rose, & Bursuck, 1994; Janiga & Costenbader, 2002). Self-advocacy skills can be taught to students of all ages and disabilities (Test, Fowler, Brewer, & Wood, 2005).

In effective student self-advocacy training, students learn their strengths and weaknesses, the potential impact of these strengths and weaknesses on their performance, the support they need to succeed, and the skills required to communicate their needs positively and assertively. Generally speaking, special educators have much of the responsibility for teaching self-advocacy directly. However, general education teachers are in a good position to teach all students about the opportunities and expectations of the adult world related to self-awareness and self-advocacy. For example, in applying the steps in INCLUDE, when Ms. Gay observed that Meredith was getting Fs on her independent work in class, Ms. Gay surmised that Meredith's problem was at least in part due to her being afraid to ask for help. Ms. Gay decided to spend five minutes with the whole class to talk about knowing when and how to ask for help. She felt this discussion would help Meredith and other students in the class be more assertive when they encountered difficulty in their work. In another situation, Cecil, a student with a vision impairment who was in Mr. Jordan's algebra class, sat in the front row but was still unable to see the problems on the board because Mr. Jordan wrote the numbers too small. However, Cecil did not feel comfortable asking Mr. Jordan to write larger. With his special education teacher, Cecil practiced asking Mr. Jordan for help. Cecil then asked Mr. Jordan directly, who responded that it would be no problem to write bigger. Mr. Jordan also gave Cecil some additional pointers on how to describe his disability and how to ask his teachers for accommodations. The Working Together stresses the importance of teachers working together as a team when helping students acquire self-advocacy skills.

INCLUDE

RESEARCH NOTE

Neale and Test (2010) successfully taught third- and fourth-grade students with high-incidence disabilities to express their learning preferences in an IEP meeting using a learning strategy called "I Can Use Effort."

Working TOGETHER

Fostering Team Communication and Self-Advocacy

Avery was a student in Mr. Katz's biology class. During the third week of school, Avery approached Mr. Katz after class. Avery said he had a learning disability and that his special education teacher said he had a legal right to receive more time to take his classroom tests. Mr. Katz was concerned. He felt that it wasn't fair to let Avery have extra time when he couldn't do that for the rest of the class. Mr. Katz also knew that the state test in science would be given soon and that getting more time to take classroom tests was not a good way to prepare Avery for them. In Mr. Katz's eyes, if Avery failed to meet standards in science, he, Avery's teacher, would be accountable. Furthermore, Mr. Katz was furious that no one had told him about this issue. He knew Avery had learning disabilities and that he might need extra help, but no one had said anything about changing how he took tests. Mr. Katz remembered that he had been unable to attend Avery's individualized education program (IEP) meeting due to a scheduling conflict, but shouldn't someone have told him about something as important as this?

Why is it important for students with disabilities to be able to advocate for themselves?

Why do you think a problem has occurred in this case?

What steps should Mr. Katz take to get the IEP team working together to support Avery?

www.resources

The following websites can be valuable resources for students as they develop self-advocacy skills:
Wrightslaw: http://www.wrightslaw.com
Disability Rights Education and Defense Fund (DREDF): http://edhd.bgsu.edu/isod

INCLUDE

How Can You Effectively Teach Independent Learning Strategies in Class?

In addition to teaching students to advocate for their own educational needs, another way you can help your students become more independent is to teach them strategies for learning how to learn (Lenz, 2006). These methods are collectively referred to as learning strategies. **Learning strategies** are techniques, principles, and rules that enable a student to learn to solve problems and complete tasks independently (Lenz, Ellis, & Scanlon, 1996; Schumaker, Deshler, & Denton, 1984). Learning strategies, which are similar to study skills, not only emphasize the steps needed to perform a strategy (for example, steps to follow in reading a textbook) but also stress why and when to use that strategy as well as how to monitor its usage. For example, when Ms. Blankenship taught her students a strategy for reading their textbook, she pointed out that the strategy would save them time yet improve their test scores. She also taught them to judge how well they were using the strategy by filling out a simple checklist as they read. The Case in Practice shows how the INCLUDE strategy can be used to select the appropriate learning strategies for your students.

An important component of teaching learning strategies effectively is that they be well-designed. As you recall from the discussions of effective materials in Chapters 5 and 9, the better your materials are designed, the greater the chance that they will work for your students with disabilities or other special needs without requiring you to make major accommodations. Some effective guidelines for designing learning strategies are presented in the Professional Edge on page 308.

For students to use learning strategies independently, they must first learn to perform them accurately and fluently. Research shows that most students benefit when the teacher directly explains how learning strategies can help them complete academic tasks (Lenz, 2006). However, students vary in the amount of structure they need to acquire learning strategies (Lenz, 2006). Some students can construct successful strategies on their own from repeatedly completing tasks in their classes (Pressley & Hilden, 2006). Other students may need simple prompts and models to develop strategies. This level of structure usually can be delivered by the general education teacher in a large-group setting. Still other students may require more intensive instruction, often in a small group, that includes explicit describing and

CASE IN PRACTICE

Using INCLUDE to Guide Instruction in Learning Strategies

Mr. Devereau taught social studies at Martin Luther King Jr. Middle School. He had a reputation for expecting a lot from his students; throughout the year, he expected them to be able to learn an increasing amount of subject matter independently.

Prior to the first day of school, Mr. Devereau was informed that his first-period class included eight students with learning disabilities and two with behavior disorders. He was also told that a special education teacher, Ms. Finch, was assigned to the class as a co-teacher. Mr. Devereau had never before had this many students with disabilities in one class; he also had never worked with a co-teacher. Still, he was hopeful that Ms. Finch would be able to help him, so he set up an appointment to meet with her.

Ms. Finch: What demands do students have to meet to be successful in your class?

Mr. Devereau: I expect students to begin to learn on their own. That is what is expected when they get to high school. I assign most of the reading of the text to be done outside of class, and I require students to take notes from class lectures and DVDs that I show. With my lectures, I use mainly PowerPoint slides. I distribute copies of the slides to students before class.

Ms. Finch: How does your grading system work?

Mr. Devereau: Grades are based on student performance on two multiple-choice tests and a five-page report on a famous person in pre–Civil War America.

Ms. Finch: Based on how your class is structured, my concern is that the students' IEPs show that they all are likely to have problems finding main ideas in both the textbook and the class lectures. But I know of some learning strategies that would help them be more successful in these areas.

Mr. Devereau: That sounds good. It's likely that other students in the class would benefit from these strategies as well.

Mr. Devereau and Ms. Finch decided to each take a strategy. Mr. Devereau would teach the note-taking strategy while he was lecturing in class. Ms. Finch would assist by modeling note taking at the board and/or monitoring student note-taking performance and providing corrective feedback as necessary. Ms. Finch was to teach the students two textbook-reading strategies: one for scanning a text and another for summarizing the big ideas in the text. She was to work on these strategies daily during the last 15 minutes of class until the students were able to perform them independently. While Ms. Finch and Mr. Devereau thought that the students with special needs also would have trouble with the multiple-choice tests and the five-page report, they decided that covering these strategies at the same time would be too much. However, they agreed to show the students how the strategies they were learning for note taking and textbook reading could also help them with their tests and research paper.

REFLECTION

How did Mr. Devereau and Ms. Finch use INCLUDE to help their students? Was it appropriate for them to teach the strategies to the entire class? Why? Which specific strategies described in this chapter might be appropriate for Mr. Devereau and Ms. Finch to use?

modeling of a specific strategy as well as extensive practice and feedback about how to apply the strategy to their course demands (Swanson, 2001). This more intensive instruction can be delivered in Tier 2 or 3 of an RtI system, depending on the degree of student need. The following steps for teaching learning strategies are research-based (Deshler et al., 1996):

1. Assess current strategy use.
2. Clarify expectations.
3. Demonstrate strategy use.
4. Encourage students to memorize strategy steps.
5. Provide guided and independent practice.
6. Administer posttests.

These steps incorporate many of the effective teaching practices described in Chapters 5 and 9, and would also qualify as evidence-based practices for RtI. Use the INCLUDE strategy to help you determine the level of structure you need to provide to students as you deliver each step. Guidelines for differentiating instruction in Tier 3 in RtI are provided in the Instructional Edge on page 309.

INCLUDE

PROFESSIONAL EDGE

Developing Your Own Learning Strategies

You can use the guidelines here either to create your own learning strategies or to evaluate ones that are commercially produced. By following these suggestions, you can develop learning strategies tailored for the students in your class.

1. Identify skill areas that are problematic for most of your students, such as taking multiple-choice tests or writing lecture notes.

2. For each skill area, specify student outcomes, such as scoring at least 10 percent higher on multiple-choice tests or writing down key main ideas and details from a lecture.

3. List a set of specific steps students need to follow to reach the identified outcomes. You may want to ask other students who have good test-taking and note-taking skills what they do. Presented here is a sample reading comprehension strategy called *RAP* (Ellis & Lenz, 1987):

   R　*Read* a paragraph.

   A　*Ask* yourself what were the main idea and two details.

   P　*Put* the main idea and details in your own words.

4. Your strategy should contain no more than eight steps. Having more steps makes the strategy difficult to remember.

5. Your steps should be brief; each should begin with a verb that directly relates to the strategy.

6. To help students remember the steps, encase the strategy in a mnemonic device (for example, the acronym RAP for the reading strategy just presented).

7. The strategy should cue students to perform behaviors for thinking (remembering), for doing (reading), and for self-evaluation (surveying or checking their work).

8. A textbook-reading strategy developed by teachers (Bartelt, Marchio, & Reynolds, 1994) that meets the guidelines for developing an effective learning strategy follows:

   R　*Review* headings and subheadings.

   E　*Examine* boldface words.

   A　*Ask,* "What do I expect to learn?"

   D　*Do* it—Read!

   S　*Summarize* in your own words.

Source: Adapted from "Generalization and Adaptation of Learning Strategies to Natural Environments: Part 2. Research into Practice," by E. Ellis, K. Lenz, and E. Sabornie, 1987, *Remedial and Special Education, 8*(2), pp. 6–23. Copyright © 1987 by Hammill Institute on Disability. Reprinted with permission.

Assess Current Strategy Use

INCLUDE

Students often are receptive to instruction when they can clearly see what problems they are having and how the strategy you are teaching can help them overcome these problems. Therefore, learning-strategy instruction begins with an assessment of how well your students can currently perform a skill, a part of the N and C steps of INCLUDE. As you learned in Chapter 4, specific learning strategies can be assessed using direct observation checklists, analyses of student products, and student self-evaluations.

You also need to assess whether your students have the preskills necessary to perform the strategy. For example, students who can discriminate between main ideas and details in a lecture are ideal candidates for learning a note-taking strategy; students who can read all the words on a test and understand the class content will benefit most from a test-taking strategy. In contrast, students who cannot identify most of the words in their texts are not logical candidates for learning a textbook-reading strategy; students whose assignments are too difficult for them will not benefit from a strategy to help them organize their independent practice activities.

As you have learned, students with special needs often lack critical preskills. Before you decide to teach a particular strategy, you should identify its preskills and assess them separately. If most students lack the preskills, they can be taught as part of your everyday instruction. If only a few have problems with preskills, these students need to receive additional instruction in class, with a peer or adult tutor, through co-taught lessons, or in a learning center, Tier 2, Tier 3, or special education setting.

Clarify Expectations

Learning strategies have the potential of empowering your students because they enable them to learn and succeed in and out of school on their own, without undue help from others. When you introduce learning strategies to students, you need to

INSTRUCTIONAL **EDGE**

Providing Differentiated Instruction in Tier 3 in RtI

You have learned that in RtI, professionals accommodate individual differences using instruction of varying intensities called tiers, and that students who fail to make adequate progress in the least intensive tier, Tier 1, receive extra practice on targeted foundational skills in Tier 2. A smaller number of students continue to struggle, despite well-delivered evidence-based Tier 2 instruction. These students need even more intensive instruction in Tier 3.

What is Tier 3 instruction?
In Tier 3, students receive highly intensive instruction matched to their individual needs (Reschley, 2007). Tier 3 can be special education, but not always. Tier 3 instruction is more concentrated than Tiers 1 and 2, focusing on a small set of foundational skills, usually in math, reading, writing, and behavior, that may or may not be at grade level (Lemons, 2007). Intensity in Tier 3 is addressed through (a) more frequent sessions, often of longer duration, (b) smaller groups, and (c) highly systematic and explicit instruction characterized by control of task difficulty, careful sequencing of tasks, frequent teacher modeling, guided practice and feedback, a mastery learning orientation (whereby students don't move to the next skill, lesson, or activity until the previous one is learned), and motivators to help students regulate their attention and behavior and work hard (Gersten et al., 2009a; Gersten et al., 2009b). Prepackaged and/or commercially produced programs can be used for Tier 3 as long as they are highly systematic, explicit, and evidence based (Bursuck & Damer, 2011). One example of such a program is the University of Kansas Strategic Instruction Model (SIM) learning strategy materials (http://www.ku-crl.org/sim/).

Who is eligible for Tier 3 instruction?
Students enter Tier 3 when the results of their progress monitoring show a clear lack of progress towards meeting specified benchmarks. If special education is involved, then a comprehensive evaluation to determine special education needs and eligibility is required. Tier 3 typically includes approximately 2–6% of students (Lyon, 2009). In a class of 25 students this would amount to 1 or 2 students, though this figure may be higher in some high-poverty schools (Bursuck et al., 2004).

Where, when, and for how long does Tier 3 instruction take place?
Tier 3 instruction usually takes place outside the general education classroom. In middle or high school, Tier 3 can occur during time scheduled for elective classes or study halls (Mellard & Prewett,

2010). On average, students participating in Tier 3 receive interventions daily, totaling from 45–120 extra minutes of instruction per week in addition to time spent in their core general education program (Gersten et al., 2009a). In many instances Tier 3 time in high school is longer because in areas such as reading there is no core general education program. Length is dependent on multiple issues including problem severity, subject, intervention method, and scheduling. Sometimes Tier 3 instruction is delivered in the form of a "double dose," whereby student daily time in instruction is doubled. With regard to group size, one-to-one instruction appears to be most effective (Gersten et al., 2009a), although groups as large as 3 are used in situations of limited resources and middle and high schools.

Who teaches Tier 3 groups?
Tier 3 groups are most commonly taught by special education teachers, even when Tier 3 is not special education, although Tier 3 groups can be taught by general educators, speech and language pathologists, and Title 1 teachers. Tier 3 interventions involving behavior are likely to involve the school psychologist.

How long do students remain in Tier 3 groups?
Because the skill deficits of students receiving Tier 3 services are very significant, Tier 3 groups are longer term than Tier 2 groups, extending for as long as one or two years (Reschley, 2007). While in Tier 3, students' progress is monitored continually; the results are used to change instruction as needed as well as determine eventual readiness to exit Tier 3 and reenter Tiers 1 and 2.

What is the role of the general education teacher in teaching Tier 3 students?
Even though general education teachers do not usually teach Tier 3 groups, they teach Tier 3 students at other times during the day. By applying the INCLUDE strategy, teachers can readily find out how well their Tier 3 students are meeting their classroom demands. This "window on reality" is an important part of progress monitoring for the RtI team as they continually evaluate the extent to which the gap between Tier 3 students and their peers is narrowing. Of course, information gathered using INCLUDE also can help teachers successfully accommodate Tier 3 students in their classrooms. Keep in mind that when RtI is implemented, all teachers are responsible for all students, regardless of tier. Also, the fact that students require intensive instruction in one area does not mean they cannot be successful in other areas of the general education curriculum.

---

point out their potential benefits clearly and specifically. Carefully explained expected outcomes can be motivating, particularly as students get older and teacher encouragement alone may no longer be enough to keep them interested.

The first step in getting and keeping students motivated to learn is to provide a strong rationale for why learning the strategy is important. This rationale should be directly tied to current student performance as well as to the demands of your class, two essential pieces of information derived from the INCLUDE process. For example, when introducing a new note-taking strategy, Mr. Washington pointed out that

INCLUDE

Demonstrating the use of a learning strategy involves explaining both the thinking and the doing parts of a process, showing examples and nonexamples of effective strategy use, and checking learners' understanding. How do these steps help students with special needs acquire learning strategies?

the class was able to identify on average only half of the main ideas presented on a note-taking pretest. He also told his class that half of the material on his tests would come from information presented during his lectures. Finally, Mr. Washington explained that taking good notes can help students outside school as well; in many job situations, employers give directions that need to be written down.

The next step in clarifying expectations is to explain specifically what students should be able to accomplish when they have learned the skill. For example, Ms. Thompson told her class that after learning a textbook-reading strategy, they would be able to do their homework faster. Also, give students an idea of how long it will take them to learn the strategy. You could make a chart showing the instructional activities to be covered each day and the approximate number of days it will take to learn the strategy. The advantage of presenting the information on a chart is that steps can be checked off as completed. The act of checking off completed activities can be very motivating for students, and it is also a way of demonstrating self-monitoring, an effective independent learning skill discussed later in this chapter.

Demonstrate Strategy Use

In demonstrating strategies, keep in mind three important points. First, remember that the process one goes through in performing a task or solving a problem should be carefully explained. For example, demonstrate both thinking and doing behaviors. Talking aloud to yourself while performing the skill is particularly important for many students with disabilities, who often do not develop spontaneously organized thinking patterns.

Second, present both positive and negative examples of appropriate strategy use, carefully explaining why they are positive or negative. This explanation can help students tell the difference between doing a strategy the right way and doing it incorrectly, a distinction that can be difficult for students with special needs to make without direct instruction. For example, Mr. Washington demonstrated effective and ineffective notetaking strategies using a Smartboard ©. As students listened to a short videotaped lecture, he took notes systematically, writing down key ideas and details. Next, using the same lecture, he demonstrated ineffective note taking by trying to write down every word.

Third, after you demonstrate, ask frequent questions to monitor student understanding and determine whether more demonstration is needed. Keep in mind that for many students, including those with disabilities, one demonstration may not be enough.

Encourage Students to Memorize Strategy Steps

The purpose of having students memorize the steps in the strategy is to make it easier for them to recall the strategy when they need to use it. To help students learn the steps, you can post them prominently in your classroom at first so that you and your students can refer to them throughout the class or day. Students also may need to be drilled on saying the strategy steps. To practice, students could pair off and quiz each other, or you could ask students the strategy steps before and after class. For example, each day during the last several minutes of class, Ms. Henry quizzed four of her social studies students on the steps of a strategy for paraphrasing text. This type of help also can be given in a Tier 2 RtI group.

Even though memorizing a strategy can help students recall it, you may not want to spend too much time on this step, particularly for some of your students with learning disabilities, who may have memory problems. For these students, you might include the steps to all the strategies they are learning in a special section of their assignment notebooks. For strategies used most often, cue cards listing strategy steps can be taped to the inside cover of textbooks or notebooks.

Provide Guided and Independent Practice

Because students must learn how to perform strategies accurately and fluently before they can attempt them independently, they need considerable practice. Five ways of providing practice on learning strategies are suggested. One way is to have students use controlled materials when they are first learning a strategy. **Controlled materials** generally are materials at the student's reading level, of high interest, and relatively free of complex vocabulary and concepts. Because controlled materials remove many content demands on the learner, they allow students to focus all their energy on learning the strategy. Controlled materials also foster initial success, which is important for motivation. For example, Mr. Bernard was teaching his students a strategy for taking essay tests in current events. At first, he had his students practice this strategy on simply worded, one-part essay questions about material familiar to the students, such as people and events in the areas of rock music, movies, television, and sports. As students became better at using the strategy, Mr. Bernard gradually introduced more complex questions on less familiar topics, such as the AIDS epidemic in Africa and the drug war in Mexico. Finally, he used sample test questions.

A second way to provide students with practice is first to guide them and then to allow them to perform independently. *Guided practice* means giving students verbal cues when they are first attempting a skill. For example, before and while her students were practicing a strategy, Ms. Waters asked them questions such as, "What will you do first?" "Why did you do that?" "What should you do after you are done with the strategy steps?" "Which key words are you going to look for in the questions?" "How will you know which are the main ideas?" and "Was the sentence I just read a main idea? Why?" Once most students seem able to answer your reminder questions, you can gradually stop asking them so that students are eventually performing independently. Some students may need little guided practice or none at all and can be allowed to work independently right away.

A third practice technique is to give feedback that is specific and encourages students to evaluate themselves (Lenz, 2006; Lenz et al., 1996). For example, Dominique has just performed the steps of a proofreading strategy in front of the class. Her teacher says, "Good job, Dominique! I knew you could do it." Denise performed the same strategy in front of her class and her teacher asked, "How do you think you did? What do you need to focus on most the next time?" The feedback Dominique received does not clearly tell her what she did right, nor does it encourage self-evaluation. The feedback given to Denise encourages self-evaluation, a critical part of independent learning. Of course, if Denise cannot evaluate her own performance at first, the key parts of good performance have to be pointed out to her and practice on self-evaluation provided.

A fourth aspect of practicing learning strategies is to praise students only when they have produced work that is praiseworthy. Praise that is not tied to student performance or is exaggerated, often for the purpose of enhancing student self-image, may only reinforce the student's sense of inadequacy. For example, because of a history of failure in learning situations, students with special needs often see little relationship between their efforts and classroom success. When you give nonspecific praise to these students, it is easier for them to attribute your praise to something other than competence, such as sympathy ("I'm so bad at this, she has to pretend I did well").

Fifth, encourage students to reinforce themselves and to take responsibility for both their successes and their failures. For example, after doing well on a note-taking strategy, Alicia was encouraged by her teacher to say, "I did a good job. This time I paid attention and wrote down all the main ideas. I need to do the same the next time." Alicia's teacher was showing her how to attribute her success to factors under her control. This approach can help her become a more active, independent learner.

Administer Posttests

When it appears from your practice sessions that most students have acquired the strategy, give them the pretest again, this time as a posttest, to test their mastery. If, according to your posttest, students have not acquired the strategy, identify where the breakdown occurred and then provide additional instruction and/or practice. If more than 20 percent of the students need extra practice or instruction, they can receive additional help in a large or small group. If your school is using RtI, the extra help could be provided in a Tier 2 group. If fewer than 20 percent of the students require more assistance, they can be provided with more individualized practice by the teacher before or after school, by a special education teacher or other support staff, or in a Tier 3 group.

What Are Some Examples of Successful Learning Strategies?

There is a growing number of research-based learning strategies that work for students who are at risk or who have special needs. These strategies cover many areas, including reading and reading comprehension, listening and note taking, written expression, math-problem solving, and time and resource management. An array of strategies that incorporate many of these effective practices are summarized in the following sections. Many of these strategies can be used with students at all levels—elementary, middle, and high school.

Word-Identification and Reading Fluency Strategies

Students cannot always depend on the teacher to help them figure out difficult words. They also need to read fluently enough so that they can understand what they are reading and finish assignments in a timely manner. The next two strategies are designed to help students help themselves in the important areas of word identification and reading fluency.

Identifying Words in Textbook Reading   Middle and high school students are likely to encounter technical words in their content-area textbooks that have multiple syllables, making them difficult for some students to identify. One strategy designed to help students with special needs identify difficult words in their textbook reading (Archer, Gleason, & Vachon, 2003, p. 95) helps students break apart words and then put them back together. First, teach your students to break words apart on paper by having them do the following:

1. Circle the word parts at the beginning of the word (prefixes).
2. Circle the word parts at the end of the word (suffixes).
3. Underline the letters representing vowel sounds in the rest of the word.
4. Say the parts of the word.
5. Say the parts fast.
6. Make it a real word.

Here is an example of this strategy:

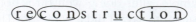

Once your students can perform all of these steps by writing them, they are gradually encouraged to perform the steps in their heads, as follows (Archer et al., 2003, p. 95):

1. Look for word parts at the beginning and end of the word, and vowel sounds in the rest of the word.
2. Say the parts of the word.
3. Say the parts fast.
4. Make it a real word.

To be successful with this strategy, students need to be able to perform two critical preskills. They need to know sounds the vowels make, and they need to be able to pronounce prefixes and suffixes. Students lacking these preskills need to be taught them prior to strategy instruction. With RtI, preskill training can take place in Tier 2. For words that have parts difficult to decode, encourage students to say the parts they know and then use the strategy described next for using the context to figure out the word. Of course, it is fair to get help from a classmate or the teacher if all of these strategies have been tried and students are still unable to figure out the word.

WARF   To be successful in understanding content-area textbooks, students need to read quickly enough so that they can think about word meaning rather than squander their energy on word identification. Students also may have to adjust their rate of reading, depending on their purpose for reading (Mercer & Pullen, 2009). Minskoff and Allsopp (2003) suggest a strategy to help students who can read accurately at least at the third-grade level but need to increase and/or adjust their reading speed. It is called *WARF:*

W   *Widen* your eye span.
A   *Avoid* skip-backs.
R   *Read* silently.
F   *Flex* your reading rate.

Students first are taught to widen their eye span and not read word by word. They are taught to group words, not reading the articles (for example, *the* or *a*) or auxiliary words (for example, *is* or *are*), so they can focus on words that give meaning. As part of this **W** step, they also are taught to try to group words meaningfully (for example, for the words *a sunny day,* focus on *sunny* and *day*). In the **A** step, avoiding skip-backs, students are taught to keep reading if they do not understand something, using context clues to gain understanding. They are told to go back only if this is unsuccessful. In the **R** step, students are taught to read silently, avoiding reading aloud in a whisper by pressing their lips together. In the final step, **F,** students learn to change their reading rate depending on the difficulty and/or familiarity of the material. For example, when students are looking for information, they need to know to read quickly as they search for key words on the page. When students read important information they must understand or memorize, they need to be aware to read more slowly. Conversely, if students are reading information they know well, they can adjust their rate and read faster.

Vocabulary Strategies

In addition to being able to identify technical vocabulary, students also must know what words mean if they are to understand what they read. Strategies for using direct instruction to teach new vocabulary were covered in Chapter 9. Realistically, however, teachers have the time to teach only about two vocabulary words per day (Armbruster, Lehr, & Osborn, 2001).

A strategy that your students can use to help them figure out the meaning of words independently is shown in Figures 10.1 and 10.2. To perform this strategy, students must first learn the meaning of common morphemes.

FIGURE 10.1 Word-Part Clues

1. Look for the *root word,* which is a single word that cannot be broken into smaller words or word parts. See if you know what the root word means.
2. Look for a *prefix,* which is a word part added to the beginning of a word that changes its meaning. See if you know what the prefix means.
3. Look for a *suffix,* which is a word part added to the end of a word that changes its meaning. See if you know what the suffix means.
4. Put the meaning of the *root word* and any prefix or suffix together and see if you can build the meaning of the word.

Source: "Vocabulary Tricks: Effects of Instruction in Morphology and Context on Fifth-Grade Students' Ability to Derive and Infer Word Meanings," by J. Baumann, E. Edwards, E. Boland, S. Olejnik, & E. Kame´enui, 2003, *American Educational Research Journal, 40*(2), pp. 447–494.

FIGURE 10.2 Vocabulary Clues

When you come to a word and you don't know what it means, use these clues:

1. *Context clues:* Read the sentences around the word to see if there are clues to its meaning.
2. *Word-part clues:* See if you can break the word into a root word, prefix, or suffix to help figure out its meaning.
3. *Context clues:* Read the sentences around the word again to see if you have figured out its meaning.

Source: "Vocabulary Tricks: Effects of Instruction in Morphology and Context on Fifth-Grade Students' Ability to Derive and Infer Word Meanings," by J. Baumann, E. Edwards, E. Boland, S. Olejnik, & E. Kame´enui, 2003, *American Educational Research Journal, 40*(2), pp. 447–494.

Reading Comprehension Strategies

Reading comprehension strategies are intended to help students meet the independent reading demands of content-area classes, particularly in the middle and upper grades. Although reading primarily involves textbooks, students must be able to read and understand a variety of source books as well. The following are examples of proven reading comprehension strategies for students of all grade levels.

SCROL One example of a reading comprehension strategy is *SCROL* (Grant, 1993). The SCROL strategy enables students to take notes while they are reading, an important study strategy, and to use text headings to aid their comprehension and help them find and remember important information. The SCROL strategy has five steps:

S *Survey* the headings. In the assigned text selection, read each heading and subheading. For each heading and subheading, try to answer the following questions: What do I already know about this topic? What information might the writer present?

C *Connect.* Ask yourself, How do the headings relate to one another? Write down key words from the headings that might provide connections between them.

R *Read* the text. As you read, look for words and phrases that express important information about the headings. Mark the text to point out important ideas and details. Stop to make sure that you understand the major ideas and supporting details. If you do not understand, reread.

O *Outline.* Using indentations to reflect structure, outline the major ideas and supporting details in the heading segment. Write the heading and then try to outline each heading segment without looking back at the text.

L *Look* back. Now look back at the text and check the accuracy of the major ideas and details you wrote. Correct any inaccurate information in your outline. If you marked the text as you read, use this information to help you verify the accuracy of your outline.

Advise students to follow steps 3–5 (**R–L**) every time they encounter a section with headings in the text they are reading. Taking notes using SCROL improves student comprehension while also providing students with a product that can help them study more effectively for tests.

Students often struggle with the R step of SCROL that involves marking the important ideas and details. Mariage, Englert, and Okolo (2009) developed the *Highlight It!* and *Mark It!* strategies to help students identify and then elaborate on main ideas and details. Cue cards used to guide students through the *Highlight-It!* and *Mark-It!* steps are shown in Figures 10.3 and 10.4 *Highlight It!* focuses on the meaning in the text, while in *Mark-It!* students elaborate on the meaning by questioning the author's ideas and themselves, making personal connections, predicting

FIGURE 10.4

FIGURE 10.3

Highlight It!

1. Read section.

2. Pause and Think.

3. Highlight.

4. Re-read Highlighting.

5. Self-Check:
   Does it make sense?
   Do I have the main idea(s)?
   Do I have several key details?

6. Pair/Share/Compare
   "I highlighted . . ."
   "I highlighted this because . . ."
   (Justify and Explain Thinking)

7. Discussion: How is our highlighting similar and different?

8. Community Share: Report Out

Source: From "Teaching Organizational Skills to Promote Academic Achievement in Behaviorally Challenged Students," by D. H. Anderson, V. H. Munk, K. R. Young, L. Conley, and P. Caldarella, 2008, *Teaching Exceptional Children*, 40(4), 6–13.

Mark It!

1. Read and **highlight.**
2. **Mark** the text with symbols. Make notes in the margins to record your thoughts and strategies.
3. Pause and Think.
4. Self-Check:
   Do my marks and notes make sense?

5. Pair/Share/Compare
   Here's what I marked. . . ."
   "I made these marks because . . ."
   "The **strategy** I used was . . ."
   "I was thinking. . . ."
   (Justify and Explain Thinking)
   "Questions or comments?"

6. Discussion: How are we similar or different?

7. Community Share: Report Out

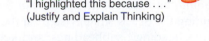

Mark-It Symbols

PK: Prior knowledge
Q: Question
CL: Clarify (idea or word)
P: Predict
S: Summarize
I: Imagery
C: Connect (self, text, world)
MI: Main Idea
D: Detail
**   Key point
?   Confusing part

Source: From "Teaching Organizational Skills to Promote Academic Achievement in Behaviorally Challenged Students," by D. H. Anderson, V. H. Munk, K. R. Young, L. Conley, and P. Caldarella, 2008, *Teaching Exceptional Children*, 40(4), 6–13.

ideas, using imagery, and clarifying text. To teach both strategies, first model the strategies. Then perform the strategies with your students, focusing on a section of text. Last, have your students collaborate with partners on performing the strategies and share the results with the class.

PARS *PARS* is a simplified textbook-reading strategy that is good for younger students and students without much experience using textbook-reading strategies (Cheek & Cheek, 1983). The four steps of PARS follow:

P *Preview* the material by scanning the chapter and surveying the introductory statement, headings, graphic aids, and chapter summary to identify main ideas.
A *Ask* questions that relate to the main ideas discovered when surveying the chapter.
R *Read* the chapter to answer the questions developed.
S *Summarize* the main ideas in the chapter.

Remember that just telling students the steps of a learning strategy is not enough. Letting students watch you perform the strategy and then carefully guiding students as they learn to perform it are essential if students are to learn to use PARS to gain access to the content of their textbooks more independently.

CAPS You have learned that students who can comprehend stories are able to identify key parts of stories called story grammars (see the Case in Practice in Chapter 4). *CAPS* is a self-questioning strategy that guides students as they look for these important story elements (Leinhardt & Zigmond, 1988). The strategy is composed of the following steps:

C Who are the *characters?*
A What is the *aim* of the story?
P What *problem* happens?
S How is the problem *solved?*

CAPS is particularly effective for students in elementary school, where key reading demands involve understanding stories.

SLiCK A common accommodation for students with reading disabilities is the bypass strategy of providing them with an oral text. However, some students still struggle to understand a text, even when they no longer have to read it. *SLiCK* (Boyle et al., 2002) is a strategy designed to help students comprehend digitally recorded textbooks. It involves the following steps:

S *Set* it up.
L *Look* ahead through the chapter.
C *Comprehend.*
K *Keep* it together.

In the **S** step, the student sets it up by opening the textbook to the start of the assigned section; readying a worksheet containing the SLiCK strategy steps at the top, with spaces to record key information such as headings, subheadings, and key vocabulary words. In the **L** step, the student looks ahead through the chapter using the recorded book, player, and print textbook. The student notes keywords, headings, and subheadings and records them on the worksheet. In the comprehend, or **C,** step, the student reads along with the recording, pausing to record important details under the headings and subheadings previously identified. The student is encouraged to think of big ideas by writing minisummaries as he or she reads. In the final step, **K,** the student combines all of the minisummaries to get the big picture about what the section of text means. Boyle et al., (2002) report that students acquire the **S** and **L** steps quickly, while the **C** and **K** steps require considerable teacher modeling and practice before they are learned.

RUDPC You have learned that successful comprehension requires an understanding of how information in stories and expository text is organized and that students with learning disabilities and attention deficit–hyperactivity disorder (ADHD) often have trouble identifying organizational patterns. While we typically think of organizational patterns as applying to written text, information presented on computer screens has an organizational scheme as well (Minskoff & Allsopp, 2003). Assignments in school routinely require students to access information on the Internet. Research shows that students need to learn how to navigate the different parts of a website to acquire efficiently the information sought (Kuiper, Volman, & Terwel, 2005). Often this involves ignoring the many distractions that can appear on the computer screen.

Minskoff and Allsopp (2003) developed the *RUDPC* strategy for helping students derive important information from a webpage. The steps are as follows:

R *Read* the title and headings.
U *Use* the cursor to skim the page.
D *Decide* whether you need the page.
P *Print* the page.
C *Copy* the bibliographic information.

When reading a website, students need to make quick decisions about whether a given section of a webpage provides information they are looking for. Reading everything on the screen is inefficient. Students with special needs may need explicit instruction on the **D** step in order to learn to make these judgments. Minskoff and Allsopp (2003) also suggest that for some students, printing pages prevents them from being distracted by graphics or frustrated by small fonts.

POSSE Another reading comprehension strategy is *POSSE* (Englert, 2009; Englert & Mariage, 1991). This strategy includes many reading practices that have been shown to aid reading comprehension, such as graphic organizers, text structures, stimulation of student background knowledge, and self-monitoring. The steps in this strategy are as follows:

P *Predict* ideas.
O *Organize* the ideas.
S *Search* for the structure.
S *Summarize* the main ideas.
E *Evaluate* your understanding.

When students are predicting, they can be given a sentence starter such as *I predict that . . .* For this step, students are taught to use signals from a variety of sources, including title, headings in bold, pictures, keywords, and so on. Brainstorming is very important in this step. A technique used for teaching the POSSE strategy steps is a process called reciprocal teaching. **Reciprocal teaching** is a way to teach students to comprehend reading material by providing them with teacher and peer models of thinking behavior and then allowing them to practice these thinking behaviors with their peers (Palincsar & Brown, 1988). At first, the teacher leads the dialogue, demonstrating how the strategies can be used during reading. As instruction goes on, the teacher gives the students more and more responsibility for maintaining the dialogue. Eventually, students are largely responsible

These students are engaged in a structured dialogue about the test they are reading, a peer-mediated comprehension strategy called reciprocal teaching. What strategies must students be taught before they can practice reciprocal teaching?

for the dialogue, though the teacher still provides help as necessary. The most important part of the technique is the teacher's releasing control and turning the dialogue over to the students (Englert & Mariage, 1991).

A sample dialogue for reciprocal teaching is presented in the Case in Practice. After reading it, think of the reasons reciprocal teaching is such a powerful technique for teaching reading comprehension to students who are at risk or who have other special needs. In what other areas could reciprocal teaching be used? The Technology Notes feature describes an electronic textbook geared to students' individual reading levels that teaches students the same reading comprehension strategies stressed in POSSE, and more.

RESEARCH NOTE

Kim et al. (2006) improved the reading comprehension skills of middle school students with disabilities using reciprocal teaching adapted for use with a computer.

Listening and Note-Taking Strategies

Students in all grades need to be able to understand information presented orally by their teachers. In elementary school, students are required to follow many oral directions and listen when the teacher is reading aloud or presenting information. In middle school, junior high, and high school, where lecturing is a common way for teachers to present subject-area content, students are required to discern and record key information in lectures so they can study it later. As you have already learned, students with special needs may have problems understanding information presented orally. These problems can make access to the general education curriculum more difficult for them.

CASE IN PRACTICE

Teaching Script for Demonstrating POSSE

The students in this class have just read a section of text that focuses on Loch Ness. They are now applying the search, summarize, and evaluate steps of POSSE.

Teacher: What is the main topic the text is talking about?

Peg: The Loch Ness monster.

Teacher: What was this section about? What was the main idea?

Peg: Oh, the lake. I have two questions: "What is a lake?" and "What lives in it?"

Teacher: Do you mean this particular lake or any lake?

Peg: This lake. Joe?

Joe: It's foggy, it's deep, and it's long and narrow.

Peg: Don?

Don: The land beside the lake, you don't know if it is real soft and you could fall through it.

Teacher: So it could be soft and swampy.

Ann: I think the Loch Ness monster lives there.

Teacher: Is Ann answering your question, Peg?

Peg: No.

Teacher: What was your question?

Peg: I had two: "What is a lake?" and "What lives in the lake?"

Joe: But the book never answered that. I have a question about the main idea. Aren't we supposed to do a question about the main idea?

Teacher: Just about what we read.

Joe: Yes, but Peg asked us, "What lives in the lake?" but it doesn't really mention that in the book.

Teacher: That's true. The major idea has to do with Loch Ness and what it looks like. A minor idea that we really inferred rather than directly read in the article was that the Loch Ness monster lives in the lake.

Peg: Are there any clarifications?

Students: [No response.]

Teacher: I have a clarification. You had trouble reading some of these words and I wondered if you know what some of them mean. What does *ancestors* mean?

[The teacher continues discussing vocabulary.]

Sources: From "Making Students Partners in the Comprehension Process: Organizing the Reading 'POSSE,'" by C. S. Englert and T. V. Mariage, 1991, *Learning Disability Quarterly, 14,* pp. 133–134. Used by permission of Council for Learning Disabilities.

Thinking Reader: The Textbook of the Future

Textbooks are the most common method of delivering subject-area information to students of all grades but particularly to those who are in middle school or high school. Yet many students with and without special needs experience problems comprehending their textbooks. Whereas some of these problems are due to reading slowly and/or inaccurately, students also lack strategies for locating and retaining important information in their texts. Unfortunately, standard textbooks provide teachers and students with little support in teaching and learning important comprehension strategies. Enter the Thinking Reader.

The Thinking Reader incorporates a variety of supports into electronic text in order to teach research-based reading comprehension strategies such as summarizing, questioning, clarifying, predicting, and visualizing. The supports can be customized to accommodate individual student reading abilities by systematically reducing the level of structure as students become more proficient in the reading comprehension strategies. The goal is for students to select independently the strategy that best fits their comprehension needs.

The specific supports in the program include a human voice feature that reads the text while highlighting it and natural intonation to support the finding of main ideas and the development of fluency. Comprehension is supported through a series of strategy prompts that guide students as they practice the comprehension strategies. For example, at the end of each passage, students might be asked to predict what will happen in the story, clarify something that they find confusing, summarize the passage, or visualize what is happening. Students respond to the prompts in three formats: open-ended, fill-in-the-blank, and oral. There are also supports for vocabulary development,

FIGURE 10.5 Sample Daily Lesson Plan Format

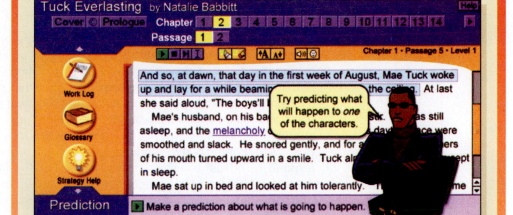

including a contextual glossary with Spanish translations for English-language learners.

Perhaps the most helpful aspect of the Thinking Reader is the availability of supports to help students think about the passage. The program employs an *agent* who provides hints for each strategy (for example, "Try predicting what will happen to one of the characters") or think-alouds (for example, "I remembered that both Winnie's grandmother and the stranger are very interested in music. She is excited to hear the music again, and he seems to find it meaningful that she has heard it before. So I predict that the music will be important in some way"). A sample screen display is shown in Figure 10.5.

Note: The Thinking Reader was developed by Dr. David Rose and Dr. Bridget Dalton at the Center for Applied Special Technology (CAST). The program is based on research cited in this text, including a report of the National Reading Panel (2000), principles of universal design (Dalton & Pisha, 2001), and reciprocal teaching (Palincsar & Brown, 1988). The Thinking Reader has been used successfully to teach comprehension strategies to students with learning disabilities (Dalton & Pisha, 2001).

The listening and note-taking strategies described in the next section were designed to help all students learn more successfully from their teachers' presentations.

SLANT   Students who are engaged in class are more likely to be successful (Larkin & Ellis, 1998). The *SLANT* strategy is designed to increase student involvement in class lectures or discussions. Greater student involvement increases the likelihood that students will listen more carefully and take better notes. *SLANT* includes the following steps:

S *Sit* up.
L *Lean* forward.
A *Activate* your thinking.
N *Name* key information.
T *Track* the talker.

In the **S** step, Sit up, remind students that slouching or putting their heads down in class makes their bodies want to fall asleep and causes them to miss a lot of information. For **L**, tell students that leaning forward shows they are interested in the information, even when they are not, and that often they can train their minds to follow their bodies. **A**ctivating your thinking involves having your students ask themselves question such as, "What is this about?" or "What is important to remember?" This step also involves asking the teacher a question when they don't understand (Vaughn & Bos, 2008). For the **N** step, students answer teacher questions, share their ideas, and respond to others' comments (Ellis, 1991). For the final step **T**, Track the talker, encourage students to keep their eyes on the teacher or whomever else is talking because this prevents them from daydreaming or being distracted by other things.

TASSELL   As students move into the upper grades, they are required to take notes for longer periods of time. Longer lectures require sustained attention, a skill that is often problematic for students with disabilities (Smith, 2004). The *TASSELL* strategy is recommended for students who have trouble maintaining their level of attention (Minskoff & Allsopp, 2003). It includes the following steps:

T *Try* not to doodle.
A *Arrive* at class prepared.
S *Sit* near the front.
S *Sit* away from friends.
E *End* daydreaming.
L *Look* at the teacher.

For the **E** step, encourage students to monitor their attention. When they find they are daydreaming, they should immediately change their position, sit forward, and make eye contact with the teacher. Then they should write down whatever the teacher is saying, regardless of its importance (Minskoff & Allsopp, 2003). For the **L** step, encourage students to keep their eyes on the teacher when they are not taking notes or looking at the chalkboard, overhead, PowerPoint presentation, or computer screen (Minskoff & Allsopp, 2003).

CALL UP   *CALL UP* is a research-based strategy for taking lecture notes. It has the following steps (Czarnecki, Rosko, & Fine, 1998):

C *Copy* from the board or PowerPoint.
A *Add* details.
L *Listen* and write the question.
L *Listen* and write the answer.
U *Utilize* the text.
P *Put* in your own words.

When copying from the board, a transparency, or a PowerPoint slide, students listen and look for cue words and phrases that identify main ideas, copy them down in the margin, and underline them. Students also listen for details, writing them 1 inch from the margin with a dash (—) in front of each detail. Students listen for teacher or student questions that they think can inform their understanding and write them, indented, under the appropriate main ideas. Students also record answers under the main ideas. The last two steps can be carried out at home or in study hall. Students first read about the main ideas in their textbooks and then paraphrase the information under each main idea in a space previously left blank. Students record relevant text pages in the margins so they can refer to the text at a later time if needed. Try posting the CALL UP steps prominently in your classroom. As you lecture, model the various steps while explicitly telling your students which steps you are performing and why. For example, Mr. Sauter was lecturing his class on the topic of the respiratory system. He wrote *respiratory system* on the board and directed his students to write down this main idea of the lecture. He then told them to add the details of the parts of the respiratory system (for example, *nose, lungs, mouth,* and *windpipe*) to their notes. Mr. Sauter posed important questions as he lectured such as "What is the purpose of the bronchial tubes?" He directed students to copy down these questions as he raised them. Finally, Mr. Sauter asked students to answer all questions raised for homework.

Of course, to learn this or any other note-taking strategy, students need the preskill of being able to tell the difference between main ideas and details. Some students choose key words that represent main ideas, but others attempt to write down everything and should be taught directly how to differentiate main ideas and details. For example, Mr. Abeles discovered that many students in his world history class were unable to identify the main ideas in his lectures. First, he explained the difference between main ideas and details: A *main idea* is what a whole section or passage is about; a *detail* is what just one part of a section or passage is about. For several weeks he stopped after presenting a section of material and put three pieces of information on the board—one main idea and two details. He asked the students which was the main idea and why. When his students were doing well at these tasks, Mr. Abeles had them write their own main ideas for a section of a lecture, which were shared with the class, and then he provided corrective feedback as necessary.

Writing Strategies

Another area that requires student independence is writing and proofreading papers. Several research-based strategies are useful to help students in this area.

POWER   One strategy that helps students organize all the steps in the writing process is called *POWER* (Englert et al., 1988). The process involves the use of self-questioning, graphic organizers, and peer editing using the following steps:

P	*Planning*
O	*Organizing*
W	*Writing*
E	*Editing*
R	*Revising*

The POWER strategy teaches students four different organizational structures for writing papers: stories, comparison/contrast, explanations, and problem/solution (Englert et al., 1988). When writing stories, students use key story elements—Who? When? Where? What happened? How did it end?—to organize their papers. A comparison/contrast structure includes information on what subjects are being compared (for example, atoms and molecules), on what characteristic of those subjects is being compared (size), and on how the subjects are alike and/or different in relation to that characteristic (atoms are the smallest particles; molecules are composed of two or more atoms). Explanations involve telling how to do something, such as explaining the steps in changing a tire. In a problem/solution structure, a problem is identified (for example, it took too long to travel from the East to the West in the early 1800s in the United States), the cause of the problem is explained (the only way to go from the East to the West was by stagecoach), and the solution is stated (the transcontinental railroad was built).

For the *planning* stage, students focus on the audience for the paper, the purpose, and the background knowledge that is necessary to write the paper. In the *organizing* step, students decide which organizational pattern fits their paper (for example, story, comparison/contrast) and then complete a pattern guide to help them organize their ideas. A **pattern guide** is a graphic organizer designed to help students organize their papers. A sample pattern guide for a comparison/contrast paper is shown in Figure 10.6. Notice that the words not in boxes—*Both same, In contrast to, Similarly,* and *However*—are key words frequently used when making comparisons. These words help students make the transition to writing sentences. For example, in Figure 10.6, two kinds of pizza are being compared and contrasted. The student might write, "The crusts of deep dish and regular pizza are the same in that they both are made of white flour. This is in contrast to their thickness; deep dish pizza crust is much thicker."

In the *writing* stage, the teacher demonstrates and thinks aloud to show students how to take the information gathered in the planning and organizing steps and produce a first draft. For example, you can compose an essay comparing two kinds of pizza using an overhead projector, thinking out loud as you write. You can involve students by asking questions such as, "What would a good topic sentence be? Is this a good example? How do you think I should end this? Why?" You could also have students write the paper along with you.

The *editing* step teaches students to critique their own writing and to identify areas in which they need clarification or assistance, an important self-evaluation skill. Editing is a two-step process involving student self-evaluation and peer editing. For self-evaluation, students reread and evaluate their drafts, starring sections of the

www.resources

Your students can research their papers more independently by accessing Kids Web (http://www.npac.syr.edu/), a digital library specifically designed for children.

FIGURE 10.6 Pattern Guide for Comparison/Contrast Paper

Compare/Contrast

What is being compared and contrasted?

Deep dish pizza and regular pizza

On what characteristics?

Crust

Both same | Alike? White flour | Different? Deep dish is thicker | In contrast to

On what characteristics?

Similarly | Alike? | Different? | However

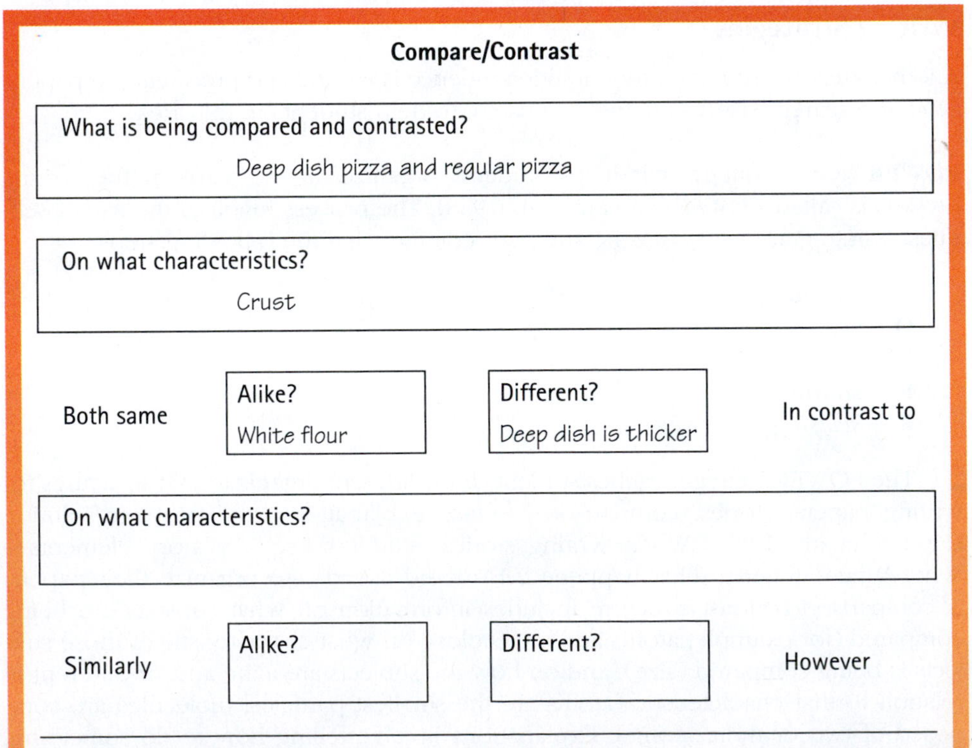

Source: From "A Case for Writing Intervention: Strategies for Writing Informational Text," by C. S. Englert, T. E. Raphael, L. M. Anderson, H. M. Anthony, K. L. Fear, and S. L. Gregg, 1988, *Learning Disability Quarterly, 3*(2), p. 108. Reprinted with permission.

paper they like best and putting question marks in the margins beside passages they think may be unclear. Finally, students think of two questions to ask their peer editors. For example, Jorge asked his peer editor whether he had used capital letters and punctuation correctly. He was also concerned about whether his paper was long enough and asked for suggestions on how to add information.

For **peer editing,** several steps are followed. First, the writer reads the paper to a peer editor while the editor listens. The peer editor then summarizes the paper. Next, the editor evaluates the paper, sharing with the writer an analysis of salient features of the writing that might guide a revision or lead to improvement. For example, the peer editor might suggest that the writer add key words or reorganize the paper for clarity. Then the peer editor and the writer brainstorm ways to improve the paper.

A research-based strategy called *TAG* also can help students with the peer-editing process (Carlson & Henning, 1993; MacArthur & Stoddard, 1990). The TAG strategy involves three simple steps:

T   *Tell* what you like.
A   *Ask* questions.
G   *Give* suggestions.

As with all strategies, students need to be provided with models and guided practice for doing these steps prior to doing them independently. In the *revising* step, students decide on changes to be made using their self-evaluation marks and peer feedback. Englert et al. (1988) suggest that the teacher model how to insert or change the order of information, providing a rationale for any changes. All modifications are made directly on the first draft. Last, the teacher and student have a conference, and changes in writing mechanics are suggested. Following this conference, a final draft is composed on clean sheets of paper.

COPS   When students have to proofread their papers independently, they might use a strategy called *COPS* (Alley, 1988). In the COPS strategy, students question themselves as follows:

C   Have I *capitalized* the first word and proper nouns?
O   How is the *overall appearance* of my paper? Have I made any handwriting, margin, or messy errors?
P   Have I used end *punctuation,* commas, and semicolons carefully?
S   Do words look like they are *spelled* right? Can I sound them out or use the dictionary?

Although COPS has been shown to be effective, students need preskills to perform this strategy adequately. Before teaching COPS, consider the following questions: Can the students recognize misspelled words? Do the students know rules for using capital letters and punctuation? Can they apply these rules? Can the students use a dictionary? If the answer to any of these questions is no, teach these skills directly before teaching students the COPS strategy.

W-W-W What=2 How=2   This strategy was developed and researched by Harris, Graham, and Mason (2003) to help elementary-age students write stories:

W   *Who* is the main character?
W   *When* does the story take place?
W   *Where* does the story take place?
W   *What* does the main character do or want to do? What do other characters do?
W   *What* happens then? What happens with other characters?
H   *How* does the story end?
H   *How* does the main character feel? How do the other characters feel?

dimensions of DIVERSITY

Cohen and Riel (1989) studied the effects of writing for authentic audiences of peers from different cultures using the Internet. They found that essays written for distant peers were more explicit and detailed than essays written to be graded by their teachers.

INCLUDE

www.resources

Inspiration is a software program designed to help students plan and organize research projects through outlines and concept maps. For more information about this program, go to http://www.inspiration.com.

Students with weak writing skills and other language difficulties will require more support with the vocabulary and concepts. Their instruction can be differentiated by giving them more practice or by using a graphic organizer and picture cues, such as the one in Figure 10.7.

Report Writing   Report writing is something many students prefer to avoid, largely because they lack a systematic way of writing successfully. Graham, Harris, and MacArthur (2006) report success teaching students a six-step report-writing strategy originally developed by MacArthur et al. (1996). The steps in the strategy are as follow:

1. Choose a topic.
2. Brainstorm all you know and would like to know about the topic.
3. Organize your ideas by main points and details on a web-type graphic organizer, where main ideas and subordinate ideas are linked together through the use of lines and arrows.
4. Read to find new information and verify the accuracy of information already generated. (Add, delete, and modify items on the Web as necessary.)

FIGURE 10.7 **Practice Cue Cards for W-W-W What=2 HOW=2**

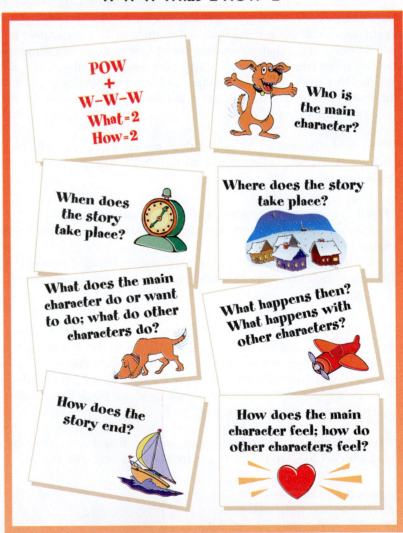

Source: Adapted from "Self-Regulated Strategy Development in the Classroom: Part of a Balanced Approach to Writing Instruction for Students with Disabilities," by K. R. Harris, S. Graham, and L. H. Mason, *Focus on Exceptional Children, 35*(7),1–17.

5. Write your report using the information you organized on the Web, but continue planning as you write.
6. Check to be sure you used everything you wanted from the Web (p. 291).

In Graham et al. (2006), the report-writing strategy was co-taught by general and special educators using many of the suggestions for teaching a learning strategy described earlier in the chapter. First, they clarified expectations by carefully describing the qualities of a good report and showing the students actual examples of well-written reports. Next the teachers encouraged students to memorize the strategy, and then the special education teacher demonstrated how to use the strategy while holding a running dialogue with herself. For example, to show the students how to keep themselves focused, she asked herself, "What do I need to do?" To show the students how to keep themselves on task, the teacher said to herself, "Keep going." To demonstrate how to self-monitor, the teacher said, "Does this part make sense?" To show students how to cope with frustration, she said, "I can do this."

For guided practice, the teachers differentiated instruction. The special education teacher co-wrote reports with some of the students with special needs in a small group, while the general education teacher worked with the remainder of the class in a large group, providing reduced support. Once students were writing independently, the teachers required them to reflect on what they were doing in a daily journal. Students were also reminded to continue to manage the writing process by talking to themselves. In all, it took the students six weeks to master the report-writing strategy—time that the teachers felt was well spent, given the improvement in student reports that resulted.

Learning Spelling Words   A study strategy can help students learn unknown spelling words (Graham & Freeman, 1986). Students are required to carry out the following five steps:

1. Say the word.
2. Write and say the word.
3. Check the word.
4. Trace and say the word.
5. Write the word from memory and check your spelling.

If students misspell the word in step 5, they need to repeat all five steps.

Strategies for Using Technology to Improve Student Writing

Revising Essays   This strategy uses a word processor for revising essays (Graham & Harris, 1987). Students instruct themselves using the following six steps:

1. Read your essay.
2. Find the sentence that tells you what you believe—is it clear?
3. Add two reasons why you believe it.
4. SCAN each sentence:

   S   Does it make *sense?*
   C   Is it *connected* to your belief?
   A   Can you *add* more?
   N   *Note* errors.

5. Make changes on the computer.
6. Reread your essay and make final changes.

Using Spell Checkers Effectively   Spell checkers can help students identify misspelled words and correct them. However, one problem with spell checkers is that the correctly spelled version of a word that the student is attempting to write

fyi

You can see a writing strategy co-taught in a videotape published by the Association of Supervision and Curriculum Development (Alexandria, Virginia) titled *Teaching Students with Learning Disabilities: Using Learning Strategies* (2002).

www.resources

The Write Site (http://www.writesite.org) allows students to take on the roles of journalists and editors to research, write, and publish their own newspaper. The site provides unit outlines, handouts, exercises, downloadable teaching materials, information about how to write, and more.

is not always presented as an alternative. This happens when the combination of letters that the student has typed does not approximate closely enough the intended word for the software to offer the needed choices. Because the correct word does not appear on the first attempt, students often click on "Go to Next Word" or "Skip Word" without making a change. The result can be a paper with many misspelled words.

Ashton (1999) describes the *CHECK* strategy, a sequence of steps designed to help students use any spell checker more effectively. The sequence of steps in the strategy is as follows:

C **Check** *the beginning sounds.* Most spell checkers search for similar words beginning with the same letter as the word typed. Therefore, the correctly spelled version of the word is more likely to appear when at least the first letter is correct. For this step, students check the beginning sound of the word and ask themselves what other letter could make that beginning sound. For example, if the student is attempting to spell the word *elephant* but has begun the word with *ul,* teach him or her to ask what other letter(s) make that beginning sound.

H **Hunt for** *the correct consonants.* If trying a new beginning sound does not help, have students change other consonants in the word. Ashton (1999, p. 26) tells of a boy who was writing about Egypt and wanted to use the word *pyramid.* His first spelling attempt was *perament,* but the only suggested word was *per.* The boy continued to sound out the word and changed the spelling to *peramed.* This still did not produce the word he was looking for, so he changed his spelling again to *peramid. Pyramid* then appeared in the suggested word list, and the student recognized it as being the correct spelling.

E **Examine** *the vowels.* Selecting the correct vowel when spelling is especially difficult because vowels make so many sounds. Spell checkers can help students figure out which sound to use for a particular vowel or vowel combination. For example, a student spelled the place where she ate lunch as *cafitirea.* After substituting other possible vowels in the word, she came close enough to the actual spelling to elicit the word *cafeteria* on the suggested list.

C **Changes** *in word lists give hints.* Sometimes students can use words in the suggested word list to find the correct spelling. For example, a student trying to spell the word *favorite* first tried *fovoriute.* When this spelling did not produce the correct alternative, she changed her original spelling to *foariute,* then *fovaritue,* then *favaritue.* After the last try, the word *favor* was given as a suggested spelling. Using that word, she typed *favorite,* which brought *favorite* to the list—the correct spelling, which she recognized.

K **Keep repeating** *steps 1 through 4.* The most important aspect of using this strategy effectively is to give it repeated chances, students trying as many different letter combinations as they can. However, at some point students may want to use another source, such as a dictionary, personalized word list (a continually updated list of words students have looked up before), classmate, teacher, or parent.

Strategies for Problem Solving in Math

Increasingly, teachers are focusing on problem solving as a major component of the math curriculum. This concentration is consistent with the math standards developed by the National Council of Teachers of Mathematics (2000) as well as the recommendations of the more recent report of the National Mathematics Advisory Panel (2008), which stress the importance of teaching problem solving. However, research indicates that if students with special needs are to become good problem solvers, they must be taught how to problem solve directly. A common (but by no means

PROFESSIONAL EDGE

The Key Word Strategy for Solving Math Word Problems: Is There a Better Way?

The key word strategy is an example of an ineffective strategy that many students with special needs use or are taught to use in solving math word problems (Kelly & Carnine, 1996). In this approach, students associate key words such as *more, in all, gave away,* and *left over* with certain mathematical operations. The key word strategy is attractive to teachers and students because sometimes it works. For example, the word *more* is commonly associated with subtraction, as in the following problem:

Jose has 15 cents. Carmen has 10 cents. How much *more* money does Jose have?

Unfortunately, many times the word *more* appears in word problems that call for addition, as in the following problem:

Charmaine had 15 cents. Her mother gave her 10 *more* cents. How many cents does she have now?

Kelly and Carnine (1996) suggest teaching students with special needs a more effective strategy for solving math word problems using problem maps and math fact families. Their strategy for teaching single-operation addition and subtraction problems follows:

For any addition/subtraction situation, there are two "small" numbers and a "big" number (the sum).

An addition/subtraction number family is mapped this way:

$$\xrightarrow{\quad 7 \quad 9 \quad} 16$$

The preceding family represents the following addition/subtraction facts:

$$7 + 9 = 16 \qquad 16 - 9 = 7$$
$$9 + 7 = 16 \qquad 16 - 7 = 9$$

A missing *big* number implies addition:

$$\xrightarrow{\quad 8 \quad 22 \quad} \square \qquad 8 + 22 = \square$$

A missing *small* number implies subtraction:

$$\xrightarrow{\quad \square \quad 22 \quad} 30 \qquad 30 - 22 = \square$$

or

$$\xrightarrow{\quad 8 \quad \square \quad} 30 \qquad 30 - 8 = \square$$

These maps can then be applied to a variety of addition and subtraction word problems. Kelly and Carnine (1996, p. 6) give the following example involving comparison problems:

In comparison problems, the difference between two values being compared may be information given in a problem (for example, Marco sold 57 fewer subscriptions than Lui) or the unknown in a problem (for example, How much heavier was Mary?). Because of the words *sold fewer* in the following problem, many students with LD will subtract.

Marco sold 57 fewer magazine subscriptions than Lui. Marco sold 112 subscriptions. How many subscriptions did Lui sell?

Students can use number families to avoid this confusion. The first step is to represent the problem using a number family; students must determine whether each of the two numbers given in the problem is a small number or the big number. The students are shown a simple way to do this:

They find the sentence that tells about the comparison and read it without the difference number. For example, students are taught to read the first sentence without the 57: "Marco sold fewer subscriptions than Lui." Because Marco sold fewer subscriptions, Marco is represented by a small number. By default, Lui is the big number. The students write M for Marco and L for Lui:

$$\xrightarrow{\qquad M \qquad} L$$

The word problem also gives a number for the difference between Marco and Lui. That number always has to be a small number. Marco sold 57 fewer, so 57 is the other small number:

$$\xrightarrow{\quad 57 \quad M \quad} L$$

Next, the students read the rest of the problem. The problem asks about Lui and gives a number for Marco, so the students draw a box around L and replace the M with 112:

$$\xrightarrow{\quad 57 \quad \overset{112}{\cancel{M}} \quad} L$$

Because the problem gives both small numbers, the students write an addition problem.

$$\begin{array}{r} 57 \\ +112 \\ \hline \end{array}$$

The answer tells how many magazine subscriptions Lui sold.

Stein, Kinder, Silbert, and Carnine (2005) and Seethaler, Powell, and Fuchs (2010) offer similar word problem strategies as applied to multiplication, division, and multistep word problems.

Source: Excerpt from "The 'Key Word' Strategy for Solving Math Story Problems," by B. Kelly and D. Carnine, 1996, reprinted by permission of Council for Learning Disabilities.

fyi

See Seethaler, Powell, and Fuchs (2010) to learn about PIRATES, a research-based strategy for solving word problems.

the only) way to introduce problem solving to students in a classroom context is through word problems. An effective technique for teaching word problems for students with special needs is presented in the Professional Edge on page 327.

STAR The *STAR* strategy has been used successfully to teach older students with disabilities to solve math problems, including algebra (Gagnon & Maccini, 2001, p. 10). It consists of the following steps:

S *Search* the word problem, reading the problem carefully and writing down knowns or facts.

T *Translate* the word problem into an equation in picture form by choosing a variable, identifying the operation, and representing the problem through manipulatives or picture form.

A *Answer* the problem.

R *Review* the solution by rereading the problem and checking the reasonableness of the answer.

Examples of how STAR can be used to solve division problems with integers are shown in Figure 10.8.

FIGURE 10.8 Using the STAR Strategy to Solve Division Problems with Integers

Sample problem: Suppose the temperature changed by an average of –2°F per hour. The total temperature change was –16°F. How many hours did it take for the temperature to change?

Phase of Instruction

⭐ **Star Strategy**

1. Concrete Application

Students use blocks to represent the problem. General guidelines: inverse operation of multiplication.

Algebra tiles: ▪ = 1 unit

Prompts students to:

Search problem (read carefully, ask questions, write down facts); translate the problem using blocks; answer the problem using the tiles; and review the solution (reread the problem, check reasonableness and calculations).

1)
Students begin with no tiles on the workmat.

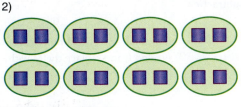

2)

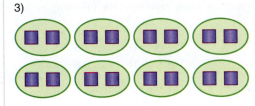

3)

a. Count the number of sets of –2 needed to obtain –16.

b. Students add 8 sets.

c. Students count the number of sets needed (8).

2. Semiconcrete Application

Students draw pictures of the representations.

Prompts students to:

Search problem (read carefully, ask questions, write down facts); translate (represent) the problem via drawings and write down the equation; answer the problem using drawings and write the answer; and review the solution (reread the problem, check reasonableness and calculations).

3. Abstract Application

Students first write numerical representations:

$-16 \div 2 = x$, apply the rule for dividing integers to obtain $x = +8$, and reread and check the answer.

Prompts students to:

Search problem (read carefully, ask questions, write down facts); translate the problem into an equation; answer the problem (apply the rule for division integers); and review the solution (reread the problem, check reasonableness and calculations).

Source: "Preparing Students with Disabilities for Algebra," by J. C. Gagnon and P. Maccini, 2001, *Teaching Exceptional Children, 34*(1), 8–15. Copyright 2001 by the Council for Exceptional Children Reprinted with permission.

Note how the teacher moves students beyond the concrete application phase and into semiconcrete and abstract phases. For example, she starts with blocks (concrete) and moves to pictures (semiconcrete) and then to numerals (abstract). Moving students beyond concrete representations is important for students with special needs, because if they are to become independent learners, they must be able to work at an abstract level. While these students benefit from working with manipulatives and other concrete representations, teachers must make sure to move them to more abstract levels as soon as they are able.

LAMPS   The *LAMPS* strategy (Reetz & Rasmussen, 1988) can be used as an aid to help remember the steps in regrouping or carrying in addition:

L   *Line up* the numbers according to their decimal points.
A   *Add* the right column of numbers and ask . . .
M   "*More* than 9?" If so, continue to the next step.
P   *Put* the 1s below the column.
S   *Send* the 10s to the top of the next column.

SLOBS   To help with borrowing in subtraction, teach students to follow the steps in the *SLOBS* strategy (Reetz & Rasmussen, 1988):

S   *Smaller:* Follow steps.
L   *Larger:* Leap to subtract.
O   *Cross off* the number in the next column.
B   *Borrow* by taking one 10 and adding to the next column.
S   *Subtract.*

For the problem

$$\begin{array}{r} 72 \\ -46 \\ \hline \end{array}$$

students look at the top number on the right to see whether it is smaller or larger than the bottom right number. If it is smaller, the students follow the rest of the steps. They cross off the number in the next column to the left to borrow one unit from that column (reducing that number by one) and add it to the other column. In the problem shown, they borrow 10 from the left column and then subtract. If the number is larger, students proceed directly to the subtract step. They repeat the steps if more digits are to be subtracted.

FOIL   The *FOIL* strategy (Crawford, 1980) helps prevent algebra students from missing one of the four products needed to calculate multiplication of a binomial by another binomial. Students follow these four steps:

F   Multiply *first* terms.
O   Multiply *outermost* terms.
I   Multiply *innermost* terms.
L   Multiply *last* terms.

For example, the FOIL strategy can be applied to the following problem:

$$(x + 4)(x + 3)$$
$$A \quad B \quad C \quad D$$

In the **F** step, the student multiplies the first two factors in each binomial, $x \times x = x^2$, or using the letters, *AC*. Next, in the **O** step, the student multiplies the first factor in the first binomial and the second factor in the second binomial, $x \times 3 = 3x$, or *AD*. Then, in the **I** step, the student multiplies the second factor of the first binomial and the first factor of the second binomial, $4 \times x = 4x$, or *BC*. Finally, in the **L** step, the second factors of both binomials are multiplied: $4 \times 3 = 12$, or *BD*. This strategy applies only to the special case of multiplying two binomials.

RESEARCH NOTE

Fuchs et al. (2008) identified seven evidence-based principles of effective instruction for students with math disabilities: instructional explicitness, instructional design to minimize the learning challenge, strong conceptual basis, drill and practice, cumulative review, motivators to help students regulate their attention and behavior to work hard, and ongoing progress monitoring.

Strategies for Managing Time and Resources

A lack of organization is a common characteristic of students with disabilities (Lerner & Johns, 2009; Silver, 2006), as is true for Ron, one of the students introduced at the beginning of the chapter. Organizing study materials involves having the appropriate school supplies, making sure these supplies are brought to class when they are needed, and having an organized notebook to ensure easy access to information. First, you can make sure that students obtain the appropriate school supplies by requiring that they tell their parents what materials they need daily, because you will not be able to call each of their parents individually each day to remind them. In many cases, teachers tell their students what to bring and assume that the students will do the rest on their own. However, this method may not be structured enough for some students who, like Ron, are likely to forget what you said.

Second, you can encourage students to write the information down rather than try to remember it. Having the information on the board or projected helps ensure that their lists are accurate. You may also want to duplicate the list and distribute it to students who cannot easily write it themselves.

Finally, encourage your students to ask themselves the following or similar questions, which can help them remember school supplies as well as assignments throughout the school year:

- What is due tomorrow in school?
- What do I need to do to get it done tonight?
- What materials or other things do I need to get the job done?
- Whom can I ask for help in doing this?

These questions can at first be posted on the board to help students remember them and to prompt their use. You can help motivate students to bring needed materials by providing positive recognition for those who do bring their supplies to school. For example, Mr. Gutierrez gave school pencils to students who had all their supplies in school. Ms. Habner put the names of her students on a "responsible students" list, from which she chose people for classroom jobs.

You may need to make accommodations for students with special needs. For example, students with complex physical disabilities may need a classmate or parent

Strategies for managing time and organizing materials help provide the structured routines that many students need to succeed in school. What are the three steps in teaching students how to use weekly assignment calendars?

to carry their supplies into school. Students who live in poverty might be unable to afford supplies other than materials the school or teacher provides.

Besides having to organize their materials, students also need to organize their time, particularly as they get older and the demands made on their time increase. More schools are teaching students to use schedule books to help them arrange their time (Bryan, Burstein, & Bryan, 2001; Jenson, Sheridan, Olympia, & Andrews, 1994; Patton, 1994). Anderson, Munk, Young, Conley, & Caldarella (2008) developed an organizational skills form for this purpose. A sample form is shown in Figure 10.9. Students are taught to use one form for each of their classes using these steps.

- Students organize their notebooks by inserting divider tabs and blank notebook paper for each class.
- Students are introduced to the activity forms for each class and given a rationale for their use such as: "These will help you get your work done on time and get better grades."

www.resources

TimeLiner is a software program designed to help students organize information for research projects using a timeline. For more information, go to http://www.teachtsp.com.

FIGURE 10.9 Organizational Skills Form

Student Name _____ Subject_____ Week _____ Term _____

Day/ Date	On time or Absent (Step 3)	*Prepared (Step 3)	**Tests and/or Assignments (Steps 4 and 5)	*** ✓ = "Completed" and Turned in (Step 6)	% Correct (Teacher) (Step 7)	Components Complete (Step 8)
MON	OT	Binder				
		Pencil				
		Pouch				
	A	Form	---------------			
		Labels				
		Paper				
		Correct sections				
Tue	OT	Binder				
		Pencil				
		Pouch				
	A	Form	---------------			
		Labels				
		Paper				
		Correct sections				

*Prepared	**Tests and Assignments	***Turned In
1. Binder	W = worksheet, assignments listed	Check mark (✓) = assignment handed to teacher
2. Pencil daily in class	T = test, tests listed	Estimated grade for this term _____
3. Form for the week	V = video	I could improve my grade by:
4. Divider labels for each subject	L = lecture	
5. Paper, 5 sheets behind each label	N/A = nothing due	
6. Papers in correct sections		
7. Pencil pouch		

- Students begin to use the form by self-recording in column 2 whether they have the necessary materials for class by turning the terms in column 3 into self-questions such as, "Do I have a pencil?" or "Are the papers for this class in the right section of my binder?"
- Students record their assignments for the day; if there are no written assignments, using a code, they record what was covered in class that day such as a "V" for video, "L" for lecture, etc.
- Students check whether the assignment was completed and turned in, thus providing themselves with self-reinforcement for finishing the assignment. The teacher can initial students' boxes when work is turned in to provide additional accountability.
- Students record their scores on the assignment, thus providing themselves with written records of their grades so there are no surprises at the end of the grading period.
- Students record the number of items completed. This helps the teacher monitor students' use of the form, and the students self-monitor their performance.

How Can Students Learn to Use Strategies Independently?

Some students may have trouble using a learning strategy independently, even after they have learned how to do it. Their problem could be that they do not know when to use a strategy or how to keep track of how well they are using it, and how to change their behavior, if necessary.

Three strategies that can help students perform tasks more independently are self-instruction, self-monitoring, and self-questioning. Like all learning strategies, these "self" strategies may need to be carefully taught using the teaching practices described in this chapter.

Self-Instruction

In **self-instruction,** learners are taught to use language to guide their performance. In essence, students are taught to talk themselves through a task. The idea is that if they can talk themselves through a task, they will not need help from anyone else. Self-instruction has been successfully used to teach students with disabilities strategies for math, test taking, reading comprehension, and writing (Uberti, Mastropieri, & Scruggs, 2004).

The first step to teach students self-instruction techniques is to explain that self-instruction involves giving oneself directions on how to do a task. For example, self-instruction can be used to help get seatwork done or to remember to use a strategy for a multiple-choice test. Next, ask students to identify a situation that requires the use of a specific skill, such as getting their seatwork done in reading or taking a 10-minute science quiz on Friday. Demonstrate how to write down the steps needed to perform that task. For example, to get independent classwork done, the student first decides how much effort to put into this task. Next, he or she decides what is supposed to be done. Finally, the student decides what the first step in completing the task should be, what the next step should be, and so forth, until the assignment is done. When students are finished, they praise themselves for a job well done. Ask students to rehearse the steps through self-talk or peer review, going over all the steps involved in completing a written classwork task from beginning to end.

After you have demonstrated how to apply self-instruction, have the students practice in a role-play situation, and give them feedback. In the independent classwork task, for example, you could project a sample reading task and demonstrate the steps by thinking out loud. The students could then practice in pairs and give

FIGURE 10.10 Sample Reading Strategies Notebook

Alonzo's Reading Strategies Notebook
Table of Contents

	Page
Identifying hard words	
Using word parts	3
Reading fluency	
WARF	4
Reading comprehension	
SCROL	5
Highlight It!	6
Mark It!	7

Source: Adapted from "Supporting Self-Regulated Learning with Exceptional Children," by J. J. Wery and J. L. Niefield. *Teaching Exceptional Children, 42*(4), 70–78.

each other feedback, with you monitoring and also giving feedback. Even after all of this careful instruction, students still can forget the purpose of certain strategies, forget to use the strategies, or not understand when and where to use the strategies. Wery and Niefield (2010) developed the form shown in Figure 10.10 to guide students as they try to independently use learning strategies they have been taught to perform in class.

Self-Monitoring

In **self-monitoring,** students watch and check themselves to make sure they have performed targeted behaviors. Self-monitoring has been shown to be effective in making positive changes in the academic and social behavior of students with disabilities (Daly & Ranalli, 2003). It is a critical aspect of independent learning, which often requires students to check their performance to see whether it is effective and make a change when a particular strategy is not working (Hallahan et al., 2005; Reid, 1996). Self-monitoring also can be a strong motivator for students by providing them concrete evidence of their progress.

In teaching self-monitoring to your students, first explain to them that it is a way they can check their own behavior to make sure they are doing the right thing. Ask the students to identify a learning strategy they need to use in class. For example, students may select a strategy such as the COPS proofreading strategy described earlier in the chapter.

The next step is to select a practical and expedient way for students to measure the behavior. One possibility is to have them use a checklist of strategy steps and then record the percentage of steps completed. For example, Yashika recorded the steps of the SCROL strategy he completed when reading a section in his science text.

Teach students to use the measurement system through demonstration, practice, and feedback, and continue to encourage and reinforce the use of self-monitoring in your class. Self-monitoring can be applied to any learning strategy.

Self-Questioning

Self-questioning is a form of self-instruction in which students guide their performance by asking themselves questions. The idea behind self-questioning is that if students can guide their own behavior by asking themselves questions, then they will not always need a teacher or other adult present to perform.

Brimijoin et al. (2003) report a teacher using a car windshield metaphor to teach students to monitor their understanding. The teacher asked, "How many [of you] are clear as glass about how greatest common factor works? How many have bugs on your windshields? How many have windshields covered with mud?" (p. 70).

RESEARCH NOTE

Wehmeyer et al. (2003) studied the use of self-monitoring with students with developmental and intellectual disabilities. They found that the use of "self" strategies improved the students' class participation and decreased their rate of problem behaviors.

Math-Problem Solving

Read (for understanding)

Say:	Read the problem. If I don't understand it, read it again.
Ask:	Have I read and understood the problem?
Check:	For understanding as I solve the problem.

Paraphrase (in your own words)

Say:	Underline the important information.
	Put the problem in my own words.
Ask:	Have I underlined the important information?
	What is the question? What am I looking for?
Check:	That the information goes with the question.

Visualize (a picture or a diagram)

Say:	Make a drawing or a diagram.
Ask:	Does the picture fit the problem?
Check:	The picture against the problem information.

Hypothesize (a plan to solve the problem)

Say:	Decide how many steps and operations are needed.
	Write the operations symbols $(+, -, \times, \div)$
Ask:	If I do . . . , what will I get?
	If I do . . . , then what do I need to do next?
	How many steps are needed?
Check:	That the plan makes sense.

Estimate (predict the answer)

Say:	Round the numbers, do the problem in my head, and write the estimate.
Ask:	Did I round up and down?
	Did I write the estimate?
Check:	That I use the important information.

Compute (do the arithmetic)

Say:	Do the operations in the right order.
Ask:	How does my answer compare with my estimate?
	Does my answer make sense?
	Are the decimals or money signs in the right places?
Check:	That all the operations are done in the right order.

Check (make sure everything is right)

Say:	Check the computation.
Ask:	Have I checked every step?
	Have I checked the computation?
	Is my answer right?
Check:	That everything is right. If not, go back.
	Then ask for help if I need it.

Source: From "Solve It! Strategy Instruction to Improve Mathematical Problem Solving," by M. Montague, C. Warger, and T. H. Morgan, 2000, *Learning Disabilities: Research and Practice,* *15*(2), pp. 110–116. Reprinted by permission of Blackwell Publishing.

In teaching students self-questioning, have them first identify the duties or tasks that are required in class. For example, students can identify steps needed to proofread a written paper, such as checking the correct use of capital letters, punctuation, spelling, and appearance. Have students write these tasks in question form, asking, for example, "Have I capitalized all words correctly? Have I used the right punctuation marks in the right places? Have I spelled all the words correctly? Is my paper neat?"

As in self-monitoring, the next step is to select a practical and expedient way for students to measure the behavior, such as recording behaviors as they occur using a checklist. Students might practice self-questioning in pairs for feedback. Other practical measures include keeping task questions on index cards and putting them in a convenient place. For example, students might put the proofreading questions on an index card and tape it to the inside cover of their notebooks. Recall that in the classroom organization form just described, students were taught to use self-questioning to prompt themselves about whether they had the necessary materials for class.

Montague, Warger, and Morgan (2000) taught students with disabilities to solve math word problems using a strategy that included elements of self-instruction, self-monitoring, and self-questioning. The strategy is shown in Figure 10.11.

WRAPPING IT UP
BACK TO THE CASES

This section provides opportunities for you to apply the knowledge gained in this chapter to the cases described at the beginning of this chapter. The questions and activities that follow demonstrate how these principles, along with other concepts that you have learned about in this chapter, connect to the everyday activities of all teachers.

GERALD has problems in written expression including organization and mechanical errors. Mr. McCrae has determined that organization is most important, because the mechanical errors can be corrected after Gerald has produced an organized written product. Mr. McCrae has selected the POWER strategy to teach Gerald. You are interested in applying this strategy in your teaching, so you work with Mr. McCrae to develop a script for teaching it. (See the Case in Practice "Teaching Script for Demonstrating POSSE" on page 318 for a sample script.) In the planning portion of POWER, you may want to consider an editing strategy such as COPS and a graphic organizer from Chapter 9. After you have written your script, compare scripts with a peer partner from your class.

TRACI, as you may recall, struggled with solving word problems. After helping her with a strategy for solving such problems, Ms. Cord reflects on Traci's skills in other academic areas. Traci often cannot answer comprehension questions regarding main ideas and details in short passages of text or storybooks. Ms. McCord wonders whether Traci's difficulties in reading might be similar to the ones she experienced in word problems. What do you think? Explain your thinking. Suppose that she does discover that the difficulties are similar. What strategies would you teach Traci that would be useful for reading word problems? Provide a reason for each of your choices.

RON often came unprepared to class. However, after several weeks of his teachers working with him, he now is coming to class with all of the books and materials he needs. In fact, he completed his homework assignments every day this week. He is proud that he has been remembering to check his schedule book and the checklist in his locker. However, he still experiences difficulty getting to school and work on time, and on four days last week, he missed the bus that takes him home. After deciding that the next step is to teach Ron to use self-instruction and self-monitoring strategies for the home and work situations, you have learned about a website (http://coe.jmu.edu/Learningtoolbox/index .html) where you can find a strategy that will help Ron manage time when he is away from the school environment. Once you are at this website, enter as a teacher and select the "Strategy List" from the column on the left. Select two strategies that you think will work for Ron and share your choices with two peers. After all of you have shared your strategies and the reasons for your choices, select two you would present to Ron so that he can choose the one he wants to use.

SUMMARY

- General education teachers can help all their students, including students with disabilities and other special needs, become independent learners. One way teachers can build student independence is to encourage student self-awareness, self-advocacy, and self-determination.

- Another way to help your students become more independent is to design and teach effective learning strategies in class. Methods of teaching learning strategies to students include assessing current strategy use, clarifying expectations, demonstrating strategy use, encouraging students to memorize strategy steps,

providing guided and independent practice, and administering posttests.

- Many successful strategies that can help students become independent learners are available in the areas of reading and reading comprehension, listening and note taking, writing, problem solving in math, and managing time and resources.

- Three strategies that can help students learn to use learning strategies independently are self-instruction, self-monitoring, and self-questioning.

APPLICATIONS IN TEACHING PRACTICE

DESIGNING STRATEGIES FOR INDEPENDENCE

Latasha is a student who has a moderate hearing loss. Although her hearing aid helps, she still has to depend on speech reading to communicate. She also speaks slowly and has trouble saying high-frequency sounds such as *sh* and *t*. Latasha has a poor self-image and is reluctant to interact with her peers and teachers. Design a self-advocacy program for Latasha.

QUESTIONS

1. What skills would you teach Latasha to use for self-advocacy?
2. How would you get Latasha to use these skills in your class and in other in-school and out-of-school situations?

Cal is a student with organizational problems; he is chronically late for class and rarely finishes his homework. Design an organizational strategy for Cal using the guidelines for developing strategies covered in this chapter.

QUESTIONS

1. How would you teach the organizational strategy you have designed using the guidelines covered in this chapter for effectively teaching a learning strategy?
2. How would you teach Cal to apply the strategy independently using self-instruction? Self-monitoring? Self-questioning?

Evaluate the design of any one of the learning strategies in the chapter using the guideline in the Professional Edge on page 308.

QUESTIONS

1. Is there anything you would change about the strategy? How would you teach the strategy using the six steps described in this chapter?
2. How would you help students apply the strategy independently using the three "self" strategies discussed in this chapter?

Go to Topics 10: Instructional Practices and Learning Strategies, 11: Reading Instruction, and 12: Content Area Teaching in the MyEducationLab (www.myeducationlab.com) for your course, where you can:

- Find learning outcomes for Instructional Practices and Learning Strategies, Reading Instruction, and Content Area Teaching along with the national standards that connect to these outcomes.
- Complete Assignments and Activities that can help you more deeply understand the chapter content.
- Apply and practice your understanding of the core teaching skills identified in the chapter with the Building Teaching Skills and Dispositions learning units.
- Examine challenging situations and cases presented in the IRIS Center Resources. (optional)
- Access video clips of CCSSO National Teachers of the Year award winners responding to the question, "Why Do I Teach?" in the Teacher Talk section. (optional)
- Check your comprehension on the content covered in the chapter by going to the Study Plan in the Book Resources for your text. Here you will be able to take a chapter quiz, receive feedback on your answers, and then access Review, Practice, and Enrichment activities to enhance your understanding of chapter content. (optional)

chapter

11

Evaluating Student Learning

LEARNING Objectives

After you read this chapter, you will be able to

1. Identify and describe accommodations that can be made before, during, and after testing students with special needs.
2. Describe grading practices that can benefit all of your students.
3. Explain how accommodations in report card grading can be made for students with special needs.
4. Explain the potential benefits of using performance-based and portfolio assessments with students with disabilities, including accommodations that may need to be made.

STACI is a student in Ms. Stevens's earth science class. Staci has a learning disability that causes her to have trouble reading textbooks. Staci also has difficulty figuring out multiple-choice test questions, the kind that Ms. Stevens uses on her exams and quizzes. Staci says that she knows the material but just needs more time to take the tests because she reads slowly. During the past marking period, Ms. Stevens gave four multiple-choice tests, each worth 20 percent of the final grade. Scores on homework assignments counted for the remaining 20 percent. Staci earned a grade of B on her homework, but she had two Ds, one C, and one F on the tests. Ms. Stevens assigned her a grade of D for the marking period. Ms. Stevens felt this was a fair grade because most of Staci's peers scored much higher on the tests. Ms. Stevens is also committed to keeping her reputation as a teacher with high standards. When Staci received her grade for the marking period, she asked her parents why she should work so hard when she couldn't seem to get good grades anyway. Staci's parents felt that she had improved during the last marking period but that her grade did not show it. They were afraid that Staci would stop trying and eventually drop out of school.

What testing and grading issues are evident here? How can Ms. Stevens accommodate Staci without lowering her standards?

JENNIFER is in Ms. Robinson's third-grade class. She has a hearing loss and has some trouble in reading but is doing well in Ms. Robinson's classroom reading program. Ms. Robinson is pleased with her progress and has given her As in reading for the first two grading periods. Recently, Jennifer's parents became very upset when they learned that Jennifer was reading only at the first-grade level according to district standardized tests. They wondered how she could have done so poorly on the standardized tests when she has been bringing home As on her report card.

What would you tell Jennifer's parents if she were in your class? How could you change your grading procedures to prevent communication problems like this from occurring?

LUCILLE is a student with a mild intellectual disability who is in Mr. Henry's fourth-grade math class. On the basis of her current performance in math, which is at the first-grade level, Lucille's individualized education program (IEP) team set math goals for her in the areas of basic addition and subtraction. The rest of the class is working on more difficult material based on the fourth-grade math standards. Lucille's IEP objective for the second marking period was to compute in writing, within 20 minutes, 20 two-digit by two-digit addition problems with regrouping with 80 percent accuracy. She received direct instruction on these problems from Mr. Brook, her special education teacher, who was co-teaching with Mr. Henry. As a result, she met her goal for the marking period.

School policy mandates letter grades. How should Mr. Henry grade Lucille?

PEARSON
myeducationlab

To check your comprehension on the content covered in Chapter 11, go to the Book Resources in the MyEducationLab for your course, select your text, and complete the Study Plan. Here you will be able to take a chapter quiz, receive feedback on your answers, and then access review, practice, and enrichment activities to enhance your understanding of chapter content.

While high-stakes tests have become the predominant method of evaluating student learning, teachers continue to play an important role. The information teachers collect during classroom evaluation activities can indicate whether their teaching has been effective and can help them alter instruction as needed. Classroom evaluations also are helpful in giving students (and their parents) an idea of how well they are performing in school.

Even though evaluation activities are very important, the ways in which students are evaluated most frequently—testing and grading—can be problematic for students with disabilities, their teachers, and their parents. For example, Staci and her earth science teacher have a problem because Staci's test scores more often reflect her learning disability than her knowledge of earth science. Jennifer's teacher has a problem in communicating the meaning of Jennifer's grades to her parents. She graded Jennifer based on Jennifer's progress and effort in class. Jennifer's parents, however, thought she was being graded in comparison with her peers and therefore expected their daughter to be performing at or above grade level, not below. Lucille's teacher needs to give Lucille a grade even though she has different curricular goals than the other students in the class. Further complicating these problems is the current climate of accountability and the related expectation that most students with disabilities will meet standards. This expectation makes it imperative that accommodations in evaluation be done without compromising students' ability to meet standards on high-stakes tests. As you work with students with disabilities or other special needs, you will experience these and other challenges in evaluating their learning. In this chapter, you learn a number of ways to address these dilemmas.

How Can Accommodations Be Made for Students with Special Needs When Giving Classroom Tests?

Although testing has always been a major part of U.S. education, the current emphasis on school reform, with its dominant theme of raising educational standards, promises to make educators rely even more on tests in the future (Koretz, 2008; Nolet & McLaughlin, 2005). This increasing emphasis on test performance focuses concerns about the test performance of students with disabilities. As described in the vignette about Staci at the beginning of this chapter, testing can be a very trying experience for many of these students and their families.

Most important in testing students with disabilities is ensuring that test results reflect their knowledge and skills, not their disabilities. Fortunately, classroom tests can be designed or modified in ways that help you test students with disabilities fairly and with a reasonable amount of accuracy. As shown in Table 11.1, accommodations for students with special needs can be made in three contexts: before the test, during the test administration, and after the test as part of the grading procedures. Many of these accommodations also can benefit students who do not have disabilities.

TABLE 11.1 Examples of Testing Accommodations

Before the Test	During the Test	After the Test
Study guide	Alternative forms of questions	Changed letter or number grades
Practice test	Alternative ways of administering tests	Changed grading criteria
Individual tutoring		Alternatives to letter and number grades
Teaching test-taking skills Modified test construction		

Accommodations Before the Test

You can do a number of things before a test to help students with disabilities. First, you can prepare a *study guide* that tells students what to study for the test. A study guide can help students avoid wasting valuable time studying everything indiscriminately and instead help them concentrate on the most important information. For example, Acrey, Johnstone, & Milligan (2005) suggest using a "countdown study guide." A week prior to the test, give students a blank one-week organizer with enough blank space for each day. At the beginning of each class have the students write down what they will do that day to prepare for the test. Roditi et al. (2005) recommend providing students with a list of the major topics to be covered on the exam along with four columns: (a) "I am missing this information; I need to get it," (b) "I don't know this," (c) "I remember this topic but need to read it over one more time," and (d) "I know this well enough to answer questions on a test." The columns help students decide how much time to spend on each topic included on the test (Lagares & Connor, 2010, p. 64).

Students can help each other prepare effectively for tests using directly taught study strategies. What strategies might these students be using to prepare for an upcoming test?

Second, you can give a *practice test*. This test can clarify your test expectations and also benefits the class by familiarizing students with the test format. Practice tests are also helpful to students who have trouble following directions and to those who are anxious about taking tests and often fail to cope immediately with an unfamiliar test format. Finally, many students with disabilities also benefit from *tutoring* before tests. Tutoring can be offered before or after school and may be carried out by peer tutors or paraprofessionals. Tutors can provide guidelines for what to study or can help directly with particularly difficult content.

Another option is to teach students *test-taking skills*. This option can help students take your classroom tests and state high-stakes tests as well. Students may need a number of test-taking skills, including ones for studying for tests, taking objective tests, and writing essay tests.

When studying for tests, students often are required to remember a lot of material. This can be difficult for students with learning or intellectual disabilities, who may have memory problems. Students can benefit from strategies that help them remember important content for tests. For example, Georgia uses a memorization technique called **chunking.** After she studies a chapter in her text, she tries to recall five to seven key ideas. These key thoughts help trigger her recall of more significant details. After reading a chapter about the life of Harriet Tubman, for example, she remembers information in chunks—Tubman's early years, her experiences with the underground railroad, and so on. These general ideas help her remember details such as when Harriet Tubman was born and how many slaves she helped to free.

Mnemonic devices also can help students remember information for tests. **Mnemonics** impose an order on information to be remembered using words, poems, rhymes, jingles, or images to aid memory. For example, Mr. Charles wants his class to remember the six methods of scientific investigation. He tells the students to think of the word *chrome* (Cermak, 1976). The following six steps make up the *CHROME* strategy:

C   Categorization
H   Hypothesis
R   Reasoning
O   Observation
M   Measurement
E   Experimentation

fyi

Planning tests and test accommodations at the beginning of instruction helps you clarify what is essential to teach and achieve a good match between your tests and instruction.

www.resources

The Study Guides and Strategies website (http://www.studygs.net) provides study guides as well as strategies for preparing for and taking tests. The site provides study skills resources including several links to study skills guides and interactive tutorials.

RESEARCH NOTE

Robinson et al. (1998) found that students who studied for tests using graphic organizers and delayed reviewing their notes by two days performed better on tests than students using traditional outlines who studied their notes immediately after recording them.

dimensions of DIVERSITY

Research shows that 5–14 hours of instruction in test wiseness spread over 5–7 weeks improves African-American, Hispanic, and Native American students' test scores (Casanova & Berliner, 1986; Grossman, 1995). Strategies for teaching test wiseness and other independent learning skills are covered in this chapter.

Another mnemonic device that can help students remember definitions and factual information is called the keyword method, not to be confused with the keyword method used to teach math word problems that was referred to in Chapter 10 (Mastropieri, 1988; Uberti, Scruggs, & Mastropieri, 2003). The **keyword method** uses visual imagery to make material more meaningful to students and hence easier to remember. First, a vocabulary word or fact is changed into a word that sounds similar and is easy to picture. For example, to help remember that the explorer Hernando de Soto came from Spain, students might be shown the picture in Figure 11.1, a bull (to symbolize Spain) at a counter sipping a soda (the keyword for *de Soto*) (Carney, Levin, & Levin, 1993). When students are asked to name an explorer who came from Spain, they are told to think of the keyword for de Soto. Next, they are told to think back to the picture the keyword was in and remember what was happening in the picture. Finally, they are told to answer the question. (Who was an explorer from Spain?)

Many students do poorly on tests because they do not study for tests systematically. Teach students to organize their materials so that they avoid wasting time searching for such items as notes for a particular class or the answers to textbook exercises. Making random checks of students' notebooks is one way to find out how well organized they are. For example, Ms. Barber stresses note taking in her fifth-grade social studies class. Every Friday afternoon, she checks the notebooks of five students. She gives students bonus points if they have notes for each day and if their notes are legible and include key information. Also teach students strategies for how to process material when they are studying. For example, Ms. Treacher shows her third graders a verbal **rehearsal strategy** for learning spelling words. She says the word, spells it out loud three times, covers the word, writes the word, and then compares her spelling to the correct spelling. Another effective rehearsal strategy is for students to ask themselves questions about the most important information to be learned.

Students, including those with special needs, may not test well because they lack strategies for actually taking the tests. For example, Sal rarely finishes tests in science because he spends too much time on questions that he finds difficult. Laura has trouble with true–false questions because she does not pay attention to key words such as *always, never, usually,* and *sometimes.* Lewis's answers to essay questions contain

FIGURE 11.1 Keyword for de Soto

Source: From "Mnemonic Strategies: Instructional Techniques Worth Remembering," by R. N. Carney, M. E. Levin, and J. R. Levin, 1993. *Teaching Exceptional Children, 25*(4), p.27. Reprinted by permission of the Council for Exceptional Children.

PROFESSIONAL **EDGE**

Teaching Test-Taking Strategies for Taking Objective Tests

You can help your students approach their objective tests more systematically by teaching them the following six rules for responding to multiple-choice and true–false items based on a comprehensive review of the research literature (Scruggs & Mastropieri, 1988):

1. *Respond to the test maker's intention.* Answers to test questions should take into account the way material is treated in class. For example, Rob had this item on his social studies test:
During the occupation of Boston, the British received their most severe losses at Bunker Hill.
True
False
Even though Rob had learned at a recent trip to the museum that the Battle of Bunker Hill was actually fought on Breed's Hill, his teacher had not brought up this point in class. Therefore, Rob responded by circling *true*.

2. *Anticipate the answer.* Before students attempt to answer the question, they should fully understand its meaning. Therefore, they should try to figure out the answer before they read the possible answers. For example, Armand was answering the following multiple-choice item:
What does an astronomer study?
a. plants
b. music
c. history
d. stars
After he read the question, Armand thought about the word *astronomy* and what his teacher had talked about in class, such as the fact that astronomers use telescopes and that they look at stars and planets. He then read all the possible choices and circled *d, stars,* as the correct answer.

3. *Consider all alternatives.* Many students with special needs, such as students with learning or intellectual disabilities or ADHD, tend to answer too quickly, choosing the first available choice. Students should be encouraged to read all the choices before responding. Students can monitor their behavior by putting a check mark next to each choice after they have read it.

4. *Use logical reasoning strategies to eliminate unlikely answers.* Even if students do not know the answer to a question, they can improve their chances of getting it right by using what knowledge they do have to eliminate unlikely choices. For example, Dolores read the following item:
In which country would it be impossible to use a sled in the winter?
a. Guatemala
b. Canada
c. Zimbabwe
d. Norway
Dolores did not know the geographical locations of Guatemala or Zimbabwe, but she did know that Canada and Norway were countries where it snowed often. She then took a guess between *a* and *c* and chose *a*, the correct answer. By eliminating two of the items, she improved her chance of getting the question right by 25 percent.

5. *Use time wisely.* As already mentioned, a frequent test-taking problem is failing to budget time. While taking tests, students should check the time periodically to make sure they have enough time left to answer the remaining questions. You can assist students by writing the time remaining on the chalkboard several times during the testing period or by displaying an electronic countdown timer. Students also can be taught to estimate the amount of time they should spend on each question. For example, if students are taking a 100-item test in a 50-minute period, they should figure on spending no more than one-half minute per question. After 25 minutes, they can then check to see that they have completed at least 50 items. Finally, teach students to spend more time on items on which they have at least partial knowledge and less time on questions for which they have no knowledge.

6. *Guess, if all else fails.* Most tests do not have a penalty for guessing. On standardized tests especially, tell your students that if they do not answer a question, they have no chance of getting it right, but if they guess, they have a 50 percent chance of getting true–false questions right and a 25 percent chance of getting most multiple-choice questions right.

STRATEGIES USING THINK-ALOUDS

Teaching test-taking strategies explicitly and systematically can help ensure students will be able to apply the strategies in completing actual classroom tests. Once you have selected a strategy aligned with your tests, show your students how to use it. Be sure your demonstration includes thinking aloud about what the strategy is, why it is important, and when and where to use it. Provide students with both guided and independent practice using the strategy and offer systematic corrections, as needed. Notice how the teacher in this example uses a think-aloud to teach the strategy of *anticipating the answer* that you just read about:

OK. The question is asking me what an astronomer studies. I'm going to try to figure out the answer before I even look at the choices, because that will make picking the right answer easier. This is helpful for Ms. Busey's tests because she always tests us on things she's talked about in class. So, let's see. What has Ms. Busey said in class about astronomy? Well, she's been telling us about how astronomers use these powerful telescopes to look at stars and planets. So the answer probably will have something to do with stars and planets. In looking at the possible answers, the choices of plants, music, and history don't make sense, but choice *d* is stars. That must be the right answer.

much irrelevant information and do not focus on what the questions are asking. The Professional Edge on page 343 offers suggestions for teaching students strategies for taking objective tests. These strategies work for taking high-stakes tests too.

Students also need strategies for taking essay tests. Performing well on essay tests requires that students know the content covered; can follow directions, including identifying and understanding key words; and can organize their ideas. All these areas can be problematic for students with disabilities. Thierreen, Hughes, Kapelski, and Mokhtari (2009) successfully taught seventh- and eighth-grade students with learning and writing disabilities to answer essay questions using the ANSWER strategy described here.

1. **A**nalyze the action words in the question by reading the question carefully and underlining the key words.
2. **N**otice the requirements of the question. Mark each and change the question into your own words.
3. **S**et up an outline listing your main ideas for the essay question.
4. **W**ork in detail by adding important details to the outline that you plan to include in your essay.
5. **E**ngineer your answer by writing your answer including an introductory sentence and detailed senetences about each of the main ideas in your outline.
6. **R**eview your answer by checking that all parts of the question have been answered and edit your essay. (p. 17)

All students benefit from tests that are written clearly and assess pertinent knowledge or skills. Thus, everything that you have learned about writing good tests in your teacher-education program applies here. Still, test items can be reasonably well written but constructed in a way that results in problems for students with special needs. When this situation occurs, *modified test construction* is necessary. For example, Carmen has difficulty reading tests that are visually cluttered. She might benefit from triple spacing between test items and extra space between lines. Juan scores poorly on tests because the items contain complex sentences with many words that are above his reading level and that his teacher did not use while teaching.

Practical ways of constructing objective tests that allow you to measure student knowledge more accurately are shown in the Professional Edge. Strategies for constructing test items for English-language learners are shown in the Instructional Edge.

Accommodations During the Test

If changes in test construction are intended for the whole class, they can be incorporated into the original master before duplicating. However, when changes are intended only for one or two students, you can make them as students take the test. For example, Ms. Minter's co-teacher, Ms. James, was working with Barry on his test-taking skills. She was helping Barry consider each choice in multiple-choice questions carefully, rather than always picking the first choice. Ms. James began by using an alternative form of question for Barry. When using **alternative forms of questions,** the teacher changes the type of question asked (for example, multiple-choice instead of essay questions) or the construction of the question (for example, adding a word bank for fill-in-the-blank questions). Ms. James used an alternative form of question by decreasing the number of choices on Barry's test items from four to two to make it easier to apply the strategy; on Barry's tests, she blackened two of the four choices. Eventually, however, she added choices to be sure that Barry was able to take the same tests as his classmates. Ms. James used this type of accommodation for another student with reading comprehension difficulties by underlining key words in each question. She gradually eliminated the underlining as the student showed he was able to identify the key words in questions without them.

The way that tests are given to students with disabilities can affect the accuracy of the results. Students, like Staci from the chapter-opening case, who have reading comprehension problems, might do better on tests if given more time to finish them or if allowed to take them orally. Students with written expression problems might

RESEARCH NOTE

Holzer et al. (2009) reduced the test anxiety of 4 out of 5 college students with learning disabilities by teaching them a strategy designed to assist them with test preparation and evaluating and keeping a positive mindset when taking tests.

www.resources

Ways to apply principles of universal design to constructing tests can be found at the website for the National Center on Educational Outcomes (NCEO): http://www.education.umn.edu/nceo/OnlinePubs/Policy15.htm.

PROFESSIONAL **EDGE**

Modifications in Test Construction for Students with Disabilities

All of your students will do better on clearly written tests that ask questions pertaining specifically to the material covered in class and in the textbook. But your students with disabilities especially require well-phrased and visually accessible tests if they are to succeed at test taking.

1. Tests should be typewritten and photocopied.
2. Make tests visually uncluttered by leaving sufficient space between items (3 spaces) and between lines within items (1½ spaces). Do not crowd pages with items; keep wide margins.
3. Use symmetrical spacing. For multiple-choice tests, align possible responses vertically rather than horizontally, and type the question and possible responses on the same page. Permit students to circle the letter of the correct answer rather than write it in front of the item.
4. Provide additional spacing between different types of test questions. Provide separate directions and a sample item for each type of test question.
5. For completion, short-answer, and essay questions, leave sufficient space to write the answer. Students do not do as well when they must continue their answers on the back of the page or on the next page.
6. Leave space for students to answer on the test rather than using machine scoring or answer sheets. Some students have difficulty transferring answers from one page to another.
7. For students who have difficulty with multiple-choice questions, reduce the number of possible answers. Students might choose the correct answer from three possible responses, for example, rather than from four or five.
8. For students who read slowly and students who have organizational problems, avoid the following constructions in matching items: long matching lists—keep lists to five or six items and group by concepts; lengthy items; and drawing lines to the correct answer, which can be confusing for students with visual–motor problems (Wood, Miederhoff, & Ulschmid, 1989). Lists with 10 to 15 entries in the first column can be simplified by preselecting three to four choices from the second column for each item in the first column. Record these choices beside the item in the first column and have the student select the correct answer from the smaller pool.

Consider the following example:

Match the definition on the left with the word on the right by writing the letter for the word in the blank next to the definition.

1. in a sudden way _____	a. brightness
2. not able _____	b. visitor
3. to make bright _____	c. suddenly
4. one who visits _____	d. happiness
5. in a happy way _____	e. rearrange
6. to tell again _____	f. brighten
7. to arrange beforehand _____	g. retell
8. state of being happy _____	h. prearrange
9. to arrange again _____	i. unable
10. state of being bright _____	j. happily

These questions will be less confusing for your students with disabilities if you modify them using the guidelines just described:

1. in a sudden way _____	a. brightness
	b. visitor
	c. suddenly
	d. retell
2. to make bright _____	a. happily
	b. unable
	c. brighten

9. Change fill-in-the-blank items to a multiple-choice format, providing three or four choices for the blank. Students select the correct answer only from the choices given. This modification changes the task from one of recall (memory) to one of recognition.
10. For essay questions, review the questions, keywords, and tasks with students individually and help students develop answer outlines. Permit dictated or recorded responses when appropriate.
11. Consider color-coding, underlining, enlarging, or highlighting key words and mathematical symbols.

Source: Adapted from *Accommodations for Secondary Learning Disabled/Mainstreamed Students on Teacher-Made Tests,* by J. N. Williams, 1986, unpublished manuscript, Wheaton, MD: Wheaton High School.

---

benefit from a dictionary or a handheld spell checker or by dictating their answers. Seating students with attention problems near you when they take a test might help them stay on task longer. These are all examples of **alternative ways of administering tests.**

Students also might benefit from the use of an alternative test site. An **alternative test site** is a type of testing accommodation that involves changing the location where a student with a disability is tested to make sure the results of the test are accurate. For example, testing in the resource room might help students with attention problems (by allowing them to take their tests in a setting with fewer distractions) and students with written language problems (by permitting them to

dimensions of DIVERSITY

Some African-American, Brazilian-American, Filipino-American, and Hawaiian students are accustomed to working at a measured pace. These students may benefit from extended time when taking tests (Grossman, 1995).

INSTRUCTIONAL **EDGE**

Testing English-Language Learners in Math-Problem Solving

Recent research reveals two important findings about English-language learners (ELLs) and tests. The bad news is that the test scores of English-language learners in all subject areas, including math, are much lower than those of native English speakers (Abedi, Hofstetter, & Lord, 2004). The poorer test performance of ELLs in math occurs not because they know less about the math content but because they have a hard time understanding the language used in test items. In effect, the language demands of the test render the test invalid and unfair. However, the good news is that test scores for English-language learners can be improved by decreasing the complexity of the language (Abedi et al., 2004). In fact, simplifying the language of test items is more helpful to ELLs than translating the items into their native language (American Institutes for Research, 1999). Here are some examples of how you can simplify language when writing math problems for your students (Abedi et al., 2004):

- Change unfamiliar or infrequently used nonmath vocabulary. For example, the phrase "a certain business concern" is unfamiliar and difficult to understand; the substituted phrase "Acme Company" is more common and easier to understand.
- Change the voice of verbs from passive to active. For example, change "If a marble is taken from the bag" to "if you take a marble from the bag."
- Shorten the length of noun phrases. For example, the phrase "the pattern of the puppy's weight gain" can be changed to "the pattern above."
- Replace conditional clauses with separate sentences or change the order of the conditional and main clauses. For example, consider the sentence "If two batteries in the sample were found to be dead, then the workers had to inspect all of the batteries."

This sentence can be simplified by changing it into two sentences: "The workers found two dead batteries in the sample. Because of this, they had to inspect all of the batteries." You could also change the order of the clauses: "The workers had to inspect all of the batteries when they found that two batteries in the sample were dead."

- Remove or change relative clauses. For example, change "What is the total number of newspapers that Lee delivers in 5 days?" to "How many papers does Lee deliver in 5 days?"
- Change complex question phrases to simple question words. For example, change "which is the best approximation of the number . . . ?" to "approximately how many . . . ?"
- Make abstract wordings more concrete. For example, change "2,675 radios sold" to "2,675 radios that Mr. Jones sold."

Examine the following word problem from the Massachusetts Comprehensive Assessment System (at http://www.doe.mass.edu/mcas/2003/release):

Students in Mr. Jacob's English class were giving speeches. Each student's speech was 7–10 minutes long. Which of the following is the best estimate for the total number of student speeches that could be given in a 2-hour class?

a. 4 speeches
b. 8 speeches
c. 13 speeches
d. 19 speeches

What problems do you think an English-language learner might have with this question? How would you change the item to make it more understandable?

---

answer test questions orally). Changing the test site also protects students who are taking the test in a different way from being embarrassed. However, before sending a student out of class to take a test, you should first try other options.

For example, Ms. Edwards allows her students to choose whether to have a test read to them. Those who do not want the test read aloud can work independently while she reads the test to the rest of the students. She also gives the students to whom she reads the test more help with directions and the meanings of key vocabulary or difficult questions without, of course, giving the answers away. Mr. Collins and Ms. Klein are co-teaching. Mr. Collins supervises students taking the test silently while Ms. Klein reads the test to another group of students. If a student's IEP specifies that testing must occur in a separate setting, be sure to coordinate your plans in advance with the special education teacher to avoid scheduling problems.

Accommodations After the Test

You also may need to use alternative test-grading procedures for students including changing letter or number grades, changing the grading criteria, and using alternatives to traditional letters and numbers.

Changing letter or number grades by adding written comments or symbols or by giving multiple grades can help clarify what a grade means. For example, Seth, a

www.resources

You can create online quizzes on the Quiz Center page of the Discovery-School website (http://school.discovery.com/quizcenter/quizcenter.html).

PROFESSIONAL EDGE

Using Grading Rubrics with Students

The use of grading guidelines called *rubrics* helps students do the following:

- better understand their teachers' expectations
- monitor their progress
- judge the quality of their work (Jackson & Larkin, 2002)

Jackson and Larkin (2002) created the *RUBRIC* strategy to help students with special needs use rubrics to assess the quality of their work. To teach students to carry out the strategy, explain what rubrics are by showing students some examples. Internet resources for finding rubrics include RubiStar (http://rubistar.4teachers.org); the rubrics page of Teachnology (http://www.bestteachersites.com/web_tools/rubrics); Kathy Schrock's guide to assessment and rubric information (http://school.discovery.com/schrockguide/assess.html#rubrics); and Project Based Learning (http://pblchecklist.4teachers.org).

Once students know what rubrics are, they are ready to apply the RUBRIC strategy. In general, follow the same steps described in Chapter 10 for teaching learning strategies, including clarifying expectations, demonstrating strategy use, and providing guided and independent practice.

R: Encourage students to familiarize themselves with the criteria to be applied to each component of the task. Getting the "big picture" prevents students from diving into the task without thinking, a common problem for students with disabilities.

U: Students work individually and apply the rubric to one of their products, giving it a score. They should ask questions about the clarity of the scoring guidelines as well as verbalize their thought processes to someone else, receiving feedback as needed.

B: Students select a buddy to help them rate the product again.

R: The student and the buddy then review the material, forming a team to compare scores and ideas. They then present their scores to the larger group of students, explaining how they used the rubric and why they agreed or disagreed. Next, the group gives the team feedback on how they applied the rubric.

I: The team uses the feedback to identify and award a new set of scores.

C: Students check their work.

Source: Adapted from Goodrich, as cited in "Rubric: Teaching Students to Use Grading Rubrics," by C. W. Jackson and M. J. Larkin, 2002, *Teaching Exceptional Children, 35*(1), 40–45.

---

student with a moderate intellectual disability, was tested only on questions covering standards stressed on his IEP. His teacher, Mr. Grassley, placed an asterisk next to his grade of B indicating that his test covered less content than that given to the rest of the class. Giving multiple grades can also be helpful on tests that require written responses. For example, on an English test, Jacinto is required to write an essay on the character Boo Radley in the novel *To Kill a Mockingbird*. When his teacher grades his essay, she assigns him one grade based on the quality of his analysis of the character and another grade for writing mechanics. Having *grading rubrics,* or guidelines, to follow when evaluating student performance helps students understand the criteria by which their work is judged. A strategy designed to help students use grading rubrics to improve their performance is described in the Professional Edge. A sample rubric designed for English-language learners to evaluate their effort is shown in Figure 11.2.

A second option is to change the **grading criteria,** or the standards on which the grade is based. For example, Seth's teacher could give him a grade of B by basing his grade on fewer questions. In some cases you may also want to base a student's grade on the percentage correct of the items tried instead of on the total number of questions. This adjustment may help students who work accurately but slowly. Giving partial credit is another possible option. For example, when Ms. Jordan grades student answers to math word problems, she gives students points for underlining key words in the question and setting up the equation correctly even if they still get the final answer wrong. These points can motivate students who are improving but do not increase their test scores significantly. Students also can be allowed to retake tests. They can then be graded using their score on the retake or averaging their original score with their retake score.

A third grading option is using **alternatives to letter and number grades,** such as pass/fail grades and checklists of skill competencies. For example, Matt could be given a grade of P (pass) because he mastered 7 of 10 key concepts in the chapter, or

RESEARCH NOTE

Grading based on rubrics with clear descriptors results in a more accurate representation of students' learning at the end of a grading period. In addition, basing a grade primarily on mathematical averages often distorts the accuracy of grades (Marzano, 2000).

www.resources

EdWeb: Exploring Technology and School Reform (http://edwebproject.org) is a website that includes education-focused discussion groups in which you can discuss testing, grading, and many other educational issues.

FIGURE 11.2 Effort Rubric Adapted for English-Language Learners

4		I worked until I finished. I tried even when it was difficult. This lesson helped me learn more English.
3		I worked until I finished. I tried even when it was difficult.
2		I tried, but I stopped when it was too difficult.
1		I didn't try.

Source: From "Classroom Instruction That Works with English Language Learners," by J. D. Hall and K. M. Flynn, Alexandria, VA: ASCD

he could be rated on a **competency checklist** showing which key concepts in the chapter he learned. While all of these test-grading accommodations allow students to be more successful, remember that grades or percentages do not constitute feedback; learners need specific feedback if they are to improve on future work (Munk, 2009). In addition, care must be taken to assure that students are prepared to meet state standards. For example, Matt's teacher needs to be certain that the content for which Matt is held responsible reflects state standards and that reducing the content for which he is held responsible will not interfere with his attainment of state standards.

How Can Accommodations in Report-Card Grading Be Made for Students with Special Needs?

Report-card grading is perhaps the most prevalent and controversial evaluation option used in schools. The practice of grading by letters and percentages began in the early twentieth century, a time of great faith in the ability of educational measures to assess students' current levels of learning accurately and also predict future levels of learning. High grades were seen as a sign of accomplishment, intended to spur students on to even greater achievements. Those who received low grades were either placed in basic-level or special classes or were encouraged to join the workforce (Cohen, 1983).

Times certainly have changed. Laws have been passed guaranteeing that our evaluations do not discriminate on the basis of disability, race, or ethnicity. These laws also guarantee an appropriate education for all students, not just those who can succeed with minimal intervention. Furthermore, our ability to compete in the global economy depends on better educational outcomes for all citizens, not just a privileged few. These changes have led to new demands that go beyond the relatively simple matter of identifying good and poor students. For example, how can evaluations be modified to ensure that they do not discriminate against students with disabilities? How can they be used to motivate students to stay in school, to communicate educational competence and progress to parents and students, and to guide our teaching as we strive to meet the needs of an increasingly diverse student body?

Report-card grades for students with disabilities and other students with special needs must be carefully explained to prevent misunderstandings. What grading accommodations or modifications might these people be discussing?

Although answers to these and other questions about grading are beginning to emerge, in large part professionals continue to use a grading system that was intended to fulfill a purpose much more narrow in scope. The use of traditional letter and number grades has caused problems for teachers, who must communicate with many audiences, including parents, students, administrators, and legislators. These audiences often are looking for information that is not readily communicated using a single number or letter (Guskey, 2006; Munk & Bursuck, 2001, 2003). For example, students may be interested in how much progress they have made, whereas their parents want to know how their children compare to their classmates as well as to children nationwide. Principals, on the other hand, may need to provide college admissions offices with indicators of student potential to do college work. Teachers also are increasingly left with many conflicting concerns about grading, including upholding the school's standards, maintaining consistency with other teachers' evaluations, being honest with students, justifying grades with other students, motivating students for better future performance, communicating accurately to the students' next teachers, and avoiding the reputation of being an "easy" teacher (Munk & Bursuck, 2003).

Increased inclusion in schools has put even more burdens on grading systems. As illustrated in the vignettes at the beginning of the chapter, grading can present serious challenges for students with disabilities and their teachers. Staci was not a good test taker, yet 80 percent of her report-card grade in earth science was based on her test performance. She was concerned that her grade did not accurately reflect her effort or progress in class. Jennifer's parents were surprised to find that their daughter had received As in reading all year but was reading below grade level on a recent standardized achievement test. Lucille was working on math skills that were more basic than those the rest of the class covered, and her teacher was unsure how to grade her performance. Add to these problems the concern that grades need to relate to student performance on state high-stakes assessments or universal screening and progress-monitoring measures used in RtI.

Despite these challenges, a number of reasons support the continued use of grades. First, many parents want to see how their children compare to other students, and they demand grades. In addition, grades are efficient and can make decision making easier, particularly for schools making decisions about promotion to the next grade level and for colleges and universities making admissions decisions (Munk & Bursuck, 2001). Despite their many limitations, grades are likely to be used by teachers and schools for many years to come. Teachers need to recognize the limitations, however, and, when necessary, differentiate grading systems to ensure they are fair to all students.

The next section is divided into two topics. First, grading practices that benefit all students, including students with disabilities, will be described. Second, strategies for individualized grading will be covered. Individualized grading is carried out only with students with disabilities as specified in their IEPs.

Grading Practices That Benefit All Students

Grading practices that benefit all of your students include using differentiated report cards, avoiding grades of zero, and reporting student progress frequently.

Differentiated report cards are report cards that have individualized provisions for students to clarify the meaning of their grades. Differentiated report cards can be used with most students in your class and are appropriate for students with disabilities (1) who are working toward the same learning standards as the rest of the class, (2) whose progress is being appropriately monitored, and (3) who are receiving accommodations that result in reasonable access to the general education curriculum (Munk, 2007). You can differentiate report-card grades for your students in several ways. Three of the most practical of these include making changes to letter and number grades, reporting separate grades, and standards-based grading.

Changes to letter and number grades clarify report-card grades by supplementing them with other ways of evaluating and reporting student progress, such as written or verbal comments, logs of student activities, and portfolios. Written or verbal comments can be used to clarify areas such as student performance levels as compared with peers and the extent of student effort. For example, Robert scored below standard for the grading period; his teacher commented that he had read more trade books but that these books were below grade level.

Comments about student performance levels can prevent misunderstandings, particularly when parents find their children are performing below standard on state tests or on RtI universal screening assessments. For instance, in the chapter-opening vignette, Jennifer's mother thought her daughter's high grade in reading meant that she was reading at grade level. An explanation on Jennifer's report card would have put her grade in context. Keep in mind, however, that students sometimes compare report cards with their classmates and might be embarrassed by comments that indicate they are working below grade level. To prevent this situation, you might use an alternative procedure, such as talking to parents or sending them a separate note of clarification. In addition, report-card comments should never state that the student is receiving special services; this would be a violation of student confidentiality.

Finally, the basis for arriving at number or letter grades on report cards is often not clear. For example, does the grade represent a student's performance in comparison with his or her classmates, or is it based on the student's progress toward meeting objectives on his or her IEP? Failure to clarify the basis for grades can lead to issues of fairness raised by students, as shown in the Case in Practice, as well as communication problems with parents, as shown in the Working Together.

Because report-card grades are primarily summaries of student performance, they provide few specifics about student achievement over a period of time. You can use **daily activity logs** of student activities and achievement to provide ongoing information for students and their parents. Daily observations of students can be recorded in a notebook or journal, directly on a calendar, or on self-sticking notes.

Whatever type of daily activity log is used, entries should at least include the date, the student's name, the classroom activity, and a brief description of the observation. For example, Ms. Parks was concerned about the progress of one of her students, Carrie, in the area of word-identification skills. Each day during an hour-long literature class, Ms. Parks observed how Carrie approached the trade books she was reading. One day she recorded that Carrie spontaneously used the parts of a multisyllable word to figure out its pronunciation and meaning. Information taken from the logs can be summarized periodically. These summaries can then be shared with parents as often as necessary to clarify student grades.

Another way to differentiate report-card grading is to report **separate grades,** each based on a different grading element and corresponding set of criteria (Guskey,

CASE IN PRACTICE

Fairness

Ms. Rodriguez had never questioned her decision to become a middle school science teacher—that is, not until last week. She has always had students with disabilities as class members and felt comfortable being able to meet their individual needs while maintaining high standards. This year, she has three such students: one with learning disabilities, another who has an emotional disability, and a third with a mild intellectual disability. All three students have testing or grading accommodations written into their IEPs. To complicate matters, for the first time this year, her students without disabilities are complaining. Tricia wants to know why Tyrell is allowed extra time to take his tests. She feels she would do better, too, if given extra time. Monikee questions why Maya receives extra points for coming to class but she does not. Even Dayrone, who never complains about anything, wants to know why Garrett has to learn fewer vocabulary words than the rest of the class.

Ms. Rodriguez has always believed that fairness means everyone should receive what he or she needs, which is not necessarily the same thing. Still, she has to think carefully about how best to respond to her students' concerns about fairness. She believes she can likely appeal to Tricia's independence and sense of right and wrong if she can get her to think more clearly about the situation. So Ms. Rodriguez tells Tricia, "You don't think it's fair. Please write me a note about your point of view, and we'll talk about it later." Monikee will require a different approach. Because she thrives on Ms. Rodriguez's attention, Ms. Rodriguez concludes that she is complaining because she needs something special, too. Ms. Rodriguez tells her, "Maya is getting extra points because she is working on something that is really hard for her. Do you want to work on something that is hard for you?" Ms. Rodriguez is concerned that students like Dayrone complain when they feel the teacher is unsure about a classroom policy. Ms. Rodriguez believes that, in general, it is important to respond to complaints of unfairness consistently and without explanation. Therefore, she says to Dayrone, "I can't make comments about anyone else's work. May I help you with your own?" (Welch, 2000, p. 37).

REFLECTION

What are the different ways Ms. Rodriguez responds to her students' complaints about fairness? Is each approach appropriate? Can you think of other ways she could have responded to her students' complaints? What could Ms. Rodriguez do in the future to prevent complaints about fairness?

Working TOGETHER

Communicating with Parents about Grades

Mr. and Mrs. Washington's son Delarnes is in Mr. Campbell's junior English class. Delarnes received an F in English for the last marking period, and Mr. and Mrs. Washington are upset. They know Delarnes is working hard in the class because they are spending a lot of time helping him with his English homework at night. They schedule a meeting with Mr. Campbell to learn more about the problem.

When Mr. and Mrs. Washington arrive at the meeting, Mr. Campbell is seated at a table with the chairperson of the English department, Dr. West. The Washingtons hadn't expected someone else to be at the meeting, and it makes them fear that Delarnes has done something terrible. After asking the Washingtons to sit down, Mr. Campbell introduces Dr. West, who talks for what seems like forever on the state English standards and on how the state "seems to be setting the bar higher every year."

The Washingtons aren't sure how the state standards affect Delarnes' English grade but are afraid to ask. Mr. Washington is beginning to grow impatient. He had expected the meeting to be about helping Delarnes. Next Mr. Campbell says that while Delarnes seems to be working hard, he has failed both of the grammar tests during the quarter, and his essay on Frederick Douglass has received a score of D–. Mrs. Washington helped Delarnes outline that paper but hasn't heard anything about it since. Delarnes hasn't told his parents about the grammar tests. When Mr. Campbell asks the Washingtons if they will help Delarnes more at home, Mr. Washington explodes, saying that they *have* been helping him at home, asking why they haven't been told about Delarnes's problem in English before, and demanding that the school do something to help him.

Why is it sometimes difficult to communicate with parents about the meaning of their children's grades?

What can Mr. Campbell do to prevent this problem from happening again?

How did the way Mr. Campbell conducted the meeting contribute to the problem? How could he have conducted the meeting differently?

2006). As we have said, teachers become frustrated when they have to communicate multiple messages using a single grade. For example, Ms. Lsu wanted to tell her parents which standards her students had met by reporting on the quality of the products they had produced, such as tests, reports, and projects. However, she also wanted to tell parents about the processes involved in developing the products, such as the effort that went into creating them and the work habits her students had displayed. In addition, Ms. Lsu wanted to communicate how much her students had progressed. Fortunately Ms. Lsu's school had just adopted an individualized grading report format, (Bailey & McTighe, 1996) such as the one shown in Figure 11.3 for Ms. Lsu's student Taylor. Note that Ms. Lsu used a number grade to evaluate Taylor's products for the marking period, thus providing a realistic assessment of his performance on state standards. Ms. Lsu was also able to communicate Taylor's level of effort using the three-point scale of *Outstanding, Satisfactory,* and *Needs Improvement.* Finally, Taylor's progress was communicated by reporting his grades for the previous marking period.

Educators have voiced several concerns about differentiated report cards. The first is that factoring elements such as effort and progress into students' grades diminishes grades' accuracy as indicators of the mastery of standards (Wormeli, 2006) and accounts for discrepancies between students' high school course grades and their performance on state high-stakes tests (Guskey, 2006). In our view, the strategies for differentiating report-card grades described here represent realistic ways for teachers to minimize this problem.

Some teachers also question whether students who receive instructional accommodations should be graded in the same manner as students who do not receive accommodations. It is important to remember that the curricular expectations for

FIGURE 11.3 Individualized Grading Report

The class has worked toward meeting standards in geometry including applying and using concepts of indirect measurement, and representing problem situations with geometric models. Geometry is difficult for Taylor, and handing in incomplete assignments three times, being absent, and coming late to class on numerous occasions has only made things worse. Attending extra tutoring sessions I conduct before school could help him better understand and complete his assignments. Attending class more regularly and being on time is a must if he is to meet the geometry standards, which are quite difficult.

Grade as of 12 / 5 / 2010	65
Previous Grade	75
Effort	
Outstanding	
Satisfactory	
Needs Improvement	✓
Absences	5
#Times Tardy	3

In English 2 we have stressed writing personal narratives as well as responding reflectively to a variety of expressive texts including memoirs, monologues, and diaries. Taylor loves English and is performing well. He is always in class and has completed all of his assignments. Of particular note is that he takes the initiative to get feedback on his writing, the quality of which is very good.

Grade as of 12 / 5 / 2010	95
Previous Grade	90
Effort	
Excellent	✓
Satisfactory	
Needs Improvement	
Absences	0
#Times Tardy	0

students receiving accommodations are the same as for all students. As you have learned, the purpose of accommodations is to maximize access to the general education curriculum by reducing or minimizing the interaction between a student's disability and classroom demands and by allowing for the valid assessment of learning that is not affected by disability. Thus, students' accommodations do not signify reduced expectations, and most students receiving accommodations do not require a different grading system (Munk, 2007).

Jung & Guskey (2007) recommend a **standards-based grading model** as a way of differentiating report card grades. In standards-based grading, the IEP team first reviews grade-level standards to determine whether an accommodation or modification is needed. Since accommodations merely involve access to the general education curriculum, if a standard only requires an accommodation, there is no need to modify the grade level standard or the grading process. As long as the appropriate accommodations are in place for both instruction and assessment, students with disabilities can be graded on the grade level standard the same as everyone else. For example, Juan, a student with learning disabilities, is enrolled in Biology. Juan has a reading disability, but with a digital text, recorder, and oral tests as accommodations, he can meet the same biology standards as his classmates without disabilities. Therefore, in grading whether he met the standard for comparing and contrasting the structure and function of the organic molecules of carbohydrates, proteins, and lipids, there is no need for a grading accommodation. The expectations are the same for Juan as for everyone else. If modifications are required, then the IEP team needs to modify the standards. Modified standards must be clearly linked to grade-level standards, but be more developmentally appropriate for the student. The student is then graded on the modified standards. Germaine is a student with an intellectual disability who requires a modification in standards. His IEP team decided that he could meet the standard related to comparing organic molecules just described for Juan by identifying foods in the grocery store that consisted primarily of proteins, carbohydrates, and lipids, and comparing their respective nutritional benefits. Standards-based grading may need to be combined with the other ways to differentiate report card grades just described. For example, Jung & Guskey (2007) recommend marking grades based on modified standards with an asterisk to make it clear that the student is not performing at grade level. In addition, since standards-based grading does not take effort or progress into account, a separate grade for these dimensions of student performance may need to be provided.

Another effective grading practice for all of your students is to **avoid giving zeroes** for work not submitted or tests missed due to unexcused absences. Some teachers give zeroes for missing assignments on the grounds that it teaches students personal responsibility (Munk, 2007). The truth is that the practice of giving zeroes for work not submitted is full of problems. First, a grade of zero distorts the final grade and diminishes its value as an indicator of what was learned (Wormeli, 2006). For example, Cherise had the following scores on six classroom quizzes: 100, 100, 100, 95, 100, 0. She received a zero on quiz 6 because of an unexcused absence. Cherise's average score for the quizzes with a score of zero figured in was 83 percent. She received a grade of B despite the fact that she earned an A on every quiz she took. Not only does giving Cherise a zero for the quiz she missed distort the evidence of what she learned, but it could also undermine her motivation. Missing work and missed tests may also result from organizational problems related to a learner's disability or life circumstances beyond her control. For example, Cherise is involved in family child care. On the day of the quiz, she had to take her younger brother to the doctor because her mother was working.

Wormeli (2006) suggests giving a grade of 60 percent rather than zero as a way of lessening the impact of a missed assignment or test. While this practice would lessen the numerical impact of a zero (Cherise would have averaged 93 percent, rather than 83 percent), in our view, there are more proactive ways to solve the problem of giving zeroes. First, make sure all students understand your grading policies for late or missed work. Second, allow students to turn in late work for full or partial credit. Third, increase the level of communication regarding assignments, tests, and due dates.

INSTRUCTIONAL EDGE

Using Progress Monitoring to Evaluate Student Performance in RtI

What are progress monitoring assessments?

Progress monitoring assessments are brief assessments given during the school year that inform teachers whether students are making adequate progress toward meeting grade-level performance benchmarks so support can be provided if they aren't (Bursuck & Damer, 2011).

What is the purpose of using progress monitoring assessments in RtI?

The RtI process begins with effective instruction in Tier 1 in the general education classroom using evidence-based practices. However, as much as we know about evidence-based instruction, we still cannot predict how each student will respond to any given instructional practice. That is why monitoring student progress is such an important part of RtI. Progress monitoring can help make important instructional decisions in RtI such as whether a student should remain in a tier, enter a more intensive tier, or exit into a less-intensive tier.

What are the qualities of effective progress monitoring measures?

Progress monitoring measures must be able to forecast later achievement, be given by real teachers in real classrooms, and provide results in a timely fashion so that appropriate support can be provided before too much time is lost (Jenkins, 2009). Progress monitoring assessments also must directly reflect the curriculum, and, because they are given repeatedly over time, must be of approximately equal difficulty. That is why curriculum-based measurements (CBM), a type of curriculum-based assessments described in Chapter 4, are ideally suited for progress monitoring.

What is the process for using progress monitoring to make decisions in RtI?

The process of progress monitoring involves these steps: set student goals, select progress-monitoring assessments of approximately equal difficulty, assess regularly to determine growth rates, and adjust instruction when growth is unsatisfactory (Jenkins, 2009). Generally, students in Tier 1 are assessed a minimum of three times per year, while Tier 2 and Tier 3 students can be assessed every 3–4 weeks, or more often if desired (Jenkins, 2009). Progress

monitoring uses research-based decision rules to interpret progress monitoring data and determine whether instruction is sufficient (Mellard & McKnight, 2008). A commonly used decision rule is the "four and above" rule. According to this rule:

- If the last four data points are above the aimline, keep the current program and consider raising the goal if appropriate.
- If the last four data points are below the line, make a change in intervention, tier, or both.
- If some data points are above the line and some are below, keep the current program and goal in place (Fuchs, Fuchs, Hintze, & Lembke, 2007).

To see progress monitoring in action, consider this case. Mr. Henley, a fifth-grade general education teacher, is monitoring Maura's progress in reading comprehension. Mr. Henley is using the Maze (Parker, Hasbrouck, & Tindal, 1992), a CBM measure where students read a grade level passage from which every seventh word is deleted and replaced by three words in parentheses, one of which makes sense in the passage. Students circle the correct words as they read the passage silently for 3 minutes. The number of correct responses per minute (RC) is recorded. The MAZE has norms established for each grade level for fall, winter, and spring.

As shown in Figure 11.4, Maura's score at the beginning of the year was 10 RC. While this score is at the 25th percentile, Mr. Henley didn't want to place Maura into Tier 2 until he first saw how well she performed in his Tier 1 reading instruction. Mr. Henley set an end-of-the-year goal for Maura of 24 RC, the 50th percentile for Grade 5, and drew an aimline from Maura's beginning score of 10 RC to her annual goal of 24 RC. Mr. Henley decided to monitor Maura's performance in Tier 1 twice per month using a different fifth-grade Maze passage of equal difficulty each time. He used the recommended "four and below" rule to decide whether Maura would stay in Tier 1 or move to Tier 2 for additional support. As shown in the figure, Maura made some progress, but all four of her data points were below the line. At this rate, she is unlikely to meet her goal of 24 RC by the end of the year. Mr. Henley decided to form

---

Fourth, have students complete projects in segments with separate scores for each segment. Finally, for students with disabilities, consider setting an IEP goal for improving time management, including the self-monitoring of work completion (Munk, 2007).

A final grading practice that can benefit all of your students is to **report student progress more frequently.** Report-card grades come out only four times a year. Students as well as parents need more frequent feedback than that. Of course, the frequency with which you provide student progress reports will vary depending on the student as well as the time demands made on you as a teacher. Such frequent progress monitoring is a regular part of RtI, the subject of the Instructional Edge.

Using Individualized Grading with Students with Disabilities

Researchers have identified two general types of **individualized grading**: (1) grading accommodations that involve changing the grading elements, or what counts toward earning a grade; and (2) grading accommodations that involve changing the value of

a Tier 2 group with Maura and three other students in the class who were also struggling with reading comprehension. He assessed them further using a curriculum-based assessment to see what type of comprehension questions he needed to cover in the group. He planned to continue monitoring Maura's progress twice monthly to evaluate the effectiveness of the Tier 2 instruction.

FIGURE 11.4 Progress Monitoring for Maura

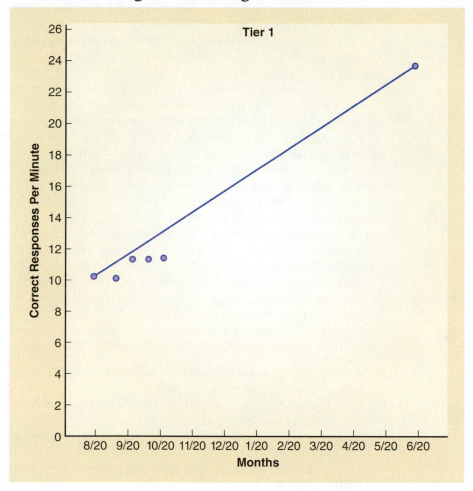

the grading elements, or how much each element counts toward the final grade. Individualized grading is called for when a learner has a moderate to severe disability and modified curricular expectations. It is also called for when a learner has a high-incidence disability and receives a series of low or failing grades despite the delivery of appropriate classroom accommodations. Merely having an IEP, trying hard, failing because of missed work, or receiving poorly administered accommodations or modifications is not enough to qualify a student for individualized grading (Munk, 2007).

Individualized grading involves making judgments in a systematic way. It is done in conjunction with the student's IEP. That makes individualized grading legally binding and prevents problems such as the ones described at the beginning of the chapter for Jennifer and Lucille. Accommodations that involve changing the grading elements include basing all or part of the grade on progress on IEP objectives; basing all or part of the grade on performance on prioritized content and assignments; and emphasizing learning strategies and effort in a balanced grading system (Guskey & Bailey, 2001;

Munk, 2003). Changing the value of the grading elements includes basing part of the grade on improvement over past performance and modifying grading weights and scales. These types of individualized grading are summarized and described in the sections that follow.

Basing All or Part of the Grade on Progress on IEP Objectives For this type of individualized grading, **progress on IEP objectives** is used as the basis for part or all of a student's report-card grade (Munk, 2003). Grading on the basis of progress on IEP objectives would have been appropriate for Lucille, the student in the opening vignettes whose math curriculum was modified on her IEP. Whereas the rest of the class was working on decimals, she was working on two-digit by two-digit addition problems with regrouping. Because her IEP objective was to score 80 percent or better when given 20 of these problems, her fourth-grade teacher and special education teacher agreed to give her an A if she met her objective, a B if she scored between 70 and 80 percent, a C if she scored between 60 and 70 percent, and so forth. To ensure that Lucille's mother had an accurate picture of Lucille's standing in relation to her peers, Lucille's teacher included a written comment on Lucille's report card indicating that her grade was based on different curricular objectives as agreed to on her IEP.

Basing grades on progress on IEP objectives also can be helpful for students who are in special education but do not have modified curricular expectations. For example, Manny is a student with a learning disability who is included in Mr. Ottens's middle school science class. Manny receives pullout services in writing but is still expected to meet the same curriculum standards in science as his classmates. During Manny's IEP conference, it was decided that 10 percent of his science grade would be determined by progress on an IEP objective stating that "Manny will write complete sentences using correct spelling, grammar, and sentence structure." Mr. Ottens agreed to evaluate Manny's written work in science using these criteria. Mr. Ottens would give a writing grade along with a regular grade for each assignment Manny submitted. Manny's average writing grade would count 10 percent toward his report-card grade in science.

Basing all or part of a student's daily work grade or report-card grade on IEP objectives, as was done for Lucille and Manny, is advantageous in several ways. It

1. allows the team to consider how and when IEP objectives can be addressed in the general education classroom.
2. informs students, parents, and teachers which objectives are important and how supports can be provided.
3. ensures that a student's grade reflects progress on skills that have been identified as most important for him by the team.
4. eliminates the redundancy of reporting grades separately from progress on IEP objectives.
5. improves communication among parents, students, and teachers about grading in the general education classroom.

Of course, basing grades or progress on IEP objectives carries the risk that students with disabilities will be evaluated using criteria unrelated to expectations in general education. When curricular objectives in general and special education are out of sync, student access to the general education curriculum is compromised. That is why, to the maximum extent possible, IEP objectives should be based on the general education curriculum.

Basing All or Part of the Grade on Performance on Prioritized Content and Assignments Another type of individualized grading bases all or part of a student's grade on his performance on prioritized curriculum content and assignments deemed most important by the teacher (Munk, 2003). **Prioritization of curriculum** benefits students for whom remembering, organizing, and accessing the content in the general education curriculum is a difficult and time-consuming process. Limiting the content load and assignments to the essentials for these students can make learning success more likely. First and foremost, curriculum prioritization must be based on state standards. Other considerations include local curriculum guidelines, skills or content needed for future classes or postsecondary education, relevance to students' lives, or other criteria established by the IEP team (Munk, 2003). Claudia is included in Mr. Gonzales's middle school science class. She has learning disabilities; she has difficulty remembering factual material, reads quite slowly, and has problems organizing what she reads into main ideas. Claudia's IEP team decided that content prioritization would help her access the science curriculum more efficiently, particularly since the science textbook was hard to read and very content dense. Mr. Gonzales agreed to prioritize the content for the next grading period when he was covering the topic of cells. He identified the following content as most important based on state learning standards (Munk, 2003, p. 74):

1. Identify nine major parts of all cells.
2. Use a microscope to view cells of different organisms.
3. Describe the stages in photosynthesis.
4. Describe the functions of cells.
5. Describe the similarities and differences between cells of animals and plants.
6. Identify parts of cells as viewed under a microscope.

Mr. Gonzales assured the team that this content reflected the major information in the state standards pertaining to cells. He explained that content ideas 1, 3, and 4 would be evaluated using short-answer tests and ideas 2, 5, and 6 would be evaluated based on Claudia's performance on submitted lab reports. The team decided that her labs and tests would be graded based on the percentage correct on all items pertaining to her prioritized content. The resulting number grade would be converted to a letter grade using the same grading scale used schoolwide. Mr. Gonzales said that Claudia would be encouraged to participate in all of the other class activities for the grading period, including answering end-of-chapter questions in the textbook, but that the activities related to her prioritized content would be emphasized in arriving at her grade.

Using prioritization for individualized grading has a number of advantages. It

1. directs the team to focus the need for supports on the most important content and assignments. For example, Claudia needed the most support on completing lab reports related to her curricular objectives and preparing for short-answer tests. Less support was needed for producing lab reports on other topics.
2. reduces the risk that students' performance on less important content and activities will pull down their grade. For example, end-of-chapter questions are difficult for Claudia because they take her so long. In the past, she never completed them, and her low grades on these activities reduced her overall grade for the marking period.
3. helps teachers identify the most important elements of the curriculum. Knowing and communicating what is most important about the curriculum benefits all students, not just those with disabilities.

A problem that could arise when using prioritization involves the choice of what content to stress and which information to deemphasize. This decision is best made collaboratively by the student, parents, and teachers as part of the IEP process and, of course, while keeping state standards clearly in mind.

Emphasizing Learning Strategies and Effort in a Balanced Grading System

Traditionally, grading has focused on the evaluation of student products without taking into account the learning strategies and effort required to come up with the products. For example, in Mr. Kellogg's tenth-grade English class, students write a five-page persuasive essay and are graded on various qualities of the essay submitted, such as length, organization, mechanics, and the integration of elements essential to persuasive writing. When grading his students, Mr. Kellogg does not consider the amount of

www.resources

Find out about testing and grading policies being used around the country by visiting the website of the Council of Chief State School Officers (CCSSO) (http://www.ccsso.org.)

effort students put into the paper or the extent to which the students employ learning strategies. Brad is a student included in Mr. Kellogg's class. He is receiving help from his special education teacher, Ms. Laslow, in writing, but he feels discouraged. His grades in Mr. Kellogg's class have remained at D−, despite all his hard work with Ms. Laslow on learning strategies for writing such as outlining key essay elements, proofreading, self-monitoring, and using word processing. Mr. Kellogg has indicated that he has seen no changes in Brad's writing since the beginning of the year. In order to encourage Brad to use the strategy he was learning in Ms. Laslow's class, his IEP team decided to use **balanced grading** that took into account his learning-strategy performance and effort. The team decided to give Brad credit for performing the writing strategies that he was learning from Ms. Laslow. When Brad submitted the final draft of his paper, he also gave Mr. Kellogg a copy of his paper outline and a completed self-monitoring checklist of all of the writing steps he followed. The team agreed that the quality of the outline and checklist would count 25 percent toward Brad's final grade on the paper. As a way of recognizing Brad's effort, the team also agreed to give him bonus points for submitting his paper early to Mr. Kellogg for feedback and for getting the final paper in on time.

Balanced grading has a number of advantages. First, including student performance on academic learning skills as part of the grading process helps focus students' attention on applying them in their general education classes. Balanced grading also leads to greater collaboration and coordination between general education and special education teachers. Once Brad's individualized grading approach was agreed to, Mr. Kellogg took a greater interest in Brad in class. For example, he began to remind Brad to perform the skills present on his self-monitoring checklist. As a result, Brad was better able to apply what he had learned from Ms. Laslow to meeting the requirements in Mr. Kellogg's class.

While rewarding effort is a key part of balanced grading and a potentially effective way to sustain student motivation, it is a type of individualized grading that must be done with great care. First, effort is much more difficult to assess than academic progress (Gersten et al., 1996). Also, the relationship between effort and achievement is not always predictable; a student may work hard but master little of the content (Munk, 2003). Munk (2003) advises IEP teams to ask the following questions when considering incorporating effort into a student's grade:

- Do you have evidence that when the student tries harder, he performs better on assignments?
- Can the team agree on how to measure effort?
- Will the student perceive the accommodation as an incentive to keep working hard? (p. 90)

In Brad's case, based on input from his mother, the committee felt that rewarding him for effort was necessary and would be effective. The team also agreed that they could measure his level of effort by noting whether he handed in an early draft of the paper to Mr. Kellogg for feedback and whether he submitted the final draft of the paper on time.

Basing Part of the Grade on Improvement over Past Performance
Improvement grades involve basing part of a grade on improvement. They can be incorporated into a traditional grading system by assigning extra points for improvement or by moving students up a grade on the scale if they improve, particularly if they are on the border between grades. Consider the case of Aretha, whose average on spelling tests in her general education classroom for the last marking period was 77 percent, an improvement of more than 40 percentage points over the preceding marking period. Although her true grade for spelling was technically a C, Aretha's IEP team had agreed in advance that her teacher would raise her grade a letter if she were to bring her test average up to at least 75 percent. The team also agreed, however, that once she reached 75 percent, she would be graded using the same scale as the rest of the class for the remaining grading periods.

In another example, Roberto's IEP team agreed that if he read a minimum of five trade books during the grading period—an improvement of four over his performance for the previous grading period—he would receive a grade of O (outstanding) in reading because he read so many more books than before. The team felt that even though other students in the class were reading more books at a more difficult level, Roberto deserved an O if he improved that much. His teacher did note on Roberto's report card, however, that the books he read were one to two years below grade level. The team also decided that Roberto would have to improve his performance by at least one book per marking period if he were to continue to receive a grade of O in reading.

Perhaps the greatest benefit of grading based on improvement is that it motivates students to try harder. In fact, basing part of report-card grades on improvement can motivate students to take better advantage of available supports or attempt more work than they would do ordinarily. In the preceding examples, Aretha worked more conscientiously during her instructional support time in the resource room because she thought it would improve her spelling grade in general education. Roberto read even more books than the minimum of five required in his IEP.

One potential drawback of grading on the basis of improvement is the risk that students will become dependent on special contingencies. For example, when Aretha finally reaches 75 percent on her spelling tests, will she balk when asked to perform better to receive a grade of B next time? Will Roberto expect that he will always be able to receive an O in reading by reading just five trade books? As was done for Aretha and Roberto, teachers need to continue to increase the criteria for successful performance until students are performing under the same conditions as their classmates without disabilities. Another problem can arise if students do not possess the skills needed to show improvement. For example, if Aretha's knowledge of sound–spelling relationships is well below that needed to spell her weekly spelling words correctly, no level of incentive will be enough to improve her performance. If there are no books in the classroom library that Roberto can read, he will be unable to reach his objective of reading five books and answering comprehension questions, regardless of the grading incentive. Teachers should select improvement as a grading accommodation only when the student's performance clearly demonstrates the presence of the prerequisite skills needed to meet the goal.

Modifying Grading Weights and Scales   Yet another type of individualized grading involves changing the grading scale used to assign a specified letter grade or changing the weights assigned to different requirements when determining a report-card grade. In the case of Staci from the chapter-opening vignettes, for example, her teacher, Ms. Stevens, counted tests as 80 percent of the grade and homework as 20 percent. Staci's IEP team decided that they could help her become less discouraged by using **modified weights and scales** grading. The team decided to reduce the percentage Ms. Stevens counted for tests from 80 to 50 percent, while keeping homework at 20 percent. However, the team also added a new assignment: Staci would be required to make a taped summary of responses to a study guide at the end of each text chapter. This assignment would count for 20 percent of Staci's grade. The remaining 10 percent of her grade would comprise other accomplishments, such as being prepared, attempting all class activities, and participating during instruction. Ms. Stevens defined these other accomplishments as the percentage of school days for which Staci had her materials for class, completed in-class assignments, and asked at least one question in class. Because Staci's IEP team members were concerned that she would drop out of school, they also decided to make a temporary change in the grading scale for her. Staci's modified scale would be as follows: A = 90–100%; B = 80–89%; C = 70–79%; and so on. The regular school scale was this: A = 93–100%; B = 85–92%; C = 77–84%, and so on. Staci's IEP team planned to move her back to the school grading scale when her grades improved for two consecutive marking periods.

Teacher interviews consistently reveal that graphs documenting student progress are far more understandable to students than are numerical averages of scores over an entire semester (Gersten, Vaughn, & Brengelman, 1996).

dimensions of
DIVERSITY

Many metropolitan school districts provide teachers the service of having testing information translated into languages as diverse as Chinese, Korean, Tagalog, and Arabic.

As an alternative to pencil-and-paper tests, performance-based tests allow students to demonstrate their knowledge and skills through application in real-world contexts. What are some of the ways to support students with special needs as they participate in performance-based assessment?

The benefit of changing the grading scale or weights is that doing so may motivate students to keep trying because they can earn a higher grade that seemed out of reach before. This was certainly the case for Staci, who was in need of a motivator because she had been trying hard but with little success to show for it. However, changing the grading scale and/or the weights for class requirements must be implemented cautiously because these accommodations do not require a change in the student's performance. This lack of increased performance expectations may send a message to students that they have no need to improve. Changing the weights and/or the grading scale may also be perceived by classmates and other teachers as unfair. Because of this we do not recommend changing the grading scale unless other instructional accommodations are used as well. For Staci, a number of accommodations were used in conjunction with changing weights and the grading scale. While Staci's tests counted less toward her grade, she was still expected to learn key content by submitting an orally completed study guide for each chapter in the text. She was also expected to be prepared for class, attempt all class activities, and ask questions in class. Often changing weights is perceived to be fairer if weight is shifted to alternative ways to assess student learning, not simply away from a requirement that is particularly difficult for a student (Munk, 2003). Finally, the IEP team planned to reestablish the regular grading scale as soon as Staci showed signs of success in class.

Legalities of Individualized Grading

Individualizing grading is legal for students with disabilities as long as the accommodations and modifications that comprise them appear on students' IEPs. Individualized grading should not be used with students without IEPs unless it is available to all students in the class or school (Salend & Duhaney, 2002). All school districts have some grading policy, and you should check to see whether individualized grading is covered by your policy. The Professional Edge presents a more in-depth discussion of the legalities of grading students with disabilities.

How Can Performance-Based Assessment Benefit Students with Special Needs?

Ms. Johnson is just completing a unit on persuasive writing and has her students write letters to the editor of a local newspaper, trying to persuade readers to support the building of a new county facility for elderly people. Mr. Repp is teaching drawing to scale as part of a map-reading unit and has his students make a map of the neighborhood that could be used by visitors from Japan. Ms. Overton's class is working on basic bookkeeping skills and has her students plan a budget for a fund-raiser to earn money to build a new swing set for the playground.

All these teachers are checking their students' progress with a method of evaluation called performance-based assessment. **Performance-based assessment** "provides students with opportunities to demonstrate their mastery of a skill or concept through performance of a task" (Haager & Klingner, 2005, p. 66). Performance-based assessment measures learning processes rather than focusing only on learning products. It frequently involves using **authentic learning tasks,** or

PROFESSIONAL EDGE

The Legalities of Grading Students with Disabilities

Report-card grades often are used to make important educational decisions about students such as eligibility for honors awards, graduation, and admission to postsecondary education. Because of the importance of grades, teachers need to exert great care when modifying grading systems for students with and without disabilities. While most schools have a written grading policy containing guidelines for giving and interpreting grades, many such policies focus on the grading scale and the schedule for reporting grades to parents, not on judgments required for grading students with disabilities (Munk, 2003).

The following are some commonly asked questions and answers about grading students with disabilities (LRP Publications, 1997; Salend & Duhaney, 2002). As legal guidelines for grading are constantly being refined, you should consult your school policies and your building administrator prior to modifying your grading system. It is also important to document all grading accommodations and modifications for students with disabilities on their IEPs.

1. *May I give modified grades to a student with a disability who is in my classroom and receiving accommodations?* Using alternative grading systems for students with disabilities is appropriate but only if you make the same ones available for your students without disabilities as well. You do not need to make grading modifications available to all students when they are specified on a student's IEP.

2. *If a student enrolled in my class has alternative curricular objectives specified on her IEP, can I exclude her from my regular grading system and evaluate her based on her IEP objectives?* In effect, students in an alternative, more basic curriculum are usually not considered to be officially enrolled in your class for credit. Therefore, you may grade them solely on the basis of their IEP objectives.

3. *May I collaborate with a student's special education teacher to decide how to assign the student a grade?* Collaborating with a student's special education teacher is entirely appropriate (and desirable).

4. *If I want to communicate to parents and employers that a student in my class has a modified curriculum, may the student's transcript reflect that the class was a special education class?* No. It is illegal to specify that a class is *special education*. However, there is general agreement that alternative terms can be used to communicate curricular differences, although as yet no terms have been officially sanctioned by the courts. Use a term such as *basic, level 1,* or *modified curriculum,* as long as this term is also used in courses besides those for students with disabilities, such as classes within gifted and talented programs. Asterisks or other symbols can also be used to communicate a modified curriculum as long as courses for all students are handled in a similar way. Transcripts sent to postsecondary schools can contain courses designated as modified when families and students are informed and give their written consent (Salend, 2005).

5. *May we include grades earned in separate special education classes or general education classes taken with support when we calculate districtwide GPAs and rank students for purposes of creating an honor roll or assigning scholarships?* Grades earned by students in special education classes or general education classes taken with support cannot be dismissed arbitrarily or categorically by the district. However, districts can implement a system of weighted grades that assigns points to grades depending on the difficulty of the subject matter. Weighted systems are permissible as long as they are fair and simple to understand. Districts also can establish a list of core courses that must be completed to be eligible for honors, class rankings, or participation in certain activities. Again, the important consideration is that all students are similarly affected, not just students with disabilities.

---

tasks that are presented within real-world contexts and lead to real-world outcomes.

Mr. Repp could have asked his students to compute the mileage between several cities using a mileage key, a more traditional map-reading assignment. Instead, he has them create their own maps within a real context because he wants to see how well they can apply what they have learned to an actual problem. Not only does Mr. Repp evaluate students' maps, but he also evaluates parts of the learning process, such as how well his students select and implement learning strategies and collaborate with their classmates during problem solving.

Using performance-based assessment can be very helpful for students with disabilities and other special needs who may be members of your classroom. Performance-based assessment can offer students options for demonstrating their knowledge that do not rely exclusively on reading and writing, areas that often impede the successful testing performance of students with disabilities. For example, Calvin, a struggling reader in Mr. Repp's class, completed the map activity successfully but would have had trouble with a traditional paper-and-pencil test of the same material.

Performance-based tests also are not subject to the same time constraints as traditional tests. This flexibility can benefit students who need more time, such as those with reading fluency problems, or students who need to work for shorter time periods, such as those with attention deficit–hyperactivity disorder. Again using the example of Mr. Repp's map-drawing activity, students had some time limits (they had to finish in one week), but they did not have to do the entire project in one sitting.

Students with disabilities also may have particular difficulty making the connection between school tasks and tasks in the real world. Performance-based assessment can help them understand this connection, particularly if an assessment is followed up with instruction directly geared to skill applications. For example, Ms. Johnson, whose students were required to write letters to the editor, discovered that many of her students were unable to support their arguments directly with specific examples. She therefore spent some class time demonstrating to students how they could support their arguments and guiding them through several practice activities.

As you can see, using performance-based assessment has many potential benefits for students with special needs. Nonetheless, you may still need to make accommodations for students with disabilities when they participate in performance-based assessments. For example, Gregory is a student with cerebral palsy in Mr. Repp's social studies class. Gregory has very little control over fine motor movements in his hands. As a result, he is unable to write or draw. Gregory obviously needs to have the drawing-to-scale map task adapted. One possible accommodation would be to have Gregory make an audiotape to accompany the map that would provide the Japanese visitors with a self-guided tour. Or consider Rhonda, a student with a learning disability who has difficulty expressing herself in writing. Rhonda is included in Ms. Johnson's class. The class is writing letters to the editor as a way of practicing persuasive writing skills. As an accommodation, Ms. Johnson has Rhonda develop an oral editorial that is sent to the local public radio channel. In some cases then, accommodations for performance-based tests can be made just as readily as those made for traditional tests.

Some students with special needs may have problems with performance-based tests that are more difficult to accommodate. For instance, students might have difficulty making the connection between school tasks and real-world tasks. You need to teach these students directly how to make those connections. For example, Ms. Riley's class is learning to compute subtraction problems. As a performance-based test, Ms. Riley has her class compare prices of various brands of the same products in the grocery store and compute price differences using subtraction. Cleo, a student in the class who has a mild intellectual disability, is unable to perform the task because he has never used subtraction as it applies to money or products in the grocery store. The next day in class, Ms. Riley includes examples of subtracting amounts of money in her daily instruction. She also includes word problems dealing with the subtraction of money, some of which involve grocery store products. This accommodation helps Cleo make the connection between money, subtraction, and the supermarket.

Students with special needs also may lack important preskills necessary for problem solving. You need either to teach these preskills or allow such students to bypass the preskills altogether to carry out performance-based tasks. For example, Sam has a learning disability in math; he does not know basic math facts and as a result cannot get Ms. Riley's product comparisons correct. Ms. Riley allows him to perform the task with a calculator. She also requires that he spend five minutes per day using a computer-based math fact program until he learns basic math facts. Anna has visual disabilities; another student reads to her the prices of the brands and she writes them down.

For students with moderate to severe intellectual disabilities, you may need to modify or scale down performance-based tasks by using the guidelines for developing alternate assessments described in Chapter 4 and the environmental inventory process described in Chapter 9. For example, Derek has a severe intellectual disability and lacks basic math skills other than simple number identification. Ms. Riley has Derek participate in the same task as the other students but has him perform an easier step. She has Derek pick groups of products that students are to compare. This task is more consistent with Derek's IEP goal of being able to classify similar objects, such as three kinds of cola or two types of bread.

Finally, students with disabilities or other special needs may have trouble meeting the problem-solving demands of performance-based tests. For example, Peter has attention deficits and approaches problems impulsively; he rushes to find an answer and fails to consider all the options. For Peter, performance-based tests are important because they give him the opportunity to learn critical self-control and problem-solving skills. Nonetheless, for students like Peter to succeed, performance-based tasks need to be modified and problem-solving skills need to be taught directly. For example, Mr. Kelsey's class is applying work they have done in computing areas and perimeters to the task of planning a garden. Before having students design their own gardens, Mr. Kelsey carefully demonstrates how he would design his. This demonstration is very helpful for students in the class such as Peter, who are not natural problem solvers and need a model to guide them. Mr. Kelsey also scales down Peter's assignment, asking him to design only one section of a smaller garden. Finally, before allowing Peter to construct his design, Mr. Kelsey has Peter verbally explain it to him to ensure that Peter has carefully thought through his idea.

As you can see, the use of performance-based tests with students with disabilities can be helpful, but it can also be problematic. For this reason, use performance-based tests in conjunction with other classroom-based and standardized tests.

How Can Portfolio Assessment Benefit Students with Special Needs?

Portfolio assessment is a method of evaluation in which a purposeful collection of student work is used to determine student effort, progress, and achievement in one or more areas (Montgomery, 2001). A portfolio collection typically contains the observable evidence or products of performance assessment, evidence that may or may not reflect authentic tasks (Poteet, Choate, & Stewart, 1993). This evidence includes many different sources of information, such as anecdotal records, interviews, work samples, and scored samples such as curriculum-based assessment probes.

Portfolios can be very helpful for teachers working with students with disabilities. Portfolios can assist teachers in evaluating student progress toward IEP objectives and in guiding instruction. For example, Ms. Pohl is interested in finding out whether the extra math practice sheets she is sending home with Robert are improving his scores on weekly math computation tests. She consults Robert's portfolio and finds that his performance has improved quite a bit over the last two months. Ms. Pohl tells Robert's parents of his progress. They agree to continue the extra practice for at least another month. Portfolios also emphasize student products rather than tests and test scores. This emphasis benefits students with special needs, many of whom are poor test takers. Portfolios also may highlight student strengths better than traditional tests, which tend to have a narrow academic focus. For example, Leshonn's teacher uses portfolios to evaluate her social studies students. Leshonn has problems in reading and writing but has good artistic ability and excellent oral language skills. During the last marking period, his class studied the growth of suburban areas after World War II, subject matter based on the state standards. Leshonn designed a scale model of Levittown, one of the first planned communities. He also developed a recorded explanation to go with the model that explained the key features of the community. His performance on these projects was excellent and enabled him to raise his overall grade for the class because his scores on the two tests given during the marking period were low.

Finally, a key component of portfolio assessments is student self-evaluation. As you have already learned, students with special needs often are described as not being involved in their own learning; they can benefit greatly from self-evaluation. For example, students might complete a self-assessment after they have finished a unit

RESEARCH NOTE

Johnson and Arnold (2004) examined the validity of one state's alternate assessment portfolio system using commonly accepted professional standards and found serious shortcomings. While portfolios are potentially valuable evaluation tools, they should supplement, not supplant, standardized achievement, psychological, and curriculum-based measures.

of instruction. This evaluation can then become a part of the students' portfolios. The Technology Notes features the use of assistive technology in helping students with severe intellectual disabilities construct their own portfolios.

You may have to make accommodations when using portfolios with students with disabilities, particularly in selecting and evaluating portfolio pieces. For example, Jerome was asked to select an example of his best work in written expression for his portfolio. However, he was uncertain what "best work" meant: Was it the paper that he tried his hardest on? Was it the paper that was the hardest to write? Or was it the one that he or his teacher liked best? Because he did not know, Jerome simply selected one paper at random. Similarly, when Thanh was asked to evaluate his efforts to solve a word problem in math for his portfolio, all he could come up with was whether he had the correct answer. You need to teach students such as Jerome and Thanh how to select and evaluate portfolio pieces.

TECHNOLOGY NOTES

Conducting Alternative Assessments Using Electronic Portfolios

Denham and Lahm (2001) described four students who used assistive technology to make their portfolios. All four students had moderate to severe disabilities and were unable to use the standard computer keyboard effectively. They used the IntelliKeys keyboard as an adaptation.

IntelliKeys is an enlarged keyboard that enables users with physical, visual, or intellectual disabilities to easily type, enter numbers, navigate on-screen displays, and execute menu commands. IntelliKeys helps students produce artifacts for their portfolios related to their IEP objectives and can be customized for specific students using individually designed overlays. The overlay for Amanda, a student with severe intellectual disabilities, is shown in Figure 11.5.

Amanda's teacher constructed this overlay using Overlay Maker 3, a software program. The response keys were grouped according to color and were used to facilitate making correct choices. The overlay provided response choices that Amanda was to use to complete an activity sheet shown on the computer. Amanda's activity sheet is shown in Figure 11.6.

For Amanda, questions on the activity sheet were related to her performance on her IEP goals, such as loading a soda machine, recycling cans, and shopping at the store. The activity sheet and overlay were designed to allow Amanda to read the text with text-reading software and construct a variety of sentences in response to the questions asked on the activity sheet using the overlay. By pressing a response choice on the overlay, Amanda caused the text programmed into that cell to be entered into the activity sheet. All answers were read back to Amanda, allowing her to confirm the correctness of her answers. Note that some of the questions

FIGURE 11.5 Amanda's IntelliKeys Overlay

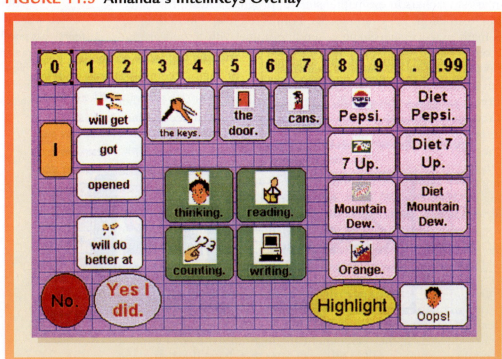

required a yes or no response while others required a more open-ended answer. The complexity of these questions was based on what Amanda was able to do. Amanda was assisted in her effort by a classroom peer without disabilities. The peer provided prompts and assistance when needed. When Amanda answered with assistance, her answer was shown in a different color, allowing her teacher to monitor her level of independent performance.

According to Denham and Lahm (2001, p. 13), "Before using the IntelliKeys, Amanda was limited to handwriting her responses, which was painstakingly slow. The IntelliKeys system allowed her to write 56 words in 20 minutes, a feat she could not have accomplished without it. Amanda's reaction to the IntelliKeys system was, 'This is neat.'"

Sources: "Using Technology to Construct Alternate Portfolios of Students with Moderate and Severe Disabilities," by A. Denham and E. Lahm, 2001, *Teaching Exceptional Children, 33*(5), pp. 10–17; and Overlay Maker (Version 3) (computer software), 2004, Petaluma, CA: IntelliTools.

FIGURE 11.6 Amanda's Soda Machine Activity Sheet

Prompt	Response			
Did I use my schedule?				
Did I use my sheet so I know what to do next?				
Did I write what sodas were needed?				
How many cans did we need?				
Did I put the can in the right place?				
Did I do a good job?				
Next time I will do better at . . .				

WRAPPING IT UP
BACK TO THE CASES

This section provides opportunities for you to apply the knowledge gained in this chapter to the cases described at the beginning of this chapter: Staci, Jennifer, and Lucille. The questions and activities that follow demonstrate how these standards and principles, along with other concepts that you have learned about in this chapter, connect to the everyday activities of all teachers.

STACI, as you may recall, struggled during tests because of her reading problem, a common concern for students with learning disabilities. Many teachers face the same dilemma as Ms. Stevens: How can she provide Staci with an opportunity to demonstrate her learned knowledge and skills that will not be affected by her reading disability? Review the information in your text regarding accommodations that can be made before, during, and after a test. In addition, consider what you have learned throughout this text about technology. Develop plans for working with Staci to improve her test-taking skills as she prepares for and takes an exam. Share your plan with a peer and discuss its pros and cons.

JENNIFER reads at a lower level than her classmates but receives As. Her parents have questions about her grade in reading, and so do some of her classmates. Jennifer shared her report card with a classmate, who then reported Jennifer's A to several other classmates.

Three of those classmates are distressed because they did not earn As and believe they are reading much harder books than Jennifer. The teacher overheard two of the students taunting Jennifer by calling her the "teacher's pet" and laughing about the "baby books" she read. When the teacher stopped the girls and asked them why they were being cruel to Jennifer, they complained about the unfairness of Ms. Robinson's grading system. What could the teacher have done to avoid situations such as this one? How might you have responded to the girls?

LUCILLE will be in your classroom this year. Her previous teachers used one of the five types of individualized grading accommodations identified by researchers: progress based on IEP objectives. You have thought carefully about the issue of modifying your grading procedures to reflect Lucille's learning and progress in your class. You are planning a conference with her guardian and the special education teacher to discuss a change in the grading procedures. You would like to use another of the five individualized grading accommodations that you believe would also be helpful for your grade and content area. To prepare for the conference, outline your plan for using one of the other grading accommodations in your content area and list your reasons for selecting this alternative individualized grading procedure.

SUMMARY

- Testing accommodations can be made before testing, during testing, and after testing. Accommodations before the test include study guides, practice tests, tutoring, teaching test-taking skills and strategies, and modifying test construction. During the test, you can make alternative forms of questions and allow alternative ways of administering tests. Accommodations after the test involve grading tests and include changing letter or number grades, changing the criteria on which grades are based, and using alternatives to letter and number grades.

- Practices in report-card grading that can benefit all students include using differentiated report cards, avoiding the use of zeroes, and reporting progress frequently.

- Individualized grading involves changing the grading elements and/or changing the value of the elements. Changing the grading elements involves grading on the basis of IEP objectives, prioritizing educational content and assignments, and balanced grading. Changing the value of grading elements includes grading on the basis of improvement and using modified grading weights and scales.

- Performance-based assessment measures learning processes rather than focusing exclusively on learning products and frequently involves authentic, or real-world, tasks. This type of assessment can be helpful in evaluating the performance of students with special needs because it does not rely exclusively on formats that create problems for students with disabilities. However, accommodations may need to be made for students with special needs.

- Portfolio assessment can also benefit students with special needs. Portfolios typically contain the observable evidence or products of performance assessment, such as anecdotal records, interviews, work samples, and scored samples. Students with disabilities may need to be taught how to select and evaluate their portfolio pieces.

APPLICATIONS IN TEACHING PRACTICE

MAKING ACCOMMODATIONS WHEN EVALUATING STUDENTS WITH SPECIAL NEEDS

Eugene is a high school student who is included in Ms. Howard's American history class. Eugene has a specific learning disability that affects his written expression, spelling, reading fluency, and organization. He is receiving a number of accommodations in Ms. Howard's class, including a recorded text with accompanying study guide, help with organizing an assignment notebook from his special education teacher, and use of an electronic speller in class. The grading elements in Ms. Howard's class are multiple-choice/essay tests (60%), 2-page research reports (25%), and end-of-chapter questions for homework (15%). Eugene is trying very hard but is barely passing Ms. Howard's class, having received a D– for the last grading period.

QUESTIONS

1. What factors might be responsible for Eugene getting such a low grade?
2. What individualized grading accommodations might be helpful for him?

Tara and Jamie are students in your fourth-grade class. Tara has a learning disability and receives intensive reading instruction in the resource room. Her short-term objectives for this marking period include reading a first-grade literature book at a rate of 20 words correct per minute with four or fewer errors per minute and discerning who the main character of the story is, what the main problem in the story is, and how the problem is solved.

Jamie is a student with mild intellectual disabilities. You are about to start a unit on adding and subtracting fractions. The IEP objective for Jamie is to identify and demonstrate the meaning of the fractions $\frac{1}{4}$, $\frac{1}{3}$, and $\frac{1}{2}$.

QUESTIONS

1. At the end of the marking period, should you give Tara a grade in reading? Why or why not?
2. Assuming that Tara has met her short-term objectives in reading, what do you think her grade for the marking period should be? Should her grade be modified in any way?
3. Describe a performance-based test that you could use to measure Jamie's knowledge of her target fractions.
4. What problems might Jamie have with your performance-based tests? What accommodations and modifications might you need to make to accommodate her?

Go to Topic 8: Assessment in the MyEducationLab (www.myeducationlab.com) for your course, where you can:

- Find learning outcomes for Assessment along with the national standards that connect to these outcomes.
- Complete Assignments and Activities that can help you more deeply understand the chapter content.
- Apply and practice your understanding of the core teaching skills identified in the chapter with the Building Teaching Skills and Dispositions learning units.
- Examine challenging situations and cases presented in the IRIS Center Resources. (optional)
- Access video clips of CCSSO National Teachers of the Year award winners responding to the question, "Why Do I Teach?" in the Teacher Talk section. (optional)
- Check your comprehension on the content covered in the chapter by going to the Study Plan in the Book Resources for your text. Here you will be able to take a chapter quiz, receive feedback on your answers, and then access Review, Practice, and Enrichment activities to enhance your understanding of chapter content. (optional)

chapter
12

Responding to Student Behavior

LEARNING Objectives

After you read this chapter, you will be able to

1. Outline classroom strategies teachers should implement to promote students' positive behavior and prevent misbehavior.

2. Explain simple techniques for responding to individual student misbehavior.

3. Describe the purpose of a functional behavior assessment and its steps for deciding how to respond to chronic, inappropriate individual student behavior.

4. Outline systematic approaches for increasing individual students' positive behaviors and decreasing their negative behaviors.

5. Identify how to help students manage their own behavior.

6. Articulate your beliefs regarding your responsibilities for fostering appropriate student behavior and addressing student behavior problems in positive ways, describing how your beliefs and actions may influence student outcomes.

JOSEPH, a high school junior with a learning disability, comes late to his algebra class at least twice each week. He seldom participates in class discussions, and he does not ask questions. Unless Mrs. Akers repeatedly asks him not to, Joseph sits with his head down on his desk. When discussing Joseph with the special education teacher, Mrs. Akers describes his demeanor as "sullen." Mrs. Akers has been teaching high school math for many years, and she believes it is students' responsibility to be interested in the subject, attend class, and participate. She knows Joseph is heading toward a failing grade for this grading period, even though she thinks he could do the work with a little more effort. She believes Joseph has given up on learning since he failed to pass the high-stakes math achievement test and refused to enroll in an after-school tutoring program that might have helped him pass it when he takes it again.

What is Joseph's responsibility for his learning? What is Mrs. Akers's responsibility for making instruction appealing to students like Joseph? What strategies could help Joseph meet Mrs. Akers's class expectations for him?

J.R. is a seventh-grade student with an emotional disability who is transitioning from a self-contained special education class to a blend of services in general education and a resource class setting. Mr. George, his social studies teacher, is concerned about two problems that are having a negative impact on J.R.'s learning. First, J.R. tends to display behaviors the school psychologist termed *oppositional:* He directly and loudly refuses to complete some assignments, he challenges Mr. George's directions, and he criticizes the way Mr. George teaches. The second issue concerns other students' interactions with J.R. Mr. George overheard a group of students discussing J.R., and they mentioned several incidents that happened in the past, one in elementary school. The students were agreeing that they did not want to work with J.R. or socialize with him away from school. Mr. George

has asked Ms. Rogers, the special educator, to schedule at least one observation in his class so that she sees J.R.'s behaviors in the general education classroom firsthand in preparation for revising J.R.'s behavior intervention plan (BIP).

What are your responsibilities for addressing the social interaction and behavior problems of students such as J.R.? What is a behavior intervention plan, and what is your role in implementing it? How can general education teachers help to ensure that students with disabilities have positive interactions with their classmates and other peers?

WHEN MS. WRIGHT was informed that her kindergarten class would include three students with disabilities, she welcomed the opportunity to make a positive difference in the lives of these as well as all her other students. But Ms. Wright did not envision a student like Jaden. Although the teacher from Jaden's early childhood program reported that he had made tremendous progress both academically and socially, he is still quite different from other kindergarteners. Ms. Wright is not concerned about academic skills. It is his behavior that worries her. Jaden gets frustrated easily and seems to express his frustration through his behavior. He has had several tantrums that included crying and kicking that lasted for longer than 15 minutes. Sometimes he also runs from the class, a clear safety issue. In addition, Jaden has "shut down" while at school, crawling under a desk, hiding his face, and refusing to interact with teachers or peers. Ms. Wright is looking forward to this afternoon's meeting about Jaden. She needs assistance in reaching Jaden when he is upset, preventing some of the situations that lead to his challenging behaviors, and creating a plan to help him learn behaviors that will enable him to succeed in school.

What purpose might Jaden's behavior be serving for him? How could Ms. Wright constructively respond to Jaden's behavior? What is a teacher's responsibility for making accommodations for a student like Jaden?

PEARSON
myeducationlab

To check your comprehension on the content covered in Chapter 12, go to the Book Resources in the MyEducationLab for your course, select your text, and complete the Study Plan. Here you will be able to take a chapter quiz, receive feedback on your answers, and then access review, practice, and enrichment activities to enhance your understanding of chapter content.

Behavior is a concern for all teachers. Whether you teach 5-year-olds in a kindergarten class or 17-year-olds in eleventh-grade English, the environment you create in your classroom affects whether students' inappropriate behaviors escalate or improve, and your response to such behaviors significantly influences students' learning (Westling, 2010). The public is concerned about student behavior, too. Despite the fact that total incidents of school violence have decreased by half over the past 20 years (U.S. Department of Justice, 2007), disruptive behavior has increased (Centers for Disease Control and Prevention, 2007), and Americans still list lack of discipline and fighting among the top five problems facing public schools (Bushow & McNee, 2009). The Professional Edge takes a brief look at the topic of school violence and related student warning signs.

To begin a discussion of preventing student behavior problems and responding to inappropriate behavior, we present three key concepts that provide a context for the rest of the chapter. First, remember that the root word of *discipline* is *disciple*, meaning "a follower of a teacher." Even though discipline often is associated with obedience, **discipline** mostly is about learning. It is a means of ensuring that students have the maximum opportunity to learn from their teachers. Discipline is never an end in and of itself, nor is it about control or power. In this chapter, you will be

PROFESSIONAL **EDGE**
Preventing School Violence

As a school professional, you have a responsibility to be alert for students who are at high risk for committing acts of violence against themselves or others. Most of these students display early warning signs that should signal to you a need for help. As you review the warning signs listed here, which have been identified through research, keep in mind that if you have serious concerns about a student, you should ask for assistance from your colleagues, including school counselors, social workers, and administrators, and, with their support, work with parents and the student to address the issues at hand.

EARLY WARNING SIGNS OF POTENTIAL FOR VIOLENCE

- *Social withdrawal:* Some students gradually withdraw from social contact because of depression, rejection, or a lack of confidence.
- *Excessive feelings of isolation:* Although most students feel isolated occasionally, a sense of isolation sometimes is associated with aggression and violence.
- *Excessive feelings of rejection:* Some aggressive students who are rejected by peers seek out other aggressive students who in turn reinforce their aggressive tendencies.
- *Victimization by others:* Students who have been physically or sexually abused are at risk of becoming violent.
- *Feelings of being picked on and persecuted:* Students who believe they are teased, bullied, or humiliated at home or at school may vent their feelings through aggression or violence.
- *Low school interest and poor academic performance:* A drastic change in school performance or poor school achievement accompanied by frustration can be a warning sign for acting out.
- *Expression of violence in writings and drawings:* When violent themes are directed at specific individuals (for example, teachers, peers), a student should be referred to a counselor or another professional for assistance.

- *Uncontrolled anger:* Getting angry is natural, but if a student is frequently and intensely angry in response to minor incidents, it may signal a potential for violence.
- *Patterns of impulsive and chronic hitting, intimidating, and bullying behavior:* If behaviors such as these are not addressed, they can escalate to violence.
- *History of discipline problems:* Chronic behavior problems sometimes signal underlying emotional needs that are unmet.
- *Past history of violent and aggressive behavior:* Unless a student with a history of aggressive and violent acts receives counseling, the behaviors are likely to continue and even escalate.
- *Intolerance for differences and prejudicial attitudes:* Intense prejudice (regarding, for example, race, ethnicity, religion, gender, or sexual orientation) may lead to violence against individuals perceived to belong to the targeted group.
- *Drug and alcohol use:* The use of drugs and alcohol tends to reduce self-control, thus increasing the chance of being either a perpetrator or victim of violence.
- *Affiliation with gangs:* Students who are members of gangs that support antisocial values may act on group beliefs.
- *Inappropriate access to, possession of, and use of firearms:* Students who have a history of aggression, impulsiveness, or other serious emotional problems should not have access to firearms and other weapons.
- *Serious threats of violence:* One of the most reliable indicators that a student is likely to commit a violent act is a specific and detailed threat.

Sources: Adapted from *Early Warning, Time Response: A Guide to Safe Schools*, by U.S. Department of Education, Special Education and Rehabilitative Services, 1998, Washington, DC: Author. Retrieved August 10, 2007, from http://www.ed.gov/about/offices/list/osers/osep/gtss.html.

finding ways to enhance your students' learning and help them to reach their potential by preventing and responding to behavior problems, that is, by fostering appropriate classroom discipline.

Second, teacher beliefs about discipline have a strong cultural basis, and some evidence suggests that a teacher is far more likely to refer students for discipline problems when they are from a culture other than the teacher's (Lee, 2008; Skiba, Michael, Nardo, & Peterson, 2002). In addition, teachers may unintentionally vary their use of discipline techniques (for example, talking to the student versus taking away a privilege) depending on the student's culture or ethnicity (Jensen, 2004; Rausch & Skiba, 2006). All teachers have an obligation to monitor their behavior to ensure that their responses are not biased.

Third, over the past decade, researchers have worked to identify interventions for preventing behavior challenges as well as techniques for addressing common and intense behavior problems. Their work has been collected at the U.S. Office of Special Education Programs (OSEP) National Technical Assistance Center on Positive Behavioral Interventions and Supports (PBIS) (U.S. Department of Education, 2009). **Positive behavioral interventions and supports (PBIS),** and variations of this specific work sometimes called the more general term **positive behavior supports (PBS),** are research-based, systemic approaches designed to enhance the learning environment and improve outcomes for students.

PBS interventions are grouped by their intensity. The first level is called *primary prevention* and is considered a universal level of intervention. That is, it is designed to create schoolwide and classroom environments that address the needs of approximately 80 percent of students (Lewis, Jones, Horner, & Sugai, 2010; Handler, Rey, Connell, Their, Feinberg, & Putman, 2007). The second level, *secondary prevention* or group level, is designed to quickly and efficiently address student behavior problems in order to prevent them from becoming more serious, and it addresses an additional 15 percent or so of students (Filter, McKenna, Benedict, Horner, Todd, & Watson, 2007), usually through small-group interventions. The final level, *tertiary prevention* or individual level, includes intensive interventions for the 5 percent or so of students whose behavior problems are chronic or exceptionally serious.

The PBS structure is similar in important ways to that used for response to intervention (RtI) for student problems related to reading and other academic areas. In the Professional Edge on page 372 you can learn how some school professionals are incorporating interventions related to behavior into their RtI procedures.

Many issues are beyond a teacher's control—you do not have the power to increase the financial support available to schools, nor can you remove the public pressures that surround many school reform initiatives. However, teachers ultimately are accountable for student outcomes, and those who actively, carefully, and creatively apply approaches to create a positive learning environment, build students' skills as members of their classroom community, and effectively address student behavior challenges will have a positive influence on student learning (Carr, 2007; Jones, Jones, & Vermette, 2009; Nelson, Hurley, Synhorst, Epstein, Stage, & Buckley, 2009). The sections that follow present a wide array of procedures grounded in the three key concepts just outlined to assist you to reach that goal.

How Can You Use Positive Behavior Supports to Prevent Discipline Problems?

The beginning point for addressing student behavior problems is to focus on how to *prevent* them (Ervin et al., 2007; McIntosh, Filter, Bennett, Ryan, & Sugai, 2010); these are the primary prevention strategies addressed in PBS. In nearly all situations, you can create a caring and positive instructional environment conducive to learning (Fairbanks, Sugai, Guardino, & Lathrop, 2007) and avoid teaching in a classroom in which the stress level is high and "keeping control" is a constant struggle.

dimensions of DIVERSITY

An important type of diversity to monitor in your interactions with students is gender. You need to ensure that you interact with boys and girls equitably and that you respond to their behavior needs without bias.

www.resources

http://www.pbis.org/
To learn more about PBIS, including explanations of primary, secondary, and tertiary interventions, visit the National Technical Assistance Center on Positive Behavioral Interventions and Supports.

PROFESSIONAL EDGE

Response to Intervention and Positive Behavior Supports

Response to intervention, with its focus on increasingly intensive interventions carefully monitored by frequent data collection, is being extended in some schools to address social and behavioral concerns as well as academic ones. Here are examples of how three tiers of interventions may apply to student behaviors.

Tier 1: Universal interventions (effective for 80–90 percent of students)

- Clear schoolwide rules and expectations, including procedures for the lunchroom, procedures for entering and leaving the building as school begins and ends, and so on.
- Clear classroom rules and expectations
- Character-building programs for all students
- Social skills instruction for all students
- Procedures for deescalating disruptive behavior by establishing cooling off times for student reflection
- Monitoring of student behavior using naturally occurring measures, such as discipline referrals

Tier 2: Selected interventions (effective for an additional 10–20 percent of students)

- Structured social skills training designed for small groups
- Group counseling
- Mentoring programs
- Daily behavior report card
- Use of structured reward programs for appropriate behavior
- Progress monitoring at least every two weeks

Tier 3: Targeted interventions (effective for the remaining 1–5 percent of students)

- Implementation of functional behavior assessment (described later in this chapter)
- Involvement of agencies outside the school, possibly including juvenile justice, mental, and social services
- Individual counseling, possibly including the family and possibly delivered at the student's home
- Individually designed behavior intervention plan (described later in this chapter)
- Frequent progress monitoring, as often as daily or weekly

Research on the use of RtI procedures for student behavior concerns indicates that it has many benefits. Pavri (2010) interviewed special education teachers about its use in urban school districts. They reported that a behavior-focused RtI procedure assisted with data collection, encouraged communication with parents, emphasized student strengths, fostered reflection about effective instructional practices, and encouraged student goal setting. However, these educators expressed skepticism concerning whether adequate resources could be available for ongoing implementation. In another study, Nelson, Hurley, Synhorst, Epstein, Stage, & Buckley (2009) found that a 3-tier approach was effective in increasing social skills and reducing inappropriate behaviors in many (but not all) children.

Clear rules and direct discussions about expectations foster a classroom climate that encourages appropriate behavior.

Instructional Environments Conducive to Learning

In Chapter 5, you learned that many factors contribute to creating an instructional environment that fosters student learning. Many of these same factors also promote appropriate classroom behavior. For example, you learned that teachers need to set clear expectations in their classrooms through rules that students understand and follow (Conroy, Sutherland, Snyder, & Marsh, 2008; George, White, & Schlaffer, 2007).

Another key factor related to the instructional environment and discipline is establishing clear classroom routines. Routines should be established for beginning the school day or class period, transitioning from one activity to another, moving about in the classroom, and ending the school day or class period. Students who have routines are less likely to misbehave because they can meet classroom expectations for behavior. In classes such as art, music, drama, and physical education, in which students may be very active participants, routines are especially important.

Effective Classroom Communication   Teachers who treat their students with respect and trust are more successful than other teachers in creating a positive classroom environment in which fewer behavior problems occur (Partin, Robertson, Maggin, Oliver, & Wehby, 2010; Rimm-Kaufman & Chiu, 2007). Communication between teacher and students is integral to fostering this trust and respect. However, teacher–student communication is a complex matter, and problems often arise. For example, sometimes teachers provide students with too much information or information that is not clear, and students become confused. And sometimes teachers give one message with words but convey another message with their tone of voice or nonverbal behaviors.

Another dimension of teacher–student communication concerns language differences. When students struggle to understand English, their behaviors may at first appear to be challenging. For example, a first-grader is asked to complete several directions at one time and has a tantrum as a result of the frustration of not understanding. Similarly, a high school student apparently ignores a teacher's direction to put away project supplies and spend any remaining time beginning the homework assignment. When the teacher addresses this behavior, the student pushes everything off his desk. Is this a behavior problem or an example of misunderstanding and frustration? Teachers working with students who are not proficient English speakers should take care to distinguish problems that result from language differences from misbehavior.

The overall quality of your communication with your students is built in numerous small ways. For example, finding time each week to speak privately with students lets them know that you value them as individuals. Asking older students sincere questions about their friends, out-of-school activities, and part-time jobs also conveys that you care. Taking the time to write positive comments on papers shows students that you appreciate their strengths and are not focusing only on their needs. Using nonverbal signals instead of, or in addition to, verbal communication also can facilitate understanding (Jamie & Knowlton, 2007).

Effective Teaching Methods   Another critical strategy for preventing behavior problems is to provide instruction that is relevant, interesting, individualized, and active (Lane, Little, Redding-Rhodes, Phillips, & Welsh, 2007; Lingo, Slaton, & Jolivette, 2006). Recall from Chapters 9 and 10 that learning is enhanced through the use of clear and systematic instructional approaches that actively engage students in learning. We remind you of this information because effective instruction plays a critical role in classroom behavior management. Students who are given boring or outdated materials, who are asked to complete seemingly endless worksheets with little instructional value, who have few opportunities to create their own learning through projects or activities, or who seldom see their own culture reflected in their learning tasks are likely to misbehave (Trussel, 2008).

Fostering Positive Student Interactions   Another key to preventing behavior problems is to foster positive student interactions; simply mixing students with and without

Do you need to review examples of effective classroom rules? If so, refer to page 144 in Chapter 5.

Zero-tolerance policies exclude students from school for serious behavior infractions. Suggested alternatives include (1) in-school suspension, (2) school or community service in addition to academic work and tutoring, and (3) structured problem solving to state specifically what students need to do to address their behavior problems (Brownstein, 2010).

disabilities in single classrooms may not result in an integrated social system for them (Odom, Zercher, Li, Marquart, Sandall, & Brown, 2006). To develop respect for one another, an appreciation for diversity, and sensitivity to others who are not exactly like themselves could be among the most important lessons you teach your students.

One way to promote positive interactions among students with and without disabilities is to provide opportunities for them to interact in meaningful ways. In both elementary and secondary classrooms and regardless of the academic content being addressed, this means structuring activities and assigning students to groups so that interacting becomes part of classroom instruction. Formal strategies for doing this are introduced in the next section of this chapter. Arranging service-learning activities in which students with and without disabilities all participate is another way to encourage interactions (Kleinert et al., 2007; Scott, 2006). For instance, students might work together to pick up debris from a local park, visit a senior citizen center, or contact local government officials to support a new recycling initiative.

Creating special programs is yet another way to accomplish the goal of meaningful interactions. For example, in one high school, peer buddies were assigned to provide students with significant intellectual disabilities with more and better opportunities to participate in general education classes (Copeland et al., 2004). In this program, students without disabilities were paired with students with disabilities to provide academic and social support. Group interviews of participating nondisabled students revealed that these students discovered many ways that their classmates with disabilities were socially isolated in schools. They also learned that they could foster social interaction by advocating for their buddies, facilitating interactions with other students, and modeling appropriate social interactions.

You may be able to identify many other strategies for fostering interactions between students with and without disabilities, interactions that build positive social relationships. How could you do this in an elementary classroom? A middle school class? A high school class? Even a small amount of attention on your part to arranging such interactions can benefit all your students (Macy & Bricker, 2007). The Case in Practice illustrates the importance of fostering positive student interactions.

Schoolwide Strategies

One additional prevention strategy goes beyond your classroom. PBS supports the use of schoolwide prevention strategies that are developed in a systematic way (for example, Hendley, 2007; Warren et al., 2006), often by a committee of several teachers and administrators. These schoolwide strategies require a commitment to implementation from every teacher, specialist, and other staff member in the school. For example, a common schoolwide expectation is that students will be respectful of themselves, of others, and of property. In the lunchroom, the specific expectations might include these:

- Use a soft voice at all times.
- Ask for assistance if something is spilled or dropped.
- Remove all trays and dispose of all trash when you are finished eating.

What might the specific applications be for a locker room? A student commons area? On the bus?

How Can You Promote Positive Group Behavior?

In effective classrooms, teachers and students respect each other, and students are busily engaged in learning (Maag, 2004); a clear sense of classroom community exists. Students attend to their work, interact with each other politely and without verbal or physical fighting, and ignore the occasional misbehavior of classmates instead of encouraging it. You can promote positive behaviors such as these by using

CASE IN PRACTICE

Intervening to Promote Positive Social Interactions

Ms. Giano, a middle school teacher, is in a quandary. This afternoon she received a phone call from Ms. Perez concerning Jesse, her son. Ms. Perez related that Jesse had come home from school looking disheveled, carrying torn books and papers. At first he wouldn't tell his mother what had happened, but eventually he related the story. Jesse has albinism. He has very little pigment in his skin, hair, and eyes. His skin is very pale, and his hair seems almost white. In addition, Jesse has a serious vision problem related to his albinism, and he also has been identified as having a learning disability. He told his mother that several of his classmates had begun making fun of him on the walk to the bus and then continued on the bus. They had been doing this almost since the beginning of the school year, but things had been getting worse lately. Today, Jesse explained, he couldn't stand it anymore and he lunged at the boys. The bus driver intervened, but all the boys now were to be brought back to school by their parents for fighting.

Ms. Perez was upset. She also mentioned to Ms. Giano that Jesse had asked her not to call school, saying that he would deal with the situation and accept the discipline for fighting on the bus. He was afraid that his classmates' teasing would become even worse if it was made an issue. Ms. Perez is not satisfied; she wants something done to stop the teasing and protect her son. She is concerned that Jesse is becoming discouraged and has read about the association between such teasing and depression, especially among middle and high school students.

REFLECTION

How does this story relate to the topic of bullying? If you were Ms. Giano, what would you say to Ms. Perez? What is the role of the general education teachers in ensuring that students are treated respectfully? How would you address this issue with Jesse? With the other boys? If you think they should have an additional consequence, what should it be? What might you try as an all-homeroom activity to foster better understanding among your diverse students? Would your response to the situation and interventions be significantly different if you plan to teach elementary students? High school students? How so?

---

behavior management strategies designed specifically for the whole class (Lannie & McCurdy, 2007; Murphy & Korinek, 2009). For example, all students might participate in discussing classroom discipline issues, helping each other monitor their behavior, and earning privileges or rewards as individuals or as members of learning groups (Rimm-Kaufman & Chiu, 2007; Sobel & Taylor, 2006). The following sections describe additional effective whole-group strategies: peer-mediated instruction and group contingency systems.

Implement Peer-Mediated Instruction

Peer-mediated instruction is the term for structured and interactive systems in which students teach each other. It enables teachers to change from traditional whole-group teaching approaches, and a strong research base demonstrates that peer-mediated instruction improves students' social relationships, decreases student behavior problems, and improves students' academic outcomes (for example, Anderson, 2007; Harper & Maheady, 2007; Kroeger, Burton, & Preston, 2009). J.R., whom you met at the beginning of the chapter, might benefit from peer-mediated instruction.

Peer Tutoring   In **peer tutoring,** pairs of students are given formal roles for promoting each other's achievement (Bond & Castagnera, 2006; Mastropieri, Scruggs, & Berkeley, 2007; McMaster, 2010). The tutor role most often is held by a peer in the same class, but the tutor could also be from another class or school. *Tutees* are the students who receive the instruction from peer tutors.

One example of a highly structured peer tutoring program is **Peer-Assisted Learning Strategies (PALS).** It has been repeatedly demonstrated through research to be effective for students with learning and behavioral disabilities (McMaster, Fuchs, & Fuchs, 2006; Sporer & Brunstein, 2009) and English-language learners

(Sáenz, Fuchs, & Fuchs, 2005). For example, a group of first-grade teachers implemented PALS for their students with and without disabilities (Baker, Gersten, Dimino, & Griffiths, 2004). Several years after the initial successful research study, the teachers were still using the peer-tutoring program effectively at least twice each week in math. Because the program includes a built-in data collection system, they were able to report that the effect on student academic achievement was highly positive. The teachers also noted that PALS had a positive impact on student social development. They found that the program taught students to work effectively with many different peers, instead of just their friends, by helping them to learn how to say positive things to one another. This result carried far beyond the math instructional period and is a specific example of how peer-mediated instructional approaches facilitate positive behaviors.

Developing Peer-Tutoring Programs   Developing a peer-tutoring program can be as simple or complex as you want it to be. You can create your own system within your classroom, partner some or all of your students with another group of students, or help coordinate a schoolwide tutoring program. Alternatively, you may decide to use a research-based approach, such as PALS, mentioned above, or **Classwide Peer Tutoring (CWPT)** (for example, Burks, 2004; Greenwood et al., 2001; Maheady, Mallette, & Harper, 2006), in which all the students in a class take on the roles of tutor and tutee in turn and follow a set of clear steps for helping each other learn. CWPT is described in Figure 12.1.

Generally, the steps for setting up a peer-tutoring program of your own are these:

1. *Selecting tutors:* To create a **same-age tutoring** program in your classroom, consider pairing students who are both high-achievers rather than pairing a high-achiever with a low-achiever. Then pair other students whose understanding of the topic at hand is fairly similar. This arrangement reduces the problem of high-achievers becoming impatient with low-achievers and the concern about high-achieving students missing their own opportunities for learning. Another approach is to pair students randomly and use a **reciprocal tutoring** approach, in which both students alternate between the tutor and tutee roles. To create a **cross-age tutoring** approach, older students tutor younger ones, either within a school, or across school levels (e.g., older elementary students tutor younger ones, middle school students tutor elementary students, or high school students tutor middle school students) (Dopp & Block, 2004). Seniors might be paired with freshmen or sophomores in this way. Remember, sometimes students with disabilities can serve as tutors to their classmates. An older student without a disability can be an ideal tutor for a younger student with a disability. Also, an older student who has a learning or intellectual disability or who is at risk for school failure can be an effective tutor for a younger student with or without a disability. In other words, you can structure a tutoring

FIGURE 12.1 **Steps in Classwide Peer Tutoring**

1. Assign all students to tutoring pairs that change weekly or biweekly.
2. Assign each tutoring pair to one of two classroom teams.
3. Teach all students a specific series of steps for presenting and practicing content.
4. Teach all students specific strategies for correcting tutees and rewarding correct responses.
5. Provide tutoring pairs with daily assignments.
6. Instruct tutors to keep score: When a tutee answers a question correctly, a point is scored for the team.
7. Announce the winning team and post point totals.
8. Reward the winning team with a privilege or class applause.
9. Reverse the tutor/tutee arrangement each session, or have both students take the tutor role within each session.

program in many ways. What is important is making deliberate decisions about structure based on the strengths and needs of the students.

2. *Deciding how much tutoring should occur:* The specific time allocated to peer tutoring depends on the needs of the students and the structure of the program. In many cases tutoring in elementary schools occurs two to four times each week for 20 or 30 minutes and as often as daily for one class period in high schools (Baker et al., 2004; Calhoon & Fuchs, 2003; Mortwect et al., 1999). Tutoring, of course, should not detract from the rest of tutors' or tutees' educational programs.

3. *Providing time for peer tutoring:* Peer tutoring can occur as part of independent work time or as a periodic activity in which an entire class participates (Hawkins, Musti-Rao, Hughes, Berry, & McGuire, 2009). Cross-age tutoring needs to occur on a schedule that accommodates both the tutor and the tutee. In some middle schools and high schools, peer tutoring is a service-learning activity that is an elective course or a course for students hoping one day to be teachers. In such cases, tutoring occurs during the class period available for the tutor, and it might occur in the tutee's classroom, the library or media center, or a study hall or advisory classroom.

4. *Selecting content and format for tutoring:* Effective peer-tutoring programs provide practice on skills already taught by the teacher and use standard formats that help tutors know how to do their job (Bowman-Perrott, 2009; Bond & Castagnera, 2006). For example, many elementary peer-tutoring programs have tutors and tutees working on basic math facts, spelling or vocabulary words, and comprehension questions from social studies and science concepts already taught. In middle and high schools, peer tutoring may occur to review vocabulary, concepts, and skills or to provide assistance to a student in a core academic class (for example, algebra or biology) that the tutor has successfully completed. Further, tutors should be given explicit directions to follow so that the tutoring format is highly structured. For example, tutors might be instructed to begin a vocabulary session by reviewing all eight words from last time and then showing each new word, waiting for a response, and marking the response as correct or incorrect. The tutor praises correct responses, corrects errors, and asks the tutee to repeat the corrected responses. Having well-defined procedures helps keep participants in tutoring sessions on task.

5. *Training tutors:* Professionals generally agree that effective peer-tutoring programs carefully prepare tutors for their teaching roles. Tutor training should provide procedures for tutoring, give tutors a way to track tutee learning, teach positive interaction skills, and include problem solving so that tutors know what to do if the tutoring is not working.

Supporting Peer-Tutoring Programs   A training program for peer tutors should include follow-up and assessment. For example, in a cross-age tutoring program, it is important to bring tutors together periodically to discuss how they are doing and how they have resolved problems and to thank them for their work. When tutoring extends beyond your own class group, it is a nice touch to provide tutor appreciation certificates or other recognition. Sometimes paraprofessionals or parent volunteers can assist with the management and supervision of peer-tutoring programs, taking that burden off you and other teachers.

Keep in mind that support for peer-tutoring programs often depends on communication with your principal or other administrators as well as parents and other community members. If you implement a peer-tutoring program, you should invite your principal or the appropriate administrator to observe the program in action. You also

Peer-mediated instruction, including cooperative learning, can help improve students' academic skills while also preventing student behavior problems.

should alert parents and explain your instructional approach. Periodic notes, class newsletters, or updates provided by your home–school hotline, website, or newsletter can keep parents informed of the accomplishments of the program. In middle schools and high schools, where peer tutoring might be an elective course, information on the program can be added to the school website, possibly with a list of frequently asked questions and information for signing up as a tutor or tutee.

Cooperative Learning   Another peer-mediated instructional approach is **cooperative learning.** It has been employed as a strategy for achieving racial and cultural integration, assisting socially isolated learners, fostering inclusive education for students with disabilities and other special needs, and accommodating culture-based learning styles.

Cooperative learning generally has four essential characteristics:

1. Students in the groups have *positive interdependence*. Either they reach their goal together, or no one is able to achieve it. For example, in Mr. Reilly's classroom, the students earn points when all the members in their cooperative groups get at least 70 percent on their weekly spelling test. Group members work very hard to help all members learn the spelling words.
2. Cooperative learning requires face-to-face interactions. In Mr. Sutter's class, students have opportunities to work directly with their group members to accomplish learning goals related to reviewing the use of advertising approaches in magazines.
3. Members of cooperative groups have individual accountability. On the weekly vocabulary test in Ms. Mather's chemistry class, students who have difficulty learning are not excused from taking the test, nor are high-achievers permitted to answer for all group members. Each member is required to make a contribution.
4. Cooperative learning stresses student interpersonal skills, such as how to ask questions, praise classmates, and help another student learn. When Ms. Bolter notices positive interpersonal interactions among her seventh-grade English students, she gives them "Bolter Bucks" to spend on a variety of privileges and rewards.

These social and interactive components of cooperative learning make it unique. They are not possible in traditional classroom procedures in which students compete against one another (for example, a classroom game that can have only one winner) nor in individualistic approaches in which students are compared only to themselves, as is common in special education settings. That means that this approach is especially important in inclusive schools. It helps students learn to work together, which, in turn, prevents behavior problems.

Developing Cooperative Learning Programs   To achieve the best results with cooperative learning, several ideas should be kept in mind. First, the makeup of the groups should be based on the age, abilities, maturity, and needs of your students, and they generally should reflect the heterogeneity of your students. The number of students in each group may range from three to six, depending on student characteristics. Second, students should be taught cooperative skills that include how to speak positively to each other and how to provide feedback to peers (Cooper, 2002). Third, students should be assigned to specific roles in their groups. Common roles include *leader, recorder, encourager*, and *timekeeper*.

The next step in cooperative learning is to select a specific program to guide student interactions. Many options exist. Some programs can be used for any subject matter. Some give students specific roles for learning part of the material being covered and teaching it to other group members. Yet other programs have clear reward structures to all group members succeeding in their learning. Two examples of specific cooperative learning programs are included in the Instructional Edge.

Supporting Cooperative Learning Programs   Once students are established in cooperative groups, your role becomes one of monitoring and managing your class (Cooper, 2002). For example, if you notice that a student is having difficulty in a

www.resources

http://olc.spsd.sk.ca/de/pd/instr/strats/coop/index.html
At Instructional Strategies Online, you will find a brief explanation of cooperative learning and many resources for making it successful in your classroom. The site includes links to sample lessons, forms for assessing students' social interactions, and others.

INSTRUCTIONAL **EDGE**

Cooperative Learning in Action

Many cooperative learning programs have been developed that provide effective ways to foster student interactions, prevent behavior problems, and increase student learning. Here are two examples.

NUMBERED HEADS TOGETHER

Numbered Heads Together (Kagan, 1990; Maheady, Michielli-Pendl, Harper, & Mallette, 2006) has these steps:

1. Students are assigned to cooperative groups (usually four or five in a group) and count off by number.
2. The teacher then poses a question to the group and students are asked to "put their heads together" to be sure all group members know the answer.
3. After a brief time, the teacher reconvenes the whole class and calls out a number.
4. All the students with that number stand and one student responds to the question, or they all write the answer on slates and hold them up for the teacher to see.
5. Students responding correctly score points for their teams.

This simple cooperative learning approach can be used for questions with single correct answers as well as for those with many responses.

JIGSAW CLASSROOM

Jigsaw Classroom (Aronson, 2005) uses these steps:

1. Students are assigned to heterogeneous work groups.
2. Each member of the work group also is assigned to a separate expert group.

3. Work groups meet and decide which member to assign to which expert group. For example, in a unit on the Midwest, experts might be assigned for four topics: geography, economy, culture, and cities.
4. All team members then read the material, with each member focusing on his expert topic.
5. After reading, team members join their respective expert groups, which are composed of all students in the room who share the same expert topic.
6. The expert groups review their portion of the instructional material and then return to teach it to their work-group members.
7. Group members ask each expert questions to help clarify the information being presented.
8. After all the group members have taught their segments of the information and the groups have had an opportunity to review their learning, a quiz or other evaluation procedure is used, and each group member is graded individually on this assessment.

Several variations of this popular cooperative learning approach have been developed (for example, Holliday, 2002), with changes such as giving the expert groups a quiz prior to their teaching information to their peers.

---

group, you might decide to join that group briefly to judge whether students can resolve the problem themselves or need your assistance. If a student seems to be struggling because of the complexity of the lesson content, you can make an on-the-spot adaptation to help the student and the group. If a student is being disruptive, your proximity might be sufficient to settle that student. As you monitor, you also can observe students' use of cooperative skills and check the progress of their learning.

By applying the INCLUDE strategy, you quickly can see that many of the teaching strategies presented in this text can be incorporated into cooperative learning experiences. Cooperative groups provide a constructive classroom structure, one that builds self-esteem, engages students in order to build group spirit and prevent behavior problems, and provides opportunities for adapting instruction for individual needs.

INCLUDE

Use Group Contingencies

Another straightforward way to prevent behavior problems in your classroom is to use group contingency systems (Hulac & Benson, 2010; Kaff, Zabel, & Milham, 2007). In these systems, the goal is to promote positive behavior by allowing students to earn a group reward based on the performance of particular students. Many group contingencies options exist. Here are two examples:

- *Small-group contingency:* In small-group contingency, the class is rewarded based on the performance of a selected group of students. For example, if four selected students complete the assigned work, the entire class will earn 5 minutes of an instructional game at the end of the class. This approach is helpful if one or two students tend to have behavior problems. It avoids placing too much pressure on one student, as would happen if the reward was based on just that student's performance, but at the same time it fosters desired student behavior.

- *All-group contingency:* In whole-group contingency, reward is based on the performance of all class members. For example, if 80 percent of all the students in an algebra class complete their assigned in-class work during the week, on Friday no homework will be assigned.

Group contingencies can be powerful classroom tools for teachers, but care must be taken in developing them. For example, one or two students may sabotage the group by deliberately misbehaving. Or one student may not be capable of performing at the level required for the group to be rewarded. In such cases, this may not be the most effective strategy to implement, and other approaches—those already discussed and those in the sections that follow—should be considered.

What Are Positive Behavior Strategies for Responding to Minor Individual Behaviors?

INCLUDE

For some students, including students with special needs, the steps you take to create a positive and productive learning environment may not be sufficient to eliminate behavior problems. These students may need much more specialized approaches—secondary prevention strategies—and you will find it helpful to follow the steps of the INCLUDE model outlined in Chapter 5 when planning and implementing these strategies. However, before you decide to use that approach, try a number of simpler strategies. Teachers long have relied on the principle of least intervention in addressing student behavior needs. The strategies described in the following sections include minimal interventions, such as "catch 'em being good," and techniques for managing students' surface behaviors.

Use Minimum Interventions

Teachers sometimes contribute unintentionally but significantly to student misbehavior. They do this by inadvertently bringing out negative student behaviors and responding too strongly to minor misbehaviors, actions that sometimes cause students to misbehave more. For example, when asked directly to begin work, a student might refuse. However, when given a choice regarding which assignment to do first, the student might comply. Similarly, when reprimanded for using profanity in the classroom, some students will use the reprimand as a signal to continue the language to get further attention. Ignoring occasional inappropriate language might lessen the problem.

When working with students with special needs, it is essential to stay alert to how you might be contributing to a student's behaviors, either through your own responses to the behavior or through your classroom structure and lesson format (Kern & Clemens, 2007). Two examples of minimum interventions teachers use to address minor student misbehavior follow.

"Catch 'Em Being Good"   A versatile and long-recognized strategy for reducing inappropriate student behavior and increasing appropriate behavior is called "catch 'em being good." In short, when a student is behaving according to expectations, you acknowledge and reward the behavior. For example, if third-grader Connor enters the room

Teachers sometimes can use minimum interventions to prevent minor behavior problems from becoming more serious.

and immediately begins his work, you might say to him, "I like the way you went right to your desk, Connor. That's exactly what you're supposed to do!" This comment has the effect of rewarding Connor's behavior. At the same time, it clearly lets other students know that going directly to one's seat is a behavior they should do, too. In a middle school or high school social studies class, a teacher might privately say to a student who is chronically late, "I noticed you were at your seat with materials ready when the bell rang. Nice going." Although the privacy of the comment eliminates its potential positive impact on other students, it has the benefit of preventing student embarrassment.

Make High-Probability Requests First Banda and Kubina (2006) describe a successful strategy for helping students with autism who have difficulty transitioning between activities in the classrooms, such as halting work on a language arts assignment to get ready to leave the classroom to go to physical education. With this approach, make several simple requests the student is likely to complete prior to making the targeted request. For example, if it is time for first-grader Angel to put away his crayons and join a group reading a story, first get Angel's attention by saying something like, "Angel, give me five." Follow this with asking Angel to tell you his address (or another appropriate piece of personal information that he is learning and likely to share). Next, ask him to shake hands, another behavior he knows and usually readily does. Finally, request that Angel leave his coloring and join the reading group. Each request should be followed by verbal praise (for example, "Right" or "Good job"). How could this approach be used with an older student? With a student with an intellectual or emotional disability?

Manage Students' Surface Behaviors

Another relatively simple strategy for responding to student behaviors is managing their **surface behaviors** (Maag, 2001; Redl, 2007). Long and Newman (1971) proposed long ago that a teacher's initial response to student behavior often determines whether a problem situation develops and how intense it is. If a teacher treats a minor misbehavior as a major infraction, the result might be a strong negative student response followed by a stronger teacher response and, ultimately, a serious behavior incident. For example, if a student mutters under her breath something negative about an assignment and the teacher responds by asking in a stern voice, "What did you say?" the situation will likely escalate. The student might reply, "Nothing," the teacher may repeat the request, and the student may eventually say something that requires a negative consequence.

Such interactions can be avoided if teachers are prepared to shift the focus of the interaction. Suggestions for heading off such problems include purposefully ignoring minor incidents and using humor to defuse tense classroom situations. Examples of additional initial response techniques are outlined in the following Professional Edge.

These low-intrusion techniques are most suited to minor misbehaviors and unlikely to resolve serious discipline issues. Also, responding to students' surface behaviors sometimes can have the effect of increasing them. For example, if you use humor with a student and she responds by talking back, then your humor may be increasing rather than decreasing the inappropriate behavior. If this happens, switch to another approach or work with colleagues to examine the behavior more carefully and devise a more individualized response to it, as described in the remainder of this chapter.

dimensions of DIVERSITY

Mmari, Blum, & Teufel-Shone (2010) studied risk and protective factors for delinquency among American Indian youth. In addition to factors in the family, they found that teacher bias and peer pressure to underperform at school increased risk while the availability of mentors reduced risk.

How Can Functional Behavior Assessment and Behavior Intervention Plans Help You Respond to Serious Individual Behaviors?

When students with disabilities have chronic and significant behavior problems, you are not expected to design and use tertiary prevention, that is, individual, strategies by yourself. You will find that the Individuals with Disabilities Education Act (IDEA)

PROFESSIONAL EDGE

Strategies for Managing Students' Surface Behaviors

You sometimes will be faced with the dilemma of how to respond to students' *surface behaviors*—minor inappropriate behaviors that students display, such as refusing to work, sitting with head down, and calling out answers. In some cases, these behaviors may be symptoms of serious problems that need the careful attention of a functional behavior assessment (described later in this chapter). However, a first approach can be to use simple techniques, such as the following, to deal with problem behaviors as soon as they occur:

1. *Planned ignoring:* If a student's behavior will not likely harm others or spread to others, you might decide to ignore it. For example, a student who repeatedly sighs loudly could be signaling a loss of interest; instead of responding to the sighing, recognize that the student needs to change activities soon. If you ignore inappropriate behavior, you should be sure to give the student attention for appropriate behavior.

2. *Signal interference:* Use nonverbal signals, such as eye contact and gestures (for example, putting your finger to your lips to request silence) to communicate with students.

3. *Proximity control:* Sometimes simply moving closer to a misbehaving student will resolve the problem. However, if the behavior continues, it may mean that your nearness actually is rewarding the student and a different technique should be used.

4. *Interest boosting:* If a student appears to be losing interest in a task or activity, refocus attention immediately by asking a specific question about her progress or otherwise paying specific attention to her work.

5. *Tension reduction through humor:* For some minor misbehavior, try humor. For example, suppose a student who was frustrated with an assignment tossed a textbook into the trash can. Instead of scolding or lecturing, the teacher exclaimed "Two points!" and then went on to assist the student with the assignment. Care must be taken, though, that the humor is not perceived as a way to embarrass or criticize the student.

6. *Hurdle help:* Beginning an assignment can be overwhelming for some students. You can help them begin and avoid a behavior issue by assisting with the first example, asking questions to facilitate their thinking, prompting them to follow steps, or literally cutting an assignment into parts and giving them one small part at a time.

7. *Support from routine:* Creating more structure in the classroom can avert discipline problems. For example, expecting all students to enter class, sit down, and begin the warm-up work by the time the bell rings may help some students avoid being disruptive. Displaying the schedule and using clear patterns for classroom activities also will help eliminate disruptions.

8. *Direct appeal to valued areas:* Students sometimes see their schoolwork as irrelevant. If you can identify a meaningful context for assigned work, students may be more likely to complete it. For example, work with decimals can be related to sports statistics.

9. *Removing seductive objects:* When students bring distracting items to school (for example, the latest electronic gadget), teachers usually should hold them for safekeeping. Other objects in the classroom environment also can become a focus for misbehavior. For example, if you set up an intriguing science lab, cover the materials until it is time to use them.

10. *Antiseptic bouncing:* When behavior is starting to become an issue or you see signals that a behavior problem is likely to occur (for example, a student seems to be angry as she comes into the classroom), consider giving the student the opportunity to move to a quiet corner of the classroom or to step outside the room to reduce tension. Doing so will help some students calm down and avoid trouble. Similarly, some students will benefit from being sent on a simple errand that takes them out of the classroom and provides them with a purposeful activity.

Source: Adapted from "Management of Surface Behavior: A New Look at an Old Approach," by J. W. Maag, 2001, *Counseling and Human Development,* 33(9), pp. 1–10.

---

contains many provisions that guide how teachers and other school personnel should respond to serious student behaviors (Etscheidt, 2006; Lo & Cartledge, 2006; Ryan, Katsiyannis, Peterson, & Chmelar, 2007; Zilz, 2006). These procedures, addressing everything from contacting parents to guidelines related to suspension and expulsion, are summarized in Figure 12.2.

In addition, you will work with a team of colleagues to complete a more detailed analysis of the behaviors of concern and to plan, carry out, and evaluate systematically the effectiveness of a range of interventions (Kamps, Wendland, & Culpepper, 2006). This legislatively mandated approach, referred to as **functional behavior assessment (FBA),** is a problem-solving process implemented for any student with a disability who has chronic, serious behavior problems.

FBA is a detailed and documented set of procedures designed to improve educators' understanding of exactly what a problem behavior looks like: where it occurs,

FIGURE 12.2 IDEA Provisions Related to Discipline

IDEA includes a number of provisions for addressing issues that relate to students with disabilities and their behavior. The following list is a sample of those provisions:

- Parents must be given an opportunity to participate in all meetings with respect to the identification, evaluation, and educational placement of the student and the provision of a free appropriate public education. This provision applies to behavior problems as well as academic problems.
- School personnel can consider on a case-by-case basis unique circumstances that may affect decisions about a change in placement for a student who violates a school's student conduct code.
- When a student's placement is changed because of her behavior, her education must continue so that progress can continue toward the accomplishment of IEP goals and, for some students, objectives. Access to the general curriculum must be assured, and any behavior intervention plan must continue.
- Within 10 school days of a decision to change the placement of a student because of a behavior code infraction, school officials must hold a special meeting to complete *manifestation determination*, that is, a decision about whether the behavior is related to the student's disability a or poor implementation of the IEP. If the behavior is related to the disability, a functional behavior assessment (FBA) must be completed and a behavior intervention plan (BIP) must

be created and implemented. (Details on these topics are included later in this chapter.)

- School officials can remove a student to an appropriate interim alternative educational setting or suspend him for not more than 10 days in the same year (to the extent that such alternatives are applied to students without disabilities) if he violates the school's student conduct code.
- Parents have to be notified of all procedural rights under IDEA, including expanded disciplinary rights, not later than the day on which the decision to take disciplinary action is made.
- School personnel may remove a student with disabilities to an interim alternative educational setting for up to 45 school days if the student has brought a weapon to school or a school function, knowingly possesses or uses illegal drugs or sells or solicits the sale of a controlled substance while at school or a school function, or causes serious bodily injury to another person. This action may be taken whether or not the behavior is found to be related to the student's disability, and it may extend beyond 45 days if that policy is in effect for other students and the student's behavior is not related to the disability.
- In the case of a student whose behavior impedes her learning or that of others, the IEP team must consider, when appropriate, strategies to address that behavior. FBA must look across contexts to include school, home, and community.

Sources: Adapted from *Highlights of New Legislation to Reauthorize the Individuals with Disabilities Education Act (IDEA), PL 108–466: The Individuals with Disabilities Education Improvement Act of 2004*, by J. West, L. Pinkus, and A. Singer, January 2005, Washington, DC: Washington Partners; and *What Every Teacher Should Know about IDEA 2004*, by M. Madlawitz, 2006, Boston: Allyn & Bacon.

when it occurs, and what function it serves for the student. FBA leads to ideas about how to change the behavior and a specific plan for doing so (Kamps et al., 2006; Scott & Caron, 2005). An FBA and *behavior intervention plan (BIP)* must be included as part of a student's individualized education program (IEP) whenever it is needed; these procedures are not only for students whose disability is emotional or based in behavior (Zirkel, 2009). For example, a student with autism might need these procedures to address her difficulty in transitioning from one school activity to another. It is likely that the professionals meeting about Jaden, the kindergarten student described in the chapter opening, will undertake writing an FBA for him.

Rationale for Functional Behavior Assessment

When a student displays behaviors that are especially aggravating or seem directed at purposely causing a classroom disruption, it is tempting to respond simply by trying to stop the behavior and get back to the business of educating the student. However, if you do not understand why the behavior is occurring and how to address that underlying cause, the behavior will likely recur.

In FBA, inappropriate behaviors are viewed as serving a function or purpose for the student. Understanding this function will help you identify the actual problem the student is experiencing and decide how to respond to it instead of the

RESEARCH NOTE

Warren et al. (2006) reported that the use of PBIS strategies in an urban middle school had significant positive results in just one year, including a 20 percent decrease in office discipline referrals, 23 percent decrease in time-outs, and 57 percent decrease in out-of-school suspensions.

symptomatic behavior (Frey & Wilhite, 2005; Gongola & Daddario, 2010). Functions of behavior include avoiding something (for example, assignments, people) or obtaining something (for example, attention, help). Put simply, this conceptualization of student behaviors suggests that before you respond, you should ask, "Why is the student doing this?" Table 12.1 describes in more detail some common student behaviors and their possible functions.

An example can help clarify the idea of identifying the function of behaviors. Daniel is in the sixth grade. When the sixth-grade teaching team meets to discuss student problems, Mr. Adams expresses concern that Daniel often uses profanity in class. Ms. Jefferson adds that Daniel picks fights with other students several times each week. Dr. Hogue agrees that Daniel is having problems and recounts a recent incident in which he was sent to the office. As the teachers talk, they begin to look past Daniel's specific behaviors and focus instead on the function the behaviors are serving. They realize that in one class, Daniel was disruptive when a difficult assignment was being given; in another, the problem was occurring as quizzes were being returned; and in the third, the incident happened immediately before Daniel's turn to give an oral book report. The teachers agree that Daniel's intent has been to escape situations in which he fears he might fail.

Once you identify the function of a problem behavior, you can assist the student in changing the behavior. In Daniel's case, it would be easy for the teachers to decide on a reward system to get Daniel to swear less in Mr. Adams's class. However, that solution would have more to do with the teachers' need to have well-mannered students than with Daniel's need to avoid the possibility of failing. An alternative approach would be to permit Daniel to receive his quizzes before the start of class or perhaps to participate in the after-school homework club that includes a group that studies for quizzes. Thus, the question of intervening to address Daniel's behavior has shifted from "How can we get Daniel to be less disruptive in the classroom?" to "How can we help Daniel use more appropriate strategies to avoid situations in which he fears he will fail?"

This approach to understanding student behavior requires looking for patterns in a student's behavior and describing them clearly in concrete terms (Dieterich,

TABLE 12.1 Possible Functions of Student Behaviors

Function	Goal	Example of Behavior
Power/control	Control an event or a situation	Acts to stay in the situation and keep control: "You can't make me!"
Protection/escape	Avoid a task or activity; escape a consequence; stop or leave a situation	Has a tantrum at the start of every math lesson; skips social studies class
Attention	Become the center of attention; focus attention on self	Puts self in the forefront of a situation or distinguishes self from others—for example, burps loudly during class instruction
Acceptance/affiliation	Become wanted or chosen by others for mutual benefit	Hangs out with troublemakers; joins a clique or gang
Self-expression	Express feelings, needs, or preoccupations; demonstrate knowledge or skill	Produces inappropriate drawings—for example, of aerial bombings, body parts, occult symbols
Gratification	Feel good; have a pleasurable experience; reward oneself	Acts to get or maintain a self-determined reward—for example, hoards an object, indulges in self-gratifying behavior at others' expense
Justice/revenge	Settle a score; get or give restitution, apology, or punishment	Destroys others' work; meets after school to fight; commits acts of vandalism

Source: From "Our Five Basic Needs: Application for Understanding the Function of Behavior," by L. M. Frey and K. Wilhite, 2005, *Intervention in School and Clinic, 40,* pp. 156–160.

Villani, & Bennett, 2003; Shippen, Simpson, & Crites, 2003). It takes more time and effort, but it greatly increases the likelihood that you and your colleagues will be able to design an effective intervention to assist the student. In addition, you should keep in mind that although many of the students involved in functional assessment and the development of a behavior plan have high-incidence disabilities, this method of addressing behavior was first used with individuals with significant intellectual disabilities, primarily to develop appropriate social and communication behavior. Certainly, this method also can be used appropriately to help students with those disabilities succeed in your classroom. The Case in Practice explores using functional assessment for such students, and the following sections present in more detail the process of completing FBAs. The procedure includes seven specific steps (Lee & Jamison, 2003; Ryan, Halsey, & Matthews, 2003):

1. verifying the seriousness of the problem
2. defining the problem behavior in concrete terms
3. collecting data to better understand the behavior
4. analyzing the data and forming hypotheses about function
5. developing a behavior intervention plan (BIP)
6. implementing the plan and gathering data on its impact on the behavior
7. monitoring intervention effectiveness and proceeding to appropriate next actions

Verifying the Seriousness of the Problem

A first step in functional assessment is to determine whether supportive strategies such as those already introduced in this chapter have been implemented in the student's classroom(s). For example, if you have a student who is bullying others, a topic addressed in the Professional Edge on page 387, your team might ask you to complete a questionnaire about the tactics you have used to address the student's behavior, and a psychologist, special education teacher, or other educator may observe and interview the student. In cases of acting-out behavior, other students may be observed. The latter approach is used to determine whether the student's behavior is typical or significantly different from that of classmates.

CASE IN PRACTICE

Supporting a Student with Autism Using Functional Behavior Assessment

Mary Elizabeth, a student with autism, just moved to the area. At her previous school, she spent most of her day in the general education classroom with the support of an instructional assistant and a special educator. She was nearly at grade level in math and just a year or so behind in reading.

In her first week at John Glenn Elementary School, however, Mary Elizabeth repeatedly tried to bite and hit staff and students, had several noisy tantrums, and refused to attempt any academic tasks. On two different days, it took two adults to remove her from the general education classroom. Ms. Lieberman, the third-grade teacher, was astonished at this disastrous beginning, especially because she had carefully prepared her other students for their new classmate and had

done some quick reading about what to expect of a student with autism.

Within the week, Ms. Lieberman was distraught and became more so when the instructional assistant quit. Mr. Poulos, the school psychologist, quickly called together the team, including Ms. Lieberman and himself as well as special education teacher Ms. Daugherty, principal Dr. Cook, and Mary Elizabeth's parents, Mr. and Mrs. O'Toole. Mary Elizabeth refused to be part of the meeting, but Ms. Daugherty spoke with her individually about the problems and ideas to address them.

The team's task was to complete the FBA checklist included here. Although occasional incidents still occurred, the

(continued)

team was successful in addressing Mary Elizabeth's behavior problems and helping her adjust to her new school.

REFLECTION

Working with your classmates, complete as many items on the checklist as possible (for example, write a definition of the behavior, identify replacement behaviors, and so on). What aspects of the FBA and BIP process seem straightforward? Which seem challenging? If you were Ms. Lieberman, what types of assistance would you request during the transition time as the behavior plan was being implemented? What expectations would you have for all the other people at this meeting to participate in implementing an intervention?

Source: Adapted from *Functional Behavior Assessment/Behavior Intervention Plan Checklist,* Center for Effective Collaboration and Practice, 2000. Retrieved August 12, 2007, from http://cecp.air .org/fba/problembehavior3/appendixa.htm.

Functional Behavior Assessment/Behavior Intervention Plan Checklist

Student _____ Date _____

Team leader _____ Grade _____

Behavior(s) of concern _____
_____

Yes   No

1. Is the student behavior of concern clearly defined?
2. Have replacement behaviors that serve the same function (or result in the same outcome) for the student been identified, along with the circumstances under which they should occur?
3. Are multiple sources of information available that have been collected from various individuals (for example, teachers, parents, classmates, student)? At least two separate indirect measures and multiple direct measures (for example, ABC charts, scatterplots) that capture multiple occurrences/nonoccurrences of the behavior (and its context) should be in agreement.
4. Does the information gathered by the team indicate a consistent behavior pattern?
5. Is the hypothesis statement written according to the three-term contingency (that is, Under *x* conditions, the student does *y* in order to achieve *z*) so that an intervention plan can be easily produced?

Yes   No

6. Is the plan aligned with student needs and assessment results?
7. Does the plan address all aspects of the social/environmental contexts in which the behavior of concern has occurred?
8. Is there a strategy to verify the accuracy of the hypothesis statement?
9. Does the plan address both short-term and long-term aspects of student behavior (and its social/environmental context), including procedures to eliminate reliance on unacceptable behavior?
10. Does the plan include practical ways to monitor both its implementation (for example, checklist) and effectiveness as a behavior intervention plan?
11. Does the plan include ways to promote the maintenance and generalization of positive behavior changes in student behavior?
12. Is the plan consistent with systems of student behavior change and support available in the school?

Defining the Problem Behavior

The second step of FBA is to ensure that the behaviors of concern are defined and described in a specific way. Teachers working with students with serious behavior problems often use a type of verbal shorthand to describe their concerns. They may refer to a student as "disruptive," "always off task," or "unmotivated." Although these general statements may have specific meaning to the teachers making them, they are too vague and tend to be too subjective to be useful in addressing the student's

PROFESSIONAL EDGE

Bullying: The Problems and Some Interventions

Bullying is a serious problem. Some 32 percent of students ages 12 to 18 report having been bullied at some point at school (National Center for Education Statistics, 2010), whether through being made fun of; being pushed, shoved, or tripped; threatened with harm, purposely excluded; pressed to do things they didn't want to do; or victimized through destruction of their property.

WHAT IS BULLYING?

Bullies generally consider themselves bigger, stronger, more popular, or in some other way more powerful than their victims. Bullying can take several forms and may occur in face-to-face or electronic interactions:

- physical violence
- verbal taunts, name-calling, put-downs
- threats and intimidation
- extortion or stealing money or possessions

Students who are bullied often are perceived as different for various reasons:

- appearance (for example, overweight, clothing, presence of a disability)
- intellect (too smart or not smart enough)
- racial or ethnic heritage
- socioeconomic background
- cultural or religious background
- sexual orientation

WHAT CAN EDUCATORS AND SCHOOLS DO?

Teachers and other school professionals can help all students feel safe using strategies such as these:

- Ensure that students understand what bullying means, what behaviors it includes, and how it makes people feel.
- Develop and post class rules against bullying (for example, "Treat others as you would like to be treated").
- Establish appropriate consequences for bullying (for example, student pays for damaged belongings, apologizes).
- Encourage students to discuss bullying and positive ways to interact with others.
- Discuss the dangers of online and other electronic interactions and the seriousness of bullying using that type of communication.
- Take immediate action when bullying is witnessed or reported.
- Administer a bullying survey to students.
- Praise prosocial and helpful student behavior.
- Pay close attention for bullying during recess and other unstructured times.
- Take student reports of bullying seriously.
- Involve parents in terms of sharing information and enlisting their assistance.
- Interview bullies, victims, and witnesses separately.

Source: Adapted from "Bullying: What's New and What to Do" (electronic version), by J. Rosiak, 2004, *Be Safe & Sound, 1*(4), pp. 3–6. Copyright 2004 by the National Crime Prevention Council. Reprinted with permission.

---

behaviors. The alternative is to describe behaviors in specific and concrete terms: "Yesterday during the first 30 minutes of language arts, Michael left his desk six times"; "When I ask Chenille a direct question, she looks away and does not answer"; "Juan talks out three to five times each class period—he does not raise his hand." If several behaviors are identified, it often is most helpful to prioritize the one that should be addressed first instead of trying to design interventions for several behaviors at one time.

Collecting Data to Better Understand the Behavior

The third step in FBA requires systematically gathering information about a behavior's occurrence and the situation in which it occurs (Killu, 2008). By doing this, team members are able to judge more accurately whether the behavior follows a particular pattern, for example, occurring during certain types of activities or at certain times of the day. Identifying a pattern will assist team members in understanding the function and seriousness of the behavior in relation to teachers' classroom expectations. At the same time, by measuring the behavior when it becomes a concern and continuing to do so after a plan for addressing it has been implemented, team members can decide whether their efforts to change the behavior have been successful. Sometimes you may be able to observe and record student behavior yourself. However, if this is not feasible, a school psychologist, special education teacher, administrator, paraprofessional, or another professional may help to

www.resources

http://www.specialconnections.ku
.edu/cgi-bin/cgiwrap/specconn/
index.php
At the University of Kansas Special Connections website, you can find many tools for gathering data as part of monitoring a behavior intervention plan. This site also contains many teacher-friendly links for working with students with special needs.

www.resources

http://www.wrightslaw.com/info/
discipl.index.htm
The Wrightslaw website, on the
Behavior Problems and Discipline
page, has links to important topics
such as guidelines on suspension
and expulsion of students with disabilities, controversy surrounding the
use of seclusion or restraint with
these students, and the increasing
incidence of violent behavior among
young children.

complete this task. Examples of commonly used behavioral data collection strategies include these:

Anecdotal Recording   When you keep written notes of a student's actions or
words, gathered while they happen or shortly thereafter, you are completing
anecdotal recording. One valuable use of this strategy involves recording specific incidents, including what happened immediately before the behavior (antecedents)
and what happened as a result of the behavior (consequences). This approach is
called an *antecedents–behaviors–consequences (ABC) analysis*. For example, whenever Ms. Carlisle directs the class to form cooperative groups (antecedent), Carlos
gets up from his seat and heads for the pencil sharpener (behavior). Ms. Carlisle then
tells Carlos to join his group (consequence). By observing Carlos and keeping an ongoing ABC log of Carlos's behaviors in the classroom, Ms. Carlisle has found out that
whenever the class is transitioning from one activity to another, Carlos is likely to be
off task. A sample ABC analysis is shown in Figure 12.3.

Event Recording   One straightforward way to measure a behavior is to count how
many times it occurs in a given period of time. This approach, called *event recording*, is appropriate when the behavior is discrete—that is, when it has a clear starting and stopping point. For example, it might be appropriate to count the number
of times John is late to class during a week or the number of times David blurts out
an answer during a 30-minute large-group social studies lesson. Conversely, event
recording probably will not be helpful in measuring Jane's tantrum or Jesse's delay
in starting his assignment, because these behaviors have more to do with how long
they last than with the number of times they occur.

Permanent Product Recording   If your concern about student behavior relates
to academics, it may be simplest to keep samples of work as a means of measuring
behavior, a strategy called *permanent product recording*. For example, if students in
a U.S. history class regularly have to respond to ten discussion questions during a
single class session, you might keep Sam's completed work to document the percentage of questions he is attempting or the percentage of his responses that are
correct.

Duration Recording   For some behaviors, the concern is the length of time the
behavior lasts. The strategy of *duration recording* might be used with a young

FIGURE 12.3 Sample ABC Analysis

Student Name: Denton R.		Date: 2/25/11
Location: Math—Mr. B		Observer: Mr. D
Start Time: 1:02		Stop Time: 1:15

Antecedents	Behaviors	Consequences
1:03 Students get out books and open to begin class.	D. pulls out his cap and puts it on.	Students around D. start laughing and saying "Hey".
1:05 Teacher notices D. and tells him to remove cap.	D. stands, slowly removes cap, and bows.	Students applaud.
1:14 Teacher asks D. a question.	D. says, "Man, I don't know."	Another student says "Yeah, you're stupid." Others laugh.

student who cries each morning at the start of the school day, a middle school student who takes an extraordinary amount of time to locate all her learning materials, or a high school student who delays beginning assignments.

Time Sampling *Time sampling* involves periodic observation of a student. For example, if you wanted to observe whether Patricia interacted with classmates during a 20-minute group assignment, you could divide the time period into ten 2-minute observations. At the end of each 2-minute interval, you would glance to see whether Patricia was interacting at that moment and record your observation accordingly. This system also can help you to observe several students at one time: By glancing at three different students and immediately recording the behavior of each one, you can look at the behavior patterns of each student during a single observational period. The risk in time sampling is that the behaviors you observe at each sampling are not typical of what has occurred until that moment. Usually this is not a problem if the length of the interval is kept brief enough. Teachers who use time sampling often need a signal to alert them to observe and record the behavior. For example, they might wear an earphone that enables them to hear a prerecorded tone after each interval. Time sampling is most easily accomplished through collaboration with a colleague or teaching assistant.

Other Data Sources Functional behavior assessment rarely consists of just classroom observations. Most likely, team members will ask questions about your perceptions of how the student's behavior has developed or changed and your attempts to contact the parents and otherwise address the behavior. Family members may be interviewed, and an analysis of the structure, length, and characteristics of the student's entire school day may be considered, as may the physical classroom environment and classroom climate. The student also is likely to be interviewed; her perspective can add important information to other data gathered (Kinch, Lewis-Palmer, Hagan-Burke, & Sugai, 2001). Any factor that might contribute to the behavior may be explored.

Professionals sometimes say that such precise behavior measurement and exhaustive consideration of the causes of the behavior are not realistic. It is true that you would not routinely have the time to use these strategies. However, when you are faced with a student whose behavior is particularly persistent and puzzling, the time you and the team take to analyze it systematically can give you a clearer picture of how to address the problem and effectively alleviate it (Newcomer & Lewis, 2004).

Analyzing the Data and Forming Hypotheses

At the fourth step in FBA, all the pieces come together. Consider, for example, Kyle, whose middle school teachers had expressed concern about his frequent loud and profane outbursts during class. Conducting five 20-minute observation sessions

Gathering data about student behavior, often in collaboration with colleagues, is essential for understanding it, designing a strategy to address it, and later for monitoring the effectiveness of that strategy.

revealed that Kyle spoke loudly using profanity an average of 2.2 times per session (event recording) during large-group instruction (classroom environment). An ABC analysis illustrated that the talking out occurred when the teacher asked the whole class group to read a paragraph in the book, review a chart or graph, or complete some other reading-related task (anecdotal recording). The other students looked at and laughed at Kyle after the talk-outs. The teacher nearly always corrected Kyle, and in just over half the instances, he challenged the teacher's reprimand, saying for example, "I did not," or pounding his fists on his desk and then putting his head down. In an interview, Kyle said that he got called on in class only when he did not know the answer, and he said he knew more than teachers gave him credit for.

In analyzing these data, Kyle's teacher and other team members hypothesized that his talking out served two functions: First, it was a means of avoiding being called on when the question required a reading task, an area of significant academic difficulty for Kyle. Second, it was a means of getting attention from both peers and the teacher. This step in the process is something like detective work. With the data collected, team members try to identify patterns in the behavior, purposes it might serve for the student, and factors that might make the behavior better or worse. In Kyle's case, the teachers recognized that instead of responding to the profanity and outbursts, they needed to address his fear and need for positive attention.

Developing a Behavior Intervention Plan

Once hypotheses have been generated, team members can develop a **behavior intervention plan (BIP)** based on them (Scott, Anderson, & Spaulding, 2008). This fifth step in functional behavior assessment may include any number of interventions. For example, the BIP might include modifying the physical or instructional arrangement of the classroom (seating Kyle nearer to where the teacher usually stands or using more cooperative groups); changing antecedents (permitting students to ask each other for help while reading the material being discussed); altering consequences (the teacher ignoring at least some occurrences of the talking out); teaching alternative behaviors to the student (having Kyle record his own behaviors and reward himself for raising his hand); or modifying curricular materials (using fewer questions for which reading is required) (Gongola & Daddario, 2010; Gresham, Van, & Cook, 2006; Wheeler & Richey, 2005). Different types of rewards and consequences that you might incorporate into a BIP are presented later in this chapter.

Implementing the Plan

Once the BIP has been developed, you and the team, often including the student, reach the sixth step in functional behavior assessment: implementing your plan. Teachers and other professionals implementing the BIP should monitor the consistency with which they implement the plan. In addition, if peers or family members have implementation responsibilities, every effort should be made to ensure that their roles are reasonable, that they understand and can carry out their parts of the plan, and that any concerns they have are addressed (Peck-Peterson, Derby, Berg, & Horner, 2002). Throughout implementation, data on the BIP's impact should be gathered so that monitoring, described next, will be facilitated.

Monitoring the Plan's Effectiveness

You began the process of FBA gathering information about the student's behavior prior to thinking about how to respond to it. The behavior records you keep as you implement the BIP enable you to determine whether the plan is working (Fairbanks, Sugai, Guarding, & Lathrop, 2007). To proceed with the seventh step, monitoring the plan, you and the team use the same recording strategies presented in the third step of FBA. Remember that behavior does not change rapidly; the team should be committed to following the plan for a specified period of time—perhaps two or three weeks or even more—before deciding whether it is effective.

As you monitor the plan, you may observe any of a number of effects. First, the inappropriate behavior may stop completely or the desired behavior may be displayed consistently. If this happens, you may decide to gradually withdraw the plan. For example, if you are intervening to eliminate a student's profane language use in class and no profane language is occurring, then you can gradually increase the length of time without profanity required to earn a reward and then move to using just verbal praise. This is called *fading out* a reward system.

Second, the plan you are implementing may have value but need modification. Perhaps it requires too much time to implement or the rewards need adjustment. Such alterations are not unusual; simply modify the plan and continue to monitor its effectiveness. For example, if you created a point system for your sophomore keyboarding student that includes earning points for being seated when the bell rings, turning homework in at the beginning of class, and having an assignment notebook and pen in class, you might discover that the system is too difficult to monitor. You might then eliminate the points for everything except homework for a student who chronically fails to come to class on time with assignments in hand.

Third, the plan may not be working. As you track the number and duration of tantrums for one of your students, you might learn that they are occurring more often and lasting longer. When a situation like this occurs, the team needs to analyze what is happening and create an alternative plan, again following the steps that have been outlined. If other options do not seem appropriate, a more significant change, such as a change in the student's placement, may need to be considered.

Finally, it is imperative that you work closely with parents to resolve student behavior problems. Parents sometimes can clarify reasons a student suddenly is behaving in a particular way (for example, a death in the family, a divorce, an unusually exciting weekend trip, a cultural response to a school activity). In addition, they can reinforce school messages at home and help provide rewards at home earned by appropriate behavior during the school day. Parents are likely to be members of the team completing the functional behavior assessment and behavior intervention plan, and their contributions cannot be emphasized enough. You increase options for responding to student behavior by creating partnerships with parents, even when you may disagree with their perceptions, a topic addressed in the Working Together.

What Are Effective Strategies for Responding to Serious Individual Behaviors?

The FBA procedure provides educators with clear guidelines for assisting students with significant behavior problems. The strategies that are part of that process usually are carried out across time in a consistent and well-documented manner. They also may involve the use of contracts, in which the expectations for behavior are specified and rewards and consequences are clearly spelled out. The interventions covered in the following sections include increasing desirable behaviors, decreasing undesirable behaviors, and using behavior contracts.

Increasing Desirable Behaviors

All students, even those who display challenging behaviors, have some appropriate behaviors you should increase. The primary strategy for increasing appropriate behavior is called *reinforcement.* Reinforcement is any response or consequence that increases a behavior (Jones & Jones, 2004; Shumate & Wills, 2010).

It is important for you to keep in mind that reinforcement can increase negative as well as positive behaviors. For example, when a teacher puts a sticker on a student's chart because the student completed his assignment without calling out for unneeded help, the student has been rewarded and is more likely in the future to

Working TOGETHER

When Differences of Opinion Occur

Few people would disagree that collaboration is essential for working with students with disabilities, and most professionals enjoy their interactions with colleagues and parents. However, collaboration can be challenging when differences of opinion occur. Think about conflicts such as the one described here. Consider role-playing this interaction with your classmates to practice using the suggestions offered.

Ms. Bonnet requests a meeting with you. She is quite upset, accusing you of treating her daughter Taylor unfairly. She says Taylor has told her that other students are misbehaving more than she is but that you discipline only her. Ms. Bonnet wants you to stop and apologize to Taylor.

- It is tempting in this type of interaction to become defensive, explaining that you have been fair and that Taylor is not telling the whole story. Instead, first be sure that Ms. Bonnet has relayed her story. When she finishes speaking, paraphrase what she has said, succinctly summarizing the information without making any judgments—for example, "Taylor has told you that other students misbehave but that I discipline only her." Notice that you are not necessarily agreeing with this perspective, only restating it.
- Try asking Ms. Bonnet for a specific example of what Taylor has described. That may help you to understand more about the situation.

- If Taylor is not present, it probably would be best to leave this matter unresolved and to arrange a meeting that includes her. That way, the situation can be more fully explored.
- As you discuss the situation with Taylor and her mother, ask Taylor what she thinks would make things more fair. You do not necessarily have to agree with her perspective, but it is important to know what she thinks should occur.
- Develop a strategy to address Taylor's concerns, and try it for a week. This might include touching base momentarily with Taylor each day or keeping a record of your interactions with her. Even if you believe that Taylor's accusations are wildly inaccurate, trying to verbally reinforce her appropriate behavior can help to ease the tension.
- Consider the possibility that Taylor may be accurate in her perception. Are you inadvertently noticing her because her voice tends to be louder than the voices of other students? Could you be responding to a cultural difference? Are you especially watchful of her because you know that she has a behavior intervention plan?

Situations that involve conflict can be stressful, but with careful communication and a willingness to consider others' opinions, you can successfully address them.

continue to work independently; a positive behavior has been increased or reinforced. However, when a teacher says "Sit down!" to a student who is wandering around the classroom, the student also has been rewarded, this time by gaining the teacher's attention. The student is more likely in the future to be out of her seat, and so an undesirable behavior has been increased or reinforced.

Positive and Negative Reinforcement   Anytime you respond to a behavior with a consequence that makes it more likely for the behavior to occur again, you are using **positive reinforcement** (Price & Nelson, 2011). When you reward a student for appropriate behavior and that behavior increases, positive reinforcement has occurred. For instance, if you tell a student that she may use the classroom computer after she completes five math problems and she completes all the problems, you are positively reinforcing math problem completion through computer rewards.

Negative reinforcement operates somewhat differently. Suppose you set up a system with your ninth-grade English students whereby they must have their homework signed each night by their parents until they have brought it back to school on time at least 9 out of 10 times. Because students see having their homework signed by their parents as an undesirable consequence, they will increase their promptness in turning in homework to avoid the consequence. Any increase in behavior to avoid a consequence is the result of **negative reinforcement** (Wheeler & Richey, 2005). Although negative reinforcement can be effective, positive reinforcement usually should be tried first because having students work toward a positive outcome is preferable to having them work under the threat or perceived threat of a negative consequence.

Some professionals object to using positive reinforcement with students, because they fear it teaches students they are entitled to a payoff for appropriate behavior. These professionals contend that students should complete their school-work and behave appropriately simply because these are the right things to do. This discussion often is addressed as one of external versus internal motivation (for example, Kohn, 2006). Although learning and behaving appropriately because of internal motivation, rather than the expectation of external rewards, certainly is preferable, some students who struggle to learn and behave as expected are simply not able or likely to do so. These students may behave and respond appropriately in school because of internal motivation only when they are extremely interested in a subject or topic or experience repeated success over an extended period of time. Additional strategies, including reinforcement, provide the support they need to succeed in their learning.

Types of Reinforcers   To ensure that positive reinforcement is successful for students with special needs, keep in mind that many different types of rewards can be used. Four of these types include the following:

1. *Social reinforcers* are various types of positive consequences that a teacher, parent, or peer can give a student to reward appropriate behavior and increase it (Gable, Hester, Rock, & Hughes, 2009). These reinforcers might include a positive phone call home to parents, a pat on the back or hug, verbal praise, or selection as Classroom Citizen of the Month. Social reinforcers, especially clear and specific verbal praise, always should be tried before other positive reinforcers because they are the most natural type of reward in a school environment. If you find it necessary to employ other types of rewards, you should use them only in conjunction with social reinforcers. Your long-term goal should always be to have students respond to rewards that occur naturally in their classroom environment.

2. *Activity reinforcers* involve activities such as playing games, having extra recess, helping a teacher in another class, and participating in other coveted individual or group pastimes. Generally, activities that directly relate to a student's educational goals (for example, practicing math skills on the computer) are preferable to those that are solely recreational (for example, playing a noneducational computer game).

3. *Tangible reinforcers* are prizes and other objects that students can earn as symbols of achievement and that students want to obtain. A student who is earning baseball cards for completing assignments is receiving a tangible reinforcer. Putting stickers on papers is another example of this type of reinforcer. When tangible reinforcers are used, the amount must be appropriate for the amount of positive behavior required (that is, small rewards for short periods of relatively simple behaviors; greater rewards for longer periods of more difficult appropriate behavior).

4. *Primary reinforcers* are foods and other items related to human needs that a student finds rewarding. They are much more basic than secondary reinforcers, which comprise the three types just described. Primary reinforcers used in schools often are edible and might include a piece of candy or a piece of fruit. Although you might occasionally employ primary reinforcers, generally you should use them only if a student is incapable of understanding more natural rewards or other types of rewards are not effective. This is important for two reasons. First, the potential negative impact of food reinforcers on student health is a concern, and second, food reinforcers are not a natural part of the school learning process. If you plan to use primary reinforcers, such as food, check with a school administrator to find out about local policies governing their use. Also check with parents, both for permission and about possible student food allergies. Keep in mind nutritional issues as well.

dimensions of DIVERSITY

Sheets (2002) reported that many Latino students perceived teachers' disciplinary actions as unfair and discriminatory, which resulted in the students feeling isolated. She found that students did not conform to expected behaviors but instead chose to follow their internal values and verbally challenged their teachers.

Effective Use of Positive Reinforcers   In addition to understanding the different types of positive reinforcers, you need to know some principles for using them effectively (Walker, Shea, & Bauer, 2003). Three principles are key:

1. *Make sure that the positive reinforcers are clear and specific and that students understand the relationship between their behavior and rewards:* The rewards students earn need to be specific. For example, rewarding a student with time on the computer is not precise enough. If it is a reward, the amount of computer time for the specific behavior displayed should be clarified. Clarity and specificity are especially important when you use verbal praise. Saying to a student "Good job!" is far less effective than saying "Good job! You asked three other students for help before you asked me."

2. *Vary how much and how often you reward students:* If a student displays very little positive behavior, you may reward it heavily at first just to increase it. As the student learns to use the appropriate behavior more readily, you should decrease the amount and intensity of the reward. For example, if at first you were rewarding a student with free-choice reading time for every two assignments completed, you might gradually change the reward so the student must complete four assignments—and get at least 90 percent on each—to earn the free-reading reward.

3. *Make sure a student desires the reward selected:* If you propose to make a positive phone call home when a student participates in group work but the student does not care what his parents think, then your reward is unlikely to work. Instead the student may be far more motivated to choose three homework problems *not* to do. You can determine your students' preferences for rewards by asking them what types of incentives they like or having them rank their preferences from a list of rewards you provide.

Related to the concept of reward desirability is that of *satiation*. That is, a student who receives the same reward over a period of time eventually may no longer find it rewarding (Contrucci-Kuhn, Lerman, & Vondran, 2006). If five minutes of free time is given repeatedly, after a while the student may come to expect the free time and not work to receive it. When this happens, it is important to change the reward. You often can avoid the problem of satiation by using a *reinforcement menu*, which is a list of rewards from which students may choose. The menu can be posted in the classroom, or students can keep individual lists. Some rewards might be reserved for extraordinary performance. Many websites provide ideas for rewards and other ways to increase student behavior. Some of these are outlined in the Technology Notes.

Decreasing Undesirable Behaviors

Many teachers find that some students with special needs have inappropriate classroom behaviors that need to be decreased. These might include aggressive behaviors such as calling classmates names and poking, pinching, and hitting others; verbal outbursts such as using profanity and making nonsense statements during large-group instruction; and other behaviors such as copying others' work and refusing to work. Just as some strategies increase desirable behaviors, other strategies are designed to decrease undesirable behaviors.

Decreasing behavior generally is accomplished through one of these four strategies (Jones & Jones, 2004; Kauffman et al., 2002):

1. differential reinforcement of behaviors that are incompatible with the undesirable behavior
2. extinction, or ignoring the behavior until the student stops it
3. removing something desirable from the student
4. presenting a negative or aversive consequence

fyi

School districts that allow corporal punishment usually have clear guidelines, including obtaining advance parent permission, specifying how punishment is administered, and requiring the presence of a witness.

•◦•● **TECHNOLOGY NOTES**

Help on the Web for Responding to Student Behavior

The Internet is a valuable resource for information about fostering positive behavior and responding to misbehavior. Here is a sampling of particularly valuable websites:

DR. MAC'S (MCINTYRE'S) AMAZING BEHAVIOR MANAGEMENT ADVICE SITE

http://www.behavioradvisor.com

This website lives up to its name. It offers basic information for new teachers related to setting up positive classroom behavior management systems, strategies for addressing common student behavior problems, examples and explanations of interventions such as contracts and token economies, and links to hundreds of additional websites. This site also provides a teacher bulletin board for posting problems and receiving assistance.

CENTER FOR EFFECTIVE COLLABORATION AND PRACTICE

http://cecp.air.org/

This organization is dedicated to improving the lives of students with emotional and behavior problems, and its website contains valuable information regarding school violence, prevention of behavior problems, and related topics. Of particular interest is the detailed but easy-to-read information on completing a functional behavior assessment and creating and implementing a behavior intervention plan.

KENTUCKY DEPARTMENT OF EDUCATION BEHAVIOR HOME PAGE

http://www.state.ky.us/agencies/behave/interact/interaction.html

This webpage is a portal to a variety of links about responding to student behavior. Information addresses the law and legal requirements, positive behavior supports, bullying, time-out, and safe schools. Also included are several forums/blogs about student behavior and information on fostering positive student interactions by teaching social skills.

NORTH CAROLINA DEPARTMENT OF JUVENILE JUSTICE AND DELINQUENCY PREVENTION, CENTER FOR THE PREVENTION OF SCHOOL VIOLENCE

http://www.ncdjjdp.org/cpsv

This webpage provides information about making schools into safe environments conducive to learning. It features specific sections for topics not frequently addressed, including ideas related to physical education and foreign language as well as specific locations in schools, such as restrooms. It has a page called Teacher's Lounge with links to many valuable discipline resources.

TEACHING SOCIAL SKILLS THROUGH THE LANGUAGE ARTS CURRICULUM

http://www.cccoe.net/social/opening.htm

Developed by teachers at El Dorado Middle School in Concord, California (but applicable to students across age groups), this website includes more than 100 lessons, student activities, and other resources for teaching social skills through language arts, especially by using literature. The site also includes ideas for evaluating the effectiveness of your social skills instruction and simple forms for record-keeping.

•◦•●

The latter two strategies—removing something desirable and presenting a negative or aversive consequence—are considered *punishment*. Punishment occurs when a consequence applied has the effect of decreasing a behavior. Punishment violates the principles of PBS and should be employed only when accompanied by strategies that increase desired behaviors. Each of the four strategies for decreasing undesirable behaviors is explained in the following sections.

Differential Reinforcement of Incompatible and Other Behaviors   Inappropriate behaviors can be decreased by increasing related appropriate behaviors through reinforcement. Perhaps you have a student like Patrick in your classroom. Patrick has a severe learning disability. He tends

When students' behavior problems are serious and persistent, you will work with a team to design an effective behavior intervention plan (BIP).

to be very dependent on you for affirmation that he is doing his work correctly; he seems to be constantly at your elbow asking, "Is this right?" To change this behavior, you might want to try praising Patrick when you can catch him working independently at his desk. This technique is called **differential reinforcement of incompatible behaviors.** You are reinforcing a positive behavior that is preferred—working independently at the student's own desk—that is incompatible with the negative behavior—being at your desk asking for affirmation (Conyers et al., 2003; Wheatley, West, Charlton, Sanders, Smith, & Taylor, 2009). You also could decide to reward Patrick for asking a classmate for assistance—that is, by reinforcing other behaviors incompatible with dependence.

Extinction   Another approach to decreasing negative behavior is **extinction.** To extinguish a behavior, you stop reinforcing it; eventually, the behavior decreases (Walker et al., 2003; Wright-Gallo, Higbee, & Reagon, 2006). This strategy often is appropriate when a student has a minor but annoying undesirable behavior, such as tapping a pencil or rocking a chair, which you inadvertently have been reinforcing by calling attention to it or otherwise responding to it. However, extinction is appropriate only when the behavior is minor and does not threaten student well-being. Also, before an ignored behavior will decrease, it will likely increase; that is, at first the student might tap the pencil more loudly or rock more rapidly before stopping. If you respond to the behavior at this higher level (by telling the student to stop the noise or to keep still), you can inadvertently reward the student for the exaggerated behavior through your response. If you think you cannot ignore a behavior while it increases, then extinction is not the strategy to use.

Removing Reinforcers   In some instances, you can decrease inappropriate behavior by taking away from the student something desired, a strategy called **removal punishment.** One example of removal punishment is **response cost,** which involves taking away a privilege, points, or some other reward (Price & Nelson, 2011). An informal use of response cost occurs when a teacher takes away recess, a field trip, or attendance at an assembly because of misbehavior. More systematically, a student may lose the privilege of helping in the classroom because she refuses to begin assigned tasks. If you are considering using response cost, keep in mind that it is effective only if the student currently has reinforcers you can remove. For example, denying a student access to a special school program will decrease his negative behavior only if he wants to attend the program. Also, response cost sometimes fails because the negative behavior is being reinforced so strongly that the response cost is not effective. For example, every time Laquan uses profanity or makes a rude remark during class he loses a point toward the reward available to every student: a homework-free weekend. However, Laquan's classmates usually give him considerable attention for his colorful language by laughing, calling out to him, or giving him a thumbs-up. Laquan's use of profanity is so strongly reinforced by his peers' reactions to it that the loss of points is not a powerful enough response cost to cause him to change his behavior. Finally, because response cost teaches a student only what *not* to do, it is essential that you simultaneously teach the student desired behaviors—what she *should* do.

Another removal punishment strategy you may have heard of is **time-out,** which involves removing a student from opportunities for reward (Wolfgang, 2001). Many elementary school teachers use a simple form of time-out when they require students who are misbehaving on the playground to spend a few minutes in a "penalty box." The reward from which students are removed is playtime with classmates. Time-out can be used in a number of ways depending on the age of the student, the nature of the inappropriate behaviors, and the student's response to isolation. For example, it may be sufficient in a kindergarten or first-grade classroom to have a time-out chair in a quiet corner of the classroom. When Heather pushes another child, she is told

dimensions of DIVERSITY

Punishments vary from culture to culture. Your students may come from families that use punishments such as shame, ostracism, and physical punishment. Your knowledge of how students are punished at home should help you understand how they respond to punishment in school.

to sit in time-out, where she can observe other students in the reading circle but cannot interact with them. If this is not effective, then placing a carrel on the student's desk or using a screen (possibly made from a large box) around a chair might be the next step. For older students and for those with more challenging behaviors, the time-out may need to be in a location totally removed from the student's class. For example, when Louis swears at his teacher, he is sent to the time-out room, a small, undecorated room with just a desk and chair that adjoins the counselor's office. However, for Cherri, time-out means going to Ms. Eich's room across the hall, where she doesn't know the students.

Several factors must be kept in mind if time-out is being considered as a behavior intervention. First, you should think about an appropriate length of time for the time-out. Generally, it should be brief, just a few minutes for young students and never for an extended period of time, even for older students. Second, time-out is effective only if the student was being reinforced by the activities in your classroom. If the student was not engaged, time-out is unlikely to have the desired effect. Finally, the location of the time-out should not be reinforcing. For example, if Jadyn is accompanied by a paraprofessional to a time-out setting located in an empty classroom, but the paraprofessional talks with Jadyn and helps him create geometric patterns on the whiteboard, the attention and activity are likely to be strong reinforcers. Instead of decreasing Jadyn's inappropriate classroom behavior, this poorly designed time-out may actually increase the behavior.

Time-out, especially time-out that removes students from their learning environment, has become controversial (Ryan, Peterson, Tetreault, & Hagen, 2007). Many professionals note that the negative effects of this punishment strategy on students can be significant and that it sometimes is used excessively and inappropriately (Council for Children with Behavior Disorders, 2009). For example, some students who prefer to be alone may find time-out rewarding. Other strategies that teach appropriate behavior are strongly preferred as an alternative, and some school districts now prohibit the use of time-out.

Presenting Negative Consequences   The final strategy for decreasing undesirable student behavior, **presentation punishment,** is the least preferable, because it involves presenting negative consequences to students (Rubin, 2005). For example, when a teacher verbally reprimands a student, the *reprimand* is a negative consequence intended to decrease student misbehavior. It is a mild punisher, one of the most common used in schools.

Another type of presentation punishment is *overcorrection*, in which a student is directed to restore a situation to its original condition or a better condition. This strategy is useful when a student has damaged classroom property or otherwise created a mess. For example, a student who scribbles on a chalkboard might be assigned to erase and wash all the boards in the room. A student who writes on a desktop might be required to stay after school to clean all the desktops in the classroom. This strategy can make clear the undesirable consequences of negative behaviors, but it is not without problems. First, the student must be willing to complete the overcorrection activity. In fact, it might be extremely difficult to get the student to comply. If a student refuses to complete the task, a confrontation might occur. In addition, the overcorrection requires close teacher supervision. A student should not be left alone to complete the assigned task, which could translate into a significant time commitment from the teacher.

Physical punishment is another traditional presentation punishment. Although corporal punishment, carried out within specific guidelines, still is permitted in schools in many states, most educators strongly oppose its use because of its negative effects (Cameron, 2006; Dupper & Montgomery-Dingus, 2008). For example, punishment often suppresses a student's undesirable behavior but does not change it, and the behavior may recur when the student perceives a chance to "get away with it" or another negative behavior may occur in place of the original, punished behavior. Some students may learn to associate school with punishment, causing

www.resources

http://www.youtube.com
If you visit the YouTube site and type in "classroom management" or "behavior management," you will find advice from experienced teachers on using positive approaches to preventing behavior problems and addressing those that occur.

them to dislike school or even to avoid attending. Further, when students crave attention, no matter the cost, punishment can actually increase inappropriate student behavior. Finally, when teachers punish students, they are modeling negative behavior themselves.

In general, then, the message for you as a teacher responding to student behaviors in class is this: Increasing positive behaviors through the use of reinforcers, especially when these desirable behaviors can substitute for undesirable behaviors, is the preferred approach to behavior management. If you find it necessary to decrease undesirable behaviors, the preferred strategies are reinforcing positive incompatible behaviors and extinction. Removal or presentation punishment should be a last resort, used only as part of an ongoing behavior intervention plan and involving a team decision.

Using Behavior Contracts

Using behavior contracts is one straightforward way to apply the strategies for increasing and decreasing behavior. A **behavior contract** is an agreement between the teacher and student that clearly specifies the expectations for the student, the rewards for meeting those expectations, the consequences of not meeting them, and the timeframe for which the agreement is valid (Mruzek, Cohen, & Smith, 2007; Wright, 2007).

Contracts are best used with students like Joseph and perhaps J. R. from the chapter-opening vignettes, who are old enough to understand the purpose of a contract and its specific requirements and whose disabilities either do not affect their cognitive functioning or affect it only marginally. However, simple contracts can be used with almost any student (Jones & Jones, 2004). As you review the sample contract in Figure 12.4, notice that it has more detail than some student contracts you may have seen. For students with special needs who have behavior challenges, contracts with less detail often are ineffective in changing behavior.

The original and still most comprehensive information on how to write student behavior contracts comes from Homme (1970). He stressed the following points:

1. The reward that goes with the contract should be immediate, that is, as close in time as possible to the performance of the desired behavior.
2. An initial contract should call for and reward small amounts of the desired behavior. For example, requiring a student to read an entire book to earn a reward probably would be too frustrating a task for a student with a reading problem. Instead, the student could be rewarded for each chapter (or even each chapter section or page) completed.
3. Rewards should be distributed frequently in small amounts. This approach has been proven more effective than using fewer but larger rewards.
4. A contract should call for and reward accomplishments rather than obedience. That is, it should reward the completion of assigned work or appropriate behavior rather than teacher-pleasing behaviors such as staying in one's seat.
5. The performance should be awarded only after it has occurred. This rule seems obvious but is often overlooked. Students who are allowed privileges or rewards before or during assigned work are far less likely to complete it successfully than those who are rewarded after it.
6. The contract must be fair. The amount of work required of the student and the payoff for completing the work must be balanced.
7. The terms of the contract should be clear to the student. The contract should be put in writing in language the student understands and discussed with the student. If the student is not able to understand a contract, this strategy is probably not appropriate. Both the student and the teacher should sign the contract.

www.resources

http://kittyk70.tripod.com/
printmaterials.htm#
Assessment & Classroom
Management
This page, at tripod.com, links
teachers to dozens of sites with
helpful materials to address behavior
management, including letter templates for communicating with parents, behavior charts, good behavior
certificates, and more.

FIGURE 12.4 Sample Student Contract

For <u>Mia</u>   Class <u>History—Mr. Lee</u>

   (Student name)

I agree to do these things (what, how much, how well, how often, how measured):

<u>Every day when the bell rings, I will be in my seat with my book, notebook, and a pen ready.</u>
<u>During class, I will answer questions only when called on (2 warnings per class for calling out).</u>

For doing them I will receive (what, how much, how often, when):

<u>1 point/day for being prepared, 1 point/day for appropriate class participation. Every time</u>
<u>I accumulate 8 points, I may earn 5 extra-credit points toward my course grade.</u>

Outstanding performance will be if I

Keep my contract 5 days in a row (10 points in a 5-day week)

My bonus for outstanding performance is

The option of skipping 1 homework assignment during the week after the bonus is earned

If I don't meet the terms of my contract, this is the consequence:

If fewer than 5 points are earned in a week, I forfeit participating in the History Jeopardy!
competition the following Monday.

This contract will be renegotiated on

October 19, 2011

<u>Mia</u>   <u>Mr. Lee</u>
Student signature   **Teacher signature**

<u>September 15, 2011</u>   <u>September 15, 2011</u>
Date   **Date**

8. The contract must be honest. The teacher should be willing to carry out the terms of the contract as written and do so immediately. In practice, this means that you should be sure you can deliver on the promises you make.
9. The contract should be positive. It should specify student accomplishments and rewards rather than restrictions and punishments.
10. The contract should be used systematically. If the contract is enforced only occasionally, the result may be worse (or at least very confusing) for the student than not using one at all.

How Can You Help Students Manage Their Own Behavior?

The strategies just outlined for increasing positive and decreasing negative student behavior rely on the teacher providing rewards or consequences to the student. Another set of strategies, far less teacher directed, involves having students take an active role in regulating their own behavior (Banks & Zionts, 2009; Sebag, 2010). These strategies are preferred because they promote student independence by giving students skills they can use in many school settings and outside school as well. They have been used with young children; with students who have learning disabilities, emotional disabilities, autism, and intellectual disabilities, as well as other special needs; and with a wide range of academic and social behaviors.

When students learn to manage their own behavior, they are acquiring skills that can help them be successful throughout their lives.

fyi

For students with autism, social stories—brief vignettes that directly address situations encountered by students—can provide a basis for teaching social skills (Scattone, Tingstrom, & Wilczynski, 2006).

Cognitive Behavior Management Strategies

In **cognitive behavior management (CBM),** students are taught to monitor their own behavior, make judgments about its appropriateness, and change it as needed (for example, Sebag, 2010; Meichenbaum, 1977; Patton, Jolivette, & Ramsey, 2006). Many elements of CBM were introduced in Chapter 10 as a means of increasing student independence in academic learning and organization. In this chapter, they are applied to helping students manage their own classroom conduct and social behavior in a variety of situations. For example, Joseph, the student with a learning disability introduced at the beginning of this chapter, might be able to use CBM to manage his own classroom behavior. Two specific CBM strategies are commonly used to teach students how to manage their own behavior. These are self-monitoring and self-reinforcement.

Self-Monitoring   Students learn to monitor and record their own behavior in *self-monitoring*. For example, a student might keep a daily tally of the number of assignments completed or the number of times he waited until the teacher was between instructional groups to ask a question. A student might also use self-monitoring to track the rate at which she completes and turns in homework assignments or any other behavior (Daly & Ranalli, 2003; Toney, Kelley, & Lanclos, 2003). Students with more advanced skills could even wear headphones to listen to prerecorded signals and record whether they are on task at the sound of each tone. Students also can self-record their nonacademic behaviors. For instance, they can tally the number of times they leave their seat without permission or ask permission before leaving the classroom.

Self-Reinforcement   Another CBM strategy, *self-reinforcement*, often is used in conjunction with self-monitoring. In this approach, students self-evaluate and then judge whether they have earned a reward. For example, Eric might award himself three points for a high self-monitoring score, two points for an average score, and no points for a low score. When he accumulates 20 points, he chooses a reward from his personal reinforcement menu. His favorite reward might be working on a timeline for critical events of the twentieth century. The teacher periodically checks the accuracy of Eric's self-evaluation and self-reinforcement. He earns a bonus point for being accurate in his assessment of himself, even if that assessment is occasionally negative. If Eric has to give himself no points for a low score and his teacher checks his accuracy that day, he receives a bonus point because he accurately assessed his work.

Teaching Cognitive Behavior Management Strategies

Generally, teaching a CBM strategy to a student with special needs involves three main steps:

1. *Discuss the strategy with the student and present a rationale for its use:* If you cannot clarify for the student what the strategy is or how it works, he might not be a good candidate for CBM. To check understanding, ask the student to explain the approach back to you. You can even summarize the goal of the strategy and the rewards and consequences in a contract.

2. *Model for the student what you expect:* For example, you might use an old sample of the student's work and walk through the strategy you plan to use, such as showing the amount of completed work that represents a high score or a low score. Alternatively, you might use a brief role-play to demonstrate to the student how to self-monitor behavior and record it.

3. *Provide practice and feedback:* For this step, the teacher rewards the student for correctly using the strategy until the student is confident enough to use it without such support. If you are teaching a student to use CBM, use reinforcers with the student until she has mastered the strategy. Even after mastery, it is helpful to reward the student periodically for successfully self-managing behavior. This step can be enhanced by helping the student develop a personal reinforcement menu so rewards are meaningful. Parents and colleagues sometimes can assist in implementing this step.

Although CBM is not appropriate for every student behavior problem, it has the advantage of teaching a student to monitor and take responsibility for his own behavior (Niesyn, 2009). Because of increased student responsibility, cognitive behavior management is a far more effective long-term strategy for some students than are more traditional classroom rewards. Students can transfer self-management strategies to other classrooms and teachers and even into adult life. By collaborating with special education teachers and other school professionals, you can design a CBM program that could have a long-lasting positive student impact.

Final Thoughts About Including Students with Special Needs and the INCLUDE Strategy

With your understanding of strategies and approaches for responding to student behavior, you now have the final ingredient for making your classroom a place where students want to come and want to learn. You know about the foundations of special education and the procedures followed for identifying students with disabilities. You have a strategy—INCLUDE—for guiding your decisions about student needs and interventions. You know about the importance of having the support and assistance of colleagues and parents, whether for planning an instructional program for a student, teaching with you in the classroom, or problem solving when concerns arise. You also understand some of the most important characteristics and needs of students with disabilities and other special needs. You have learned many strategies for helping students succeed in your classroom, including creating a positive instructional environment, assessing student needs, implementing instructional interventions, helping students be independent, and evaluating their learning. And you have learned several approaches for responding to students' discipline and behavior needs.

What is most important, however, is the statement that appeared in the first chapter of this text: Students with disabilities and other special needs are children and youth first. If you keep that in mind and use the knowledge you have gained, you will positively touch the lives and learning of all the students who call you *teacher*. You will help all your students reach their potential so that they can become productive individuals who contribute to their communities, living happy, constructive, and fulfilled lives. And those former students will remember that you were that special teacher who made all the difference.

www.resources

http://iris.peabody.vanderbilt.edu/ The IRIS Center aims to provide high-quality resources for learning about students with disabilities. Its resources are free, online, and interactive, translating research about educating students with disabilities into practice. If you have questions about working with students with disabilities, IRIS probably has a module that will help you find answers.

WRAPPING IT UP
BACK TO THE CASES

This section provides opportunities for you to apply the knowledge gained in this chapter to the cases described at the beginning of the chapter. The questions and activities that follow demonstrate how the concepts that you have learned about in this chapter, connect to the everyday activities of all teachers.

JOSEPH, as you may remember, seems to have given up trying to learn. Mrs. Akers is sure that Joseph has the potential to be successful in her class. In addition, she is concerned that her beliefs about his behavior have limited her ability to support his needs. Based on her concern and desire to help him achieve, Mrs. Akers has spent several hours reading about behavior management techniques and discussing Joseph's individual needs with the special education teacher. She has decided that using a contract will work best with Joseph. She requests your help, and her questions are these:

■ What behaviors should I target first for Joseph? Should he decide this or should I?

■ What types of rewards would be likely to appeal to Joseph? (Make a list of items that you think would be most likely to motivate adolescents.)

■ How can I explain this to Joseph in a way that will encourage him to participate? Should I explain this to his parents?

J.R., as you may recall, frequently disrupts his class with oppositional behavior. Mr. George is concerned about these disruptions, but he also knows that some of J.R.'s classmates socially reject him.

Mr. George will meet tomorrow with teachers from the seventh-grade team, the special education teacher, J.R.'s mother, and J.R. They will discuss a plan to use CBM to teach J.R. to monitor and change his behavior. As a member of the team, you have been asked to come to the meeting with your written responses to the following concerns. (Of course, the team will want to hear your rationale for all of your answers.)

■ What functions might J.R.'s behaviors be serving? How would this knowledge affect the intervention designed to address them?

■ What could the team plan to do to help J.R. learn skills to interact more effectively with his peers? What should a teacher do when she overhears students making negative comments about J.R.?

■ How would you teach J.R. to self-monitor this behavior? To change it?

MS. WRIGHT has discovered that Jaden's behavior is more challenging than she had anticipated. She cannot allow it to continue. She is aware that there are simple and effective responses to student behavior, but she is not sure which to use. She has asked you to list the pros and cons for using each of the responses addressed in this chapter with Jaden. In addition, she is particularly interested in which of the techniques for managing surface behaviors, you would recommend. Include the rationales for all of your decisions.

SUMMARY

- *Positive behavioral interventions and supports (PBIS)* is a systematic approach for addressing prevention as well as the more intensive interventions needed by some students with disabilities or other special needs.

- Responding to student behavior begins with prevention: By setting clear expectations, fostering respect and communication, and establishing effective teaching methods, teachers can create a positive classroom learning environment that encourages appropriate behavior and discourages inappropriate behavior.

- Group techniques, such as peer-mediated instruction, also can promote positive student behavior. Peer tutoring and cooperative learning help students learn social skills, prevent behavior problems, build classroom community, and enhance student learning. Some students need additional supports and may respond to low-intrusion strategies such as "catch 'em being

good," managing surface behaviors, and direct instruction in social skills.

- When behavior problems are serious and persistent, you may participate in functional behavior assessment (FBA) with your team to prepare and follow a behavior intervention plan (BIP) tailored to the student's needs. Such a plan may be part of the IEP if the need arises for any student with a disability.

- A behavior intervention plan may include one or more strategies for increasing desirable student behavior (for example, reinforcement) or decreasing undesirable student behavior (for example, extinction, removal punishment); it also may be presented to the student in the form of a behavior contract.

- For some students, cognitive behavior management strategies such as self-monitoring and self-reinforcement also can be employed. Such techniques help students learn to manage their own behavior.

APPLICATIONS IN TEACHING PRACTICE
DEVELOPING STRATEGIES FOR RESPONDING TO INDIVIDUAL STUDENT BEHAVIOR

Ms. Caldwell is a second-year teacher who is very concerned about the behavior of Russell, a student identified as having a learning disability and behavior problems. Russell tends to be the class clown. He makes flippant remarks that border on being disrespectful of other students and Ms. Caldwell. He often is reprimanded for chatting with other students instead of listening and then complaining that he doesn't know how to do the assignment that was just explained. The other students generally like Russell, and they sometimes directly or indirectly, through their laughter, urge him to engage in more classroom antics.

Ms. Caldwell is not alone in her concern about Russell's behavior. Other teachers report a similar pattern. All are concerned that, unless his behavior improves, his troubling behaviors may develop into more serious ones that could jeopardize his learning and his relationships with peers, teachers, and others. Ms. Caldwell's tally of classroom incidents from the last week suggests that Russell was reprimanded at least six times in a single 45-minute period. The reprimands tend to occur when the class is transitioning from one activity to another—for example, from a large-group lecture to an individual assignment.

Ms. Caldwell, special education teacher Mr. Clark, counselor Ms. Lassaux, and parent Ms. Pinelli have been meeting about Russell. The first step in their functional behavior assessment was to think about whether any simple strategies have been effective and about the intent of Russell's behavior. They decide that the behaviors he has been displaying probably have to do with seeking attention from both peers and teachers, but they conclude that current interventions are inadequate. Using observational data from the classroom and interview information from other teachers, the lunchroom supervisor, and Russell himself, they spend considerable time discussing what sources of appropriate attention are available to Russell, and they weigh the pros and cons of various alternatives for responding to Russell's behavior. They also engage in a conversation about the impact other students are having on maintaining Russell's behavior when they encourage him. Ms. Caldwell is convinced that if Russell's peers were not providing him with an audience, many of his problems might take care of themselves.

QUESTIONS

Before you answer the questions that follow, decide the grade level you wish to attribute to Russell—elementary, middle, or high school.

1. What strategies could Ms. Caldwell and other teachers use to address the group response to Russell's behavior? What cautions would you have for them in trying these strategies?
2. What simple strategies outlined early in this chapter could Ms. Caldwell use to help Russell behave more appropriately in class? For each strategy, identify potential positive outcomes that could occur, as well as potential problems.
3. What information about Russell do you think the team gathered? How can this information be used to help them create a behavior intervention plan? What additional information might be needed?
4. What types of reinforcement might work for Russell? How can Ms. Caldwell decide which reinforcers to use if reinforcement is the strategy selected? Which types of reinforcers would you avoid in this case?
5. Is Russell a good candidate for cognitive behavior management? Why or why not? If you decided to try a CBM strategy, how would you go about it?
6. How should Russell and his mother be involved in the discussion about his behavior? What contributions could each make?

PEARSON
myeducationlab

Go to Topic 9: Classroom/Behavior Management in the MyEducationLab (www.myeducationlab .com) for your course, where you can:

- Find learning outcomes for Classroom/Behavior Management along with the national standards that connect to these outcomes.
- Complete Assignments and Activities that can help you more deeply understand the chapter content.
- Apply and practice your understanding of the core teaching skills indentified in the chapter with the Building Teaching Skills and Dispositions learning units.
- Examine challenging situations and cases presented in the IRIS Center Resources. (optional)
- Access video clips of CCSSO National Teachers of the Year award winners responding to the question, "Why Do I Teach?" in the Teacher Talk section. (optional)
- Check your comprehension on the content covered in the chapter by going to the Study Plan in the Book Resources for your text. Here you will be able to take a chapter quiz, receive feedback on your answers, and then access Review, Practice, and Enrichment activities to enhance your understanding of chapter content. (optional)

Appendix
CEC Knowledge and Skill Standards Common Core

Standard I: *Foundations*

ICC1K1: Models, theories, and philosophies, and research methods that provide the basis for special education practice.

ICC1K2: Laws, policies, and ethical principles regarding behavior management planning and implementation.

ICC1K3: Relationship of special education to the organization and function of educational agencies.

ICC1K4: Rights and responsibilities of students, parents, teachers, and other professionals, and schools related to exceptional learning needs.

ICC1K5: Issues in definition and identification of individuals with exceptional learning needs, including those from culturally and linguistically diverse backgrounds.

ICC1K6: Issues, assurances, and due process rights related to assessment, eligibility, and placement within a continuum of services.

ICC1K7: Family systems and the role of families in the educational process.

ICC1K8: Historical points of view and contributions of culturally diverse groups.

ICC1K9: Impact of the dominant culture on shaping schools and the individuals who study and work in them.

ICC1K10: Potential impact of differences in values, languages, and customs that can exist between the home and school.

ICC1S1: Articulate personal philosophy of special education.

Standard II: *Development and Characteristics of Learners*

ICC2K1: Typical and atypical human growth and development.

ICC2K2: Educational implications of characteristics of various exceptionalities.

ICC2K3: Characteristics and effects of the cultural and environmental milieu of the individual with exceptional learning needs and the family.

ICC2K4: Family systems and the role of families in supporting development.

ICC2K5: Similarities and differences of individuals with and without exceptional learning needs.

ICC2K6: Similarities and differences among individuals with exceptional learning needs.

ICC2K7: Effects of various medications on individuals with exceptional learning needs.

Standard III: *Individual Learning Differences*

ICC3K1: Effects an exceptional condition(s) can have on an individual's life.

ICC3K2: Impact of learner's academic and social abilities, attitudes, interests, and values on instruction and career development.

ICC3K3: Variations in beliefs, traditions, and values across and within cultures and their effects on relationships among individuals with exceptional learning needs, family, and schooling.

ICC3K4: Cultural perspectives influencing the relationships among families, schools, and communities as related to instruction.

ICC3K5: Differing ways of learning of individuals with exceptional learning needs including those from culturally diverse backgrounds and strategies for addressing these differences.

Standard IV: *Instructional Strategies*

ICC4K1:   Evidence-based practices validated for specific characteristics of learners and settings.

ICC4S1:   Use strategies to facilitate integration into various settings.

ICC4S2:   Teach individuals to use self-assessment, problem-solving, and other cognitive strategies to meet their needs.

ICC4S3:   Select, adapt, and use instructional strategies and materials according to characteristics of the individual with exceptional learning needs.

ICC4S4:   Use strategies to facilitate maintenance and generalization of skills across learning environments.

ICC4S5:   Use procedures to increase the individual's self-awareness, self-management, self-control, self-reliance, and self-esteem.

ICC4S6:   Use strategies that promote successful transitions for individuals with exceptional learning needs.

Standard V: *Learning Environments and Social Interactions*

ICC5K1:   Demands of learning environments.

ICC5K2:   Basic classroom management theories and strategies for individuals with exceptional learning needs.

ICC5K3:   Effective management of teaching and learning.

ICC5K4:   Teacher attitudes and behaviors that influence behavior of individuals with exceptional learning needs.

ICC5K5:   Social skills needed for educational and other environments.

ICC5K6:   Strategies for crisis prevention and intervention.

ICC5K7:   Strategies for preparing individuals to live harmoniously and productively in a culturally diverse world.

ICC5K8:   Ways to create learning environments that allow individuals to retain and appreciate their own and each other's respective language and cultural heritage.

ICC5K9:   Ways specific cultures are negatively stereotyped.

ICC5K10: Strategies used by diverse populations to cope with a legacy of former and continuing racism.

ICC5S1:   Create a safe, equitable, positive, and supporting learning environment in which diversities are valued.

ICC5S2:   Identify realistic expectations for personal and social behavior in various settings.

ICC5S3:   Identify supports needed for integration into various program placements.

ICC5S4:   Design learning environments that encourage active participation in individual and group settings.

ICC5S5:   Modify the learning environment to manage behaviors.

ICC5S6:   Use performance data and information from all stakeholders to make or suggest modifications in learning environments.

ICC5S7:   Establish and maintain rapport with individuals with and without exceptional learning needs.

ICC5S8:   Teach self-advocacy.

ICC5S9:   Create an environment that encourages self-advocacy and increased independence.

ICC5S10: Use effective and varied behavior management strategies.

ICC5S11: Use the least intensive behavior management strategy consistent with the needs of the individual with exceptional learning needs.

ICC5S12: Design and manage daily routines.

ICC5S13: Organize, develop, and sustain learning environments that support positive intracultural and intercultural experiences.

ICC5S14: Mediate controversial intercultural issues among students within the learning environment in ways that enhance any culture, group, or person.

ICC5S15: Structure, direct, and support the activities of paraeducators, volunteers, and tutors.

ICC5S16: Use universal precautions.

Standard VI: *Communication*

ICC6K1:   Effects of cultural and linguistic differences on growth and development.

ICC6K2:   Characteristics of one's own culture and use of language and the ways in which these can differ from other cultures and uses of languages.

ICC6K3:   Ways of behaving and communicating among cultures that can lead to misinterpretation and misunderstanding.

ICC6K4:   Augmentative and assistive communication strategies.

ICC6S1:   Use strategies to support and enhance communication skills of individuals with exceptional learning needs.

ICC6S2:   Use communication strategies and resources to facilitate understanding of subject matter for students whose primary language is not the dominant language.

Standard VII: *Instructional Planning*

ICC7K1: Theories and research that form the basis of curriculum development and instructional practice.
ICC7K2: Scope and sequences of general and special curricula.
ICC7K3: National, state or provincial, and local curricula standards.
ICC7K4: Technology for planning and managing the teaching and learning environment.
ICC7K5: Roles and responsibilities of the paraeducator related to instruction, intervention, and direct service.
ICC7S1: Identify and prioritize areas of the general curriculum and accommodations for individuals with exceptional learning needs.
ICC7S2: Develop and implement comprehensive, longitudinal individualized programs in collaboration with team members.
ICC7S3: Involve the individual and family in setting instructional goals and monitoring progress.
ICC7S4: Use functional assessments to develop intervention plans.
ICC7S5: Use task analysis.
ICC7S6: Sequence, implement, and evaluate individualized learning objectives.
ICC7S7: Integrate affective, social, and life skills with academic curricula.
ICC7S8: Develop and select instructional content, resources, and strategies that respond to cultural, linguistic, and gender differences.
ICC7S9: Incorporate and implement instructional and assistive technology into the educational program.
ICC7S10: Prepare lesson plans.
ICC7S11: Prepare and organize materials to implement daily lesson plans.
ICC7S12: Use instructional time effectively.
ICC7S13: Make responsive adjustments to instruction based on continued observations.
ICC7S14: Prepare individuals to exhibit self-enhancing behavior in response to societal attitudes and actions.
ICC7S15: Evaluate and modify instructional practices in response to ongoing assessment data.

Standard VIII: *Assessment*

ICC8K1: Basic terminology used in assessment.
ICC8K2: Legal provisions and ethical principles regarding assessment of individuals.
ICC8K3: Screening, prereferral, referral, and classification procedures.
ICC8K4: Use and limitations of assessment instruments.
ICC8K5: National, state or provincial, and local accommodations and modifications.
ICC8S1: Gather relevant background information.
ICC8S2: Administer nonbiased formal and informal assessments.
ICC8S3: Use technology to conduct assessments.
ICC8S4: Develop or modify individualized assessment strategies.
ICC8S5: Interpret information from formal and informal assessments.
ICC8S6: Use assessment information in making eligibility, program, and placement decisions for individuals with exceptional learning needs, including those from culturally and/or linguistically diverse backgrounds.
ICC8S7: Report assessment results to all stakeholders using effective communication skills.
ICC8S8: Evaluate instruction and monitor progress of individuals with exceptional learning needs.
ICC8S9: Develop or modify individualized assessment strategies.
ICC8S10: Create and maintain records.

Standard IX: *Professional and Ethical Practice*

ICC9K1: Personal cultural biases and differences that affect one's teaching.
ICC9K2: Importance of the teacher serving as a model for individuals with exceptional learning needs.
ICC9K3: Continuum of lifelong professional development.
ICC9K4: Methods to remain current regarding research-validated practice.
ICC9S1: Practice within the CEC Code of Ethics and other standards of the profession.
ICC9S2: Uphold high standards of competence and integrity and exercise sound judgment in the practice of the professional.
ICC9S3: Act ethically in advocating for appropriate services.
ICC9S4: Conduct professional activities in compliance with applicable laws and policies.
ICC9S5: Demonstrate commitment to developing the highest education and quality-of-life potential of individuals with exceptional learning needs.

ICC9S6: Demonstrate sensitivity for the culture, language, religion, gender, disability, socioeconomic status, and sexual orientation of individuals.

ICC9S7: Practice within one's skill limit and obtain assistance as needed.

ICC9S8: Use verbal, nonverbal, and written language effectively.

ICC9S9: Conduct self-evaluation of instruction.

ICC9S10: Access information on exceptionalities.

ICC9S11: Reflect on one's practice to improve instruction and guide professional growth.

ICC9S12: Engage in professional activities that benefit individuals with exceptional learning needs, their families, and one's colleagues.

ICC9S13: Demonstrate Commitment to engage evidence-based practice.

Standard X: *Collaboration*

ICC10K1: Models and strategies of consultation and collaboration.

ICC10K2: Roles of individuals with exceptional learning needs, families, and school and community personnel in planning of an individualized program.

ICC10K3: Concerns of families of individuals with exceptional learning needs and strategies to help address these concerns.

ICC10K4: Culturally responsive factors that promote effective communication and collaboration with individuals with exceptional learning needs, families, school personnel, and community members.

ICC10S1: Maintain confidential communication about individuals with exceptional learning needs.

ICC10S2: Collaborate with families and others in assessment of individuals with exceptional learning needs.

ICC10S3: Foster respectful and beneficial relationships between families and professionals.

ICC10S4: Assist individuals with exceptional learning needs and their families in becoming active participants in the educational team.

ICC10S5: Plan and conduct collaborative conferences with individuals with exceptional learning needs and their families.

ICC10S6: Collaborate with school personnel and community members in integrating individuals with exceptional learning needs into various settings.

ICC10S7: Use group problem-solving skills to develop, implement, and evaluate collaborative activities.

ICC10S8: Model techniques and coach others in the use of instructional methods and accommodations.

ICC10S9: Communicate with school personnel about the characteristics and needs of individuals with exceptional learning needs.

ICC10S10: Communicate effectively with families of individuals with exceptional learning needs from diverse backgrounds.

ICC10S11: Observe, evaluate, and provide feedback to paraeducators.

Glossary

ABC analysis Systematic recording of antecedents, behaviors, and consequences as a strategy for analyzing student behavior.

absence seizure Seizure that is brief and often characterized by momentary lapses of attention. Also called a *petit mal seizure*.

academic learning time The time students are meaningfully and successfully engaged in school.

academic survival skills Skills needed to succeed in school, including regular and punctual attendance, organization, task completion, independence, motivation, and appropriate social skills.

acceleration Approach for educating gifted and talented students based on allowing them to move through all or part of the curriculum at their own, accelerated pace.

accuracy The extent to which a student's academic performance is without errors.

acquired immune deficiency syndrome (AIDS) Disease that results when students are infected with the human immunodeficiency virus (HIV) and their bodies lose the ability to fight infection.

activity reinforcer Positive activity that causes a behavior to increase. An example of an activity reinforcer is a student being rewarded with extra time to work on the computer.

ADA *See* Americans with Disabilities Act.

adaptive physical educator Specialist with expertise in assessing students' motor needs and designing and delivering physical education programs that accommodate those needs.

ADD *See* attention deficit disorder.

adequate yearly progress (AYP) The minimum level of improvement, set by each state, that schools and districts must achieve toward reaching the goals of the No Child Left Behind Act of 2001.

ADHD *See* attention deficit–hyperactivity disorder.

administrator Professional responsible for managing some aspect of schools; includes principals, assistant principals, department chairpersons, team leaders, special services coordinators, district administrators, and others.

advance organizer Information, often presented as organizational signals, that makes content more understandable by putting it within a more general framework.

advocate Individual who works to ensure that parents understand their rights and that school professionals provide an appropriate education for parents' children with disabilities.

AIDS *See* acquired immune deficiency syndrome.

alternate assessment A form of functional assessment for students with severe disabilities who are unable to participate in the standard state and district-wide assessment programs.

alternative forms of questions Testing adaptations that involve changing the construction of a test item or substituting one kind of test item for another. Examples of alternative forms of questions include reducing the choices on a multiple choice item from four to two or adding a word bank to fill-in-the-blank items.

alternatives to letter and number grades Ways to evaluate student test performance using pass-fail grades and/or checklists of student skills.

alternative teaching Co-teaching option in which students are divided into one large and one small group. The large group receives the planned instruction. The small group receives reteaching, preteaching, enrichment, or other special instruction.

alternative test site A type of testing accommodation that involves changing the location where a student with a disability is tested to make sure the results of the test are accurate. An example is testing a student with attention problems in a room having fewer distractions.

alternative ways of administering tests Testing adaptations that involve changing the ways students respond on tests and/or the ways teachers give tests. An example of changing the way students respond on tests is responding orally to written test items. An example of changing the way teachers give tests is giving a test orally.

American Sign Language (ASL) A sign language not based on the grammar or structures of English; used by some people with hearing impairments.

Americans with Disabilities Act (ADA) Civil rights law passed in 1990 that protects individuals with disabilities from discrimination and requires building and transportation accessibility and reasonable accommodations in the workplace.

anecdotal recording Strategy for recording behavior in which incidents before and after a behavior are recorded along with a description of the behavior.

annual goal Broad statement describing estimated yearly outcomes for a student with a disability. Annual goals address areas of identified needs.

annual review Yearly process of convening a team that includes a parent, teacher, administrator, and others as needed to review and update a student's IEP.

anticipation guide Series of statements, some of which may not be true, related to material that is about to be presented during instruction, given to students as a way of activating their knowledge by making predictions about the topic.

anxiety Condition in which an individual experiences extraordinary worry in some situations or worries excessively about future situations.

articulation Production of speech sounds.

Asperger syndrome Mild form of autism in which an individual develops speech but has gross motor problems, intense interests in a narrow range of topics, and chronic difficulty in forming and sustaining social relationships.

assessment Process of gathering information to monitor progress and make educational decisions.

assistive technology (AT) Any of a wide variety of technology applications designed to help students with disabilities learn, communicate, and otherwise function more independently by bypassing their disabilities.

asthma Physical condition in which an individual experiences difficulty breathing, especially during physically or psychologically stressful activities.

at risk Term used to describe students who have characteristics, live in conditions, or have experiences that make them more likely than others to experience failure in schools.

attention deficit disorder (ADD) Term sometimes used as a synonym for attention deficit–hyperactivity disorder.

attention deficit–hyperactivity disorder (ADHD) Medical condition in which students have significant inability to attend, excessive motor activity, and/or impulsivity.

attribution retraining Teaching program that increases student task persistence and performance by convincing them that their failures are due to effort and can therefore be overcome.

augmentative and alternative communication (AAC) Ways other than speech to send a message to another individual, including nonaided communication such as using sign language or gestures and facial expressions and aided communication such as using computers or other simple or complex devices as communication tools.

authentic learning tasks Tasks used in performance-based assessment that are based on real-world contexts and lead to real-world outcomes.

autism Condition in which an individual lacks social responsiveness from a very early age, has a high need for structure and routines, and demonstrates significant language impairments. These characteristics interfere with learning.

autism spectrum disorder (ASD) Contemporary term used to convey the diversity of autism and related disorders, from classic autism that usually includes intellectual disabilities, to Asperger syndrome in which individuals may be intellectually gifted.

balanced grading A type of grading adaptation that considers effort and/or the performance of individualized learning strategies along with products of performance when determining a student's grade.

basal textbook A book used for instruction in basic-skills areas that contains all key components of the curriculum to be taught for that subject. Often called a *basal*.

basic-skills instruction Instruction in the tool skills of reading, writing, and math.

behavior contract Agreement between a teacher (or other adult) and student that clearly specifies student performance expectations, rewards for meeting expectations, consequences of not meeting expectations, and the time frame for which the agreement is valid.

behavior intervention plan (BIP) A detailed strategy, developed on the basis of a functional behavior assessment, to address significant behavior problems being experienced by a student with a disability. The plan typically includes detailed descriptions of interventions, persons responsible, a timeline, and methods for data collection. This plan is required by federal law when a student with a disability has significant behavior problems.

big ideas Important principles that help learners understand the connections among facts and concepts they learn.

bilingual education program Education approach in which students with limited English skills learn core subjects in a separate setting in their native language and spend the remainder of their school day with English-speaking peers.

bilingual special education program Special education approach in which students with disabilities with limited English skills learn core subjects in a separate setting in their native language.

bilingual special education teacher Teacher who works with students with disabilities whose native language is not English.

bilingual teacher Teacher who teaches students whose native language is not English.

blind Condition in which an individual has little or no vision and relies on auditory and other input for learning.

Braille Writing system, used by individuals who have vision impairments, that uses various combinations of six raised dots punched on paper read with the fingertips.

brainstorming Strategy for generating solutions to problems in which participants call out ideas, building on one another's responses, deferring all evaluation.

Brown v. Board of Education Supreme Court decision in 1954 that established that it is unlawful and discriminatory to create separate schools for African American students. This "separate cannot be equal" concept was later applied to students with disabilities.

bypass strategies Ways of receiving or expressing information that allow students to gain access to or demonstrate mastery of the curriculum in alternate ways. For examples, a bypass strategy for a student with a reading disability would be a digitized book.

CALL UP Learning strategy for taking lecture notes. The steps are: copy from board or slide, add details, listen and write the question, listen and write the answer, utilize the text, and put in your words.

CAPS Four-step learning strategy for helping a student decide what is important in a story: ask who the characters are; identify the aim of the story; decide what problem happens; and determine how the problem is solved.

catch 'em being good Behavior management strategy in which a teacher notices appropriate student behavior and positively comments on it, either privately to the student or publicly to the class.

CBA *See* curriculum-based assessment.

CBM *See* cognitive behavior management or curriculum-based measurement.

cerebral palsy Most common type of orthopedic impairment among public school students, caused by brain injury before or during birth and resulting in poor motor coordination and abnormal motor patterns.

changing letter or number grades A way of clarifying letter and number grades by supplementing them with other ways of evaluating and reporting learner progress such as written or verbal comments, logs of student activities, and portfolios.

CHECK Learning strategy for using spell checkers more effectively. The steps are: check the beginning sound of the word; hunt for the correct consonants; examine the vowels; check changes in suggested word lists for hints; and keep repeating steps 1–4.

child abuse Situation in which a parent or other caregiver inflicts or allows others to inflict injury on a child, or permits a substantial risk of injury to exist.

child neglect Situation in which a parent or other caregiver fails to provide the necessary supports for a child's well-being.

CHROME Mnemonic for remembering the six methods of scientific investigation: categorization, hypothesis, reasoning, observation, measurement, and experimentation.

chunking Memorization strategy in which students are taught to remember five to seven key ideas at one time.

CIRC *See* Cooperative Integrated Reading and Composition.

Circle of Friends Program designed to help students without disabilities understand how important it is to have friends with disabilities and to encourage them to form friendships with classmates with disabilities.

classroom climate The overall atmosphere of a classroom, including whether it is friendly and pleasant, based on the expectations of teachers and their interactions with students.

classroom grouping Various grouping arrangements, such as teaching the whole class at once or in small groups, that modify the classroom environment. Classroom grouping may be teacher centered or peer mediated, and based on same or mixed-skills configurations.

classroom instruction Strategies through which a teacher presents curriculum content to students.

classroom organization Strategies through which a teacher establishes and maintains order in a classroom.

classwide peer tutoring (CWPT) Peer-mediated instruction in which all students in a class are partnered. Both students serve as the tutor and tutee following a clear procedure, and they are rewarded for demonstrating appropriate social behaviors.

cluster programs Special education service delivery system in which students with similar needs from several schools or an entire district attend a single school to receive special education services.

cognitive behavior management (CBM) Behavior management strategy in which students learn to monitor and change their own behavior.

collaboration A style of interaction professionals use in order to accomplish a goal they share, often stressed in inclusive schools.

community-based education Approach to instruction in which what is learned in school is related to activities that occur in the community.

compensatory strategies *See* bypass strategies.

competency checklist Evaluation technique in which student learning is checked against a listing of key concepts, ideas, or skills being taught.

comprehension Reading skill involving understanding the meaning of what has been read.

concept diagram Specific type of graphic organizer used to present vocabulary words that includes definitions and characteristics.

concept map Graphic organizer showing relationships among concepts of instruction as well as essential characteristics of the concepts.

constructivistic teaching Type of teaching based on the belief that students are capable of constructing meaning on their own, in most cases, without explicit instruction.

consultant Specialist who provides particular expertise to teachers and others when an extraordinary student need arises.

consultation Specialized problem-solving process in which one professional with particular expertise assists another professional or parent who needs the benefit of that expertise; used as an instructional approach for some students with disabilities.

consulting teacher Special education teacher who meets with general education teachers to problem solve and monitor student progress but who typically has little or no direct contact with students.

content-area textbook A book used for instruction in science, social studies, or other content areas.

controlled materials Instructional materials at the student's reading level, of high interest and free of complex vocabulary and concepts; often used while teaching students a learning strategy.

cooperative integrated reading and composition (CIRC) Cooperative learning program for teaching reading, writing, and other language arts to students in upper elementary grades.

cooperative learning Student-centered instructional approach in which students work in small, mixed-ability groups with a shared learning goal.

COPS Learning strategy for proofreading papers with these steps: Have I capitalized the first word and proper nouns? How is the overall appearance of my paper; have I made any handwriting, margin, or messy errors? Have I used end punctuation, commas, and semicolons carefully? Do words look like they're spelled right; can I sound them out or use a dictionary?

co-teaching Instructional approach in which two or more teachers or other certified staff share instruction for a single group of students within a single classroom setting.

counselor Specialist with expertise in meeting students' social and affective needs.

credit/no credit grading system *See* pass/fail grading system.

cross-age tutoring Peer tutoring approach in which older students tutor younger ones.

cross-categorical approach Instructional approach in which the cognitive, learning, affective, and social and emotional needs of students, not their disability labels, form the basis for planning and delivering instruction.

cue words Words that make patterns of information more conspicuous for students, such as the words "similar" and "different," signalling the presence of a compare/contrast pattern.

curriculum-based assessment (CBA) Method of measuring the level of achievement of students in terms of what they are taught in the classroom.

curriculum-based measurement A particular kind of curriculum-based assessment characterized by a research base establishing its technical adequacy as well as standardized measurement tasks that are fluency based.

curriculum placement Type of assessment decision concerning where to begin instruction for students.

CWPT *See* classwide peer tutoring.

cystic fibrosis Genetically transmitted disease in which the body produces excessive mucus that eventually damages the lungs and causes heart failure.

daily activity log Strategy for providing ongoing information for students and their parents about learning by noting daily observations of student work, effort, and outcomes.

deaf Hearing impairment in which the individual cannot process linguistic information through hearing with or without the use of hearing aids and relies on visual and other input for learning.

deaf–blind Condition in which an individual has both significant visual and hearing impairments that interfere with learning.

decibel (dB) Unit for measuring the loudness of sounds.

decoding Reading skill involving accurately identifying words and fluently pronouncing them.

depression Condition in which an individual is persistently and seriously unhappy, with a loss of interest or pleasure in all or almost all usual activities. Symptoms of depression include changes in appetite or weight, sleep disturbances, loss of energy, feelings of worthlessness, and thoughts of death or suicide.

developmental delay Significant delay in one or more of the following areas leading to the need for special education and related services: physical development, cognitive development, communication development, social or emotional development, or adaptive development. Applicable only for children ages 3–9.

developmental disability A significant, chronic condition, typically physical, cognitive, or a combination of both, that results in the need for special education and related services. IDEA permits the use of this term in lieu of a more specific disability label for children until age 9.

diabetes Disease in which the body does not produce enough insulin to process the carbohydrates eaten.

diagnosis Type of assessment decision concerning whether or not a student meets established federal guidelines for being classified as having a disability and, if so, the nature and extent of the disability.

diagnostic teaching Sample lessons and other instructional activities carried out with students experiencing extreme academic or behavioral difficulty as part of screening.

differential reinforcement of incompatible behaviors Reinforcing an appropriate behavior that is incompatible with another undesirable behavior in order to increase the positive behavior.

differentiated instruction A form of instruction that meets students' diverse needs by providing materials and tasks of varied levels of difficulty, with varying degrees of support, through multiple instructional groups and time variations.

differentiated report cards Report cards that have individualized provisions for students, including additional information to clarify grades and separate grades for different grading elements such as progress and effort.

direct instruction Research-based instructional approach in which the teacher presents subject matter using a review of previously taught information, presentation of new concepts or skills, guided practice, feedback and correction, independent student practice, and frequent review.

disability Condition characterized by a physical, cognitive, psychological, or social difficulty so severe that it negatively affects student learning. In the Americans with Disabilities Act, a disability is defined as a condition that limits some major life activity.

discipline Term to describe the set of classroom expectations, including rules for behavior, that serves as a means for facilitating student learning.

discovery learning *See* inquiry learning.

Down syndrome Most prevalent type of biologically caused cognitive disability, caused by the failure of one pair of chromosomes to separate at conception.

drill-and-practice programs A form of computer-assisted instruction in which students learn in small steps, are given systematic feedback, and engage in a lot of practice until mastery is attained.

due process Procedures outlined in IDEA for ensuring that parents' and children's rights are protected and for resolving disputes between parents and school district personnel concerning any aspect of special education.

duration recording Strategy for recording behavior in which the length of time a behavior occurs is recorded.

dyslexia A word used to refer to the condition of a severe reading disability.

echolalic speech Occurs when an individual communicates by repeating what others have said instead of producing original speech.

ED *See* emotional disturbance.

Education for All Handicapped Children Act (EHCA) *See* Public Law 94-142.

emotional disturbance (ED) Condition in which an individual has significant difficulty in the social and emotional domain, so much so that it interferes with learning.

English-language learners (ELLs) Students whose native language is not English and who are developing their English skills while in school.

enrichment Approach for educating gifted and talented students based on helping them elaborate on or extend concepts being presented to all students.

environmental inventory Assessment procedure, often used for students with moderate or severe disabilities, designed to find out what adaptations or supports are needed to increase student participation in classroom and community environments.

epilepsy Physical condition in which the brain experiences sudden but brief changes in its functioning leading to seizures.

evaluation Procedures used to determine whether teaching is effective, to provide feedback to students and their parents about student learning, and to inform school boards and communities about school effectiveness.

event recording Strategy for recording behavior in which each occurrence of the behavior is counted.

evidence-based practice Instructional techniques that have been shown by research to be most likely to improve student outcomes in a meaningful way.

example selection Teacher choice of examples during instruction. Example selection directly affects student understanding of instruction.

example sequence Order of presentation of examples during instruction. Example sequence directly affects student understanding of instruction.

exemplar A sample student performance designed to specify a level of achievement in authentic learning evaluation. For example, a writing sample of an "average" seventh-grader is an exemplar against which other students' writing can be compared.

expressive language An individual's ability to communicate meaning clearly through speech.

extinction Strategy for decreasing negative behavior by no longer reinforcing it; most effective when the undesirable behavior has been inadvertently reinforced by the teacher.

facilitated communication Method of assisting individuals with autism and other disabilities to communicate by gently supporting the wrist, arm, or shoulder on a typewriter or computer keyboard. This method is controversial.

fading out Gradual process for decreasing the use of behavioral strategies to support appropriate student behavior.

FAE *See* fetal alcohol effects.

family-centered practices Approach for working with families based on the notion that outcomes are best for students when their families' perspectives are respected, family input is sincerely sought, and families gain information that can assist them to make the best decisions for their children.

FAS *See* fetal alcohol syndrome.

FBA *See* functional behavior assessment.

fetal alcohol effects (FAE) Mild form of fetal alcohol syndrome (FAS), often without physical characteristics. Students with FAE often experience a variety of learning and behavior problems in school.

fetal alcohol syndrome (FAS) Medical condition caused by prenatal maternal abuse of alcohol, often resulting in slight physical abnormalities and learning, cognitive, or emotional disabilities.

finger spelling Communication system in which each alphabet letter is assigned a specific hand position. Finger spelling is often used to communicate proper names or technical words for which no other sign language signs exist.

fluency The rate at which a student performs an academic task such as calculating math problems or reading.

FOIL Four-step learning strategy for multiplying binomials in algebra: multiply the first terms; multiply the outermost terms; multiply the innermost terms; and multiply the last terms.

frame of reference An individual's predisposition to respond to a situation in a certain way based on his background, education, experiences, and work history.

functional behavior assessment (FBA) The process of gathering detailed data on a student's behavior and the context in which it occurs for the purpose of determining the reasons for it and creating a behavior intervention plan. This process is required by federal law when a student with a disability has significant behavior problems.

functional curriculum Instructional approach in which goals and objectives are based on real-life skills needed for adulthood. Examples of skills addressed in a functional curriculum include shopping and making purchases; reading common signs such as exit, stop, and sale; riding public transportation; and interacting with peers and adults.

general education teacher Elementary, middle school, junior high, or high school teacher whose primary responsibility is teaching one or more class groups.

generalized tonic-clonic seizure Seizure involving the entire body. Also called a *grand mal seizure.*

gifted and talented Demonstrated ability far above average in one or several areas including overall intellectual ability, leadership, specific academic subjects, creativity, athletics, or the visual or performing arts.

Good Behavior Game Strategy for reducing disruptive behavior and promoting positive behavior in the classroom in which students work on teams to earn points for appropriate behavior toward a reward.

grading contract Agreement between a teacher and student that specifies the quantity, quality, and timeliness of work required to receive a specific grade.

grading criteria The standard on which a student's academic performance is evaluated and graded.

grand mal seizure *See* generalized tonic-clonic seizure.

graphic organizer Visual format that helps students to organize their understanding of information being presented or read and the relationships between various parts of the information.

group-administered standardized achievement test Standardized achievement test given to large groups of students at one time, usually administered by general education teachers, useful as a screening measure.

group roles Assigned roles for students in cooperative groups that help the group function effectively. Roles commonly assigned include encourager, monitor, leader, and recorder.

guided practice A teaching technique where students are given verbal cues when first attempting a skill.

handicap Term, generally no longer preferred, to describe disabilities.

hard of hearing Hearing impairment in which an individual has some hearing through which to process linguistic information, possibly with the assistance of hearing aids or other assistive devices.

hearing impairment Condition in which an individual has the inability or limited ability to receive information auditorily such that it interferes with learning.

hemophilia Genetically transmitted disease in which blood does not properly coagulate.

hertz (Hz) Unit for measuring the pitch or tone of sounds.

heterogeneous grouping *See* mixed-skill grouping.

high-incidence disability Any of the most common disabilities outlined in IDEA, including learning disabilities, speech or language impairments, mild mental retardation, and serious emotional disturbance.

highly qualified teacher Term from both NCLB and IDEA and defined by each state; specifies that a professional has met rigorous requirements documenting qualifications to teach in a specific academic area (e.g., math, English) or special education. Some teachers are highly qualified in both academic content areas and special education.

high-stakes tests Assessments designed to measure whether students have obtained state learning standards.

HIV *See* human immunodeficiency virus.

homework The most common form of student practice.

homogeneous grouping *See* same-skill grouping.

human immunodeficiency virus (HIV) Viral disease in which the body loses its ability to fight off infection. Individuals with HIV often become infected with AIDS.

hyperactive-impulsive disorder Type of ADHD characterized by excessive movement and other motor activity including fidgeting, a need to move around a room even when others are seated, and rapid changes in activities.

individualized grading Accommodations made for individual students that are included on students' IEPs. Individualized grading includes accommodations that involve changing either the elements being graded such as curriculum content, class participation, and homework, or the value or weights assigned to these elements.

Individuals with Disabilities Education Improvement Act (IDEA) Public Law 101-476. Current federal special education law.

IEP *See* individualized education program.

IFSP *See* Individualized Family Service Plan.

improvement grade Giving credit in evaluation of student performance for progress made, based on the student's level of learning prior to instruction.

impulsivity The extent to which an individual acts before thinking; often a characteristic of students with high-incidence disabilities or ADHD.

INCLUDE A strategy for accommodating students with special needs in the general education classroom.

inclusion *See* inclusive practices.

inclusion specialist Special education teacher responsible for providing a wide variety of supports to students with disabilities and general education teachers who teach them. Inclusion specialists most often work with students with low-incidence disabilities; sometimes called a *support facilitator.*

inclusive practices Term to describe a professional belief that students with disabilities should be integrated into general education classrooms whether or not they can meet traditional curricular standards and should be full members of those classrooms.

independent learning skills Skills students need to manage their own learning, including note taking, textbook reading, test taking, written expression, and time management.

indirect instruction A type of teaching based on the belief that children are naturally active learners and that given the appropriate instructional environment, they actively construct knowledge and solve problems in developmentally appropriate ways.

individualized education program (IEP) Document prepared by the multidisciplinary team or annual review team that specifies a student's level of functioning and needs, the instructional goals and objectives for the student and how they will be evaluated, the nature and extent of special education and related services to be received, and the initiation date and duration of the services. Each student's IEP is updated annually.

individualized family service plan (IFSP) Education plan for children receiving services through P.L. 99-457. Similar to an IEP.

individualized instruction Instruction designed to meet the specific needs of a student with a disability; a requirement of IDEA.

individually administered diagnostic test Diagnostic achievement test given to one student at a time, often administered by a special education teacher or school psychologist, useful as a diagnostic measure. These tests provide more specific information than group-administered achievement tests do.

Individuals with Disabilities Education Act (IDEA) Federal education law that updates the 1975 Education for All Handicapped Children Act and ensures that students with disabilities receive special education and related services through prescribed policies and procedures.

inquiry learning The most common method of nondirect instruction. *See also* nondirect instruction.

instructional accommodations Services or supports provided to help students gain full access to class content and instruction, and to help them demonstrate accurately what they know.

instructional adaptation Any strategy for adapting curriculum materials, teacher instruction, or student practice activities that increases the likelihood of success for students with special needs.

instructional assistance team (IAT) Team of teachers, specialists, and administrators that solves problems about students experiencing academic or behavior difficulty and decides whether students should be individually assessed for possible special education services.

instructional evaluation Type of assessment decision concerning whether to continue or change instructional procedures that have been initiated with students.

instructional materials The textbooks, manipulatives, models, and technology used as part of instruction.

instructional methods The ways in which teachers present content or skills to students and evaluate whether learning has occurred.

instructional modifications Changes in classroom instruction that involve altering student content expectations and performance outcomes.

integration The physical, social, and instructional assimilation of students with disabilities in general education settings.

intellectual disability Term sometimes used as a synonym for *mental retardation.*

intensive instruction Intensive instruction in RtI is instruction that takes place for longer periods of time, in smaller groups, using highly scaffolded teaching procedures.

intent The purpose or goal of a student's behavior; not always clear from the behavior itself. An example of an intent occurs when a student repeatedly calls out in class to gain the teacher's attention; that is, the intent is teacher attention.

interval recording Strategy for recording behavior in which observation occurs for brief segments of time and any occurrence of the behavior during the segment is noted.

intervention assistance team Group of professionals, including general education teachers, that analyzes the strengths and problems of referred students to identify strategies to address the problems. If not successful this team may recommend that a student be assessed to determine special education eligibility.

itinerant teacher Special education teacher who provides services to students with disabilities and teaches in two or more schools.

Jigsaw Classroom Cooperative learning program in which work group team members are assigned to expert groups to master part of the assigned material to which no other group has access. In the work group, each team member has an opportunity to present his or her part of the material. Students are then assessed for mastery individually.

job coach A special education professional who accompanies students with disabilities to job sites and helps them master the skills needed to perform the job.

keyword method Mnemonic for remembering definitions and factual information in which visual imagery is used to enhance recall.

LAMPS Learning strategy for remembering the steps for regrouping in addition with these steps: line up the numbers according to their decimal points; add the right column of numbers; if more than nine continue to the next step; put the 1s below the column; and send the 10s to the top of the next column.

LD *See* learning disability.

learned helplessness Characteristic of some students with disabilities in which they see little relationship between their own efforts and school or social success, often resulting in a belief that they cannot perform challenging tasks.

learning and behavior disabilities Term used to describe collectively learning disabilities, emotional disturbance, and mild intellectual disabilities.

learning disability (LD) Condition in which a student has dysfunction in processing information typically found in language-based activities, resulting in interference with learning. Students with learning disabilities have average or above-average intelligence but experience significant problems in learning how to read, write, and/or do math.

learning outcomes Specific goals or outcomes students are expected to accomplish as a result of a unit of instruction.

learning strategies Techniques, principles, or rules that enable a student to solve problems and complete tasks independently.

Learning Together Cooperative learning program in which groups of two to six members learn specific skills for interacting with one another and then work together in various formal and informal group structures to learn material.

least restrictive environment (LRE) The setting as similar as possible to that for students without disabilities in which a student with a disability can be educated, with appropriate supports provided. For most students, the LRE is a general education classroom.

legal blindness Visual impairment in which an individual's best eye, with correction, has vision of 20/200 or less, or the visual field is 20 percent or less.

lesson organizer routine A teaching method that helps teachers convert content into understandable formats that meet the diverse needs of students. The method has three components: the lesson organizer device, linking steps, and cue-do-review sequence.

low demand request Behavior management strategy in which the teacher helps a student transition from one activity to another by making a series of simple requests of the student that are unrelated to the targeted task.

low-incidence disability Any of the less common disabilities outlined in IDEA, including multiple disabilities, hearing impairments, orthopedic impairments, other health impairments, visual impairments, deaf-blindness, autism, and traumatic brain injury.

LRE *See* least restrictive environment.

mainstreaming Term for placing students with disabilities in general education settings when they can meet traditional academic expectations with minimal assistance, or when those expectations are not relevant.

manipulatives Concrete objects or representational items used as part of instruction. Examples of commonly used manipulatives include blocks and counters.

MDT *See* multidisciplinary team.

mediation Process in which a neutral professional assists parents and school district personnel in resolving disputes concerning any aspect of a student's special education.

mental retardation Condition in which an individual has significant limitations in intellectual ability and adaptive behaviors that interfere with learning. Also referred to as a *intellectual disability*.

mild intellectual disabilities Condition in which students have some difficulty meeting the academic and social demands of general education classrooms due in large part to below-average intellectual functioning (55–70 on an IQ test).

minimum intervention Strategy for promoting positive behavior that is nonintrusive and often spontaneous instead of systematic and long term. Examples of minimum interventions include noticing positive student behavior and commenting on it and moving students from one activity to another by making unrelated but easily accomplished requests first.

mixed-skill grouping Classroom grouping arrangement in which students are clustered for instruction without focusing on specific skill needs. Also referred to as *heterogeneous grouping*.

mnemonic A device or code used to assist memory by imposing an order on the information to be remembered.

mobility specialist Specialist who helps students with visual impairments learn to be familiar with their environments and able to travel from place to place independently and safely.

model Concrete representation that can help students make connections between abstractions and real-life physical objects or processes.

modified test construction Individualized changes made to tests to make them more accessible for students with disabilities. For example, triple spacing a test for a student with a learning disability who has difficulty reading tests that have lots of clutter.

modified weights and scales A type of individualized grading accommodation that involves changing the number of points or the percentages required to earn a specified grade or changing the weights assigned to different performance areas.

multicultural education Approaches to education that reflect the diversity of society.

multidisciplinary team (MDT) Team including teachers, specialists, administrators, and parents who assess a student's individual needs, determine eligibility for special education, and develop the IEP.

multimedia software Computer programs that combine written words, graphics, sound, and animation.

multiple disabilities Condition in which individuals have two or more of the disabilities outlined in IDEA, although no one can be determined to be predominant.

multiple intelligences Concept proposed by Howard Gardner (1993) that suggests there are seven types of intelligence, not just one.

multisensory approach Instructional approach that emphasizes the use of more than one modality for teaching and learning. For example, having a student read a vocabulary word, spell it out loud, and then write it on paper is a multisensory approach to teaching vocabulary.

muscular dystrophy Disease that weakens muscles, causing orthopedic impairments. This disease is progressive, often resulting in death during the late teenage years.

negative example Instructional stimulus that does not illustrate the concept being taught, used with examples to ensure that students understand the instruction. Also called *nonexample*.

negative reinforcement A potential negative consequence to a behavior that causes the behavior to increase.

No Child Left Behind Act of 2001 (NCLB) Reauthorization of the Elementary and Secondary Education Act of 1965; this law set high standards for student achievement and increased accountability for student learning and criteria by which teachers are considered highly qualified.

novelty Approach for educating gifted and talented students based on allowing students to learn traditional content using alternative or unusual strategies that might include working with an adult mentor, creating materials for other students to use, or using a problem-based learning approach.

Numbered Heads Together Cooperative learning program in which students number off. The teacher poses a question; the students work together to ensure all members know the answer, and then the teacher calls a number. Students with the number stand, and one is called upon to respond to the question, with correct responses scoring points for the team.

nurse Specialist who has expertise in understanding and responding to students' medical needs and who sometimes serves as a liaison between medical and school professionals.

occupational therapist Specialist with expertise in meeting students' needs in the area of fine motor skills, including self-help skills such as feeding and dressing.

one-to-one instruction Classroom grouping arrangement in which individual students work with either a teacher or computer in materials geared to their level and at their own pace.

organizational patterns Ways in which content area texts are written to reflect main ideas such as compare-contrast, cause-effect, and problem solution.

orthopedic impairments (OI) Physical conditions that seriously impair the ability to move about or to complete motor activities and interfere with learning.

other health impairments (OHI) Medical or health conditions such as AIDS, seizure disorders, cancer, juvenile diabetes, and asthma that are serious enough that they negatively affect a student's educational performance.

overcorrection Type of presentation punishment in which a student makes restitution for misbehavior. An example of overcorrection is a student cleaning all the desks in a room as a consequence for writing on one desk.

parallel teaching Co-teaching option in which students are divided into small groups and each group receives the same instruction from one of the teachers in the room.

paraprofessional Noncertified staff member employed to assist certified staff in carrying out education programs and otherwise help in the instruction of students with disabilities.

PARS Learning strategy for reading textbooks with these steps: preview the material, ask questions, read the chapter, and summarize the main ideas.

partially sighted Condition in which an individual has a significant visual impairment but is able to capitalize on residual sight using magnification devices and other adaptive materials.

passive learner Learner who does not believe in his or her own ability, has limited knowledge of problem-solving strategies, and is unable to determine when to use a strategy.

pattern guide A graphic organizer designed to help students organize their written papers.

peer-assisted learning strategies (PALS) Research-based form of reciprocal classwide peer tutoring designed to assist struggling students across all grade levels to learn key math and reading skills.

peer comparison A component of curriculum-based assessment in which a student's performance is compared to that of classmates as a means of determining whether a learning problem exists.

peer editing Component of student writing in which students review, evaluate, and provide feedback to each other about their written work.

peer tutoring Student-centered instructional approach in which pairs of students help one another and learn by teaching.

performance-based assessment Method of evaluation that measures what students can do with knowledge rather than measuring specific bits of knowledge the student possesses.

permanent product recording Strategy for recording behavior in which samples of student work and other permanent evidence of student behavior are collected and evaluated.

personal assistant Paraprofessional specially trained to monitor and assist a particular student with a disability.

personal role One of the roles individuals bring to a team, consisting of characteristics, knowledge, skills, and perceptions based on life experiences broader than those in the professional area.

petit mal seizure *See* absence seizure.

physical punishment Type of presentation punishment, not recommended for use by teachers, that involves a negative physical consequence for misbehavior.

physical therapist Specialist with expertise in meeting students' needs in the area of gross motor skills.

placement Location in which education will occur for a student with a disability.

planning think sheet Set of questions to which students respond as a strategy for assisting them to help writers focus on background knowledge as well as on the audience and purpose of a paper, in preparation for writing.

portfolio assessment Method of evaluation in which a purposeful collection of student work is used to determine student effort, progress, and achievement in one or more areas.

positive behavioral interventions and supports (PBIS) Strategies for preventing behavior challenges as well as techniques for addressing common and intensive behavior problems; PBIS is based on clearly defined outcomes, behavioral and biomedical science, research-validated practices, and systematic approaches.

positive reinforcement A consequence to a behavior that causes it to increase. Also called a *reward*.

POSSE Learning strategy for reading comprehension with these steps: predict ideas, organize the ideas, search for the structure, summarize the main ideas, and evaluate your understanding.

POWER Learning strategy for writing with these steps: planning, organizing, writing, editing, and revising.

practice test An accommodation used before students take tests. Students are given a test with the same format and content but different questions. Practice tests clarify test expectations and familiarize students with test content.

PReP (PreReading Plan) strategy Strategy for determining how much background information students have about a topic.

prereferral assistance team *See* instructional assistance team.

present level of functioning Information about a student's current level of academic achievement, social skills, behavior, communication skills, and other areas that is included on an IEP.

presentation punishment Presenting negative consequences as a strategy for decreasing behavior.

preskill Basic skill necessary for performing a more complex skill.

primary reinforcer Food or other items related to human needs that cause a behavior to increase; used only occasionally in schools. An example of a primary reinforcer is a piece of licorice earned for appropriate behavior.

prioritization of curriculum A type of individualized grading accommodation in which a student's grade is based on specific content determined to be most important by the teacher.

probe Quick and easy measure of student performance (accuracy and fluency) in the basic-skill areas of reading, math, and written expression consisting of timed samples of academic behaviors.

probe of basic academic skills *See* probe.

probe of prerequisite skills Specific type of probe designed to assess whether a student has the prerequisite skills needed to succeed in the planned instruction.

professional role One of the roles individuals bring to a team, including knowledge, skills, and perceptions based on professional training and experience.

program evaluation Type of assessment decision concerning whether a special education program should be terminated, continued as is, or modified.

program placement Type of assessment decision concerning where a student's special education services will take place.

progress on IEP objectives A type of individualized grading accommodation in which a student's grade is based on the measurable goals and objectives and progress monitoring components of the IEP.

progress monitoring assessments Brief assessments given during the school year that inform teachers whether students are making adequate progress toward meeting grade-level performance benchmarks so support can be provided if they aren't.

psychological test Test designed to measure how efficiently students learn in an instructional situation; often used to assess intelligence and to determine whether learning disabilities exist.

psychologist *See* school psychologist.

psychometrist Specialist with expertise in assessment who in some states completes much of the individual assessment required to determine eligibility for special education services.

Public Law 94-142 Education for All Handicapped Children Act; first federal special education law that incorporated many of the rights captured today in the Individuals with Disabilities Education Improvement Act (IDEA).

pullout model Instructional approach in which students with disabilities leave the general education classroom once or more each day to receive special education services.

punishment Any response or consequence that has the effect of decreasing a behavior.

rate of skill introduction The pace at which new skills are introduced during instruction.

RAP Reading comprehension strategy consisting of three steps: read the paragraph; ask yourself "What was the main idea and what were two details?"; put the main idea and details in your own words.

READS Textbook-reading strategy consisting of five steps: review headings and subheadings; examine boldfaced words; ask, "What do I expect to learn?"; do it—read!; summarize in your own words.

reasoning A range of important learning skills, including comprehension, generalization, induction, and sequencing.

receptive language An individual's ability to understand what people mean when they speak.

reciprocal teaching Teaching students to comprehend reading material by providing them with teacher and peer models of thinking behavior and then allowing them to practice these thinking behaviors with their peers.

reciprocal tutoring Same-age tutoring approach in which students in the same class are randomly assigned and take turns teaching each other. *See also* reciprocal teaching.

regular class One placement for students with disabilities. Also referred to as a *general education class.*

rehearsal strategy Test-taking strategy that involves saying information out loud, repeating it, checking it for accuracy, and repeating it again as part of studying.

reinforcement Any response or consequence that causes a behavior to increase.

reinforcement menu List of rewards from which students may choose; often most effective if students participate in its development.

related services Services students with disabilities need to benefit from their educational experience. Examples of related services include transportation, speech therapy, physical therapy, and counseling.

removal punishment Taking away from a student something that is desired as a strategy for decreasing inappropriate behavior.

residential facility Placement for students with disabilities when their needs cannot be met at a school. Students attend school and live at a residential facility.

resource room Special education setting in which a special education teacher works with groups of students with disabilities for parts of the school day.

resource teacher Special education teacher who provides direct services to students with disabilities either in a special education or general education classroom and who also meets to solve problems with teachers. Resource teachers most often work with students with high-incidence disabilities.

response cost Type of removal punishment in which a student loses privileges or other rewards as a consequence of inappropriate behavior.

response to intervention (RtI) An approach for the identification of learning disabilities based on whether student learning progress improves or fails to improve after the student receives increasingly intense, research-based interventions; the latter may be an indication of a learning disability.

retention Ability to remember information after time has passed.

Ritalin Psychostimulant medication commonly prescribed for individuals with ADHD.

RUDPC Learning strategy to help students derive important information from a webpage. The steps are read the title and headings, use the cursor to skim the page, decide whether you need the page, print the page, and copy the bibliographic information.

same-age tutoring Peer-tutoring approach in which students in the same class or grade level tutor one another, typically with higher-achieving students assisting lower-achieving students.

same-skill grouping Classroom grouping arrangement in which all students needing instruction on a particular skill are clustered for that instruction. Also referred to as *homogeneous grouping.*

satiation Situation in which a positive reinforcer, used repeatedly, loses its effectiveness.

scaffolding Instructional approach for teaching higher-order thinking skills in which the teacher supports student learning by reviewing the cognitive strategy to be addressed, regulating difficulty during practice, providing varying contexts for student practice, providing feedback, increasing student responsibility for learning, and creating opportunities for independent student practice.

school psychologist Specialist with expertise to give individual assessments of students in cognitive, academic, social, emotional, and behavioral domains. This professional also designs strategies to address students' academic and social behavior problems.

SCAN Self-questioning strategy for proofreading sentences. The questions are: Does it make sense? Is it connected to my belief? Can I add more? and Are there any errors to note?

screening Type of assessment decision concerning whether or not a student's academic or behavior performance is different enough from that of his or her peers to merit further, more in-depth assessment. See also universal screening.

SCROL Learning strategy for teaching students to use text headings to aid their comprehension with these steps: survey the headings, connect, read the text, outline, and look back.

Section 504 The section of the Vocational Rehabilitation Act of 1973 that prohibits discrimination against all individuals with disabilities in programs that receive federal funds.

self-advocacy Extent to which a student can identify supports needed to succeed and communicate that information effectively to others, including teachers and employers.

self-awareness Extent to which a student has an accurate perception of his or her learning strengths, learning needs, and ability to use strategies to learn independently.

self-control training A strategy in which students who lack self-control are taught to redirect their actions by talking to themselves.

self-determination Providing meaningful opportunities for students with disabilities to express their needs and goals so that their wishes guide decision making.

self-image Individual's perception of his or her own abilities, appearance, and competence.

self-instruction Strategy in which students are taught to talk themselves through tasks.

self-monitoring Strategy in which students are taught to check whether they have performed targeted behaviors.

self-questioning Strategy in which students are taught to guide their performance by asking themselves relevant questions.

sensory impairment Disability related to vision or hearing.

separate class Classroom in which students with disabilities spend 50 percent or more of the school day.

separate grades Differentiating report cards by assigning grades for different grading elements such as effort and progress.

separate school School serving only students with disabilities.

shared problem solving Process used by groups of professionals, sometimes including parents, for identifying problems, generating potential solutions, selecting and implementing solutions, and evaluating the effectiveness of solutions.

short-term objective Description of a step followed in order to achieve an annual goal.

sickle-cell anemia Inherited disorder occurring most often in African Americans in which red blood cells are abnormally shaped and weakened.

sign language interpreter Specialist who listens to instruction and other communication and relays it to students with hearing impairments through sign language.

simulation Activity in which students experience what it might be like to have a disability; in a technology context, simulations are computer programs that teach problem solving, decision making, and risk taking by having students react to real-life and imaginary situations.

SLANT Learning strategy to help student stay engaged while the teacher is talking. The steps are: sit up straight, lean forward, ask questions, nod your head, and track the teacher with your eyes.

SLICK A learning strategy for helping students comprehend digitized textbooks. The steps in using a digitized text include: set it up, look ahead through the chapter, comprehend, and keep it together.

SLOBS Learning strategy to help students with regrouping in subtraction with these steps: if smaller, follow the steps; if larger, leap to subtract; cross off the number in the next column; borrow by taking one 10 and adding to the next column; subtract.

slow learner Student whose educational progress is below average, but not so severe as to be considered an intellectual disability, and is consistent with the student's abilities.

social cues Verbal or nonverbal signals people give that communicate a social message.

social reinforcer Positive interpersonal interaction that causes a behavior to increase. An example of a social reinforcer is a teacher praising a student's appropriate behavior.

social skills Behaviors that help students interact successfully with their peers, teachers, and others and that help them win social acceptance.

social skills training Strategies for improving students' social interaction skills through modeling and guided and independent practice with feedback.

social worker Specialist with expertise in meeting students' social needs and fostering working relationships with families.

sophistication Approach for educating gifted and talented students based on helping students learn complex principles about subject matter being presented to the entire class.

special education Specially designed instruction provided by the school district or other local education agency that meets the unique needs of students identified as disabled.

special education teacher Teacher whose primary responsibility is delivering and managing the delivery of special education services to students with disabilities.

Special Friends Program designed to promote friendships between students with disabilities and those without disabilities.

special services coordinator Administrator responsible for interpreting guidelines related to educating students with disabilities and assisting other school district personnel in carrying out those guidelines.

speech articulation The ability to produce sounds correctly at the age where they would normally be expected to develop.

speech or language impairment Condition in which student has extraordinary difficulties in communicating with others due to causes other than maturation and that interferes with learning.

speech reading Strategy used by individuals with hearing impairments to gain information by watching a person's lips, mouth, and expression. Only a small proportion of a spoken message can typically be discerned through speech reading.

speech/language therapist Specialist with expertise in meeting students' communication needs, including articulation and language development.

spina bifida Birth defect in which there is an abnormal opening in the spinal column, often leading to partial paralysis.

spinal cord injury Condition in which the spinal cord is damaged or severed because of accident or injury, leading to orthopedic impairments.

standardized achievement test Norm-referenced test designed to measure academic progress, or what students have retained in the curriculum.

standards-based education Education that is based on meeting state expectations of what students should know or be able to do as a result of public education.

STAR Learning strategy that helps older students solve math problems, including algebra. The steps are: search the word problem, translate the word problem, answer the problem, and review the solution.

station teaching Co-teaching option in which students are divided into small groups and each group receives part of its instruction from each teacher.

stereotypic behavior An action or motion repeated over and over again. Examples of stereotypic behaviors include spinning an object, rocking the body, and twirling.

story grammar Description of the typical elements of stories, including theme, setting, character, initiating events, attempts at resolution, resolution, and reactions.

story map Graphic organizer for narrative material.

student evaluation Determination of the extent to which students have mastered academic skills or other instructional content, frequently communicated through grades.

student self-evaluation Assessment approach in which students are asked to perform a task, are given a checklist of strategy steps for the task, and then are asked to tell which of these steps they did or did not use.

study guide General term for outlines, abstracts, or questions that emphasize important information in texts.

stuttering Speech impairment in which an individual involuntarily repeats a sound or word, resulting in a loss of speech fluency.

supplementary aids and services Term in IDEA for a range of supports provided in general education classes and other education-related settings that enable students with disabilities to be educated with students who are not disabled to the maximum extent appropriate.

support facilitator *See* inclusion specialist.

surface behaviors Initial student behaviors that teachers could interpret as misbehavior. Responding appropriately to surface behaviors can prevent them from escalating into more serious discipline problems.

TAG Learning strategy for peer editing with these steps: tell what you like, ask questions, and give suggestions.

tangible reinforcer Prizes or other objects students want and can earn through appropriate behavior and that cause that behavior to increase. An example of a tangible reinforcer is a school pencil earned for appropriate behavior.

task analysis Six-step strategy for managing time: decide exactly what you must do; decide how many steps are needed to complete the task; decide how much time each step will take; set up a schedule; get started; finish the task.

task goal Type of goal teams set that describes the business the team was formed to accomplish.

TASSEL A learning strategy that helps students sustain their attention during longer lectures. The steps include: try not to doodle, arrive at class prepared, sit near the front, sit away from friends, end day dreaming, and look at the teacher.

TBI *See* traumatic brain injury.

teacher-centered instruction Classroom instructional arrangement in which the pattern of interaction is between teacher and student, with the teacher as the central figure.

team Formal work group that has clear goals, active and committed members, leaders, clear procedures followed in order to accomplish goals, and strategies for monitoring effectiveness.

team role One of the formal or informal roles individuals bring to a team, consisting of contributions made to help ensure effective team functioning. Examples of formal team roles include team facilitator, recorder, and timekeeper. Examples of informal team roles include compromiser, information seeker, and reality checker.

team teaching Co-teaching option in which students remain in one large group and teachers share leadership in the instructional activity of the classroom.

test administration The conditions under which a test is given to students.

test construction The way in which test items are worded, ordered on the test, and formatted.

test site The location in which a test is given.

test-taking skills Learning strategies taught to students to help them succeed in studying for and taking tests.

thinking reader An enhanced electronic version of a textbook designed to offer support for students in word identification, comprehension, and study skills.

three-year reevaluation Triannual process of reassessing the needs of a student with a disability, carried out by a multidisciplinary team.

tier 1 instruction Instruction in RtI that is evidence-based and provided to all students in a class.

tier 2 instruction Tier 2 in RtI consists of instruction provided in Tier 1 plus additional small groups sessions that provided extra practice of targeted skills and content covered in Tier 1.

tier 3 instruction Tier 3 in RtI consists of highly intensive instruction matched to the individual needs of students who continue to struggle, despite well delivered, evidence-based instruction in Tier 2.

time-out Type of removal punishment in which a student is removed from opportunities for reward. An example of time out is a "penalty box" for misbehavior on the playground.

time sampling Strategy for recording behavior in which a behavior is periodically observed and measured during a specified time period.

token economy Group behavior management procedure in which students earn a representative or token currency for appropriate behavior that can later be exchanged for rewards.

tracking Educational practice of grouping students for instruction by their perceived ability level.

transition plan Document for students with disabilities who are as young as 14 years old that describes strategies for assisting them to prepare to leave school for adult life.

transition specialist Special educator who helps prepare students with disabilities for postschool activities, including employment, vocational training, or higher education.

transition time The time it takes a group of students to change from one classroom activity to another.

traumatic brain injury (TBI) Condition in which an individual experiences a significant trauma to the head from an accident, illness, or injury and that affects learning.

Treatment fidelity Carrying out the teaching practice the same way it was done in the research.

tutorial Computer program designed to present new material to students in small sequential steps and/or to review concepts.

unison responding All students responding at once to teacher questions or other instruction.

universal design The design of instructional materials, methods, and assessments that are compatible with a diverse range of student needs and minimize the need for labor-intensive adaptations.

universal screening The process used in RtI to assess all students to identify those who are having difficulty learning despite evidence-based Tier 1 instruction.

video self-modeling A form of instruction in which students learn by watching themselves successfully perform a behavior.

visual impairment Condition in which an individual has an inability or limited ability to receive information visually, so much so that it interferes with learning.

wait time Amount of time a teacher gives a student to respond to a question.

written language difficulties Problems that students with learning and behavior disabilities have with skills related to handwriting, spelling, and written expression.

References

Abedi, J., Hofstetter, C. H., & Lord, C. (2004). Assessment accommodations for English language learners: Implications for policy-based empirical research. *Review of Educational Research, 74*(1), 1–28.

Abell, M. M., Bauder, D. K., & Simmons, T. J. (2005). Access to the general curriculum: A curriculum and instruction perspective for educators. *Intervention in School and Clinic, 41,* 82–86.

Acrey, C., Johnstone, C., & Milligan, C. (2005). Using universal design to unlock the potential for academic achievement of at-risk learners. *Teaching Exceptional Children, 35,* 22–31.

Adcock, J., & Cuvo, A. (2009). Enhancing learning for children with autism spectrum disorders in regular education by instructional modifications. *Research in Autism Spectrum Disorders, 3,* 319–328.

Adreon, D., & Durocher, J. S. (2007). Evaluating the college transition needs of individuals with high-functioning autism spectrum disorders. *Intervention in School and Clinic, 42,* 271–279.

Affleck, J. Q., Lowenbraun, S., & Archer, A. (1980). *Teaching the mildly handicapped in the regular classroom.* Columbus, OH: Merrill.

Agran, M., Blanchard, C., Wehmeyer, M., & Hughes, C. (2002). Increasing the problem-solving skills of students with developmental disabilities participating in general education. *Remedial and Special Education, 23,* 279–288.

Agran, M., Cavin, M., Wehmeyer, M., & Palmer, S. (2006). Participation of students with moderate to severe disabilities in the general curriculum: The effects of the self-determined learning model of instruction. *Research and Practice for Persons with Severe Disabilities, 31,* 230–241.

Akram, G., Thomson, A. H., & Boyter, A. C. (2009). ADHD and the role of medication: Knowledge and perceptions of qualified and student teachers. *European Journal of Special Needs Education, 24,* 423–436.

Al Otaiba, S., & Pappamihiel, N. E. (2005). Guidelines for using volunteer literacy tutors to support reading instruction for English language learners. *Teaching Exceptional Children, 37*(6), 6–11.

Al-Hassan, S., & Gardner, R. (2002). Involving immigrant parents of students with disabilities in the educational process. *Teaching Exceptional Children, 34*(5), 52–59.

Alberto, P. A., & Trautman, A. C. (2005). *Applied behavior analysis for teachers* (7th ed.). Upper Saddle River, NJ: Prentice Hall.

Alberto, P. A., & Troutman, A. C. (2008). *Applied behavior analysis for teachers* (8th ed.). Upper Saddle River, NJ: Merrill/Pearson.

Albrecht, S., & Jones, C. (2003). Accountability and access to opportunity: Mutually exclusive tenets under a high-stakes testing mandate. *Preventing School Failure, 47,* 86–91.

Alexander, R., & Cooray, S. (2003). Diagnosis of personality disorder in learning disability. *The British Journal of Psychiatry, 182,* 28–31.

Algozzine, B., Ysseldyke, J. E., & Campbell, P. (1994). Strategies and tactics for effective instruction. *Teaching Exceptional Children, 26*(3), 34–36.

Alley, G. R. (1988). Effects of generalization instruction on the written language performance of adolescents with learning disabilities in the mainstream classroom. *Reading, Writing, and Learning Disabilities, 4,* 291–309.

Allinder, R. M., Bolling, R. M., Oats, R. G., & Gagnon, W. A. (2000). Effects of teacher self-monitoring on implementation of curriculum-based measurement and mathematics computation achievement of students with disabilities. *Remedial and Special Education, 21,* 219–226.

Allport, G. (1954). *The nature of prejudice.* Cambridge, MA: Addison-Wesley.

Ambrose, R. (2002). Are we overemphasizing manipulatives in the primary grades to the detriment of girls? *Teaching Children Mathematics, 9*(1), 16–22.

American Academy of Pediatrics. (2000). Clinical practice guideline: Diagnosis and evaluation of the child with attention-deficit/hyperactivity disorder. *Pediatrics, 105,* 1158–1170.

American Academy of Pediatrics. (1999). The treatment of neurologically impaired children using patterning. Retrieved November 6, 2007, from http://aappolicy.aappublications.org/cgi/reprint/pediatrics;104/5/1149.pdf

American Association on Mental Retardation. (2002). *Mental retardation: Definition, classification, and systems of supports* (10th ed.). Washington, DC: Author.

American Cancer Society. (2007). *Detailed guide: Cancer in children: What is childhood cancer?* Retrieved July 9, 2007, from www.cancer.org/docroot/CRI/content/CRI_2_4_1X_Introduction_7.asp?sitearea=

American Institutes for Research. (1999, February). *Voluntary national tests in reading and math: Background paper reviewing laws and regulations, current practice, and research relevant to inclusion and accommodation for students with limited English proficiency.* Palo Alto, CA: Author.

American Psychiatric Association. (2000). *Diagnostic and statistical manual of mental disorders* (4th ed., text rev.). Washington, DC: Author.

Anderson, D. H., Munk, J. H., Young, K. R., Conley, L., & Caldarella, P. (2008). Teaching organizational skills to promote academic achievement in behaviorally challenged students. *Teaching Exceptional Children, 40*(4), 6–13.

Anderson, J. A., Kutash, K., & Duchnowski, A. J. (2001). A comparison of the academic progress of students with EBD and students with LD. *Journal of Emotional and Behavioral Disorders, 9,* 106–115.

Anderson, K. M. (2007). Differentiating instruction to include all students. *Preventing School Failure, 51*(3), 49–54.

Anderson, L. B. (2007). A special kind of tutor. *Teaching PreK-8, 37*(5). Retrieved August 25, 2007, from www.teachingk-8.com/archives/articles/a_special_kind_of_tutor_by_linda_brown_anderson.html

Anderson, L. W., & Krathwohl, D. R. (Eds.). (2001). *A taxonomy for learning, teaching and assessing: A revision of Bloom's taxonomy of educational objectives: Complete edition.* New York: Longman.

Angelle, P., & Bilton, L. (2009). Confronting the unknown: Principal preparation training in issues related to special education. *AASA Journal of Scholarship & Practice, 5*(4), 5–9.

Antia, S., Jones, P., Reed, S., & Kreimeyer, K., (2009). Academic status and progress of deaf and hard-of-hearing students in general education classrooms. *Journal of Deaf Studies and Deaf Education, 14,* 293–311.

Antshel, K. M., Faraone, S. V., Stallone, K., Nave, A., Kaufmann, F. A., Doyle, A., et al. (2007). Is attention deficit hyperactivity disorder a valid diagnosis in the presence of high IQ? Results from the MGH longitudinal family studies of ADHD. *Journal of Child Psychology and Psychiatry, 48,* 687–694.

Aprile, D., & Mistry, R. S. (2007). Congruence of mother and teacher educational expectations and low-income youth's academic competence. *Journal of Educational Psychology, 99,* 140–153.

Archer, A. L., Gleason, M. M., & Vachon, V. L. (2003). Decoding and fluency: Foundation skills for struggling older readers. *Learning Disability Quarterly, 26,* 89–101.

Archer, A., & Gleason, M. (2010). Direct instruction in content-area reading. In D. W. Carnine, J. Silbert, E. J. Kame'enui, & S. G. Tarver (Eds.), *Direct instruction reading* (5th ed., pp. 273–318), Upper Saddle River, NJ: Merrill/Pearson.

Arends, R. I. (2004). *Learning to teach* (6th ed.). New York, NY: McGraw-Hill.

Arivett, D. L., Rust, J. O., Brissie, J. S., & Dansby, V. S. (2007). Special education teachers' perceptions of school psychologists in the context of individualized education program meetings. *Education, 127,* 378–388.

Armbruster, B. B. (1984). The problem of "inconsiderate text." In G. G. Duffy, L. R. Roehler, & J. Mason (Eds.), *Comprehensive instruction: Perspectives and suggestions* (pp. 202–217). New York: Longman.

Armbruster, B. B., & Anderson, T. H. (1988). On selecting "considerate" content area textbooks. *Remedial and Special Education, 9*(1), 47–52.

Armbruster, B., Lehr, F., & Osborn, J. (2001). *Put reading first: The research building blocks for teaching children to read.* Washington, DC: Partnership for Reading.

Arms, E., Bickett, J., & Graf, V. (2008). Gender bias and imbalance: Girls in U.S. special education programmes. *Gender and Education, 20,* 349–359.

Arndt, S. A., Konrad, M., & Test, D. W. (2006). Effects of the self-directed IEP on student participation in planning meetings. *Remedial and Special Education, 27,* 194–207.

Aronson, E. (2005). *Jigsaw in 10 easy steps.* Middletown, CT: Social Psychology Network. Retrieved February 8, 2005, from www.jigsaw.org/index.html

Arroyos-Jurado, E., & Savage, T. (2008). Intervention strategies for serving students with traumatic brain injury. *Intervention in School and Clinic, 43,* 252–254.

Artiles, A. J., Harris-Murri, N., & Rostenberg, D. (2006). Inclusion as social justice: Critical notes on discourses, assumptions, and the road ahead. *Theory into Practice, 45,* 260–268.

Artiles, A. J., Rueda, R., Salazar, J. J., & Higareda, I. (2005). Within-group diversity in minority disproportionate representation: English language learners in urban school districts. *Exceptional Children, 71,* 283–300.

Artiles, A., Kozleski, E., Trent, S., Osher, D., & Ortiz, A. (2010). Justifying and explaining disproportionality, 1968–2008: A critique of underlying views of culture. *Exceptional Children, 76,* 279–299.

Ashton, T. M. (1999). Spell checking: Making writing meaningful in the inclusive classroom. *Teaching Exceptional Children, 32*(2), 24–27.

Assouline, S., Nicpon, M., & Whiteman, C. (2010). Cognitive and psychosocial characteristics of gifted students with written language disability. *Gifted Child Quarterly, 54,* 102–115.

Asthma and Allergy Foundation of America. (2007). *Asthma facts and figures.* Retrieved July 8, 2007, from www.aafa.org/display.cfm?id=8&sub=42

August, D., & Shanahan, T. (Eds.). (2006). *Developing literacy in second-language learners: Report of the national literacy panel on language-minority children and youth.* Mahwah, NJ: Lawrence Erlbaum Associates.

Avcioğlu, H. (2007). Examining the effectiveness of a program developed to teach social skills to hearing impaired students based on cooperative learning. *Educational Sciences: Theory and Practice, 7,* 340–347.

AVERT. (2007). *United States statistics summary.* Retrieved July 8, 2007, from www.avert.org/statsum.htm

Babkie, A. A. (2006). Be proactive in managing classroom behavior. *Intervention in School and Clinic, 41,* 184–187.

Bahamonde, C., & Friend, M. (1999). Bilingual education: An alternative approach for collaborative service delivery. *Journal of Educational and Psychological Consultation, 10,* 1–24.

Bahr, M., & Kovaleski, J. (2006). The need for problem-solving teams. *Remedial and Special Education, 27*(1), 2–5.

Bailey, J., & McTighe, J. (1996). Reporting achievement at the secondary level: What and how. In T. R. Guskey (Ed.), *Communicating student learning: 1996 Yearbook of the Association for Supervision and Curriculum Development* (pp. 119–140). Alexandria, VA: ASCD.

Baker, D., & Bettino, C. (1988). *Easy English dictionary.* In D. McCarr, J. McCarr, L. Eckert, & S. Natwick (Eds.) Austin, Texas: Pro-Ed.

Baker, J. M., & Zigmond, N. (1995). The meaning and practices of inclusion for students with learning disabilities: Implications from the five cases. *The Journal of Special Education, 29,* 163–180.

Baker, S., Gersten, R., Dimino, J. A., & Griffiths, R. (2004). The sustained use of research-based instructional practice: A case study of peer-assisted learning strategies in mathematics. *Remedial and Special Education, 25,* 5–24.

Baker, S. K., Kame'enui, E. J., Simmons, D. C., & Simonsen, B. (2007). Characteristics of students with diverse learning and curricular needs. In M. D. Coyne, E. J. Kame'enui, & D. W. Carnine (eds.). *Effective teaching strategies that accommodate diverse learners.* Upper Saddle River, NJ: Merrill/Pearson.

Banda, D. R., & Kubina, R. M. (2006). The effects of a high-probability request sequencing technique in enhancing transition behaviors. *Education and Treatment of Children, 29,* 507–515.

Banda, D., Grimmit, E., & Hart, S. (2009). Activity schedules: Helping students with autism spectrum disorders in general education classrooms manage transition issues. *Teaching Exceptional Children, 41*(4), 16–21.

Bandura, A. (1969). *Principles of behavior modification.* New York: Holt, Rinehart, and Winston.

Banks, J. A. (2001). *Cultural diversity in education: Foundations, curriculum and teaching.* Boston: Allyn and Bacon.

Banks, J. (2007). *Educating citizens in a multicultural society* (2nd ed.). New York: Teachers College Press.

Banks, J. A., & Banks, C. A. (2007). *Multicultural education: issues and perspectives,* (6th ed.). Hoboken, NJ: John Wiley & Sons, Inc.

Banks, T., & Zionts, P. (2009). Teaching a cognitive behavioral strategy to manage emotions: Rational emotive behavior therapy in an educational setting. *Intervention in School and Clinic, 44*(5), 307–313.

Barkley, R. (1995). *Taking charge of ADHD: The complete authoritative guide for parents.* New York: Guilford Press.

Barkley, R. A. (2004). Adolescents with attention-deficit/hyperactivity disorder: An overview of empirically based treatments [Electronic version]. *Journal of Psychiatric Practice, 10,* 39–56.

Barkley, R. A. (2006). *Attention-deficit hyperactivity disorder: A handbook for diagnosis and treatment* (3rd ed.). New York: Guilford Press.

Barootchi, N., & Keshavarz, M. H. (2002). Assessment of achievement through portfolios and teacher-made tests. *Educational Research, 44,* 279–288.

Barrie, W., & McDonald, J. (2002). Administrative support for student-led individualized education programs. *Remedial and Special Education, 23,* 116–121.

Barron, A. M., & Foot, H. (1991). Peer tutoring and tutor training. *Educational Research, 33,* 174–185.

Bartelt, L., Marchio, T., & Reynolds, D. (1994). *The READS strategy.* Unpublished manuscript. Northern Illinois University.

Barth, R. S. (2006). Improving relationships within the schoolhouse. *Educational Leadership, 63*(6), 8–13.

Barton-Arwood, S., Morrow, L., Lane, K., & Jolivette, K. (2005). Project IMPROVE: Improving teachers' ability to address students' social needs. *Education and Treatment of Children, 28,* 430–443.

Bateman, B. D., & Herr, C. M. (2006). *Writing measurable IEP goals and objectives.* Verona, WI: IEP Resources.

Bateman, B. D., & Linden, M. A. (2006). *Better IEPs: How to develop legally correct and educationally useful programs* (4th ed.). Verona, WI: IEP Resources.

Bateman, B. E. (2004). Achieving affective and behavioral outcomes in culture learning: The case for ethnographic interviews. *Foreign Language Annals, 37*(2), 240–253.

Bateman, B., Warner, J., Hutchinson, E., Dean, T., Rowlandson, P., Gant, C., Grundy, J., Fitzgerald, C., & Stevenson, J. (2004). The effects of a double blind, placebo controlled, artificial food colourings and benzoate preservative challenge on hyperactivity in a general population sample of preschool children. *Archives of Disease in Childhood, 89,* 506–511.

Bateman, D. (2009). Due process hearing case study. *Teaching Exceptional Children, 41*(4), 73–75.

Bauminger, N., & Kimhi-Kind, I. (2008). Social information processing, security of attachment, and emotion regulation in children with learning disabilities. *Journal of Learning Disabilities, 41*(4), 315–332.

Bausch, M., & Hasselbring, T. (2004). Assistive technology: Are the necessary skills and knowledge being developed at the preservice and inservice levels? *Education and Special Education, 27*(2), 97–104.

Baxendell, B. W. (2003). Consistent, coherent, creative: The 3 C's graphic organizers. *Teaching Exceptional Children, 35*(3), 46–53.

Beck, I. L., & McKeown, M. G. (2002). *Bringing words to life.* New York: Guilford.

Behrmann, M., & Jerome, M. K. (2002). Assistive technology for students with mild disabilities: Update 2002 (ERIC Digest No. E623). Arlington, VA: ERIC Clearinghouse on Disabilities and Gifted Education. (ERIC Document Reproduction Service No. ED463595)

Beigel, A. R. (2000). Assistive technology assessment: More than the device. *Intervention in School and Clinic, 35,* 237–245.

Benner, A. D., & Mistry, R. S. (2007). Congruence of mother and teacher educational expectations and low-income youth's academic competence. *Journal of Educational Psychology, 99,* 140–153.

Bennett, A. (1932). *Subnormal children in elementary grades.* New York: Columbia University, Teacher's College, Bureau of Publications.

Bennett, C. I. (2003). *Comprehensive multicultural education: Theory and practice* (5th ed.). Boston: Allyn and Bacon.

Bentley, J. (2008). Lessons from the 1%: Children with labels of severe disabilities and their peers as architects of inclusive education. *International Journal of Inclusive Education, 12,* 543–561.

Berger, K. S. (2007). Update on bullying at school: Science forgotten? *Developmental Review, 27,* 90–126.

Berliner, D. (1990). What's all the fuss about instructional time? In M. Ben-Peretz & R. Bromme (Eds.), *The nature of time in schools: Theoretical concepts, practitioner perceptions.* New York: Teachers College Press. Retrieved Date, from http://courses.ed.asu.edu/berliner/readings/fuss/fuss.htm

Berliner, D. C. (1984). The half-full glass: A review of research on teaching. In P. L. Hosford (Ed.), *Using what we know about teaching (1984 yearbook)* (pp. 69–83). Alexandria, VA: Association for Supervision and Curriculum Development.

Birdsall, P., & Correa, L. (2007, March/April). Gifted underachievers. *Leadership,* 21–23.

Bisagno, J. M., & Haven, R. M. (2002, Spring). Customizing technology solutions for college students with learning disabilities. International Dyslexia Association quarterly newsletter, *Perspectives,* 21–26. Retrieved February 10, 2010, from LDONLINE: http://www.ldonline.org/ld_indepth/technology/customizing_technology.html

Bishop, V. E. (2004). *Teaching visually impaired children* (3rd ed.). Springfield, IL: Charles C. Thomas.

Blackman, B. A. (Ed.). (1997). *Foundations of reading acquisition and dyslexia: Implications for early intervention.* Mahwah, NJ: Lawrence Erlbaum Associates.

Blackman, B. A. (2000). Phonological awareness. In M. L. Kamil, P. B. Mosenthal, P. D. Pearson, & R. Barr (Eds.), *Handbook of reading research: Volume III* (pp. 483–502). Mahwah, NJ: Lawrence Erlbaum Associates.

Blanchett, W. J., Brantlinger, E., & Shealey, M. W. (2005). Brown 50 years later—Exclusion, segregation, and inclusion. *Remedial and Special Education, 26,* 66–69.

Blankenship, C., & Lilly, M. (1981). *Mainstreaming students with learning and behavior problems.* New York: Holt, Rinehart & Winston.

Blatt, B. (1958). The physical, personality, and academic status of children who are mentally retarded attending special classes as compared with children who are mentally retarded attending regular class. *American Journal of Mental Deficiency, 62,* 810–818.

Blatt, B. (1987). *The conquest of mental retardation.* Austin, TX: PRO-ED.

Bloom B., & Cohen, R. A. (2007). *Summary health statistics for U.S. children: National health interview survey, 2006* [vital health stat 10(234)]. Washington, DC: National Center for Health Statistics.

Blue-Banning, M., Summers, J. A., Frankland, H. C., Nelson, L. L., & Beegle, G. (2004). Dimensions of family and professional partnerships: Constructive guidelines for collaboration. *Exceptional Children, 70,* 167–184.

Blue-Banning, M., Turnbull, A. P., & Pereira, L. (2002). Hispanic youth/young adults with disabilities: Parents' visions for the future. *Journal of the Association for Persons with Severe Handicaps (JASH), 27,* 204–219.

Boaler, J. (2006). Promoting respectful learning. *Educational Leadership, 63*(5), 74–78.

Bond, R., & Castagnera, E. (2006). Peer supports and inclusive education: An underutilized resource. *Theory into Practice, 45,* 224–229.

Bonner, F. A. (2003). To be young, gifted, African American, and male [Electronic version]. *Gifted Child Today, 26*(2), 26–34.

Bos, C. S., & Vaughn, S. (2005). *Strategies for teaching students with learning and behavior problems* (6th ed.). Boston: Allyn and Bacon.

Bouck, E. (2007). Co-teaching . . . Not just a textbook term: Implications for practice. *Preventing School Failure, 51*(2), 46–51.

Bouck, E. C., & Flanagan, S. M. (2010). Virtual manipulatives: What they are and how teachers can use them. *Intervention in School and Clinic, 45,* 186–192.

Bovey, T., & Strain, P. (2003). *Promoting positive peer social interactions. What works briefs.* Champaign, IL: Center on the Social and Emotional Foundations for Early Learning, University of Illinois. (ERIC Document Reproduction Service No. ED481996)

Bowen, J. M. (2005). Classroom interventions for students with traumatic brain injuries. *Preventing School Failure, 49*(4), 34–41.

Bowen, S. (n.d.). *Daily story problem.* Retrieved November 23, 2004, from www.pacificnet.net/~mandel/math.html

Bowman-Perrott, L. (2009). Classwide peer tutoring: An effective strategy for students with emotional and behavioral disorders. *Intervention in School and Clinic, 44,* 259–267.

Boyle, E. A., Washburn, S. G., Rosenberg, M. S., Connelly, V. J., Brinckerhoff, L. C., & Banerjee, M. (2002). Reading's SLiCK with new audio texts and strategies. *Teaching Exceptional Children, 35*(2), 50–55.

Boyle, J. R., & Weishaar, M. (2001). The effects of strategic notetaking on the recall and comprehension of lecture information for high school students with learning disabilities. *Learning Disabilities: Research and Practice, 16,* 133–141.

Bracken, B. A., & Brown, E. F. (2006). Behavioral identification and assessment of gifted and talented students. *Journal of Psychoeducational Assessment, 24,* 112–122.

Brady, K. P. (2004). Section 504 student eligibility for students with reading disabilities: A primer for advocates. *Reading & Writing Quarterly, 20,* 305–329.

Brain Injury Association of America. (2004). *Causes of brain injury.* McLean, VA: Author. Retrieved March 13, 2004, from www.biausa.org/Pages/causes_of_brain_injury.html

Branding, D., Bates, P., & Miner, C. (2009). Perceptions of self-determination by special education and rehabilitation practitioners based on viewing a self-directed IEP versus an external-directed IEP meeting. *Research in Developmental Disabilities: A Multidisciplinary Journal, 30,* 755–762.

Brandon, R., Higgins, K., Pierce, T., Tandy, R., & Sileo, N. (2010). An exploration of the alienation experienced by African American Parents from their children's educational environment. *Remedial and Special Education, 31,* 208–222.

Brandwein, P. F., & Bauer, N. W. (1980). *The United States, living in our world: Research, evaluation, and writing.* Barton R. Clark et al., consulting social scientists. San Francisco and New York: Center for the Study of Instruction/Harcourt Brace Jovanovich.

Brigham, N., Morocco, C. C., Clay, K., & Zigmond, N. (2006). What makes a high school a good high school for students with disabilities. *Learning Disabilities Research & Practice, 21*(3), 184–190.

Brimijoin, K., Marquisse, E., & Tomlinson, C. A. (2003). Using data to differentiate Instruction, *Educational Leadership, 60*(5), 70–73.

Brinckerhoff, L. (1994). Developing effective self-advocacy skills in college-bound students with learning disabilities. *Intervention in School and Clinic, 29*(4), 229–237.

Broderick, A., Mehta-Parekh, H., & Reid, D. K. (2005). Differentiating instruction for disabled students in inclusive classrooms. *Theory into Practice, 44*(3), 194–202.

Brooke, V., Revell, G., & Wehman, P. (2009). Quality indicators for competitive employment outcomes: What special education teachers need to know in transition planning. *Teaching Exceptional Children, 41*(4), 58–66.

Brophy-Herb, H. E., Lee, R. E., Nievar, M. A., & Stollak, G. (2007). Preschoolers' social competence: Relations to family characteristics, teacher behaviors and classroom climate. *Journal of Applied Developmental Psychology, 28,* 134–148.

Browder, D. M., Wakeman, S. Y., & Flowers, C. (2006). Assessment of progress in the general curriculum for students with disabilities. *Theory into Practice, 45*(3), 249–259.

Browder, D. M., Wakeman, S. Y., Spooner, F., Ahlgrin-Delzell, L., & Algozzine, B. (2006). Research on reading instruction for individuals with significant cognitive disabilities. *Exceptional Children, 72,* 392–408.

Brown, G. M., Kerr, M. M., Zigmond, N., & Harris, A. L. (1984). What's important for student success in high school? "Successful" and "unsuccessful" students discuss school survival skills. *High School Journal, 68,* 10–17.

Brown, T. E. (2007, February). A new approach to attention deficit disorder. *Educational Leadership,* 22–27.

Brownell, M. T., Adams, A., Sindelar, P., & Waldron, N. (2006). Learning from collaboration: The role of teacher qualities. *Exceptional Children, 72*(2), 169–185.

Brownstein, R. (2010). Pushed out. *Education Digest: Essential Readings Condensed for Quick Review, 75*(7), 23–27.

Bruce, S. M. (2007). Teacher preparation for the education of students who are deafblind: A retrospective and prospective view. *Deaf-Blind Perspectives, 14*(2), 9–12.

Bruce, S., Godbold, E., & Naponelli-Gold, S. (2004). An analysis of communicative functions of teachers and their students who are congenitally deafblind. *RE:view: Rehabilitation Education for Blindness and Visual Impairment, 36*, 81–90.

Bryan, T. (2005). Science-based advances in the social domain of learning disabilities. *Learning Disability Quarterly, 28*(2), 119–121.

Bryan, T. H., & Bryan, J. H. (1986). *Understanding learning disabilities* (3rd ed.). Palo Alto, CA: Mayfield.

Bryan, T., Burstein, K., & Bryan, J. (2001). Students with learning disabilities: Homework problems and promising practices. *Educational Psychologist, 36*(3), 167–180.

Buchholtz, K., & Helming, M., (2005). Making history come alive through technology. *Phi Delta Kappan, 87*(2), 174.

Buck, G. H., Polloway, E. A., Smith-Thomas, A., & Cook, K. W. (2003). Pre-referral intervention processes: A survey of state practices. *Exceptional Children, 69*, 349–360.

Bulgren, J. A., Schumaker, J. B., & Deshler, D. (1988). Effectiveness of a concept teaching routine in enhancing the performance of LD students in secondary-level mainstream classes. *Learning Disability Quarterly, 11*, 3–17.

Bullara, D. T. (1993). Classroom management strategies to reduce racially-biased treatment of students. *Journal of Educational and Psychological Consultation, 4*(4), 357–368.

Bullock, L. M., Gable, R. A., & Mohr, J. D. (2005). Traumatic brain injury: A challenge for educators. *Preventing School Failure, 49*, 6–10.

Burks, M. (2004). Effects of classwide peer tutoring on the number of words spelled correctly by students with LD. *Intervention in School and Clinic, 39*, 301–304.

Burns, M. K. (2004). Empirical analysis of drill ratio research: Refining the instructional level for drill tasks. *Remedial and special education, 25*(3), 167–173.

Burns, P. C., Roe, B. D., & Ross, E. P. (2001). *Teaching reading in today's elementary schools* (8th ed.). Boston: Houghton Mifflin.

Burris, C. C., Heubert, J. P., & Levin, H. M. (2006). Accelerating mathematics achievement using heterogeneous grouping. *American Educational Research Journal, 43*, 105–136.

Burstein, N., Sears, S., Wilcoxen, A., Cabello, B., & Spagna, M. (2004). Moving toward inclusive practices. *Remedial and Special Education, 25*, 104–116.

Bursuck, B., Damer, M., & Dickson, S. (2005, May). Translating reading research to practice in three urban schools: An account of successful school-wide change. Presented at Annual Convention of the Association for Behavioral Analysis, Chicago, IL.

Bursuck, W. D., & Damer, M. (2011). *Teaching reading to students who are at-risk or have disabilities: A multi-tier approach.* Upper Saddle River, NJ: Pearson Education

Bursuck, W. D., & Lessen, E. (1987). A classroom-based model for assessing students with learning disabilities. *Learning Disabilities Focus, 3*(1), 17–29.

Bursuck, W. D., Harniss, M. K., Epstein, M. H., Polloway, E. A., Jayanthi, M., & Wissinger, L. M. (1999). Solving communication problems about homework: Recommendations of special education teachers. *Learning Disabilities Research and Practice, 14*, 149–158.

Bursuck, W. D., Polloway, E. A., Plante, L., Epstein, M. H., Jayanthi, M., & McConeghy, J. (1996). Report card grading and adaptations: A national survey of classroom practices. *Exceptional Children, 62*, 301–318.

Bursuck, W. D., Smith, T., Munk, D., Damer, M., Mehlig, L., & Perry, J. (2004). Evaluating the impact of a prevention-based model of reading on children who are at risk. *Remedial and Special Education, 25*, 303–313.

Bushaw, W. J., & McNee, J. A. (2009). *Americans speak out—Are educators and policy makers listening? The 41st annual Phi Delta Kappa/Gallup poll of the public's attitudes toward the public schools.* Retrieved July 1, 2010 from http://www.pdkintl.org/kappan/docs/k0909pol.pdf.

Byrnes, M. A., & Majors, M. (2004). No teacher left behind: Training teachers to meet the challenge of accessing the general curriculum for deaf-blind students. *Deaf-Blind Perspectives, 11*(3), 1–5.

Byrnes, M. (2008). Educators' interpretations of ambiguous accommodations. *Remedial and Special Education, 29* (5), 306–315.

Byrnes, M. (2008). Writing explicit, unambiguous accommodations. *Intervention in School and Clinic, 44*(1), 18–24.

Byrnes, M. (2010). Writing explicit, unambiguous accommodations. *Intervention in School and Clinic, 44* (1), 18–24.

Calderon, M. E. (1999). *Promoting language proficiency and academic achievement through cooperation.* Washington, DC: ERIC Clearinghouse on Languages and Linguistics. (ERIC Document Reproduction Service No. ED436983)

Calhoon, M. B. (2005). Effects of a peer-mediated phonological skill and reading comprehension program on reading skill acquisition for middle school students with reading disabilities. *Journal of Learning Disabilities, 38*, 424–433.

Calhoon, M. B., & Fuchs, L. S. (2003). The effects of peer-assisted learning strategies and curriculum-based measurement on the mathematics performance of secondary students with disabilities. *Remedial and Special Education, 24*, 235–245.

Callahan, C. M., (2005). Identifying gifted students from underrepresented populations. *Theory into Practice, 44*, 98–104.

Callins, T. (2006). Culturally responsive literacy instruction. *TEACHING Exceptional Children, 39*(2), 62–65.

Cameron, M. (2006). Managing school discipline and implications for school social workers: A review of the literature. *Children and Schools, 28*, 219–227.

Camp, B. W., & Bash, M. A. (1985). *Think aloud.* Champaign, IL: Research Press.

Canney, C., & Byrne, A. (2006). Evaluating circle time as a support to social skills development—reflections on a journey in school-based research. *British Journal of Special Education, 33*, 19–24.

Cardona, C. (2009). Teacher education students' beliefs of inclusion and perceived competence to teach students with disabilities in Spain. *Journal of the International Association of Special Education, 10*(1), 33–41.

Carey, T. A., & Bourbon, W. T. (2006). Is countercontrol the key to understanding chronic behavior problems? *Intervention in School and Clinic, 42*, 5–13.

Carlo, M. S., August, D., Mclaughlin, B., Snow, C. E., Dressler, C., Lippman, D. N., Lively, T. J., & White, C. E. (2004). Closing the gap: Addressing the vocabulary needs of English-language learners in bilingual and mainstream classrooms. *Reading Research Quarterly, 39*, 188–215.

Carlson, C., & Henning, M. (1993). *The TAG peer editing procedure.* Unpublished manuscript, Northern Illinois University.

Carlson, E., Chen, L., Schroll, K., & Klein, S. (2002). *SPeNSE: Study of Personnel Needs in Special Education* [final report of the paperwork substudy]. Gainesville: University of Florida. (ERIC Document Reproduction Service No. ED479674)

Carnahan, C., Hume, K., & Clarke, L. (2009). Using structured work systems to promote independence and engagement for students with autism spectrum disorders. *Teaching Exceptional Children, 41*, 6–14.

Carnahan, C., Williamson, P., Clarke, L., & Sorensen, R. (2009). A systematic approach for supporting paraeducators in educational settings: A guide for teachers. *Teaching Exceptional Children, 41*(5), 34–43.

Carnes, S. L., & Quinn, W. H. (2005). Family adaptation for brain injury: Coping and psychological distress. *Families, Systems, and Health, 23*, 186–203.

Carney, R. N., Levin, M. E., & Levin, J. R. (1993). Mnemonic strategies: Instructional techniques worth remembering. *Teaching Exceptional Children, 25*(4), 24–30.

Carnine, D. W. (1981). High and low implementation of direct instruction teaching techniques. *Education and Treatment of Children, 4*, 42–51.

Carnine, D. W., Silbert, J., Kame'enui, E. J., & Tarver, S. G. (2010). *Direct instruction reading* (5th ed.). Upper Saddle River, NJ: Merrill/Pearson.

Carolan, J., & Guinn, A. (2007). Differentiation: Lessons from master teachers. *Educational Leadership, 64*(5), 44–47.

Carr, E. G. (2007). The expanding vision of positive behavior support: Research perspectives on happiness, helpfulness, hopefulness. *Journal of Positive Behavior Interventions, 9*, 3–14.

Carr, M., & Jessup, D. L. (1997). Gender differences in first grade mathematics strategy use: Social and metacognitive influences. *Journal of Educational Psychology, 89,* 318–328.

Carter, E. W., & Kennedy, C. H. (2006). Promoting access to the general curriculum using peer support strategies. *Research and Practice for Persons with Severe Disabilities, 31,* 284–292.

Carter, E. W., & Wehby, J. H. (2003). Job performance of transition-age youth with emotional and behavioral disorders. *Exceptional Children, 69,* 449–465.

Carter, E., & Pesko, M. (2008). Social validity of peer interaction intervention strategies in high school classrooms: Effectiveness, feasibility, and actual use. *Exceptionality, 16,* 156–173.

Carter, E., O'Rourke, L., Sisco, L., & Pelsue, D. (2009). Knowledge, responsibilities, and training needs of paraprofessionals in elementary and secondary schools. *Remedial and Special Education, 30,* 344–359.

Carter, N., Prater, M., Jackson, A., & Marchant, M. (2009). Educators' perceptions of collaborative planning processes for students with disabilities. *Preventing School Failure, 54,* 60–70.

Cartledge, G., & Kourea, L. (2008). Culturally responsive classrooms for culturally diverse students with and at risk for disabilities. *Exceptional Children, 74,* 351–371.

Casanova, U., & Berliner, D. (1986). Should students be made test-wise? *Instructor 95*(6), 22–23.

Casella, R. (2003). Zero tolerance policy in schools: Rationale, consequences, and alternatives [Electronic version]. *Teachers College Record, 105,* 872–892.

Cass, M., Cates, D., Smith, M., & Jackson, C. (2003). Effects of manipulative instruction on solving area and perimeter problems by students with learning disabilities. *Learning Disabilities Research & Practice, 18*(2), 112–120.

Cassidy, V. M., & Stanton, J. E. (1959). *An investigation of factors involved in the educational placement of mentally retarded children: A study of differences between children in special and regular classes in Ohio.* (U.S. Office of Education Cooperative Research Program, Project No. 43). Columbus: Ohio State University. (ERIC Document Reproduction Service No. ED002752)

Catts, H. W., & Kamhi, A. G. (2005). *Language and reading disabilities.* (2nd ed.). Boston: Allyn and Bacon (Pearson).

Causton-Theoharis, J., & Malmgren, K. (2005). Building bridges: Strategies to help paraprofessionals promote peer interaction. *Teaching Exceptional Children, 37*(6), 18–24.

Cawley, J. F., Miller, J., & School, B. (1987). A brief inquiry of arithmetic word problem solving among learning disabled secondary students. *Learning Disabilities Focus, 2*(2), 87–93.

Cawley, J., Hayden, S., Cade, E., & Baker-Kroczynski, S. (2002). Including students with disabilities into the general education science classroom. *Exceptional Children, 68,* 423–436.

Cawley, J., Parmar, R., Foley, T. E., Salmon, S., Roy, S. (2001). Arithmetic performance of students: Implications for standards and programming. *Exceptional Children, 67,* 311–328.

Celce-Murcia, M. *Discourse and context in language teaching: A guide for language teachers.* New York: Cambridge University Press.

Center for the Study of Reading. (1988). *A guide to selecting basal reading programs: Workbooks.* Cambridge, MA: Bolt, Beraneck, and Newman.

Centers for Disease Control and Prevention. (2002). *AIDS in the United States.* Retrieved November 15, 2004, from www.cchs.net/health/health-info/docs/1100/1171.asp?index=5905

Centers for Disease Control and Prevention. (2004a). Prevalence of overweight among children and adolescents: United States, 2003–2004. Retrieved May 15, 2007, from www.cdc.gov/nchs/products/pubs/pubd/hestats/overweight/overwght_child_03.htm

Centers for Disease Control and Prevention. (2004b). *Tourette syndrome.* Retrieved November 20, 2004, from www.cdc.gov/ncbddd/tourette/default.htm

Centers for Disease Control and Prevention. (2005, September). Mental health in the United States: Prevalence of diagnosis and medication treatment for attention-deficit/hyperactivity disorder—United States, 2003. *Morbidity and Mortality Weekly Report, 54,* 842–847. Retrieved

August 2, 2007, from www.cdc.gov/mmwr/preview/mmwrhtml/mm5434a2.htm

Centers for Disease Control and Prevention. (2006). Youth risk behavior surveillance—United States, 2005. *Morbidity & Mortality Weekly Report 2006, 55,* 1–108. Retrieved October 18, 2007, from www.cdc.gov/mmwr/PDF/SS/SS5505.pdf

Centers for Disease Control and Prevention. (2007, Summer). *Youth violence: Facts at a glance.* Washington, DC: Author. Retrieved August 7, 2007, from www.cdc.gov/ncipc/dvp/YV_DataSheet.pdf

Centers for Disease Control and Prevention, U.S. Department of Health and Human Services. (2002, May). *MMR vaccine and autism (measles–mumps–rubella): Fact sheet.* Retrieved February 6, 2004, from www.cdc.gov/nip/vacsafe/concerns/autism/autism-mmr-facts.htm

Centers for Disease Control and Prevention. (2008). *Food allergy among U.S. children: Trends in prevalence and hospitalizations.* Washington, DC: National Center for Health Statistics. Retrieved June 15, 2010 from http://www.cdc.gov/nchs/data/databriefs/db10.htm.

Centers for Disease Control and Prevention. (2010, June). How many children have autism? Washington, DC: National Center on Birth Defects and Developmental Disabilities. Retrieved June 14, 2010 from http://www.cdc.gov/ncbddd/features/counting-autism.html.

Centers for Disease Control and Prevention. (2010, March). *Childhood overweight and obesity.* Atlanta: Author. Retrieved from http://www.cdc.gov/obesity/childhood/index.html.

Centers for Disease Control and Prevention. (2010a, June). *Childhood obesity.* Retrieved June 26, 2010 from http://www.cdc.gov/HealthyYouth/obesity/.

Centers for Disease Control and Prevention. (2010b, May). *Attention-deficit/hyperactivity disorder data and statistics (ADHD).* Retrieved June 23, 2010 from http://www.cdc.gov/ncbddd/adhd/data.html.

Cermak, L. S. (1976). *Improving your memory.* New York: Norton.

Cesaroni, L., & Garber, M. (1991). Exploring the experience of autism through firsthand accounts. *Journal of Autism and Developmental Disorders, 21,* 303–313.

Chadsey, J., & Han, K. G. (2005). Friendship-facilitation strategies: What do students in middle school tell us? *Teaching Exceptional Children, 38*(2), 52–57.

Chaffin, J. (1975). Will the real "mainstreaming" program please stand up! (Or . . . should Dunn have done it?). In E. L. Meyen, G. A. Vergason, & R. J. Whelan (Eds.), *Alternatives for teaching exceptional children.* Denver, CO: Love.

Chambers, C. R., Wehmeyer, M. L., Saito, Y., Lida, K. M., Lee, Y., & Singh, V. (2007). Self-determination: What do we know? Where do we go? *Exceptionality, 15*(1), 3–15.

Chard, D., & Dickson, S. V. (1999). Phonological awareness: Instructional and assessment guidelines. *Intervention in School and Clinic, 5,* 261–270.

Cheek, E. H., Jr., & Cheek, M. C. (1983). *Reading instruction through content teaching.* Columbus, OH: Merrill.

Chen, F., Planche, P., & Lemonnier, E. (2010). Superior nonverbal intelligence in children with high-functioning autism or Asperger's syndrome. *Research in Autism Spectrum Disorders, 4,* 457–460.

Child abuse characteristics. (2000). Retrieved September 13, 2000, from www.angelfire.com/fl2/ChildAbuse/Characteristics.html

Children's Defense Fund. (2003). *2002 facts on child poverty in America.* Washington, DC: Author. Retrieved December 4, 2004 from www.childrens-defense.org/familyincome/childpoverty/basicfacts.asp

Choate, J. S., Enright, B. E., Miller, L. J., Poteet, J. A., & Rakes, T. A. (1995). *Curriculum-based assessment and programming.* Boston: Allyn and Bacon.

Chopra, R. V., Sandoval-Lucero, E., Aragon, L., Bernal, C., De Balderas, H. B., & Carroll, D. (2004). The paraprofessional role of connector. *Remedial and Special Education, 25,* 219–232.

Christopolos, F., & Renz, P. (1969). A critical examination of special education programs. *Journal of Special Education, 3,* 371–379.

Clarke, B., Baker, S., Smolkowski, K., & Chard, D. J. (2008). An analysis of early numeracy curriculum-based measurement: Examining the role of growth in student outcomes. *Remedial and Special Education, 29,* 46–57.

Clayton, J., Burdge, M., Denham, A., Kleinert, H. L., & Kearns, J. (2006). A four-step process for accessing the general curriculum for students with significant cognitive disabilities. *Teaching Exceptional Children, 38*(5), 20–27.

Cobuild, C. (2005). *Collins COBUILD dictionary.* Florence, KY: Heinle ELT.

Cohen, M., & Riel, M. M. (1989). The effect of distant audiences on students' writing. *American Educational Research Journal, 26,* 143–159.

Cohen, S. B. (1983). Assigning report card grades to the mainstreamed child. *Teaching Exceptional Children, 15,* 186–189.

Coker, D. L., & Ritchey, K. D. (2010). Curriculum-based measurement of writing in kindergarten and first grade: An investigation of production and qualitative scores. *Exceptional Children, 76,* 175–193.

Colangelo, N. (2002, Fall). Counseling gifted and talented students. *National Research Center on the Gifted and Talented Newsletter.* Storrs, CT: National Research Center on the Gifted and Talented. (ERIC Document Reproduction Service No. ED447662)

Colangelo, N., & Davis, G. A. (Eds.). (2003). *Handbook on gifted education* (3rd ed.). Boston: Allyn and Bacon.

Colangelo, N., Assouline, S., Marron, M., Castellano, J., Clinkenbeard, P., Rogers, K., et al. (2010). Guidelines for developing an academic acceleration policy. *Journal of Advanced Academics, 21,* 180–203.

Cole, C. M., Waldron, N., & Majd, M. (2004). Academic progress of students across inclusive and traditional settings [Electronic version]. *Mental Retardation, 42,* 136–144.

Coleman, M. C., & Webber, J. (2002). *Emotional and behavioral disorders: Theory and practice* (4th ed.). Boston: Allyn and Bacon.

Coleman, R. J. (2005). Academic strategies that work for gifted students with learning disabilities. *Teaching Exceptional Children, 38*(1), 28–32.

Colvin, G., Flannery, K., Sugai, G., & Monegan, J. (2009). Using observational data to provide performance feedback to teachers: A high school case study. *Preventing School Failure, 53,* 95–104.

Conderman, G., & Bresnahan, V. (2010). Study guides to the rescue. *Intervention in School and Clinic, 45*(3), 169–176.

Conderman, G., & Johnston-Rodriguez, S. (2009). Beginning teachers' views of their collaborative roles. *Preventing School Failure, 53,* 235–244.

Conners, N. A., Bradley, R. H., Mansell, L. W., Liu, J. Y., Roberts, T. J., Burgdorf, K., et al. (2004). Children of mothers with serious substance abuse problems: An accumulation of risks. *American Journal of Drug & Alcohol Abuse, 30,* 85–100.

Connor, D. J. (2006). Michael's story: "I get into so much trouble just by walking": Narrative knowing and life at the intersctions of learning disability, race, and class. *Equity & Excellence in Education, 39,* 154–165.

Connor, D. J., & Ferri, B. A. (2007). The conflict within: Resistance to inclusion and other paradoxes in special education. *Disability & Society, 22,* 63–77.

Conoley, J. C., & Conoley, C. W. (2010). Why does collaboration work? Linking positive psychology and collaboration. *Journal of Educational and Psychological Consultation, 20,* 75–82.

Conroy, M., Sutherland, K., Snyder, A., & Marsh, S. (2008). Classwide interventions: Effective instruction makes a difference. *Teaching Exceptional Children, 40*(6), 24–30.

Contrucci-Kuhn, S. A., Lerman, D. C., & Vondran, C. M. (2006). Analysis of factors that affect responding in a two-response chain in children with developmental disabilities. *Journal of Applied Behavior Analysis, 39,* 263–280.

Conyers, C., Miltenberger, R., Romaniuk, C., Kopp, B., & Himle, M. (2003). Evaluation of DRO schedules to reduce disruptive behavior in a preschool classroom [Electronic version]. *Child and Family Behavior Therapy, 25,* 1–6.

Cook, B. G., Semmel, M. I., & Gerber, M. M. (1999). Attitudes of principals and special education teachers toward the inclusion of students with mild disabilities. *Remedial and Special Education, 20,* 199–207, 243.

Cook, B. G., Tankersley, M., Cook, L., & Landrum, T. J. (2008a). Evidence-based practices in special education: Some practical considerations. *Intervention in School and Clinic, 44,* 69–75.

Cook, L., & Friend, M. (2010). The state of the art of collaboration on behalf of students with disabilities. *Journal of Educational and Psychological Consultation, 20,* 1–8.

Cook, L., Cook, B. G., Landrum, T. J., & Tankersley, M. (2008b). Examining the role of group experimental research in establishing evidence-based practices. *Intervention in School and Clinic, 44*(2), 76–82.

Cooper, H. (1989). Synthesis of research on homework. *Educational Leadership, 47*(3).

Cooper, S. M. A. (2002). Classroom choices for enabling peer learning. [Electronic version]. *Theory into Practice, 41*(1), 53–57.

Copeland, S. R., Hughes, C., Carter, E. W., Guth, C., Presley, J. A., Williams, C. R., et al. (2004). Increasing access to general education: Perspectives of participants in a high school peer support program. *Remedial and Special Education, 25,* 342–352.

Correa-Torres, S. M., & Howell, J. J. (2004). Facing the challenges of itinerant teaching: Perspectives and suggestions from the field. *Journal of Visual Impairment & Blindness, 98,* 420–433.

Correa-Torres, S. (2008). The nature of the social experiences of students with deaf-blindness who are educated in inclusive settings. *Journal of Visual Impairment & Blindness, 102,* 272–283.

Cott, A. (1977). *The orthomolecular approach to learning disabilities.* New York: Huxley Institute.

Cott, A. (1985). *Help for your learning disabled child: The orthomolecular treatment.* New York: Time Books.

Council for Children with Behavioral Disorders. (2009, May). *CCBD position summary: The use of seclusion in school settings.* Arlington, VA: Council for Exceptional Children.

Council for Exceptional Children. (2000). *Transition specialist competencies: Fact sheet.* Arlington, VA: Author.

Council of State Directors of Programs for the Gifted. (2001). *The 1999–2000 state of the states gifted and talented education report.* Longmont, CO: Author.

Council of State Directors of Programs for the Gifted. (2007). *Gifted education: State of the nation.* Washington, DC: National Association for Gifted Children. Retrieved September 10, 2009 from http://www.nagc.org/index .aspx?id=1051.

Coutinho, M. J., & Oswald, D. P. (2000). Disproportionate representation in special education: A synthesis and recommendations. *Journal of Child and Family Studies, 9*(2), 135–156.

Cowen, E. L., Pederson, A., Babijian, H., Izzo, L. D., & Trost, M. A. (1973). Long-term follow-up of early detected vulnerable children. *Journal of Consulting and Clinical Psychology, 41,* 438–446.

Coyne, M. D., Kame'enui, E. J., & Carnine, D. W. (2007). *Effective teaching strategies that accommodate diverse learners.* Upper Saddle River, NJ: Merrill/Pearson.

Crawford, C. G. (1980). *Math without fear.* New York: New Viewpoints/Vision Books.

Cullinan, D. (2007). *Students with emotional and behavioral disorders: An introduction for teachers and other helping professionals* (2nd ed.). Upper Saddle River NJ: Pearson Merrill/Prentice Hall.

Cullinan, D., Epstein, M. H., & Lloyd, J. (1983). *Behavior disorders of children and adolescents.* Upper Saddle River, NJ: Prentice-Hall.

Cummings, R., & Maddux, C. (1985). *Parenting the learning disabled: A practical handbook.* Springfield, IL: Charles C Thomas.

Cunningham, M. M., & Wodrich, D. L. (2006). The effect of sharing health information on teachers' production of classroom accommodations. *Psychology in the Schools, 43,* 553–564.

Curry, C. (2003). Universal design: Accessibility for all learners. *Educational Leadership, 61*(2), 55–60.

Curtin, D. F., Pisecco, S., & Hamilton, R. J. (2006). Teacher perceptions of classroom interventions for children with ADHD: A cross-cultural comparison of teachers in the United States and New Zealand. *School Psychology Quarterly, 21,* 171–196.

Czarnecki, E., Rosko, D., & Fine, F. (1998). How to CALL UP notetaking skills. *Teaching Exceptional Children, 30*(6), 14–19.

D'Angelo, A., Lutz, J. G., & Zirkel, P. A. (2004). Are published IDEA hearing officer decisions representative? *Journal of Disability Policy Studies, 14,* 241–252.

Dabkowski, D. M. (2004). Encouraging active parent participation in IEP team meetings. *Teaching Exceptional Children, 36*(3), 34–39.

Dalton, B., & Pisha, B. (2001). Developing strategic readers: A comparison of computer-suggested versus traditional strategy instruction on struggling readers' comprehension of quality children's literature. Paper presented at the 51st annual meeting of the National Reading Conference, San Antonio, TX.

Dalton, B., Sable, J., & Hoffman, L. (2006, September). Characteristics of the 100 largest public elementary and secondary school districts in the United States: 2003–2004 [statistical analysis report]. Washington, DC: National Center for Education Statistics. (ERIC Document Reproduction Service No. ED493585)

Daly, B., Kral, M., & Brown, R. (2008). Cognitive and academic problems associated with childhood cancers and sickle cell disease. *School Psychology Quarterly, 23,* 230–242.

Daly, P. M., & Ranalli, P. (2003). Using countoons to teach self-monitoring skills. *Teaching Exceptional Children, 35*(5), 30–35.

Damore, S., & Murray, C. (2009). Urban elementary school teachers' perspectives regarding collaborative teaching practices. *Remedial and Special Education, 30,* 234–244.

D'Angelo, A., Lutz, J. G., & Zirkel, P. A. (2004). Are published IDEA hearing officer decisions representative? *Journal of Disability Policy Studies, 4*(14), 241–252.

Danneker, J., & Bottge, B. (2009). Benefits of and barriers to elementary student-led individualized education programs. *Remedial and Special Education, 30,* 225–233.

Darch, C., & Gersten, R. (1985). The effects of teaching presentation and praise on LD students' oral reading performance. *British Journal of Educational Psychology, 55,* 295–303.

Dardig, J. C. (2005). The McClurg monthly magazine and 14 more practical ways to involve parents. *Teaching Exceptional Children, 38*(2), 46–51.

Davern, L. (2004). School-to-home notebooks. *Teaching Exceptional Children, 36*(5), 22–28.

Davies, D. M., Stock, S., & Wehmeyer, M. L. (2002). Enhancing independent time management and personal scheduling for individuals with mental retardation through use of a palmtop visual and audio prompting system. *Mental Retardation, 40,* 358–365.

Davis, L. J. (2007). Deafness and the riddle of identity. *Chronicle of Higher Education, 53*(19), B6.

Daviss, W., Diler, R., & Birmaher, B. (2009). Associations of lifetime depression with trauma exposure, other environmental adversities, and impairment in adolescents with ADHD. *Journal of Abnormal Child Psychology, 37,* 857–871.

Day-Vines, N. L., Patton, J. M., & Baytops, J. L. (2003). Counseling African American adolescents: The impact of face, culture, and middle class status [Electronic version]. *Professional School Counseling, 7,* 40–51.

de Boo, G. M., & Prins, P. J. M. (2007). Social incompetence in children with ADHD: Possible moderators and mediators in social-skills training. *Clinical Psychology Review, 27,* 78–97.

DeBettencourt, L. U. (2002). Understanding the differences between IDEA and Section 504. *Teaching Exceptional Children, 34*(3), 16–23.

Deidrick, K. K., & Farmer, J. E. (2005). School reentry following traumatic brain injury. *Preventing School Failure, 49*(4), 23–33.

Deitz, D. E. D., & Ormsby, D. (1992). A comparison of verbal social behavior of adolescents with behavioral disorders and regular class peers. *Behavioral Modification, 16,* 504–524.

DeLaPaz, S. (1999). Composing via dictation and speech recognition systems: Compensatory technology for students with learning disabilities. *Learning Disabilities Quarterly, 22,* 173–182.

Delgado, R. (2010). "Poco a poquito se van apagando": Teachers' experiences educating Latino English language learners with disabilities. *Journal of Latinos and Education, 9,* 150–157.

Demchak, M. A. (n.d.). *Fact Sheet: Circles of friends.* Reno: Nevada Dual Sensory Impairment Project, University of Nevada, Reno. Retrieved February 9, 2005, from www.unr.edu/educ/ndsip/factsheets/circle.friends.pdf

Denham, A., Hatfield, S., Smethurst, N., Tan, E., & Tribe, C. (2006). The effect of social skills interventions in the primary school. *Educational Psychology in Practice, 22,* 33–51.

Denham, A., & Lahm, E. A. (2001). Using technology to construct alternate portfolios of students with moderate and severe disabilities. *Teaching Exceptional Children, 33*(5), 10–17.

Denning, C. B. (2007). Social skills interventions for students with Asperger syndrome and high-functioning autism: Research findings and implications for teachers. *Beyond Behavior, 16*(3), 16–23.

Dennison, P. E., & Dennison, G. E. (1994). *Brain Gym™ teacher's edition: Revised.* Ventura, CA: Edu-Kinesthetics.

Deno, S. L. (1985). Curriculum-based measurement: The emerging alternative. *Exceptional Children, 52,* 219–232.

Deno, S. L. (2003). Developments in curriculum-based measurement. *Journal of Special Education, 37,* 184–192.

Deno, S. L., Reschly-Anderson, A., Lembke, E., Zorka, H., & Callender, S. (2002). *A model for school wide implementation: A case example.* Paper presented at the annual meeting of the National Association of School Psychology, Chicago, IL.

DePaepe, P., Garrison-Kane, L., & Doelling, J. (2002). Supporting students with health needs in schools: An overview of selected health conditions. *Focus on Exceptional Children, 35*(1), 1–24.

DeRosier, M. E., & Marcus, S. R. (2005). Building friendships and combating bullying: Effectiveness of S.S. GRIN at one-year follow-up. *Journal of Clinical Child and Adolescent Psychology, 34,* 140–150.

Deshler, D., Ellis, E., & Lenz, B. (Eds.). (1996). *Teaching adolescents with learning disabilities: Strategies and methods* (2nd ed.). Denver: Love.

DeSimone, J. R., & Parmar, R. S. (2006). Middle school mathematics teachers' beliefs about inclusion of students with learning disabilities. *Learning Disabilities Research and Practice, 21,* 98–110.

Dettmer, P., Thurston, L. P., & Dyck, N. J. (2005). *Consultation, collaboration, and teamwork for students with special needs* (5th ed.). Englewood Cliffs, NJ: Prentice-Hall.

Dettmer, P., Thurston, L. P., Knackendoffel, A., & Dyck, N. J. (2009). *Collaboration, consultation and teamwork for students with special needs* (6th ed.). Boston: Allyn & Bacon.

deValenzuela, J., Copeland, S., Huaquing Qi, C., & Park, M. (2006). Examining educational equity: Revisiting the disproportionate representation of minority students in special education. *Exceptional Children, 72,* 425–441.

DeVito, J. A. (2005). *Messages, building interpersonal communication skills* (6th ed). Boston: Allyn & Bacon.

DeVito, J. A. (2009). *The interpersonal communication book* (12th ed.). Boston: Allyn & Bacon.

Devlin, P. (2008). Create effective teacher-paraprofessional teams. *Intervention in School and Clinic, 44,* 41–44.

Dexter, D., Hughes, C., & Farmer, T. (2008). Responsiveness to intervention: A review of field studies and implications for rural special education. *Rural Special Education Quarterly, 27*(4), 3–9.

Dickson, S. V., & Bursuck, W. D. (1999). Implementing a model for preventing reading failure. *Learning Disabilities Research and Practice, 14*(4), 191–202.

Dickson, S. V., & Bursuck, W. D. (2003). Implementing an outcomes-based collaborative partnership for preventing reading failure. In D. L. Wiseman & S. L. Knight (Eds.), *Linking school-university collaboration and K–12 student outcomes* (pp. 131–146). Washington, DC: AACTE.

Dieterich, C. A., Villani, C. J., & Bennett, P. T. (2003). Functional behavioral assessments: Beyond student behavior [Electronic version]. *Journal of Law and Education, 32,* 357–368.

Dietz, S., & Montague, M. (2006). Attention deficit hyperactivity disorder comorbid with emotional and behavioral disorders and learning disabilities in adolescents. *Exceptionality, 14*(1), 19–33.

Dinnebeil, L., McInerney, W., & Hale, L. (2006). "Shadowing" itinerant ECSE teachers: A descriptive study of itinerant teacher activities. *Journal of Research in Childhood Education, 21*(1), 41–52.

Disability Films. (2007). *Films involving disabilities.* Retrieved August 20, 2007, from www.disabilityfilms.co.uk

Dole, R. L. (2004). Collaborating successfully with your school's physical therapist. *Teaching Exceptional Children, 36*(5), 28–35.

Doman, G., & Delacato, D. (1968). Doman–Delacato philosophy. *Human Potential, 1,* 113–116.

Donne, V., & Zigmond, N. (2008). An observational study of reading instruction for students who are deaf or hard of hearing in public schools. *Communications Disorders Quarterly, 29,* 219–235.

Dopp, J., & Block, T. (2004). High school peer mentoring that works? *Teaching Exceptional Children, 37*(1), 56–62.

Doré, R., Dion, E., Wagner, S., & Brunet, J. P. (2002). High school inclusion of adolescents with mental retardation: A multiple case study. *Education and Training in Mental Retardation and Developmental Disabilities, 37,* 253–261.

Dover, W. F. (2005). 20 ways to . . . Consult and support students with special needs in inclusive classrooms. *Intervention in School and Clinic, 41*(1), 32–35.

Downing, J. A. (2004). Related services for students with disabilities: Introduction to the special issue. *Intervention in School and Clinic, 39,* 195–208.

Downing, J. E. (2002). *Including students with severe and multiple disabilities in typical classrooms: Practical strategies for teachers* (2nd ed.). Baltimore: Brookes.

Downing, J. E. (2005). Inclusive education for high school students with severe intellectual disabilities: Supporting communication. *Alternative and Augmentative Communication, 21,* 132–148.

Downing, J. E., & Eichinger, J. (2003). Creating learning opportunities for students with severe disabilities in inclusive classrooms. *Teaching Exceptional Children, 36*(1), 26–31.

Dowrick, P. W., Kim-Rupnow, W.S., & Power, T. J. (2006). Video feedforward for reading. *The Journal of Special Education, 39*(4), 194–207.

Doyle, W. (1986). Classroom organization and management. In M. Wittrock (Ed.), *Handbook of research on teaching* (pp. 392–431). New York: Macmillan.

Doyle, W. (1990). Classroom management techniques. In O. C. Moles (Ed.), *Student discipline strategies* (pp. 83–105). Albany, NY: State University of New York Press.

Drasgow, E., Yell, M. L., & Robinson, T. R. (2001). Developing legally correct and educationally appropriate IEPs. *Remedial and Special Education, 22,* 359–373.

DuFour, R., DuFour, R., Eaker, R., & Many, T. (2006). *Learning by doing: A handbook for professional learning communities at work.* Bloomington, IN: Learning Tree.

Duhaney, L. M. G. (2003). A practical approach to managing the behaviors of students with ADD. *Intervention in School and Clinic, 38*(5), 267–279.

Duhon, G., Mesmer, E., Gregerson, L., & Witt, J. (2009). Effects of public feedback during RtI team meetings on teacher implementation integrity and student academic performance. *Journal of School Psychology, 47,* 19–37.

Duke, N. K. (2000). 36 minutes per day: The scarcity of informational texts in first grade. *Reading Research Quarterly, 35,* 202–224.

Dukes, C., & Lamar-Dukes, P. (2009). Inclusion by design: Engineering inclusive practices in secondary schools. *Teaching Exceptional Children, 41*(3), 16–23.

Dunn, C., Chambers, D., & Rabren, K. (2004). Variables affecting students' decisions to drop out of school. *Remedial and Special Education, 25,* 314–323.

Dunn, L. M. (1968). Special education for the mildly handicapped—Is much of it justifiable? *Exceptional Children, 35,* 5–22.

Dunn, R. (1983). Learning style and its relation to exceptionality at both ends of the spectrum. *Exceptional Children, 49*(6), 496–506.

Dunst, C. J. (2002). Family-centered practices: Birth through high school. *Journal of Special Education, 36,* 139–147.

DuPaul, G. J., & Stoner, G. (2003). *ADHD in the schools: Assessment and intervention strategies* (2nd edition). New York: Guilford.

DuPaul, G. J., Jitendra, A. K., Volpe, R. J., Tresco, K. E., Lutz, J. G., & Vile Junod, R. E. (2006). Consultation-based academic interventions for children with ADHD: Effects on reading and mathematics achievement. *Journal of Abnormal Child Psychology, 34*(5), 633–646.

DuPaul, G. J., & Wyeandt, L. L. (2006). School-based intervention for children with attention deficit hyperactivity disorder: Effects on academic, social and behavioural functioning. *International Journal of Disability, Development and Education, 53,* 161–176.

Dupper, D., & Montgomery Dingus, A. (2008). Corporal punishment in U.S. public schools: A continuing challenge for school social workers. *Children & Schools, 30,* 243–250.

Durlak, C. M., Rose, E., & Bursuck, W. (1994). Preparing high school students with learning disabilities for the transition to postsecondary education: Teaching the skills of self-determination. *Journal of Learning Disabilities, 27,* 51–59.

Dykeman, B. F. (2009). Response to intervention: The functional assessment of children returning to school with traumatic brain injury. *Education, 130,* 295–300.

Dyson, B. (2002). The implementation of cooperative learning in an elementary physical education program [Electronic version]. *Journal of Teaching in Physical Education, 22,* 69–85.

Dyson, L. (2005). Kindergarten children's understanding of and attitudes toward people with disabilities. *Topics in Early Childhood Special Education, 25,* 95–104.

Dyson, L. (2010). Unanticipated effects of children with learning disabilities on their families. *Learning Disability Quarterly, 33,* 43–55.

Easterbrooks, S. (1999). Improving practices for students with hearing impairments. *Exceptional Children, 65,* 537–554.

Echevarria, J. C. (1998). Preparing text and classroom materials for English-language learners: Curriculum adaptations in secondary school settings. In R. Gersten & R. Jimenez (Eds.), *Promoting learning for culturally and linguistically diverse students: Classroom applications from contemporary research.* Belmont, CA: Wadsworth.

Eckstein, M. (2009). Enrichment 2.0-Gifted and talented education for the 21st century. *Gifted Child Today, 32*(1), 59–63.

Edgemon, E. A., Jablonski, B. R., & Lloyd, J. W. (2006). Large-scale assessments: A teacher's guide to making decisions about accommodations. *Teaching Exceptional Children, 38*(3), 6–11.

Egyed, C. J., & Short, R. J. (2006). Teacher self-efficacy, burnout, experience and decision to refer a disruptive student. *School Psychology International, 27,* 462–474.

Ehri, L. C. (2004). Teaching phonemic awareness and phonics: An explanation of the National Reading Panel meta-analyses. In P. McCardle & V. Chhabra (Eds.), *The voice of evidence in reading research* (pp. 153–186). Baltimore, MD: Brookes.

Eigenbrood, R. (2004). IDEA requirements for children with disabilities in faith-based schools: Implications for practice. *Journal of Disability Policy Studies, 15,* 2–8.

Elbaum, B., Moody, S. W., & Schumm, J. S. (1999). Mixed-ability grouping for reading: What students think. *Learning Disabilities Research and Practice, 14,* 61–66.

Elhoweris, H., & Alsheikh, N. (2006). Teachers' attitudes toward inclusion. *International Journal of Special Education, 21,* 115–118.

Eli Lilly. (2003). *The history of ADHD.* Retrieved June 28, 2003, from www.strattera.com/1_3_childhood_adhd/1_3_1_1_2_history.jsp

Elliot, L. B., Stinson, M. S., McKee, B. G., Everhart, V.S., & Francis, P. J. (2001). College students' perceptions of the C-print speech-to-text transcription system. *Journal of Deaf Studies and Deaf Education, 6,* 285–298.

Elliott, S. N., & Roach, A. T. (2002). *The impact of providing testing accommodations to students with disabilities.* Retrieved from www.wcer.wisc.edu/testacc/Publications/aera2002.doc

Ellis, A., & Ryan, A. (2003). Race and cognitive ability test performance: The mediating effects of test preparation, test-taking strategy use and self-efficacy. *Journal of Social Psychology, 33,* 2607–2629.

Ellis, E. (1991). *SLANT: A starter strategy for participation.* Lawrence, KS: Edge Enterprises.

Ellis, E. (1996). Reading strategy instruction. In D. Deshler, E. Ellis, & K. Lenz (Eds.), *Teaching adolescents with learning disabilities: Strategies and methods* (2nd ed., pp. 61–125). Denver, CO: Love.

Ellis, E. S., & Colvert, G. (1996). Writing strategy instruction. In D. Deshler, E. Ellis, and B. Lenz (Eds.), *Teaching adolescents with learning disabilities: Strategies and methods* (2nd ed., pp. 127–207). Denver, CO: Love.

Ellis, E., & Lenz, B. K. (1996). Perspectives on instruction in learning strategies. In D. Deshler, E. Ellis, & B. K. Lenz (Eds.), *Teaching adolescents with learning disabilities: Strategies and methods* (2nd ed., pp. 9–60). Denver: Love.

Ellis, E. S., & Sabornie, E. S. (1990). Strategy-based adaptive instruction in content-area classes: Social validity of six options. *Teacher Education and Special Education, 13,* 133–144.

Ellis, E., Lenz, B. K., & Sabornie, E. (1987a). Generalization and adaptation of learning strategies to natural environments: Part 1: Critical agents. *Remedial and Special Education, 8*(2), 6–24.

Ellis, E., Lenz, B. K., & Sabornie, E. (1987b). Generalization and adaptation of learning strategies to natural environments: Part 2: Research into practice. *Remedial and Special Education, 8*(2), 6–23.

Emmer, E. T., & Gerwels, M. C. (2002). Cooperative learning in elementary classrooms: Teaching practices and lesson characteristics [Electronic version]. *Elementary School Journal, 103,* 76–91.

Emmer, E. T., Evertson, C. M., Sanford, J. P., Clements, B. S., & Worsham, M. E. (1983). *Organizing and managing the junior high classroom.* Austin: Research and Development Center for Teacher Education, University of Texas.

Engelmann, S., & Bruner, E. C. (2003). *Reading mastery classic.* Columbus, OH: SRA/McGraw-Hill.

Englert, C., & Mariage, T. (1991). Making students partners in the comprehension process: Organizing the reading "POSSE." *Learning Disability Quarterly, 14,* 123–138.

Englert, C. S., Raphael, T. E., Anderson, L. M., Anthony, H. M., Fear, K. L., & Gregg, S. L. (1988). A case for writing intervention: Strategies for writing informational text. *Learning Disabilities Focus, 3*(2), 98–113.

Englert, C. S., Zhao, Y., Dunsmore, K., Collings, N. Y., & Wolbers, K. (2007). Scaffolding the writing of students with disabilities through procedural facilitation: Using an internet-based technology to improve performance. *Learning Disability Quarterly, 30,* 9–29.

Englert, C. S. (2009). Connecting the dots in a research program to develop, implement, and evaluate strategic literacy interventions for struggling readers and writers. *Learning Disabilities Research & Practice, 24*(2), pp. 104–120.

Epilepsy Foundation. (n.d.). *Understanding epilepsy: Epilepsy and seizure statistics.* Retrieved July 8, 2007, from www.epilepsyfoundation.org/about/statistics.cfm

Epstein, M. H. (2004). *Behavioral and emotional rating scale*(2nd ed.). Austin, TX: PRO-ED.

Epstein, M. H., Polloway, E. A., Buck, G. H., Bursuck, W. D., Wissinger, L., Whitehouse, F., & Jayanthi, M. (1997). Homework-related communication problems: Perspectives of general education teachers. *Learning Disabilities Research and Practices, 12,* 221–227.

Epstein, M. H., Rudolph, S., & Epstein, A. (2000). Using strength-based assessment in transition planning. *Teaching Exceptional Children, 32*(6), 50–55.

Erchul, W. P., & Martens, B. K. (2002). *School consultation: Conceptual and empirical bases of practice* (2nd ed.). New York: Kluwer Academic/Plenum Publishers.

Erion, J. (2006). Parent tutoring: A meta-analysis. *Education and Treatment of Children, 29*(1), 79–106.

Ervin, R. A., Schaughency, E., Matthews, A., Goodman, S. D., & McGlinchey, M. T. (2007). Primary and secondary prevention of behavior difficulties: Developing a data-informed problem-solving model to guide decision making at a school-wide level. *Psychology in the Schools, 44,* 7–18.

Espin, C., Shin, J., & Busch, T. (2005). Curriculum-based measurement in the content areas: Vocabulary matching as an indicator of progress in social studies learning. *Journal of Learning Disabilities, 38*(4), 353–363.

Espin, C., Wallace, T., Campbell, H., Lembke, E. S., Long, J. D., & Ticha, R. (2008). Curriculum-based measurement in writing: Predicting the success of high-school students on state standards tests. *Exceptional Children, 74,* 174–193.

Estell, D. B., Jones, M. H., Pearl, R., Van Acker, R., Farmer, T. W., & Rodkin, P. C. (2008). Peer groups, popularity, and social preference. *Journal of Learning Disabilities, 41*(1), 5–14.

Etscheidt, S. (2006). Behavioral intervention plans: Pedagogical and legal analysis of issues. *Behavioral Disorders, 31,* 223–243.

Etscheidt, S. K. (2006). Progress monitoring: Legal issues and recommendations for IEP teams. *Teaching Exceptional Children, 38*(3), 56–60.

Etscheidt, S., & Knesting, K. (2007). A qualitative analysis of factors influencing the interpersonal dynamics of a prereferral team. *School Psychology Quarterly, 22,* 264–288.

Etzel-Wise, D., & Mears, B. (2004). Adapted physical education and therapeutic recreation in schools. *Intervention in School and Clinic, 39,* 223–232.

Evertson, C. M., Emmer, E. T., Clements, B. S., Sanford, J. P., Worsham, M. E., & Williams, E. L. (1983). *Organizing and managing the elementary school classroom.* Austin: Research and Development Center for Teacher Education, University of Texas.

Fagan, M., & Pisoni, D. (2010). Hearing experience and receptive vocabulary development in deaf children with cochlear implants. *Journal of Deaf Studies and Deaf Education, 15,* 149–161.

Fairbanks, S., Sugai, G., Guardino, D., & Lathrop, M. (2007). Response to intervention: Examining classroom behavior support in second grade. *Exceptional Children, 73,* 288–310.

Farmer, T. W., Goforth, J. B., Clemmer, J. T., & Thompson, J. H. (2004). School discipline problems in rural African American early adolescents: Characteristics of students with major, minor, and no offenses. *Behavioral Disorders, 29,* 317–336.

Farmer, T. W., Farmer, E. M. Z., & Brooks, D. S. (2010). Recasting the ecological and developmental roots of intervention for students with emotional and behavior problems: The promise of strength-based perspectives. *Exceptionality, 18,* 53–57.

Fairbanks, S., Sugai, G., Guardino, D., & Lathrop, M. (2007). Response to intervention: Examining classroom behavior support in second grade. *Exceptional Children, 73,* 288–310.

Feingold, B. F. (1975). *Why your child is hyperactive.* New York: Random House.

Fennema, E., Carpenter, T. P., Jacobs, V. R., Franke, M. L., & Levi, L. (1998). A longitudinal study of gender differences in young children's mathematical thinking. *Educational Researcher, 27*(5), 6–11.

Ferguson, P. M. (2002). A place in the family: An historical interpretation of research on parental reactions to having a child with a disability. *Journal of Special Education, 36,* 124–130.

Ferrell, K. A. (2005). The effects of NCLB. *Journal of Visual Impairment & Blindness, 99,* 681–683.

Fiedorowicz, C. (2005). Neurobiological basis of learning disabilities: An overview. Retrieved from www.ldac-taac.ca/Research/neurobiological-e.asp

Field, S., Sarver, M. D., & Shaw, S. F. (2003). Self-determination: A key to success in postsecondary education for students with learning disabilities. *Remedial and Special Education, 24,* 339–349.

Fighting Autism. (2004, November). *U.S. and outlying areas public schools autism prevalence report school years, 1992–2003.* Gibsonia, PA: Author. Retrieved July 1, 2007, from www.fightingautism.org/idea/reports/US-Autism-Statistics-Prevalence-Incidence-Rates.pdf

Fighting Autism. (2010). Autism: Statistics, incidence, prevalence. Retrieved June 14, 2010 from http://www.fightingautism.org/idea/index.php.

Filter, K. J., McKenna, M. K., Benedict, E. A., Horner, R. H., Todd, A. W., & Watson, J. (2007). Check in/check out: A post-hoc evaluation of an efficient, secondary-level targeted intervention for reducing problem behaviors in schools. *Education and Treatment of Children, 30,* 69–84.

Finstein, R. F., Yang, F. Y., & Jones, R. (2007). Build organizational skills in students with learning disabilities. *Intervention in School and Clinic, 42*(3), 174–178.

Fitch, F. (2003). Inclusion, exclusion, and ideology: Special education students' changing sense of self [Electronic version]. *Urban Review, 35,* 233–252.

Fitzgerald, J. L., & Watkins, M. W. (2006). Parents' rights in special education: The readability of procedural safeguards. *Exceptional Children, 72,* 497–510.

Fleischer, D. Z., & Zames, F. (2001). *The disability rights movement: From charity to confrontation.* Philadelphia: Temple University Press.

Fleming, J. L., & Monda-Amaya, L. E. (2001). Process variables critical for team effectiveness: A Delphi study of wraparound team members. *Remedial and Special Education, 22,* 158–171.

Foegen, A. (2008). Algebra progress monitoring and interventions for students with learning disabilities. *Learning Disability Quarterly, 31,* 65–78.

Fombonne, E. (2003). The prevalence of autism. *Journal of the American Medical Association, 289,* 87–89.

Foorman, B. R. (Ed.). (2003). *Preventing and remediating reading difficulties: Bringing science to scale.* Baltimore, MD: York.

Foorman, B. R., Goldenberg, C., Carlson, C. D., Saunders, W. M., & Pollard-Durodola, S. D. (2004). How teachers allocate time during literacy instruction in primary-grade English language learner classrooms. In P. McCardle & V. Chhabra (Eds.), *The voice of evidence in reading research* (pp. 289–322). Baltimore, MD: Paul H. Brookes.

Fore, C., Riser, S., & Boon, R. (2006). Implications of cooperative learning and educational reform for students with mild disabilities. *Reading Improvement, 43*(1), 3–12.

Forest, M., Pierpoint, J., & O'Brien, J. (1996). MAPS, Circles of Friends, and PATH: Powerful tools to help build caring communities. In S. Stainback & W. Stainback (Eds.), *Inclusion; A guide for educators*. Baltimore, MD: Paul H. Brookes.

Forness, S. R., & Kavale, K. A. (2001). ADHD and a return to the medical model of special education. *Education and Treatment of Children, 24*, 224–247.

Forness, S., & Knitzer, J. (1992). *A new proposed definition and terminology to replace "serious emotional disturbance" in individuals with disabilities education act*. Alexandria, VA: The National Mental Health and Special Education Coalition.

Foster, M. (1997). *Black teachers on teaching*. New York: New Press.

Foster, M. (1995) African American teachers and culturally-relevant pedagogy. In J. A. Banks & C. A. M. Banks (Eds.), *Handbook of research on multicultural education* (pp. 570–581). New York: Macmillan.

Francis, D. J., Shaywitz, S. E., Stuebing, K. K., Fletcher, J. M., & Shaywitz, B. A. (1996). Developmental lag vs. deficit models of reading disability: A longitudinal individual growth curves analysis. *Journal of Educational Psychology, 1*, 3–17.

Frattura, E., & Capper, C. A. (2006). Segregated programs versus integrated comprehensive service delivery for all learners: Assessing the differences. *Remedial and Special Education, 27*(6), 355–364.

Frattura, E. M., & Capper, C. A. (2007). New teacher teams to support integrated comprehensive services. *Teaching Exceptional Children, 39*(4), 16–21.

Frea, W. (2010). Preparing adolescents with autism for successful futures. *Exceptional Parent, 40*(4), 26–29.

Freeman, J. (2000). Teaching for talent: Lessons from the research. In C. M. F. van Lieshout & P. G. Heymans (Eds.), *Developing talent across the life span* (pp. 231–248). Philadelphia: Psychology Press.

Freeman, R., Eber, L., Anderson, C., Irvin, L., Horner, R., Bounds, M., et al. (2006). Building inclusive school cultures using school-wide positive behavior support: Designing effective individual support systems for students with significant disabilities. *Research & Practice for Persons with Severe Disabilities, 31*, 4–17.

Freeman, S. F. N., & Alkin, M. C. (2000). Academic and social attainments of children with mental retardation in general education and special education settings. *Remedial and Special Education, 21*(1), 3–18.

French, N. K. (2003). *Managing paraeducators in your school: How to hire, train, and supervise non-certified staff*. Thousand Oaks, CA: Corwin.

Frey, L. M., & Wilhite, K. (2005). Our five basic needs: Application for understanding the function of behavior. *Intervention in School and Clinic, 40*, 156–160.

Friedland, E. S., & Truesdell, K. S. (2006). "I can read to whoever wants to hear me read": Buddy readers speak out with confidence. *Teaching Exceptional Children, 38*(5), 36–42.

Friend, M. (2000). Perspective: Myths and misunderstandings about professional collaboration. *Remedial and Special Education, 21*, 130–132, 160.

Friend, M. (2008). *Co-Teach! A manual for creating and sustaining effective classroom partnerships in inclusive schools*. Greensboro, NC: Marilyn Friend, Inc.

Friend, M. (2011). *Special education: Contemporary perspectives for school professionals* (3rd edition). Upper Saddle River, NJ: Merrill/Pearson.

Friend, M., & Cook, L. (2004). Collaborating with professionals and parents without being overwhelmed: Building partnerships and teams. In J. Burnette, & C. Peters-Johnson (Eds.), *Thriving as a special educator: Balancing your practices and ideals* (pp. 29–39). Arlington, VA: Council for Exceptional Children.

Friend, M., & Cook, L. (2007). *Interactions: Collaboration skills for school professionals* (5th ed.). Boston: Allyn and Bacon.

Friend, M., Cook, L., Hurley-Chamberlain, D., & Shamberger, C. (2010). Co-teaching: An illustration of the complexity of collaboration in special education. *Journal of Educational and Psychological Consultation, 20*, 9–27.

Friend, M., & Shamberger, C. (2008). Inclusion. In T. L. Good (Ed.), *Twenty-first century education: A reference handbook* (Volume II, Part XI, Ch 64; pp. 124–131). Thousand Oaks, CA: Sage.

Frye, H. (2005). How elementary school counselors can meet the needs of students with disabilities. *Professional School Counseling, 8*, 442–450.

Fuchs, D., & Deshler, D. D. (2007). What we need to know about responsiveness to intervention (and shouldn't be afraid to ask). *Learning Disabilities Research and Practice, 22*, 129–136.

Fuchs, D., Fuchs, L. S., & Stecker, P. M. (2010). The "blurring" of special education in a new continuum of general education placements and services. *Exceptional Children, 76*, 301–323.

Fuchs, L. S., & Fuchs, D. (2001). Helping teachers formulate sound test accommodation decisions for students with learning disabilities. *Learning Disabilities Research and Practice, 16*, 174–181.

Fuchs, L. S., & Fuchs, D. (2006). A framework for building capacity for responsiveness to intervention. *School Psychology Review, 35*, 621–626.

Fuchs, L. S., Fuchs, D., Hamlett, C., Philips, N., & Bentz, J. (1994). Classwide curriculum-based measurement: Helping general educators meet the challenge of student diversity. *Exceptional Children, 60*, 518–537.

Fuchs, L. S., Fuchs, D., Hamlett, C. L., Hope, S. K., Hollenbeck, K. N., Capizzi, A.M., Craddock, C.F., & Brothers, R.L. (2006). Extending responsiveness-to-intervention to math problem-solving at third grade. *TEACHING Exceptional Children, 38*(4), 59–63.

Fuchs, L. S., Fuchs, D., Hamlett, C. L., & Stecker, P. M. (1991). Effects of curriculum-based measurement and consultation on teacher planning and student achievement in mathematics operations. *American Educational Research Journal, 28*, 617–641.

Fuchs, L. S., Fuchs, D., Kazdan, S., Karns, K., Calhoon, M. B., Hamlett, C. L., & Hewlett, S. (2000). Effects of workgroup structure and size on student productivity during collaborative work on complex tasks. *Elementary School Journal, 100*, 201–210.

Fuchs, L. S., Hamlett, C. L., & Fuchs, D. (1997). *Monitoring basic skills progress: Basic reading* (2nd ed.) [Computer software, manual, and blackline masters]. Austin TX: PRO-ED.

Fuchs, L. S., Hamlett, C. L., & Fuchs, D. (1998). *Monitoring basic skills progress: Basic math computation* (2nd ed.) [Computer software, manual, and blackline masters]. Austin TX: PRO-ED.

Fuchs, L. S., Hamlett, C. L., & Fuchs, D. (1999). *Monitoring basic skills progress: Basic math concepts and applications* [Computer software, manual, and blackline masters]. Austin TX: PRO-ED.

Fuchs, L. S., Fuchs, D., Hintze, J., & Lembke, E. (2007). *Progress monitoring in the context of response to intervention*. Presentation at the National Center on Student Progress Monitoring Summer Institute: Nashville.

Fuchs, L. S., Fuchs, D., Powell, S. R., Seethaler, P. M., Cirino, P. T., & Fletcher, J. M. (2008). Intensive intervention for students with mathematics disabilities: Seven principles of effective practice. *Learning Disability Quarterly, 31*(2), 79–92.

Fuchs, L. S., Hamlett, C. L., & Fuchs, D. (1998). Monitoring basic skills progress: Basic math computation (2nd ed.). Austin, TX: Pro-Ed.

Fuchs, L. S., Hamlett, C. L., & Fuchs, D. (1999). *Monitoring basic skills progress: Basic math concepts and applications*. Austin, TX: Pro-Ed.

Fulk, B. M. (1996). The effects of combined strategy and attribution training on LD adolescents' spelling performance. *Exceptionality, 6*(1), 13–27.

Furlong, M., & Morrison, G. (2000). The *school* in school violence: Definitions and facts. *Journal of Emotional and Behavioral Disorders, 8*, 71–82.

Fusell, J. J., Macias, M. M., & Saylor, C. F. (2005). Social skills and behavior problems in children with disabilities with and without siblings. *Child Psychiatry and Human Development, 36*, 227–241.

Gabe, J., Bury, M., & Ramsay, R. (2002). Living with asthma: The experiences of young people at home and at school [Electronic version]. *Social Science and Medicine, 55*, 1619–1633.

Gable, R. A., Mostert, M. P., & Tonelson, S. W. (2004). Assessing professional collaboration in schools: Knowing what works. *Preventing School Failure, 48*(3), 4–8.

Gable, R., Hester, P., Rock, M., & Hughes, K. (2009). Back to basics: Rules, praise, ignoring, and reprimands revisited. *Intervention in School and Clinic, 44*, 195–205.

Gagnon, J. C., & Maccini, P. (2001). Preparing students with disabilities for algebra. *Teaching Exceptional Children, 34*(1), 8–15.

Ganz, J. B., Cook, K. E., & Earles-Vollrath, T. L. (2007). A grab bag of strategies for children with mild communication deficits. *Intervention in School and Clinic, 42*(3), 179–187.

Garcia, S., & Ortiz, A. (2006). Preventing disproportionate representation: Culturally & linguistically prereferral interventions [Electronic version]. *Teaching Exceptional Children, 38*(4), 64–68.

Gardner, H. (1993). *Multiple intelligences: The theory in practice*. New York: Basic Books.

Gardner, H. E. (2006). *Multiple intelligences: New horizons in theory and practice*. New York: Basic Books.

Gartin, B. C., & Murdick, N. L. (2005). IDEA 2004: The IEP. *Remedial and Special Education, 26,* 327–331.

Gay, G. (2002). Culturally responsive teaching in special education for ethnically diverse students: Setting the stage. *Qualitative Studies in Education, 15*(6), 613–629.

Gehrling, A. (2006). Classroom management and teaching strategies for students with attention deficit hyperactivity disorder. *Law & Disorder, 1,* 43–48.

Geisthardt, C. L., Brotherson, M. J., & Cook, C. C. (2002). Friendships of children with disabilities in the home environment. *Education and Training in Mental Retardation and Developmental Disabilities, 37,* 235–252.

George, M. P., White, G. P., & Schlaffer, J. J. (2007). Implementing schoolwide behavior change: Lessons from the field. *Psychology in the Schools, 44*(1), 41–51.

Germinario, V., Cervalli, J., & Ogden, E. H. (1992). *All children successful: Real answers for helping at risk elementary students.* Lancaster, PA: Technomic.

Gersten, R., Baker, S. K., & Marks, S. U. (1998). *Teaching English language learners with learning difficulties.* Eugene, OR: Eugene Research Institute.

Gersten, R., Beckmann, S., Clarke, B., Foegen, A., Marsh, L., Star, J. R., & Witzel, B. (2009b). *Assisting students struggling with mathematics: Response to Intervention (RtI) for elementary and middle school. A practice guide* (NCEE 2009–4060) [Electronic version]. Washington, DC: National Center for Education Evaluation and Regional Assistance, Institute of Education Sciences. Retrieved July 5, 2010, from http://ies.ed.gov/ncee/wwc/publications/practiceguides/

Gersten, R., Compton, D., Connor, C. M., Dimino, J., Santoro, L., Linan-Thompson, S., & Tilly, W. D. (2009). *Assisting students struggling with reading: Response to Intervention and multi-tier intervention for reading in the primary grades, A practice guide (NCEE 2009–4045)* [Electronic version]. Washington, DC: National Center for Education Evaluation and Regional Assistance, Institute of Education Sciences, U.S. Department of Education. Retrieved May 28, 2009, from http://ies.ed.gov/ncee/wwc/publications/practiceguides/

Gersten, R., Fuchs, L. S., Williams, J. P., & Baker, S. (2001). Teaching reading comprehension strategies to students with learning disabilities: A review of research. *Review of Educational Research, 71,* 279–320.

Gersten, R., Jordan, N. C., & Flojo, J. R. (2005). Early identification and interventions for students with mathematics difficulties. *Journal of Learning Disabilities, 38*(4), 293–304.

Gersten, R., Vaughn, S., & Brengelman, S. U. (1996). Grading and academic feedback for special education students and students with learning difficulties. In T. R. Guskey (Ed.), *Communicating student learning.* Alexandria, VA: Association for Supervision and Curriculum Development.

Gersti-Pepin, C. I. (2006). The paradox of poverty narratives: Educators struggling with children left behind. *Educational Policy, 20*(1), 143–162.

Getty, K. C., & Erchul, W. P. (2009). The influence of gender on the likelihood of using soft social power strategies in school consultation. *Psychology in the Schools, 46,* 447–458.

Getty, L. A., & Summy, S. E. (2004). The course of due process. *Teaching Exceptional Children, 36*(3), 40–43.

Ghere, G., & York-Barr, J. (2007). Paraprofessional turnover and retention in inclusive programs. *Remedial and Special Education, 28*(1), 21–32.

Giangreco, M. F. (2007). Extending inclusive opportunities. *Educational Leadership, 64*(5), 34–37.

Giangreco, M. F., & Broer, S. M. (2005). Questionable utilization of paraprofessionals in inclusive schools: Are we addressing symptoms or causes? *Focus on Autism and Other Developmental Disabilities, 20*(1), 10–26.

Giangreco, M. F., & Doyle, M. B. (2002). Students with disabilities and paraprofessional supports: Benefits, balance, and band-aids [Electronic version]. *Focus on Exceptional Children, 34*(7), 1–12.

Giangreco, M. F., Edelman, S. W., & Broer, S. M. (2003). Schoolwide planning to improve paraeducator supports. *Exceptional Children, 70,* 63–80.

Giangreco, M. F., Suter, J. C., & Doyle, M. B. (2010). Paraprofessionals in inclusive schools: A review of recent research. *Journal of Educational and Psychological Consultation, 20,* 41–57.

Gibb, G. S., & Dyches, T. T. (2007). *Guide to writing quality individualized education programs* (2nd ed.). Boston: Allyn and Bacon.

Gillette, Y. (2006). Assistive technology and literacy partnerships. *Top Lang Disorders, 26*(1), 70–81.

Gillies, R. M. (2007). *Cooperative learning: Integrating theory and practice.* Thousand Oaks, CA: Sage.

Gillies, R. M., & Ashman, A. F. (2000). The effects of cooperative learning on students with learning difficulties in the lower elementary school. *Journal of Special Education, 34,* 19–27.

Ginsberg, M. B. (2005). Cultural diversity, motivation, and differentiation. *Theory into Practice, 44,* 218–225.

Giovacco-Johnson, T. (2007). Twice-exceptional children: Paradoxes and parenting. *Childhood Education, 83*(3), 175–176.

Goetz, L., & O'Farrell, N. (1999). Connections: Facilitating social supports for students with deaf-blindness in general education classrooms. *Journal of Visual Impairment and Blindness, 92,* 704–715.

Golden, S. M. (2009). Does childhood use of stimulant medication as a treatment for ADHD affect the likelihood of future drug abuse and dependence? A literature review. *Journal of Child & Adolescent Substance Abuse, 18,* 343–358.

Goldstein, A. P., Sprafkin, R. P., Gershaw, N. J., & Klein, P. (1980). *Skillstreaming the adolescent.* Champaign, IL: Research Press.

Goldstein, H., Moss, J. W., & Jordan, L. J. (1965). *The efficacy of special class training on the development of mentally retarded children* (U.S. Office of Education Cooperative Research Program Project No. 619). Urbana: University of Illinois Institute for Research on Exceptional Children. (ERIC Document Reproduction Service No. ED002907)

Gong, B., & Marion, S. (2006). *Dealing with flexibility in assessments for students with significant cognitive disabilities* (Synthesis Report 60). Minneapolis, MN: University of Minnesota, National Center on Educational Outcomes. Retrieved May 27, 2007, from http://cehd.umn.edu/nceo/OnlinePubs/Synthesis60.html

Gongola, L. C., & Daddario, R. (2010). A practitioner's guide to implementing a differential reinforcement of other behaviors procedure. *Teaching Exceptional Children, 42*(6), 14–20.

Good, R. (2002, April). *Catching kids before they fall: What schools can do.* Presentation at the Illinois branch of the International Dyslexia Association, Lincolnwood, IL.

Good, R. H., Gruba, J., & Kaminki, R. A. (2002). Best practices in using dynamic indicators of basic early literacy skills (DIBELS) in an outcomes-driven model. In A. Thomas & J. Grimes (Eds.), *Best practices in school psychology IV* (pp. 699–720). Bethesda, MD: National Association of School Psychologists.

Good, T. L., & Brophy, I. E. (1986). School effects. In M. C. Wittrock (Ed.), *Handbook of research on teaching* (3rd ed., pp. 570–602). Upper Saddle River, NJ: Prentice Hall.

Goodenow, C., Szalacha, L., & Westheimer, K. (2006). School support groups, other school factors, and the safety of sexual minority adolescents. *Psychology in the Schools, 43,* 573–589.

Goodman, H., Gottlieb, J., & Harrison, R. H. (1972). Social acceptance of EMR children integrated into a non-graded elementary school. *American Journal of Mental Deficiency, 76,* 412–417.

Graetz, J. E., Mastropieri, M. A., & Scruggs, T. E. (2006). Show time: Using video self-modeling to decrease inappropriate behavior. *Teaching Exceptional Children, 38*(5), 43–48.

Graham, S. (1999). Handwriting and spelling instruction for students with learning disabilities: A review. *Learning Disability Quarterly, 22,* 77–98.

Graham, S., & Freeman, S. (1986). Strategy training and teacher- vs. student-controlled study conditions: Effects on LD students' spelling performance. *Learning Disability Quarterly, 9,* 15–22.

Graham, S., & Harris, K. R. (1987). Improving composition skills of inefficient learners with self-instructional strategy training. *Topics in Language Disorders, 7*(4), 66–77.

Graham, S., & Harris, K. R. (2005). Improving the writing performance of young struggling writers. *The Journal of Special Education, 39*(1), 19–33.

Graham, S., Harris, K. R., & MacArthur, C. (2006). Explicitly teaching struggling writers: Strategies for mastering the writing process. *Intervention in School and Clinic, 41*(5), 290–294.

Graham-Day, K., Gardner, R., & Hsin, Y. (2010). Increasing on-task behaviors of high school students with attention deficit hyperactivity disorder: Is it enough? *Education and Treatment of Children, 33,* 205–221.

Grandin, T. (2002). *Teaching tips for children and adults with autism.* Salem, OR: Center for the Study of Autism. Retrieved November 22, 2004, from www.autism.org/temple/tips.html

Grandin, T. (2007). Autism from the inside. *Education Leadership, 64*(5), 29-32.

Grant, R. (1993). Strategic training for using text headings to improve students' processing of content. *Journal of Reading, 36,* 482-488.

Gratz, D. (2009). The problem with performance pay. *Educational Leadership, 67*(3), 76-79.

Green, T. (2005). Using technology to help English language students develop language skills: A home and school connection. *Multicultural Education, 13*(2), 56-59.

Greenfield, R., Rinaldi, C., Proctor, C. P., & Cardarelli, A. (2010). Teachers' perceptions of a response to intervention (RTI) reform effort in an urban elementary school: A consensual qualitative analysis. *Journal of Disability Policy Studies, 21,* 47-63.

Greenwood, C. R., Arreaga-Mayer, C., Utley, C. A., Gavin, K. M., & Terry, B. J. (2001). Classwide peer tutoring learning management system: Applications with elementary-level English language learners. *Remedial and Special Education, 22,* 34-47.

Gresham, F. M., Van, M. B., & Cook, C. R. (2006). Social skills training for teaching replacement behaviors: Remediating acquisition deficits in at-risk students. *Behavior Disorders, 31*(4), 363-377.

Gringel, M., Neubert, D. A., Moon, M. S., & Graham, S. (2003). Self-determination for students with disabilities: Views of parents and teachers. *Exceptional Children, 70,* 97-111.

Grossen, B. J. (2002). The BIG accommodation model: The direct instruction model for secondary schools. *Journal of Education for Students Placed At Risk, 7,* 241-263.

Grossman, H. (1995). *Special education in a diverse society.* Boston: Allyn and Bacon.

Gubbins, E. J. (Ed.). (2002, Fall). *National Research Center on the Gifted and Talented Newsletter.* Storrs: University of Connecticut, National Research Center on the Gifted and Talented. (ERIC Document Reproduction Service No. ED477662)

Guiberson, M. (2009). Hispanic representation in special education: Patterns and implications. *Preventing School Failure, 53*(3), 167-176.

Gul, S., & Vuran, S. (2010). An analysis of studies conducted video modeling in teaching social skills. *Educational Sciences: Theory and Practice, 10,* 249-274.

Gunter, P. L., Miller, K. A., Venn, M. L., Thomas, K., & House, S. (2002). Self-graphing to success. *Teaching Exceptional Children, 35*(2), 30-35.

Guskey, T. R. (2006). Making high school grades meaningful. *Phi Delta Kappan, 87*(9), 670-675.

Guskey, T. R., & Bailey, J. M. (2001). *Developing grading and reporting systems for student learning.* Thousand Oaks, CA: Corwin.

Gyamfi, P., Walrath, C., Burns, B., Stephens, R., Geng, Y., & Stambaugh, L. (2010). Family education and support services in systems of care. *Journal of Emotional and Behavioral Disorders, 18,* 14-26.

Haager, D., & Klinger, J. K. (2004). *Differentiating instruction in inclusive classrooms: The special educator's guide.* Boston: Allyn & Bacon.

Hackett, P. (2009). Everybody wins: How to be an effective member of your child's IEP team. *Exceptional Parent, 39*(3), 30-32.

Hall, H. I., Song, R., Rhodes, P., Prejean, J., An, Q., Lee, L. M., et al. (2008). Estimation of HIV incidence in the United States. *Journal of the American Medical Association, 300,* 520-529.

Hallahan, D. P., Lloyd, J. W., Kauffman, J. M., Weiss, M. P., & Martinez, E. A. (2005). *Learning disabilities: Foundations, characteristics, and effective teaching* (3rd ed.). Boston: Allyn and Bacon.

Hallahan, D. P., Kauffman, J. M., & Pullen, P. C. (2009). *Exceptional learners: An introduction to special education.* (11th ed.). Upper Saddle River, NJ: Pearson.

Hammill, D. (1990). On defining learning disabilities: An emerging consensus. *Journal of Learning Disabilities, 23*(2), 74-84.

Handler, B. R. (2003, April). *Special education practices: An evaluation of educational environmental placement trends since the regular education initiative.* Paper presentation at the Annual meeting of the American Educa-

tional Research Association, Chicago. Retrieved October 4, 2004, from www.eric.ed.gov/contentdelivery/servlet/ERICServlet?accno= ED480184

Handler, M., W., Rey, J., Connell, J., Their, K., Feinberg, A., & Putman, R. (2007). Practical considerations in creating school-wide positive behavior support in public schools. *Psychology in the Schools, 44*(1), 29-39.

Hang, Q., & Rabren, K. (2009). An examination of co-teaching: Perspectives and efficacy indicators. *Remedial and Special Education, 30,* 259-268.

Hanline, M. F., & Daley, S. (2002). "Mom, will Kaelie always have possibilities?" The realities of early childhood inclusion. *Phi Delta Kappan, 84,* 73-76.

Hansuvadha, N. (2009). Compromise in collaborating with families: Perspectives of beginning special education teachers. *Journal of Early Childhood Teacher Education, 30,* 346-362.

Hänze, M., & Berger, R. (2007). Cooperative learning, motivational effects, and student characteristics: An experimental study comparing cooperative learning and direct instruction in 12th grade physics classes. *Learning and Instruction, 17,* 29-41.

Hardman, M. L., Drew, C. J., & Egan, M. W. (2005). *Human exceptionality: School, community, and family, IDEA 2004 Update Edition* (8th ed.). Boston: Allyn and Bacon.

Harlacher, J. E., Roberts, N. E., & Merrell, K. W. (2006). Classwide interventions for students with ADHD: A summary of teacher options beneficial for the whole class. *Teaching Exceptional Children, 39*(2), 6-12.

Harley, D. A., Nowak, T. M., Gassway, L. J., & Savage, T. A. (2002). Lesbian, gay, bisexual, and transgender college students with disabilities: A look at multiple cultural minorities. *Psychology in the Schools, 39,* 525-538.

Harniss, M. K., Caros, J., & Gersten, R. (2007). Impact of the design of U.S. history textbooks on content acquisition and academic engagement of special education students: An experimental investigation. *Journal of Learning Disabilities, 40*(2), 100-110.

Harniss, M. K., Epstein, M. H., Bursuck, W. D., Nelson, J., & Jayanthi, M. (2001). Resolving homework-related communication problems: Recommendations of parents of children with and without disabilities. *Reading and Writing Quarterly, 17,* 205-225.

Harper, G., & Maheady, L. (2007). Peer-mediated teaching and students with learning disabilities. *Intervention in School and Clinic, 43,* 101-107.

Harpin, V. A. (2005). The effect of ADHD on the life of an individual, their family, and community from preschool to adult life. *Archives of Disease in Childhood, 90,* i2-i7.

Harris, K. R., Graham, S., Mason, L. H. (2003). Self-regulated strategy development in the classroom: Part of a balanced approach to writing instruction for students with disabilities. *Focus on Exceptional Children, 35*(7), 1-16.

Harris, S. F., Prater, M. A., Dyches, T. T., & Heath, M. A. (2009). Job stress of school-based speech-language pathologists. *Communication Disorders Quarterly, 30,* 103-111.

Harry, B. (2002). Trends and issues in serving culturally diverse families of children with disabilities. *Journal of Special Education, 36,* 131-138.

Harry, B. (2008). Collaboration with culturally and linguistically diverse families: Ideal versus reality. *Exceptional Children, 74,* 372-388.

Harry, B., & Klingner, J. K. (2005). Why are so many minority students in special education?: Understanding race and disability in schools. New York: Teachers College Press.

Harry, B., & Klingner, J. (2007). Discarding the deficit model. *Educational Leadership, 64*(5), 16-21.

Hartas, D. (2004). Teacher and speech-language therapist collaboration: Being equal and achieving a common goal? *Child Language Teaching and Therapy, 20,* 33-54.

Hartman, M. (2009). Step by step: Creating a community-based transition program for students with intellectual disabilities. *Teaching Exceptional Children, 41*(6), 6-11.

Hartwig, E. P., & Ruesch, G. M. (2000). Disciplining students in special education. *Journal of Special Education, 33,* 240-247.

Hasbrouck, J. E., & Tindal, G. (2006). Oral reading fluency norms: A valuable assessment tool for reading teachers. *The Reading Teacher, 59*(7), 636-644.

Hattie, J. (2009). *Visible learning: A synthesis of over 800 meta-analyses relating to achievement.* London: Routledge.

Hauge, J. M., & Babkie, A. M. (2006). Develop collaborative special educator-paraprofessional teams: One para's view. *Intervention in School and Clinic, 42*(1), 51–53.

Hawkins, R., Musti-Rao, S., Hughes, C., Berry, L., & McGuire, S. (2009). Applying a randomized interdependent group contingency component to classwide peer tutoring for multiplication fact fluency. *Journal of Behavioral Education, 18*, 300–318.

Hazelkorn, M., Packard, A., & Douvanis, G. (2008). Alternative dispute resolution in special education: A view from the field. *Journal of Special Education Leadership, 21*(1), 32–38.

Heath, D. (1993). Using portfolio assessment with secondary LED students yields a cross-cultural advantage for all. *BeOutreach, 4*(1), 27.

Hehir, T. (2007). Confronting ableism. *Education Leadership, 64*(5), 8–14.

Hendley, S. L. (2007). Use positive behavior support for inclusion in the general education classroom. *Intervention in School and Clinic, 42*(4), 225–228.

Henley, M. (2003). *Teaching self-control: A curriculum for responsible behavior.* (2nd ed.). Bloomington, IN: National Education Service.

Heron, T. E., Villareal, D. M., & Yao, M. (2006). Peer tutoring systems: Applications in classroom and specialized environments. *Reading and Writing Quarterly, 22*, 27–45.

Hertberg-Davis, H. (2009). Myth 7: Differentiation in the regular classroom is equivalent to gifted programs and is sufficient—classroom teachers have the time, the skill, and the will to differentiate adequately. *Gifted Child Quarterly, 53*, 251–253.

Hessler, T., Konrad, M., & Alber-Morgan, S. (2009). 20 ways to assess student writing. *Intervention in School and Clinic, 45*, 68–71.

Hetzroni, O. E., & Shrieber, B. (2004). Word processing as an assistive technology tool for enhancing academic outcomes of students with writing disabilities in the general classroom. *Journal of Learning Disabilities, 37*, 143–154.

Hill, J., & Flynn, K. (2006). *Classroom instruction that works with English language learners.* Alexandria, VA: Association for Supervision and Curriculum Development.

Hinchey, P. H. (2003). Corporal punishment: Legalities, realities, and implications [Electronic version]. *Clearing House, 76*, 127–131.

Hines, J. (2008). Making collaboration work in inclusive high school classrooms: Recommendations for principals. *Intervention in School and Clinic, 43*, 277–282.

Hinkelman, L., & Bruno, M. (2008). Identification and reporting of child sexual abuse: The role of elementary school professionals. *Elementary School Journal, 108*, 376–391.

Hitchcock, C. H., Dowrick, P. W., & Prater, M. A. (2003). Video self-modeling intervention in school-based settings. *Remedial and Special Education, 24*, 36–45.

Hitchcock, C., Meyer, A., Rose, D., & Jackson, R. (2002). Providing new access to the general curriculum: Universal Design for Learning. *Teaching Exceptional Children, 35*(2), 8–17.

Hitti, M. (2005, September). New numbers on ADHD in U.S. kids. *WebMD Medical News.* Retrieved July 25, 2007, from www.webmd.com/add-adhd/news/20050901/new-numbers-on-adhd-in-us-kids

Hobbs, N. (1975). *The futures of children.* San Francisco: Jossey-Bass.

Hodges, D., Mandlebaum, L. H., Boff, C., & Miller, M. (2007). Instructional strategies online database (ISOD). *Intervention in School and Clinic, 42*(4), 219–224.

Hodgkinson, H. (2000/2001). Educational demographics: What teachers should know. *Educational Leadership, 58*(4), 6–11.

Holliday, D. C. (2002). *Jigsaw IV: Using student/teacher concerns to improve Jigsaw III.* (ERIC Document Reproduction Service No. ED465687)

Holverstott, J. (2005). Promote self-determination in students. *Intervention in School and Clinic, 41*(1), 39–41.

Holzer, L. H., Madaus, J. W., Bray, M. A., & Kehle, T. J. (2009). The test-taking strategy for college students with learning disabilities. *Learning Disabilities Research & Practice, 24*(1), 44–56.

Homme, L. (1970). *How to use contingency contracting in the classroom.* Champaign, IL: Research Press.

Hooper, S. R. (2006). Myths and misconceptions about traumatic brain injury: Endorsements by school psychologists. *Exceptionality, 14*, 171–182.

Hoover, J. J., & Patton, J. R. (2005). Differentiating curriculum and instruction for English-language learners with special needs. *Intervention in School and Clinic, 40*, 231–235.

Horne, P., & Timmons, V. (2009). Making it work: Teachers' perspectives on inclusion. *International Journal of Inclusive Education, 13*, 273–286.

Horrocks, J., White, G., & Roberts, L. (2008). Principals' attitudes regarding inclusion of children with autism in Pennsylvania public schools. *Journal of Autism and Developmental Disorders, 38*, 1462–1473.

Horton, S. V. (1987). *Study guides: A paper on curriculum modification.* Unpublished manuscript, University of Washington.

Hosp, J. L., & Reschly, D. J. (2002). Predictors of restrictiveness of placement for African-American and Caucasian students. *Exceptional Children, 68*, 225–238.

Hosp, J. L., & Reschly, D. J. (2003). Referral rates for intervention or assessment: A meta-analysis of racial differences. *Journal of Special Education, 37*, 67–80.

Hosp, J. L., & Reschly, D. J. (2004). Disproportionate representation of minority students in special education: Academic, demographic, and economic predictors. *Exceptional Children, 70*, 185–199.

Hosp, J. L. (2008). Best practices in aligning academic assessment with instruction. In A. Thomas & J. Grimes (Eds.), *Best practices in school psychology* (5th ed., pp. 363–376). Bethesda, MD: National Association of School Psychologists.

Hosp, M. K., & Hosp, J. (2003). Curriculum-based measurement for reading, spelling, and math: How to do it and why. *Preventing School Failure, 48*(1), 10–17.

Hosterman, S., DuPaul, G., & Jitendra, A. (2008). Teacher ratings of ADHD symptoms in ethnic minority students: Bias or behavioral difference? *School Psychology Quarterly, 23*, 418–435.

Howell, K. M., & Morehead, M. K. (1993). *Curriculum-based evaluation for special and remedial education* (2nd ed.). Columbus, OH: Merrill.

Huefner, D. S. (2000). The risks and opportunities of the IEP requirements under IDEA '97. *Journal of Special Education, 33*, 195–204.

Hughes, J, & Kwok, O. (2007). Influence of student-teacher and parent-teacher relationships on lower achieving readers' engagement and achievement in the primary grades. *Journal of Educational Psychology, 99*, 39–51.

Hughes, M., & Greenhough, P. (2006). Boxes, bags, and videotape: Enhancing home-school communication through knowledge exchange activities. *Educational Review, 58*, 471–487.

Hughes, C., & Dexter, D. D. (2010). Universal screening within a response to intervention model. http://www.rtinetwork.org/learn/research/universal-screening-within-a-rti-model

Hulac, D., & Benson, N. (2010). The use of group contingencies for preventing and managing disruptive behaviors. *Intervention in School and Clinic, 45*, 257–262.

Hunt, P., Soto, G., Maier, J., & Doering, K. (2003). Collaborative teaming to support students at risk and students with severe disabilities in general education classrooms. *Exceptional Children, 69*, 315–332.

Hyatt, K. J. (2007). Brain Gym™ building stronger brains or wishful thinking? *Remedial and Special Education, 28*(2), 117–124.

Hyatt, K. J. (2007). The new IDEA: Changes, concerns, and questions. *Intervention in School and Clinic, 42*, 131–136.

Iano, R. P., Ayers, D., Heller, H. B., McGettigan, J. F., & Walker, V. S. (1974). Sociometric status of retarded children in an integrative program. *Exceptional Children, 40*, 267–271.

Idol, L. (2006). Toward the inclusion of special education students in general education: A program evaluation of eight schools. *Remedial and Special Education, 27*, 77–94.

Ingersoll, B., Dvortcsak, A., Whalen, C., & Sikora, D. (2005). The effects of a developmental, social-pragmatic language intervention on rate of expressive language production in young children with autistic spectrum disorders. *Focus on Autism and Other Developmental Disabilities, 20*, 213–222.

Institute of Education Sciences, National Center for Education Statistics (2007, July). *Percentage of high school dropouts (status dropouts) among persons 16 through 24 years old, by sex and race/ethnicity: Selected years, 1960 through 2005* [Table 104]. Retrieved July 31, 2007, from http://nces.ed.gov/programs/digest/d06/tables/dt06_104.asp?referrer=list

Ira, V. B. (2000). Safe and secure on the web: Pointers on determining a web site's credibility. *Exceptional Parent, 30*(1), 148.

Irlen, H. (1991). *Reading by the colors: Overcoming dyslexia and other reading disabilities through the Irlen method.* Garden City Park, NY: Avery.

Isaacson, S. (2001). Written language. In P. J. Schloss, M. A. Smith, & C. N. Schloss (Eds.), *Instructional methods for secondary students with learning and behavior problems* (3rd ed., pp. 222–245). Boston: Allyn and Bacon.

Ives, B., & Hoy, C. (2003). Graphic organizers applied to higher-level secondary mathematics. *Learning Disabilities: Research and Practice, 18,* 36–51.

Ivey, J., & Ward, A. (2010). Dual familial roles: An Asperger's syndrome case story. *Teaching Exceptional Children Plus, 6*(3).

Jackson, C. W., & Larkin, M. J. (2002). RUBRIC: Teaching students to use grading rubrics. *Teaching Exceptional Children, 35*(1), 40–45.

Jaffee, S. R., Caspi, A., & Moffitt, T. E. (2007). Individual, family, and neighborhood factors distinguish resilient from non-resilient maltreated children: A cumulative stressors model. *Child Abuse & Neglect: The International Journal, 31,* 231–253.

Jamie, K., & Knowlton, E. (2007). Visual supports for students with behavior and cognitive challenges. *Intervention in School and Clinic, 42*(5), 259–270.

Janiga, S. J., & Costenbader, V. (2002). The transition from high school to postsecondary education for students with learning disabilities: A survey of college service coordinators. *Journal of Learning Disabilities, 35,* 462–468.

Janisch, C., & Johnson, M. (2003). Effective literacy practices and challenging curriculum for at-risk learners: Great expectations [Electronic version]. *Journal of Education for Students Placed at Risk, 8,* 295–308.

Jarolimek, J., Foster, C. D., & Kellough, R. D. (2004). *Teaching and learning in the elementary school* (8th ed.). Upper Saddle River, NJ: Prentice Hall.

Jenkins, J. R., Antil, L. R., Wayne, S. K., & Vadasy, P. F. (2003). How cooperative learning works for special education and remedial students. *Exceptional Children, 69,* 279–292.

Jenkins, J. (2009). Measuring reading growth: New findings on progress monitoring. *New Times for DLD, 27,* 1–2.

Jenkins, J., & Johnson, E. (2010). Universal screening for reading problems: Why and how should we do this? http://www.rtinetwork.org/essential/assessment/screening/ReadingProblems

Jensen, R. J. (2004). Discipline preferences and styles among Latino families: Implications for special educators. *Multiple Voices, 7*(1), 60–73.

Jenson, W. R., Sheridan, S. M., Olympia, D., & Andrews, D. (1994). Homework and students with learning disabilities and behavior disorders: A practical, parent-based approach. *Journal of Learning Disabilities, 27,* 538–549.

Johns, B. H., Crowley, E. P., & Guetzloe, E. (2005). The central role of teaching social skills. *Focus on Exceptional Children, 37*(8), 1–8.

Johnson, D., Johnson, R., & Holubec, E. (1998). *Cooperation in the classroom.* Boston: Allyn and Bacon. Retrieved February 11, 2005, from www.intime.uni.edu/coop_learning/ch5/teaching.htm

Johnson, D. W., Johnson, R. T., & Maruyama, G. (1983). Interdependence and interpersonal attraction among heterogeneous and homogeneous individuals: A theoretical formulation and a meta-analysis of the research. *Review of Educational Research, 53,* 5–54.

Johnson, E. S. (2000). The effects of accommodations on performance assessments. *Remedial and Special Education, 21,* 261–267.

Johnson, E., & Arnold, N. (2004). Validating an alternate assessment. *Remedial and Special Education, 25,* 266–275.

Johnson, G. O., & Kirk, S. A. (1950). Are mentally handicapped children segregated in the regular grades? *Exceptional Children, 17,* 65–68, 87–88.

Johnson, J., & Duffett, A. (2002). *When it's your own child: A report on special education from the families who use it.* New York: Public Agenda Foundation. (ERIC Document Reproduction Service No. ED471033)

Johnson, L. R., & Johnson, C. E. (1999). Teaching students to regulate their own behavior. *Teaching Exceptional Children, 31*(4), 6–10.

Johnson, D. R., Stout, K. E., & Thurlow, M. L. (2009). Diploma options and perceived consequences for students with disabilities. *Exceptionality, 17,* 119–134.

Johnston, J., Knight, M., & Miller, L. (2007). Finding time for teams: Student achievement grows as district support boosts collaboration. *Journal of Staff Development, 28*(2), 14–18.

Jones, J. L., Jones, K. A., & Vermette, P. J. (2009, Summer). Using social and emotional learning to foster academic achievement in secondary mathematics. *American Secondary Education.*

Jones, J. M. (2007). Exposure to chronic community violence: Resilience in African American children. *Journal of Black Psychology, 33,* 125–149.

Jones, V. F., & Jones, L. S. (1990). *Comprehensive classroom management.* Boston: Allyn and Bacon.

Jones, V. F., & Jones, L. S. (2004). *Comprehensive classroom management: Creating communities of support and solving problems* (7th ed.). Boston: Allyn and Bacon.

Juel, C. (1988). Learning to read and write: A longitudinal study of 54 children from first through fourth grades. *Journal of Educational Psychology, 80*(4), 437–447.

Juel, C. (1988). Retention and nonretention of at-risk readers in first grade and their subsequent reading achievement. *Journal of Learning Disabilities, 21,* 571–580.

Jung, L., & Guskey, T. R. (2007). Standards-based grading and reporting: A model for special education. *Teaching Exceptional Children, 40*(2), 48–53.

Kaff, M. S., Zabel, R. H., & Milham, M. (2007). Revisiting cost-benefit relationships of behavior management strategies: What special educators say about usefulness, intensity, and effectiveness. *Preventing School Failure, 51*(2), 35–45.

Kagan, S. (1990). A structural approach to cooperative learning. *Educational Leadership, 47*(4), 12–15.

Kalyva, E., & Avramidis, E. (2005). Improving communication between children with autism and their peers through the 'Circle of Friends': A small-scale intervention study. *Journal of Applied Research in Intellectual Disabilities, 18,* 253–261.

Kame'enui, E. J., Carnine, D. W., Dixon, R. C., Simmons, D. C., & Coyne, M. D. (2002). *Effective teaching strategies that accommodate diverse learners* (2nd ed.). Upper Saddle River, NJ: Merrill/Prentice Hall.

Kaminski, R. A., & Good, R. H. (1996). Toward a technology for assessing basic early literacy skills. *School Psychology Review, 25,* 215–227.

Kampfer, S. H., Horvath, L. S., Kleinert, H. L., & Kearns, J. F. (2001). Teachers' perceptions of one state's alternative assessment implications for practice and preparation. *Exceptional Children, 67,* 361–374.

Kamps, D., Wendland, M., & Culpepper, M. (2006). Active teacher participation in functional behavior assessment for students with emotional and behavioral disorders: Risks in general education classrooms. *Behavioral Disorders, 31*(2), 128–146.

Kampwirth, T. J. (2005). *Collaborative consultation in the schools* (3rd ed.). Upper Saddle River, NJ: Merrill.

Kaniuka, M. (2009). Blueprint III: Is the third time the charm? *Journal of Educational and Psychological Consultation, 19,* 224–235.

Karger, J. (2004). *Access to the general curriculum for students with disabilities: The role of the IEP.* Washington, DC: National Center on Accessing the General Curriculum. Retrieved August 15, 2004, from www.cast.org/ncac/index.cfm?i=5312

Kats-Gold, I., & Priel, B. (2009). Emotion, understanding, and social skills among boys at risk of attention deficit hyperactivity disorder. *Psychology in the Schools, 46,* 658–678.

Kauffman, J. M. (2005). *Cases in emotional and behavioral disorders of children and youth.* Upper Saddle River, NJ: Merrill/Prentice Hall.

Kauffman, J. M., Mostert, M. P., Trent, S. C., & Hallahan, D. P. (2002). *Managing classroom behavior: A reflective, case-based approach* (3rd ed.). Boston: Allyn and Bacon.

Kauffman, J. M., & Landrum, T. J., (2009). *Characteristics of emotional and behavioral disorders of children and youth.* Upper Saddle River, NJ: Merrill/Pearson.

Kavale, K. (2002). Mainstreaming to full inclusion: From orthogenesis to pathogenesis of an idea [Electronic version]. *International Journal of Disability, Development, and Education, 49,* 201–214.

Kavale, K. A., & Forness, S. R. (2000). History, rhetoric, and reality: Analysis of inclusion debate. *Remedial and Special Education, 21,* 279–296.

Kavale, K.A., Hirshoren, A., & Forness, S.R. (1998). Meta-analytic validation of the Dunn and Dunn Model of learning-style preferences: A critique of what was Dunn. *Learning Disabilities Research and Practice, 13*(2), 75–80.

Kazdin, A. E. (1977). *The token economy: A review and evaluation.* New York: Plenum.

Kearns, J., Kleinert, H., Clayton, J., Burdge, M., & Williams, R. (1998). Inclusive educational assessments at the elementary school level: Perspectives from Kentucky. *Teaching Exceptional Children, 31*(2), 16–23.

Keefe, E. B., Moore, V., & Duff, F. (2004). The four "knows" of collaborative teaching. *Teaching Exceptional Children, 36*(5), 36–43.

Keefe, E. B., Moore, V. M., & Duff, F. R. (2006). *Listening to the experts: Students with disabilities speak out.* Baltimore: Paul H. Brookes.

Kern, L., & Clemens, N. H. (2007). Antecedent strategies to promote appropriate classroom behavior. *Psychology in the Schools, 44*(1), 65–75.

Kerr, M. M., & Nelson, C. M. (2009). *Strategies for managing behavior problems in the classroom* (6th ed.). Upper Saddle River, NJ: Merrill/Pearson.

Kerschner, J. R. (1990). Self-concept and IQ as predictors of remedial success in children with learning disabilities. *Journal of Learning Disabilities, 23,* 368–374.

Khisty, L. L. (2002). Mathematics learning and the Latino student: Suggestions from research for classroom practice. *Teaching Children Mathematics, 9*(1), 32–36.

Khorsheed, K. (2007). Four places to dig deep: To find more time for teacher collaboration. *Journal of Staff Development, 28*(2), 43–45.

Killu, K. (2008). Developing effective behavior intervention plans: Suggestions for school personnel. *Intervention in School and Clinic, 43,* 140–149.

Kim, A., Vaughn, S., Klinger, J. K., Woodruff, A. L., Reutebuch, C. K., & Kouzekanani, K. (2006). Improving the reading comprehension of middle school students with disabilities through computer-assisted collaborative strategic reading. *Remedial and Special Education, 27*(4), 235–249.

Kim, K., Lee, Y., & Morningstar, M. (2007). An unheard voice: Korean American parents' expectations, hopes, and experiences concerning their adolescent child's future. *Research and Practice for Persons with Severe Disabilities, 32,* 253–264.

Kinch, C., Lewis-Palmer, T., Hagan-Burke, S., & Sugai, G. (2001). A comparison of teacher and student functional behavior assessment interview information from low-risk and high-risk classrooms [Electronic version]. *Education and Treatment of Children, 24,* 480–494.

Kindler, A. L. (2002). *Survey of states' limited English proficient students and available educational programs and services 1999–2000 summary report.* Washington, DC: National Clearinghouse for English Acquisition and Language Instruction Educational Programs.

King, E. W. (2005). Addressing the social and emotional needs of twice-exceptional students. *Teaching Exceptional Children, 38*(1), 16–20.

King, M. A., Sims, A., & Osher, D. (2007). *How is cultural competence integrated in education?* Retrieved June 1, 2007, from www.mayoclinic.com/health/childhood-obesity/DS00698

King, M. B., & Youngs, P. (2003). *Classroom teachers' views on inclusion (Riser Brief No. 7).* Madison: University of Wisconsin-Madison, Research Institute on Secondary Education Reform for Youth with Disabilities (RISER). (ERIC Document Reproduction Service No. ED477878)

King-Sears, M. E. (2007). Designing and delivering learning center instruction. *Intervention in School and Clinic, 42*(3), 137–147.

King-Sears, M. E. (2001). Three steps for gaining access to the general education curriculum for learners with disabilities. *Intervention in School and Clinic, 37,* 67–76.

King-Sears, M. E., Burgess, M., & Lawson, T. L. (1999). Applying curriculum-based assessment in inclusive settings. *Teaching Exceptional Children, 32*(1), 30–38.

Kleinert, H., & Kearns, J. (2001). Accountability for all students: Kentucky's alternate portfolio system for students with moderate and severe cognitive disabilities. *Journal of the Association for Persons with Severe Handicaps (JASH), 22,* 88–101.

Kleinert, H., & Kearns, J. (2004). Alternate assessments. In F. Orelove, D. Sobsey, & R. Silberman (Eds.), *Educating children with multiple disabilities: A collaborative approach* (4th ed., pp. 115–149). Baltimore: Paul Brookes.

Kleinert, H. L., Miracle, S., & Sheppard-Jones, K. (2007). Including students with moderate and severe intellectual disabilities in school extracurricular and community recreation activities. *Intellectual and Developmental Disabilities, 45,* 46–55.

Klingner, J. K., & Harry, B. (2006). The special education referral and decision-making process for English language learners: Child study team meetings and placement conferences. *Teachers College Record, 108*(11), 2247–2281.

Klingner, J. K., & Vaughn, S. (2002). The changing roles and responsibilities of an LD specialist [Electronic version]. *Learning Disability Quarterly, 25,* 19–31.

Kluth, P. (2003). *"You're going to love this kid": Teaching students with autism in the inclusive classroom.* Baltimore: Brookes.

Knackendoffel, E. A. (2005). Collaborative teaming in the secondary school. *Focus on Exceptional Children, 37*(5), 1–16.

Knight, J. (2002). Crossing boundaries: What constructivists can teach intensive-explicit instructors and vice versa. *Focus on Exceptional Children, 35*(4), 1–15.

Knotek, S. (2003). Bias in problem solving and the social process of student study teams: A qualitative investigation of two SSTs. *Journal of Special Education, 37,* 2–14.

Kode, K. (2002). *Elizabeth Farrell and the history of special education.* Arlington, VA: Council for Exceptional Children.

Kohn, A. (2004). Challenging students . . . and how to have more of them. *Phi Delta Kappan, 86,* 184–193.

Kohn, A. (2006). *Beyond discipline: From compliance to community* (10th anniversary edition). Alexandria, VA: Association for Supervision and Curriculum Development.

Kolb, S. M., & Hanley-Maxwell, C. (2003). Critical social skills for adolescents with high incidence disabilities: Parental perspectives. *Exceptional Children, 69,* 163–180.

Kollins, S. H., Barkley, R. A., & DuPaul, G. J. (2001). Use and management of medications for children diagnosed with attention deficit disorder. *Focus on Exceptional Children, 33*(5), 1–24.

Koretz, D. (2008). *Measuring up: What educational testing really tells us.* Cambridge: Harvard University Press.

Kozen, A. A., Murray, R. K., & Windell, I. (2006). Increasing all students' chance to achieve: Using and adapting anticipation guides with middle school learners. *Intervention in School and Clinic, 41*(4), 195–200.

Kozik, P., Cooney, B., Vinciguerra, S., Gradel, K., & Black, J. (2009). Promoting inclusion in secondary schools through appreciative inquiry. *American Secondary Education, 38*(1), 77–91.

Kozik, P., Cooney, B., Vinciguerra, S., Gradel, K., & Black, J. (2009). Promoting inclusion in secondary schools through appreciative inquiry. *American Secondary Education, 38,* 77–91.

Kroeger, S., Burton, C., & Preston, C. (2009). Integrating evidence-based practices in middle science reading. *Teaching Exceptional Children, 41*(3), 6–15.

Kroesbergen, E. H., Van Luit, J. E. H., & Maas, C. J. M. (2004). Effectiveness of explicit and constructivist mathematics instruction for low-achieving students in the Netherlands. *The Elementary School Journal, 104*(3), 233–251.

Kuiper, E., Volman, M., & Terwel, J. (2005). The web as an information resource in K–12 education: Strategies for supporting students in searching and processing information. *Review of Educational Research, 75*(3), 285–328.

Kunsch, C. A., Jitendra, A. K., & Sood, S. (2007). The effects of peer-mediated instruction in mathematics for students with learning problems: A research synthesis. *Learning Disabilities Research & Practice, 22,* 1–12.

Ladson-Billings, G. (1994). *The dreamkeepers: Successful teachers for African American children.* San Francisco: Jossey-Bass.

Lagares, C. L., & Connor, D. J. (2010). Help students prepare for high school examinations. *Intervention in School and Clinic, 45*(1), 63–67.

Lambert, M. A., & Nowacek, J. (2006). Help high school students improve their study skills. *Intervention in School and Clinic, 41*(4), 241–243.

Landrum, T. J., & McDuffie, K. A. (2010). Learning styles in the age of differentiated instruction. *Exceptionality, 18*(1), 6–17.

Lane, K. L., Givner, C. C., & Pierson, M. R. (2004). Teacher expectations of student behavior: Social skills necessary in elementary school classrooms. *Journal of Special Education, 38,* 104–110.

Lane, K. L., Little, M. A., Redding-Rhodes, J., Phillips, A., & Welsh, M. T. (2007). Outcomes of a teacher-led reading intervention for elementary students at risk for behavioral disorders. *Exceptional Children, 74,* 47–70.

Lane, K. L., Mahdavi, J. N., & Borthwick-Duffy, S. (2003). Teacher perceptions of the prereferral intervention process: A call for assistance with school-based interventions. *Preventing School Failure, 47,* 148–155.

Lane, K. L., Pierson, M. R., & Givner, C. C. (2004). Secondary teachers' views on social competence: Skills essential for success. *Journal of Special Education, 38,* 174–187.

Lane, K. L., Wehby, J., & Barton-Arwood, S. M. (2005). Students with and at risk for emotional and behavioral disorders: Meeting their social and academic needs. *Preventing School Failure, 49*(2), 6–9.

Lane, K. L., Wehby, J. H., & Cooley, C. (2006). Teacher expectations of students' classroom behavior across the grade span: Which social skills are necessary for success? *Exceptional Children, 72*(2), 153–167.

Lange, A., Mulhern, G., Wylie, J., & McPhillips, M. (2006). Assistive software tools for secondary-level students with literacy difficulties. *Journal of Special Education Technology, 21*(3), 13–22.

Langer, J. (1984). Examining background knowledge and text comprehension. *Reading Research Quarterly, 19,* 468–481.

Lannie, A. L., & McCurdy, B. L. (2007). Preventing disruptive behavior in the urban classroom: Effects of the good behavior game on student and teacher behavior. *Education and Treatment of Children, 30*(1), 85–98.

Larkin, M. J. (2001). Providing support for student independence through scaffolded instruction. *Teaching Exceptional Children, 34*(1), 30–34.

Larkin, M. J., & Ellis, E. S. (1998). Adolescents with learning disabilities. In B. Y. L. Wong (Ed.), *Learning about learning disabilities* (2nd ed., pp. 557–584), San Diego, CA: Academic Press.

Lasky, B., & Karge, B. D. (2006). Meeting the needs of students with disabilities: Experience and confidence of principals. *NASSP Bulletin, 90,* 9–36.

Laushey, K. M., Hefflin, L. J., Shippen, M., Alberto, P. A., & Fredrick, L. (2009). Concept mastery routines to teach social skills to elementary children with high functioning autism. *Journal of Autism and Developmental Disorders, 39,* 1435–1448.

Lavoie, R. (1991). *How difficult can this be? Understanding learning disabilities* [Videotape]. Portland, OR: Educational Productions.

Lavoie, R. D. (1989). *Mainstreaming: A collection of field-tested strategies to help make the mainstreaming classroom more successful for learning disabled children, their classmates . . . and their teachers.* Norwalk: Connecticut Association for Children with Learning Disabilities.

Lawton, M. (1995, Nov. 8). Students post dismal results on history test. *Education Week, 1,* 12.

Lazarus, S. S., Thurlow, M. L., Lail, K. E., & Christensen, L. (2009). Longitudinal analysis of state accommodations policies: Twelve years of change, 1993-2005. *Journal of Special Education, 43,* 67–80.

Leach, D., & Duffy, M. (2009). Supporting students with autism spectrum disorders in inclusive settings. *Intervention in School and Clinic, 45*(1), 31–37.

Lee, S. W., & Jamison, T. R. (2003). Including the FBA process in student assistance teams: An exploratory study of team communications and intervention selection. *Journal of Educational and Psychological Consultation, 14,* 209–239.

Lee, S., Wehmeyer, M. L., Soukup, J. H., & Palmer, S. B. (2010). Impact of curriculum modifications on access to the general education curriculum for students with disabilities. *Exceptional Children, 76,* 213–233.

Lee-Tarver, A. (2006). A survey of teachers' perceptions of the function and purpose of student support teams. *Education, 126*(3), 525–533.

LeFever, G. B., Villers, M. S., Morrow, A. L., & Vaughn, E. S. (2002). Parental perceptions of adverse educational outcomes among children diagnosed and treated for ADHD: A call for improved school/provider collaboration. *Psychology in the Schools, 39,* 63–71.

Leinhardt, G., & Zigmond, N. (1988). The effects of self-questioning and story structure training on the reading comprehension of poor readers. *Learning Disabilities Research,4*(1), 41–51.

Lemanek, K. L. (2004). Adherence. In R. T. Brown (Ed.), *Handbook of pediatric psychology in school settings* (pp. 129–148). Mahwah, NJ: Erlbaum.

Lembke, E., McMaster, K., & Stecker, P. (2010). The prevention science of reading research within a response-to-intervention model. *Psychology in the Schools, 47,* 22–35.

Lemons, C. (2007). *Response to intervention (RTI): Important aspects of effective implementation.* Presented at 29th International Conference on Learning Disabilities, Myrtle Beach, SC.

Lenz, B. K. (1983). Using the advance organizer. *Pointer, 27,* 11–13.

Lenz, B. K., Ellis, E. S., & Scanlon, D. (1996). *Teaching learning strategies to adolescents and adults with learning disabilities.* Austin, TX: PRO-ED.

Lenz, K. (2006). Creating school-wide conditions for high-quality learning strategy classroom instruction. *Intervention in School and Clinic, 41*(5), 261–266.

Lerner, J., & Johns, B. (2008). *Learning disabilities and related mild disabilities: Characteristics, teaching strategies and new directions* (11th ed.). Boston, MA: Houghton Mifflin.

Lessen, E., Sommers, M., & Bursuck, W. (1987). *Curriculum-based assessment and instructional design.* DeKalb, IL: DeKalb County Special Education Association.

Levy, F., Hay, D. A., & Bennett, K. S. (2006). Genetics of attention deficit hyperactivity disorder: A current review and future prospects. *International Journal of Disability, Development & Education, 53,* 5–20.

Lewis, T., Jones, S., Horner, R., & Sugai, G. (2010). School-wide positive behavior support and students with emotional/behavioral disorders: Implications for prevention, identification and intervention. *Exceptionality, 18,* 82–93.

Licht, B. G., Kistner, J. A., Ozkaragoz, T., Shapiro, S., & Clausen, L. (1985). Causal attributions of learning disabled children: Individual differences and their implications for persistence. *Journal of Educational Psychology, 77,* 208–216.

Lilly, M. S. (1971). A training model for special education. *Exceptional Children, 37,* 740–749.

Lindamood, P., & Lindamood, P. (1998). *LiPS: The Lindamood phoneme sequencing program for reading, spelling, and speech: LiPS teacher's manual for the classroom and clinic* (3rd ed.). Austin, TX: PRO-ED.

Lindquist, T. (1995). *Seeing the whole through social studies.* Portsmouth, NH: Heinemann.

Lindstrom, L., Doren, B., Metheny, J., Johnson, P., & Zane, C. (2007). Transition to employment: Role of the family in career development. *Exceptional Children, 73,* 348–366.

Lingo, A. S., Slaton, D. B., & Jolivette, K. (2006). Effects of corrective reading on the reading abilities and classroom behaviors of middle school students with reading deficits and challenging behavior. *Behavioral Disorders, 31*(3), 265–283.

Little, J. W. (1993). Teachers' professional development in a climate of educational reform. *Educational Evaluation and Policy Analysis, 15,* 129–151.

Lo, Y., & Cartledge, G. (2006). FBA and BIP: Increasing the behavior adjustment of African American boys in schools. *Behavioral Disorders, 31*(2), 147–161.

Lohmeier, K., Blankenship, K., & Hatlen, P. (2009). Expanded core curriculum: 12 years later. *Journal of Visual Impairment & Blindness, 103,* 102–112.

Lohmeier, K. L. (2005). Implementing the expanded core curriculum in specialized schools for the blind. *RE:view: Rehabilitation Education for Blindness and Visual Impairment, 37,* 126–133.

Long, N. J., & Newman, R. G. (1971). Managing surface behavior of children in school. In N. J. Long, W. C. Morse, & R. G. Newman (Eds.), *Conflict in the classroom: The education of children with problems* (2nd ed., pp. 442–452). Belmont, CA: Wadsworth.

Lopez, V., & Sotillo, M. (2009). Giftedness and social adjustment: Evidence supporting the resilience approach in Spanish-speaking children and adolescents. *High Ability Studies, 20*(1), 39–53.

Lorenzi, D. G., Horvat, M., & Pellegrini, A. D. (2000). Physical activity of children with and without mental retardation in inclusive recess settings. *Education and Training in Mental Retardation and Developmental Disabilities, 35,* 160–167.

Lortie, D. C. (1975). *Schoolteacher: A sociological study.* Chicago: University of Chicago Press.

Lott, B. (2003). Recognizing and welcoming the standpoint of low-income parents in the public schools. *Journal of Educational and Psychological Consultation, 14,* 91–104.

Love, A., & Kruger, A. C. (2005). Teacher beliefs and student achievement in urban schools serving African American students. *The Journal of Educational Research, 99*(2), 87–98.

Lovitt, T. C., Rudsit, J., Jenkins, J., Pious, C., & Benedetti, D. (1985). Two methods of adapting science materials for learning disabled and regular seventh graders. *Learning Disability Quarterly, 8,* 275–285.

Lowell-York, J., Doyle, M. E., & Kronberg, R. (1995). *Module 3. Curriculum as everything students learn in school: Individualizing learning opportunities.* Baltimore, MD: Paul H. Brookes.

LRP Publications. (1997). *Grading individuals with disabilities education law report, 25*(4), 381–391.

Luckner, J. L., & Muir, S. (2001). Successful students who are deaf in general education settings. *American Annals of the Deaf, 146,* 450–461.

Luecking, R. (2004). *In their own words: Employer perspectives on youth with disabilities in the workplace: Essential tools.* Minneapolis: National Center on Secondary Education and *Transition,* University of Minnesota (NCSET). (ERIC Document Reproduction No. ED484254)

Luster, J. N., & Durrett, J. (2003, November). *Does educational placement matter in the performance of students with disabilities?* Paper presented at the annual meeting of the Mid-South Educational Research Association, Biloxi, MS. (ERIC Document Reproduction Service No. ED482518)

Lyon, R. (2009). *Reading difficulties: Prevention, early intervention, and remediation. Presented at the Dallas Branch of the International Dyslexia Association Annual Conference.* [Electronic version] Dallas, Texas: Synergistic Education Solutions. Retrieved July 5, 2010 from http://www.google.com/search?q=students+in+tier+3+typically+represent+2-6%25+of+the+student+population&rls=com.microsoft:en-us&ie=UTF-8&oe=UTF-8&startIndex=&startPage=1&rlz=1I7RNTN_en

Lytle, R. K., & Bordin, J. (2001). Enhancing the IEP team: Strategies for parents and professionals. *Teaching Exceptional Children, 33*(5), 40–45.

Lytle, R., & Todd, T. (2009). Stress and the student with autism spectrum disorders: Strategies for stress reduction and enhanced learning. *Teaching Exceptional Children, 41*(4), 36–42.

Maag, J. (2004). *Behavior management: From theoretical implications to practical applications* (2nd ed.). Belmont, CA: Wadsworth.

Maag, J. (2006). Social skills training for students with emotional and behavioral disorders: A review of reviews. *Behavioral Disorders, 32*(1), 5–17.

Maag, J. W. (2001). Management of surface behavior: A new look at an old approach. *Counseling and Human Development, 33*(9), 1–10.

Maag, J. W. (2005). Social skills training for youth with emotional and behavioral disorders and learning disabilities: Problems, conclusions, and suggestions. *Exceptionality, 13,* 155–172.

Maag, J. W., & Katsiyannis, A. (2006). Behavioral intervention plans: Legal and practical considerations for students with emotional and behavioral disorders. *Behavioral Disorders, 31*(4), 348–362.

Maag, J. W., & Reid, R. (2006). Depression among students with learning disabilities: Assessing the risk. *Journal of Learning Disabilities, 39*(1), 3–10.

Mabbot, D. J., & Bisanz, J. (2008). Computational skills, working memory, and conceptual knowledge in older children with mathematics learning disabilities. *Journal of Learning Disabilities, 41*(1), 15–28.

MacArthur, C., Schwartz, S., Graham, S., Malloy, D., & Harris, K. R. (1996). Integration of strategy instruction into a whole language classroom: A case study. *Learning Disabilities Research and Practice, 11,* 168–176.

MacArthur, C. A., & Stoddard, B. (1990, April). *Teaching learning disabled students to revise: A peer editor strategy.* Paper presented at the Annual Meeting of the American Education Research Association, Boston.

Macy, M. G., & Bricker, D. D. (2007). Embedding individualized social goals into routine activities in inclusive early childhood classrooms. *Early Child Development and Care, 177,* 107–120.

Madden, J. A. (2000). Managing asthma at school. *Educational Leadership, 57*(6), 50–52.

Maheady, L., Mallette, B., and Harper, G. F. (2006). Four classwide peer tutoring models: Similarities, differences, and implications for research and practice. *Reading and Writing Quarterly, 22*(1), 65–89.

Maheady, L., Michielli-Pendl, J., Harper, G. F., & Mallette, B. (2006). The effects of Numbered Heads Together with and without an incentive package on the science test performance of a diverse group of sixth graders. *Journal of Behavioral Education, 15,* 25–39.

Maher, J., Burroughs, C., Dietz, L., & Karnbach, A. (2010). From solo to ensemble: Fine arts teachers find a harmonious solution to their isolation. *Journal of Staff Development, 31*(1), 24–29.

Mandlebaum, L. H., & Wilson, R. (1989). Teaching listening skills. *LD Forum, 15*(1), 7–9.

Margolis, H. (2005). Resolving struggling learners' homework difficulties: Working with elementary school learners and parents. *Preventing School Failure, 50*(1), 5–12.

Marino, M. T., Marino, E. C., & Shaw, S. F. (2006). Making informed assistive technology decisions for students with high incidence disabilities. *Teaching Exceptional Children, 38*(6), 18–25.

Maroney, S. A., Finson, K. D., Beaver, J. B., & Jensen, M. M. (2003). Preparing for successful inquiry in inclusive science classrooms. *Teaching Exceptional Children, 36*(1), 18–25.

Marschark, M., Convertino, C., & LaRock, D. (2006). Optimizing academic performance of deaf students: Access, opportunities, and outcomes. In D. F. Moores & D. S. Martin (Eds.), *Deaf learners: Developments in curriculum and instruction.* (pp. 179–200). Washington, DC: Gallaudet University Press.

Marsh, L. G., & Cooke, N. L. (1996). The effects of using manipulatives in teaching math problem solving to students with learning disabilities. *Learning Disabilities Research and Practice, 11,* 58–65.

Marston, D. B. (1989). A curriculum-based measurement approach to asesssing academic performance: What it is and why do it. In M. R. Shinn (Ed.), *Curriculum-based measurement: Assessing special children* (pp. 18–78). New York: Guilford Press.

Marston, D. B. (1996). A comparison of inclusion only, pull-out only, and combined service models for students with mild disabilities. *Journal of Special Education, 30*(2), 121–132.

Marston, D. B., Tindal, G., & Deno, S. (1984). Eligibility for learning disability services: A direct and repeated measurement approach. *Exceptional Children, 50,* 554–556.

Marston, D., Muyskens, P., Lau, M., & Canter, A. (2003). Problem-solving model for decision making with high-incidence disabilities: The Minneapolis experience. *Learning Disabilities Research and Practice, 18*(3), 187–200.

Martin, B. N., Johnson, J. A., Ireland, H., & Claxton, K. (2003). Perceptions of teachers on inclusion in four rural Midwest school districts [Electronic version]. *Rural Educator, 24*(3), 3–10.

Martin, J. E., Marshall, L. H., & Sale, P. (2004). A 3-year study of middle, junior high, and high school IEP meetings. *Exceptional Children, 70,* 285–298.

Martin, J. E., Van Dycke, J. L., Christensen, W. R., Greene, B. A., Gardner, J. E., & Lovett, D. L. (2006). Increasing student participation in IEP meetings: Establishing the self-directed IEP as an evidenced-based practice. *Exceptional Children, 72,* 299–316.

Marzola, E. S. (1987). Using manipulatives in math instruction. *Reading, Writing, and Learning Disabilities, 3,* 9–20.

Marzano, R. J. (2003). *What works in schools: Translating research into action.* Alexandria, VA: Association for Supervision and Curriculum Development.

Marzano, R. J. (2004). *Building background knowledge for academic achievement.* Alexandria, VA: Association for Supervision and Curriculum Development.

Marzano, R. J., & Marzano, J. S. (2003). The key to classroom management. *Educational Leadership, 61*(1), 6–13.

Mason, C. Y., McGahee-Kovac, M., & Johnson, L. (2004). How to help students lead their IEP meetings. *Teaching Exceptional Children, 36*(3), 18–25.

Mason, L. H., Snyder, K. H., Sukhram, D. P., Kedem, Y. (2006). TWA + PLANS strategies for expository reading and writing: Effects for nine fourth-grade students. *Exceptional Children, 73*(1), 69–89.

Massat, C. R. (2006). The many faces of school social work [Letter]. *School Social Work, 30*(2), vii–viii.

Mastropieri, M. A. (1988). Using the keyword method. *Teaching Exceptional Children, 20*(4), 4–8.

Mastropieri, M. A., Scruggs, T. E., & Berkeley, S. L. (2007). Peers helping peers. *Educational Leadership, 64*(5), 54–58.

Mastropieri, M., Scruggs, T., Graetz, J., Norland, J., Gardizi, W., & McDuffie, K. (2005). Case studies in co-teaching in the content areas: Successes, failures, and challenges. *Intervention in School and Clinic, 40*(5), 260–270.

Mastropieri, M. A., Scruggs, T. E., Norland, J. J., Berkeley, S., McDuffie, K., Tornquist, E. H., & Connors, N. (2006). Differentiated curriculum enhancement in inclusive middle school science: Effects on classroom and high-stakes tests. *Journal of Special Education, 40,* 130–137.

Mastropieri, M. A., Scruggs, T. E., Spencer, V., & Fontana, J. (2003). Promoting success in high school world history: Peer tutoring versus guided notes. *Learning Disabilities: Research and Practice, 18,* 52–65.

Mathur, S., & Smith, R. M. (2003). 20 ways to collaborate with families of children with ADD. *Intervention in School and Clinic, 38*(5), 311–315.

Mattox, R., & Harder, J. (2007) Attention deficit hyperactivity disorder (ADHD) and diverse populations. *Child and Adolescent Social Work Journal, 24*(2), 195–207.

Matuszny, R. M., Banda, D. R., & Coleman, T. J. (2007). A progressive plan for building collaborative relationships with parents from diverse backgrounds. *Teaching Exceptional Children, 39*(4), 24–31.

McCardle, P., & Chhabra, V. (Eds.). (2004). *The voice of evidence in reading research.* Baltimore, MD: Brookes.

McClanahan, B. (2009). Help! I have kids who can't read in my world history class! *Preventing School Failure, 53,* 105–112.

McCleary, L. (2002). Parenting adolescents with attention deficit hyperactivity disorder: Analysis of the literature for social work practice [Electronic version]. *Health and Social Work, 27,* 285–292.

McCollin, M., & O'Shea, D. (2005). Increasing reading achievement of students from culturally and linguistically diverse backgrounds. *Preventing School Failure, 50,* 41–46.

McCord, K., & Watts, E. (2010). Music educators' involvement in the individual education program process and their knowledge of assistive technology. *Update: Applications of Research in Music Education, 28*(2), 79–85.

McDonnell, J., Thorson, N., Disher, S., Mathot-Buckner, C., Mendel, J., & Ray, L. (2003). The achievement of students with developmental disabilities and their peers without disabilities in inclusive settings: An exploratory study [Electronic version]. *Education and Treatment of Children, 26,* 224–236.

McDougall, D., & Brady, M. P. (1998). Initiating and fading self-management interventions to increase math fluency in general education classes. *Exceptional Children, 64,* 151–166.

McDuffie, K., Mastropieri, M., & Scruggs, T. (2009). Differential effects of peer tutoring in co-taught and non-co-taught classes: Results for content learning and student-teacher interactions. *Exceptional Children, 75,* 493–510.

McGinnis, E., & Goldstein, A. P. (2005). *Skills-streaming: Teaching prosocial skills to the elementary-school child.* Champaign, IL: Research Press.

McGrath, M. Z., Johns, B. H., & Mathur, S. R. (2004). Is history repeating itself? Services for children with disabilities endangered. *Teaching Exceptional Children, 37*(1), 70–71.

McGuire, J. M., Scott, S. S., & Shaw, S. F. (2006). Universal design and its applications in educational environments. *Remedial and Special Education, 27,* 166–175.

McIntosh, K., Filter, K., Bennett, J., Ryan, C., & Sugai, G. (2010). Principles of sustainable prevention: Designing scale-up of school-wide positive behavior support to promote durable systems. *Psychology in the Schools, 47,* 5–21.

McLaughlin, M. J. (2002). Examining special and general education collaborative practices in exemplary schools. *Journal of Educational and Psychological Consultation, 13,* 279–284.

McLaughlin, M. J. (2010). Evolving interpretations of educational equity and students with disabilities. *Exceptional Children, 76,* 265–278.

McLeskey, J., & Waldron, N. L. (2007a). Comprehensive school reform and inclusive schools. *Theory into Practice, 45,* 269–278.

McLeskey, J., & Waldron, N. L. (2007b). Making differences ordinary in inclusive classrooms. *Intervention in School and Clinic, 42,* 162–168.

McLeskey, J., Waldron, N. L., So, T. H., Swanson, K., & Loveland, T. (2001). Perspectives of teachers toward inclusive school programs. *Teacher Education and Special Education, 24,* 108–115.

McMaster, K. L., Fuchs, D., & Fuchs, L. S. (2006). Research on peer-assisted learning strategies: The promise and limitations of peer-mediated instruction. *Reading and Writing Quarterly, 22,* 5–25.

McMaster, K. N., & Fuchs, D. (2002). Effects of cooperative learning on the academic achievement of students with learning disabilities: An update of Tateyama-Sniezek's review. *Learning Disabilities: Research and Practice, 17,* 107–117.

McNaughton, D., & Vostal, B. (2010). Using active listening to improve collaboration with parents: The LAFF don't CRY strategy. *Intervention in School and Clinic, 45,* 251–256.

McNeil, J. (2001). *Disability.* Retrieved October 24, 2007, from www.census.gov/population/www/pop-profile/disabil.html

Meadan, H., & Monda-Amaya, L. (2008). Collaboration to promote social competence for students with mild disabilities in the general classroom: A structure for providing social support. *Intervention in School and Clinic, 43,* 158–167.

Meichenbaum, D. (1977). *Cognitive behavior modification: An integrative approach.* New York: Plenum.

Mellard, D. F., & McKnight, M. A. (2008). *RTI implementation tool: Best practices for grades K–5.* Lawrence, KS: National Center on Response to Intervention.

Mellard, D., McKnight, M., & Woods, K. (2009). Response to intervention screening and progress-monitoring practices in 41 local schools. *Learning Disabilities Research & Practice, 24,* 186–195.

Mellard, D., & Prewett, S. (2010). *RTI in middle schools.* [Electronic version] Lawrence, Kansas and Nashville, Tennessee: National Center on Response to Intervention. Retrieved June 30, 2010, from http://www.rti4success.org/images/stories/webinar/RTI_in_Middle_Schools_TranscriptFINAL.pdf

Meo, B. (2008). Curriculum planning for all learners: Applying universal design for learning (UDL) to a high school reading comprehension program. *Preventing School Failure, 52*(2), 21–30.

Mercer, C. D., Mercer, A. R., & Pullen, P. C. (2011). *Teaching students with learning problems* (8th ed.). Upper Saddle River, NJ: Pearson.

Mercer, C. D., & Pullen, P. C. (2005). *Students with learning disabilities* (6th ed.). Upper Saddle River, NJ: Pearson.

Mercer, C. D., & Pullen, P. C. (2009). *Students with learning disabilities* (7th ed.). Upper Saddle River, NJ: Merrill/Pearson.

Mercier Smith, J., Fien, H., Basaraba, D., & Travers, P. (2009). Planning, evaluating and improving tiers of support in beginning reading. *Teaching Exceptional Children, 41*(5), 16–22.

Miles-Bonart, S. (2002, March). A look at variables affecting parent satisfaction with IEP meetings. In *No Child Left Behind: The vital role of rural schools.* Annual national conference proceedings of the American Council on Rural Special Education (ACRES) (22nd, Reno, Nevada, March 7–9, 2002) (pp. 180–187). Logan, UT: ACRES. (ERIC Document Reproduction Service No. ED463119)

Miller, G., & Hall, T. (2005). *Classroom management.* Wakefield, MA: National Center on Accessing the General Curriculum. Retrieved from www.cast.org/publications/ncac/ncac_classroom.html

Miller, M. C., Cooke, N. L., Test, D. W., & White, R. (2003). Effects of friendship circles on the social interactions of elementary age students with mild disabilities [Electronic version]. *Journal of Behavioral Education, 12,* 167–184.

Miller, R. V. (1956). Social status of socioempathic differences. *Exceptional Children, 23,* 114–119.

Miller, S. P., & Hudson, P. J. (2007). Using evidence-based practices to build mathematics competence related to conceptual, procedural, and declarative knowledge. *Learning Disabilities Research & Practice, 22*(1), 47–57.

Miller, S. P. (1996), Perspectives on mathematics instruction. In D. D. Deshler, E. S. Ellis, & B. K. Lenz (Eds.), *Teaching adolescents with learning disabilities: Strategies and methods* (2nd ed., pp. 313–367). Denver, CO: Love.

Milsom, A., & Hartley, M. (2005). Assisting students with learning disabilities transitioning to college: What school counselors should know. *Professional School Counseling, 8,* 436–441.

Minskoff, E., & Allsopp, D. (2003). *Academic success strategies for adolescents with learning disabilities and ADHD.* Baltimore, MD: Paul H. Brookes.

Miranda, A., & Guerrero, M. (1986). The funny farola. In *Adventures* (pp. 42–53). Boston: Houghton Mifflin.

Miranda, A., Jarque, S., & Tárraga, R. (2006). Interventions in school settings for students with ADHD. *Exceptionality, 14*(1), 35–52.

Mitcham, M., Portman, T., & Dean, A. (2009). Role of school counselors in creating equitable educational opportunities for students with disabilities in urban settings. *Urban Education, 44,* 465–482.

Mitchell, S., Foulger, T., & Wetzel, K. (2009). Ten tips for involving families through Internet-based communication. *Young Children, 64*(5), 46–49.

Mittan, R. J. (2005). S.E.E. program parents manual: How to raise a child with epilepsy. Part two: Coping with stigma. *Exceptional Parent, 35*(11), 58–66.

Mmari, K., Blum, R., & Teufel-Shone, N. (2010). What increases risk and protection for delinquent behaviors among American Indian youth?: Findings from three tribal communities. *Youth & Society, 41*, 382–413.

Moats, L. (2007). Whole-language high-jinks: How to tell when "scientifically-based reading instruction" isn't. Thomas B. Fordham Institute. Retrieved from www.fordhaminstitute.org/doc/Moats2007.pdf

Moats, L. C. (2007). *Language essentials for teaching of reading and spelling. Module 6: Digging for meaning: Teaching text comprehension.* Boston, MA: Sopris West.

Mock, D. R., & Kauffman, J. M. (2002). Preparing teachers for full inclusion: Is it possible? [Electronic version]. *Teacher Educator, 37*, 202–215.

Montague, M., Warger, C. L., & Morgan, H. (2000). Solve It! Strategy instruction to improve mathematical problem solving. *Learning Disabilities Research and Practice, 15*, 110–116.

Montgomery, K. (2001). *Authentic assessment: A guide for elementary teachers.* New York: Longman.

Monuteaux, M., Mick, E., Faraone, S., & Biederman, J. (2010). The influence of sex on the course and psychiatric correlates of ADHD from childhood to adolescence: A longitudinal study. *Journal of Child Psychology and Psychiatry, 51*, 233–241.

Moody, J. D., & Gifford, V. D. (1990). *The effect of grouping by formal reasoning ability, formal reasoning ability levels, group size, and gender on achievement in laboratory chemistry.* (ERIC Document Reproduction Service No. ED326443)

Moore, J. L., Ford, D. Y., & Milner, H. R. (2005). Underachievement among gifted students of color: Implications for educators. *Theory into Practice, 44*, 167–177.

Moreno, R., & Duran, R. (2004). Do multiple representations need explanations? The role of verbal guidance and individual differences in multimedia mathematics learning. *Journal of Educational Psychology, 96*(3), 492–503.

Morgan, S. A. (2006). Introduction: Four classwide peer tutoring programs—research, recommendations for implementation, and future directions. *Reading and Writing Quarterly, 22,* 1–4.

Morgan, P. L., Farkas, G., Tufis, P. A., & Sperling, R. A. (2008). Are reading and behavior problems risk factors for each other? *Journal of Learning Disabilities, 41*(5), 417–436.

Morgan, P. L., Fuchs, D., Compton, D. L., Cordray, D. S., & Fuchs, L. S. (2008). Does early reading failure decrease children's reading motivation? *Journal of Learning Disabilities, 41* (5), 387–404.

Mortweet, S. L., Utley, C. A., Walker, D., Dawson, H. L., Delquadri, J. C., Reddy, S. S., et al. (1999). Classwide peer tutoring: Teaching students with mild mental retardation in inclusive classrooms. *Exceptional Children, 65*, 524–536.

Mosteller, F., Light, R., & Sachs, J. (1996). Sustained inquiry in education: Lessons from skill grouping and class size. *Harvard Educational Review, 66*, 797–828.

Mruzek, D. W., Cohen, C., & Smith, T. (2007). Contingency contracting with students with autism spectrum disorders in a public school setting. *Journal of Developmental and Physical Disabilities, 19*(2), 103–114.

MTA Cooperative Group. (2004). National Institute of Mental Health multimodal treatment study of ADHD follow-up: 24-month outcomes of treatment strategies for attention-deficit/hyperactivity disorder [Electronic version]. *Pediatrics, 113,* 754–761.

Mueller, T. (2009). Alternative dispute resolution: A new agenda for special education policy. *Journal of Disability Policy Studies, 20*(1), 4–13.

Mulloy, A., Lang, R., O'Reilly, M., Sigafoos, J., Lancioni, G., & Rispoli, M. (2010). Gluten-free and casein-free diets in the treatment of autism spectrum disorders: A systematic review. *Research in Autism Spectrum Disorders, 4*, 328–339.

Munk, D. (2009). Grading students with disabilities: FAQs. *CEC Today.* Retrieved from: http://www.cec.sped.org/AM/Template.cfm?Section=Home&CONTENTID=12679&TEMPLATE=/CM/ContentDisplay.cfm

Munk, D. D. (2003). *Solving the grading puzzle for students with disabilities.* Whitefish Bay, WI: Knowledge by Design.

Munk, D. D. (2007). Equitable, effective, and meaningful grading practices for students with disabilities/exceptionalities. Retrieved September 14, 2007, from http://icdd.idaho.gov/pdf/Parent%20League/GradingWebinarMar07Handout.pdf

Munk, D. D., & Bursuck, W. D. (2001). Personalized grading plans: A systematic approach to making the grades of included students more accurate and meaningful. In L. Denti & P. Tefft-Cousin (Eds.), *Looking at learning disabilities in new ways: Connections to classroom practice* (pp. 111–127). Denver, CO: Love.

Munk, D. D., & Bursuck, W. D. (2003). Grading students with disabilities. *Educational Leadership, 61*(2), 38–43.

Munk, D. D., & Bursuck, W. D. (2005). *Personalized grading plans for students with disabilities.* [Manuscript in preparation.]

Munk, D. D., Bursuck, W. D., Epstein, M. H., Jayanthi, M., Nelson, J., & Polloway, E. A. (2001). Homework communication problems: Perspectives of special and general education parents. *Reading and Writing Quarterly, 17*(3), 189–203.

Munk, J., Gibb, G., & Caldarella, P. (2010). Collaborative preteaching of students at risk for academic failure. *Intervention in School and Clinic, 45*, 177–185.

Munoz, M. A., Dossett, D., & Judy-Gullans, K. (2003). *Educating students placed at risk: Evaluating the impact of Success for All in urban settings.* (ERIC Document Reproduction Service No. ED480178)

Murphy, S., & Korinek, L. (2009). It's in the cards: A classwide management system to promote student success. *Intervention in School and Clinic, 44*, 300–306.

Murray, C. (2004). Clarifying collaborative roles in urban high schools: General educators' perspectives. *Teaching Exceptional Children, 36*(5), 44–51.

Murray, D., Ruble, L., & Willis, H. (2009). Parent and teacher report of social skills in children with autism spectrum disorders. *Language, Speech, and Hearing Services in Schools, 40*, 109–115.

Myles, B. S. (2005). *Children and youth with Asperger syndrome: Strategies for success in inclusive settings.* Thousand Oaks, CA: Corwin.

Myles, B. S., & Adreon, D. (2001). *Asperger syndrome and adolescence: Practical solutions for school success.* Shawnee Mission, KS: Autism Asperger Publishing.

Myles, B. S., Ferguson, H., & Hagiwara, T. (2007). Using a personal digital assistant to improve the recording of homework assignments by an adolescent with Asperger syndrome. *Focus on Autism and Other Developmental Disabilities, 22*, 96–99.

Myles, B. S., & Southwick, J. (1999). *Asperger syndrome and difficult moments: Practical solutions for tantrums, rage, and meltdowns.* Lawrence, KS: Autism Asperger Publishing.

Nabors, L., Little, S., Akin-Little, A., & Iobst, E. (2008). Teacher knowledge of and confidence in meeting the needs of children with chronic medical conditions: Pediatric psychology's contribution to education. *Psychology in Schools, 45*, 217–226.

Nansel, T., Overpeck, M., Pilla, R., Ruan, W., Simons-Morton, B., & Scheidt, P. (2001). Bullying behaviors among US youth: Prevalence and association with psychosocial adjustment. *Journal of the American Medical Association, 285*, 2094–2100.

Nash, J. M., & Bonesteel, A. (2002, May 6). The geek syndrome. *Time, 159* (18), 50–51.

National Association of School Psychologists. (2002). *Position statement on inclusive programs for students with disabilities.* Retrieved September 5, 2004, from www.nasponline.org/information/pospaper_ipsd.html

National Association for Gifted Children. (2008). *Frequently asked questions.* Retrieved June 23, 2010 from http://www.nagc.org/index2.aspx?id=548.

National Cancer Institute. (2009). A snapshot of pediatric cancer. Bethesda, MD: Author. Retrieved June 16, 2010 from http://www.cancer.gov/aboutnci/servingpeople/snapshots/pediatric.pdf

National Center for Children in Poverty. (2006, September). *Basic facts about low-income children: birth to age 18.* New York: Author. Retrieved August 3, 2007, from www.nccp.org/publications/pdf/text_678.pdf

National Center for Children in Poverty. (2010). *Basic facts about low-income children: Children under age 18.* Retrieved June 25, 2010 from http://www.nccp.org/publications/pub_892.html.

National Center for Education Statistics. (2004). *Crime and safety in America's public schools: Selected findings from the school survey on crime and safety*. Retrieved December 30, 2004, the school survey on crime and safety website, from http://nces.ed.gov/surveys/ssocs

National Center for Education Statistics. (2010). *Indicators of school crime and safety: 2009*. Washington, DC: U.S. Department of Education. Retrieved July 10, 2010 from http://nces.ed.gov/programs/crimeindicators/crimeindicators2009/index.asp

National Center for Education Statistics. (2007, June). *Dropout rates in the United States, 2005*. Retrieved October 18, 2007, from http://nces.ed.gov/Pubsearch/pubsinfo.asp?pubid=2007059

National Center for Education Statistics (NCES). (2007, June). *Dropout rates in the United States: 2005*. Washington, D.C.: Author. Retrieved August 3, 2007, from http://nces.ed.gov/pubSearch/pubsinfo.asp?pubid =2007059

National Center on Secondary Education and Transition. (2002). *Age of majority: Preparing your child for making good choices*. Minneapolis, MN: Author. (ERIC Document Reproduction Service No. ED467248)

National Clearinghouse for Professions in Special Education. (2003). *School counselor: Making a difference in the lives of students with special needs* [Brochure]. Arlington, VA: Author. Retrieved April 19, 2003, from www.special-ed-careers.org/pdf/schcoun.pdf

National Coalition for the Homeless. (2006, June). How many people experience homelessness? [NCH fact sheet #2]. Washington, DC: Author. Retrieved August 1, 2007, from www.nationalhomeless.org/publications/facts/How_Many.pdf

National Council of Teachers of Mathematics. (2000). *Principles and standards for school mathematics*. Reston, VA: Author.

National Council on Disability. (2006, November). *National disability policy: A progress report*. Washington, DC: Author.

National Center for Education Statistics. (2010, June). *The condition of education 2010—Section 1: Participation in education*. Retrieved June 23, 2010 from http://nces.ed.gov/pubsearch/pubsinfo.asp?pubid =2010028.

National Coalition for the Homeless. (2009, July). Who is homeless? Retrieved June 26, 2010 from http://www.nationalhomeless.org/factsheets/who.html.

National Dissemination Center for Children with Disabilities. (2006). *Traumatic brain injury fact sheet*. Retrieved July 9, 2007, from www.nichcy.org/pubs/factshe/fs18txt.htm

National Dissemination Center for Children with Disabilities. (2010). Traumatic brain injury. Retrieved June 16, 2010 from http://www.nichcy.org/Disabilities/Specific/Pages/TBI.aspx.

National Dissemination Center for Children with Disabilities. (n.d.). *All about the IEP—Contents of the IEP—Related services*. Retrieved May 3, 2010 from http://www.nichcy.org/educatechildren/iep/pages/related services.aspx

National Early Literacy Panel. (2008). *Developing early literacy: Report of the National Early Literacy Panel*. Washington, DC: National Institute for Literacy.

National High School Center, National Center on Response to Intervention, and Center on Instruction. (2010). *Tiered interventions in high schools: Using preliminary "lessons learned" to guide ongoing discussion*. Washington, DC: American Institutes for Research.

National Institute of Mental Health. (2003). *Attention deficit hyperactivity disorder*. Bethesda, MD: Author. Retrieved December 3, 2004, from www.nimh.nih.gov/publicat/adhd.cfm

National Institute of Mental Health (NIMH). (2006). *Attention deficit hyperactivity disorder: A detailed booklet that describes the symptoms, causes, and treatments, with information on getting help and coping*. Bethesda, MD: Author. Retrieved August 2, 2007, from www.nimh.nih.gov/publicat/adhd.cfm#intro

National Institute of Mental Health (NIMH). (2007). *Autism spectrum disorders: Pervasive developmental disorders*. Bethseda, MD: Author. Retrieved July 6, 2007, from www.eric.ed.gov/ERICDocs/data/ericdocs2sql/content_storage_01/0000019b/80/27/fe/bb.pdf

National Institute of Neurological Disorders and Stroke. (2007). *NINDS muscular dystrophy information page*. Retrieved July 8, 2007, from www.ninds.nih.gov/disorders/md/md.htm

National Institute on Deafness and Other Communication Disorders. (2006). *What are communication considerations for parents of deaf and hard-of-hearing children?* [NIDCD fact sheet]. Bethesda, MD: Author. Retrieved July 10, 2007, from www.eric.ed.gov/ERICDocs/data/ericdocs2sql/content_storage_01/0000019b/80/28/0c/98.pdf

National Institute on Drug Abuse. (2006, December). *NIDA infofacts: High school and youth trends*. Washington, DC: Department of Health and Human Services. Retrieved July 5, 2007, from www.nida.nih.gov/infofacts/HSYouthtrends.html

National Institutes of Health. (2010). *What are the signs and symptoms of sickle cell anemia?* Washington, DC: National Heart, Lung, and Blood Institute. Retrieved June 16, 2010 from http://www.nhlbi.nih.gov/health/dci/Diseases/Sca/SCA_SignsAndSymptoms.html.

National Institutes of Mental Health. (2009a, January). *How is ADHD diagnosed?* Retrieved June 23, 2010 from http://www.nimh.nih.gov/health/publications/attention-deficit-hyperactivity-disorder/how-is-adhd-diagnosed.shtml.

National Institutes of Mental Health. (2009b, June). *Attention deficit hyperactivity disorder (ADHD)*. Retrieved June 23, 2010 from http://www.nimh.nih.gov/health/publications/attention-deficit-hyperactivity-disorder/what-causes-adhd.shtml.

National Mathematics Advisory Panel (2008). Foundations for Success: The final report of the national mathematics advisory panel. Washington, DC: US Department of Education.

National Organization on Fetal Alcohol Syndrome. (2004). *What are the statistics and facts about FAS and FASD?* Washington, DC: Author. Retrieved December 4, 2004, from www.nofas.org/faqs.aspx?ID=1

National Reading Panel (2000). *Teaching children to read: An evidence-based assessment of the scientific research literature on reading and its implications for reading instruction*. Washington, DC: National Institute of Child Health and Human Development.

National Resource Center on ADHD. (2004). *Managing medication for children and adolescents with AD/HD*. Retrieved October 18, 2007, from www.help4adhd.org/en/treatment/medical/WWK3

National Spinal Cord Injury Association. (2004). *Factsheet on spinal cord injury*. Bethesda, MD: Author. Retrieved March 9, 2004, from www.spinalcord.org/html/factsheets/spinstat.php

National Spinal Cord Injury Statistical Center. (2009). *Spinal cord injury: Facts and figures at a glance*. Birmingham, AL: Author. Retrieved September 3, 2009 from http://www.spinalcord.uab.edu/show.asp?durki=119513.

Nazzal, A. (2002). Peer tutoring and at-risk students: An exploratory study. *Action in Teacher Education, 24,* 68–80.

Neal, J., Bigby, L., & Nicholson, R. (2004). Occupational therapy, physical therapy, and orientation and mobility services in public schools. *Intervention in School and Clinic, 39,* 218–222.

Neal, L. V. I., McCray, A. D., Webb-Johnson, G., & Bridgest, S. T. (2003). The effects of African American movement styles on teachers' perceptions and reactions. *Journal of Special Education, 37,* 49–57.

Neile, M. H., & Test, D. W. (2010). Effects of the "I can use effort" strategy on quality of student verbal contributions and individualized education program participation with third-and fourth-grade students with disabilities. *Remedial and Special Education, 31*(3), 184–194.

Nelson, B. (2005). Creating positive outcomes for deafblind youth and young adults: A personal futures planning transition model. *RE:view: Rehabilitation Education for Blindness and Visual Impairment, 36,* 173–177.

Nelson, J., Hurley, K., Synhorst, L., Epstein, M., Stage, S., & Buckley, J. (2009). The child outcomes of a behavior model. *Exceptional Children, 76,* 7–30.

Nelson, J. S., Epstein, M. H., Bursuck, W. D., Jayanthi, M., & Sawyer, V. (1998). The preferences of middle school students for homework adaptations made by general education teachers. *Learning Disabilities: Research and Practice, 13,* 109–117.

Nelson, L. G. L., Summers, J. A., & Turnbull, A. P. (2004). Boundaries in family-professional relationships: Implications for special education. *Remedial and Special Education, 25,* 153–166.

Neuman, R. J., Sitdhiraksa, N., Reich, W., Ji, T. H-C., Joyner, C. A., & Todd, R. D, (2005). Estimation of prevalence of DSM-IV and latent class ADHD subtypes in a population based sample of child and adolescent twins. *Twin Research and Human Genetics, 8,* 392–401.

Newcomer, L. L., & Lewis, T. J. (2004). Functional behavioral assessment: An investigation of assessment reliability and effectiveness of function-based interventions. *Journal of Emotional and Behavioral Disorders, 12,* 168–181.

Niesyn, M. (2009). Strategies for success: Evidence-based instructional practices for students with emotional and behavioral disorders. *Preventing School Failure, 53,* 227–233.

Nieto, S. M. (2002/2003). Profoundly multicultural questions. *Educational Leadership, 60*(4), 6–10.

Nolet, V., & McLaughlin, M. J. (2005). *Accessing the general curriculum: Including students with disabilities in standards-based reform* (2nd ed.). Thousand Oaks, CA: Corwin.

Nomi, T. (2010). The effects of within-class ability grouping on academic achievement in early elementary years. *Journal of Research on Educational Effectiveness, 3*(1), 56–92.

Núñez, R. G., González-Pienda, J. A., González-Pumariega, S., Roces, C., Alvarez, L., González, P., (2005). Subgroups of attributional profiles in students with learning difficulties and their relation to self-concept and academic goals. *Learning Disabilities Research and Practice, 20*(2), 86–97.

Nunn, G., & Jantz, P. (2009). Factors within response to intervention implementation training associated with teacher efficacy beliefs. *Education, 129,* 599–607.

Oakes, J., & Lipton, M. (2003). *Teaching to change the world.* Boston: McGraw-Hill.

Oakland, T., Black, J. L., Stanford, G., Nussbaum, N. L., & Balise, R. R. (1998). An evaluation of the dyslexia training program: A multisensory method for promoting reading in students with reading disabilities. *Journal of Learning Disabilities, 31,* 140–147.

O'Connor, E. (2010). Teacher-child relationships as dynamic systems. *Journal of School Psychology, 48,* 187–218.

O'Connor, R. (2000). Increasing the intensity of intervention in kindergarten and first grade. *Learning Disabilities: Research and Practice, 15,* 43–54.

Obiakor, F. E. (2007). Multicultural special education: Effective intervention for today's schools. *Intervention in School and Clinic, 42*(3), 148–155.

Obiakor, F. E., Utley, C. A., Smith, R., & Harris-Obiakor, P. (2002). The comprehensive support model for culturally diverse exceptional learners: Intervention in an age of change. *Intervention in School and Clinic, 38,* 14–27.

Odegard, T. N., Ring, J., Smith, S., Biggan, J., & Black, J. (2008). Differentiating the neural response to intervention in children with developmental dyslexia. *Annals of Dyslexia, 58,* 1–14.

Odom, S. L., Zercher, C., Li, S., Marquart, J. M., Sandall, S., & Brown, W. H. (2006). Social acceptance and rejection of preschool children with disabilities: A mixed-method analysis. *Journal of Educational Psychology, 98,* 807–823.

Office for Civil Rights. (2009, March). *Frequently asked questions about Section 504 and the education of children with disabilities.* Retrieved June 23, 2010 from http://ed.gov/about/offices/list/ocr/504faq.html.

Ogle, D. M. (1986). K. W. L.: A teaching model that develops active reading of expository text. *Reading Teacher, 39,* 565.

Ohtake, T. (2004). Meaningful inclusion of all students in team sports. *Teaching Exceptional Children, 37*(2), 22–27.

Okolo, C. M. (2000). Features of effective instructional software. In J. Lindsey (Ed.), *Technology and exceptional individuals* (3rd ed.). Austin, TX: PRO-ED.

Okolo, C. M., Ferretti, R. P., & MacArthur, C. A. (2007). Talking about history: Discussions in a middle school inclusive classroom. *Journal of Learning Disabilities, 40*(2), 154–165.

Olivos, E., Gallagher, R. J., & Aguilar, J. (2010). Fostering collaboration with culturally and linguistically diverse families of children with moderate to severe disabilities. *Journal of Educational and Psychological Consultation, 20,* 28–40.

Olivos, E. (2009). Collaboration with Latino families: A critical perspective of home-school interactions. *Intervention in School and Clinic, 45,* 109–115.

Olmeda, R. E., & Trent, S. C. (2003). Social skills training research with minority students with learning disabilities [Electronic version]. *Learning Disabilities, 12*(1), 23–33.

Olson, J. L., Platt, J. C., & Dieker, L. (2007). *Teaching children and adolescents with special needs* (5th ed.). Upper Saddle River, NJ: Merrill/Prentice Hall.

Olson, R. K. (2006). Genes, environment, and dyslexia: The 2005 Norman Geschwind Memorial Lecture. *Annals of Dyslexia, 56*(2), 205–238.

Oluwole, J. (2009). A principal's dilemma: Full inclusion or student's best interests? *Journal of Cases in Educational Leadership, 12*(1), 12–25.

Operation Sickle Cell. (2007). *Prevalence.* Retrieved July 8, 2007, from www.sicklecellnc.org/disease.php

Opitz, M. (2007). Back-to-school tips: Learning centers: The first week. Excerpted from Michael Opitz's book *Learning Centers: Getting Them Started, Keeping Them Going.* Retrieved from http://teacher.scholastic.com/professional/backtoschool/learning_center.htm

Orfield, G., & Lee, C. (2004). *Brown at 50: King's dream or Plessy's nightmare?* Cambridge, MA: Harvard Civil Rights Project. Retrieved December 5, 2004, from www.civilrightsproject.harvard.edu/research/reseg04/brown50.pdf

Organ, J., & Gonzalez-DeHass, A. (2004). How to infuse social skills training into literacy instruction. *Teaching Exceptional Children, 36*(6), 24–31.

Ornstein, A. C., & Lasley, T. J. II. (2004). *Strategies for effective teaching* (4th ed.). New York, NY: McGraw-Hill.

Orosco, M., & Klingner, J. (2010). One school's implementation of RTI with English language learners: "Referring into RTI". *Journal of Learning Disabilities, 43,* 269–288.

Overton, T. (2009). *Assessing learners with special needs: An applied approach* (6th ed.). Upper Saddle River, NJ: Merrill/Pearson.

Overton, T., Fielding, C., & Simeonsson, M. (2004). Decision making in determining eligibility of culturally and linguistically diverse learners: Reasons given by assessment personnel. *Journal of Learning Disabilities, 37,* 319–330.

Owens, M., & Bergman, A. (2010). Alcohol use and antisocial behavior in late adolescence: Characteristics of a sample attending a GED program. *Journal of Child & Adolescent Substance Abuse, 19,* 78–98.

Owens, R. E., Jr., Metz, D. E., & Haas, A. (2007). *Introduction to communication disorders: A lifespan perspective.* (3rd ed.). Boston: Pearson, Allyn and Bacon.

Paese, P. C. (2003). Impact of professional development schools: Preservice through induction. *Action in Teacher Education, 25,* 83–88.

Paine, S. C., Radicchi, J., Rosellini, L. C., Deutchman, L., & Darch, C. B. (1983). *Structuring your classroom for academic success.* Champaign, IL: Research Press.

Palincsar, A., & Brown, A. (1988). Teaching and practicing thinking skills to promote comprehension in the context of group problem solving. *Remedial and Special Education, 9*(1), 53–59.

Palley, E. (2006). Challenges of rights-based law: Implementing the least restrictive environment mandate. *Journal of Disability Policy Studies, 16,* 229–235.

Parette, H. P., Hourcade, J. J., & Huer, M. B. (2003). Using assistive technology focus groups with families across cultures. *Education and Training in Developmental Disabilities, 38,* 429–440.

Parker, R., Hasbrouck, J. E., & Tindal, G. (1992). The maze as a classroom-based reading measure: Construction methods, reliability, and validity. *Journal of Special Education, 26,* 195–218.

Parmar, R. S., & Signer, B. R. (2005). Sources of error in constructing and interpreting graphs: A study of fourth- and fifth-grade students with LD. *Journal of Learning Disabilities, 38*(3), 250–261.

Parsons, L. D. (2006). Using video to teach social skills to secondary students with autism. *Teaching Exceptional Children, 39*(2), 32–38.

Partin, T., Robertson, R., Maggin, D., Oliver, R., & Wehby, J. (2010). Using teacher praise and opportunities to respond to promote appropriate student behavior. *Preventing School Failure, 54,* 172–178.

Patillo, J., & Vaughn, E. (1992). *Learning centers for child-centered classrooms.* Washington, DC: National Education Association.

Patton, B., Jolivette, K., & Ramsey, M. (2006). Students with emotional and behavioral disorders can manage their own behavior. *Teaching Exceptional Children, 39*(2), 14–21.

Patton, J. R. (1994). Practical recommendations for using homework with students with disabilities. *Journal of Learning Disabilities, 27,* 570–578.

Patton, J. R., Payne, J. S., & Beirne-Smith, M. (1986). *Mental retardation* (2nd ed.). Columbus, OH: Merrill.

Paulsen, K. (2008). School-based collaboration: An introduction to the collaboration column. *Intervention in School and Clinic, 43,* 313–315.

Pavri, S., & Monda-Amaya, L. (2001). Social support in inclusive schools: Student and teacher perspectives. *Exceptional Children, 67,* 391–411.

Pavri, S. (2010). Response to intervention in the social-emotional-behavioral domain: Perspectives from urban schools. *Teaching Exceptional Children Plus, 6*(3), article 4. Retrieved July 10, 2010 from http://escholarship.bc.edu/education/tecplus.

Pearson, P. D., & Fielding, L. (1991). Comprehension instruction. In R. Barr, M. L. Kamil, P. Mosenthal, & P. D. Pearson (Eds.), *Handbook of reading research* (Vol. 2, pp. 815–860). White Plains, NY: Longman.

Peck-Peterson, S. M., Derby, K. M., Berg, W. K., & Horner, R. H. (2002). Collaboration with families in the functional behavior assessment of and intervention for severe behavior problems [Electronic version]. *Education and Treatment of Children, 25,* 5–25.

Pedrotty-Bryant, D., Bryant, B. R., & Raskind, M. H. (1998). Using assistive technology to enhance the skills of students with learning disabilities. *Intervention in School and Clinic, 34,* 53–58.

Pertsch, C. F. (1936). *A comparative study of the progress of subnormal pupils in the grades and in special classes.* New York: Teacher's College, Columbia University, Bureau of Publications.

Peterson, J. S., & Ray, K. E. (2006). Bullying and the gifted: victims, perpetrators, prevalence, and effects. *Gifted Child Quarterly, 50,* 148–168.

Peterson, L. D., Young, K. R., Salzberg, C. L., West, R. P., & Hill, M. (2006). Using self-management procedures to improve classroom social skills in multiple general education settings. *Education and Treatment of Children, 29*(1), 1–21.

Petscher, E. S., & Bailey, J. S. (2006). Effects of training, prompting, and self-monitoring on staff behavior in a classroom for students with disabilities. *Journal of Applied Behavior Analysis, 39,* 215–226.

Peverly, S. T., Ramaswamy, V., Brown, C., Sumowski, J., Alidoost, M., & Garner, J. (2007). What predicts skill in lecture note taking? *Journal of Educational Psychology, 99*(1), 167–180.

Pewewardy, C., & Fitzpatrick, M. (2009). Working with American Indian students and families: Disabilities, issues, and interventions. *Intervention in School and Clinic, 45,* 91–98.

Pham, A., Carlson, J., & Kosciulek, J. (2010). Ethnic differences in parental beliefs of attention-deficit/hyperactivity disorder and treatment. *Journal of Attention Disorders, 13,* 584–591.

Piercy, M., Wilton, K., & Townsend, M. (2002). Promoting social acceptance of young children with moderate-severe intellectual disabilities using cooperative-learning techniques [Electronic version]. *American Journal on Mental Retardation, 107,* 352–360.

Pincus, A. R. H. (2005). What's a teacher to do? Navigating the worksheet curriculum. *The Reading Teacher, 59*(1), 75–79.

Pine, J., & Aschbacher, P. (2006). Students' learning of inquiry in 'inquiry' curricula. *Phi Delta Kappan, 88*(4), 308–313.

Pisha, B. (2003). Assistive technologies: Making a difference. *IDA Perspectives, 29*(4), 1, 4.

Pisha, B., & Coyne, P. (2001). Smart from the start: The promise of universal design for learning. *Remedial and Special Education, 22*(4), 197–203.

Pisha, B., & Stahl, S. (2005). The promise of new learning environments for students with disabilities. *Intervention in School and Clinic, 41*(2), 67–75.

Pittman, P., & Huefner, D. S. (2001). Will the courts go bi-bi? IDEA 1997, the courts, and deaf education. *Exceptional Children, 67,* 187–198.

Pivik, J., McComas, J., & Laflamme, M. (2002). Barriers and facilitators to inclusive education. *Exceptional Children, 69,* 97–108.

Ploessl, D., Rock, M., Schoenfeld, N., & Blanks, B. (2010). On the same page: Practical techniques to enhance co-teaching interactions. *Intervention in School and Clinic, 45,* 158–168.

Pogrund, R. L, & Fazzi, D. L. (Eds.). (2002). *Early focus: Working with young blind and visually impaired children and their families* (2nd ed.). New York: American Foundation for the Blind.

Polloway, E. A., Bursuck, W. D., Jayanthi, M., Epstein, M. H., & Nelson, J. S. (1996). Treatment acceptability: Determining appropriate interventions within inclusive classrooms. *Intervention in School and Clinic, 31,* 133–144.

Polloway, E. A., Epstein, M. H., Bursuck, W. D., Jayanthi, M., & Cumblad, C. (1994). Homework practices of general education teachers. *Journal of Learning Disabilities, 27,* 100–109.

Popp, P. A., Stronge, J. H., & Hindman, J. L. (2003). *Students on the move: Reaching and teaching highly mobile children and youth* (Urban Diversity Series). Washington, DC: National Center for Homeless Education and ERIC Clearinghouse on Urban Education. (ERIC Document Reproduction Service No. ED482661)

Poston, D., & Turnbull, A. (2004). Role of spirituality and religion in family quality of life for families of children with disabilities. *Education and Training in Developmental Disabilities, 39,* 95–108.

Poteet, J. A., Choate, J. S., & Stewart, S. C. (1993). Performance assessment and special education: Practices and prospects. *Focus on Exceptional Children, 26*(1), 1–20.

Powell-Smith, K. A., & Shinn, M. R. (2004). *Administration and scoring of Written Expression Curriculum-Based Measurement (WE-CBM) for use in general outcome measurement.* Eden Prairie, MN: EdFormation.

Praisner, C. L. (2003). Attitudes of elementary school principals toward the inclusion of students with disabilities. *Exceptional Children, 69,* 135–145.

Pressley, M. (2000). What should comprehension instruction be the instruction of? In M. Kamil, P. B. Mosenthal, P. D. Pearson, & R. Barr (Eds.), *Handbook of Reading Research* (Vol. 3). Mahwah, NJ: Erlbaum.

Pressley, M., & Hilden, K.R. (2006). Cognitive strategies: Production deficiencies and successful strategy instruction everywhere. In D. Kuhn & R. Siegler (Eds.), W. Damon & R. Lerner (Series Eds.), *Handbook of Child Psychology: Vol. 2. Cognition, perception, and language* (6th ed.). Hoboken, NJ: Wiley.

Price, K. M., & Nelson, K. L. (2011). *Planning effective instruction: Diversity responsive methods and management* (4th edition). Belmont, CA: Wadsworth.

Pugach, M. C., & Johnson, L. J. (2002). *Collaborative practitioners, collaborative schools* (2nd ed.). Denver, CO: Love.

Punch, R., Hyde, M., & Creed, P. A. (2004). Issues in the school-to-work transition of hard of hearing adolescents. *American Annals of the Deaf, 149,* 28–38.

Purcell, M. L., Turnbull, A., & Jackson, C. W. (2006). Linking early childhood inclusion and family quality of life: Current literature and future directions. *Young Exceptional Children, 9*(3), 10–19.

Quenemoen, R., Rigney, S., & Thurlow, M. (2002). *Use of alternate assessments results in reporting and accountability systems: Conditions for use based on research and practice* (Synthesis Report 43). Minneapolis: University of Minnesota, National Center on Educational Outcomes. Retrieved from http://education.umn.edu/NCEO/OnlinePubs/Synthesis43.html

Rafferty, Y., Piscitelli, V., & Boettcher, C. (2003). The impact of inclusion on language development and social competence among preschoolers with disabilities. *Exceptional Children, 69,* 467–480.

Raforth, M. A., & Foriska, T. (2006). Administrator participation in promoting effective problem-solving teams. *Remedial and Special Education, 27*(3), 130–135.

Ramirez, A. Y. (2005). Esperanza's lessons: Learning about education through the eyes of the innocent. *Multicultural Education, 13*(2), 47–51.

Ramsey, W. L., Gabriel, L. A., McGuirk, J. F., Phillips, C. R., & Watenpaugh, T. R. (1983). *General science.* New York: Holt, Rinehart, and Winston.

Raphael, T. E., Kirschner, B. W., & Englert, C. S. (1986). *Text structure instruction within process writing classrooms: A manual for instruction* (Occasional Paper No. 104). East Lansing: Michigan State University, Institute for Research on Teaching.

Rapp, W. H. (2005). Inquiry-based environments for the inclusion of students with exceptional learning needs. *Remedial and Special Education, 26*(5), 297–310.

Rappaport, J. (1982/1983). Effects of dietary substances in children. *Journal of Psychiatric Research, 17,* 187–191.

Rausch, K., & Skiba, R. (2006). *Discipline, disability, and race: Disproportionality in Indiana schools* (Education Policy Brief, vol. 4, no. 10). Bloomington, IN: Center for Evaluation and Education Policy. (ERIC Document Reproduction Service No. ED495751)

Ray, J., Pewitt Kinder, J., & George, S. (2009, September). Partnering with families of children with special needs: One parent's adivce. *Young Children.*

Rea, P. J. (2005). 20 ways to . . . Engage your administrator in your collaborative initiative. *Intervention in School and Clinic, 40*(5), 312–316.

Rea, P. J., McLaughlin, V. L., & Walther-Thomas, C. (2002). Outcomes for students with learning disabilities in inclusive and pullout programs. *Exceptional Children, 68,* 203–224.

Readence, J. E., Moore, D. W., & Rickelman, R. (2000). *Prereading activities for content-area reading and learning* (3rd ed.). Newark, DE: International Reading Association.

Redl, F. (2007). Rethinking youthful defiance [Reprint]. *Reclaiming Children and Youth: The Journal of Strength-Based Interventions, 16*(1), 33–35.

Reetz, L., & Rasmussen, T. (1988). Arithmetic mind joggers. *Academic Therapy, 24*(1), 79–82.

Reeve, J. (2006). Teachers as facilitators: What autonomy-supportive teachers do and why their students benefit. *The Elementary School Journal, 106*(3), 231–236.

Reeves, J. R. (2006). Secondary teacher attitudes toward including English-language learners in mainstream classrooms. *Journal of Educational Research, 99,* 131–142.

Regan, K. S., Mastropieri, M. A., & Scruggs, T. E. (2005). Promoting expressive writing among students with emotional and behavioral disturbance via dialogue journals. *Behavioral Disorders, 31*(1), 33–50.

Reid, D. H., & Green, C. W. (2006). Preference-based teaching: Helping students with severe disabilities enjoy learning without problem behavior. *Teaching Exceptional Children Plus, 2*(3) Article 2. Retrieved August 10, 2007 from http://escholarship.bc.edu/education/tecplus/vol2/iss3/art2

Reid, R. (1996). Research in self-monitoring with students with learning disabilities: The present, the prospects, the pitfalls. *Journal of Learning Disabilities, 29,* 317–331.

Reid, R. (1999). Attention deficit hyperactivity disorder: Effective methods for the classroom. *Focus on Exceptional Children, 32,* 1–19.

Reid, R., Trout, A. L., & Schartz, M. (2005). Self-regulation interventions for children with attention deficit/hyperactivity disorder. *Exceptional Children, 71*(4), 361–377.

Reis, S. M. (2007). No child left bored: How to challenge gifted and talented students with a continuum of high-end learning opportunities. *School Administrator, 64*(2), 22–26.

Reis, S. M., & Renzulli, J. S. (2004a). Current research on the social and emotional development of gifted and talented students: Good news and future possibilities. *Psychology in the Schools, 41*(1), 119–130.

Reis, S. M., & Renzulli, J. S. (2004b). Curriculum compacting: A systematic procedure for modifying the curriculum for above average ability students. Storrs, CT: National Research Center on the Gifted and Talented. Retrieved April 1, 2004, from www.sp.uconn.edu/~nrcgt/sem/semart08.html

Reis, S. M., & Sullivan, E. E. (2009). Characteristics of gifted learners: Consistently varied, refreshingly diverse. In F. A. Karnes & S. M. Bean (Eds.), *Methods and materials for teaching the gifted* (3rd ed.) (pp. 3–35). Waco, TX: Prufrock.

Renzulli, J. S. (2005). Applying gifted education pedagogy to total talent development for all students. *Theory Into Practice, 44*(2), 80–89.

Renzulli, J. S., & Park, S. (2002). *Giftedness and high school dropouts: Personal, family, and school-related factors* (Research Monograph Series). Storrs, CT: National Research Center on the Gifted and Talented. (ERIC Document Reproduction Service No. 480177)

Reschly, D. J. (2007). *Overview document: Teacher quality for multi-tiered interventions.* Washington, DC: National Comprehensive Center for Teacher Quality.

Reutebuch, C. (2008). Succeed with a response-to-intervention model. *Intervention in School and Clinic, 44,* 126–128

Reys, B. J., & Reys, R. E. (2006). The development and publication of elementary textbooks: Let the buyer beware! *Phi Delta Kappan, 87*(5), 377–383.

Reyes, M. L., & Molner, L. A. (1991). Instructional strategies for second-language learners in the content areas. *Journal of Reading, 35,* 96–103.

Richards, H. V., Brown, A. F., & Forde, T. B. (2007). Addressing diversity in schools: Culturally responsive pedagogy. *Teaching Exceptional Children, 39*(3), 64–68.

Riggs, C. G. (2004). To teachers: What paraeducators want you to know. *Teaching Exceptional Children, 36*(5), 8–13.

Riley-Tillman, T. C., Chafouleas, S. M., & Briesch, A. M. (2007). A school practitioner's guide to using daily behavior report cards to monitor student behavior. *Psychology in the Schools, 44*(1), 77–89.

Rimm-Kaufman, S. E., & Chiu, Y. I. (2007). Promoting social and academic competence in the classroom: An intervention study examining the contribution of the responsive classroom approach. *Psychology in the Schools, 44*(4), 397–413.

Rimm-Kaufman, S. E., La Paro, K. M., Downer, J. T., & Pianta, R. C. (2005). The contribution of classroom setting and quality of instruction to children's behavior in kindergarten classrooms. *The Elementary School Journal, 105*(4), 377–394.

Roach, V., & Salisbury, C. (2006). Promoting systemic, statewide inclusion from the bottom up. *Theory into Practice, 45,* 279–286.

Robinson, B. L., & Lieberman, L. J. (2004). Effects of visual impairment, gender, and age on self-determination. *Journal of Visual Impairment and Blindness, 98,* 315–366.

Robinson, D. H., Katayama, A. D., DuBois, N. F., & DeVaney, T. (1998). Interactive effects of graphic organizers and delayed review in concept acquisition. *Journal of Experimental Education, 67,* 17–31.

Roblyer, M. D., Edwards, J., & Havriluk, M. A. (2004). *2004 Update: Integrating education technology into teaching* (3rd ed.). Upper Saddle River, NJ: Merrill/Prentice-Hall.

Roditi, B. N., Steinberg, J. L., Bidale, K. R., Taber, S. E., Caron, K. B., & Kniffin, L. (2005). *Strategies for success: Classroom teaching techniques for students with learning differences.* Austin, TX: Pro-Ed.

Roe, B., Smith, S. H., & Burns, P. C. (2005). *Teaching reading in today's elementary schools* (10th ed.). Boston: Houghton Mifflin.

Roeber, E. D. (2002, November). *Appropriate inclusion of students with disabilities in state accountability systems.* Retrieved August 3, 2004, from Education Commission of the States website, www.ecs.org/clearinghouse/40/11/4011.htm

Rogers-Adkinson, D. L., Ochoa, T. A., & Delgado, B. (2003). Developing cross-cultural competence: Serving families of children with significant developmental needs [Electronic version]. *Focus on Autism and Other Developmental Disabilities, 19,* 4–8.

Rojas, N. L., & Chan, E. (2005). Old and new controversies in the alternative treatment of attention-deficit hyperactivity disorder. *Mental Retardation and Developmental Disabilities Research Reviews, 11*(2), 116–130.

Rose, D. (2000). Universal design for learning. *Journal of Special Education Technology, 15*(1), 67–70.

Rose, L. C., & Gallup, A. M. (2006). The 38th annual Phi Delta Kappa/Gallup Poll of the public's attitudes. *Phi Delta Kappan, 88,* 41–53.

Rosenshine, B. (1997). Advances in research on instruction. In E. J. Lloyd, E. J. Kameanui, & D. Chard (Eds.), *Issues in educating students with disabilities* (pp. 197–221). Mahwah, NJ: Lawrence Erlbaum.

Rosenshine, B., & Meister, C. (1992). The use of scaffolds for teaching higher-level cognitive strategies. *Educational Leadership, 49,* 26–33.

Rosenshine, B., & Stevens, R. (1986). Teaching functions. In M. C. Wittrock (Ed.)., *Handbook of research on teaching* (pp. 376–391). New York: Macmillan.

Ross, R., & Kurtz, R. (1993). Making manipulatives work: A strategy for success. *Arithmetic Teacher, 40*(5), 254–257.

Rowland, A. S., Umbach, D. M., Stallone, L., Naftel, A. J., Bohlig, E. M., & Sandler, D. P. (2002). Prevalence of medication treatment for attention deficit-hyperactivity disorder among elementary school children in Johnston County, North Carolina [Electronic version]. *American Journal of Public Health, 92,* 231–234.

Rubin, R. (2005). A blueprint for a strengths-based level system in schools. *Reclaiming Children and Youth: The Journal of Strength-Based Interventions, 14,* 143–145.

Rubinson, F. (2002). Lessons learned from implementing problem-solving teams in urban high schools. *Journal of Educational and Psychological Consultation, 13,* 185–217.

Rudd, F. (2002). *Grasping the promise of inclusion.* (ERIC Document Reproduction Service No. ED471855)

Ruddell, R. B. (2006). *Teaching children to read and write: Becoming an effective literacy teacher* (4th ed.). Boston: Allyn and Bacon.

Rueda, R., & Genzuk, M. (2007). Sociocultural scaffolding as a means toward academic self-regulation: Paraeducators as cultural brokers. *Focus on Exceptional Children, 40*(3), 1–7.

Rueda, R., Klingner, J. K., Velasco, A., & Sager, N. (2008). Reducing the disproportionate representation of culturally and linguistically diverse students in special education. In T. C. Jiménez and V. L. Graf (Eds.), *Education for ALL.* San Francisco: Jossey-Bass.

Ryan, A. L., Halsey, H. N., & Matthews, W. J. (2003). Using functional assessment to promote desirable student behavior in schools. *Teaching Exceptional Children, 35*(5), 8–15.

Ryan, J., Katsiyannis, A., Peterson, R., & Chmelar, R. (2007). IDEA 2004 and disciplining students with disabilities. *NASSP Bulletin, 91,* 130–140.

Ryan, J., Peterson, R., Tetreault, G., & Hagen, E. (2007). Reducing seclusion timeout and restraint procedures with at-risk youth. *Journal of At-Risk Issues, 13*(1), 7–12.

Ryan, J. B., Reid, R., & Epstein, M. H. (2004). Peer-mediated intervention studies on academic achievement for students with EBD: A review. *Remedial and Special Education, 25,* 330–341.

Ryan, J. B., Sanders, S., Katsiyannis, A., and Yell, M. L. (2007). Using time-out effectively in the classroom. *Teaching Exceptional Children, 39*(4), 60–67.

Ryndak, D. L., & Alper, S. (2003). *Curriculum and instruction for students with significant disabilities in inclusive settings* (2nd ed.). Boston: Allyn and Bacon.

Ryndak, D., Ward, T., Alper, S., Storch, J. F., & Montgomery, J. W. (2010). Long-term outcomes of services in inclusive and self-contained settings for siblings with comparable significant disabilities. *Education and Training in Autism and Developmental Disabilities, 45*, 38–53.

Sabatino, C. (2009). School social work consultation models and response to intervention: A perfect match. *Children & Schools, 31*, 197–206.

Sabornie, E. J., & deBettencourt, L. U. (2009). *Teaching students with mild and high-incidence disabilities at the secondary level* (3rd ed.). Upper Saddle River, NJ: Merrill/Pearson.

Sabornie, E. J., Evans, C., & Cullinan, D. (2006). Comparing characteristics of high-incidence disability groups. *Remedial and Special Education, 27*(2), 95–104.

Sáenz, L. M., Fuchs, L. S., & Fuchs, D. (2005). Peer-assisted learning strategies for English language learners with learning disabilities. *Exceptional Children, 71*, 231–247.

Safran, S. P., & Oswald, K. (2003). Positive behavior supports: Can schools reshape disciplinary practices? *Exceptional Children, 69*, 361–373.

Sale, P., & Carey, D. M. (1995). The sociometric status of students with disabilities in a full-inclusion school. *Exceptional Children, 62*, 6–19.

Salend, S. J. (2005). Report card models that support communication and differentiation of instruction. *TEACHING Exceptional Children, 37*(4), 28–34.

Salend, S. J. (2006). Explaining your inclusion program to families. *Teaching Exceptional Children, 38*(4), 6–11.

Salend, S. J., & Duhaney, L. M. G., (2002). Grading students in inclusive settings. *Teaching Exceptional Children, 34*(3), 8–15.

Salend, S. J., & Duhaney, L. M. G. (2005). Understanding and addressing the disproportionate representation of students of color in special education. *Intervention in School and Clinic, 40*, 213–221.

Salend, S. J., & Rohena, E. (2003). Students with attention deficit disorders: An overview. *Intervention in School and Clinic, 38*(5), 259–266.

Salend, S. J., & Taylor, L. S. (2002). Cultural perspectives: Missing pieces in the functional assessment process. *Intervention in School and Clinic, 38*, 104–112.

Salend, S. J., Duhaney, D., Anderson, D. J., & Gottschalk, C. (2004). Using the internet to improve homework communication and completion. *Teaching Exceptional Children, 36*(3), 64–74.

Salisbury, C. L., & McGregor, G. (2002). The administrative climate and context of inclusive elementary schools. *Exceptional Children, 68*, 259–274.

Salvia, J., Ysseldyke, J., & Bolt, S. (2010). *Assessment in special and inclusive education* (11th ed.). Boston, MA: Houghton-Mifflin.

Samuels, C. A. (2007, June). Team teaching key to turnaround: Classroom partnerships on behavior, instruction helped produce gains. *Education Week, 26*(42), 34–37. Retrieved July 2, 2007, from www.edweek.org/ew/articles/2007/06/20/42speeds1.h26.html

Sánchez, S. Y. (1999). Learning from the stories of culturally and linguistically diverse families and communities. *Remedial and Special Education, 20*, 351–359.

Santangelo, T. (2009). Collaborative problem solving effectively implemented, but not sustained: A case for aligning the sun, the moon, and the stars. *Exceptional Children, 75*, 185–209.

Saunders, W. M., Foorman, B. R., & Carlson, C. D. (2006). Is a separate block of time for oral English language development in programs for English language learners needed? *The Elementary School Journal, 107*(2), 181–198.

Sayeski, K. (2009). Defining special educators' tools: The building blocks of effective collaboration. *Intervention in School and Clinic, 45*, 38–44.

Scanlon, D., & Mellard, D. F. (2002). Academic and participation profiles of school-age dropouts with and without disabilities. *Exceptional Children, 68*, 239–258.

Scattone, D., Tingstrom, D. H., & Wilczynski, S. M. (2006). Increasing appropriate social interactions of children with autism spectrum disorders using social stories. *Focus on Autism and Other Developmental Disabilities, 21*, 211–222.

Scheerenberger, R. C. (1983). *A history of mental retardation.* Baltimore, MD: Paul H. Brookes.

Schifini, A. (1994). Language, literacy, and content instruction: Strategies for teachers. In K. Spangenberg-Unbschat & R. Pritchard (Eds.), *Kids come in all languages: Reading instruction for ESL students* (pp. 158–179). Newark, DE: International Reading Association.

Schmitz, M. F., & Velez, M. (2003). Latino cultural differences in maternal assessments of attention deficit/hyperactivity symptoms in children [Electronic version]. *Hispanic Journal of Behavior Sciences, 25*(1), 110–122.

Schoen, S. F., & Nolen, J. (2004). Action research: Decreasing acting-out behavior and increasing learning. *Teaching Exceptional Children, 37*(1), 26–31.

Schuler, P. (2002). Gifted kids at risk: Who's listening? New York: Advocacy for Gifted and Talented Education in New York. Retrieved March 3, 2004, from http://washougalhicap.virtualave.net/gifted.htm

Schulte, A. C., & Osborne, S. S. (2003). When assumptive worlds collide: A review of definitions of collaboration in consultation. *Journal of Educational and Psychological Consultation, 14*(2), 109–138.

Schumaker, J. B., Deshler, D. D., & Denton, P. (1984). *The learning strategies curriculum: The paraphrasing strategy.* Lawrence: University of Kansas.

Schunk, D. (1989). Self-efficacy and cognitive achievement: Implications for students with learning disabilities. *Journal of Learning Disabilities, 22*, 14–22.

Schwarz, P. A. (2007). Special education: A service, not a sentence. *Educational Leadership, 64*(5), 39–42.

Scott, P. B., & Raborn, D. T. (1996). Realizing the gifts of diversity among students with learning disabilities. *LD Forum, 21*(2), 10–18.

Scott, T. M., & Caron, D. B. (2005). Conceptualizing functional behavior assessment as prevention practice within positive behavior support systems. *Preventing School Failure, 50*(1), 13–20.

Scott, T. M., McIntyre, J., Liaupsin, C., Nelson, C. M., & Conroy, M. (2004). An examination of functional behavior assessment in public school settings: Collaborative teams, experts, and methodology. *Behavioral Disorders, 29*, 384–395.

Scott, T. M., Nelson, C. M., & Liaupsin, C. J. (2001). Effective instruction: The forgotten component in preventing school violence. *Education and Treatment of Children, 24*, 309–322.

Scott, V. G. (2006). Incorporating service learning into your special education classroom. *Intervention in School and Clinic, 42*(1), 25–29.

Scott, T., Anderson, C., & Spaulding, S. (2008). Strategies for developing and carrying out functional assessment and behavior intervention planning. *Preventing School Failure, 52*(3), 39–49.

Scruggs, T., & Mastropieri. M. (1988). Are learning disabled students "test-wise"? A review of recent research. *Learning Disabilities Focus, 3*(2): 87–97.

Scruggs, T., Mastropieri, M., & McDuffie, K. (2007). Co-teaching in inclusive classrooms: A metasynthesis of qualitative research. *Exceptional Children, 73*, 392–416.

Sebag, R. (2010). Behavior management through self-advocacy: A strategy for secondary students with learning disabilities. *Teaching Exceptional Children, 42*(6), 22–29.

Seeley, K. I. (2004). Gifted and talented students at risk. *Focus on Exceptional Children, 37*(4), 1–8.

Seethaler, P. M., Powell, S. R., & Fuchs, L. S. (2010). *Help students solve word problems with "Pirate Math."* [Electronic version]. Reston, Virginia: Council for Exceptional Children CEC Today. Retrieved July 4, 2010 from http://www.cec.sped.org/AM/Printer1&TEMPLATE=/...

Seferian, R. (1999). *Design and implementation of a social-skills program for middle school students with learning and behavioral disabilities.* (ERIC Document Reproduction Service No. ED436863)

Selekman, J. (Ed.). (2006). *School nursing: A comprehensive text.* Philadelphia: F. A. Davis.

Sever, K., & Bowgren, L. (2007). Shaping the workday: District professional learning into the classroom. *Journal of Staff Development, 28*(2), 20–23.

Severson, H. H., Walker, H. M., & Hope-Doolittle, J. (2007). Proactive, early screening to detect behaviorally at-risk students: Issues, approaches, emerging innovations, and professional practices. *Journal of School Psychology, 45*, 193–223.

Shapiro, D. R., & Sayers, L. K. (2003). Who does what on the interdisciplinary team regarding physical education for students with disabilities? *Teaching Exceptional Children, 35*(6), 32–38.

Sharan, S., Kussell, P., Hertz-Lazarowitz, R., Bejarano, Y., Raviv, S., & Sharan, Y. (1984). *Cooperative learning in the classroom: Research in desegregated schools.* Hillsdale, NJ: Lawrence Erlbaum.

Shaywitz, S. (2003). *Overcoming dyslexia: A new and complete science-based program for reading problems at any level.* New York: Knopf.

Shaywitz, S., Morris, R., & Shaywitz, B. (2008). The education of dyslexic children from childhood to young adulthood. *Annual Review of Psychology, 59,* 451–475.

Shaywitz, S. E., & Shaywitz, B. A. (2007). What neuroscience really tells us about reading instruction. *Educational Leadership, 64*(5), 74–76.

Sheets, R. H. (2002). "You're just a kid that's there"—Chicano perception of disciplinary events [Electronic version]. *Journal of Latinos and Education, 1,* 105–122.

Shepard, M. P., & Mahon, M. M. (2002). Family considerations. In L. L. Hayman, M. M. Mahon, & J. R. Turner (Eds.), *Chronic illness in children: An evidence-based approach* (pp. 143–170). New York: Springer.

Shin, J., Deno, S. L., & Espin, C. (2000). Technical adequacy of the maze task for curriculum-based measurement of reading growth. *Journal of Special Education, 34,* 164–172.

Shinn, M. R., Collins, V. L., & Gallagher, S. (1998). Curriculum-based measurement and problem solving assessment. In M. R. Shinn (Ed.), *Advanced applications of curriculum-based measurement* (pp. 143–174). New York: Guilford Press.

Shinn, M. R., & Hubbard, D. (1992). Curriculum-based measurement and problem-solving assessment: Basic procedures and outcomes. *Focus on Exceptional Children, 24,* 1–20.

Shippen, M. E., Simpson, R. G., & Crites, S. A. (2003). A practical guide to functional behavioral assessment. *Teaching Exceptional Children, 35*(5), 36–44.

Short, D., & Echevarria, J. (2004/2005). Teacher skills to support English language learners. *Educational Leadership, 62*(4), 8–13.

Shumate, E., & Wills, H. (2010). Classroom-based functional analysis and intervention for disruptive and off-task behaviors. *Education and Treatment of Children, 33,* 23–48.

Sideridis, G. S., & Scanlon, D. (Eds.). (2006). Motivational issues in learning disabilities. *Learning Disability Quarterly, 29*(3), 131–135.

Siegal, L. S. (2005). IQ is irrelevant to the definition of learning disabilities. *Journal of Learning Disabilities, 22,* 469–486.

Siegle, D., & McCoach, D. B. (2005). Making a difference: Motivating students who are not achieving. *Teaching Exceptional Children, 38*(1), 22–27.

Sigafoos, J., & Littlewood, R. (1999). Communication intervention on the playground: A case study on teaching requesting to a young child with autism. *International Journal of Disability, Development, and Education, 46,* 421–429.

Silva, M., Munk, D. D., & Bursuck, W. D. (2005). Grading adaptation for students with disabilities. *Intervention in School and Clinic, 41*(2), 87–98.

Silver, L. B. (2006). *The misunderstood child: Understanding and coping with your child's learning disabilities.* (4th ed.). New York: Three Rivers Press.

Silverman, S. K., Hazelwood, C., & Cronin, P. (2009, July). *Universal education: Principles and practices for advancing achievement of students with disabilities.* Columbus, OH: Center for School Improvement and Office for Exceptional Children, Ohio Department of Education. Retrieved from http://www.ohioregion14.org/perspectives/wp-content/uploads/2009/08/Universal_Ed_Report_Aug_09.pdf.

Simmons, R., & Magiera, K. (2007). Evaluation of co-teaching in three high schools within one school district: How do you know when you are TRULY co-teaching? *Teaching Exceptional Children Plus, 3*(3), Article 4. Retrieved July 1, 2007, from http://escholarship.bc.edu/education/tecplus/vol3/iss3/art4

Simos, P. G., Fletcher, J. M., Sarkari, S., Billingsley-Marshall, R. L., Denton, C. A., & Papanicolaou, A. C. (2007). Intensive instruction affects brain magnetic activity associated with oral word reading in children with persistent reading disabilities. *Journal of Learning Disabilities, 40*(1), 37–48.

Simpson, R. L., de Boer-Ott, S., & Smith-Myles, B. (2003). Inclusion of learners with autism spectrum disorders in general education settings. *Topics in Language Disorders, 23,* 116–33.

Sindelar, P. T., Shearer, D. K., Yendol-Hoppey, D., & Liebert, T. W. (2006). The sustainability of inclusive school reform. *Exceptional Children, 72,* 317–331.

Sinha, D., & Efron, D. (2005). Complementary and alternative medicine use in children with attention deficit hyperactivity disorder. *Journal of Paediatrics and Child Health, 41*(1–2), 23–26.

Skiba, R. J., Michael, R. S., Nardo, A. B., & Peterson, R. L. (2002). The color of discipline: Sources of racial and gender disproportionality in school punishment [Electronic version]. *Urban Review, 34,* 317–342.

Skiba, R., Poloni-Staudinger, L., Gallini, S., Simmons, A., & Feggins-Azziz, R. (2006). Disparate access: The disproportionality of African American students with disabilities across educational environments [Electronic version]. *Exceptional Children, 72,* 411–424.

Skiba, R. J., Poloni-Staudinger, L. P., Simmons, A., Feggins-Assiz, L. R., & Chung, C. (2005). Unproven links: Can poverty explain ethnic disproportionality in special education? *Journal of Special Education, 39,* 130–144.

Skiba, R. J., Simmons, A. B., Ritter, S., Gibb, A. C., Rausch, M. K., Cuadrado, J., & Chung, C. (2008). Achieving equity in special education: History, status, and current challenges. *Exceptional Children, 74,* 264–288.

Skilton-Sylvester, E., & Slesaransky-Poe, G. (2009). More than a least restrictive environment: Living up the civil covenant in building inclusive schools. *Perspectives on Urban Education, 6,* 32–37.

Slavin, R. E. (1994). *Cooperative learning* (2nd ed.). Boston: Allyn and Bacon.

Slavin, R. E. (1999). Comprehensive approaches to cooperative learning [Electronic version]. *Theory into Practice, 38,* 74–79.

Slonski-Fowler, K. E., & Truscott, S. D. (2004). General education teachers' perceptions of the prereferral intervention team process. *Journal of Educational and Psychological Consultation, 15,* 1–39.

Smith, C. R. (2004). *Learning disabilities: The interaction of students and their environments* (5th ed.). Boston: Allyn and Bacon.

Smith, K., & Weitz, M. (2003). Problem solving and gifted education: A differentiated fifth-grade fantasy unit [Electronic version]. *Gifted Child Today, 26*(3), 56–60.

Smith, S., Boone, R., & Higgins, K. (1998). Expanding the writing process to the web. *Teaching Exceptional Children, 30*(5), 22–26.

Smith, T. E. C. (2002). Section 504: What teachers need to know. *Intervention in School and Clinic, 37,* 259–266.

Smith-Arrezzo, W. M. (2003). Diversity in children's literature: Not just a black and white issue [Electronic version]. *Children's Literature in Education, 34,* 75–94.

Snell, M., Chen, L., Allaire, J., & Park, E. (2008). Communication breakdown at home and at school in young children with cerebral palsy and severe disabilities. *Research & Practice for Persons with Severe Disabilities, 33,* 25–36.

Snider, V. E. (1997). Transfer of decoding skills to a literature basal. *Learning Disabilities Research and Practice, 12*(1), 54–62.

Snow, C. E., & Biancarosa, G. (2003). *Adolescent literacy and the achievement gap: What do we know about where do we go from here?* New York: Carnegie Corporation of New York.

Snow, C. E., Burns, M. S., & Griffin, P. C. (1998). *Preventing reading difficulties in young children.* Washington, DC: National Academy Press.

Sobel, D. M., & Taylor, S. V. (2006). Blueprint for the responsive classroom. *Teaching Exceptional Children, 38*(5), 28–35.

Solish, A., Perry, A., & Minnes, P. (2010). Participation of children with and without disabilities in social, recreational and leisure activities. *Journal of Applied Research in Intellectual Disabilities, 23,* 226–236.

Solorzano, R. W. (2008). High stakes testing: Issues, implications, and remedies for English Language learners. *Review of Educational Research, 78*(2), 260–329.

Sparks, N. M. (2000). *Assistive technology criteria.* Paper presented at International Special Education Congress, July.

Spaulding, L. S., Mostert, M. P., & Beam, A. P. (2010). Is Brain Gym an effective educational intervention? *Exceptionality, 18,* 18–30.

Spencer, V. G., & Balboni, G. (2003). Can students with mental retardation teach their peers? *Education and Training in Mental Retardation and Developmental Disabilities, 38,* 32–61.

Sporer, N., & Brunstein, J. (2009). Fostering the reading comprehension of secondary school students through peer-assisted learning: Effects on strategy knowledge, strategy use, and task performance. *Contemporary Educational Psychology, 34,* 289–297.

Stainback, S., & Stainback, W. (1988). Educating students with severe disabilities in regular classes. *Teaching Exceptional Children, 21*(1), 16–19.

Stang, K., Carter, E., Lane, K., & Pierson, M. (2009). Perspectives of general and special educators on fostering self-determination in elementary and middle schools. *Journal of Special Education, 43,* 94–106.

Stanovich, K., & Siegel, L. S. (1994). Phenotypic performance profile of children with reading disabilities: A regression-based test of the phonological-core variable-difference model. *Journal of Educational Psychology, 86,* 24–53.

Stanovich, P. J., & Jordan, A. (2002). Preparing general educators to teach in inclusive classrooms: Some food for thought [Electronic version]. *Teacher Education, 37,* 173–185.

Starr, E. M., Foy, J. B., Cramer, K. M., & Singh, H. (2006). How are schools doing? Parental perceptions of children with autism spectrum disorders, Down syndrome, and learning disabilities: A comparative analysis. *Training in Developmental Disabilities, 41,* 315–332.

Stein, M., Kinder, D., Silbert, J., & Carnine, D. G. (2005). *Designing effective mathematics instruction: A direct instruction approach.* (4th ed.). Upper Saddle River, NJ: Prentice Hall.

Steiner, H. H. (2006). A microgenetic analysis of strategic variability in gifted and average-ability children. *Gifted Child Quarterly, 50*(1), 62–75.

Stevenson, J., McCann, D., Watkin, P., Worsfold, S., & Kennedy, C. (2010). The relationship between language development and behaviour problems in children with hearing loss. *Journal of Child Psychology and Psychiatry, 51,* 77–83.

Stichter, J. P., Conroy, M. A., & Kauffman, J. M. (2007). *An introduction to students with high-incidence disabilities.* Upper Saddle River, NJ: Pearson.

Stichter, J. P., Stormont, M., & Lewis, T. J. (2008). Instructional practices and behavior during reading: A descriptive summary and comparison of practices in Title One and Non-Title elementary schools. *Psychology in the Schools, 46,* 172–183.

Stillwell, R. (2010, June). *Public school graduates and dropouts from the common core of data: School Year 2007–08* (NCES 2010-341). Washington, DC: National Center for Education Statistics, Institute of Education Sciences, U.S. Department of Education. Retrieved June 25, 2010 from http://nces.ed.gov/pubsearch/pubsinfo.asp?pubid=2010341.

Stinson, M., Elliot, L., Kelly, R., & Yufang, L. (2009). Deaf and hard-of-hearing students' memory of lectures with speech-to-text and interpreting/note taking services. *Journal of Special Education, 43,* 52–64.

Stipek, D. (2006). Relationships matter. *Educational Leadership, 64*(1), 46–49.

Stivers, J. (2008). Strengthen your coteaching relationship. *Intervention in School and Clinic, 44,* 121–125.

Strang, J. D., & Rourke, B. P. (1985). Arithmetic disability subtypes: The neuropsychological significance of specific arithmetical impairment in childhood. In B. P. Rourke (Ed.), *Neuropsychology of learning disabilities* (pp. 167–182). New York: Guilford Press.

Straus, M. A. (2001). New evidence for the benefits of never spanking [Electronic version]. *Society, 38*(6), 52–60.

Stronge, J. H. (2002). *Qualities of effective teachers.* Alexandria, VA: Association of Supervision and Curriculum Development.

Substance Abuse and Mental Health Services Administration. (2009, November). *Results from the 2008 national survey on drug use and health: National findings* [Office of Applied Studies, NSDUH Series H-36, HHS Publication No. SMA 09-4434]. Rockville, MD: Author. Retrieved June 26, 2010 from http://www.oas.samhsa.gov/nsduh/2k8nsduh/2k8Results.cfm#2.2.

Sugai, G., & Horner, R. H. (2008). What we know and need to know about preventing problem behavior in schools. *Exceptionality, 16,* 67–77.

Summers, J. A., Hoffman, L., Marquis, J., Turnbull, A., Poston, D., & Nelson, L. L. (2005). Measuring the quality of family-professional partnerships in special education services. *Exceptional Children, 72*(1), 65–81.

Supovitz, J., Sirinides, P., & May, H. (2010). How principals and peers influence teaching and learning. *Educational Administration Quarterly, 46*(1), 31–56.

Sutherland, K. S., Lewis-Palmer, T., Stichter, J., & Morgan, P. L. (2008). Examining the influence of teacher behavior and classroom context on the behavioral and academic outcomes for students with emotional and behavior disorders. *The Journal of Special Education, 41,* 223–233.

Swain, K. D., Friehe, M. M., & Harrington, J. M. (2004). Teaching listening strategies in the inclusive classroom. *Intervention in School and Clinic, 40,* 48–54.

Swanson, H. L. (2000). What instruction works for students with learning disabilities? Summarizing the results from a meta-analysis of intervention studies. In R. Gersten, E. Schiller, & S. Vaughn (Eds.), *Contemporary special education research: Syntheses of the knowledge based on critical instructional issues* (pp. 1–30). Mahwah, NJ: Lawrence Erlbaum Associates.

Swanson, H. L. (2001). Reading intervention research outcomes and students with learning disabilities: What are the major instructional ingredients for successful outcomes? *Perspectives, 27*(2), 18–20.

Swanson, H. L., & Deshler, D. (2003). Instructing adolescents with learning disabilities: Converting a meta-analysis to practice. *Journal of Learning Disabilities, 36,* 124–135.

Swanson, H. L., & Jerman, O. (2006). Math disabilities: A selective meta-analysis of literature. *Review of Educational Research, 76*(2), 249–274.

Swanson, H. L., Zheng, X., & Jerman, O. (2009). Working memory, short-term memory, and reading disabilities: A selective meta-analysis of the literature. *Journal of Learning Disabilities, 42*(3), 260–287.

Sze, S. (2009). A literature review: Pre-service teachers' attitudes toward students with disabilities. *Education, 130*(1), 53–56.

Tankersley, M., Harjusola-Webb, S., & Landrum, T. J. (2008). Using single-subject research to establish the evidence base of special education. *Intervention in School and Clinic, 44,* 83–90.

Tannock, M. (2009). Tangible and intangible elements of collaborative teaching. *Intervention in School and Clinic, 44,* 173–178.

Taub, D. J. (2006). Understanding the concerns of parents of students with disabilities: Challenges and roles for school counselors. *Professional School Counseling, 10*(1).

Terman, L. (1925). *Genetic studies of genius: Vol. 1. Mental and physical traits of 1000 gifted children.* Stanford, CA: Stanford University Press.

Test, D. W., & Ellis, M. F. (2005). The effects of LAP fractions on addition and subtraction of fractions with mild disabilities. *Education and Treatment of Children, 28*(1), 11–24.

Test, D. W., Fowler, C. H., Brewer, D., & Wood, W. M. (2005). A content and methodological review of self-advocacy intervention studies. *Exceptional Children, 72*(1), 101–125.

Test, D. W., Mason, C., Hughes, C., Konrad, M., Neale, M., & Wood, W. M. (2004). Student involvement in individualized education program meetings. *Exceptional Children, 70,* 391–412.

Therrien, W. J., Hughes, C., Kapelski, C., & Mokhtari, K. (2009). Effectiveness of a test-taking strategy on achievement in essay tests for students with learning disabilities. *Journal of Learning Disabilities, 41*(1), 14–23.

Thompson, S., & Thurlow, M. (2003). *2003 state special education outcomes: Marching on.* Minneapolis, MN: University of Minnesota, National Center on Educational Outcomes. Retrieved January 31, 2005, from http://education.umn.edu/NCEO/OnlinePubs/2003StateReport.htm

Thurlow, M. L., Elliott, J. L., & Ysseldyke, J. F. (2003). *Testing students with disabilities: Practical strategies for complying with district and state regulations* (2nd ed.). Thousand Oaks, CA: Corwin Press, Inc.

Tindal, G. A., & Marston, D. B. (1990). *Classroom-based assessment: Evaluating instructional outcomes.* Columbus, OH: Merrill.

Tindal, G., Mcdonald, M., Tedesco, M., Glasgow, A., Almond, P., Crawford, L., & Hollenbeck, K. (2003). Alternate assessments in reading and math: Development and validation for students with significant disabilities. *Exceptional Children, 69,* 481–494.

Titus, D. N. (2007). Strategies and resources for enhancing the achievement of mobile students. *NASSP Bulletin, 91*(1), 81–97.

Tomlinson, C. A. (2000). Reconcilable differences? Standards-based teaching and differentiation. *Educational Leadership, 58*(1), 6–11.

Tomlinson, C. A. (2001). *How to differentiate instruction in mixed-ability classrooms* (2nd ed.). Alexandria, VA: Association for Supervision and Curriculum Development.

Tomlinson, C. A. (2004). The Möbius effect: Addressing learner variance in schools. *Journal of Learning Disabilities, 37,* 516–524.

Tomlinson, C. A. (2005). Quality curriculum and instruction for highly able students. *Theory into Practice, 44,* 160–166.

Tomlinson, C. A., & Jarvis, J. (2006). Teaching beyond the book. *Educational Leadership, 64*(1), 16–21.

Toney, L. P., Kelley, M. L., & Lanclos, N. F. (2003). Self- and parental monitoring of homework in adolescents: Comparative effects on parents' perceptions of homework behavior problems [Electronic version]. *Child and Family Behavior Therapy, 25,* 35–51.

Topping, K. J. (2005). Trends in peer learning. *Educational Psychology, 25,* 631–645.

Torgesen, J. (1991). Learning disabilities: Historical and conceptual issues. In B. Wong (Ed.), *Learning about learning disabilities* (pp. 3–39). San Diego, CA: Academic Press.

Torgesen, J. K. (2000). Increasing the intensity of interventions in reading: The lingering problem of treatment resisters. *Learning Disabilities: Research and Practice, 15*(1), 55–64.

Toth, K., Munson, J., Meltzoff, A. N., & Dawson, G. (2006). Early predictors of communication development in young children with autism spectrum disorder: Joint attention, imitation, and toy play. *Journal of Autism and Developmental Disorders, 36,* 993–1005.

Tournaki, N. (2003). The differential effects of teaching addition through strategy instruction versus drill and practice to students with and without learning disabilities. *Journal of Learning Disabilities, 36,* 449–458.

Tournaki, N., & Criscitiello, E. (2003). Using peer tutoring as a successful part of behavior management. *Teaching Exceptional Children, 36*(2), 22–29.

Towles-Reeves, E., Kleinert, H., & Muhomba, M. (2009). Alternate assessment: Have we learned anything new? *Exceptional Children, 75,* 233–252.

Trainor, A. (2010). Diverse approaches to parent advocacy during special education home-school interactions: Identification and use of cultural and social capital. *Remedial and Special Education, 31,* 34–47.

Trautman, M. L. (2004). Preparing and managing paraprofessionals. *Intervention in School and Clinic, 39,* 131–138.

Troen, V., & Boles, K. (2010). Team spirit: Teachers work together to establish and achieve key goals. *Journal of Staff Development, 31*(1), 59–62.

Trumbull, E., & Pacheco, M. (2005). Leading with diversity: Cultural competencies for teacher preparation and professional development. Providence, RI: Brown University. (ERIC Document Reproduction Service No. ED494221)

Trussell, R. (2008). Classroom universals to prevent problem behaviors. *Intervention in School and Clinic, 43,* 179–185.

Tucker, J. A. (1985). Curriculum-based assessment: An introduction. *Exceptional Children, 52,* 199–204.

Turnbull, A. P., Blue-Banning, M., & Pereira, L. (2000). Successful friendships of Hispanic children and youth with disabilities: An exploratory study. *Mental Retardation, 38,* 138–153.

Turnbull, A. P., Pereira, L., & Blue-Banning, M. J. (2000). Teachers as friendship facilitators. *Teaching Exceptional Children, 32*(5), 66–70.

Turnbull, H. R., Turnbull, A. P., Wehmeyer, M. L., & Park, J. (2003). A quality of life framework for special education outcomes. *Remedial and Special Education, 24,* 67–74.

Turnbull, R., Huerta, N., & Stowe, M. (2006). *The Individuals with Disabilities Education Act as amended in 2004.* Upper Saddle River, NJ: Merrill.

Turnbull, A., Turnbull, R., Erwin, E. J., Soodak, L. C., & Shogren, K. A. (2011). *Families, professionals, and exceptionality: Positive outcomes through partnerships and trust* (6th ed.). Upper Saddle River, NJ: Merrill/Pearson.

U.S. Department of Education. (2004a). PBIS goals. Retrieved December 19, 2004, from the U.S. Office of Special Education Programs, National Technical Assistance Center on Positive Behavioral Interventions and Supports (PBIS) website, www.pbis.org

U.S. Department of Education. (2004b). *26th annual report to Congress on the implementation of the Individuals with Disabilities Education Act.* Washington, DC: Author.

U.S. Department of Education. (2006). *28th annual report to Congress on the implementation of the Individuals with Disabilities Education Act.* Washington, DC: Author.

U.S. Department of Education. (2007, February). Bilingual cooperative integrated reading and composition (pp. 1–12). *What Works Clearinghouse Intervention Report.* (ERIC Document Reproduction Service No. ED495727). Retrieved August 31, 2007, from www.eric.ed.gov/ERICDocs/data/ericdocs2sql/content_storage_01/0000019b/80/29/e3/b6.pdf

U.S. Department of Education. (2007). *Final regulations on modified academic achievement standards.* Retrieved October 23, 2007, from Special Education and Rehabilitative Services website www.ed.gov/policy/speced/guid/modachieve-summary.html

U.S. Department of Education. (2010, March). *A blueprint for reform: The reauthorization of the Elementary and Secondary Education Act.* Washington, DC: Author. Retrieved from http://www2.ed.gov/policy/elsec/leg/blueprint/blueprint.pdf.

U.S. Department of Health and Human Services. (2007, April). *Results from the 2005 national survey on drug use and health: National findings.* Washington, DC: Author. Retrieved August 2, 2007, from www.oas.samhsa.gov/NSDUH/2k5NSDUH/2k5results.htm#Ch2

U.S. Department of Health and Human Services, Children's Bureau. (2006, June). *Child maltreatment 2004.* Washington, DC: Author. Retrieved July 31, 2007, from www.acf.hhs.gov/programs/cb/pubs/cm04/index.htm

U.S. Department of Health and Human Services, Office of Civil Rights. (2006, June). *Fact sheet: Your rights under Section 504 of the Rehabilitation Act.* Retrieved October 18, 2007, from www.hhs.gov/ocr/504.pdf

U.S. Department of Justice, Bureau of Justice Statistics. (2005). *School crime supplement (SCS) to the National Crime Victimization Survey* [Table 17.1]. Retrieved August 10, 2007, from http://nces.ed.gov/pubs2006/2006001.pdf

U.S. Department of Justice, Bureau of Justice Statistics. (2007). *National crime victimization survey (NCVS), 2007.* Retrieved July 2, 2010 from http://www.childstats.gov/americaschildren/surveys.asp#ncvs.

Uberti, H. Z., Mastropieri, M. A., & Scruggs, T. E. (2004). Check it off: Individualizing a math algorithm for students with disabilities via self-monitoring checklists. *Intervention in School and Clinic, 39,* 269–275.

Uberti, H. Z., Scruggs, T. E., & Mastropieri, M. A. (2003). Keywords make the difference! Mnemonic instruction in inclusive classrooms. *Teaching Exceptional Children, 35*(3), 56–61.

Ulrich, M. E., & Bauer, A. M. (2003). Levels of awareness: A closer look at communication between parents and professionals. *Teaching Exceptional Children, 35*(6), 20–25.

United Cerebral Palsy (n.d.). *Cerebral palsy—facts and figures.* Retrieved November 26, 2004, from www.ucp.org/ucp_generaldoc.cfm/1/9/37/37-37/447

United Cerebral Palsy. (2001). *Cerebral palsy: Facts and figures.* Washington, DC: Author. Retrieved June 15, 2010 from http://www.ucp.org/ucp_generaldoc.cfm/1/9/37/37-37/447.

United Federation of Teachers. (2007, August). *Child abuse: Questions and answers for New York City's educators* (7th ed.). New York: Author. Retrieved August 2, 2007 from www.uft.org/member/education/development/brochure/article3

Vacca, R. T., & Vacca, J. L. (2007). *Content area reading: Literacy and learning across the curriculum* (9th ed.) Boston: Little Brown.

Valle, J. W., & Conner, D. J. (2011). *Rethinking disability: A disability studies approach to inclusive practices.* New York: McGraw-Hill.

Vandercook, T., York, J., & Forest, M. (1989). The McGill Action Planning System (MAPS): A strategy for building the vision. *Journal of the Association for Persons with Severe Handicaps (JASH), 14*(3), 205–218.

Vannest, K., Temple-Harvey, K., & Mason, B. (2009). Adequate yearly progress for students with emotional and behavioral disorders through research-based practices. *Preventing School Failure, 53,* 73–84.

VanTassel-Baska, J. L., Cross, T., & Olenchak, F. R. (Eds.). (2009). *Social-emotional curriculum with gifted and talented students.* Waco, TX: Prufrock.

VanTassel-Baska, J., Feng, A., Swanson, J., Quek, C., & Chandler, K. (2009). Academic and affective profiles of low-income, minority, and twice-exceptional gifted learners: The role of gifted program membership in enhancing self. *Journal of Advanced Academics, 20,* 702–739.

VanTassel-Baska, J., Feng, A., Swanson, J., Chandler, K., & Quek, C. (2009). *Patterns of development to the special needs of gifted learners.* Denver: Love.

VanTassel-Baska, J. (2003). *Curriculum planning and instructional design for gifted learners.* Denver, CO: Love.

Vaughan, W. (2002). Effects of cooperative learning on achievement and attitudes among students of color. *Journal of Educational Research, 95,* 359–364.

Vaughn, B. S., Roberts, H. J., & Needelman, H. (2009). Current medications for the treatment of attention-deficit/hyperactivity disorder. *Psychology in the Schools, 46,* 846–856.

Vaughn, S. (2003, December). *How many tiers are needed for response to intervention to achieve acceptable prevention outcomes?* Paper presented at the National

Research Center on Learning Disabilities Responsiveness-to-Intervention Symposium, Kansas City, MO.

Vaughn, S., & Bos, C. S. (2009). *Strategies for teaching students with learning and behavior problems* (7th ed.). Upper Saddle River, NJ: Merrill/Pearson.

Vaughn, S., & Haager, D. (1994). Social competence as a multifaceted construct: How do students with learning disabilities fare? *Learning Disability Quarterly, 2*, 253–266.

Vaughn, S., Linan-Thompson, S., Kouzekanani, K., Bryant, D. P., Dickson, S., & Blozis, S. A. (2003). Reading instruction grouping for students with reading difficulties. *Remedial and Special education, 24*, 301–315.

Vaughn, S., Cirino, P., Tolar, T., Fletcher, J., Cardenas-Hagan, E., Carlson, C., et al. (2008). Long-term follow-up of Spanish and English interventions for first-grade English language learners at risk for reading problems. *Journal of Research on Educational Effectiveness, 1*, 179–214.

Verte, S., Geurts, H. M., & Roeyers, H. (2006). Executive functioning in children with an autism spectrum disorder: Can we differentiate within the spectrum? *Journal of Autism and Developmental Disorders, 36*, 351–372.

Villa, R. A., Thousand, J. S., Nevin, A., & Liston, A. (2005). Successful inclusive practices in middle and secondary schools. *American Secondary Education, 33*(3), 33–50.

Voix, R. G. (1968). *Evaluating reading and study skills in the secondary classroom: A guide for content teachers.* Newark, DE: International Reading Association.

Volpe, R. J., DuPaul, G. J., Jitendra, A. K., & Tresco, K. E. (2009). Consultation-based academic interventions for children with attention deficit hyperactivity disorder: Effects on reading and mathematics outcomes at 1-year follow-up. *School Psychology Review, 38*, 5–13.

Vukovic, R. K., & Siegel, L. S. (2010). Academic and cognitive characteristics of persistent mathematics difficulty from first through fourth grade. *Learning Disabilities Research and Practice, 25* (1), 25–38.

Wade, S. L., Stancin, T., & Taylor, H. G. (2004). Interpersonal stressors and resources as predictors of parental adaptation following pediatric traumatic injury. *Journal of Consulting and Clinical Psychology, 72*, 776–784.

Wade, S., Carey, J., & Wolfe, C. (2006). An online family intervention to reduce parental distress following pediatric brain injury. *Journal of Consulting and Clinical Psychology, 74*, 445–454.

Wagner, M., Cadwallader, T. W., Garza, N., & Cameto, R. (2004, March). *Social activities of youth with disabilities* (NLTS2 Data Brief). Retrieved November 20, 2004, from www.ncset.org

Waitoller, F., Artiles, A., & Cheney, D. (2010). The miner's canary: A review of overrepresentation research and explanations. *Journal of Special Education, 44*, 29–49.

Wakeman, S. Y., Browder, D. M., & Flowers, C. (2006). Principals' knowledge of fundamental and current issues in special education. *NASSP Bulletin, 90*, 153–174.

Waldron, N. L., & McLeskey, J. (2010). Establishing a collaborative school culture through comprehensive school reform. *Journal of Educational and Psychological Consultation, 20*, 58–74.

Walker, C. J. (2006). Adequate access or equal treatment: Looking beyond the IDEA to Section 504 in a post-Schaffer public school. *Stanford Law Review, 58*, 1563–1622.

Walker, H. M., & Rankin, R.J. (1983). Assessing the behavioral expectations and demands of less restrictive settings [SBS inventory of teacher social behavior standards and expectations and the SBS checklist of correlates of child handicapping conditions]. *The School Psychology Review, 12*, 274–284.

Walker, J. E., Shea, T. M., & Bauer, A. M. (2003). *Behavior management: A practical approach for educators* (8th ed.). Columbus, OH: Merrill/Prentice Hall.

Walker, L. (2006). Violence prevention through cooperative learning. *Reclaiming Children and Youth, 15*(1), 32–36.

Walker-Dalhouse, D., & Risko, V. (2008). Homelessness, poverty, and children's literacy development. *Reading Teacher, 62*, 84–86.

Walker-Dalhouse, D., Risko, V., Esworthy, C., Grasley, E., Kaisler, G., McIlvain, D., Stephan, M. (2009). Crossing boundaries and initiating conversations about RTI: Understanding and applying differentiated classroom instruction. *Reading Teacher, 63*, 84–87.

Wallace, T., Anderson, A. R., & Bartholomay, T. (2002). Collaboration: An element associated with the success of four inclusive high schools. *Journal of Educational and Psychological Consultation, 13*, 349–382.

Wang, M. C., Reynolds, M. C., & Walberg, H. J. (1988). Integrating the children of the second system. *Phi Delta Kappan, 70*, 248–251.

Wang, P., & Spillane, A. (2009). Evidence-based social skills interventions for children with autism: A meta-analysis. *Education and Training in Developmental Disabilities, 44*, 318–342.

Wanzek, J., Vaughn, S., Wexler, J., Swanson, E., Edmonds, M., & Kim, A. (2006). A synthesis of spelling and reading interventions and their effects on the spelling outcomes of students with LD. *Journal of Learning Disabilities, 39*(6), 528–543.

Warren, J. S., Bohanon-Edmonson, H. M., Turnbull, A. P., Sailor, W., Wickham. D., Griggs, P., et al. (2006). School-wide positive behavior support: Addressing behavior problems that impede student learning. *Educational Psychology Review, 18*, 187–198.

Wasburn-Moses, L. (2005). Roles and responsibilities of secondary special education teachers in an age of reform. *Remedial and Special Education, 26*, 151–158.

Wasburn-Moses, L. (2006). Obstacles to program effectiveness in secondary special education. *Preventing School Failure, 50*(3), 21–30.

Watson, S. (2004). Open the science doorway: Strategies and suggestions for incorporating English language learners in the science classroom. *Science Teacher, 71*(2), 32–35.

Wehmeyer, M. (2002). *Self-determination and the education of students with disabilities* (ERIC Digest). Reston, VA: ERIC Clearinghouse on Disabilities and Gifted Education. (ERIC Document Reproduction Service No. ED470036)

Wehmeyer, M. L. (2007). *Promoting self-determination in students with developmental disabilities: What works for special-needs learners.* New York: Guilford Publications.

Wehmeyer, M. L., Lattin, D. L., Lapp-Rincker, G., & Agran, M. (2003). Access to the general curriculum of middle school students with mental retardation: An observational study. *Remedial and Special Education, 24*, 262–272.

Welch, A. B. (2000). Responding to student concerns about fairness. *Teaching Exceptional Children, 33*(2), 36–40.

Welner, K. (2006). Legal rights: The overrepresentation of culturally and linguistically diverse students in special education. *Teaching Exceptional Children, 38*(6), 60–62.

Welton, E., Vakil, S., & Carasea, C. (2004). Strategies for increasing positive social interactions in children with autism: A case study. *Teaching Exceptional Children, 37*(1), 40–46.

Werts, M. G., Harris, S., Tillery, C. Y., & Roark, R. (2004). What parents tell us about paraeducators. *Remedial and Special Education, 25*, 232–239.

Wery, J. J., & Niefeld, J. L. (2010). Supporting self-regulated learning with exceptional children. *Teaching Exceptional Children, 42*(4), 70–78.

Westling, D. (2010). Teachers and challenging behavior: Knowledge, views, and practices. *Remedial and Special Education, 31*, 48–63.

Whalen, C. K., Jamner, L. D., Henker, B., Delfino, R. J., & Lo-zano, J. (2002). The ADHD spectrum and everyday life: Experience sampling of moods, activities, smoking, and drinking. *Child Development, 73*, 209–227.

Wheatley, R., West, R., Charlton, C., Sanders, R., Smith, T., & Taylor, M. (2009). Improving behavior through differential reinforcement: A praise note system for elementary school students. *Education and Treatment of Children, 32*, 551–571.

Wheeler, J. J., & Richey, D. D. (2005). *Behavior management: Principles and practices of positive behavior supports.* Upper Saddle River, NJ: Merrill/Prentice Hall.

Whitbread, K. M., Bruder, M. B., Fleming, G., & Park, H. J. (2007). Collaboration in special education parent-professional training. *Teaching Exceptional Children, 39*(4), 6–14.

Wiggins, R. A., Follow, E. J., & Eberly, M. B. (2007). The impact of a field immersion program on pre-service teachers' attitudes toward teaching in culturally diverse classrooms. *Teaching and Teacher Education, 23*, 653–663.

Wilen, W. W., Ishler, M., Hutchinson, J., & Kindsvatter, R. (1999). *Dynamics of effective teaching* (4th ed.). Boston: Allyn and Bacon.

Willaimson, P., McLeskey, J., Hoppey, D., & Rentz, T. (2006). Educating students with mental retardation in general education classrooms. *Exceptional Children, 72*(3), 347–361.

Williams, G. J., & Reisberg, L. (2003). Successful inclusion: Teaching social skills through curriculum integration. *Intervention in School and Clinic, 38*, 205–210.

Wilson, G., & Michaels, C. (2006). General and special education students' perceptions of co-teaching: Implications for secondary-level literacy instruction. *Reading & Writing Quarterly, 22,* 205–225.

Winn, J., & Blanton, L. (2005). The call for collaboration in teacher education. *Focus on Exceptional Children, 38*(2), 1–10.

Winnick, J. P. (Ed.). (2005). *Adapted physical education and sport* (4th ed.). Champaign, IL: Human Kinetics.

Winter-Messiers, M. A., Herr, C. M., Wood, C. E., Brooks, A. P., Gates, M. A. M., Houston, T. L., & Tingstad, K. I. (2007). How far can Brian ride the Daylight 4449 Express? A strength-based model of Asperger syndrome based on special interest areas. *Focus on Autism and Other Developmental Disabilities, 22,* 67–79.

Winzer, M. A. (1993). *The history of special education: From isolation to integration.* Washington, DC: Gallaudet University Press.

Wodrich, D., & Spencer, M. (2007). The other health-impairment category and health-based classroom accommodations: School psychologists' perceptions and practices. *Journal of Applied School Psychology, 24,* 109–125.

Wolf, P. S., & Hall, T. E. (2003). Making inclusion a reality for students with severe disabilities. *Teaching Exceptional Children, 35*(4), 56–61.

Wolfgang, C. H. (2001). The many views of "time-out": Teaching strategies [Electronic version]. *Journal of Early Education and Family Review, 8*(5), 18–28.

Wolraich, M. L., Wibbelsman, C. J., Brown, T. E., Evans, S. W., Gotlieb, E. M., Knight, J. R., et al. (2005). Attention-deficit/hyperactivity disorder among adolescents: A review of the diagnosis, treatment, and clinical implications. *Pediatrics, 115*(6), 1734–1746.

Wong, H. K., & Wong, R. T. (1998). *How to be an effective teacher: The first days of school.* Mountain View, CA: Harry K. Wong Publications.

Wood, J. W., Miederhoff, J. W., & Ulschmid, B. (1989). Adapting test construction for mainstreamed social studies students. *Social Education, 53*(1), 46–49.

Woods, J., & Poulson, C. L. (2006). The use of scripts to increase the verbal initiations of children with developmental disabilities to typically developing peers. *Education and Treatment of Children, 29,* 437–457.

Wormeli, R. (2006). *Fair isn't always equal: Assessing and grading in the differentiated classroom.* Portland, ME: Stenhouse Publishers.

Wright, J. (2007). *Behavior contracts.* Retrieved August 6, 2007, from www.interventioncentral.org/htmdocs/interventions/behavior/behcontr.php

Wright, P. W. D., & Wright, P. D. (2006). *IDEA 2004.* Hartfield, VA: Harbor House Law Press.

Wright-Gallo, G. L., Higbee, T. S., & Reagon, K. A. (2006). Classroom-based functional analysis and intervention for students with emotional/behavioral disorders. *Education and Treatment of Children, 29,* 421–434.

Wright-Gallo, G. L., Higbee, T. S., Reagon, K. A., & Davey, B. J. (2006). Classroom-based functional analysis and intervention for students with emotional/behavioral disorders. *Education and Treatment of Children, 29*(3), 421–436.

Yang, Y. F. (2002). Reassessing readers comprehension monitoring. *Reading in a Foreign Language, 14,* 18–42.

Yarger, C. C. (2001). Educational interpreting: Understanding the rural experience. *American Annals of the Deaf, 146,* 16–30.

Yell, M. L. (1990). The use of corporal punishment, suspension, expulsion, and timeout with behaviorally disordered students in public schools: Legal considerations. *Behavioral Disorders, 15,* 100–109.

Yell, M. L. (2006). *The law and special education* (2nd ed.). Upper Saddle River, NJ: Merrill/Pearson.

Yell, M., Clyde, K., & Puyallup, S. K. (1995). School district: The courts, inclusion, and students with behavioral disorders. *Behavioral Disorders, 20,* 179–189.

Yell, M. L., Katsiyannis, A., & Shiner, J. G. (2006). The *No Child Left Behind Act,* adequate yearly progress, and students with disabilities. *Teaching Exceptional Children, 38*(4), 32–39.

Yell, M. L., Rogers, D., & Rogers, E. L. (1998). The legal history of special education: What a long, strange trip it's been! *Remedial and Special Education, 19,* 219–228.

Yell, M., Ryan, J., Rozalski, M., & Katsiyannis, A. (2009). The U.S. Supreme Court and special education: 2005 to 2007. *Teaching Exceptional Children, 41*(3), 68–75.

Yoder, P., & Lieberman, R. (2010). Brief report: Randomized test of the efficacy of Picture Exchange Communication System on highly generalized picture exchanges in children with ASD. *Journal of Autism and Developmental Disorders, 40,* 629–632.

York-Barr, J., Ghere, G., & Sommerness, J. (2007). Collaborative teaching to increase ELL student learning: A three-year urban elementary case study. *Journal of Education for Students Placed at Risk (JESPAR), 12,* 301–335.

Young, S., & Amarasinghe, J. (2010). Practitioner review: Non-pharmacological treatments for ADHD: A lifespan approach. *Journal of Child Psychology and Psychiatry, 51,* 116–133.

Youse, K. M., Le, K. N., Cannizzaro, M. S., & Coelho, C. A. (2002, June). Traumatic brain injury: A primer for professionals. *ASHA Leader Online.* Retrieved February 20, 2005, from www.asha.org/about/publications/leader-online/archives/2002/q2/020625a.htm

Ysseldyke, J., Algozzine, B., & Thurlow, M. L. (2000). *Critical issues in special education* (3rd ed.). Boston: Houghton Mifflin.

Ysseldyke, J., Burns, M. K., Scholin, S. E., & Parker, D. C. (2010). Instructionally valid assessment within response to intervention. *Teaching Exceptional Children, 42*(4), 54–61.

Zhang, C., & Bennett, T. (2003). Facilitating the meaningful participation of culturally and linguistically diverse families in the IFSP and IEP process [Electronic version]. *Focus on Autism and Other Developmental Disabilities, 18,* 51–59.

Zigmond, M. (2003). Where should students with disabilities receive special education services? Is one place better than another? *Journal of Special Education, 37,* 193–199.

Zilz, W. A. (2006). Manifestation determination: Rulings of the courts. *Education and the Law, 18*(2), 193–206.

Zirkel, P. A. (2004). The case law on gifted education: A new look. *Gifted Child Quarterly, 48,* 309–314.

Zirkel, P. A., & Thomas, L. B. (2010). State laws for RTI: An updated snapshot. *Teaching Exceptional Children, 42*(3), 56–63.

Zirkel, P. (2009). Section 504: Student eligibility update. *Clearing House: A Journal of Educational Strategies, Issues and Ideas, 82,* 209–211.

Zirkel, P. (2009). What does the law say? *Teaching Exceptional Children, 41*(5), 73–75.

Zirkel, P. (2009a). Section 504: Student eligibility update. *Clearing House: A Journal of Educational Strategies, Issues, Ideas, 82,* 209–211.

Zirkel, P. (2009b). What does the law say? *Teaching Exceptional Children, 42,* 73–75.

Zirkel, P., & Krohn, N. (2008). RTI after IDEA: A survey of state laws. *Teaching Exceptional Children, 40*(3), 71–73.

Zirkel, S. (2008). The influence of multicultural educational practices on student outcomes and intergroup relations. *Teachers College Record, 110,* 1147–1181.

Zuvekas, S. H., Vitiello, B., & Nordquist, G. S. (2006). Recent trends in stimulant medication use among U.S. children. *American Journal of Psychiatry, 163,* 586–593.

Name Index

Abedi, J., 109, 346
Acrey, C., 341
Adcock, J., 171
Adreon, D., 172, 173
Affleck, J. Q., 295
Agran, M., 17, 333
Aguilar, J., 38, 73, 86, 87, 181
Ahlgrin-Delzell, L., 178
Akin-Little, A., 196
Akram, G., 243
Al-Ahssan, S., 88
Alber-Morgan, S., 117
Alberto, P. A., 144, 172
Alexander, R., 223
Algozzine, B., 178, 211
Alidoost, M., 321
Alkin, M. C., 137, 225
Allaire, J., 180
Alley, G. R., 323
Allinder, R. M., 117
Allsop, D., 313, 317, 320
Almond, P., 113
Alper, S., 17, 18
Alsheikh, N., 33
Alvarez, L., 224
Amarasinghe, J., 241, 242
American Academy of
    Pediatrics, 220
American Institutes for
    Research, 346
American Psychiatric
    Association, 223, 238
American Speech-Language-Hearing
    Association, 205
An, Q., 194
Anderson, C., 390
Anderson, D. H., 315, 331

Anderson, J. A., 219
Anderson, L. M., 281, 321,
    322, 323
Anderson, L. W., 149
Anderson, T. H., 152
Andrews, D., 331
Angelle, P., 36
Anthony, H. M., 281, 321, 322, 323
Antia, S., 187
Aragon, L., 88
Archer, A. L., 151, 284, 285,
    295, 312, 313
Arends, R. I., 144, 145
Arivett, D. L., 35
Armbruster, B. B., 152, 288,
    289, 313
Arms, E., 53
Arndt, S. A., 39
Arnold, N., 364
Aronson, E., 379
Arreaga-Mayer, C., 376
Arroyo-Jurado, E., 196, 198
Artiles, A. J., 6, 250, 252
Aschunk, D., 229
Ashton, T. M., 326
Association of Supervision
    and Curriculum
    Development, 325
Assouline, S., 234, 248
Asthma and Allergy Foundation
    of America, 194
August, D., 209
Ayers, 184, 184

Babijian, H., 206
Bahr, M., 72, 79
Bailey, J., 352

Bailey, J. M., 355
Baker, J. M., 137
Baker, S., 117, 152, 376, 377
Baker, S. K., 277, 281
Baker-Kroczynski, S., 17
Balise, R. R., 213
Banda, D. R., 17, 173, 381
Banerjee, M., 316
Banks, J. A., 251, 252, 399
Barad, D., 206, 207
Barkley, R. A., 220, 238,
    239, 243
Barootchi, N., 363
Bartelt, L., 165, 308
Bartlett, L., 10
Barton-Arwood, S. M.,
    219, 225
Basaraba, D., 32
Bateman, B., 220
Bateman, B. D., 54
Bateman, B. E., 211
Bateman, D., 51
Bates, P., 38
Bauer, A. M., 394, 396
Bauer, N. W., 289
Baumann, J., 314
Bauminger, N., 222
Baush, M., 156
Baxendell, B. W., 282, 284
Beam, A. P., 220
Beaver, J. B., 160
Beck, I. L., 152
Beckmann, S., 309
Beegle, J., 73
Beigel, A. R., 156
Beirne-Smith, M., 8
Benedetti, D., 282

Subject Index

ABC (antecedents-behaviors-consequences) analysis, 388
Ability, lack of, 139
Absence seizures, 193
Academic learning time, 145–146
Academic probes. *See* Probes
Academics
  attention deficit–hyperactivity disorder and, 240, 241–242
  gifted and talented students, 246
  language disorders and, 207
  learning and behavioral disabilities and, 212–219, 224–225, 226–227
  student learning strengths/needs and, 134
Academic survival skills, 134, 219
Acceleration, 248
Acceptance, creating atmosphere of, 208
Accommodations. *See also* Differentiated instruction
  assessment, 54, 106, 109
  autism spectrum disorders, 173–174
  communication disorders, 208–209
  defined, 4
  fairness in, 351
  hearing impairments, 187–190
  instructional, 136–137, 138
  intellectual disability, 178–181
  learning and behavioral disabilities, 224–229
  modifications *versus,* 4–5
  orthopedic impairments, 191
  other health impairments, 194–195

Section 504, 237
testing, 340–348
traumatic brain injury, 197
visual impairments, 184
Accountability, shared, for outcomes, 68
Accuracy, 124
Acquired brain injury. *See* Traumatic brain injury (TBI)
Acquired immune deficiency syndrome (AIDS), 194
Activity logs, daily, 350
Activity reinforcers, 393
ADA (Americans with Disabilities Act), 11
ADAA (Americans with Disabilities Act Amendments), 11, 235
Adaptive behavior scales, 177
Adaptive physical educators, 38
Adderall (amphetamine), 243, 244
Addition learning strategies, 329
Adequate yearly progress (AYP), 13–14
ADHD. *See* Attention deficit–hyperactivity disorder (ADHD)
Administrators, role in special education, 36. *See also* Principals
Advanced Placement (AP) program, 247
Advance organizers, 282
Advice, as barrier to communication, 70
Advocates, 38
African Americans
  attention deficit–hyperactivity disorder, 243

behavior disorders, overidentification with, 210
discipline problems, 374
distrust of school professionals, 89–90
effective teachers of, 143
instruction for, 252
sickle-cell disease, 193
special education, overrepresentation in, 5
test accommodations, 345
test-taking skills, 342
Aides. *See* Paraprofessionals
AIDS (acquired immune deficiency syndrome), 194
AIMSWEB, 102
Algebra learning strategies, 329
Allergies, 194, 221, 237
All-group contingency, 380
Alternate assessments, 109–111
Alternative forms of questions, 344
Alternative teaching, 78
Alternative test sites, 345–346
Ambivalence, as reaction to child's disability, 85
American Foundation for the Blind, 185
American Indians. *See* Native Americans
American Psychological Association, 105
American Sign Language, 189
Americans with Disabilities Act (ADA), 11
Americans with Disabilities Act Amendments (ADAA), 11, 235
Amphetamine (Adderall), 243, 244